THE GERMAN
NORTHERN THEATER
OF OPERATIONS
1940-1945

BY
EARL F. ZIEMKE

FOREWORD

The Office of the Chief of Military History of the Department of the Army is currently preparing a series of studies on German military operations in World War II against forces other than those of the United States. In addition to the volumes already published dealing with Poland and the Balkans and the present volume on Norway and Finland, these monographs will cover German operations in Russia, France and the Low Countries. These campaign studies are being made available to the General Staff and to the Army schools and colleges as reference works. They will also prove of value to all who are interested in military affairs.

The German campaigns in Norway and Finland established landmarks in the evolution of military science even though they failed in the long run to influence the outcome of the war. In the invasion of Norway the Germans executed the first large-scale amphibious (in fact triphibious) operation of World War II. The subsequent German operations out of Finland provided the first, and still unique, instance of major military forces operating in the Arctic and created a precedent, at least, for the inclusion of that region, once considered almost totally inaccessible, in strategic considerations. In these respects the operations in the German Northern Theater have a direct association with concepts of warfare which have not yet reached their final stage of development and are, therefore, of current and possible future interest.

PREFACE

This volume describes two campaigns that the Germans conducted in their Northern Theater of Operations. The first they launched, on 9 April 1940, against Denmark and Norway. The second they conducted out of Finland in partnership with the Finns against the Soviet Union. The latter campaign began on 22 June 1941 and ended in the winter of 1944–45 after the Finnish Government had sued for peace.

The scene of these campaigns by the end of 1941 stretched from the North Sea to the Arctic Ocean and from Bergen on the west coast of Norway, to Petrozavodsk, the former capital of the Karelo-Finnish Soviet Socialist Republic. It faced east into the Soviet Union on a 700-mile-long front, and west on a 1,300-mile sea frontier. Hitler regarded this theater as the keystone of his empire, and, after 1941, maintained in it two armies totaling over a half million men.

In spite of its vast area and the effort and worry which Hitler lavished on it, the Northern Theater throughout most of the war constituted something of a military backwater. The major operations which took place in the theater were overshadowed by events on other fronts, and public attention focused on the theaters in which the strategically decisive operations were expected to take place. Remoteness, German security measures, and the Russians' well-known penchant for secrecy combined to keep information concerning the Northern Theater down to a mere trickle, much of that inaccurate. Since the war, through official and private publications, a great deal more has become known. The present volume is based in the main on the greatest remaining source of unexploited information, the captured German military and naval records. In addition a number of the participants on the German side have very generously contributed from their personal knowledge and experience.

CONTENTS

MAPS

ILLUSTRATIONS

Photographs are from captured German files

PART ONE

THE CAMPAIGNS IN NORWAY AND DENMARK

Chapter 1

The Background of German Operations in Norway and Denmark

The Scandinavian Dilemma

Once, in the Dark Ages, the Norsemen had been the terror of the European coasts, and their search for plunder had carried them east to Byzantium and into the interior of Russia. In the eleventh century Cnut the Great of Denmark ruled England and Norway. Later, for a time, the Danes united all of Scandinavia under their crown. Under Gustavus Adolphus, a military genius who created the world's first modern army, Sweden became a Great Power and brought the entire eastern shore of the Baltic Sea under its control.

By the nineteenth century those glories had dimmed and faded. Sweden lost Finland to the Russian Czar in 1809; and a few years later, as a consequence of its alliance with Napoleon, Denmark was forced to give up Norway which, until 1905, was joined to Sweden in an uneasy personal union under the Swedish king. With practical good sense, the Scandinavian countries then turned their energies to internal affairs and, except for a short war which Denmark lost to the German Confederation in 1866, resolutely avoided military entanglements. After the turn of the century they watched with growing concern as tension built up in Europe, and in December 1912 they formulated a set of rules for neutrality in an attempt to create a legal basis for the position they hoped to maintain in case of war.

For Scandinavia the most fateful aspect of the approaching conflict was the rising enmity between Great Britain and Germany. In a war between the great sea power and the great land power the Scandinavian states would occupy the middle ground, no comfortable spot for neutrals. Whatever course they took promised to be hazardous and might end in disaster.

In World War I it was still possible to strike a balance. The Norwegian and Swedish merchant fleets were pressed into Allied service.

1

On the other hand, the largest share of Swedish industrial production and of the iron ore from the Kiruna–Gällivare fields went to Germany, and German pressure forced Denmark to mine sections of the Great Belt to protect the German naval base at Kiel. In August 1918 the British compelled Norway to complete the North Sea minefield by mining the waters near Karmöy. Although the cost had been high, the Scandinavian countries emerged from the war more than ever convinced that neutrality had to be the major principle of their foreign policy.

On the eve of World War II it appeared that the pattern of 1914–18 might be repeated; but the Scandinavian position was only superficially the same: there had been important and dangerous changes. In Germany, the Nazi government was both daring and capricious, and militarily it was not tied down on the Continent as the Imperial government had been. The Germans had not forgotten the so-called "hunger blockade" of World War I nor the part Norway had played in it and might be forced to play again. The German Navy's poor showing during World War I still rankled, and a favorite theory was that the war at sea would have gone differently had the German Fleet been able to operate from bases outside the land-locked North Sea, bases, for instance, on the west coast of Norway. Most significant of all, as long as the Lorraine mines stayed in French hands, the German war machine was absolutely dependent on Swedish iron ore. During the warmer months the ore could be shipped through the Swedish port of Luleå on the Baltic Sea; but in winter, when ice closed the Baltic ports, the ore had to be loaded at Narvik on the Norwegian Atlantic coast. To reach Narvik in wartime the German ore ships had to use the Leads, the protected channel between the Norwegian coast and its tight fringe of offshore islands. Also, German blockade runners could take cover in the Leads and break out into the open ocean anywhere along the Norwegian coast. These were facts which had not escaped the Allies, particularly the British who were not prepared to take the offensive anywhere except at sea and saw in economic warfare a chance to avoid a second bloodletting on the scale of World War I.

On 1 September 1939 the German Foreign Ministry instructed its ministers in Norway, Sweden, and Finland to inform those governments "in clear, but decidedly friendly, terms" that Germany intended to respect their integrity—in so far as they maintained strict neutrality—but would not tolerate breaches of that neutrality by third parties. It had made a similar declaration to the Danish Government a week earlier. During the next week Ambassador Ulrich von Hassell visited the Scandinavian and Finnish capitals where he repeated the German assurances and warned the governments against accepting any restrictions imposed from the outside on their trade with Germany.[1] The

---

[1] U.S. Department of State, *Documents on German Foreign Policy, 1918–1945* (Washington, 1956), Series D, Vol. VII, pp. 392, 396–98, 502, 522, 541.

German statements to the Scandinavian governments were essentially the same as those made to the other European neutrals at the same time. The British Government had already considered a more positive approach. A week before the outbreak of war the Foreign Office had proposed intimating to the Norwegian Government that a German attack on Norway would be regarded as tantamount to an attack on Great Britain. But the communication finally sent was watered down to a promise that the British would consider it in their interest to come to Norway's assistance if Norway incurred German reprisals by showing benevolence toward the Allies in the matter of the ore traffic.[2]

A Siege of Britain

In the third week of September 1939 the German conquest of Poland was nearly completed. The Russians were marching in from the east, and the remnants of the Polish Army were being wiped out at Warsaw, Modlin, and L'vov. Great Britain and France had declared war, but they displayed no inclination to take the offensive. Contrary to the widely held belief that Hitler was following a detailed war plan, the Germans themselves had no clear idea of what to do next. During a conference with Hitler on 23 September, Grossadmiral Erich Raeder, Commander in Chief, Navy, raised the question of measures to be adopted "in case" the war against Great Britain and France had to be fought to the finish. The possibility of unrestricted submarine warfare, to be proclaimed as "a siege of Britain," came under consideration; but Hitler had not yet made up his mind. He still hoped "to drive a wedge" between Great Britain and France.[3]

On 27 September, the day Warsaw and Modlin surrendered, Hitler called the commanders in chief of the three services to the Reich Chancellery and informed them that he intended to open an offensive in the west as soon as possible, certainly before the end of the year.[4] The announcement, bombshell though it was, was received with some skepticism. It was not the first time Hitler had given too free a rein to his imagination; moreover, the prospects of peace with the Allies appeared good, and Hitler had committed himself to making an offer (which he did in the Reichstag speech of 6 October). Within two days the Army had mustered a half dozen compelling arguments against a campaign in the west, which it regarded as technically impossible before the turn of the year and unpromising, if not dangerous, at any time in the foreseeable future.[5] The following weeks of doubt and uncertainty brought

[2] J. R. M. Butler, *Grand Strategy* (London: H.M. Stationery Office, 1957), Vol. II, p. 93.
[3] *Fuehrer Conferences on Matters Dealing With the German Navy* (Washington, 1947) (hereafter cited as *Fuehrer Conferences*), 1939, p. 9.
[4] Helmuth Greiner, *Die Feldzuege gegen die Westmaechte und im Norden*, pp. 1–10. MS # C–065d. OCMH.
[5] Franz Halder, *Kriegstagebuch des Generalobersten Franz Halder* (hereafter cited as *Halder Diary*), Vol. II, p. 16. *War Diary, German Naval Staff, Operations Division, Part A* (Washington, 1948) (hereafter cited as *Naval War Diary*), Vol. 2, p. 40.

a flurry of estimates, proposals, and counterproposals from the Armed Forces High Command (*Oberkommando der Wehrmacht*—OKW) and the service commands—Army High Command (*Oberkommando des Heeres*—OKH), Navy High Command (*Oberkommando der Kriegsmarine*—OKM), and Air Force High Command (*Oberkommando der Luftwaffe*—OKL).[6]

In a Naval Staff Conference on 2 October Raeder presented a list of three possibilities for future operations which he had received from the Chief, OKW:

1. Attempt a decision by operations on land in the west. Concentrate the entire armament industry and war economy on the Army and Air Force.

2. Attempt a decision by the "siege of Britain." Concentrate efforts on the most speedy and large-scale expansion of the submarine arm and of the aircraft types required for warfare against Britain. On land: defense in the west.

3. Defense at sea and on land; delaying tactics.[7]

As Chief, Naval Staff, Raeder expressed the belief that the most effective means to accomplish the defeat of the main enemy, Great Britain, was the "siege of Britain," and he ordered supporting considerations drawn up.[8]

Since, according to the generals, the future of land operations was doubtful, it looked as if the "siege of Britain" might move into the forefront of German strategy. While Raeder obviously welcomed such a development, he had to recognize that the Navy was far from ready to carry out the greatly expanded mission that would fall to it. In the first place, the Submarine Command had only 29 Atlantic-type U-boats.[9] Secondly, the Navy was not in a favorable position to assume the offensive outside the North Sea. It had concluded, in the "Battle Instructions" of May 1939, that the English Channel would be completely blocked and that the British would spare no pains to close the northern route out of the North Sea, between the Shetland Islands and Norway.[10] Resolution of the first problem, that of the submarines, was

---

[6] The German abbreviations OKW, OKH, OKM, and OKL will be used throughout this study. The commanders in chief were Generaloberst Walter von Brauchitsch, Army; Grossadmiral Erich Raeder, Navy; and Generalfeldmarschall Hermann Goering, Air Force. The OKW, headed by the Chief, OKW, Generaloberst Wilhelm Keitel, was not organized as a true armed forces command but functioned mainly as a coordinating agency and personal military staff for Hitler, who in February 1938 had assumed command of the German Armed Forces as Supreme Commander (*Oberste Befehlshaber*). The most important of the several sections in the OKW was the Armed Forces Operations Staff (*Wehrmachtfuehrungsstab*) under Generalmajor Alfred Jodl, who in the course of the war became Hitler's closest military adviser.

[7] *Naval War Diary*, Vol. 2, p. 9.

[8] Raeder was both Commander in Chief, Navy, and Chief, Naval Staff.

[9] *Naval War Diary*, Vol. 2, p. 19.

[10] Battle Instructions for the Navy (Edition of May 1939), in *Fuehrer Directives and Other Top-Level Directives of the German Armed Forces, 1939–1941* (Washington, 1948), p. 25.

a matter of time; the second, how to achieve freedom of action outside the North Sea, Raeder turned to on 3 October. He told the Naval Staff that he believed it necessary to acquaint the Fuehrer with the considerations in extending the Navy's operational bases to the north. He asked the staff to determine whether German and Soviet diplomatic pressure could be used to acquire bases in Norway, or, if that were not possible, whether the bases could be taken by military force. The investigation was to include a selection of places in Norway which could be used as bases; estimates of the amount of construction needed; and an analysis of how the bases could be defended.[11]

Raeder was thinking in terms of two bases, one at Narvik and the other at Trondheim. Admiral Rolf Carls, Commanding Admiral, Baltic Sea Station, thought a base at Narvik was not necessary, apparently because Germany already had the use of the Soviet arctic port of Murmansk.[12] (In mid-October 1939 Germany acquired a separate base, Base North, in Zapadnaya Litsa Bay on the Murman Coast.) Konteradmiral Karl Doenitz, Commanding Admiral, Submarines, considered both Narvik and Trondheim suitable as submarine bases and recommended that Trondheim be the main base and Narvik an auxiliary.[13]

On 5 October the Chief of Staff, Naval Staff, Vizeadmiral Otto Schniewind conferred with the Chief of Staff, Army, General der Artillerie Franz Halder on the question whether the proposed bases could be secured and defended. Schniewind pointed out that, if the war against Great Britain had to be fought to the finish, the Navy and Air Force would have to take responsibility for the main effort. He asked, first, whether it would be possible for the Army by operations in the direction of the Channel–Normandy–Brittany to create a broader base for submarine operations. This, Halder replied, was beyond the power of the Army. Asked whether the Army could take the areas in central and northern Norway which had been mentioned as sites for bases, Halder again gave a negative answer, citing the probable opposition of both Norway and Sweden, difficult terrain, bad communications, and long supply lines. He believed a thrust in the west (where he doubted that the coast could be reached at all) or in Norway would require concentration of the entire war industry on Army requirements and bring the submarine program to a halt. An extension of the base, in the direction of Jutland as far as Skagen, could be promised, he thought, but he doubted

---

[11] Trials of the Major War Criminals Before the International Military Tribunal (Nuremberg, 1947) (hereafter cited as International Military Tribunal), Doc. 122–C.
[12] In a memorandum of 30 January 1944 Raeder stated that it was Carls who first called the importance of bases on the Norwegian coast to his attention. After the war, Raeder testified that Carls had also expressed concern over a British occupation of Norway. The naval records contain no evidence to support either of these contentions. International Military Tribunal, Vol. XIV, p. 99, and Doc. 066–C.
[13] International Military Tribunal, Doc. 005–C.

5

whether the advantages to the Navy would outweigh the political and economic disadvantages of such an undertaking.[14]

In its own appraisal, set down on 9 October, the Naval Staff was far from enthusiastic. A base on the Norwegian coast, it conceded, would offer great advantages for the fleet which Germany planned to have after 1945; but until then only the submarines could use it profitably. Although a base, Trondheim, for instance, would undeniably be useful for submarine warfare, the length and vulnerability of its lines of communication to Germany would greatly reduce its value. Finally, to acquire such a base by a military operation would be difficult, and, even if political pressure were enough, serious political disadvantages, among them loss of the protection which Norwegian neutrality gave German shipping, would have to be taken into account.[15]

On the day the Naval Staff completed its study Hitler put the finishing touches on a lengthy political and military analysis in which he reaffirmed his intention to launch an offensive in the west. A major objective was to be to secure bases in Holland, Belgium, and—if possible— on the French coast from which the Navy and Air Force could operate against the British Isles.[16] The next day (10 October) Raeder explained to Hitler that the conquest of the Belgian coast (at the time even Hitler believed this would be the limit of the advance) would be of no advantage for submarine warfare and then, mentioning Trondheim as a possibility, pointed out the advantages of bases on the Norwegian coast. Hitler replied that bases close to Britain were essential for the Air Force but agreed to take the question of Norway under consideration.[17]

Fuehrer Directive No. 6, issued on 9 October, placed the German main effort on land. In it Hitler called for an Army offensive on the northern flank of the Western Front, with the objectives of smashing large elements of the French and Allied armies and taking as much territory as possible in Holland, Belgium, and northern France to create favorable conditions for air and sea warfare against Great Britain and for defense of the Ruhr. The Air Force would support the Army operations, and the Navy would "make every effort to support the Army and Air Force directly or indirectly." [18] ' Of the three services, the Navy was given by far the least important mission. Its direct contribution was to consist of small operations, such as seizure of the West Frisian Islands; and it would give indirect support by employing the submarines and

---

[14] *Naval War Diary,* Vol. 2, p. 39.
[15] *OKM, SKL, Ueberlegungen zu Frage der Stuetzpunktgewinnung fuer die Nordsee-Kriegfuehrung, 9.10.39.*
[16] *Denkschrift und Richtlinien ueber die Fuehrung des Krieges im Westen, 9.10.39,* in *OKM, Weisungen OKW (Fuehrer).*
[17] *Fuehrer Conferences,* 1939, pp. 13ff.
[18] *Der Oberste Befehlshaber der Wehrmacht, OKW Nr. 172/39, WFA/L, Weisung Nr. 6 fuer die Kampffuehrung, 9.10.39,* in *OKM, Weisungen OKW (Fuehrer).*

pocket battleships in warfare against Allied merchant shipping "until such time as the siege of Britain can be carried out." [19]

The Hitler-Quisling Talks, December 1939

After 10 October Hitler was preoccupied with his plans for the offensive in the west. He showed no further interest in the question of Norwegian bases; and Raeder for the time being did not return to it; but as the Navy prepared to intensify the war against merchant shipping its attention was increasingly drawn toward northern Europe and Norway in particular. If there was one area where Germany could hope to throttle British trade completely it was the Baltic Sea. The Navy had been active there since the outbreak of war but with less success than had been expected. One source of acute concern was the firm, almost hostile, attitude of Sweden which in October and November culminated in a series of running disputes, mostly over alleged Swedish attempts to stretch their neutral rights almost to the point of provocation. Another was the continuing traffic across Sweden to the Norwegian Atlantic ports of goods from the Baltic countries and Finland. The Navy considered it essential to stop that trade, which consisted mainly of lumber to be used as pit props in British coal mines. At the end of October Raeder ordered that submarines be stationed off the north coast of Norway, but the chances of their having any effect were small since it was impossible to determine where ships bound for Britain would depart from the Leads.[20]

On 29 November Fuehrer Directive No. 9 brought the "siege of Britain" to the fore again. Declaring that the most effective way to accomplish the defeat of Great Britain was by paralyzing its economy, Hitler announced that, after the French and British armies had been annihilated in the field and parts of the Channel coast occupied, the German main effort would shift to naval and air warfare against the British economy.[21] Discussing the projected economic warfare at a Fuehrer conference on 8 December, Raeder attempted once more to turn Hitler's attention toward Norway. He pointed out that transport via Sweden and Norway through Trondheim to Britain was very active and difficult to control. It was important, he declared, to occupy Norway; the northern countries could then be forced to route their exports to Germany.[22]

In December Raeder acquired support from a new direction when he came into contact with Vidkun Quisling, leader of the Norwegian National Union Party (Nasjonal Samling)—a small and not very in-

---

[19] *Naval War Diary*, Vol. 2, p. 70.
[20] *Naval War Diary*, Vols. 2 and 3 *passim*.
[21] *Der Oberste Befehlshaber der Wehrmacht, OKW/WFA Nr. 215/39, Weisung Nr. 9, Richtlinien fuer die Kriegfuehrung gegen die feindliche Wirtschaft, 29.11.39*, in *OKM, Weisungen OKW (Fuehrer)*.
[22] *Fuehrer Conferences*, 1939, p. 46.

fluential copy of the German Nazi Party. Quisling, who had served as Norwegian Minister of War in the early 1930's, claimed to have well-placed contacts in the Norwegian Government and Army. He was convinced that the Soviet Union was the greatest menace to Europe, and before the era of the Nazi-Soviet Pact he had advocated a German-Scandinavian-British bloc to stand off the Bolshevik threat.[23] Quisling's patron in Germany was Reichsleiter Alfred Rosenberg, head of the Foreign Political Office of the Nazi Party. On a visit to Berlin in June 1939, Quisling, talking to Rosenberg, had pictured Norway as split politically between the bourgeois parties—completely under the influence of Great Britain—and the Labor Party—engaged in transforming the country into a Soviet Socialist Republic. He had emphasized the strategic importance of Norway in a war between Germany and Great Britain and the advantages that would accrue to the power gaining control of the Norwegian coast.[24] On the assumption that the Norwegian question would be of great significance for air operations, Rosenberg had secured an interview for Quisling in the Air Ministry. Subsequently, in August 1939, a group of Quisling's followers had been given a short training course by the Rosenberg organization. In September the Air Ministry had indicated willingness to take over financial support of Quisling, but the decision had been postponed during the Polish Campaign. Further urging by Rosenberg had brought no results.[25]

In December Quisling made a second trip to Berlin, where, at first, he found little encouragement. Rosenberg, who reported Quisling's presence to Hitler and briefly outlined his proposal to pave the way for a German occupation by establishing a pro-German government in Norway, was content with an explanation that "naturally" Hitler could not receive Quisling and a halfhearted promise to look into the matter further.[26] At the Foreign Ministry, Quisling's known antipathy for the Soviet Union gained him a cold reception. The officials he talked to there wanted only to bundle him off to Norway again as quickly as they could. But, on 11 December, Wiljam Hagelin, a Norwegian businessman who acted as Quisling's liaison man in Germany, introduced him to Raeder, who proved to be an interested listener. Leaving Russia somewhat in the background, Quisling chose as his theme the pro-British bias of the Norwegian Government and the danger of a British occupation. The Government, he claimed, had secretly agreed not to oppose a British invasion if Norway became involved in war with one

[23] U.S. Department of State. *Documents on German Foreign Policy, 1918–1945* (Washington, 1954), Series D, Vol. VIII, p. 56.
[24] Rosenberg, *Die politische Vorbereitung der Norwegen-Aktion, 15 Juni 1940.* EAP 250–d–18-42/2. Reichsamtsleiter Scheidt, *Aktenvermerk fuer Reichsleiter Rosenberg. Betr: Besuch des ehem. Kriegsministers, Staatsrat Quisling, 14 Juni 1939.* EAP 250–d–18–42/4.
[25] Rosenberg, *Die politische Vorbereitung der Norwegen Aktion, 15 Juni 1940.* EAP 250–d–18–42/2.
[26] Hans-Guenther Seraphim, *Das politische Tagebuch Alfred Rosenbergs aus den Jahren 1934/35 und 1939/40* (Goettingen: Musterschmidt-Verlag, 1956), p. 91.

of the other Great Powers. The National Union Party, he said, wanted to forestall a British move by placing the necessary bases at the disposal of the German armed forces. In the coastal areas men in important positions had already been bought for that purpose, but the months of unproductive negotiations with Rosenberg demonstrated that a change in the German attitude was necessary.[27]

What Quisling had to say fitted in neatly with a line of thought Raeder had recently been following. On 25 November he had told the Naval Staff that he saw a danger that, in the event of a German invasion of Holland, the British might make a surprise landing on the Norwegian coast and take possession of a base there. He had requested that further thought be given to the matter.[28]

Reporting to Hitler on 12 December, Raeder gave an account of his meeting with Quisling and added a summary of his own and the Naval Staff's thinking on the subject of a British or German occupation of Norway. To permit the British to establish themselves in Norway, he said, would be intolerable because Sweden would then fall entirely under British influence, the war would be carried to the Baltic, and German naval warfare would be completely disrupted in the Atlantic and the North Sea. On the other hand, a German occupation of bases in Norway would provoke strong British countermeasures aimed at interdicting the transport of ore from Narvik. That eventually, Raeder admitted, would remain a weak spot; but he recommended that, if Hitler's impression of Quisling was favorable, the OKW be given permission to use him as a collaborator in preparing plans for an occupation of Norway either by peaceful means—that is, by German troops being called in—or by force.[29]

During the next week Hitler saw Quisling twice. After the first meeting, on 14 December, he instructed the OKW to "investigate how one can take possession of Norway." [30] At the second interview, on 18 December, as he had at the first, Hitler expressed a personal desire to preserve Norway's neutrality. But, he stated, if the enemy prepared to extend the war, he would be obliged to take countermeasures. He promised financial support for Quisling's party and gave control of political arrangements to Rosenberg. A special staff in the OKW was to handle military matters.[31]

---

[27] *Fuehrer Conferences,* 1939, p. 56.
[28] *Naval War Diary,* Vol. 3, p. 155.
[29] *Fuehrer Conferences,* 1939, p. 54.
[30] The date, 13 December, given in the *Jodl Diary,* is apparently in error. In the *Akten Raeder, ObdM, Heft I* at the bottom of a 13 December letter from Rosenberg, explaining that he could not take Quisling to see Hitler that day, Raeder noted, "*14.XII.39. . . . Empfang von Q. und H. durch F. Raeder 14.XII.39.*" *Tagebuch General Jodl (WFA),* International Military Tribunal, Docs, 1809–PS and 1811–PS (unpublished documents in National Archives) (hereafter cited as *Jodl Diary),* 13 Dec 39.
[31] Rosenberg, *Die politische Vorbereitung der Norwegen Aktion, 15 Juni 1940.* EAP 250–d–18–42/2.

Hitler's interest in Norway was sudden and, as was soon shown, still superficial, but events were conspiring to draw him closer to Raeder's point of view. In October Hitler had said that, barring completely unforeseen developments, the neutrality of the northern states could be assumed for the future.[32] When he addressed the generals, on 23 November, his opinion had changed somewhat. He described Scandinavia as hostile to Germany because of Marxist influences "but neutral now."[33] At the end of November the Soviet attack on Finland had injected a new and potentially dangerous element into the situation. The Soviet aggression aroused immediate sympathy for Finland among the Allies and in the Scandinavian countries, but Germany, bound by the Nazi-Soviet Pact in which Finland had been declared outside the German sphere of interest, was forced to resort to strict neutrality. As a result, anti-German sentiment in Scandinavia, which had been growing since the start of the war, rose to avalanche proportions. It was this plus the fear that the Russian advance into northern Europe might not stop with Finland that brought Quisling to Berlin in December. For Germany the most serious consideration was that the Allies might use the Russo-Finnish conflict as an excuse to establish bases in Norway.[34]

The First Planning Phase

Studie Nord

In his order to the OKW on 14 December, Hitler stipulated that the planning for Norway was to be kept within a very limited circle. That same day the Chief of Staff, Army, learned that a preventive operation in Norway which would also involve Denmark was being considered and ordered Army Intelligence to supply maps and information on the two countries.[35] In the OKW, Generalmajor Alfred Jodl, Chief of the Operations Staff, took the preliminary work in hand. Entries in the *Jodl Diary* indicate that he discussed the question of Norway with the Chief of Staff, Air Force, presumably on the assumption that the Air Force role would be predominant in any operation which might result. On 19 December he reported to Hitler, who ordered that control of the planning be kept in the hands of the OKW. The next day Jodl and Generaloberst Wilhelm Keitel, Chief, OKW, discussed the possibilities of reconnaissance in Norway and considered assigning missions to the air attachés, the *Abwehr* (OKW Intelligence), and the Reconnaissance Squadron "Rowel," a special purpose air unit that was supposed to be able to escape detection from the ground by flying at extremely high alti-

[32] *Denkschrift und Richtlinien ueber die Fuehrung des Krieges im Westen, 9.10.39, in OKM, Weisungen OKW (Fuehrer)*.
[33] International Military Tribunal, Doc. 789–PS.
[34] Walther Hubatsch, *Die deutsche Besetzung von Daenemark und Norwegen 1940* (Goettingen: Musterschmidt-Verlag, 1952), pp. 11–13. *Fuehrer Conferences, 1939*, p. 56. *Naval War Diary*, Vol. 4, p. 17.
[35] *Jodl Diary*, 13 Dec. 39. *Halder Diary, Vol.* III, p. 5.

tudes.[36]   Toward the end of the month, under the title *Studie Nord*, the Operations Staff, OKW, completed a rough summary of the main military and political issues relating to Norway.   This Hitler ordered held in the OKW for the time being.[37]

In the meantime the Rosenberg organization had also gone to work. Its first task was to overcome the objections of the Foreign Ministry, which held the purse strings, and arrange financial backing for Quisling.   The Foreign Ministry and the Foreign Political Office of the Nazi Party were rivals of long standing.   The case of Quisling and Norway was particularly touchy since it might involve a danger to Soviet-German friendship, which Foreign Minister Joachim von Ribbentrop regarded as his crowning achievement.[38]   Eventually, after several weeks of negotiations, Rosenberg managed to secure an initial subvention of 200,000 gold marks to be paid out to Quisling in installments.   It was planned also to supply him with quantities of readily convertible commodities, such as sugar and coal.

While he was in Berlin, Quisling had presented a plan for bringing the Germans into Norway by so-called "political" means.   He proposed to send a detachment of picked men from among his followers to Germany for intensive military training.   Later they would be attached as interpreters and guides to a special German force which would be transported to Oslo in coal ships.   In the Norwegian capital, after the Germans and Quisling-men had captured the leading members of the government and taken possession of the administrative offices, Quisling would assume control and issue an official call for German troops.[39]

After Quisling returned to Oslo, Rosenberg detailed Reichsamtsleiter Hans-Wilhelm Scheidt to act as go-between.   In Oslo Scheidt found that the diplomats at the German Legation placed very little stock in the talk of a British invasion and wanted to steer clear of Quisling to avoid compromising themselves.   The naval attaché, on the other hand, offered his assistance and soon became Scheidt's chief collaborator. From the outset the Germans thought Quisling's proposed *coup* involved too many chances for slip-ups; they preferred to see it mature slowly and diverted Quisling's efforts toward the gathering of political and military information.   Most of the money from Germany went for propaganda and to support the National Union Party's weekly newspaper.   Quisling's reports were sent to Rosenberg who passed them on to Hitler.   Raeder kept in contact through the naval attaché; but the OKW remained indifferent and apparently neither asked Quisling's advice nor paid much attention to that which he volunteered.[40]

---

[36] *Jodl Diary*, 18–20 Dec. 39.
[37] *Halder Diary*, Vol. III, p. 13.
[38] Rosenberg, *Die politische Vorbereitung der Norwegen Aktion, 15 Juni 1940* (*Anlage 6, Schickedantz, Aktennotiz Norwegen, 22.12.39*).   EAP 250–d–18–42/2.
[39] Seraphim, *op. cit.* pp. 162 ff.   Rosenberg, *Die politische Vorbereitung der Norwegen Aktion, 15 Juni 1940.* EAP 250–d–18–42/2.
[40] *Ibid.*

At the turn of the year everything about the Norwegian project was still vague. Reporting to Hitler, on 30 December, Raeder again declared that Norway must not be allowed to fall into British hands. He saw a danger that British volunteers "in disguise" might carry out a "cold" occupation and warned that it was necessary to be ready.[41] That his feeling of urgency was not shared in other quarters was demonstrated two days later when Halder and Keitel agreed that it was in Germany's interest to keep Norway neutral and that a change in the German attitude would depend on whether or not Great Britain actually threatened the neutrality of Norway.[42] On the other hand, Hitler's interest was increasing, but slowly, stimulated by rumors and newspaper talk of an Allied intervention in Finland. It is also possible that he had some knowledge of the British attempt on 6 January 1940 to secure an agreement permitting British naval forces to operate in Norwegian territorial waters. On 10 January, after a delay of almost two weeks, he released the OKW *Studie Nord* to the service high commands.

The Naval Staff, the only one of the service staffs at that time showing any inclination to concern itself with Norway, reviewed *Studie Nord* in a meeting on 13 January 1940. As summarized in the Naval Staff minutes, *Studie Nord* proceeded from the premise that Germany could not tolerate British control of the Norwegian area and that only a German occupation which would forestall the British could prevent such a development. Because of the Russo-Finnish war, according to the OKW, anti-German opinion was on the increase in Scandinavia, working to the benefit of Great Britain, and Norwegian resistance to a British invasion was hardly to be expected. The OKW believed that the British might use the German offensive in the west as an excuse to occupy Norway. *Studie Nord* directed that a special staff, headed by an Air Force general, be created to devise a plan of operations. The Navy was to supply the chief of staff, and the Army the operations officer.

During the review of *Studie Nord* the Naval Staff, with Raeder present, argued strongly against an operation in Norway. It did not believe a British invasion of Norway was imminent, and it considered a German occupation in the absence of any previous British action as strategically and economically dangerous. At the end, Raeder agreed that to preserve the *status quo* was the best solution, but he ordered the Naval Staff to initiate additional planning because the course of the war could not be predicted and it was necessary, on principle, to include the occupation of Norway in the Navy's preparations.[43]

Between 14 and 19 January the Naval Staff worked out an expansion of *Studie Nord*. The mission it foresaw for the Navy was to support and, where necessary, execute troop landings at the major Norwegian ports from Oslo to Tromsö. Surprise was regarded as absolutely essen-

[41] *Fuehrer Conferences,* 1939, p. 62.
[42] *Halder Diary,* Vol. III, p. 13.
[43] *Naval War Dairy,* Vol. 5, pp. 62–64.

tial to the success of the operation. If surprise was achieved, no serious opposition was anticipated during the naval phase of the operation, at least not on the outbound trip. The Naval Staff regarded the Norwegian warships as "no threat, even to single German light units"; the only British ships which it thought needed to be taken into account were those that happened to be on patrol off Norway, possibly one or two cruisers. The Norwegian coastal fortifications, not manned in peacetime, were not expected to offer much opposition, but it was deemed necessary to capture them intact at the earliest possible moment in order to be able to fight off British counterattacks.

The assault force, the Naval Staff calculated, could consist of either the 22d Infantry Division (airborne) or a mountain division. Transportation would be provided by the 7th Air Division (the airborne and parachute troop command) and the Navy. The first possibility considered was to move the troops that did not go by air on merchant ships disguised as ore transports. If successful, this method would guarantee surprise, but it had disadvantages: the large number of ships required could not be assembled without attracting attention; they were slow and could not be protected; and it would be difficult to keep the troops concealed, particularly since the ships would have to pass through the Leads with Norwegian pilots aboard. A second possibility, sending the troops on warships, avoided all of these disadvantages but limited the number of troops and severely restricted the amounts of supplies and equipment that could be transported. The Naval Staff recommended a combination of the two, the first wave of troops moving by warship and a second wave of troops, supplies, and equipment following in merchant steamers.

The Naval Staff assumed that Denmark, Sweden, and the Soviet Union would be concerned in the operation in one way or another. It recommended acquisition of bases in Denmark, at the northern tip of Jutland in particular, as a means of approaching the Shetlands–Norway passage and of facilitating naval and air control of the Skagerrak. Possible objections from the Soviet Union were to be warded off by assurances to be given "without regard for actual intentions" that the northern Norwegian ports would be occupied only for the duration of the war. In the case of Sweden, it was "to be made absolutely clear that pro-German neutrality and complete fulfillment of all delivery obligations [of goods] is the sole road to preservation of its independence." [44]

The Krancke Staff

During the first weeks of January 1940 Hitler's attention was still concentrated entirely on the plan for the offensive in the west which he hoped to put into execution before the end of the month. But because the weather predictions became increasingly less favorable after the

---

[44] *OKM, SKL, I Op., 73/40, Ueberlegungen Studie Nord, 19.1.40.*

middle of the month, Hitler, on 20 January, announced that the operation could probably not begin before March. It then became necessary to look at the Scandinavian situation in a new light, since the postponement of the German offensive might give the Allies time to intervene in the north.

On 23 January Hitler ordered *Studie Nord* recalled. The creation of a working staff in the OKL was to be canceled, and all further work was to be done in the OKW. In that order he killed two birds with one stone, placing the planning for an operation in Norway on a somewhat firmer basis and, at the same time, giving an example of the more stringent security procedures he had demanded after an incident earlier in the month which had resulted in some of the plans for the invasion in the west falling into Allied hands when an Air Force major made a forced landing on Belgian territory. On the 27th, in a letter to the commanders in chief of the Army, Navy, and Air Force, Keitel stated that henceforth work on *Studie Nord* would be carried out under Hitler's direct personal guidance and in closest conjunction with the over-all direction of the war. Keitel would take over supervision of the planning, and a working staff, which would provide a nucleus for the operations staff, would be formed in the OKW. Each of the services was to provide an officer suitable for operations work, who also, if possible, had training in organization and supply. The operation was assigned the code name Weseruebung.[45]

The staff for Weseruebung assembled on 5 February, and was installed as a special section of the National Defense Branch, Operations Staff, OKW. Its senior officer was Captain Theodor Krancke, Commanding Officer of the cruiser *Scheer*. For the first time direct control of operational planning was taken out of the hands of the service commands and vested in Hitler's personal staff, the OKW. This move, although justified by the character of the operation being planned, constituted a downgrading of the service commanders in chief and their staffs. It accounts, at least in part, for the violent Army and Air Force reactions several weeks later.

Although it was widely assumed later—after the failure of Allied counteroperations in Norway—that the Germans had laid their plans and had begun gathering intelligence well in advance, probably even before the outbreak of war, such was not the case. The Krancke staff began its work with very modest resources. German military experience afforded no precedent for the sort of operation contemplated, and the preliminary work of the OKW and Naval Staff provided little more than tentative points of departure for the operational planning. A certain amount of intelligence information on the Norwegian Army and military installations was available, which, while it was useful and later proved accurate,

---

[45] *Jodl Diary*, 23 Jan 40. *Halder Diary*, Vol. III, p. 28. International Military Tribunal, Doc. 063–C.

was not of decisive importance. For maps and general background information it was often necessary at first to rely on hydrographic charts, travel guides, tourist brochures, and other similar sources. The limitation of personnel imposed by the necessity for preserving secrecy was a further handicap. The Krancke staff in the approximately three weeks of its existence, nevertheless, produced a workable operations plan.

The Krancke Plan for the first time focused clearly on the technical and tactical aspects of the projected operation. As the Naval Staff had earlier, the Krancke staff based its plan on a division of Norway into six strategically important areas:

1. The region around Oslo Fiord.
2. The narrow coastal strip of southern Norway from Langesund to Stavanger.
3. Bergen and its environs.
4. The Trondheim region.
5. Narvik.
6. Tromsö and Finnmark.

To control those fairly small areas, which contained most of Norway's population, industry, and trade, was, in effect, to control the entire country. For that reason the Krancke staff proposed to execute simultaneous landings at Oslo, Kristiansand, Arendal, Stavanger, Bergen, Trondheim, and Narvik. Tromsö and Finnmark it regarded as being of no direct interest to Germany and significant only for the two airfields located near Tromsö. Capture of the seven ports was expected to entail a loss for the Norwegians of eight of their estimated sixteen regiments, nearly all of their artillery, and almost all of their airfields.

The operation was to be executed by a corps composed of the 22d Infantry Division (airborne), the 11th Motorized Rifle Brigade, one mountain division, and six reinforced infantry regiments. The troops for the landings were to be transported by a fleet of fast warships and by the 7th Air Division, which would provide eight transport groups and approximately five battalions of parachute troops for the first wave. Planes of the 7th Air Division would bring in the second wave, consisting of the main elements of the 22d Infantry Division, in three days. The remaining troops, the third and fourth waves, would arrive by ship on about the fifth day. Under the Krancke Plan, with the exception of the troops for Narvik and Trondheim where distance precluded airborne operations, half the troops were to be transported by air and half by sea. The Air Force was also to provide bomber and fighter support.

The Krancke staff believed that the occupation could be restricted to the seven main ports. It did not expect the Norwegian armed forces to show either the desire or the ability to offer effective resistance, and it thought that, after the landings, the German position could be consolidated by diplomatic means. The Norwegian Government would be assured of "as much independence as possible" in internal affairs. Its armed forces, except for the troops on the Finnish border, would be reduced to cadre strength, and orders for mobilization would require the approval of the German commander. German troops would take over the fortresses and military supply depots.

To provide security for the supply lines from Germany, the Krancke staff proposed using the threat of a military occupation of Jutland to extract permission from the Danish Government for use of airfields in northern Jutland. To induce Sweden and the Soviet Union to remain neutral, they were to be assured that the occupation would be terminated at the end of the war and that Germany guaranteed the former boundaries of Norway. At a later date, the Krancke staff believed, it would be necessary to require from Sweden use of the Luleå–Narvik railroad for hauling supplies to Narvik.[46]

The Decision to Occupy Norway

The Appointment of Falkenhorst

In mid-February the *Altmark* Incident gave the first real sense of urgency to the preparations for WESERUEBUNG. On 14 February the German tanker *Altmark*, with 300 captured British seamen from the commerce raider *Graf Spee* aboard, entered Norwegian territorial waters on its return trip to Germany. Despite strong misgivings the Norwegian Admiralty, which suspected the nature of the *Altmark's* "cargo," permitted the ship to proceed. On 16 February, when six British destroyers put in an appearance, the *Altmark*, escorted by two Norwegian torpedo boats, took refuge in Jössing Fiord near Egersund. Disregarding protests from the Norwegian naval craft, the British destroyer *Cossack* entered the fiord and, sending a party aboard the *Altmark*, took the prisoners off after a brief skirmish.

The deliberate action of the *Cossack* convinced Hitler that the British no longer intended to respect Norwegian neutrality, and on 19 February he demanded a speed-up in the planning for WESERUEBUNG. On Jodl's suggestion he decided to turn the operation over to a corps commander and his staff. The nomination fell to General der Infanterie Nikolaus von Falkenhorst, Commanding General, XXI Corps, who had acquired some experience in overseas operations during the German intervention in Finland in 1918.[47] Talking to Rosenberg the same day, Hitler decided that Quisling's plan for bringing his party to power in Norway should be dropped. The Quisling organization, he ordered, was to stand by for the eventuality that the British might force Germany to protect its routes to Norway.[48]

At noon on 21 February Falkenhorst reported to Hitler and was given the mission of planning and, if it were to be executed, commanding the

---

[46] *OKW, WFA, Abt. III, Weisung an Oberbefehlshaber "Weseruebung," 26.2.40.*
[47] *Jodl Diary,* 19 Feb 40. *Halder Diary,* Vol. III, pp. 62, 64.
[48] Seraphim, *op. cit.,* p. 102.

operation against Norway. The plan would have two objectives: to forestall the British by occupying the most important ports and localities, in particular the ore port of Narvik; and to take such firm control of the country that Norwegian resistance or collaboration with Great Britain would be impossible.[49] The next day, after Falkenhorst had reviewed the Krancke Plan and prepared a rough preliminary estimate of his own, Hitler confirmed the appointment. On 26 February a selected staff from Headquarters, XXI Corps, began work in Berlin.

The first major question concerned Denmark. Falkenhorst's staff decided not to rely on diplomatic pressure as the Krancke plan suggested and proposed, instead, a military occupation of Jutland which might have to be followed by an operation against Sjaelland if the Danish reaction were hostile. On 28 February Falkenhorst reported the change to Keitel and asked for a provisional corps headquarters and two divisions to conduct the operation in Denmark.

On the same day, 28 February, an even more important change, one which eventually made extensive revision of the Krancke Plan necessary, was introduced. Replying to a question whether it would be better to execute WESERUEBUNG before or after the offensive in the west (Operation GELB) which Hitler had raised two days earlier, Jodl proposed to prepare WESERUEBUNG in such a fashion that it could be executed independently of GELB in terms both of time and forces employed. All of the planning up to that time had assumed that WESERUEBUNG would have to come either before or after GELB since the parachute troops and transports of the 7th Air Division would be required for both operations. The OKW now decided to reduce the commitment of parachute troops for WESERUEBUNG to four companies and to hold back one airborne regiment of the 22d Infantry Division. These changes and that concerning Denmark Hitler approved on 29 February after he had established a landing at Copenhagen as an additional requirement.[50] Satisfied with the military plan, Hitler then called in Rosenberg and told him that there would be no attempt to enlist Quisling's active support in any form.[51]

The Fuehrer Directive

On 1 March, in the "Directive for Case WESERUEBUNG," Hitler established the general requirements for the operation and authorized the start of actual operational planning. The strategic objectives were to be to forestall a British intervention in Scandinavia and the Baltic Sea area, to provide security for the sources of Swedish iron ore, and to give the Navy and Air Forces advanced bases for attacks on the British

---

[49] *Gruppe XXI, Ia, Kriegstagebuch Nr. 1*, 20.2.40–8.4.40, 21 Feb 40. AOK 20 180/5.
[50] *Gruppe XXI, Ia, Kriegstagebuch Nr. 1*, 26–29 Feb 40. *Jodl Diary*, 28 and 29 Feb 40.
[51] Seraphim, *op. cit.*, p. 102.

Isles. The idea of a "peaceful" occupation to provide armed protection for the neutrality of the Scandinavian countries was to be basic to the operation. Daring and surprise would be relied on rather than strength in terms of numbers of troops. WESERUEBUNG would consist of WESERUEBUNG NORD, the air- and sea-borne invasion of Norway, and WESERUEBUNG SUED, occupation of Jutland and Fuenen and landings on Sjaelland which could be expanded later if the Danes resisted. Charged with planning and executing WESERUEBUNG, Falkenhorst, as Commanding General, Group XXI, would be directly subordinate to Hitler.[52] The forces to be employed would be requisitioned from the three services separately. The Air Force units for WESERUEBUNG would be under the tactical control of Group XXI, and independent employment of forces by the Air Force and Navy would be worked out in close collaboration with the Commanding General, Group XXI.[53]

The appearance of the Fuehrer Directive promptly brought a wave of protests and objections from the Army and the Air Force. With the campaign in the west impending, neither wanted to divert forces to a subsidiary theater of operations. The Army had not altered the negative attitude toward the projected operation that Halder had expressed on 5 October 1939. Moreover, personal feelings were involved, since up to that time neither the OKH nor the OKL had been brought directly into the planning for WESERUEBUNG. Halder noted in his diary that as of 2 March 1940 Hitler had not "exchanged a single word" with the Commander in Chief, Army, on the subject of Norway. Above all, the Army objected to troop dispositions being made independently by the OKW.[54] The Air Force entered a protest against the subordination of Luftwaffe units to Group XXI and, on 4 March, secured a ruling from Hitler that all air units would be placed under X Air Corps, which would receive its orders, "based on the requirements of Group XXI," through the OKL. The Air Force also did not want to release the 22d Infantry Division and considered the demands on the 7th Air Division and other air units too high.[55]

In contrast to the other two service staffs, the Naval Staff endorsed the Fuehrer Directive wholeheartedly. Meeting, on 2 March, to review the directive, it decided that the problem was no longer purely military but had "become a first class question of war economy and politics." Reversing the position it had taken in January, the Naval Staff concluded:

It is no longer solely a case of improving Germany's strategic position and gaining isolated military advantages or of weighing the pros and

---

[52] In German military terminology "group" (Gruppe) was used to designate an intermediate unit, in this instance, between a corps and an army.

[53] Der Fuehrer und Oberste Befehlshaber der Wehrmacht, WFA/Abt. L Nr. 22070/40, Weisung fuer "Fall Weseruebung," 1.3.40, in German High Level Directives, March–April 1940.

[54] Halder Diary, Vol. III, p. 64. Jodl Diary, 1 Mar 40.

[55] Jodl Diary, 3 and 4 Mar 40.

cons of the possibility of executing WESERUEBUNG and of asserting military scruples, but for the Armed Forces it is a matter of accommodation at lightning speed to political conditions and necessities.

The Naval Staff recommended that Hitler be informed of the difficulties standing in the way of a successful execution of WESERUEBUNG and of the Navy's determination "to abandon all scruples and sweep aside the difficulties that arise by using all its forces." [56]

On 3 March Hitler called for "the greatest speed" in preparing WESERUEBUNG. He saw a necessity to act quickly and with force in Norway and forbade delays on the part of the individual services. He wanted the forces for WESERUEBUNG assembled by 10 March and ready for the jump-off by the 13th so that a landing would be possible in northern Norway on approximately 17 March. He decided to execute WESERUEBUNG before GELB (the offensive in the west), leaving an interval of about three days between the operations. [57]

On the afternoon of 5 March at the Reich Chancellery Falkenhorst and his chief of staff gave a progress report to Hitler and the three commanders in chief. Generalfeldmarschall Hermann Goering, angry and claiming he had been kept in the dark about the operation, condemned all the planning so far as worthless. After Goering had given vent to his feelings, Hitler explained that he expected an Allied intervention in Scandinavia under the guise of help for Finland in the near future. He insisted again on accelerating the work on WESERUEBUNG.

Two days later, after Falkenhorst had staged a private presentation at Karinhall to sooth Goering's ruffled feelings, WESERUEBUNG began to take concrete form. On 7 March Hitler signed a directive assigning the 3d Mountain Division, the 69th, 163d, 196th, and 181st Infantry Divisions, and the 11th Motorized Rifle Brigade for employment in Norway and the 170th, 198th, and 214th Infantry Divisions for Denmark. That disposition of forces he declared final and no longer subject to change. WESERUEBUNG and GELB were thereby completely divorced from each other. [58] The 7th Air Division and 22d Infantry Division were released for GELB. As a consequence, it was no longer possible to contemplate airborne and parachute landings on the scale which had been envisioned in the Krancke Plan.

Hitler's Decision

After 5 March the timing of WESERUEBUNG became the major concern at the highest command level. In a conference with Hitler on the 9th Raeder declared that prompt execution of WESERUEBUNG was urgent. The British, he maintained, had the opportunity of occupying

---

[56] *Naval War Diary*, Vol. 7, p. 10.
[57] *Halder Diary*, Vol. III, pp. 78, 81. *Jodl Diary*, 3 Mar 40.
[58] *OKW, WFA, Abt. L, Nr. 22082/40, in Anlagenband 1 zum K.T.B. 1, Anlagen 1–52.* AOK 20 E 180/7. *Gruppe XXI, Ia, Kriegstagebuch Nr. 1,* 5 Mar 40. *Jodl Diary,* 5 and 7 Mar 40.

Norway and Sweden under the pretext of sending troops to aid the Finns. Such an occupation would result in loss of the Swedish iron ore and could be decisive against Germany. He characterized WESERUE-BUNG as contradicting all the principles of naval warfare since Germany not only did not have naval supremacy but would have to carry out the operation in the face of a vastly superior British Fleet; still, he predicted, success would be attained if surprise were achieved.[59]

On 12 March, as news of progress in the Soviet-Finnish peace conference spurred the Allies on to last-minute offers of assistance for Finland, Hitler ordered a speed-up in the German preparations and instructed Group XXI to include an emergency action in its calculations.[60] The Navy had canceled all other naval operations on 4 March and on that day began holding submarines in port for WESERUEBUNG. On the 11th, long-range submarines were dispatched to the main ports on the Norwegian west coast where they were to combat Allied invasion forces or, according to the circumstances, support WESERUEBUNG.[61]

The peace treaty between Russia and Finland signed in Moscow on the night of 12 March created an entirely new situation. British submarines were observed concentrated off the Skagerrak on the 13th; and an intercepted radio message setting 14 March as the deadline for loading transports indicated that an Allied operation was getting under way; but another message, intercepted on the 15th, ordering the submarines to disperse, revealed that the peace had disrupted the Allied plan.[62] On the German side, ice in the Baltic Sea prevented the assembly and loading of the warships and transports for WESERUEBUNG.[63] The peace deprived both the Germans and the Allies of the means for justifying an invasion of Norway in world opinion; and Hitler, on 13 March, ordered the planning continued "without excessive haste and without endangering secrecy."[64]

The OKW concluded that, with their pretext gone, the Allies would not attempt to take the offensive in Norway for the time being. Hitler was inclined to agree, but he believed that the British would not abandon their strategic aim of cutting off the German ore imports and, to accomplish that, would begin by invading Norwegian territorial waters. He thought the Allies, later, might still go so far as to occupy bases and ports in Norway. In his opinion the Scandinavian area had become a decisive sphere of interest for both belligerents and would remain "a permanent seat of unrest"; therefore, he considered WESERUEBUNG still

[59] *Fuehrer Conferences,* 1940–I, p. 20.
[60] *Gruppe XXI, Ia, Kriegstagebuch Nr. 1,* 12 Mar 40.
[61] International Military Tribunal, Doc. 2265–NOKW. *Naval War Diary,* Vol. 7, p. 63.
[62] *Fuehrer Conferences,* 1940–I, p. 22. *Naval War Diary,* Vol. 7, p. 100.
[63] *Naval War Diary,* Vol. 7, p. 75.
[64] *Gruppe XXI, Ia, Kriegstagebuch Nr. 1,* 13 Mar 40.

necessary and reaffirmed his intention to carry out the operation shortly before GELB.[65]

Jodl and Raeder concurred fully in Hitler's reasoning, but other officers in the small circle associated with WESERUEBUNG began to have doubts. Jodl's deputy suggested that, since Operation GELB could be expected to tie down the British and French ground and air forces for a long time, WESERUEBUNG could be dropped.[66] Similar thoughts had, apparently, started taking root in Falkenhorst's staff. Jodl complained that Falkenhorst's "three chiefs" (Krancke and the Air Force representative on the Krancke staff had been attached as naval and air chiefs of staff) were starting to worry about things that did not concern them and that Krancke saw more drawbacks than advantages in WESERUEBUNG.[67]

It seems that even Hitler, despite his expressed determination, would have preferred at least a temporary postponement. But the time for decision had come. From the point of view of the Navy an early execution was imperative because all other naval operations had been brought to a standstill by WESERUEBUNG and because after 15 April the nights in the northern latitudes would become too short to afford proper cover for the naval forces. Reporting to Hitler on 26 March, Raeder declared that, although there was no need to anticipate a British landing in Norway in the immediate future, he believed Germany would have to face the question of carrying out WESERUEBUNG sooner or later. He advised that it be done as soon as possible. Hitler agreed and promised to set the date for some time in the period of the next new moon, which would begin on 7 April.[68]

On 1 April Hitler conducted a detailed review of the WESERUEBUNG plan. After he had heard reports from Falkenhorst, the senior naval and air officers, and the commanders of the landing teams, he gave his approval and closed the meeting with a short address. He told the officers that the days until the occupation was completed would impose on him the greatest nervous strain of his life, but he was confident of victory since the history of warfare demonstrated that well and carefully prepared operations usually succeeded with relatively small losses. The British were trying to cut Germany off from its sources of raw materials by disrupting the sea lanes along the Norwegian coast and intended, further, to assume the role of a "policeman" in Scandinavia and to occupy Norway. This he could not tolerate under any circumstances. It was high time Germany provided itself with secure routes out into the world and did not allow every new generation to be subjected to British pressure. That was the fated struggle of the German

---

[65] *Naval War Diary,* Vol. 7, p. 96.
[66] Walter Warlimont, *Gutachten zu der Kriegstagebuch-Ausarbeitung OKW/WFSt,* "Der noerdliche Kriegsschauplatz,"* p. 10. MS # C-0991. OCMH.
[67] *Jodl Diary,* 28 Mar 40.
[68] *Fuehrer Conferences,* 1940–I, p. 22. *Naval War Diary,* Vol. 7, p. 161.

people, and he was not the man to evade necessary decisions or battles.[69]

On the next day, 2 April, having been assured by the Commanders in Chief, Air Force and Navy, that flying conditions were expected to be satisfactory and ice would not impede naval movements in the Baltic, Hitler designated 9 April as WESER Day and 0515 as WESER Time.[70]

Allied Objectives and Intentions

An Allied staff paper of April 1939 on "broad strategic policy" recognized that in the first phase of a war with Germany economic warfare would be the only effective Allied offensive weapon.[71] In the light of this and the World War I experience in blockading Germany, Norway inevitably assumed a special importance for the Allies as soon as war broke out. Before mid-September 1939 the British Government had made its first attempt to secure from Norway a "sympathetic" interpretation of its rights as a neutral.[72] Winston Churchill, as First Lord of the Admiralty, was already engaged in devising more active measures. On 12 September he submitted his plan CATHERINE for sending naval forces through the straits leading into the Baltic Sea to gain control of those waters and to stop the Swedish ore traffic; but since it involved extensive alteration of several battleships to give them greater protection against aerial bombs, it could not be put into effect at an early date. At the end of the month he suggested mining Norwegian territorial waters to cut the ore route from Narvik. In December he renewed his efforts to obtain consent for the mining of the Leads but could not obtain a decision for action.[73]

During the early months of the war there was a strong tendency in the Allied camp to base hopes on the weakness of Germany in terms of strategic natural resources, with the result that Norway and the Swedish ore began to loom very large in Allied thinking. Late in November the British Ministry of Economic Warfare expressed the view that, cut off from the Swedish ore supply, Germany could not continue the war for more than twelve months and, deprived of the supply which passed through Narvik, would suffer "acute industrial embarrassment." [74] (On the other hand, Admiral Raeder believed that Germany could stand the loss of from two and a half to three and a half million tons of ore per year which came via Narvik and that, by storing ore in Sweden during the winter for summer shipment, it could probably reduce the annual loss

[69] *Gruppe XXI, Ia, Notiz fuer das Kriegstagebuch, 1.4.40,* in *Anlagenband 1 zum K.T.B. 1, Anlagen 1–52.* AOK 20 E 180/7.
[70] *Gruppe XXI, Ia, Kriegstagebuch Nr. 1,* 2 Apr 40.
[71] Butler, *op. cit.,* p. 71.
[72] T. K. Derry, *The Campaign in Norway* (London: H.M. Stationery Office, 1952), p. 9.
[73] Winston S. Churchill, *The Second World War* (Boston: Houghton Mifflin Company, 1948), Vol. I, p. 112.
[74] Derry, *op. cit.,* p. 11.

to about one million tons.) [75] Subsequent Allied planning centered on the decisive significance of the Swedish ore, often to the extent of not recognizing all of the difficulties of securing and holding both Narvik and the Kiruna–Gällivare mines against the determined German counteraction such a move would undoubtedly produce.

At the end of November the Soviet attack on Finland created new possibilities for the Allies by arousing a hope that the Scandinavian countries, out of sympathy for Finland and on the ground of their obligations as members of the League of Nations, might permit Allied troops sent to aid the Finns to cross their territory. Such an undertaking could be made to include the occupation of Narvik and Kiruna–Gällivare almost automatically, since the Narvik–Luleå railroad provided the most direct route to Finland. The French Government went so far as to think of establishing a major theater of war in Scandinavia to draw the main action away from the Franco-German frontier. However, on 19 December, when the French Premier Edouard Daladier proposed the dispatch of an expeditionary force to Finland, he met opposition from the British, who were fearful of provoking a breach with the Soviet Union.[76]

When the early successes of the Finns made it appear that the Red Army would be a weak adversary, French enthusiasm for a second front in Scandinavia grew. After Marshal Mannerheim on 29 January appealed for support, the Supreme War Council of the Allies decided to send an expedition timed for mid-March. The French wanted to blockade Murmansk and attempt landings in the Pechenga region and talked of simultaneous operations in the Caucasus in addition to the occupation of parts of Norway and Sweden.[77] The British plan, which was adopted, was more modest and, while ostensibly intended to bring Allied troops to the Finnish front, laid its main emphasis on operations in northern Norway and Sweden. The main striking force was to land at Narvik and advance along the railroad to its eastern terminus at Luleå, occupying Kiruna and Gällivare along the way. By late April two Allied brigades were to be established along that line. Another Allied brigade would then be sent on to Finland. A secondary force of five British Territorial battalions was to occupy Trondheim, Bergen, and Stavanger to provide defensive bases in southern Norway. Stavanger would be held only long enough to destroy its airfield, while Trondheim was to become the major base in the south and the port of debarkation for Allied troops sent into southern and central Sweden to meet the expected German counterattack. Eventually the British intended to put as many as 100,000 men in the field, and the French 50,000.[78]

The Allied effort moved slowly, and massive Soviet offensives in February rapidly wore down the Finnish resistance. The execution

---

[75] *Fuehrer Conferences,* 1940, I, 16–18.
[76] Carl Gustaf Mannerheim, *Erinnerungen* (Zurich: Atlantis Verlag, 1952), p. 403.
[77] International Military Tribunal, Doc. 83—Raeder.
[78] Derry, *op. cit.,* p. 13.

of the Allied plan, meanwhile, remained contingent on the willingness of the Norwegian and Swedish Governments to grant rights of transit to the Allied troops. A Finnish request to that effect was turned down on 27 February, and another by the British and French Governments was refused on 3 March. By that time the Finns had decided to open peace negotiations. On 9 March the Finnish Ministers in Paris and London were told that, if the Finns issued a call for help, the Allies would come to their aid with all possible speed. The Allies promised delivery of a hundred bombers within two weeks, but the dispatch of troops still remained dependent on the attitude of Sweden and Norway. On the same day, 9 March, Marshal Mannerheim, who regarded the Allied proposal as too uncertain, gave his government categorical advice to conclude peace.[79]

At the last minute, on 12 March, still hoping for an appeal from the Finns, the Allies decided, at the suggestion of the French, to attempt a semipeaceable invasion of Scandinavia. Assuming that the recent diplomatic responses of the Norwegian and Swedish Governments ran counter to public opinion in those countries, they proposed to "test on the Norwegian beaches the firmness of the opposition." A landing was to be made at Narvik; if it succeeded, it would be followed by one at Trondheim. Forces for Bergen and Stavanger were to be held ready. The objectives were to take Narvik, the railroad, and the Swedish ore fields; but the landing and the advance into Norway and Sweden were to take place only if they could be accomplished without serious fighting. The troops were not to fight their way through either Norway or Sweden and were not to use force except "as an ultimate measure of self-defense."[80] The treaty which Finland signed in Moscow on the night of the 12th ended the Allied hopes. The troops which had been assembled in England were released to other assignments.

On 21 March Paul Reynaud became the head of a French Government committed to a more aggressive prosecution of the war, and a week later, at a meeting of the Supreme War Council, the Scandinavian question again came under consideration.[81] The new Allied undertaking was to consist of two separate but related operations, WILFRED and PLAN R 4. WILFRED involved the laying of two minefields in Norwegian waters, one in the approaches to the Vest Fiord north of Bodö and the other between Ålesund and Bergen, with the pretended laying of a third near Molde. The laying of the minefields was to be justified in notes delivered to Norway and Sweden several days in advance protesting those nations' inability to protect their neutrality. The supposition was that WILFRED would provoke a German counteraction, and PLAN R 4 was to become effective the moment the Germans landed in Norway "or showed they intended to do so." Narvik and the railroad

[79] Mannerheim, *op. cit.*, pp. 380–87.
[80] Butler, *op. cit.*, p. 113.
[81] International Military Tribunal, Doc. 83—Raeder.

to the Swedish border were the principal objectives. The port was to be occupied by one infantry brigade and an antiaircraft battery, with the total strength to be built up eventually to 18,000 men. One battalion, in a transport escorted by two cruisers, was to sail within a few hours after the mines had been laid. Five battalions were to be employed in occupying Trondheim and Bergen and in raiding Stavanger to destroy the Sola airfield. The battalions at Trondheim and Bergen would later be reinforced by the troops from Stavanger if the movement could be managed, but otherwise they were cast on their own resources. The success of the plan depended heavily on the assumption that the Norwegians would not offer resistance, and, strangely, the possibility of a strong German reaction was left almost entirely out of account.[82]

The execution of WILFRED and PLAN R 4 was at first tied to Operation ROYAL MARINE, a British proposal for sowing fluvial mines in the Rhine, to which the French objected on the ground that it would provoke German bombing of French factories. WILFRED had been scheduled for 5 April, but it was not until that date that the British Government agreed to carry out the Norwegian operations independently of ROYAL MARINE.[83] As a result, the mines were not laid until the morning of 8 April, at which time the German ships for WESERUEBUNG were already advancing up the Norwegian coast. When it became known on the morning of the 8th that the German Fleet, which aircraft had sighted on the previous day, was at sea in the vicinity of Norway, the minelaying force was withdrawn, PLAN R 4 was abandoned, and the British Fleet was ordered to sea in an attempt to intercept the German naval force.[84]

---

[82] Derry, op. cit., p. 14.
[83] Churchill, op cit., pp. 508–10, and 575–83. International Military Tribunal, Doc. 83—Raeder.
[84] Derry, op. cit., pp. 25–26.

Chapter 2

The Plan WESERUEBUNG

The Problem

Given the risks and limitations imposed by British naval superiority, the chief task in the German planning for the occupation of Norway was to devise a scheme of operations suited to the peculiarities of the Norwegian geography. From the first the German planning centered on one feature of the country which stood out above all the others, namely, that the population and economic life were concentrated along the coast or in valleys cutting inland from the coast and that settlement was not contiguous but further concentrated in nodes relatively isolated from one another, the largest of them around Oslo, Bergen, and Trondheim.

Oslo was by far the most important. It was not only the political capital and largest city but was situated in the heart of the dominant agricultural and industrial region and was the hub of the railroad network fanning out to Trondheim, Åndalsnes, Bergen, and the cities of the south coast. Its location in the southeastern corner of the country off the narrow waters of the Skagerrak made it easily accessible from the German-controlled Baltic Sea and placed it beyond the reach of the British Navy. In the south the Danish peninsula of Jutland was virtually a land bridge from Germany to Oslo and the Norwegian south coast. Bergen, the second largest city, was strategically significant for its location close to the British Isles. Trondheim, the medieval capital of Norway, ranked next to Oslo as a center of economic activity. It dominated the land and coastal sea routes from the south into the Norwegian Arctic regions. For the Germans, is was an indispensable steppingstone to Narvik. Of the Norwegian Atlantic ports, it offered the most promise as a naval base. Also important as ports were Tromsö, Stavanger, Kristiansand, and Haugesund and, militarily at least, Bodö, Namsos, and Åndalsnes. Two of these had to be included in the German planning: Stavanger for its air base and Kristiansand because of its strategic position on the Norwegian south coast. In the case of the others the risks of leaving them open had to be weighed against the necessity to husband the limited shipping which the Navy could provide, and, in the end, they were all omitted.

The scattering and isolation of the principal centers were not accidental but were imposed by the nature of the terrain. The cities occupied the few relatively low-lying and hospitable areas of a country in which one half of the land lay at altitudes over 2,000 feet and mountains rose abruptly out of the sea all along the coast. Interior communications were poorly developed because of the expense of building roads and railroads which required hundreds of tunnels and bridges. The sea afforded the most dependable and expeditious routes of communication.

Tactically, the best solution, as the Germans quickly concluded, was to take as many of the main centers as possible in the first assault and establish contact between them later. Its correctness was confirmed by the known condition and dispositions of the Norwegian Army. The Army, a victim of years of neglect, could, as a consequence of the recent crisis, be expected to have reached approximately its authorized peacetime strength of 19,000 men, about one-fifth of full mobilization. Its six divisions (in wartime field brigades) were assigned as follows: 1st Division—Halden, 2d Division—Oslo, 3d Division—Kristiansand, 4th Division—Bergen, 5th Division—Trondheim, and 6th Division—Harstad. If Oslo, Kristiansand, Bergen, and Trondheim were taken simultaneously, it could be expected that five of the six Norwegian divisions would either be knocked out immediately or seriously crippled.

The Navy

Operation WESERUEBUNG was acutely vulnerable during its naval phase since the German Navy, even with all of its available ships committed, was no match for the British Navy. A British intervention while the ships were at sea could have resulted in both failure of the operation and annihilation of the Navy. Consequently, from the beginning, the planning had laid heavy emphasis on surprise. To achieve surprise, speed and accurate timing were essential. It was therefore decided to transport the assault troops to Norway on warships.

To execute the operation, a so-called Warship Echelon of 11 groups was organized as follows:

Group 1 (Narvik): the battleships *Scharnhorst* and *Gneisenau* with 10 destroyers (2,000 troops).

Group 2 (Trondheim): the cruiser *Hipper* and 4 destroyers (1,700 troops).

Group 3 (Bergen): the cruisers *Koeln* and *Koenigsberg,* the service ships *Bremse* and *Karl Peters,* 3 torpedo boats, 5 motor torpedo boats (1,900 troops).

Group 4 (Kristiansand–Arendal): the cruiser *Karlsruhe,* the special service ship *Tsingtau,* 3 torpedo boats, and 7 motor torpedo boats (1,100 troops).

27

Group 5 (Oslo): the cruisers *Bluecher, Luetzow, Emden,* 3 tor-
pedo boats, 2 armed whaling boats, and 8 minesweepers (2,000
troops).
Group 6 (Egersund): 4 minesweepers (150 troops).
Group 7 (Korsör and Nyborg): (1,990 troops).
Group 8 (Copenhagen): (1,000 troops).
Group 9 (Middelfart): (400 troops).
Group 10 (Esbjerg): (no troops).
Group 11 (Tyborön): (no troops).

Groups 7 to 11 consisted of the World War I battleship *Schleswig-
Holstein* (to provide artillery support for the landing at Korsör) and
miscellaneous minesweepers, submarine chasers, merchant ships, tugs,
and picket boats.

Groups 1 and 2 were to proceed together to the vicinity of Trondheim
escorted by the *Scharnhorst* and the *Gneisenau,* which carried no troops.
Group 2 would then maneuver at sea until W Time, while Group 1 continued north to Narvik. After passing the latitude of Trondheim, the
Gneisenau and the *Scharnhorst* would set a northwesterly course away
from the coast to divert British naval units in the area. The *Luetzow*
was at first scheduled to join Group 2 and, after taking troops to Trondheim, to break out into the Atlantic on a raiding mission, but when
engine trouble developed at the last minute the cruiser had to be
transferred to the Oslo Group.[1]

The warships could not carry heavy equipment or large quantities of
supplies for the troops, and the destroyers would exhaust their fuel loads
on the trips to Narvik and Trondheim. To meet these problems and
because it was expected that the British would intercept all ships moving
north along the west coast of Norway after W Day, the Tanker Echelon
and the Export Echelon (*Ausfuhrstaffel*) were created. Their ships,
disguised as ordinary merchant vessels, were to put in at Norwegian ports
before the arrival of the warships. The Tanker Echelon was made up
of eight ships, two for Narvik and one for Trondheim to reach port
before W Day, the rest to dock at Oslo, Bergen, Stavanger, and Kristiansand on W Day. The Export Echelon, carrying military equipment
and supplies, consisted of seven ships, three for Narvik, three for Trondheim, and one for Stavanger.[2]

The Krancke staff had proposed that the merchant ships leave
Germany after the warships and reach their destinations approximately
five days after the landings. But Group XXI saw very little likelihood
of any German ships being able to make port on the west coast of Norway
after W Day and returned to the device of stationing the merchant ships

---

[1] Kurt Assmann, *Deutsche Schicksalsjahre* (Wiesbaden: Eberhard Brockhaus,
1950), p. 134. Hubatsch, *op. cit.,* pp. 44, 96–98. *Verbindungsstab Marine, B. Nr.
130, Seetransportuebersicht nach dem Stande vom 22.3.40,* in *Gruppe XXI, Anlagenband 4 zum Ktb. Nr. 1, Anlage 55.* AOK 20 E 180/9b.

[2] *Verbindungsstab Marine, B. Nr. 130, loc. cit.* Assmann *Schicksalsjahre,* p. 135.

in Norwegian ports before W Day, which the Naval Staff had rejected as too dangerous in its original work on *Studie Nord*. The Navy protested that this method of operation jeopardized the secrecy of the operation.[3] To meet the Navy's objections, OKW ordered that none of the ships in the Export and Tanker Echelons were to depart before W minus 6 days. As a result, the danger of a breach of secrecy still existed, and most of the ships, after minor delays, did not have enough time to reach their destinations.[4]

The main troop and supply movement was to be carried out by eight sea transport echelons. The 1st Sea Transport Echelon, timed to reach port on W Day, was made up of 15 ships going to Oslo, Kristiansand, Bergen, and Stavanger. All succeeding echelons were to unload at Oslo. The 1st Sea Transport Echelon also aroused misgivings in the naval command since its ships, which would be at sea before the ships of the Warship Echelon, carried troops in uniform. To preserve secrecy, the 1st Sea Transport Echelon was given the code designation OSTPREUSSEN STAFFEL, and the ships' captains were given orders to proceed to East Prussia, ostensibly to relieve pressure on the railroads. Not until after they had put to sea were they given instructions concerning their actual destinations.[5] The 2d Sea Transport Echelon (11 ships) and the 3d (13 ships) were to dock at Oslo on W plus 2 and W plus 6 days, respectively. The 4th to 8th Echelons would arrive between W plus 8 and W plus 12 days, using the returned ships of the first three echelons.[6]

For the Navy, the most dangerous part of the operation, as Raeder saw it, was the return of the warships. He was confident that the landings could be executed successfully if surprise were achieved, but he believed that thereafter the ships along the west and north coasts of Norway would be exposed to attack by superior British forces. Raeder wanted the ships of the Narvik and Trondheim groups to rejoin the *Scharnhorst* and the *Gneisenau* as quickly as possible for a combined breakthrough to their home ports, while those at and south of Bergen were to return independently using the cover of the coasts as far as possible.[7] That intention met with opposition from Hitler, the OKW, and the OKL, all of whom wanted ships left at the ports, particularly at Narvik and Trondheim, to furnish artillery and antiaircraft support and to bolster the morale of the troops. Raeder, on the other hand, defended the viewpoint that not one destroyer, let alone a cruiser, could be left behind at Narvik or Trondheim at a time when the fate of the German Navy was hanging in the balance.[8] The question was debated until

[3] *Naval War Diary*, Vol. 8, pp. 18, 20.
[4] Assmann, *Schicksalsjahre*, p. 136.
[5] *Naval War Diary*, Vol. 8, p. 53. General der Infanterie a.D. Erich Buschenhagen, Comments on Part I, *The German Northern Theater of Operations, 1940–1945*, 7 Jun 56.
[6] *Verbindungsstabmarine, B. Nr. 130, loc. cit.*
[7] *Fuehrer Conferences*, 1940, I, p. 20.
[8] *Ibid.*

2 April, when Hitler declared that he personally did not approve of the decision to withdraw the ships immediately but did not want to interfere too strongly in matters pertaining purely to naval warfare.[9]

Barring accidents, only the submarines were to engage enemy naval forces. Operation HARTMUT by the submarines was planned to provide protection for the surface ships during the transport phase and to provide defense against enemy naval action at the beachheads. In all, 28 submarines were to be stationed off Narvik, Trondheim, Bergen, Stavanger, in the vicinity of the Orkney and Shetland islands, and west of the Skagerrak. Some of the units for Narvik and Trondheim had left port as early as 11 March. The main force departed between 31 March and 6 April.[10]

Group XXI

The Command Organization

The Norwegian campaign, depending for its successful execution equally on each of the three services, was the first German armed forces operation. In the "Directive for Case WESERUEBUNG" of 1 March 1940 the staff of Group XXI was made directly subordinate to Hitler. The staff operated within the OKW, receiving its instructions from Hitler and from the OKW. The Chief of the Operations Staff, OKW, General Jodl, and under him the National Defense Branch headed by Col. Walter Warlimont participated in the planning and acted as a coordinating agency in cases where the requirements of Group XXI involved demands on one or another of the services.[11]

A unified command, at least of the air and ground forces, was projected at the start; but, after Air Force protests resulted in the Air Force's retaining tactical control of its units employed in WESERUEBUNG, Falkenhorst remained in actual command only of the ground forces. The OKL and the OKM conducted their own planning independently in collaboration with Group XXI and assigned operational control to separate commands. The Air Force and Navy representatives of the Krancke staff remained with the staff of Group XXI, where they maintained liaison with their respective services. Command of the air units was given to X Air Corps under Generalleutnant Hans Geissler. For the Navy, the Naval Staff did the planning, aided by the staffs which would command the operations at sea, Naval Group West (North Sea and the Atlantic coast of Norway) and Naval Group East (Baltic Sea, Kattegat, and Skagerrak).[12]

The planning and direction of operations in Denmark were assigned to the staff of the XXXI Corps under General der Flieger Leonhard

---

[9] *Jodl Diary,* 2 Apr 40.
[10] International Military Tribunal, Doc. 151–C. Hubatsch, *op. cit.,* p. 47. Assmann, *Schicksalsjahre.,* p. 134.
[11] International Military Tribunal, Docs. 174–C and 3520–NOKW.
[12] *Jodl Diary,* 3 Mar 40. International Military Tribunal, Doc. 2265–NOKW.

Kaupisch. The XXXI Corps was to be directly subordinate to Group XXI until W plus 3 days, when it would revert to the control of OKH.[13]

To maintain liaison after the landings, the Heimatstab Nord (Home Staff North) was created. It consisted of one officer from each of the services and was attached to the OKW, where it functioned as a link between Group XXI and OKW. Its principal mission immediately after the landings was to supervise and regulate the sea transport movements for WESERUEBUNG NORD.[14]

For the operation itself, a three-way division of command was evolved. Falkenhorst commanded the ground troops. With respect to his opposite numbers in the Navy and Air Force he ranked as "the first among equals," but he had no direct authority over units of the other two services. The Navy appointed a Commanding Admiral, Norway, and Plenipotentiary of the Commander in Chief, Navy, with his head-quarters in Oslo; an Admiral of the Norwegian South Coast at Kristiansand, who had under him the port commanders at Oslo and Kristiansand; and an Admiral of the Norwegian West Coast at Bergen, with the port commanders at Stavanger, Bergen, Trondheim, and Narvik under him.[15] The X Air Corps had exclusive control of air opera-tions, and General Halder noted in his diary in mid-April that Falken-horst did not have control of a single plane.[16] In the course of the campaign a Luftgaukommando (territorial ground command of the Air Force) was formed, and then on 12 April the Fifth Air Force under Generaloberst Erhard Milch was installed to assume control of both the Luftgaukommando and the Air Corps.[17]

The three-way division of command functions was particularly in evi-dence at the time of the initial landings. During the transport phases the Navy had full command at all levels at sea and the Air Force in the air. For substantial changes in the plan the agreement of Group XXI was to be obtained. During the landings command passed to the senior Army officer at each beachhead, whose demands for naval and air support were to be met "as far as possible." At the individual beach-heads the commanding officer of the Army units was responsible for ground operations and security; the Navy appointed a port com-mander to take charge of the seaward defenses; and, where air units were available, the senior Air Force officer became responsible for air se-curity. One of the three, usually the senior officer present, was desig-nated armed forces commander. In emergencies he was empowered

[13] *Halder Diary*, Vol. III, 101.
[14] *Gruppe XXI, Ia, 191/40, Dienstanweisung fuer den "Heimatstab Nord,"* in *Anlagenband 1 zum Ktb Nr. 1, Anlagen 1–52, 20.2.–8.4.40.* AOK 20 E 180/7.
[15] *Gruppe XXI, Ia, Nr. 71/40,* in *Anlagenband 2 zum K.T.B. Nr. 1, Anlage 53.* AOK E 180/8. *WBN, Ia, Nr. 1394/41, Erfahrungsbericht ueber Aufgaben des W.B., 19.4.41,* in *Anlage zu AOK Norwegen Ia, Nr. 2179/44.* AOK 20 53295.
[16] *Halder Diary*, Vol. III, 118.
[17] Ulrich O. E. Kessler, *The Role of the Luftwaffe in the Campaign in Norway, 1940,* p. 8. MS # B–485. OCMH.

to issue orders to all three services within his district; on the whole it was assumed that each would receive his orders through his own command channels.[18]

The peculiarities of the command organization, which were in part a result of interservice jealousy, were to a large extent dictated by the German lack of experience in combined operations. The OKW was organized to coordinate rather than to command, and Falkenhorst had no substantial experience in directing either air or naval operations. The final report on experiences of the campaign submitted by Group XXI states:

That the commands and troop contingents of the three armed forces branches worked together almost without friction cannot be credited to purposeful organization of the commanding staff. It was, instead, entirely an achievement of the personalities involved who knew how to cooperate closely in order to overcome the inadequacies of organization.[19]

The Ground Forces, Norway

"Operations Order No. 1 for the Occupation of Norway," based on Hitler's directive of 1 March, was issued by Group XXI on 5 March. It was concerned with the landings and consolidation of the beachheads. Two possibilities were envisioned: (1) peaceful occupation could be achieved; (2) the landings and occupation would have to be carried out by force. If the first possibility materialized, the Norwegian Government was to be assured of extensive respect for its internal sovereignty, and the Norwegian troops were to be treated tactfully. If resistance was encountered, the landings were to be forced by all possible means, the beachheads secured, and nearby training centers of the Norwegian Army occupied. The complete destruction of the Norwegian Army was not considered possible as an immediate objective because of the size of the country and difficulty of the terrain, but it was believed that the localities selected for landings comprised the majority of the places which needed to be taken in order to prevent an effective mobilization and assembly of Norwegian forces and to control the country in general. The landing teams were to attempt operations against forces in the interior only if they could be conducted without impairing the defense of the beachheads. Attempted Allied landings were to be fought off, but unnecessary losses were to be avoided. If the enemy proved superior, the troops were to withdraw inland until a counterattack could be launched.[20]

---

[18] *Gruppe XXI, Ia, Anlage zu Ia Nr. 82/40, Unterstellungsverhaeltnisse bei "Weseruebung Nord," in Anlagenband 1 zum KTB Nr. 1, Anlagen 1–52,* 20.2-8.4.40. AOK 20 E 180/7.

[19] *Gruppe XXI, Ia, in Erfahrungsberichte der Gruppe XXI von 30.7.40.* AOK 20 E 279/15.

[20] *Gruppe XXI, Ia, Nr. 20/40, Operationsbefehl fuer die Besetzung Norwegens Nr. 1, in Anlagenband zum Ktb, Nr. 1, Anlagen 1–52.* AOK 20 E 180/7.

For Norway six divisions were assigned: the 3d Mountain Division (two infantry regiments) and the 69th, 163d, 181st, 196th, and 214th Infantry Divisions. The 3d Mountain Division had seen some action in the Polish campaign; the rest were newly formed divisions. In addition, Group XXI was given four batteries of 10-cm. guns, two batteries of 15-cm. guns, one tank company with Mark I and II tanks (the Mark I mounted two machine guns, the Mark II a 2-cm. gun), two companies of railroad construction troops and one communications battalion.[21] The Air Force supplied three parachute companies and three antiaircraft battalions, which remained under the command of X Air Corps.[22] In terms of numbers the German and Norwegian divisions were equally matched, but the Norwegian divisions, for the most part, existed only on paper.

Landings were to be made at Narvik, Trondheim, Bergen, Kristiansand, and Oslo, and landing parties of one company each sent ashore at Egersund and Arendal to take possession of the cable stations. Stavanger was to be taken in an airborne operation.[23] The size of the initial sea-borne landing force, 8,850 men, was determined by the available shipping space since the assault troops had to be moved in fast warships. No major reinforcement of the landing teams at the beachheads was contemplated until contact could be established overland with Oslo, where the main force was to debark—16,700 men (in addition to the 2,000 landed on W day) to be brought in by three sea transport echelons during the first week, and another 40,000 to be transported in shuttle movements thereafter.[24] An additional 8,000 troops were to be transported by air within three days.[25]

The first operations order was followed in March by a series of detailed orders for each of the landing teams. Separate plans were drawn up for taking the coastal fortifications on the fiords, since the passing of these fortifications was expected to be a critical point in the operation, and alternate landing sites were selected for use in the event that the coastal batteries could not be taken. The projected execution of WESERUEBUNG NORD after the landings was outlined in "Operations Order No. 2," which Group XXI issued on 2 April.

In the final plan Oslo was to be taken by elements of the 163d Infantry Division, two battalions brought in on warships and two battalions arriving by air transport after two companies of parachute troops

[21] *Ibid.*
[22] *Gen. Kdo. X Fl. K., Ia, Nr. 10058, 73, 89, 90, and 91/50,* in *Gruppe XXI, Anlagenband 3 zum Ktb, Nr. 1, Anlage 54.* AOK 20 E 180/9a.
[23] *Gruppe XXI, Ia. 20/40, loc. cit.*
[24] *Verbindungsstab Marine, B. Nr. 130, Seetransportuebersicht nach dem Stande von 22.3.40,* in *Gruppe XXI, Anlagenband 5 zum Ktb. Nr. 1, Anlage 56.* AOK 20 E 180/10. Kurt Assmann, *The German Campaign in Norway. Origin of the Plan, Execution of the Operation, and Measures Against Allied Counter-attack* (London: Naval Staff, Admiralty, 1948), p. 13.
[25] *Gruppe XXI, Ia, (2) Nr. 200/40,* in *Anlagenband 5 zum Ktb. Nr. 1, Anlage 56.* AOK 20 E 180/10.

had secured Fornebu Airfield. A reinforced battalion of the 163d would execute the landing at Kristiansand, and the division bicycle troops would take Arendal. The force at Kristiansand was to be brought up to regimental strength by the arrival at about noon on W Day of ships carrying two more battalions. As soon as troops became available at Oslo the 163d Division was to secure the rail line Oslo–Bergen as far as Hönefoss and the line Oslo–Kristiansand as far as Kongsberg.[26]

The 69th Infantry Division was to occupy the Norwegian west coast from Nordfiord (one hundred miles north of Bergen) to Egersund. Two battalions would land at Bergen, two by air at Stavanger (a third reaching Stavanger by air on W plus 1 day), and the division bicycle troop at Egersund. The remaining units of the 69th Division were to arrive at Oslo on W plus 2 and 3 days and proceed by rail to Bergen.

Trondheim was to be taken by two battalions of the 138th Regiment of the 3d Mountain Division. Its 139th Regiment and the division headquarters would land at Narvik, where they were to gain control of the railroad to the Swedish border and, later, occupy Tromsö and Harstad, the headquarters of the Norwegian 6th Division. A strong detachment was to be kept in readiness to occupy the iron mines at Kiruna in Sweden. The battalions at Trondheim and the units scheduled to follow via Oslo would be sent to Narvik when the situation permitted.

The 196th Infantry Division, upon reaching Oslo on W plus 2 days, was to create conditions for an advance by rail to Trondheim and Ándalsnes, taking and holding Lillehammer, Hamar, and Elverum north of Oslo with two regiments. The third regiment was to proceed by rail to Ándalsnes as soon as possible, and the first two regiments were to be relieved on W plus 7 days to move northward to Trondheim. From Trondheim, a regiment would advance northward to occupy Steinkjer, Grong, Namsos, and Mosjöen. The mission of the division would then be to hold the northwest coast of Norway from the 66th parallel (in the vicinity of Mosjöen) to Ålesund and to secure the interior to the Swedish border.

The 181st Infantry Division, after debarking at Oslo on W plus 6 days, was to mop up the Norwegian forces east and southeast of Oslo; the first available troops would take Fredrikstad, Sarpsborg, and Halden southeast of Oslo. One regiment would relieve the units of the 163d Division holding the area Kjeller–Lilleström, and a reinforced battalion would advance to Kongsvinger near the Swedish border. Taking advantage of the Glommen Line (fortifications which the Norwegians had built before World War I along the Glommen River), the division

[26] *Gruppe XXI, Ia, Nr. 194/40, Operationsbefehl Nr. 2, Weisungen fuer die Besetzung Norwegens nach durchgefuehrter Landung*, in *Anlagenband 1 zum Ktb. Nr. 1, Anlagen 1–52, 20.2–4.8.40*. AOK 20 E 180/7. *Gruppe XXI, Ia, Anlage 77, Kartenband zum Ktb. 1*. AOK 20 E 180/23. Hubatsch, *op. cit.*, pp. 85, 86.

would prepare to stand off any attempted Swedish intervention. Another regiment would relieve the units of the 196th Division in the Lillehammer–Hamar–Elverum area.

The 214th Infantry Division would reach Oslo on W plus 8 days. It was to provide security for the southwest coast from the Bömla Fiord (north of Stavanger) to the Söndeled Fiord (northeast of Arendal). The mass of the division would be concentrated in the Stavanger area. The 214th Division would relieve units of the 163d Division at Kristiansand and of the 69th Division at Stavanger.

At the completion of the operation the distribution of forces would be as follows: the 181st Division east of Oslo and in the zone along the Swedish border, the 163d Division in Oslo and holding the zone immediately west of Oslo from the mouth of the Oslo Fiord to Hamar, the 214th Division holding the area Stavanger–Kristiansand–Arendal, the 69th Division at Bergen, the 196th Division in the zone Åndalsnes–Trondheim–Mosjöen, and the 3d Mountain Division holding the Narvik–Tromsö area.[27]

The Ground Forces, Denmark

Group XXI issued "Operations Order No. 1 for the Occupation of Denmark" on 20 March, and the plan for WESERUEBUNG SUED was worked out in detail in "Corps Order No. 3" which the XXXI Corps completed on 21 March. The XXXI Corps, organized to take advantage of the ideal terrain conditions in Denmark for operations by mobile troops, was to be composed of the 170th (one regiment on trucks) and 198th Infantry Divisions, the 11th Motorized Rifle Brigade (with Mark I and II tanks), three motorized machine gun battalions, two batteries of heavy artillery (10-cm.), two companies of tanks (Mark I and II), and three armored trains. The Air Force supplied a company of parachute troops, a motorcycle company from the "General Goering" Regiment, and two battalions of antiaircraft guns.

The 170th Division and the 11th Motorized Rifle Brigade were to take Jutland in an advance northward from the German-Danish border. The principal objective of the operations in Jutland (in fact, the principal objective of WESERUEBUNG SUED) was Aalborg, at the northern tip of the Peninsula. Its two airfields were to be taken on W plus 2 hours by a parachute platoon and an airborne battalion. The 11th Motorized Rifle Brigade, supported on its left by the motorized regiment of the 170th Division, was to advance rapidly along the west side of the peninsula, reaching Aalborg on W Day. The remaining regiments of the 170th Division were to break any resistance which might be offered along the border or in the south and reach Aalborg, Frederikshaven, and Skagen on W plus 1 or W plus 2 days. Three reinforced companies

[27] *Gruppe XXI, Ia, Nr. 194/40, loc. cit. Gruppe XXI, Ia, Anlagen 77 and 78, Kartenband zum Ktb. 1.* AOK 20 E 180/23.

of the 170th Division were to go by sea from Kiel to Middelfart, landing at W Hour to secure the bridge across the Little Belt and subsequently advancing across Fuenen to Nyborg. On the west coast of Jutland, light naval forces were to land at Esbjerg and Tyborön.

The mission of the 198th Infantry Division was to occupy Sjaelland. One battalion was to land at Copenhagen; the division staff and a reinforced battalion were to land at Korsör on the west coast of Sjaelland and advance overland to Copenhagen; and one company would land at Nyborg to secure the crossing of the Great Belt. A battalion with an armored train, transported by train ferry from Warnemuende, was to land at Gedser and advance northward to Copenhagen across Falster via the bridge at Vordingborg, which was to be taken in advance by a parachute company (less one platoon).[28]

The Air Force

The X Air Corps, which had operated against British merchant shipping and naval forces, was reinforced with a variety of types of air units for WESERUEBUNG. Its principal units were the 4th, 26th, and 30th Bombardment Wings.[29] The 26th Bombardment Wing had one group of the 100th Bombardment Wing attached. Attached to the 30th Bombardment Wing were one dive bomber group, two twin-engine fighter groups, one single-engine fighter group, one coastal reconnaissance and naval support group, and two long-range reconnaissance squadrons.[30] Under the Transport Chief (Land) the corps had seven groups of three- and four-engine transports and the 1st Special Purpose Transport Wing (*Kampfgeschwader z.b.V. 1*) for airborne and parachute operations. Under the Transport Chief (Sea) it had the 108th Special Purpose Transport Wing (seaplane transports) and three air-traffic safety ships.[31] The number of aircraft of various types employed was approximately as follows:[32]

---

[28] *Gruppe XXI, Ia, 126/40, Operationsbefehl fuer die Besetzung von Daenemark, Nr. 1, in Anlagenband 1 zum Ktb. Nr. 1, Anlagen 1–52, 20.2–8.4.40.* AOK 20 E 180/7. *Hoeheres Kommando z.b.V. XXXI, Ia, Nr. 123/40, Korpsbefehl Nr. 3, in Befehlshaber der deutschen Truppen in Daenemark, Besetzung Daenemarks am 9. u. 10.4.40.* XXXI AOK E 290/2. *Gruppe XXI, Ia, Anlage 84, Kartenband zum Ktb, 1.* AOK 20 E 180/23.

[29] A wing (*Geschwader*) totaled about 100 aircraft organized into three groups. The group (*gruppe*), totaling about 27 aircraft, was organized into three squadrons (*Staffeln*) of 9 planes each.

[30] Assmann, *Schicksalsjahre.*, p. 136. Hubatsch, *op. cit.*, p. 415. *Generalkommando X Fl. K., Ia, B. Nr. 10053/40, Operationsbefehl fuer das X Fliegerkorps am Wesertag, in Gruppe XXI, Anlagenband 3, zum Ktb. Nr. 1, Anlage 54.* AOK 20 E 180/9a.

[31] Hubatsch *op. cit.*, p. 415. *Generalkommando des X Fl. K., Ia., Nr. 10056/40, Weisungen fuer den Transportchef (Land) fuer die Weseruebung and Nr. 10057/40, Weisungen fuer den Transportchef (Sea) fuer die Weseruebung, in Gruppe XXI, Anlagenband 3 zum Ktb. Nr. 1, Anlage 54.* AOK 20 E 180/9a.

[32] *The Rise and Fall of the German Air Force*, Great Britain, Air Ministry Pamphlet No. 248 (1948), p. 59.

Total	1,000

Bombers	290
Dive bombers	40
Single-engine fighters	30
Twin-engine fighters	70
Long-range reconnaissance	40
Coastal	30
Transports	500

The "Operations Order for the X Air Corps on WESER Day," together with detailed orders for the subordinate units, was issued on 20 March. The main bomber force, one wing plus two groups (less two squadrons), was to be held in readiness at German bases to combat British naval forces. One squadron was to land at Stavanger on W Day and operate against British naval forces from there. The remaining bombers were to stage aerial demonstrations over Norway and Denmark. Two groups were to demonstrate over Oslo (one squadron landing at Oslo as soon as Fornebu Airfield had been taken and thereafter becoming available for support of the ground troops), one group in the zone Kristiansand–Bergen, one squadron over Stavanger, one group over Copenhagen, and one group in support of the advance of the ground troops through Jutland. The units staging demonstrations were to be prepared to support the landings, by force if necessary, and had the additional missions of leaflet dropping and observation of the progress of ground operations. The dive bomber group was to transfer two squadrons to Aalborg on the morning of W Day and one squadron to Stavanger that afternoon. It would operate against British naval forces. One twin-engine fighter group, less 15 planes, after supporting the airborne operation at Aalborg, was to land there and assume responsibility for the protection of air-transport movements between Aalborg, Stavanger, and Oslo. Three flights (*Schwaerme*), of five twin-engine fighters each, were to support the landings at Oslo, Stavanger, and Copenhagen. Those at Oslo and Stavanger would land there; that over Copenhagen would land at Aalborg. The other twin-engine fighter flight would provide fighter cover for the bombers over Copenhagen and, after supporting the further operations of the 4th Bombardment Wing, proceed to Aalborg. The single-engine fighter group would support the taking of Esbjerg by ground troops and land either at Esbjerg or Oksböl, thereafter taking over the defense of the Danish west coast. It was intended to transfer the dive bombers and fighters employed in Jutland to Norway on W plus 1.[33]

[33] *Generalkommando des X Fl. K., Ia, Nr. 10053/40, loc. cit. Generalkommando des X Fl. K., Ia, Nr. 10064/40 Befehl fuer den Einsatz des Kampfgeschwaders 26 am Wesertag; Nr. 10054/40, Befehl fuer den Einsatz des Kampfgeschwaders 4–am Wesertag; Nr. 10054/40, Befehl fuer den Einsatz des Kampfgeschwaders 30 am Wesertag; Nr. 10055/40, Befehl fuer den Einsatz der I./Stukageschwader 1 am Wesertag; Nr. 10052/40, Befehl fuer den Einsatz der I./ZG 76 am Wesertag; Nr. 10051/40, Befehl fuer den Einsatz der LI./JG 77 ab Wesertag, in Gruppe XXI, Anlagenband 3 zum Ktb. Nr. 1, Anlage 54. AOK 20 E 180/9a.*

The Transport Chief (Land) was to employ seven groups in transport movements to Oslo, Stavanger, and Aalborg and the special purpose wing in the airborne and parachute operations. The Transport Chief (Sea) was to station air-traffic safety ships at Trondheim and Bergen on W Day, to transport troops to Bergen on W Day, and to begin moving troops and supplies to Trondheim and Narvik on W plus 1. The two squadrons of long-range reconnaissance planes were to reconnoiter over the North Sea beginning on W minus 1 day (one squadron) and to observe the progress of the landing on W Day. The coastal reconnaissance and naval support group was to move two squadrons to Trondheim and one to Bergen on W Day, where they would assume responsibility for reconnaissance off the Norwegian coast.[34]

Political Planning

To preserve secrecy, participation of civilian offices in the planning for WESERUEBUNG was prohibited, and political preparations were handled within the National Defense Branch of the Operations Staff, OKW, where the economic, administrative, and diplomatic measures were formulated in advance, to be transmitted to the appropriate agencies for execution at the proper time. The major political objective was to dissuade the Norwegian and Danish Governments from armed resistance and to persuade them to tolerate the German occupation. For their acquiescence, the governments were to be offered extensive retention of their internal sovereignty and economic aid. Their foreign political sovereignty was to be circumscribed. The initial demands were not to go beyond those necessary for the success of the operation in order to make their acceptance easy and on the assumption that more far-reaching demands could be put through without difficulty after the Wehrmacht had control. The troop commanders at the beachheads were to attempt to reach agreements with local governmental units before directives from the central authorities could arrive, and at the beginning of the operation the populations and armed forces were to be subjected to an intensive campaign of radio and leaflet propaganda calculated to arouse the impression that it was in the national interest not to resist the German forces.[35]

To protect the landward flank, strict neutrality was to be required of Sweden with assurances that Swedish warships would not operate outside the three-mile limit in the Kattegat, the Sound, and along the

[34] *Generalkommando des X Fl. K., Ia, Nr. 10056/40 and 10057/40, loc. cit.; Generalkommando X Fl. K., Ia, Nr. 10072/40, Befehl fuer den Einsatz der Aufklaerungsstaffel (F) 1.122 waehrend der Weseruebung; Nr. 10071/40, Befehl fuer den Einsatz der 1./F 120 am Wesertag; Nr. 10077/40, Befehl fuer den Einsatz der Kuestenfliegergruppe 506 waehrend der Weseruebung, in Gruppe XXI, Anlagenband 3 zum Ktb. 1, Anlage 54.* AOK 20 E 180/9a.
[35] *[OKW,WFA], Abt. L, Nr. 22076/40, Vortragsnotiz; Nr. 22074/40; Nr. /40, Besondere Anordnungen fuer politische und Verwaltungsmassnahmen bei "Fall Weseruebung," in Chefsachen Gruppe IV, Mappe "Weseruebung."* OKW/213.

south coast for the duration of the German operation. Subsequent demands, it was thought, might include control of the Swedish overseas cable connections and use of the Swedish railroads to transport German troops and supplies.[36] Admiral Raeder at one point thought it might also be useful to offer Tromsö and the northern tip of Norway to the Soviet Union, but Hitler did not want the Russians so near.[37]

The diplomatic moves were to be made simultaneously with the troop landings in order to preserve the element of surprise and to place the Danish and Norwegian Governments under the greatest possible pressure. At approximately 0500 on 9 April Dr. Curt Braeuer and Cecil von Renthe-Fink, the Ministers in Oslo and Copenhagen, as Plenipotentiaries of the German Reich would inform the governments of the German action and demand immediate submission. If the terms were accepted, the plenipotentiaries would remain to keep the governments under surveillance, and deputies would be assigned for the same purpose to the ministries. Since Braeuer and Renthe-Fink would have very short advance notice of the impending operation, Generalmajor Kurt Himer, Chief of Staff, XXXI Corps, and Lt. Col. Hartwig Pohlman, Operations Officer, Group XXI, were assigned to advise and assist them as Plenipotentiaries of the Wehrmacht. Two days before the operation, Himer and Pohlman would proceed to Copenhagen and Oslo in civilian clothes, their uniforms going as courier luggage. They were to perform a last-minute reconnaissance and at 2300 on 8 April were to brief the Ministers on their part in the forthcoming operation. They also carried sets of prearranged radio code letters to be used in informing Group XXI and the landing parties of the decisions made by the Danish and Norwegian Governments.[38] On 3 April the Chief of Staff, OKW, General Keitel, informed von Ribbentrop that the military occupation of Denmark and Norway had been in preparation under orders from Hitler for a long time and that the OKW had had ample opportunity to investigate all the questions relating to the operation.[39] In effect, all that remained for the Foreign Ministry was to execute the OKW plan.

---

[36] *[OKW/WFA], Abt, L, Nr. 22076/40, Politische Forderungen an die schwedische Regierung,* in *Chefsachen Gruppe IV, Mappe: "Weseruebung."* OKW/213.
[37] *Fuehrer Conferences,* I, 1940, p. 21.
[38] International Military Tribunal, Doc. 3596–PS.
[39] International Military Tribunal, Doc. 629–D.

Chapter 3

The Landings

WESERUEBUNG Begins

The ships of the Export Echelon were loaded and ready at Hamburg on 22 March, and three ships for Narvik departed on W minus 6 days (3 April) as did the first ship of the Tanker Echelon. The warship groups for Norway loaded at Wesermuende, Cuxhaven, Swinemuende, and Wilhelmshaven on the night of W minus 3 days, Groups 1 and 2 getting under way at midnight that night. By that time most of the ships of the 1st Sea Transport Echelon, which had begun to depart at 0400 on W minus 3 days, were already at sea. The time after which the operation could no longer be canceled was set at 1500 on W minus 3 days.[1]

As the day of the landings approached, the preservation of secrecy became increasingly urgent and at the same time more difficult. The circle of those who knew about the operation was kept to a minimum. An elaborate security system was devised, and troop movements were disguised as maneuvers with details left behind in the empty billets to carry on all the standard routines. The assembly of large numbers of troops and ships at the Baltic and North Sea ports presented a definite risk, but the greatest danger came in the interval between the sailing of the first ships on W minus 6 days and the landings. The Naval Staff, which, it will be remembered, objected to the dispatch of transports ahead of the warship groups, believed it would be an extraordinary stroke of luck if the transport fleet managed to pass through the entrances to the Kattegat and Skagerrak without incident and without giving the enemy warning.[2]

The German luck was to hold. On 2 April the Swedish Minister in Berlin attempted to question the German State Secretary in the Foreign Ministry concerning rumors of troop and transport concentrations in the port of Stettin. That same day the Swedish Naval Attaché reported

---

[1] *Verbindungsstab Marine, Nr. 130, Seetransportuebersicht nach dem Stande von 22.3.40.,* in *Gruppe XXI, Ia, Anlagenband zum Ktb. Nr. 1, Anlage 56.* AOK 20 E 180/10.

[2] *Gruppe XXI, Ia, Erfahrungsbericht,* in *Erfahrungsberichte der Gruppe XXI von 30.7.40.* AOK 20 E 279/15. *Naval War Diary,* Vol. 8, p. 41.

he had been told that the Germans had prepared an operation to fore-stall a British landing in Norway. On the 4th the Netherlands Military Attaché received information concerning WESERUEBUNG and GELB from an anti-Nazi German intelligence officer in the OKW. The information was passed on to the Danish and Norwegian ministers, but the Danish Military Attaché thought it might be a plant by the OKW; and neither the Danish nor the Norwegian Government was greatly impressed by the information. The Norwegian Foreign Minister thought an attack unlikely because of British command of the sea.

On 6 April, although a report reached London through Copenhagen that the Germans planned to land a division conveyed in ten ships at Narvik on the 8th, the British did not believe that the Germans could anticipate British forces so far north. They thought that, at best, the Germans might forestall them at Stavanger or possibly involve them in a race for Bergen or Trondheim; and the report was evaluated as of doubtful value, possibly only a move in the war of nerves.[3]

In Germany, for the period 7 to 9 April, all the foreign military attachés were invited to an inspection of the West Wall. On the evening of the 5th, Goering invited the diplomatic corps in Berlin to the premiere of the motion picture "Baptism of Fire," which showed the destructive effects of German aerial bombardment on Polish cities. The picture was shown that same evening at the German legation in Oslo.[4]

When the Danish Cabinet met on 8 April, the situation had changed. British ships had laid mines in Norwegian waters, and in the early morning German warships had passed through the Great Belt. The passage of the ships apparently was taken to mean that the threat was not aimed at Denmark. In the afternoon the Danish General Staff received information that a column of German troops fifty to sixty miles long was on route between Rendsburg and Flensburg near the Danish border. The General Staff wanted to order mobilization; but the Cabinet, at a late sitting, influenced by news that the German ships had passed the northern tip of Jutland, refused. At 1800 the Cabinet decided to take limited action: it declared a state of alarm for southern Jutland and a lesser state of readiness for the rest of the country.[5]

On 1 April the Norwegian Minister, in a report to his government, had mentioned that Germany might take certain measures to prevent British interference with the ore shipments from Narvik, but he believed the troop embarkations at Stettin did not concern Norway. Reporting on the information obtained through the Netherlands Legation on 4 April, he thought the operation was probably aimed at the west coast of Jutland to secure air and naval bases there. On the 7th, information reached Oslo that a fleet of fifteen to twenty transports had left Stettin

[3] International Military Tribunal, Doc. 3955–NG. Hubatsch, *op. cit.*, pp. 136–38. Derry, *op. cit.*, pp. 22, 28.
[4] Hubatsch, *op. cit.*, pp. 138, 151.
[5] *Ibid.*, p. 140.

Mountain troops boarding the cruiser Hipper.

during the night of 5 April on a westerly course. Not much importance was attached to the report; it was assumed that, since nothing further had been heard, the ships had gone through the Kiel Canal into the North Sea. Early on the 8th the British mining of the West Fiord was reported, and at 0700 the French and British Ministers submitted the justificatory notes. After that reports came in from Berlin and Copenhagen that German troop transports and warships of all classes were at sea on a northerly course. At 1400 the British Admiralty informed the Norwegian Minister in London that German ships had been sighted in the North Sea on the 7th and off the Norwegian coast early on the 8th. The Admiralty believed their most likely destination was Narvik, and they could be expected to arrive there shortly before midnight on the 8th. The report reached Oslo at 1900. During the afternoon the ship *Rio de Janeiro* of the 1st Sea Transport Echelon was sunk off Lillesand; and the survivors, many of them in uniform, said they were on the way to Bergen to aid the Norwegians. The Norwegian commanding admiral was not convinced that the transports were actually intended for Norway. Later in the afternoon a sighting of the warships of the Oslo group was reported; yet, by the evening of the 8th the Government had not reached a decision to order mobilization. At 1820 the Norwegian Admiralty Staff ordered increased preparedness of the coastal forts, but mines were only to be laid in the fiords on further orders. The length of time which passed before the danger was taken seriously is indicated by the fact that the chief communications officer of the Norwegian Admiralty Staff was a guest of the German Air Attaché on the night of the 8th and was not called away until 2330. At 0100 on the 9th, orders were given to lay mines on the line Rauöy–Bolarne in the Oslo Fiord, but the order could not be carried out because the German ships had already passed. At 0053 the forts at Rauöy and Bolarne reported that they were in action, and at 0158 a blackout was ordered in Oslo. The Government, meeting in the foreign ministry, at 0230 ordered the mobilization of four divisions and designated 11 April as the first mobilization day.[6]

After the campaign the German Navy assigned an officer to search the records of the Norwegian Admiralty for evidence of collaboration with the British. He found none. He concluded that WESERUEBUNG had taken the Admiralty Staff completely by surprise and that, as far as could be determined, it had received no reports from either Norwegian or foreign sources informing it of the nature or time of the operation. Only two warnings had reached Oslo. The first, on the night of 7 April, came from the pilot station at Kopervik where the German steamer *Skagerrak* had anchored with provision cases marked "Wehrmacht" aboard. The second, on the afternoon of the 8th, was a report that the *Rio de Janeiro* had had 100 German soldiers aboard. Neither aroused any particular concern.[7] This investigation supported observations which the German Naval Attaché made on the scene. On 8 April, as he noted in his diary, he at first believed that the sinking of the *Rio de Janeiro* had given the operation away; but later in the day he observed "reliable signs" that the Admiralty had not been alerted. On the afternoon of the 9th he concluded that neither the Norwegian Government nor the Admiralty knew of the impending invasion until late on the night of 8 April. He had been in constant contact with people who would have known if it had been otherwise.[8]

---

[6] *Ibid.*, pp. 153–57. *AOK Norwegen, O. Qu., Qu. 2, Bericht Freg. Kpt. Nieden ueber Durchsicht des beim Norwegischen Admiralstab gefundenen Materials.*
[7] *Ibid.*
[8] *Marineattache Norwegen, Kriegstagebuch, Nov. 39–Mai. 40, 8 and 9 Apr. 40.*

In the German command, tension increased after the departure of the warship echelons. The Naval Staff believed, on the 6th, that, although it could not be expected that the other side was completely in the dark about WESERUEBUNG, there were no definite indications of the Allies' having discerned the German strategic plan and, at least, there was no awareness of the great extent of the operation. Since the Allies appeared about to take steps themselves, they would probably expect the German action to take the form of a counterblow to their own operations. The Naval Staff, nevertheless, believed the greatest haste was necessary and thought that 9 April was the latest possible date for the landings. On the 8th, intercepted radio messages indicated that the British had identified Warship Groups 1 and 2, but it was assumed that the Admiralty would probably expect a breakthrough into the Atlantic by a pocket battleship rather than draw conclusions regarding WESERUEBUNG.[9]

On the morning of the 8th, German Army intelligence reported WESERUEBUNG proceeding according to plan, and the impression was that the enemy as yet knew nothing.[10] The Naval Staff believed the German plans had not yet become known, though it expected the increased traffic through the entrances to the Baltic to attract attention. As the day wore on, tension grew. Early reports disclosed that the ships of the Export Echelon were stalled off the Norwegian coast by inability to obtain pilots; and later in the day, after news of the sinking of the *Rio de Janeiro* arrived, the Naval Staff believed the element of surprise had been lost and engagements were to be expected at all points.[11] But events were to prove that the Germans still had the advantage of their enemies' indecision.

Narvik and Trondheim

At 0300 on 7 April Warship Groups 1 and 2 assembled north of Schillig Roads and at 0510 steamed into the North Sea.[12] At 0950 British reconnaissance aircraft sighted the ships heading north and at 1330 twelve Blenheim bombers attacked but without success. The British reaction was slow. Nearly seven hours had elapsed before Admiral Sir Charles Forbes, Commander in Chief of the Home Fleet, sailed from Scapa with two battleships, a battle cruiser, two cruisers, and ten destroyers. An hour later the 2d Cruiser Squadron (two cruisers and eleven destroyers) left Rosyth to join Forbes. Believing the German ships were attempting a breakout into the Atlantic, the British

---

[9] *Naval War Diary*, Vol. 8, pp. 40, 50.
[10] *Halder Diary*, Vol. III, p. 105.
[11] *Naval War Diary*, Vol. 8, pp. 60, 61.
[12] Unless otherwise noted, this section is based on the following: Assmann, *Schicksalsjahre*, pp. 137–44; Assmann, *Campaign in Norway*, pp. 19–24; Derry, *op. cit.*, pp. 25–33; Hubatsch, *op. cit.*, pp. 57–77; and S. W. Roskill, *The War at Sea 1939–1945, Vol. I, The Defensive* (London: H. M. Stationery Office, 1954), pp. 157–67.

forces took a northeasterly course, trailing behind the German warship groups—which passed through the Shetlands–Bergen narrows during the night—and leaving the central North Sea uncovered.

During the night the wind increased, making it difficult for the German destroyers to maintain twenty-six knots' speed in the heavy seas and creating a constant danger of collision for the ships traveling in close formation. By the morning of the 8th the force was badly scattered, and contact with several of the destroyers had been lost. At 0900 one of the stragglers, the destroyer *Berndt von Arnim*, met the British destroyer *Glowworm* which had fallen behind the destroyer force assigned to mine the approaches to the West Fiord. The *Glowworm* engaged the *von Arnim* in a running fight that lasted until 1024 when the *Glowworm* sank after ramming the *Hipper*, which had been ordered back to aid the *von Arnim*. The encounter with the *Glowworm* took place at about the latitude of Trondheim, and shortly thereafter the *Hipper* with its four destroyers, was detached to carry out its mission at Trondheim. The *Gneisenau* and the *Scharnhorst* stayed with the remaining ten destroyers about halfway to the West Fiord and then veered off northwestward to provide offshore cover. At 2100, in a heavy gale and with visibility poor, the destroyers reached the mouth of the West Fiord.

On 8 April it began to appear to the British that the Germans had an operation under way against Norway after all; still, the Home Fleet continued to steam northward throughout the day, leaving the way clear for other German warship groups moving up from the south. The battle cruiser *Renown*, which after escorting the minelaying force to the West Fiord was standing off the Lofotens, was ordered to set a course to head off German ships approaching Narvik. At the same time, the destroyers patrolling the minefield in the West Fiord were ordered to leave their stations and join the *Renown*, a move which resulted in leaving the entrance to the West Fiord unguarded. At 1430 a British flying boat sighted the *Hipper* and its destroyers on a westerly course. The *Hipper* was merely maneuvering until the time for the run in to Trondheim, but the information confused Admiral Forbes who altered course from northeast to north and then to northwest in an effort to intercept. By evening Forbes had decided that the force ahead of him was moving to Narvik while other strong German forces were probably at sea to the south in the Kattegat and Skagerrak. He sent a battle cruiser, a cruiser, and several destroyers north to assist the *Renown*, and he himself turned south with the main force at 2000.

High winds and heavy seas impeded the movement of the ships of both sides throughout the night of the 8th. The *Gneisenau* and the *Scharnhorst* had to reduce speed to seven knots. At dawn on the 9th off the Lofotens the *Gneisenau's* radar picked up a ship to the west which was shortly afterward revealed to be the *Renown*. The ships opened fire at about 0500, and almost immediately hits wrecked the artillery control system of the *Gneisenau* and put her forward turret out of action. The *Gneisenau* and the *Scharnhorst* atttempted to break off the action at 0528, but sporadic contact was maintained until 0700, as the *Renown* undertook a pursuit through heavy seas and rain squalls. The Germans missed a good chance to destroy the battle cruiser, which was supported only by eight destroyers unable to maintain high speed in the rough water. Gun flashes from the destroyers misled the German commander into believing other heavy ships were present.

At 2200 on the 8th nine destroyers of the Narvik group stood off the southern tip of the Lofotens. The *Erich Giese* had fallen about three hours behind. Shortly before midnight, as the ships passed into the lee of the Lofotens, the sea became more calm, and at 0400 the destroyers passed Baröy at the mouth of the Ofot Fiord where one remained behind on picket duty. Forty minutes later two more destroyers stopped to land assault groups for the capture of the supposed coastal forts at Ramnes and Havnes. At the head of the fiord, three destroyers were dispatched to land troops which were to take the Norwegian Army depot at Elvegaardsmoen on the Herjangs Fiord (eight miles north of Narvik), while the remaining three proceeded to Narvik. The latter, approaching Narvik, encountered the Norwegian coastal defense ship *Eidsvold,* which refused to surrender and was sunk by a torpedo salvo. In the harbor the *Berndt von Arnim* was fired on by the *Norge,* a sister ship of the *Eidsvold,* which was then also sunk in a torpedo attack.

The landings were accomplished without further incidents. Seasickness had been a problem throughout the voyage, but the few hours of quiet sailing before landing had given the troops time to recover. At Elvegaardsmoen the Norwegian troops were taken completely by surprise, and substantial stocks of supplies, which were later to prove extremely useful, were captured. At Narvik, Generalmajor Eduard Dietl, Commanding General, 3d Mountain Division, went ashore with the first troops and, at a meeting with the colonel commanding the troops in the city, demanded an immediate surrender. The commandant, who apparently was pro-German—Quisling had claimed him as one of his supporters—but who also was in no position to conduct a successful defense, complied. At 0810 Dietl reported that Narvik was in German hands. In the confusion immediately following the landing, a major, with 250 Norwegian troops, managed to withdraw eastward unnoticed.[13]

Despite the successful occupation of the city, the German position was precarious. Of the few guns and mortars which could be carried on the destroyers, a number were lost during the stormy passage. More serious still, the ships in the Export Echelon failed to arrive. On the morning of 9 April only the tanker *Jan Wellem* was in port at Narvik: it

---

[13] *3. Geb. Div., Ia, K.T.B. Narvik, 6.4.40–10.6.40,* pp. 2, 3. *3. Geb. Div. W 1689/a,b.* Gerda-Luise Dietl and Kurt Herrmann, *General Dietl* (Munich: Muenchner Buchverlag, 1951), pp. 60–68.

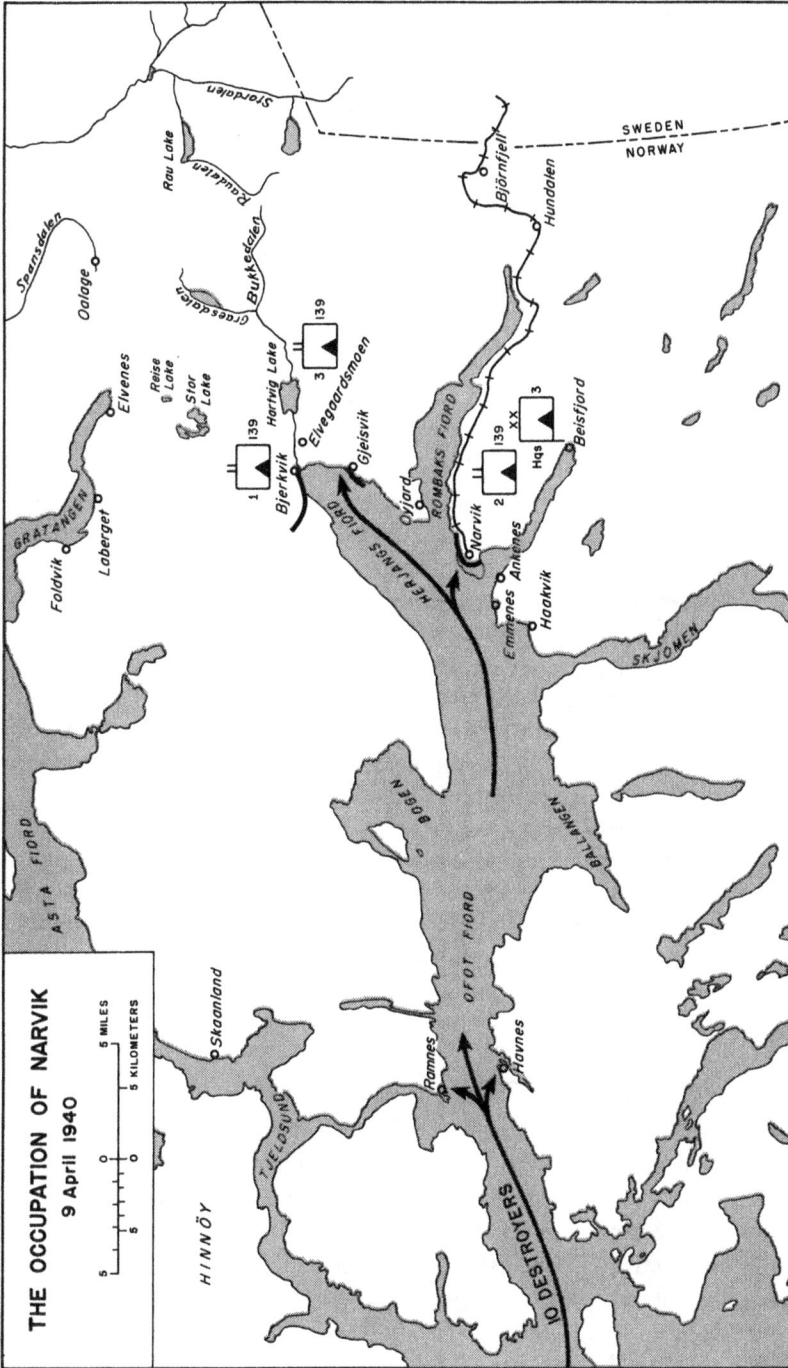

THE OCCUPATION OF NARVIK
9 April 1940

5   0   5 MILES
5   0   5 KILOMETERS

HINNÖY

TJELÖSUND

Skaanland

ASTA FIORD

Foldvik

Laberget

GRATANGEN

Elvenes

Spansdalen

Oalage

Raise Lake

Stor Lake

Rau Lake

Raudaletn

Stordalen

Buktedalen

Graesdalen

Hartvig Lake

Elvegaardsmoen

139

139

Bjerkvik

Gleisvik

1

3

Öyjord

Rombaks Fiord

ROMBAKS FIORD

Narvik

139

2

XX

Hgs

3

Beisfjord

Björnfjell

Hundalen

SWEDEN
NORWAY

Emmenes

Ankenes

Haakvik

HERJANGS FIORD

SKJOMEN

BOGEN

BALLANGEN

OFOT FIORD

Ramnes

Hovnes

10 DESTROYERS

Map 1

L. Booth

47

had sailed from the German base on the Russian Arctic coast. Of the remaining four ships one was forced to put in at Bergen, and the other three were sunk or had to be scuttled to avoid capture. The almost total loss of Dietl's equipment and supplies was to have fateful consequences for the destroyers since they had arrived at Narvik with their fuel bunkers nearly empty. A further element of danger became known in the evening when the two companies which landed to take the forts at Ramnes and Havnes arrived in Narvik and reported that no forts existed, only a few partly completed blockhouses. The Germans had counted on using the forts for defense against a British attack from the sea.[14]

Warship Group 2, after standing off the Norwegian coast throughout the day of the 8th, at 0030 on the 9th steamed in toward Trondheim at high speed. A picket boat signaled to the ships once but took no further action. At 0400, with the *Hipper* leading, they turned into the inner fiord and passed the searchlight batteries of the Brettingnes forts at 25 knots. The *Hipper* had already gone by Hysnes, farther up the fiord, when the battery there opened fire on the destroyers. One salvo from the *Hipper's* guns threw up clouds of smoke and dust which spoiled the aim of the shore guns, and with that the danger zone was passed. Three destroyers stayed behind to land troops for the assault on the forts while the *Hipper* and the remaining destroyer proceeded to Trondheim, anchoring there at 0525.

The troops encountered no resistance in the city, and the regimental commander quickly secured the cooperation of the local authorities although it was not possible to prevent numbers of men from leaving the city in response to their mobilization orders. As at Narvik, the ships of the Export Echelon were not on hand. During the day, fourteen float planes of the coastal reconnaissance group (Kuestenfliegergruppe 506) landed in the harbor. Most of them were damaged during the landing, and in any case they could not be put into operation for lack of gasoline. By nightfall the city had been secured, but the batteries at Brettingnes, Hysnes, and Agdenes and the airfield at Vaernes still were in Norwegian hands.

Bergen, Stavanger, Egersund, Kristiansand, and Arendal

The *Koeln*, the *Koenigsberg*, and the *Bremse* of Group 3 (Bergen) left Wilhelmshaven at 0040 on 8 April.[15] The advance of Group 3 was expected to be particularly dangerous since Bergen, which could be reached from Scapa in eight to nine hours sailing time, was the most likely first objective of a British counterattack. At 1700 Group 3 came within sixty miles of a British force of two cruisers and fifteen destroyers,

---

[14] *3. Geb. Div., K.T.B. Narvik, loc. cit.*, p. 3.
[15] Unless otherwise noted this section is based on Hubatsch, *op. cit.*, pp. 79–86; Assmann, *Schicksalsjahre*, pp. 144–46; and Assmann, *Campaign in Norway*, pp. 29–32.

but at that time the British forces were still all steering northward.

At 0040 on the 9th the formation set an easterly course for the approach to Kors Fiord. The night was clear, and the Norwegian coastal lights were extinguished. Passing up the fiord the ships replied to signals from patrol vessels in English. Reaching the entrance to By Fiord at 0430, the group stopped to disembark troops for the assault on the batteries at Kvarven which commanded the passage through the fiord; but the ships, in order to arrive at Bergen on time, proceeded without waiting for the capture of the batteries. At 0515, as the formation passed, the batteries opened fire, hitting the *Bremse* once and the *Koenigsberg* three times before they passed out of range. By 0620 the troops had disembarked, and Bergen was occupied with only slight resistance in the city. At 0700 four German bombers appeared. Shortly afterward the battery at Sandviken fired on the *Koeln* lying at anchor, and antiaircraft guns fired on the aircraft; but, when the *Koeln* and the *Koenigsberg* returned the fire and the aircraft dropped bombs, the forts ceased fire. At 0930 the Kvarven and Sandviken batteries were in German hands. The task of Group 3 was completed by 1100; but the captured batteries were not yet ready for action; and the *Koenigsberg,* damaged by the fire from the batteries at Kvarven, was not fit to put to sea. During the day, three German seaplane transports arrived bringing troops, and at 1930 twelve British bombers attacked the ships but failed to score any hits.[16]

After a dive-bombing attack and the landing of a company of parachute troops, two infantry battalions brought in by air occupied Stavanger. The airfield at Sola, the best in Norway, was quickly taken. The ship of the Export Echelon intended for Stavanger was sunk outside the port, but the three ships of the 1st Sea Transport Echelon arrived on time during the morning bringing troop reinforcements, supplies, and equipment. The minesweepers and troops of Group 6 took Egersund without trouble.

The ships of Group 4 (destined for Kristiansand and Arendal) began leaving Wesermuende at 0500 on 8 April, traveling in three separate formations adjusted to the speeds of the various units. When the group assembled at 0030 on the 9th the torpedo boat *Greif* with its troops had already set a course for Arendal, where it accomplished the landing without resistance but was delayed by fog until 0900. At 0345 Group 4 lay outside the fiord at Kristiansand, but could not attempt an entrance because of heavy fog. At 0600, when visibility improved, the moment of surprise had been lost, and a Norwegian aircraft had sighted the ships. Twenty minutes later the formation attempted to enter the fiord but was forced to retire under the cover of smoke after encountering fire from the batteries at Odderöy. It undertook a second ap-

---

[16] Gruppe XXI, Ia, *Durchschlaege von Abschriften eines Teils der Anlagen zum K.T.B. 2–3, 9.4.40–10.5.40.* AOK 20 E 288/1.

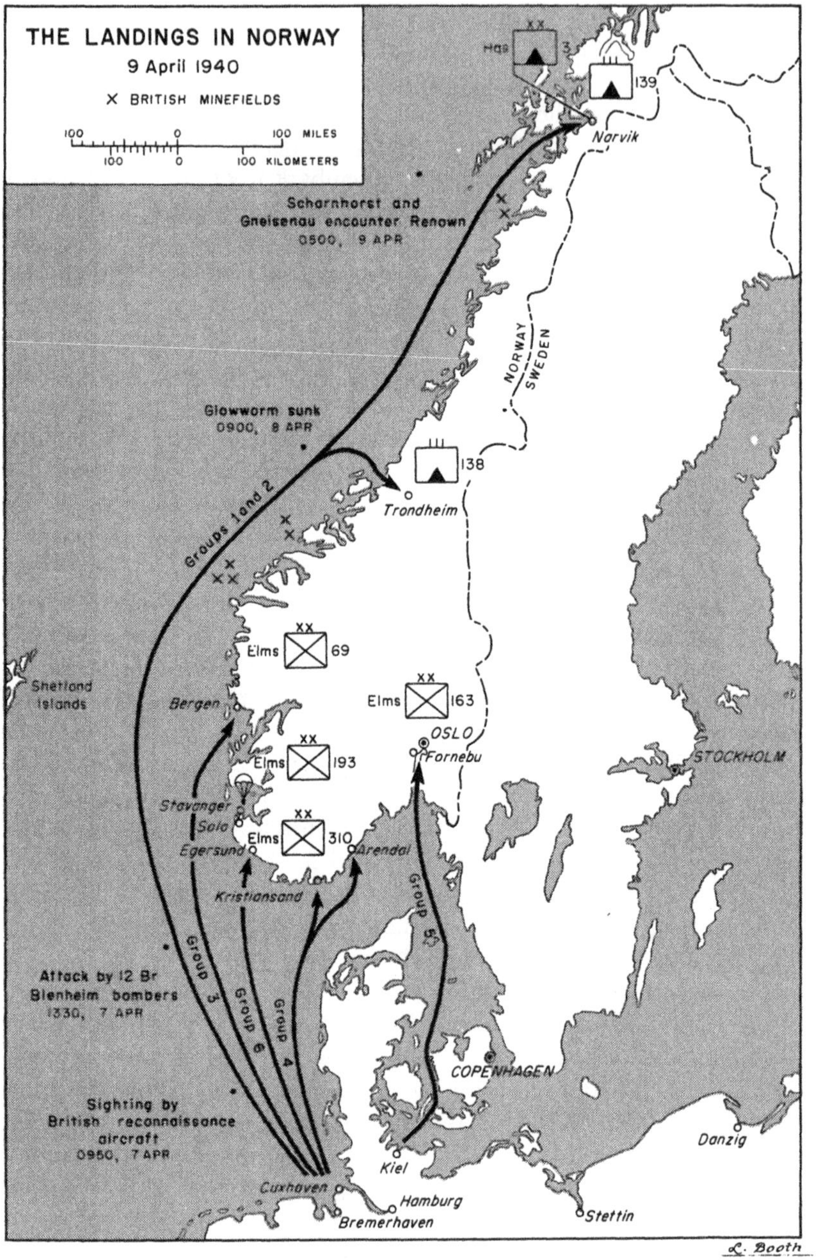

THE LANDINGS IN NORWAY
9 April 1940

X BRITISH MINEFIELDS

100   0   100 MILES
100   0   100 KILOMETERS

Schornhorst and
Gneisenau encounter Renown
0500, 9 APR

Glowworm sunk
0900, 8 APR

Groups land 2

Shetland
Islands

Bergen

Stavanger
Sola
Egersund

Kristiansand

Attack by 12 Br
Blenheim bombers
1330, 7 APR

Sighting by
British reconnaissance
aircraft
0950, 7 APR

Cuxhaven
Kiel
Hamburg
Bremerhaven

Hgs XX 3

139

Norvik

NORWAY
SWEDEN

Trondheim 138

Elms XX 69

Elms XX 163

OSLO
Fornebu

Elms XX 193

Elms XX 310

Arendal

Group 5

COPENHAGEN

Group 3
Group 6
Group 4

STOCKHOLM

Danzig

Stettin

R. Booth

Map 2

proach at 0655 after five German planes had bombed the batteries at
Odderöy and Gleodden.   The attempt failed, and the ships again had
to withdraw under the cover of smoke.   Both times the ships had approached in line, which meant that only the forward turrets of the
Karlsruhe could be brought to bear.   At 0750 a different approach

was ordered, with the torpedo boats entering under the cover of broadside fire from the *Karlsruhe*. That attempt had to be canceled because of fog. Trying to break through alone at 0930, the *Karlsruhe* nearly ran aground in the fog. In the meantime air support had been requested, and after 0930 a bomber group began to attack the forts. At 1100, after visibility had improved, the forts had ceased fire and the ships were able to enter Kristiansand without further resistance. The batteries were occupied before noon, and the city was secured in the afternoon. Three ships of the 1st Sea Transport Echelon arrived with troops and supplies in the afternoon.

Oslo

Group 5 loaded at Swinemuende and assembled on the evening of 7 April in Kiel Bay.[17] At 0300 the following morning the formation passed northward through the Great Belt and by 1900 had reached the latitude of Skagen at the tip of the Jutland Peninsula. Shortly after midnight it approached the entrance to the Oslo Fiord where the Norwegian patrol boat *Pol III*, an armed whaler, raised the alarm before being sunk by gunfire from one of the torpedo boats. Farther in, the island forts at Rauöy and Bolarne turned on their searchlights and attempted to engage the German ships, but without success because of fog. After dispatching several of the smaller vessels to land troops for the capture of the forts and the Norwegian naval base at Horten, the formation advanced up the fiord. At 0440 the ships had reached the narrows at Dröbak, about ten miles from Oslo, with the *Bluecher* in the lead, and approached the Oscarsborg fort at twelve knots in a heavy haze which reduced visibility. Since no activity could be observed in the direction of the fort (its searchlights could not be operated because the boilers of the steam generators were being cleaned), the group commander apparently assumed there would be no further resistance and a rapid advance to Oslo would be possible. When the *Bluecher* came within range, the 280-mm. guns at Oscarsborg opened fire, as did the batteries at Kaholm and Dröbak. The first hits caused severe damage, starting fires and putting the steering gear out of action; and as the ship, steering with her engines, passed Kaholm she was struck by two torpedoes from the battery there. Within three or four minutes the *Bluecher* had passed out of range, but the fires could not be brought under control, and an explosion in one of the magazines sealed her fate. At 0700 the commanding officer ordered the ship abandoned. A half hour later she capsized and sank. It was ironical that Germany's newest heavy cruiser was sunk by the guns (Krupp model 1905) of a fort built during the Crimean War and torpedoes manufactured at the turn of the

---

[17] Unless otherwise noted this section is based on Assmann, *Campaign in Norway*, pp. 33–35; Derry, *op. cit.*, pp. 35, 36; and Hubatsch, *op. cit.*, pp. 86–93.

JU 52 transports, Fornebu Airfield, 9 April 1940.

century by an Austrian firm in Fiume.[18]   The sinking entailed a heavy loss of men, including most of the staff of the 163d Infantry Division.

After the loss of the *Bluecher* command of Group 5 passed to the commanding officer of the *Luetzow,* who withdrew the rest of the ships and decided to land troops at Sonsbukten for an attack on the defenses at Dröbak from land and from the sea.   During the day waves of bombers and dive bombers attacked the outer forts and Horten, which also continued to offer resistance.   Dröbak was occupied at 1900, but negotiations for the surrender of Kaholm were protracted until the morning of 10 April when the ships were able to pass through the narrows, reaching Oslo at 1145.

In Oslo on the morning of the 9th heavy fog and antiaircraft artillery fire delayed the planned landing of parachute and airborne troops. It was only after bombers had been committed that the first infantry assault troops could land.   At 0838, more than three hours after the planned time, the transports began to land.   Even then sheer luck was all that made the landings possible.   Because of fog, the X Air Corps had ordered all the planes to land at Aalborg in Denmark.   Those carrying parachute troops had turned back, but the first transport group carrying elements of one infantry battalion had ignored the order because it was subordinate to the Transport Chief (Land), not the X Air Corps. About noon, five additional companies of infantry were brought in followed by two parachute companies.   With these forces Oslo was occupied.[19]

---

[18] *Gruppe XXI, Ia, "Uebersetzung: Die Seeschlacht von Oscarsburg am 9.4.1940, Unterredung mit dem norweg.   Lt. Bonsak,"* in *Bluecher Erlebnisberichte.*   AOK 20 E 279/2.
[19] Oberst a. D. Greffrath, *"Der Norwegen-Feldzug 1940."* USAF Historical Division, Wiesbaden.

The Return of the Warships

Throughout the night of 8 April the British main force steamed south, reaching a point somewhat below the latitude of Bergen on the morning of the 9th.[20] By that time reports were coming in of enemy landings at Norwegian ports. At 1130 Forbes detached four cruisers and seven destroyers to attack the German ships at Bergen, but the Admiralty canceled the attack in the belief that the coastal forts were already in German hands. At noon Forbes turned north again, coming under heavy German air attack during the afternoon. The display of German air superiority led Forbes to the conclusion that the southern area would have to be left to submarines and land-based aircraft. Joined early on the 10th by the aircraft carrier *Furious,* Forbes continued northward intending to launch an air attack on Trondheim.

Meanwhile, the British 2d Destroyer Flotilla (five destroyers), which had been part of the minelaying force for Narvik, entered the West Fiord at 1600 on the 9th. The following morning, at dawn in a snow storm, taking five German destroyers by surprise in the harbor at Narvik, it sank two and damaged the rest. Passing out of the Ofot Fiord the 2d Destroyer Flotilla was itself attacked by five German destroyers which had been anchored in the Herjangs and Ballangen Fiords. In the ensuing action one British destroyer was sunk, one beached, and one badly damaged.

The German destroyers had been unable to leave on the night of the 9th as had been planned because of delays in refueling; and the dawn attack was a complete surprise to the German force, since, owing to unclear orders, the destroyer on patrol had left its post shortly before the British destroyers arrived. Apparently, too, the German commander relied heavily on the four submarines posted in the fiord. The submarines, however, were unable to operate effectively because of poor visibility and torpedo failures. The incidence of torpedo failures was to hamper German submarine operations severely throughout the Norwegian campaign. It was believed that magnetic conditions in the Norwegian area affected the magnetic fuses, but the conventional torpedoes scarcely functioned better.

At 2200 on 10 April the *Hipper* left Trondheim accompanied by one destroyer which later had to turn back because of heavy seas. During the night the *Hipper* narrowly missed the force of Admiral Forbes, who was advancing for the air attack on Trondheim, an attack that eighteen torpedo bombers carried out the next morning without success. The *Scharnhorst* and the *Gneisenau* had continued northwestward after the encounter with the *Renown* until, on the 10th in the vicinity of Jan Mayen Island, they altered course southward for the return to their

---

[20] Unless otherwise noted this section is based on Assmann, *Campaign in Norway,* pp. 37–48; Hubatsch, *op. cit.,* Derry, *op. cit.,* pp. 43–53; and Roskill, *op. cit.,* pp. 171–78.

home base. Knowing from intercepted radio traffic that the British forces were concentrating in the zone from Trondheim to the Lofotens they executed a sweeping arc to the west, passing close to the Shetland Islands during the night of the 11th. At 0830 on the 12th they made contact with the *Hipper,* and at 2000 the ships entered the Jade docking at Wilhelmshaven. Two of the destroyers returned from Trondheim on 14 April, one on 10 May, and the last on 10 June.

After the attack on Trondheim failed, Admiral Forbes continued northward and arrived off the Lofotens during the afternoon of 12 April to cover and support the attack on the enemy ships at Narvik with air-craft from the *Furious.* On orders from the Admiralty the battleship *Warspite* and nine destroyers were committed in the final attack. Early on the morning of the 13th the formation advanced up the West Fiord. The first success was obtained by the *Warspite's* reconnaissance plane, which bombed and sank a German submarine while scouting ahead of the force. Two German destroyers stationed halfway up the Ofot Fiord gave a warning of the British approach. One of them was sunk where it lay at anchor. It had been damaged in the battle on 10 April and was being used as a floating gun and torpedo battery. The other escaped toward Narvik ahead of the British ships. It and the remaining six destroyers of the German flotilla engaged the British from 1300 to 1400 just outside the Narvik harbor and then, having exhausted their ammunition, retired into the Rombaks and Herjangs Fiords where some were beached and others sunk. The ten lost destroyers comprised half the total destroyer strength of the German Navy, but most of the crews were saved and formed a valuable reinforcement for General Dietl's small force in Narvik.

The return of the ships from the southern ports was carried out with varying degrees of success. At Bergen the *Koenigsberg* and the *Bremse,* damaged during the landings, were not fit to put to sea on the 9th, and the *Karl Peters,* with the motor torpedo boats, was to remain behind according to plan. The *Koeln,* with an escort of two torpedo boats, setting out on the night of the 9th, was sighted by British planes, but, after taking cover in a small fiord until the following day, was able to proceed, arriving safely at Wilhelmshaven at 1700 on the 11th. On the 10th, when British land-based bombers attacked Bergen, the *Koenigsberg* received two direct hits, capsized, and sank. The *Karlsruhe,* leaving Kristiansand with three torpedo boats on the night of the 9th, was torpedoed just outside the harbor and later had to be sunk by her own escorts. At Oslo the military situation did not permit the return of all the warships, and only the *Luetzow,* still scheduled for a raiding mission in the Atlantic, was ordered to return at once. The *Luetzow* put out from Horten on the evening of the 10th. Early the following morning, while traveling at high speed off the Swedish coast, the *Luetzow* was hit by a torpedo from a British submarine which blew off both screws and the rudder, and the ship had to be towed to Kiel.

The cost to the German Navy of the Norwegian operation ran high. It lost one heavy cruiser, two light cruisers, ten destroyers, and had three other cruisers damaged. In addition, the gunnery training ship *Brummer* was sunk on 15 April while on convoy duty. Part of this loss could be credited to the fact that the British had stationed sixteen submarines along the German approach routes through the Skagerrak and Kattegat during their own preparation for WILFRED and PLAN R 4.

Supply and Troop Transport

Of the seven ships in the Export Echelon, none arrived on time; four were sunk; one was captured; one of those for Narvik put in at Bergen on 11 April where British aircraft sank it while unloading; and one arrived at Trondheim on 13 April.[21] Of the four tankers for Narvik and Trondheim, one, the *Jan Wellem* (Narvik), reached port, and three were sunk. The loss, as has been seen, proved serious for the warships at those ports. The *Hipper,* forced to start the trip back without refueling, arrived at Wilhelmshaven with only enough fuel for two and one half hours' steaming. The four tankers for Oslo, Stavanger, and Bergen reached port on time.

The 1st Sea Transport Echelon (15 ships), its ships traveling singly, lost three ships. Another was torpedoed but could be taken in tow. The 2d Sea Transport Echelon (11 ships), traveling in convoy, lost two ships; and the 3d Transport Echelon lost one. The remaining five echelons made their runs without losses; but the submarine menace continued; and German antisubmarine measures, particularly during the first few weeks, proved singularly ineffective.[22] After the sinking of two ships in the 2d Sea Transport Echelon, which resulted in a loss of 900 troops, the Naval Staff ordered that troops were no longer to be carried on slow transports but only on fast small vessels or warships. Thenceforth the troops were routed to Frederikshaven on Jutland and from there taken to south Norwegian ports in small ships. After a while, the number of troops transported by this means was stepped up to 3,000 a day, and in the period from the middle of April to the middle of June 42,000 men were transported without losses. A similar arrangement was made for the transportation of provisions, ammunition, and equipment from Skagen to southern Norway in small boats in order to relieve the pressure on the transports. From the beginning of the Norwegian campaign to 15 June 1940 a total of 270 ships and 100 trawlers (excluding warships) carried 107,581 officers and men, 16,102 horses, 20,339 vehicles, and 109,400 tons of supplies. Twenty-one ships were lost.

---

[21] Unless otherwise noted this section is based on Assmann, *Campaign in Norway,* pp. 48–51 and Hubatsch, *op. cit.,* pp. 129–34.

[22] *Naval War Diary,* Vol. 8, p. 142.

After it became known that the Export Echelon was a failure, Hitler on 10 April ordered that the use of submarines as transports be investigated. Between 12 and 16 April three submarines, each carrying about fifty tons of ammunition and supplies, were dispatched to Narvik but, because of the uncertainty of the situation in the north, were rerouted to Trondheim. On 27 April another three boats were sent to Trondheim with aviation gasoline and aerial bombs. During the Norwegian operation the submarines carried out a total of eight transport missions.

The Air Force also played an important role in the movement of troops and matériel to Norway, especially in the crucial early weeks of the operation. In 582 transport aircraft, 21 battalions, 9 division and regimental staffs, and a number of mountain artillery batteries were moved, plus naval personnel and equipment and air force ground personnel and equipment. It was estimated that the air transport units flew 13,018 missions, carrying a total of 29,280 men and 2,376 tons of supplies.[23]

Diplomatic and Political Moves

Arriving at the foreign ministry shortly after 0500 on 9 April, the German Minister found the Norwegian Foreign Minister waiting for him. The Cabinet had been in session at the Foreign Ministry throughout the night, and the German demands were quickly presented and as quickly rejected. At 0550 Pohlman, the Military Plenipotentiary, reported to Group XXI that the Norwegian Government had declared, "We will not submit. The battle is already in progress." [24] An hour and a half later he telegraphed that there were still no warships at Oslo and no aircraft over the city.[25] While Braeuer and Pohlman awaited the arrival of their troops, the Norwegian royal family, the Cabinet, and most of the members of Parliament were able to leave the capital in a special train which took them to Hamar 70 miles inland. Later in the day the Government moved to Elverum, 50 miles from the Swedish border, where, during the night, German parachute troops made an unsuccessful attempt to capture the king.[26]

The departure of the government left the capital in a state of confusion, and the civilian population began to evacuate the city. Shortly after noon Braeuer issued an appeal to the government to stop the resistance and attempted through radio broadcasts to bring the evacuation to a halt.[27] The most serious consequence of the government's leaving

[23] Oberst a.D. Greffrath, "*Der Norwegen-Feldzug 1940.*" Hubatsch, *op. cit.*, p. 378.
[24] *Pohlman/Braeuer, Nr. 487 an das Auswaertige Amt, An Gruppe XXI, 9. April,* in *Gruppe XXI, Doppelstuecke, Durchschlaege von Abschriften eines Teiles der Anlagen zum Ktb. 2–3.* AOK 20 E 288/1.
[25] *Pohlman/Braeuer, Nr. 490, 9. April, 0720, An Auswaertiges Amt fuer Gruppe XXI,* in *Gruppe XXI, Doppelstuecke, loc. cit.*
[26] Derry, *op. cit.*, p. 37.
[27] *Telefonische Meldung des Deutschen Gesandten in Oslo an das Ministerbuero von 15.10 Uhr bis 15.30 Uhr, 9. April 1940,* in *Gruppe XXI, Doppelstuecke, loc. cit.*

was that it gave Quisling a chance to come forward with a cabinet of his own, which he did promptly on 9 April. The question of what to do with Quisling had not been decided in advance. The Germans knew that he had no popular support; and, in any event, the principal objective of Group XXI was to achieve a peaceful settlement with the existing Norwegian Government as quickly as possible. But once he had managed to appear on the scene, he received the backing of Rosenberg and Hitler, and thereafter the negotiations included a demand that the king accept a government under Quisling.

On the afternoon of the 9th the Norwegian Government agreed to reopen negotiations, and the king received Braeuer on the following day. Braeuer believed there was a strong desire to reach a settlement, but the king refused to permit Quisling to form a government. Later the Foreign Minister informed Braeuer that the resistance would continue "as far as possible." [28] After a German air attack on 11 April the Royal Headquarters was moved north and, in the course of April, was transferred to Tromsö. Braeuer made several further attempts through intermediaries to reopen conversations. On the 14th, through the Bishop of Oslo, he stated his willingness to drop Quisling; but the Norwegian Foreign Minister, by then convinced that a successful Allied counterattack would be launched, refused to enter into negotiations.[29] Several days later Braeuer, who had been saddled with most of the blame for the failure of the negotiations, was recalled. Admiral Raeder, for one, believed that a more determined and energetic man would have taken immediate steps to arrest the government at any cost.[30] Hitler had, in fact, ordered on 2 April that the kings of Norway and Denmark were under no circumstances to be permitted to leave their countries and were to be placed under guard in their residences; but it is difficult to imagine how Braeuer could have arrested the government with the forces at his disposal on the morning of 9 April.[31]

That Quisling, who was regarded as a traitor, could not form a viable government was apparent immediately. Braeuer reported that the rising unrest in the occupied areas could be traced less to the German occupation than to general opposition to Quisling. As a consequence, in an attempt to establish some sort of governing authority without completely abandoning Quisling, the so-called Administrative Council was formed on 15 April. It came into being as a result of negotiations between Braeuer and the Chief Justice of the Norwegian Supreme Court, Paal Berg. Consisting of men prominent in business and public affairs, it was to take charge of internal administration of the occupied

[28] *Telephonischer Bericht vom Gesandten Braeuer, Olso an das Buero des Reichsaussenministers, 10. April 1940, 2230 Uhr,* in *Gruppe XXI, Doppelstuecke, loc. cit.*
[29] Hubatsch, *op. cit.,* pp. 162–64.
[30] *Fuehrer Conferences,* p. 42.
[31] *OKW, WFA, Abt. L, Nr. 22125/40, Betr., Besetzung von Daenemark und Norwegen,* in *Gruppe XXI, Ia, Anlagenband 1 zum Ktb. Nr. 1, Anlagen 1–52, 20.2–8.2.1940.* AOK 20 E 180/7.

Bandsmen emplaning for Oslo, 9 April 1940.

areas, but it did not constitute a government and did not regard itself as such. Quisling, not included in the Administrative Council, was assigned a post as commissioner for demobilization. His puppet government thus terminated after an existence of less than a week.[32]

On 19 April Hitler informed Falkenhorst that a state of war existed between Norway and Germany and that the Administrative Council had no political rights or authority. He gave Falkenhorst full authority to take all the measures necessary for the rapid conquest and pacification of the country. Severity was recommended.[33] On the same day Hitler appointed Joseph Terboven, an old-line Nazi Party official, as Reichskommissar for the Occupied Norwegian Territories and in a decree of 24 April gave him the supreme governmental power in the civilian sector.[34] The latter decision ran directly counter to the accepted Ger-

[32] Braeuer, *Fernschreiben nach Berlin fuer Reichsminister* [draft telegram], *14 April*, in *Gruppe XXI, Anlagenband 3 zum K.T.B. Nr. 2.u.3., 13.4.–18.4.40.* AOK 20 E 279/3. Halvdan Koht, *Norway Neutral and Invaded* (New York, 1941), pp. 131ff. U.S. Department of State, *Documents on German Foreign Policy, 1918–1945* (Washington, 1956), Series D, Vol. IX, pp. 161, 168–72, and 195–97.
[33] *Der Fuehrer und Oberste Befehlshaber der Wehrmacht, OKW, Nr. 104/40, 19.4.40*, in *Gruppe XXI, Anlagenband 4 zum K.T.B. Nr. 2.u.3., 19.4.40–23.4.40.* AOK 20 E 279/4.
[34] Between the dismissal of Braeuer and the appointment of Terboven Gauleiter Alfred Frauenfeld held the position of Reich Plenipotentiary for a few days. After a quick look at the confused situation in Norway, Frauenfeld decided to return to the quiet of his German Gau.

man doctrine that, in a zone of operations, the commanding general of an army exercised the executive power as long as operations were in progress; and it paved the way for an endless series of disputes between the German military and civilian authorities in Norway.

The Occupation of Denmark

The operations of the XXXI Corps in Denmark were destined to go entirely according to plan. Moving up from their assembly areas in north Germany the 11th Motorized Rifle Brigade and the 170th Infantry Division bivouacked during the night of 8 April along the road Schleswig–Flensburg. Elements of the 198th Division transferred to Warnemuende, Travemuende, and Kiel so that they could begin embarkation on the night of 7 April.[35]

At 0515 on the morning of the 9th, the 11th Motorized Rifle Brigade and the 170th Infantry Division crossed the border on a broad front with the weight of the attack directed northward from Tondern and Flensburg. The weak Danish forces at the border were not capable of staging serious resistance, and German tanks quickly broke the few pockets of resistance which developed. To prevent the destruction of bridges near the border, special small units had been sent in before W Hour. At 0730 a parachute platoon and a battalion of the 69th Infantry Division transported by air took possession of the airfields at Aalborg. By 0800 the Danish Army had halted its resistance, and German forces were able to advance northward unimpeded, with elements of the 11th Motorized Rifle Brigade reaching Aalborg during the course of the day. At 1100 Group 10, composed mostly of minesweepers, put in at Esbjerg to be followed the next morning by Group 11, which landed at Tyborön. The Danish railways were taken over intact, with the result that rail contact with Aalborg could be established on the 9th.[36]

The ships of Group 7 loaded at Kiel. The staff of the 198th Infantry Division and a reinforced infantry battalion were embarked aboard the *Schleswig-Holstein* and two merchant steamers for the landing at Korsör, while a torpedo boat and two minesweepers took aboard the company for Nyborg. Before dawn on the morning of the 9th, as the formation passed through the Great Belt, the *Schleswig-Holstein* ran aground and had to be left behind. The landings were accomplished without opposition, and beachheads were quickly established. The force at Korsör was increased during the morning when merchant ships brought in

---

[35] Hubatsch, *op. cit.*, pp. 93ff.
[36] *Befehlshaber der deutschen Truppen in Daenemark (Hoeheres Kommando XXXI), Ia, Nr. 279/40, Bericht ueber die Besetzung Daenemarks am 9. und 10.4.40, und die dabei gemachten Erfahrungen,* in *Befehlshaber der deutschen Truppen in Daenemark, Besetzung Daenemarks am 9. u. 10.4.40, Abt. Ia und Ic.* XXXI AK E 290/2. Hubatsch, *op. cit.*, pp. 94, 96.

a reinforced infantry regiment; by 1300, elements had crossed Sjaelland and were in Copenhagen. On the west coast of Fuenen, Group 9 (a merchant steamer and a number of small craft) had landed a battalion at Middelfart at 0630 to secure the bridge across the Little Belt. Farther south a battalion crossed from Warnemuende to Gedser aboard two train ferries and advanced northward across Falster to Vordingborg where, with the assistance of a parachute company, it had established a secure bridgehead by 0730. On the afternoon of the 9th XXXI Corps ordered the occupation of Bornholm off the Swedish south coast—an operation which was carried out by one battalion on the following day.[37]

The mission of Group 8, consisting of the motorship *Hansestadt Danzig* carrying an infantry battalion and escorted by an icebreaker and two picket boats, was predominantly political and psychological. Hitler had ordered the landing of a "representative" force at Copenhagen to give emphasis to the diplomatic negotiations. Falkenhorst proposed having the battalion march into the city to the accompaniment of band music; but Kaupisch decided, instead, to stage an assault on the Citadel, the old fortress overlooking the harbor, and take the guards regiment quartered there prisoner.[38] On 4 April the major in command of the landing force had traveled to Copenhagen in civilian clothes, where he scouted the landing possibilities and was shown through the Citadel by a Danish sergeant. The landing, on 9 April, was accomplished without a hitch. The fort at the entrance to the harbor brought the ships under its searchlights but could not fire even a warning shot because of grease in the gun barrels. At 0735 the German commander reported the Citadel occupied without resistance.[39]

At 2300 on 8 April Minister von Renthe-Fink received his instructions from General Himer who had arrived in Copenhagen in civilian clothes on the 7th accompanied by a legation secretary from the Foreign Ministry. In coded messages to the XXXI Corps, Himer on the 8th reported the harbor ice-free and confirmed the fact that the weak point of the Citadel was at its southeast corner. On the morning of the 9th, for an hour after the landing, he was able to keep open a direct telephone connection to the headquarters of the XXXI Corps at Hamburg and give a running account of the capture of the Citadel and the progress of negotiations. The Danish Government capitulated at 0720, after Himer, to speed up the deliberations of the Ministerial Council, had

---

[37] *198. Inf. Div., Abt. Ia, Bericht ueber die Besetzung der daenischen Inseln Seeland, Fuenen, Falster und Bornholm durch die 198. Inf. Division am 9. und 10.4.40; Infanterie Regiment 308, Bericht ueber die Unternehmung der Abteilung Oberstleutnant Schultz gegen Seeland/Daenemark, in Hoeh. Kdo. z.b.V. XXXI, Sammelakte ueber die Besetzung Daenemarks, 9.4.–31.4.1940.* XXXI AK E 290/1.

[38] *Unternehmen Daenemark (am 9. April 1940), in Hoeh. Kdo. z.b.V., Sammelakte, loc. cit.*

[39] *Major Glein, Kommandeur I./I.R. 308, Bericht ueber die Landung in Kopenhagen und Besetzung der dortigen Zitadelle am 9.4.40, in Hoeh. Kdo. z.b.V., XXXI, Sammelakte, loc. cit.* Hubatsch, *op. cit.*, p. 98.

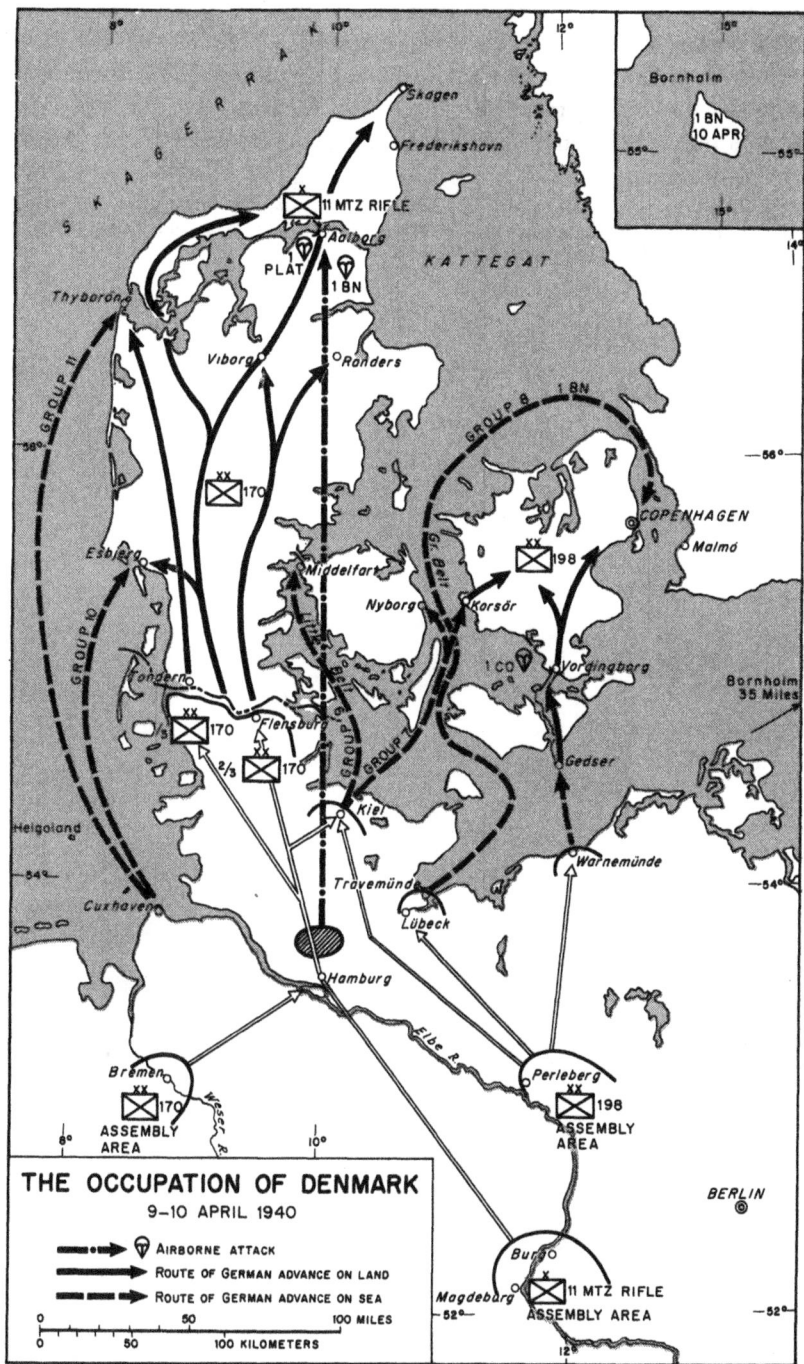

SKAGERRAK

Bornholm

1 BN
10 APR

Skagen

Frederikshavn

11 MTZ RIFLE

Aalborg

KATTEGAT

PLAT   1 BN

GROUP II

Thyborøn

Viborg   Randers

GROUP B   1 BN

GROUP 10

Esbjerg

56°

170

COPENHAGEN

Malmö

198

Middelfart

Nyborg   Korsør

Tønder

Flensburg

170

2/3   170

1 CO   Vordingborg

Bornholm
35 Miles

Heligoland

Kiel

Gedser

Cuxhaven

Travemünde

Warnemünde

Lübeck

54°

Hamburg

Elbe R.

Bremen

Perleberg

198

ASSEMBLY
AREA

Weser R.

170

ASSEMBLY
AREA

BERLIN

THE OCCUPATION OF DENMARK
9–10 APRIL 1940

AIRBORNE ATTACK
ROUTE OF GERMAN ADVANCE ON LAND
ROUTE OF GERMAN ADVANCE ON SEA

Burg

Magdeburg   11 MTZ RIFLE
52°   ASSEMBLY AREA

0   50   100 MILES
0   50   100 KILOMETERS

J. Schueren

Map 3

61

told Renthe-Fink to inform it that, unless an immediate decision were forthcoming, Copenhagen would be bombed.   Later in the day Himer requested an audience with the king in order to ascertain his attitude and to be able if necessary to prevent his leaving the country.   At 1000, negotiations regarding demobilization of the Danish armed forces began.[40]

---

[40] *Befehlshaber der Deutschen Truppen in Daenemark (Hoeheres Kommando XXXI), Ia Nr. 279/40, Anlage 2, Die diplomatische Aktion am 9.4.1940,* in *Befehlshaber der deutschen Truppen in Daenemark, loc. cit.*

Chapter 4

Operations in Southern and Central Norway

The Command Crisis

By the fourth day Operation WESERUEBUNG had entered a new phase. The enemy had reacted, isolating the regiment at Narvik; and it took no clairvoyance to envision similar developments at Trondheim or Bergen. The WESERUEBUNG plan had failed to achieve its most important objective, a Norwegian surrender that would give Group XXI control of the interior lines of communication needed to link up its landing teams. A strategy conference at Fuehrer Headquarters on 13 April decided that, if the situation in Norway deteriorated badly, the issue would not be forced there; instead the attack in the west would be launched within eight or ten days to draw off Allied pressure.[1] The weather, which continued cold and rainy, reduced the chances of applying that solution. Confronted for the first time with a possible defeat, Hitler panicked.

On the afternoon of 13 April, with results of the final British attack on the destroyers not yet known in Berlin, Hitler ordered Dietl to defend Narvik under all circumstances, but a day later he became convinced that the situation at Narvik was hopeless. On the 14th he disclosed his belief that Narvik could not be held to the Commander in Chief, Army, Generaloberst Walter von Brauchitsch, and "in a state of frightful agitation" proposed ordering Dietl to give up Narvik and withdraw southward overland.[2] The next day, after the OKH expressed opposition to the projected evacuation of Narvik, General Jodl, Chief of the Operations Staff, OKW, explained that the question of complete evacuation had not yet been decided, but the city of Narvik could not be held, and the troops were to be withdrawn into the mountains.[3]

Two days later Hitler insisted that Dietl's force either be ordered to withdraw into Sweden or be evacuated by air. Jodl maintained that a withdrawal into Sweden was "impossible," and that an air evacuation would save only part of the troops, result in a heavy loss of

---

[1] *Halder Diary*, Vol. III, p. 113.
[2] *3. Geb. Div., K.T.B. Narvik*, p. 6. *Halder Diary*, Vol. III, p. 113. *Jodl Diary*, 14 Apr 40.
[3] *Halder Diary*, Vol. III, p. 114.

planes, and shatter the morale of the Narvik force. In any case, Germany did not have enough long-range aircraft to execute the evacuation. Jodl also opposed Hitler's earlier intention of instructing Dietl to withdraw southward and brought in a professor with expert knowledge of Norway to prove that the terrain south of Narvik was impassable even for mountain troops.[4]

Nevertheless, on the afternoon of the 17th, the Operations Staff, OKW, without being previously consulted, received for transmittal an order signed by Hitler giving Dietl discretionary authority to withdraw his force into Sweden and be interned. The OKH feared that execution of the order would impair the morale of the entire Army; therefore, to counteract it, Brauchitsch dispatched a message to Dietl, congratulating him on his recent promotion to Generalleutnant and expressing "the conviction" that he would "defend Narvik even against a superior enemy."[5] In the OKW the Hitler order was held up long enough for Jodl to argue the case with Hitler once more. By evening Jodl was able to get Hitler's signature on a new order instructing Dietl to hold Narvik as long as possible and then to withdraw along the railroad into the interior. The possibility that picked troops might withdraw southward was left for further investigation.[6]

The achievement of a more rational and determined attitude with regard to the situation at Narvik did not end the crisis; and Jodl, on 19 April, complained of incipient chaos in the high-level conduct of the Norwegian operation. Goering was demanding stronger action against the population and attempted to create an impression that guerrilla warfare and sabotage were widespread in Norway. He complained, too, that the Navy was leaving the burden of troop transportation to the Air Force. The appointment of Terboven as Reichskommissar for Norway also aroused misgivings in the OKW, which doubted whether his authority could be sufficiently circumscribed to preclude interference in military affairs and saw in his appointment a shift toward repression in civilian affairs. The OKW, having no interest in fighting an extended campaign against the Norwegians, wanted to avoid stirring up either active or passive resistance.[7]

Meanwhile, Allied landings in the vicinity of Trondheim had provided a new cause for concern. The British Chiefs of Staff, having first considered a direct attack on the city, came gradually to favor an envelopment from the north and south as less risky. On 14 April a British naval party went ashore at Namsos. Two days later a British brigade, diverted from the force for Narvik, followed, and on the 19th

---

[4] *Jodl Diary,* 17 Apr 40.

[5] Generaloberst a.D. Franz Halder, Comments on Part I, *The German Northern Theater of Operations 1940–1945,* 12 Nov 56. *3. Geb. Div., K.T.B. Narvik,* p. 9. *Halder Diary,* Vol. III, p. 117.

[6] *3. Geb. Div., K.T.B. Narvik,* pp. 9, 10, 13. *Jodl Diary* 17, 18 Apr 40. Dietl, *op. cit.,* p. 107.

[7] *Jodl Diary,* 19, 20 Apr 40.

three French battalions landed.   At Åndalsnes, south of Trondheim, a British brigade debarked on 18 April, following a naval party which had landed a day earlier.   On the 19th the Allies had a total of 8,000 men ashore at Namsos and Åndalsnes.[8]

The Allied threat to Trondheim threw Hitler into a renewed state of agitation.   On 21 April the slow progress of the advance north from Oslo led him to cancel transfer of the 11th Motorized Brigade to Norway and to substitute the 2d Mountain Division.   A day later he proposed using the liners *Bremen* and *Europa* to transport a division to Trondheim but reluctantly gave way after Raeder protested that the entire fleet would be needed to escort the ships and that the probable outcome would be the loss of both transports and the fleet.   Several days later, to the dismay of the OKH, which saw its best troops being sluiced off to Norway while the campaign against France was in the offing, Hitler ordered the 1st Mountain Division readied for transport to Norway. Before that division could be dispatched, Group XXI had established land contact between Oslo and Trondheim, and the Allied evacuation had begun.[9]

The Advance Northward from Oslo

The Breakout

For the Germans Oslo was the key to the occupation of Norway.[10] Once the city was firmly in their hands they had a secure base, reasonably safe lines of communication back to Germany, and access to the important routes through the interior of the country.   Although none of those was ever in doubt, the Oslo landing, quite aside from its being the most costly and the least successful of the landings in Norway, seriously affected the whole further course of the campaign.   The WESERUEBUNG plan had been devised to exploit the effects of shock, which was expected to give the German forces command of the situation at all points and to throw the Norwegians into confusion.   At Oslo it failed.   The overwhelming attack which was supposed to paralyze the Norwegian Government and people came in driblets.   While the Norwegians had time to think, the Germans themselves were thrown off balance temporarily.   They recovered fast, but in the interval the quick victory they had gambled on had slipped out of their grasp.

In Oslo on the night of 9 April Group XXI had seven companies of infantry and two parachute companies.   The next morning, as elements

---

[8] Derry, *op. cit.,* pp. 68ff. Butler, *op. cit.,* pp. 136ff.
[9] *Jodl Diary,* 23, 29 Apr 40. *Fuehrer Conferences,* 1940, I, p. 38.
[10] In this section extensive use has been made of two articles, *"Die Kaempfe um die Landverbindung nach Drontheim im April 1940," Teil I* and *Teil II,* which appeared as parts of the three-part series *"Aus dem Feldzug in Norwegen"* published in Nos. 2, 3, and 4, *Jahrgang* 1941, of the *Militaerwissenschaftliche Rundschau* by the German Army General Staff.

of the 163d Division arrived and the airlift resumed, Group XXI considered dispatching a battalion to Bergen and another to Trondheim by rail, but it was too late for that. The Norwegian 1st and 2d Divisions were mobilizing near Oslo, and the Norwegians, both people and government, were displaying more determination than had been anticipated. As he waited another two days for the 1st and 2d Sea Transport Echelons to bring in the main forces of the 163d and 196th Divisions, Falkenhorst decided to proceed more cautiously than the WESERUEBUNG plan originally intended. He made it his first order of business to establish a secure foothold at Oslo and gain access to the main interior lines of communication.[11]

On 12 and 13 April Group XXI issued orders setting in motion an advance southeast of Oslo to the Swedish border and thrusts northward, northwestward, and westward from Oslo to take possession of the rail connections to Trondheim, Bergen, and Kristiansand. The 196th Division, assigned the sector east of Oslo, was to send two battalions southward to secure Fredrikstad, Sarpsborg, and Halden, a regiment (less one battalion) eastward to Kongsvinger, and a battalion (at the outset) northward in the direction of Hamar. The 163d Division, operating in and west of Oslo, was to provide security troops for the city, occupy the junction of the Bergen railroad at Hönefoss, and advance along the Kristiansand railline as far as Kongsberg.[12] To give the enemy as little time as possible for assembly, the striking forces were motorized, mostly by improvisation in requisitioned vehicles. As was to become characteristic of the Norwegian campaign, the divisions operated not as units but in tactical groupings which themselves varied greatly in size and composition and were subject almost daily to changes in strength as elements were detached or new troops arrived.

The advance went smoothly in all directions. Units of the 196th Division took Fredrikstad and Sarpsborg on 13 April and occupied Halden and the border fortresses at Trögstad, Mysen, and Greaaker on 14 April. Within three days the entire southeastern tip of Norway, important for its road and railroad connections with Sweden, was in German hands. One thousand Norwegian troops were captured, and 3,000, including the commanding general of the Norwegian 1st Division, were forced across the Swedish border.[13] On the east a unit advanced toward Kongsvinger, and in the north motorized troops and a mountain battalion going by rail reached the southern tip of Mjösa Lake via Eidsvoll. On the 12th, elements of the 163d Division took Kongsberg,

[11] *Gruppe XXI, Taegliche Meldungen der Gruppe XXI an OKW, 9.4.40–14.6.40*, pp. 2–14. AOK 20 E 278/3a.
[12] *Gruppe XXI, Ia, Operationsbefehl fuer die Besetzung von Suednorwegen, 12.4.1940*, in *Anlagenband 1 zum Ktb. Nr. 2 u.3, 8.4.–18.4.40*. AOK 20 E 279/1. *Gruppe XXI, Ia, Operationsbefehl fuer die Fortsetzung der Saeuberung Suednorwegens, 13.4.1940*, in *Anlagenband 3 zum Ktb. Nr. 2 u. 3, 13.4–18.4.40*. AOK 20 E 279/3.
[13] *Gruppe XXI, Taegliche Meldungen, loc. cit.*, pp. 14–16. Derry, *op. cit.*, p. 101.

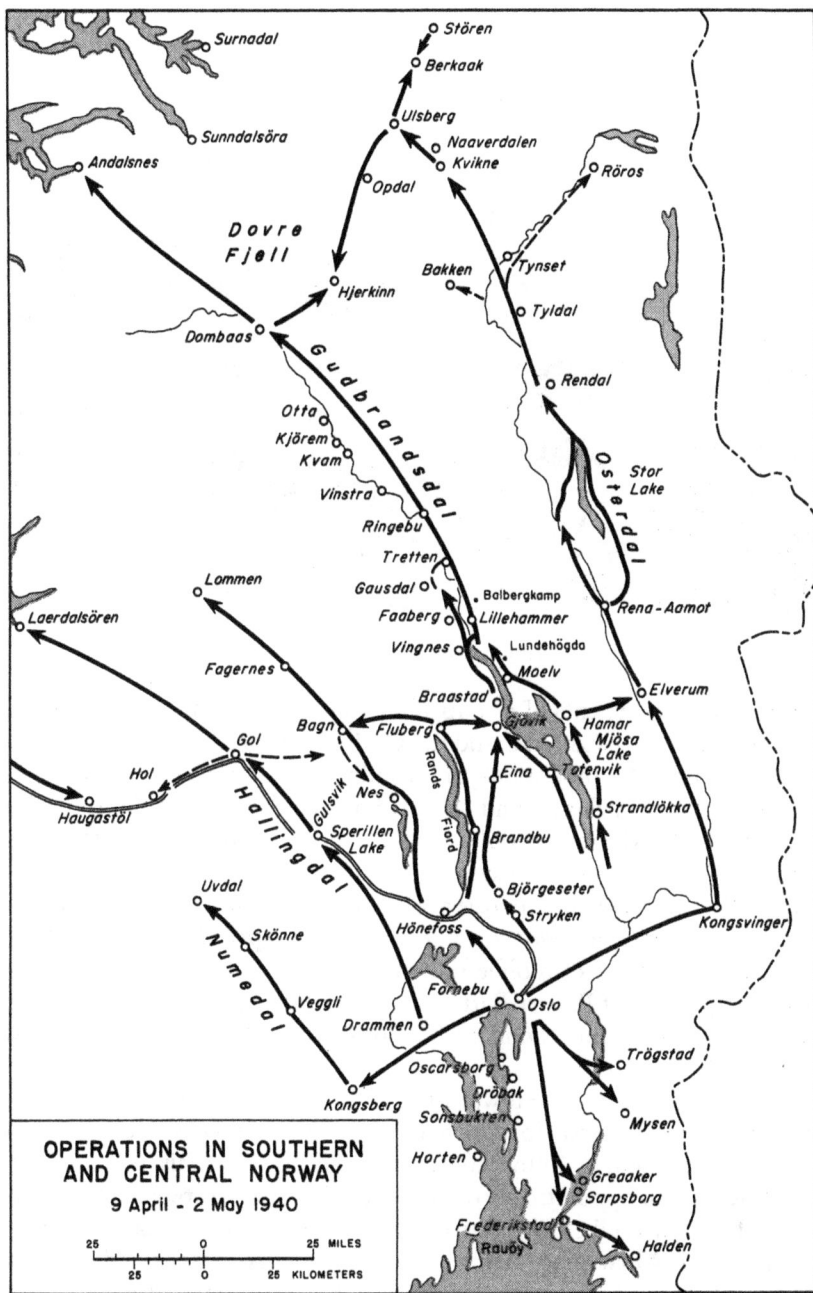

Map 4

OPERATIONS IN SOUTHERN AND CENTRAL NORWAY
9 April - 2 May 1940

Map labels: Surnadal, Sunndalsöra, Andalsnes, Stören, Berkaak, Ulsberg, Naaverdalen, Kvikne, Röros, Opdal, *Dovre Fjell*, Bakken, Tynset, Hjerkinn, Tyldal, Dombaas, *Gudbrandsdal*, Rendal, Otta, Kjörem, Kvam, *Österdal*, Stor Lake, Vinstra, Ringebu, Tretten, Lommen, Gausdal, Balbergkamp, Laerdalsören, Faaberg, Lillehammer, Rena - Aamot, Fagernes, Vingnes, Lundehögda, Braastad, Moelv, Elverum, Bagn, Fluberg, Gjövik, Hamar, Mjösa Lake, Gol, *Hallingdal*, *Rands Fjord*, Eina, Totenvik, Hol, Nes, Haugastöl, Sperillen Lake, Strandlökka, Brandbu, *Numedal*, Brandbu, Uvdal, Björgeseter, Skönne, Hönefoss, Stryken, Kongsvinger, Veggli, Fornebu, Drammen, Oslo, Oscarsborg, Trögstad, Kongsberg, Dröbak, Sonsbukten, Mysen, Horten, Greaaker, Sarpsborg, Frederikstad, Rauöy, Halden

L. Booth

where the Norwegian 3d Infantry Regiment surrendered a day later; and on the morning of the 14th Hönefoss was taken.[14]   With this, the major points in the immediate area of Oslo were secured, and the stage was set for more extensive operations into the interior.

---

[14] *Gruppe XXI, Taegliche Meldungen, loc. cit.,* pp. 15–18.

Improvised Armored Train

On 14 April elements of Group XXI were in position to strike toward the entrances to the Österdal and the Gudbrandsdal, the valley approach routes through the mountains to Trondheim. The Österdal opens in the south at Kongsvinger, and the Mjösa Lake lies astride the southern entrance to the Gudbrandsdal. In the Gudbrandsdal a road and railroad run to Åndalsnes, connecting with the Trondheim railroad at Dombaas. To complete the conquest of Norway south of Trondheim the Germans had to take these two valleys. On 13 April Group XXI began moving in a number of mobile units to aid the advance: the remainder (two companies) of Panzer Battalion 40, the 4th, 13th, and 14th Motorized Machine Gun Battalions, and a motorized battalion of the "General Goering" Regiment.[15]

The Germans' advance toward the entrances to the valleys was bringing them into the area in which the new Norwegian Commander in Chief, Generalmajor Otto Ruge, intended to stage his main effort. The last-minute appointment of Ruge, on 11 April, to replace Generalmajor Kristian Laake, who retired because of age, epitomized the condition of the Norwegian Army. Despite the six-months'-old war on the mainland and the recent conflict in Finland, very little had been done to strengthen and modernize the Army. Up to the day the Germans landed, and even afterward, Norwegian opinion at all levels was strongly influenced, on the one hand, by a conviction that war was futile and, on the other, by a single-minded, almost complacent, dedi-

---

[15] *Der Chef des Oberkommandos der Wehrmacht, WFA, Abt. L, Nr. 753/40, 13.4.40,* in *Anlagenband 3 zum Ktb. Nr. 2 u. 3, 13.4.–18.4.40.* AOK 20 E 279/3.

cation to the principle of neutrality. Even though the recent crises, particularly that in Finland, had brought a partial transition from near-total unpreparedness, the Army was still in no wise on a war footing. It had no tanks or antitank weapons, and the Army Air Force had a total of 41 combat aircraft.[16] On 9 April the coastal forts at Oslo, Kristiansand, Bergen, and Trondheim were manned at about one-third of full strength.[17] The only sizable increase in the Army's field forces was in the far north. There the 6th Division had 7,100 men stationed at and north of Narvik, most of them in the zone along the Finnish border north of Tromsö. The remaining five divisions had a total strength of 8,220 men. To those were added 950 men in the Army Air Force, 1,800 in air defense, and 300 security guards.[18] By the time mobilization began, much of the Army's supplies and equipment and the key centers of telephone and telegraph communications were in German hands.

When General Ruge arrived at the Army headquarters, then located in Rena in the Österdal, on the morning of 11 April, he had effective command of only one unit, the 2d Division, which was mobilizing north of Oslo. The Germans had already captured the supply depots closest to Oslo and were bombing the others as they located them. The division had almost no artillery, and the mobilization was hampered by snarled communications and contradictory orders being issued from the German-controlled capital. Ruge knew that an offensive or even a stationary defense was out of the question, but he had a hope that the Allies would bring effective aid quickly. He also knew that the Trondheim area offered the best possibilities for an Allied counteroperation; therefore, he decided not to risk pitched battles but to attempt to slow up the German northward advance enough to preserve for the Allied forces a favorable field for operations against Trondheim and access to the routes by which southern Norway could be reconquered. The 2d Division would begin the resistance along a line stretching roughly from the southern tip of Rands Fiord to the mouth of the Österdal.[19]

On 14 April the OKW, worried by an Air Force report that British destroyers were in the harbor at Åndalsnes, ordered Group XXI to speed up the advance, using all the means at its disposal to take possession of the railroad Oslo–Hamar–Dombaas as far as Åndalsnes and, secondarily, to Trondheim. Hitler personally ordered parachute troops committed immediately to take the railroad junction at Dombaas.[20]

[16] *OKH, GenStdH, Kriegswissenschaftlichen Abt.*, maps and charts for a study entitled *Die Eroberung Norwegens und die Besetzung Daenemarks*, Chart "*Die Wehrmacht Norwegens am 9.4.1940.*" AOK 20 85517.
[17] Ibid., chart "*Norwegens Kuestenbefestigungen am 9.4.1940 frueh.*"
[18] *Ibid.*, chart "*Die Wehrmacht Norwegens am 9.4.1940.*"
[19] O. Munthe-Kass, *Krigen I Norge 1940* (Oslo: Gyldenal Norsk Forlag, 1955), Bind I, pp. 17–20, 127, 131, 143. W. Brandt, *Krieg in Norwegen* (Zurich: Europa Verlag, 1942), pp. 62–67.
[20] *Gruppe XXI, Ia, Nr. 266/40, OKW, WFA, Nr. 88/40, 14.4.40, in Anlagenband 3 zum Ktb. Nr. 2 u. 3.13.4.–18.4.40.* AOK 20 E 279/3.

The X Air Corps landed one parachute company at Dombaas that same day, only to learn afterward that Goering thought the Air Force was already carrying too much of the burden in Norway and refused to supply any more troops. The company at Dombaas, isolated in enemy territory, had to surrender five days later.[21] Still trying for a quick solution, Group XXI planned a second airborne operation for 16 April. Its object was to bypass the Norwegian defenses in the Rands Fiord–Mjösa Lake area. A battalion of infantry and a company of parachute troops were to be landed on the ice at the northern end of Mjösa Lake and, after taking Lillehammer, were to advance up the Gudbrandsdal to Dombaas. That operation had to be canceled because the Air Force claimed "technical difficulties." [22]

While the last attempts to achieve a quick breakthrough to Trondheim were still in progress, Group XXI began positioning its forces for an advance to the north. On 14 April the 196th Division already had one column pushing east toward Kongsvinger and another at the southern tip of Mjösa Lake. On the same day a motorized battalion of the 163d Division began reconnoitering northward between Rands Fiord and Mjösa Lake.[23] When it became involved in heavy fighting with Norwegian troops defending a barricade of felled trees south of Stryken, a newly arrived regiment of the 181st Division was moved up in support.

On 15 April the 163d Division halted its advance along the Bergen railroad and began to push northward in the area between the Sperillen and Mjösa Lakes. The division formed three columns: the regiment on the right advancing from Stryken in the direction of Gjövik, two battalions in the center moving from Hönefoss along the eastern shore of Rands Fiord toward Fluberg, and two battalions on the left moving along the east shore of Sperillen Lake toward Bagn. The battalions in the center had a company of light tanks, and the battalions on the left, two tanks. As tanks and motorized forces became available they were assigned to all the forces in the northward advance, where they proved extremely valuable since the Norwegians had no tanks of their own nor any effective antitank weapons. On the 16th the right column of the 163d Division reached Björgeseter; that in the center reached the southern tip of Rands Fiord; and that on the left reached nearly to Skagnes at the northern end of Sperillen Lake.

In the sector of the 196th Division a three-pronged advance was also developing. Two battalions took Kongsvinger on the 16th, opening the

---

[21] *Gruppe XXI, Ia, Nr. 284/40, Lage in Norwegen, 18.4.40,* in *Anlagenband 4 zum Ktb. Nr. 2 u. 3, 19.4.–23.4.40.* AOK 20 E 279/4.
[22] *Gruppe XXI, Ia, Nr. 270/40, Befehl fuer Luftlandung bei Lillehammer, 16.4.40,* in *Anlagenband 3 zum Ktb. Nr. 2 u. 3, 13.4–18.4.40.* AOK 20 E 279/3. *Gruppe XXI, Ia, Nr. 270/40, 16.4.40,* in *Anlagenband 3 zum Ktb. 2 u. 3, 13.4.– 18.4.40.* AOK 20 E 279/3.
[23] *Gruppe XXIa, Ia, Nr. 265/40. Operationsbefehl, 14.4.40,* in *Anlagenband 3 zum Ktb. Nr. 2 u. 3, 13.4.–18.4.40.* AOK 20 E 279/3.

Infantry advancing north of Oslo.

way to the Österdal and gaining control of the railroad to Sweden. Two columns, each in battalion strength, were advancing along the east and west shores of Mjösa Lake. One had reached Totenvik on the west shore, but heavy resistance at Strandlökka held up the other.

From the southern tip of Rands Fiord to Kongsvinger the German units reported meeting stubborn resistance as they encountered the Norwegian 2d Division's defensive line. The terrain was becoming mountainous, and deep snow made movement off the roads nearly impossible.[24] It had been spring in Oslo, but in the highlands away from the coast winter would continue unbroken for another month or more.

On 16 April Group XXI, estimating the Norwegian strength at 15,000 men, ordered all groups to continue the advance northward and, with the exception of the battalions in the Österdal which were to proceed toward Elverum, to converge on Lillehammer at the mouth of the Gudbrandsdal. The 163d Division, which at the time had four regiments, two of its own and one each from the 69th and 181st Divisions, received the additional mission of providing security forces for the areas southeast and southwest of Oslo.[25] The OKL assigned one bomber group on the 17th to support the northward advance of Group XXI. Most of the planes continued to operate from German bases; but a squadron at the disposal of Group XXI at Oslo at least partly solved the problems raised by the separate command of the air forces.[26]

---

[24] *Gruppe XXI, Taegliche Meldungen, loc. cit.,* pp. 23–25.
[25] *Gruppe XXI, Ia, Nr. 272/40, Operationsbefehl zur Vernichtung der norweg. Kraeftsgruppe im Raum beiderseits des Mjösa Sees, 16.4.40,* in *Anlagenband 3 zum Ktb. 2 u. 3, 13.4.–18.4.40.* AOK 20 E 279/3.
[26] *Der Chef des Oberkommandos der Wehrmacht, OKW, WFA, Abt. L, Nr. 8–6/40, an Gruppe XXI, 17.4.40,* in *Anlagenband 3 zum Ktb. 2 u. 3, 14.4.–18.4.40.* AOK 20 E 279/3.

71

In the sector of the 196th Division, the battalion on the left flank along the west shore of Mjösa Lake was reinforced by the motorized battalion from Stryken and transferred to the command of the 163d Division. On the 17th, to break the resistance of the Norwegians at Strandlökka, a battalion sent up from Oslo crossed the thawing ice of Mjösa Lake from the west shore to attack the defenses from the rear. The Norwegian troops were forced to withdraw in haste, and, delayed only by roadblocks and demolished bridges, the Germans were able to take Hamar on the night of the 18th. From Hamar a battalion crossed into the Österdal to take Elverum, where, on the 20th, it met the force moving up from Kongsvinger. With that, the force in the Österdal reached full regimental strength. Two battalions remaining at Hamar (an additional battalion had been committed by the 18th) were joined by a motorized machine gun battalion. The regiment in the Österdal met strong resistance south of Rena-Aamot, which it took on the 21st. The force advancing northward from Hamar reached Moelv on the 19th but was then held up for two days by strong positions on the Lundehögda (dominating heights north of Moelv). In the fighting at the Lundehögda British troops appeared in action for the first time but could not influence the course of events. On the night of the 21st, in a daring advance, the motorized machine gun battalion took Lillehammer.

In the sector of the 163d Division the two battalions (joined by a third on the 18th) advancing along the west shore of Mjösa Lake took Gjövik on the 21st and made contact there that same day with the regiment which had been advancing via Stryken, Brandbu, and Eina.[27] The column on the east shore of Rands Fiord reached Fluberg on the 19th and turned eastward toward Gjövik on the 20th, making contact in the vicinity of Vardal with forces from Gjövik maneuvering to outflank enemy resistance on the heights at Braastad. The battalions on the far left flank reached Bagn on the 19th but encountered strong resistance and could not turn east toward Fluberg as ordered because of threats to their rear and flanks; consequently, they withdrew, leaving a security forces at Nes, and moved to Fluberg via Hönefoss and the east shore of Rands Fiord.

As the fighting moved into the Norwegian highlands the German ground tactics were forced into a uniform pattern by the nature of the terrain and the weather. Deep snow and steep valley slopes restricted movement to the roads. Taking advantage of those conditions, the Norwegians based their defense on a series of roadblocks and barricades supported by flanking fire from the heights. The German answer, which proved highly effective, was to employ reinforced infantry spearheads organized in order of march as follows: one or two tanks, two trucks carrying engineers and equipment, an infantry company with heavy weapons organized into assault detachments, a platoon of artillery,

---

[27] *Gruppe XXI, Taegliche Meldungen, loc. cit.,* 36.

a relief infantry company, relief engineers and artillery.   In action the technique was to bring a roadblock under heavy frontal fire while ski troops attempted to work their way around the defenders' flanks. Against strongly held positions small assault detachments were committed under heavy covering fire in an effort to break the line at several places.

To Trondheim

With the capture of Lillehammer and Rena-Aamot Group XXI had completed the conquest of the Oslo region, the heartland of Norway; but its advance units were still 200 miles from Trondheim, and the valley defiles of the Gudbrandsdal and the Österdal favored the defense. In the Gudbrandsdal newly arrived British forces had to be taken into account.   The British 148th Brigade, which landed at Åndalsnes on 18 April, had intended to develop an attack on Trondheim; but the speed of the German advance from the south forced it to turn into the Gudbrandsdal to support the Norwegians.   Five days later the 15th Brigade landed and also moved into the Gudbrandsdal, bringing the total of British troops to between five and six thousand.   While the appearance of British troops worried Hitler, the British from the start had their own troubles, not the least of which was the lack of a satisfactory base.   Åndalsnes was a small fishing port which larger ships visited only during the summer tourist season.   Its dock facilities were completely inadequate for handling heavy military equipment, and it was located well within range of the German Air Force.[28]

On 21 April Hitler assigned the establishment of land contact between Oslo and Trondheim as the main mission of Group XXI.   Operations against Åndalsnes were to be postponed for the time being.[29]   On the same day Group XXI prepared for the next phase of the offensive.   It withdrew the 163d Division from the northward advance and turned it west via Bagn toward the Sogne Fiord to protect the left flank.   The regiment of the 181st Division, which had been attached to the 163d Division, was to continue its advance along the west shore of Mjösa Lake and come under the command of the 196th Division on reaching the north end of the lake.[30]   The reinforced 196th Division, advancing in two columns, one in the Gudbrandsdal and the other in the Österdal, would carry out the advance to Trondheim.

On 22 April elements of the 196th Division advanced out of Lillehammer into the Gudbrandsdal, bypassing the Balbergkamp, a height commanding the entrance to the valley, and forcing the defending British and Norwegian troops into a hasty retreat.   On the following day the British and Norwegians attempted a stand at Tretten, where

[28] Derry, op. cit., pp. 67–74, 77, 104, 105, 119, 138, 143.
[29] Der Fuehrer und Oberste Befehlshaber der Wehrmacht OKW, WFA, Nr. 106/40, in Gruppe XXI, Anlagenband 4 zum Ktb. 2 u. 3, 19.4.–23.4.40.   AOK 20 279/4.
[30] Gruppe XXI, Ia, Nr. 285/40, Operationsbefehl fuer die 163. Division ab 21.4.40, in Anlagenband 4 zum Ktb. 2 u 3, 19.4.–23.4.40.   AOK 20 E 279/4.

Infantrymen taking cover behind a Mark I tank.

the valley bends and narrows to a gorge; but the troops were nearly exhausted, and the British antitank rifles failed to penetrate the German tanks which broke through the main positions along the road and cut off the defenders' forward units. For the British 148th Brigade, the action at Tretten was a disaster. A large number of its troops, including a battalion commander and other officers, were taken prisoner. At the end of the day, what was left of the brigade had to seek refuge 45 miles to the rear in one of the tributary valleys of the Gudbrandsdal.[31] At midnight on 24 April German troops entered Vinstra, halfway between Lillehammer and Dombaas.

In the light of the victory at Tretten and the rapid advance in the Gudbrandsdal, Group XXI no longer saw a need to concentrate first on reaching Trondheim. On 24 April, it ordered the 196th Division to continue its drive via Dombaas to Åndalsnes and complete the destruction of the British forces. The troops in the Österdal were to carry on the advance to Trondheim. The enemy was to be allowed no respite and no opportunity to establish new defensive positions. Henceforth, the tactical groupings were designated by the names of their commanders, Group Pellengahr (Generalleutnant Richard Pellengahr, Commanding General, 196th Division) in the Gudbrandsdal and Group Fischer (Colonel Hermann Fischer, Commanding Officer, 340th Infantry Regiment) in the Österdal. Group Fischer, transferred to the direct command of Group XXI, was composed (on 23 April) of three

---

[31] Derry, *op. cit.*, pp. 110–12.

infantry battalions, two artillery battalions, one engineer battalion, two motorized companies of the "General Goering" Regiment, one motorized machine gun company, and two platoons of tanks. Group Pellengahr (on 26 April) consisted of seven infantry battalions, a motorized machine gun battalion (less one company), two artillery battalions, a company of engineers, and a platoon of tanks.[32]

On 22 April, south of the Gudbrandsdal, the regiment of the 163d Division moving up to join Group Pellengahr pushed past Braastad on the west shore of Mjösa Lake. Encountering artillery fire at Faaberg, two battalions crossed the ice at the northern tip of the lake to Lillehammer on the 24th while one battalion pushed into the Gausdal, threw back the Norwegian troops defending the valley, and on the following day entered the Gudbrandsdal at Tretten. Several days later the 163d Division sent a battalion northward into the Gausdal from Vingnes while Group Pellengahr diverted a detachment including tanks and motorcycle troops southwestward from Tretten. Together they trapped the Norwegian troops in the Gausdal and on 29 April forced the surrender of 250 officers and 3,500 men of the Norwegian 2d Division.

On 23 April at Rena-Aamot in the Österdal, Group Fischer formed its newly arrived tank and motorized troops into a motorized advance detachment. While the mass of the group, held up by demolished bridges, remained at Rena-Aamot, the motorized detachment pushed along the east and west shores of Stor Lake reaching the northern end of the lake on the 24th. As the main force of Group Fischer followed along the eastern shore of the lake, the motorized detachment continued northward throughout the night, reaching Tynset the following morning. There a small reconnaissance party was sent east along the railroad to Röros. Part of the detachment remained in Tynset while part proceeded to Kvikne, arriving there on the same day. Meanwhile, the main force had arrived at Rendal.[33]

Group Pellengahr, moving out from Vinstra on the morning of 25 April, encountered renewed resistance at Kvam. There, at a sharp bend in the valley, the newly arrived British 15th Brigade had established a battalion in strong positions with antitank guns which were able to deal with the German armor. But this time Group Pellengahr had reached its full strength and, except for an artillery battalion held up at the mouth of the Gausdal, was echeloned in depth from Kvam to Ringebu. The fighting continued at Kvam until the night of the 26th as the German infantry attacked and attempted to work its way around

[32] *Gruppe XXI, Ia, Nr. 288/40, Operationsbefehl, 24.4.40, in Anlagenband 5 zum Ktb. Nr. 2. u. 3, 24.4.–30.4.40. AOK 20 E 279/5. 196. I.D., Gliederung der 196. Division, Stand 26.4.40 and Gruppe XXI, Anlage zur Lagenkarte der Gruppe XXI vom 27.4.40, in Anlagenband 19 zum Ktb. 2 u. 3, Kriegsgliederungen, 15.4.–25.4.40. AOK 20 E 279/19.*
[33] *v. Burstin Hauptmann u. Komp.-Chef in der Panzer-Abteilung z.b.V. 40, Bericht ueber den Einsatz der Mot. Voraus-Abteilung bei der Kampfgruppe Fischer im Norwegen Feldzug vom 23.4.40–6.5.50, pp. 1–16. 2. Geb. Div. 8358/1.*

German troops clearing fallen rocks placed as a roadblock.

the British left flank with the support of aircraft and artillery. During the night, the British troops withdrew, having placed a battalion three miles to the rear to hold a narrow spot in the valley near Kjörem while positions were to be prepared farther to the rear at Otta. The British held at Kjörem until nightfall the next day.

On the morning of the 28th the German troops encountered a British battalion in strong positions flanked by steep valley slopes at Otta. Infantry attacks, with tanks, artillery, and air support, and attempts to outflank the British positions failed during the day. In the course of the fighting, evacuation of the Ändalsnes beachhead had been ordered, and the German troops entered Otta the next morning to find the town abandoned.

The British decision to evacuate had been precipitated by German bombing of Ändalsnes and the subsidiary port of Molde on the 26th which rendered both ports practically useless. On the 28th a British battalion established positions south of Dombaas to hold the town while the force from Otta withdrew to Ändalsnes. There, during the afternoon of the 30th, it held off German infantry, advancing without its tanks and artillery which were delayed by a demolished bridge, until nightfall. At midnight the British left Dombaas for Ändalsnes by train. At 2330 on the 30th, naval units began the evacuation from Ändalsnes, which had been subjected to numerous heavy air attacks since the 26th. The evacuation was completed in the early hours of 2 May. Meanwhile, Group Pellengahr brought its rear echelons from Otta to Dombaas by rail, but the destroyed rail and road bridges west of Dombaas forced the forward elements to advance to Åndalsnes on foot. The first German troops reached Åndalsnes in the afternoon of 2 May.[34]

On 27 April the motorized advance detachment of Group Fischer in the Österdal met heavy resistance at Naaverdalen. After the Norwegian positions had been subjected to air bombardment, the Germans occupied the town during the night. During the day, the main force had moved up to Tynset and Tyldal and sent out small units on the flanks to Röros and Bakken. The next morning the motorized detachment moved into Ulsberg and turned northward toward Berkaak where, shortly before noon on the 30th, it made contact with an advance party of 181st Division troops moving southward from Trondheim. With that, the land contact Oslo–Trondheim was established.[35] On 1 May the undamaged railroad running southward from Ulsberg via Opdal to Dombaas could be used to establish contact between Group Pellengahr and Group Fischer. From Opdal a detachment was sent westward to Sunndalsöra where it reached the coast on the 2d; and on 3 May the remainder of the Norwegian 2d Division (123 officers and 2,500 men), trapped between Sundalsöra and Åndalsnes on the snow-covered Dovre Fjell, surrendered.[36]

Operations at Trondheim

On 10 April the landing team at Trondheim held the city and the batteries at the entrance to the fiord and had taken the airfield at Vaernes, 20 miles east of the city, without fighting.[37]

Mobilization of the Norwegian 5th Brigade was in large part frustrated by the capture of its supply depot and most of its artillery in Trondheim. By the 11th the airfield could accommodate transports and bombers, and on the following day seven dive bombers were based there. On the 13th a battalion of infantry was brought in by air, and the arrival of the steamer *Levante* of the Export Echelon with antiaircraft guns, 100-mm. guns, ammunition, and gasoline brought some improvement in the supply situation.[38]

Trondheim ranked next to Oslo as a political center. Located at the terminus of the railroads from Oslo and a rail line to Sweden it was strategically important for the control of central and northern Norway. To the Germans it was particularly important for air communications with Narvik. It was also, next to Narvik, the most promising target for an Allied counterthrust. The immediate German concern, then, was defense against an attack from the sea. For that purpose they manned

---

[34] Derry, *op. cit.*, pp. 119–28, 130, 134, 136, 138.

[35] *v. Burstin Hauptmann u. Komp.-Chef in der Panzer-Abteilung z.b.V. 40, Bericht,* *loc. cit.,* pp. 16–26.

[36] *v. Burstin Hauptmann u. Komp.-Chef in der Panzer-Abteilung z.b.V. 40, Bericht* *loc. cit.,* pp. 25–28. *Gruppe XXI, Taegliche Meldungen, loc. cit.,* pp. 65–69.

[37] In this section extensive use has been made of the article "*Von Drontheim bis Namsos,*" *Teil* III of the series "*Aus dem Feldzug in Norwegen*" (see footnote 10).

[38] *Gruppe XXI, Taegliche Meldungen, loc. cit.,* pp. 7–17.

the captured coastal guns and kept the main body of the landing force available in the city.

The prospect of Allied landings at Namsos and Åndalsnes posed an acute threat to the German force at Trondheim. On the 14th, when air reconnaissance mistakenly reported a British landing at Åndalsnes, the OKW informed Group XXI that its most important mission was to establish a secure beachhead at Trondheim and to smash the British landing. Hitler ordered, "with greatest emphasis," that Trondheim was to be reinforced by air; and instructed the Navy to shift the weight of its submarine operations to the area before and on either side of Trondheim.[39] Orders of the OKW and Group XXI set a twofold mission for Group Trondheim: to occupy Steinkjer and to capture the railroad running east out of Trondheim to the Swedish border. Steinkjer, located fifty miles north of Trondheim on a six-mile wide isthmus between the Beitstad Fiord and Snaasen Lake, controlled access to the Trondheim area from the north. The railroad was an important objective because the Germans believed at the time that they could secure permission to use the Swdish railroads for military transport. As soon as troops became available the northward advance was to be continued to Grong and Namsos. In place of the 196th Division, which was committed in the advance northward from Oslo, the staff and elements of the 181st Division (eventually two regiments) were to be transported to Trondheim by air from Oslo.[40]

With persistent bad weather delaying the air transport operations, Group Trondheim first decided to stage a limited offensive along the railroad to Sweden with the one battalion it had received. The advance began on the 15th with air support and an improvised armored train. By nightfall the following day the railroad up to the border was in German hands. A small but stubbornly defended fort at Hegra could not be taken and subsequently held out until 5 May.

In the meantime, Allied landings were in progress at Namsos, 127 miles north of Trondheim. On 14 April a naval party of about 350 sailors and marines landed from two cruisers, followed on the 16th by the British 146th Brigade and on the 19th by the French 5th Demi-brigade of Chasseurs Alpins. The Allied force totaled about 6,000 men, and the Norwegian troops in the vicinity, according to German estimates which were probably high, totaled another 6,000—these opposed to a German strength of about 4,000 men on 21 April and 9,500 on 30 April. Allied units, rapidly expanding their beachhead, reached Grong—the railroad junction east of Namsos—and Steinkjer on the 17th but did not

---

[39] *Gruppe XXI, Ia, Nr. 266/40, OKW, WFA, Nr. 88/40, 14.4.40,* in *Anlagenband Nr. 3 zum Ktb. 2 u. 3, 13.4.–18.4.40.* AOK 20 E 279/3.
[40] *Gruppe XXI, Ia, Nr. 268/40, Befehl fuer Operation in Raum um Drontheim, 15.4.40; OKW, L, Nr. 276/40,* and *Gruppe XXI, 14.4.40; and OKW, an Gruppe XXI, 16.4.40,* in *Gruppe XXI, Anlagenband 3 zum Ktb. 2 u. 3, 13.4.–18.4.40.* AOK 20 E 279/3.

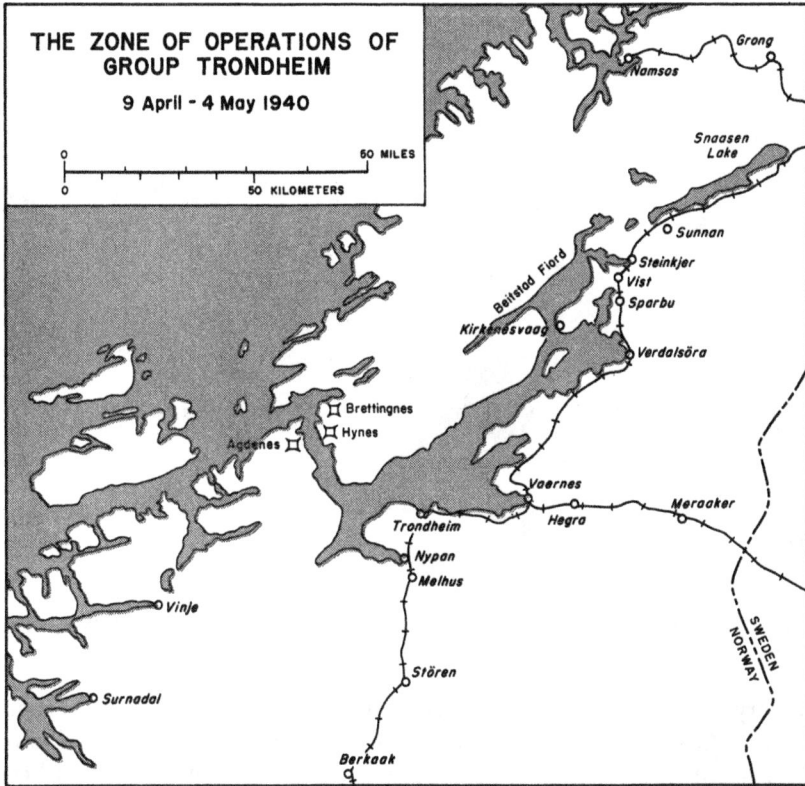

THE ZONE OF OPERATIONS OF
GROUP TRONDHEIM

9 April - 4 May 1940

Map 5

attempt to develop an attack against the German forces to the south.[41]

On 18 and 21 April Hitler established the closing of the isthmus at Steinkjer as the chief mission of Group Trondheim, and instructed Group XXI and the Air Force to move reinforcements to Trondheim as rapidly as possible.[42]   On the afternoon of the 20th Generalmajor Kurt Woytasch, commanding officer of the 181st Division, took command of Group Trondheim and ordered an advance on Steinkjer to begin the following morning.   At the time, the total forces available at Trondheim consisted of five and one-half infantry battalions, parts of two batteries of mountain artillery, and a company of engineers.   That the British had reached the Steinkjer area was not yet known.

On the morning of the 21st, elements of a mountain battalion landed from a destroyer at Kirknesvaag about 15 miles southwest of Steinkjer. To take the road and railroad bridges at Verdalsöra, a torpedo boat landed one infantry company north of the town while a company with a

[41] Derry, *op. cit.*, pp. 83–88.
[42] *OKW, WFA, Nr. 102/40, Betr: Norwegen, 18.4.40; Der Fuehrer und Oberstebefehlshaber der Wehrmacht, OKW, WFA, Nr. 106/40*, and *Gruppe XXI, 21.4.40*, in *Anlagenband 4 zum Ktb. 2 u. 3, 19.4.–23.4.40.*   AOK 20 E 279/4.

Infantrymen trudging up a snow-covered slope. Soldier resting, left foreground, carries an M.G. 34 light machine gun.

battery of mountain artillery advanced northward by rail from Trondheim. After about three hours of house-to-house fighting in a blinding snowstorm, the Germans took the town. The railroad bridge had been blown up, but the road bridge was intact.[43]

The British had established their main defensive position at Vist, about four miles south of Steinkjer. The Germans advanced on that town with a battalion moving along the shore of Beitstad Fiord and a company along the road running northward from Verdalsöra. On the morning of the 21st advance elements of the battalion from Kirknesvaag reached Vist, but the main force, depending on requisitioned vehicles, could not be brought up until nightfall. Both Vist and Steinkjer were brought under air attack. On the main road the Germans had advanced nearly to Sparbu, halfway between Verdalsöra and Vist, and at the end of the day the British were intending to withdraw northward behind Steinkjer. The next day, after fighting at Vist and Sparbu, the British at night withdrew north of Steinkjer. By the evening of the 24th, Group Trondheim had full control of the isthmus from Steinkjer to Sunnan.[44]

The British troops were not to go into action again. Bombing on the 20th and 21st had destroyed the base at Namsos, and on the 23d evacuation was being discussed. The Germans, for their part, had no

---

[43] *Gruppe Detmold, Ia, Lagenmeldung fuer die Zeit vom 20.4.1600 Uhr bis 21.4.1700 Uhr, 21.4.40 in Anlagenband 4 zum Ktb. Nr. 2 u. 3, 19.4.–23.4.40.* AOK 20 E 279/4.

[44] Derry, *op. cit.,* pp. 91–95.

intention for the time being of advancing beyond Steinkjer where their positions could be regarded as exposed so long as the Snaasen Lake remained frozen and the route along the south shore of the lake remained open to the enemy. At the end of the month the French and Norwegian units planned an offensive, but it did not materialize.[45]

On 26 April, the isthmus at Steinkjer firmly in its hands and its total strength up to seven infantry battalions and six batteries of artillery including the captured Norwegians guns, Group Trondheim ordered a push southward to meet the columns advancing from Oslo. It had taken the bridges at Nypan and Melhus, ten miles south of the city, on 22 April. Late on the night of the 27th a battalion pushing south along the railroad entered Stören, at the junction of the lines from the Gudbrandsdal and the Österdal. Three days later it made contact with elements of Group Fischer at Berkaak. Meanwhile, a battalion sent out on the 27th to secure the west flank had by the 30th pushed reconnaissance parties through to Vinje and Surnadal without encountering enemy forces.

On 1 May Group Trondheim consisted of nine infantry battalions, a battalion of engineers, and eight batteries of artillery.[46] Destroyed bridges still prevented large-scale overland transport movements from Oslo. A battalion of the 2d Mountain Division was ordered flown from Denmark to Trondheim on the 1st, and on the 3d Group XXI ordered the regiment of the 181st Division and the mountain battalion attached to Group Pellengahr dispatched to Trondheim as soon as road conditions permitted.[47]

The OKW on 2 May established destruction of the enemy forces in the Namsos area as the chief mission of Group XXI. It was to execute the operation as soon as sufficient troops were on hand, but if the enemy showed signs of withdrawing it was to carry it out immediately.[48] A day later, after reports that Namsos was being evacuated had come in, the immediate attack, to begin on the 4th, was ordered. Group Trondheim was authorized to employ all of its available forces.[49]

On the afternoon of the 3d, Group Trondheim sent out reconnaissance forces, each in battalion strength, toward Namsos and Grong. The battalion going by way of the main road reached Namsos, where the last Allied troops had embarked early on the morning of the 3d, at 1730 on the 4th. During the night 100 officers and 1,950 men of the Norwegian 5th Brigade surrendered.

---

[45] Derry, *op. cit.*, pp. 95ff.

[46] *Gruppe Trondheim, Ia, Lagenbericht, 1.5.40,* in *Anlagenband 6 zum Ktb. 2 u. 3, 1.5.–8.5.40.* AOK 20 E 279/6.

[47] *OKW, L, an Gruppe XXI, 30.4.40,* in *Anlagenband 5 zum Ktb. 2 u. 3, 24.4.–20.4.40.* AOK 20 E 279/5. *Gruppe XXI, Ia, lfd Nr. 65, an 196 I.D., 3.5.40,* in *Anlagenband 6 zum Ktb. 2 u. 3, 1.5.–8.5.40.* AOK 20 E 279/6.

[48] *OKW, WFA, Abt. L. Nr. 960/40, an Gruppe XXI, 4.5.40,* in *Anlagenband 6 zum Ktb. 2 u. 3., 1.5.–8.5.40.* AOK 20 E 279/6.

[49] *Gruppe XXI, Ia, lfd Nr. 67, an Gruppe Drontheim, 3.5.40,* in *Anlagenband 6 zum Ktb. 2 u. 3, 1.5.40–8.5.40.* AOK 20 E 279/6.

Bergen, Stavanger, Kristiansand

At Bergen immediately after the landing, the 69th Infantry Division (one regiment) found itself exposed to possible attack by British forces from the sea and by the Norwegian 4th Brigade, which was able to complete its mobilization at Voss, 45 miles northeast of the city. It therefore had to limit itself for the time being to providing security for the beachhead. On 15 April the regiment of the 69th Division which had landed at Stavanger began transferring to Bergen by air and sea; two battalions made the shift in the first week.

On 17 April the 69th Division sent out security forces ten miles east of Bergen and began reconnaissance in the direction of Voss, but it encountered resistance and reported that it could not advance farther with the troops at hand. In fact, without the knowledge of the Germans, the main body of the Norwegian 4th Brigade was, on the 18th, ordered eastward away from Voss. After a reconnaissance in force directed against Voss on 21 April the division concluded that an overland attack was not possible without seriously weakening the seaward defenses and that, for an attack through the Hardanger Fiord, the cooperation of naval units was necessary. On the basis of information from the population the division estimated the Norwegian strength at 20,000 men. Group XXI, replying that it believed there was no immediate serious threat from the sea and that the estimate of Norwegian strength was exaggerated, ordered the division to attack as soon as possible.[50]

Their weak hold on Bergen worried the Germans, and the long stretch of open coast north of the city gave them added cause for concern since the Allies might take advantage of it to strike into the flank of the German advance from Oslo to Trondheim. Hitler thought the danger great enough to justify risking another sortie into the Atlantic. He wanted to send approximately a division of troops to Bergen aboard five fast steamers with a heavy naval escort. The OKW announced that intention to Group XXI on 23 April, but canceled it three days later.[51]

In a more practical vein, Group XXI, on 21 April, diverted the 163d Division from the advance north of Oslo and gave it the missions of mopping up in the Rands Fiord–Mjösa Lake zone, advancing via Bagn to the Sogne Fiord to prevent Allied landings, and making contact with the 69th Division in the Bergen area.[52] Two days later Group XXI ordered the division to develop the attack in two columns: one, con-

---

[50] *Bergen, Ia, an Oldenburg, 21.4.40,* in *Gruppe XXI, Durchschlaege von Abschrift eines Teiles der Anlagen zum Ktb., 2 u. 3, 9.4.–10.5.40.* AOK 20 E 288/1. *von Falkenhorst an General Tittel, Bergen, 21.4.40,* in *Anlagenband 4 zum Ktb 2 u. 3, 19.4.–23.4.40.* AOK 20 E 279/4.

[51] *Chef OKW, WFA, Abt. L, Nr. 868/40, an Gruppe XXI, 23.4.40,* in *Anlagenband 4 zum Ktb. 2 u. 3, 19.4.–23.4.40.* AOK 20 E 279/4. *Jodl Diary, 23, 26 Apr 40.*

[52] *Gruppe XXI, Ia, Nr. 285/40, Operationsbefehl fuer die 163. Division ab 21.4.40,* in *Anlagenband 4 zum Ktb. 2 u. 3, 19.4.–23.4.40.* AOK 20 E 279/4.

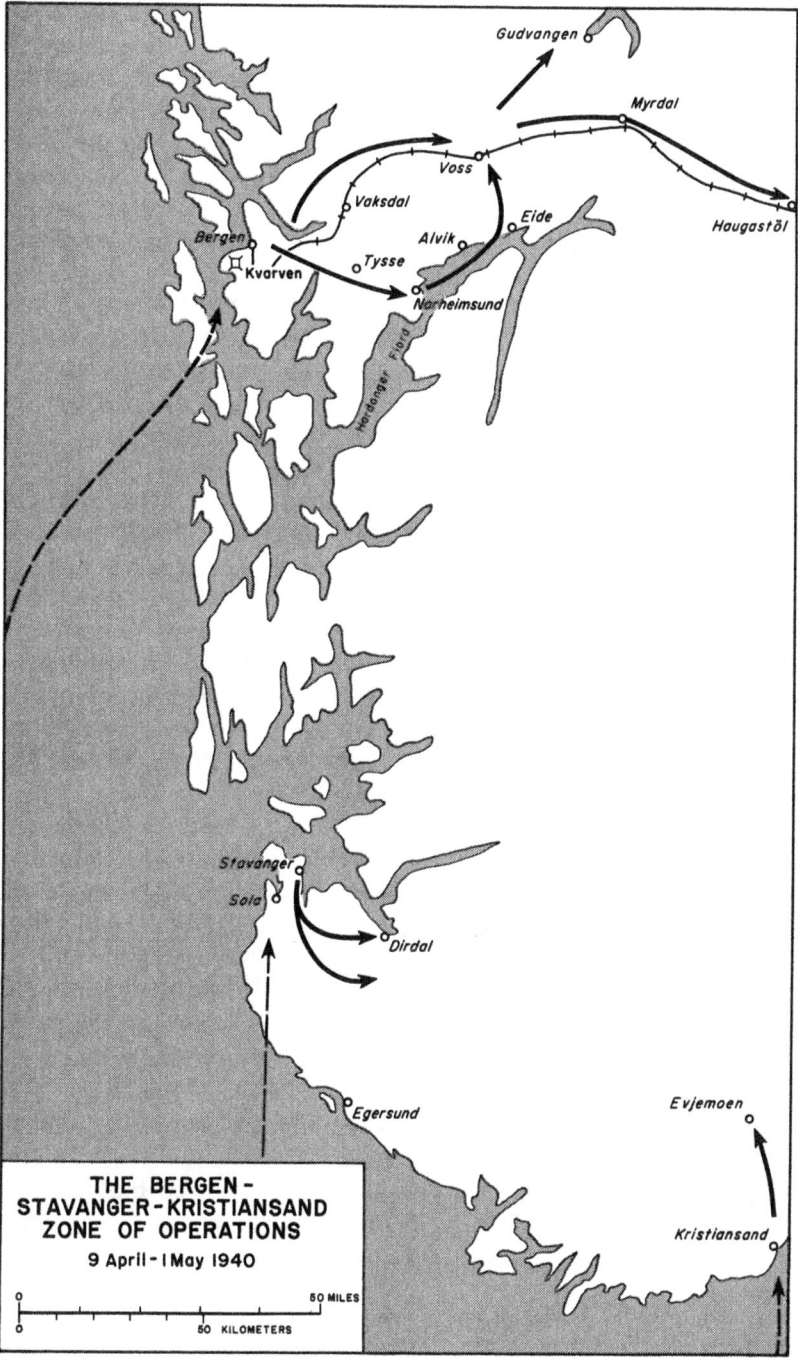

Gudvangen

Myrdal

Voss

Vaksdal

Eide

Bergen

Alvik

Kvarven

Tysse

Haugastöl

Norheimsund

Hardanger Fjord

Stavanger

Sola

Dirdal

Egersund

Evjemoen

Kristiansand

THE BERGEN-
STAVANGER-KRISTIANSAND
ZONE OF OPERATIONS

9 April - 1 May 1940

50 MILES

50 KILOMETERS

L. Booth

Map 6

sisting of four infantry battalions, a battalion of artillery, and a tank company, was to proceed via Bagn and Fagernes to Laerdalsöra on Sogne Fiord while the other, composed of two infantry battalions (later three battalions), a battery of artillery, and a tank platoon, was to advance from Drammen through the Hallingdal and along the Bergen railroad as far as Gol and from there to continue in the direction of Laerdalsöra.[53]

By 25 April the right column of the 163d Division was involved in heavy fighting at Bagn. There it encountered the Norwegian 4th Brigade which had moved east from Voss but arrived too late to influence the fighting north of Oslo. On the same day Norwegian resistance and a demolished tunnel at Gulsvik stalled the column on the left in the Hallingdal. After two days, greatly aided by strong dive bomber support, the Germans, on the 27th, broke through at Bagn and in the Hallingdal, where they advanced to within 12 miles of Gol.

The Norwegians did not succeed in making another stand. The German column in the Hallingdal, reaching Gol on the 28th, began reconnaissance in the direction of Fagernes, sent a security force along the railroad toward Hol, and continued with its main force toward Laerdalsöra. The column on the right passed through Fagernes on the 29th and reached Lommen the next day. On 28 April a third column was formed at Kongsberg on the left flank, and two days later it began an advance through the Numedal to Hol. Effective Norwegian resistance ceased on 1 May with the surrender of the Norwegian 4th Brigade (300 officers and 3,200 men) near Lommen.[54]

At Bergen the 69th Division had, on 23 April, sent one battalion out of the city along the railroad and another southeastward toward the Hardanger Fiord. The next day the division took Vaksdal on the railroad and Norheimsund on the Fiord. On the 25th it developed a three-pronged attack on Voss. Two companies advanced along the railroad; four companies pushed northeastward from the north shore of Hardanger Fiord near Alvik; and three companies landed at the eastern end of Hardanger Fiord at Eide to attack from the flank and rear.[55] The attack made rapid progress, and the Germans took Voss on the morning of the 26th. On the same day, the division issued orders to continue the advance along the railroad to Myrdal and north to Gudvangen on the Sogne Fiord.[56] On the 28th fighting began at the three-mile long Myrdal tunnel. The surrender of the Norwegian troops at Myrdal on 1 May ended organized resistance in the 69th Division sector,

---

[53] *Gruppe XXI, Ia, Vorbefehl fuer die Bildung und den Einsatz der Kampfgruppe Ritzmann, 23.4.40,* in *Anlagenband 4 zum Ktb. 2. u. 3., 19.4.–23.4.40.* AOK 20 E 279/4.

[54] *Gruppe XXI, Taegliche Meldungen,* pp. 45–68.

[55] *69. Division, Abt. Ia, Divisionsbefehl fuer Angriff auf Voss-Bomoen, 24.4.40,* in *Anlagenband 5 zum Ktb. 2 u. 3, 24.4.–30.4.40.* AOK 20 E 279/5.

[56] *69. Division, Abt. Ia, Gefechtsbericht ueber Einnahne Voss-Bomoen, 27.4.40,* in *Anlagenband 5 zum KTB. Nr. 2 u. 3, 24.4.40.* AOK 20 E 279/5.

Mark II tank and infantry column in central Norway.

and the division made contact with elements of the 163d Division on the railroad the next day.[57]

At Stavanger, after the landings, the immediate concern was with defense against a possible British landing. The airfield at Sola lay closer to the British Isles than any other German airbase and so was both a threat and an inviting target. In the first days after the landing, the beachhead was subjected to repeated air attacks, and on 17 April British cruisers shelled the airfield, doing heavy damage. On the same day troops of the 214th Division arrived by air to replace elements of the 69th Division, which were then transferred to Bergen. Orders issued on 21 April gave the 214th Division responsibility for the defense of the south coast including Stavanger and Kristiansand.[58] On the 20th elements of the 214th Division opened an attack against a Norwegian force south of the city, and on the 23d at Dirdal 50 officers and 1,250 men of the Norwegian 2d and 8th Infantry Regiments surrendered. On the 21st a motorized patrol, escorting gasoline tank trucks which had been dispatched from Oslo a week before, was able to reach Stavanger.[59]

At Kristiansand a northward advance was begun on 13 April. After dive bombers were committed at Evjemoen, the training center of the Norwegian 3d Division, Norwegian resistance collapsed, and on the 15th the commanding general offered to negotiate a surrender. Dur-

[57] *Gruppe XXI, Taegliche Meldungen,* pp. 58–65.
[58] *Gruppe XXI, Ia, Nr. 286/40, Befehl fuer den Einsatz der 214. Division in Suedwestnorwegen, 21.4.40,* in *Anlagenband 4 zum Ktb. 2 u. 3, 19.4.–23.4.40.* AOK 20 E 279/4.
[59] *Gruppe XXI, Taegliche Meldungen,* pp. 16, 35.

ing the following days 240 officers and 2,900 men of the division surrendered.[60]

In a little more than three weeks, Group XXI had taken possession of southern and central Norway north to Grong and Namsos. It had smashed the main forces of the Norwegian Army and had defeated two strong Allied landing teams. But that was merely the prelude. In the far north, at Narvik, the crucial battle of the campaign was just beginning.

---

[60] Hubatsch, *op. cit.*, p. 207. *Gruppe XXI, Taegliche Meldungen,* pp. 19, 53.

Chapter 5

Operations in Northern Norway

The Siege of Narvik

Narvik was the grand prize of the Norwegian campaign. The British conviction that, come what might, Narvik would fall to them had been the first premise of all the Allied plans concerning Scandinavia. How deep that conviction was and how painful it was to give up were demonstrated when Prime Minister Neville Chamberlain told the House of Commons twelve hours after the German landing that it was "very possible" to believe a mistake had been made in transmitting the report and, consequently, the place in question might not be Narvik at all but Larvik, a small town on the coast south of Oslo.[1] For Germans to take the rest of Norway and lose Narvik was, in effect, to lose the campaign.

Were it not for the single-track Lapland Railroad, which threads its way out of the city eastward to the Swedish ore fields, Narvik would easily have ranked among the least desirable pieces of real estate in the world. The city occupies a small area of comparatively level land at the tip of a stubby peninsula flanked on the north by the Rombaks Fiord and on the south by the Beis Fiord. The railroad follows the south shore of the Rombaks Fiord along a narrow shelf, interspersed with numerous tunnels, cut into the solid rock of the mountains which slope sharply down to the water line on both sides of the peninsula. Away from the city and railroad the arctic wilderness stretches in all directions, a tangle of hills, depressions, and irregularly shaped plateaus frequently topped by peaks reaching heights of four thousand feet and more. In winter the landscape is white except on steep slopes where the wind, blowing the snow away, exposes the bare rock underneath; in summer it is gray with narrow fringes of green along the shores of the fiords where stunted birches grow near the water and grass and mosses cover the banks to elevations of several hundred feet.

In the second week of April 1940 winter still held Narvik tightly in its grip. The snow was three to four feet deep in the city and along the shore. In the inland valleys it had accumulated to depths of eight feet and more. During the coming weeks the blizzards and later the cold

---

[1] Derry, *op. cit.*, p. 66.

spring rains were to create onerous conditions for combat; but the hardships were all in the future as the 3d Mountain Division troops marched into the prosperous, modern city which in recent years had even acquired a reputation as a winter resort. The division headquarters was set up in the top three floors of the Hotel Royal, the best of several hotels in town.

On 14 April, after the sinking of the last destroyers, Dietl had at his disposal 4,600 men, 2,600 of them members of the destroyer crews armed with Norwegian weapons from stocks captured at Elvegaardsmoen. Two battalions of mountain troops were established 17 miles north of Narvik along the line Laberget–Elvenes–Oalage. The remaining battalion took up positions in Narvik, and a company held Ankenes on the south shore of the Beis Fiord. The naval personnel were deployed along the north and east shores of the Herjangs Fiord, in Narvik, and along the railroad, which the Germans occupied up to the Swedish border on the 16th after minor skirmishes with small parties of Norwegian troops. On the 14th ten Ju 52's, which landed on the ice of Hartvig Lake, brought in a battery of mountain artillery, but four days later Hitler ordered that no new forces were to be committed.[2]

The only supplies immediately available at Narvik were those from the captured depot at Elvegaardsmoen and those which could be salvaged from the *Jan Wellem*. Two days after the landing the German Government began negotiating for permission to use the Swedish railways, and on 26 April the first train carrying rations, medical supplies, and a number of radio technicians arrived. Although repeatedly pressed, the Swedish Government did not permit the transport of ammunition but later allowed some shipments of clothing and ski equipment. In addition, 230 specialists of various kinds were brought in via Sweden in the course of the campaign. All of the ammunition and substantial quantities of rations and other supplies had to be delivered by air drops. Sea planes could land occasionally in defiance of the patrolling British warships, but after the ice on the Hartvig Lake began to thaw, which occurred before the ten Ju 52's mentioned above were able to take off, the landing of other aircraft was impossible. As the campaign progressed it developed that the difficulties of moving supplies within the 3d Mountain Division zone were almost as great as those encountered in bringing them in from outside. The divisional supply base was established at Björnfjell just west of the Swedish border, and the railroad could be used only as far as Hundalen. From there supplies for Narvik had to be carried 15 miles along the railroad right of way which was constantly exposed to shelling from British warships. After the ferry which operated between Narvik and Öyjord on the north shore

[2] *Chef OKW, WFA, Nr. 102/40, an Gruppe XXI, 18.4.40,* in *Anlagenband 3 zum Ktb. Nr. 2 u. 3, 13.4.–18.4.40.* AOK 20 E 279/3. *Gruppe XXI, Taegliche Meldungen,* loc. cit., p. 19. 3. Geb. Div. K.T.B. Narvik, loc. cit., p. 8.

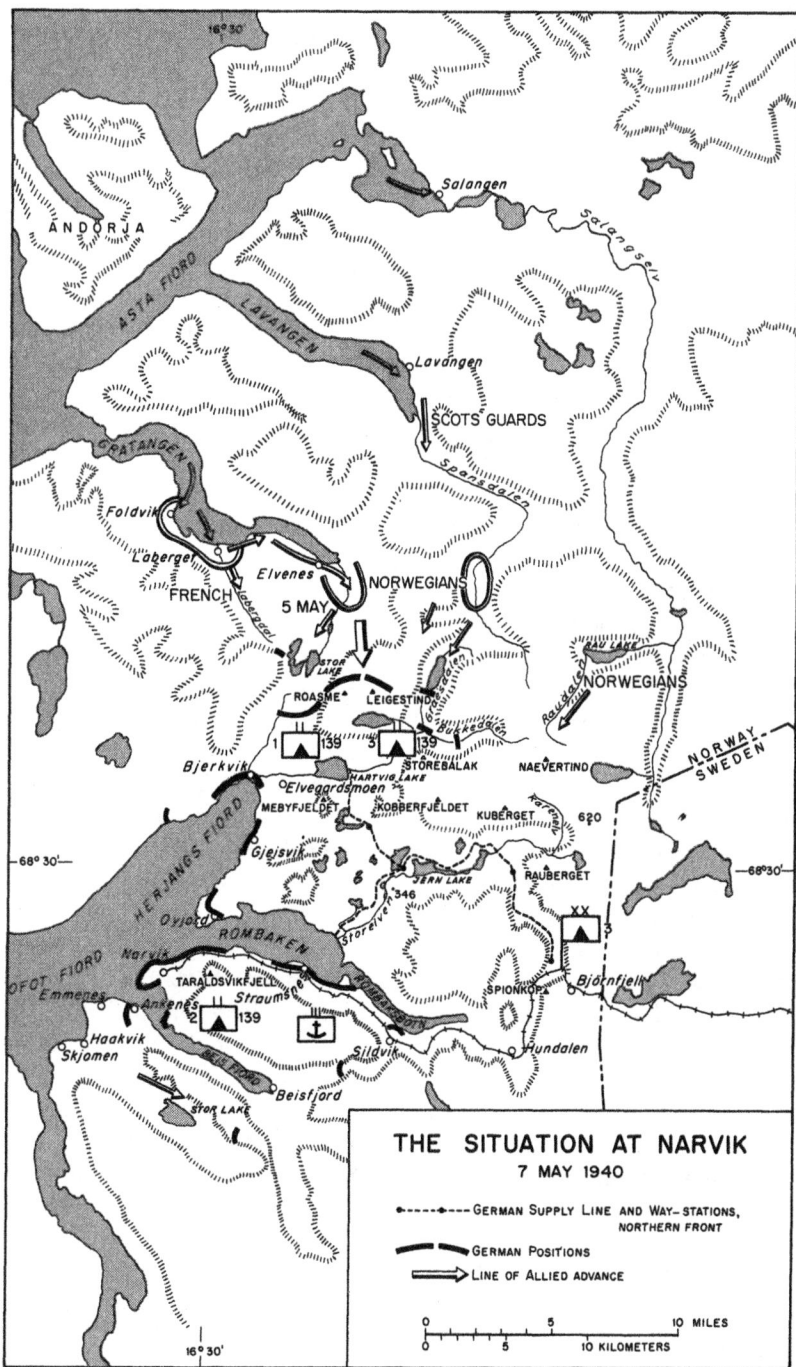

THE SITUATION AT NARVIK
7 MAY 1940

●----●----● GERMAN SUPPLY LINE AND WAY-STATIONS,
NORTHERN FRONT

━━━━━━ GERMAN POSITIONS

▭▭▭▷ LINE OF ALLIED ADVANCE

```
0          5          10  MILES
|─┴─┴─┴─┴─|─┴─┴─┴─┴─|
0       5        10  KILOMETERS
```

J. Schueren

Map 7

of Rombaks Fiord was sunk on 20 April, supplies for the troops north of Narvik had to be carried over the mountains from Björnfjell.[3]

On 14 April the British advance party of two companies of Scots Guards arrived off Narvik in the cruiser *Southhampton* and joined a naval force of cruisers and destroyers under the command of Admiral of the Fleet the Earl of Cork and Orrery. Lord Cork wanted to stage a landing at Narvik on the morning of the 15th with 350 Scots Guards and 200 sailors and marines but abandoned the idea after the Army commander, Major General P. J. Mackesy, raised objections. On the 16th Mackesy rejected a second proposal for a landing on the grounds of need to land his weapons, deep snow on the beaches, and lack of knowledge of the condition of the Germans. By the afternoon of the 17th both the Admiralty and the War Office were pressing for an immediate assault, but the general .continued to have misgivings and favored, instead, an attempt to induce the Germans to surrender by means of a naval bombardment.[4] On the morning of the 24th a battleship, two cruisers, and half a dozen destroyers shelled Narvik for three hours. At first the Germans expected a landing, and Dietl informed Group XXI that, if the city could not be held, he intended to fall back eastward along the railroad. In the end, the only tangible result of the bombardment was that Dietl decided to shift the nonessential troops out of the city and, at the urging of his staff, moved his command post to Sildvik, a railroad station near the eastern end of the Rombaks Fiord.[5]

Winston Churchill has charged Mackesy with a dilatoriness not warranted by the circumstances; on the other hand, Derry, the official British historian, is inclined to see a considerable amount of justification in the general's determination to avoid the risks of an immediate landing and develop, instead, a deliberate and scientific campaign. In view of present knowledge it seems that a landing during the first days would have had a good chance of success since Dietl had only one battalion of mountain troops in Narvik to oppose two British battalions at hand on the 15th and an additional battalion which arrived on the 16th.[6] The two German battalions stationed north of the city could not have crossed the Rombaks Fiord to enter into the fighting. Of the destroyer crews about 1,000 were being held at Hundalen, and there is no indication that many of the remainder were in Narvik or even organized and ready for combat. The opinion of the 3d Mountain Division at the end of the campaign was that in the first weeks the Allies far overestimated the German strength.[7]

---

[3] *3. Geb. Div., Ib, Bericht ueber die Erfahrungen auf dem Gebiet der Versorgung waehrend des Einsatzes in Norwegen, 7.7.40,* in *Erfahrungsberichte der Divisionen.* AOK 20 E 279/16.

[4] Derry, *op. cit.,* pp. 146–55.

[5] *Gruppe XXI, Taegliche Meldungen, loc. cit.,* p. 42. Dietl, *op. cit.,* p. 112.

[6] Derry, *op. cit.,* pp. 148, 153.

[7] *3. Geb. Div., Ia, Erfahrungsbericht,* in *Erfahrungsberichte der Divisionen, 16.7.40.* AOK 20 E 279/16.

While the possibilities of a landing were being debated, the British force established its main base and headquarters at Harstad on Hinnöy Island, already the headquarters of the Norwegian 6th Division; and the three British battalions were distributed at several points on the mainland but not in position to make contact with the Germans. The Norwegians had four battalions north of the German positions in the Elvenes area. General Mackesy planned a two-pronged drive from the north to take Öyjord and cut the railroad at Hundalen and an advance along the south shore of Ofot Fiord to Ankenes as the initial phase of his advance to Narvik.[8]

On the 24th, in the first land action of the campaign, the four Norwegian battalions attacking at Gratangen near Elvenes were repulsed and lost the better part of one battalion. The arrival on the same day of three battalions of French Chasseurs Alpins enabled Mackesy to begin developing his attack. One of the French battalions landed on the 28th in Gratangen Fiord for an advance southeastward through the Labergdal. Meanwhile, the strength of the Norwegian force had been increased, and it was organized into two brigades, one with three battalions and a mountain battery and the other with two battalions, a mountain battery, and a motorized battery. The latter, reinforced by two French companies, took up the advance from Elvenes to Bjerkvik while the former worked its way eastward into the mountains to attack on the German right flank along the Swedish border. The advance was not rapid and by 10 May had covered only five miles. South of Narvik on 29 April a British battalion, replaced several days later by one of the French mountain battalions, landed west of Haakvik to attack Ankenes. There too, the attack made little progress.[9]

On 5 May, when Dietl's force returned to the command of Group XXI after having been under the immediate command of the OKW since 15 April, the 3d Mountain Division reported that the main threat north of Narvik was seen as coming from the Norwegian brigade on the right flank. It could turn westward and cut off the two German battalions or drive straight to the south to the railroad at Björnfjell, but because of the slow and methodical character of the Norwegian operations Dietl was not greatly concerned. The additional danger of an Allied landing in the Herjangs Fiord was foreseen. Narvik was being held by a mountain battalion and approximately three naval companies while one mountain company defended Ankenes. The railroad, which provided the only route from Narvik to the rear, was held by naval personnel but was exposed day and night to fire from enemy destroyers which used their heavy guns against anything that moved along the railroad. In Narvik the Germans had blown up the piers and other installations necessary for the shipment of ore so that the city could be

---

[8] Derry, *op. cit.,* pp. 154–56.
[9] Derry, *op. cit.,* pp. 157–59.

evacuated on short notice. The impression at Dietl's headquarters was that the Allied force would not undertake a major operation against the city itself until they had completed their preparations down to the last detail and probably not until the snow had melted and the condition of the terrain had become more favorable.[10] Dietl intended to hold his advanced positions in the north and at Narvik as long as possible because of the difficulty of organizing a defense in the mountains to the rear.[11] On 6 May, however, in the light of the developing enemy attack, Group XXI viewed the position of the Narvik force as critical; and on the 8th after the loss of the Leigestind and Roasme, two commanding heights east of the Elvenes–Bjerkvik road, Dietl reported that he could hold his new positions to the rear only if reinforcements were forthcoming and if the Air Force gave strong support.[12]

In early May the build-up of the Allied force continued. Two battalions of the French Foreign Legion arrived on the 6th and a Polish brigade of four battalions on the 9th. Lord Cork had at his disposal, in addition to cruisers and destroyers, a battleship and an aircraft carrier. With five antiaircraft batteries at hand and six more due to follow, the troops investing Narvik were not as helpless in the face of German air power as the forces at Namsos and Åndalsnes had been. Nevertheless, in good weather they had to contend with several air raids a day. The first substantial German success came on 4 May with the sinking of the Polish destroyer *Grom*. Before the end of the month, the Germans had sunk the antiaircraft cruiser *Curlew* and the transport *Chrobry* and damaged a number of ships, among them the battleship *Resolution*.[13]

The next step in the Allied plan was to stage a landing at the northern end of the Herjangs Fiord which would be coupled with a renewed French and Norwegian thrust south from the Elvenes area. The Norwegian brigade operating along the Swedish border would maintain its pressure on the German right flank. The landing, to be executed by two battalions of the Foreign Legion and five light tanks, was timed for midnight on the 13th after a preliminary bombardment by a battleship, two cruisers, and five destroyers.[14]

At the German headquarters the appearance of the warships was correctly taken to indicate a landing in the Herjangs Fiord, where the only force which could be committed was the weak naval battalion already stationed at Bjerkvik and along the east shore. The possibility of a landing at Narvik was also taken into account; and the question of abandoning the city without fight arose; but Dietl decided that, although possession of the city had no decisive military significance, he

---

[10] *Gruppe XXI, Chief, Lfd. Nr. 8, Auszug aus einem Bericht der Gruppe Narvik von 5.5.40*, in *Anlagenband 12 zum Ktb. Nr. 2 u. 3.9.5.–19.5.40*. AOK 20 E 279/12.
[11] *3. Geb. Div., K.T.B., Narvik, loc. cit.*, p. 27.
[12] *Gruppe XXI, Taegliche Meldungen, loc. cit.*, pp. 80, 88.
[13] Derry, *op. cit.*, pp. 192, 206.
[14] Derry, *op. cit.*, pp. 196–99.

would have to resist for the sake of troop morale and to deny the Allies a cheap victory out of which they could make propaganda.

At Bjerkvik, where the French troops went ashore at about 0200 on 13 May, the naval battalion, badly shaken by the bombardment, gave ground quickly, abandoning most of its machine guns in the process. A small screening force of mountain troops thrown into the area west of Hartvig Lake managed to delay the enemy advance temporarily but could not prevent his taking Elvegaardsmoen.   On the Bjerkvik–Oyjord road a naval company abandoned its positions before coming under fire, thereby opening the route by which French troops occupied Öyjord before the end of the day.   During the morning Dietl ordered the mountain battalions to draw back to a line from the Mebyfjeldet to the Storebalak, but it was doubtful whether the line could be established or held because of the threat deep in the almost undefended left flank at Öyjord. Fortunately for the Germans, the Allies could not effect a junction of their forces on the Elvenes–Bjerkvik road until the afternoon of the 14th. This gave the mountain troops time to withdraw southeastward.   On the German right flank the Norwegian brigade began an advance which was to make good progress during the following days.[15]

On the evening of the 13th, Group XXI informed the OKW that the situation at Narvik was critical.   Dietl reported that for even part of his troops to retreat southward toward Bodö was out of the question because of their exhausted condition.   He intended, if the enemy offensive continued, to give up Narvik and hold a bridgehead on the railroad; but the prerequisite for that undertaking was speedy reinforcement of the front north of Narvik; otherwise, there was no other possibility than to cross the border into Sweden.   Group XXI, reporting to the OKW, requested permission for Dietl to take his troops into Sweden in case enemy action made it necessary.[16]

By the night of 13 May all that was left for the Germans at Narvik was to fight for time, on the slim chance that a miracle might yet spare them the disgrace of having to take refuge in Sweden.   The German offensive against the Low Countries and France had started three days earlier, but it was too early to predict its effect, if any, on the Allied operation at Narvik.   On 4 May Group XXI had started the 2d Mountain Division on the long march northward from the Trondheim area. The division had made surprisingly good progress, but it was still 180 miles south of Narvik.   Group XXI was almost helpless; the most it could do was send some reinforcements, not enough to turn the tide or, for that matter, even to keep the resistance alive much longer.

After the first wave of panic had subsided, Falkenhorst, on 15 May, asked Hitler for a parachute battalion to be sent to Narvik.   To justify the request, he argued that the operations of the 2d Mountain Division

[15] *3. Geb. Div., K.T.B. Narvik, loc. cit.*, pp. 38–40.   Derry *op. cit.*, p. 199.
[16] *Gruppe XXI, Ia, Nr. 2/40, an OKW, Abt. L. 13.5.40,* in *Anlagenband 12 zum Ktb. 2 u. 3, 9.5.–19.5.40.*   AOK 20 E 279/12.

north of Trondheim would become a mere waste of strength if Narvik were given up and that it was necessary to hold a beachhead in the north as long as possible for political and prestige reasons and to tie down Allied land and sea forces.[17]   On the 14th, Group XXI had sent a token reinforcement of 66 parachute troops—all it could muster in Norway.   During the remainder of the month and in the first week of June a parachute battalion and two mountain companies which had been given brief parachute training were dropped at Narvik.   The reinforcements totaled about 1,050 men, including 160 specialists who arrived by train.[18]

While the pressure for reinforcements was greatest, Group XXI, through a misunderstanding, was making arrangements for evacuation of the destroyer crews via Sweden.   Partly because the end was believed near in Narvik and partly because Dietl, after the events of 13 May, had described the naval personnel as "useless for combat and a danger to our troops," permission was secured from Sweden on the 19th for the crews to be evacuated as shipwrecked sailors.   During the following weeks Group XXI persistently urged the evacuation while Dietl, who in the meantime had changed his mind, argued that the sailors were indispensable for the movement of supplies within the division zone.[19]

On the 15th the 3d Mountain Division viewed its situation as becoming increasingly doubtful because of the threat to the northern front.   It saw the only possibility of improvement in effective air support directed against the land and sea targets.   Dietl also reported that unless reinforcements were made available immediately he would be compelled to allow his troops in the north to fall back, which would inevitably lead to the loss of Narvik.[20]   Two days later the situation on the right flank along the Swedish border was still completely confused, with the Norwegians pushing across the tactically important Kuberg Plateau and enemy pressure continuing strong all along the front.   South of Narvik, where three Polish battalions replaced the French and British battalions in the Ankenes area on 16 May, defense was becoming increasingly difficult.

On the 21st, judging that an Allied breakthrough was possible at any moment, Dietl decided to withdraw his north front and take up positions in a shortened line.   The withdrawal was executed the next day, and the line was anchored near the Swedish border 7 miles north of the Björnfjell and on the Rombaks Fiord 12 miles west of the Björnfjell.[21]

[17] v. Falkenhorst, an Fuehrerhauptquartier, Generaloberst Keitel, 15.5.40, in Anlagenband 12 zum Ktb. 2 u. 3, 9.5.–19.5.40.   AOK 20 E 279/12.
[18] 3. Geb. Div., K.T.B. Narvik, loc. cit., passim.
[19] Dietl, an Gruppe XXI, 15.5.40, in Anlagenband 7 zum Ktb. 2 u. 3, 9.5.–16.5.40. AOK 20 E 279/7.   Gruppe XXI, Ia, Nr. 595/40 and Nr. 673/40, an Oberst Buschenhagen, Drontheim, 18 and 19.5.40, in Anlagenband 8 zum Ktb. Nr. 2 u. 3, 17.5.–26.5.40.   AOK 20 E 279/8.
[20] 3. Geb. Div., K.T.B. Narvik, loc. cit., p. 42.   Dietl an Gruppe XXI, 15.5.40, in Anlagenband 7 zum Ktb. Nr, 2 u. 3, 9.5.40.   AOK 20 E 279/7.
[21] 3. Geb. Div., K.T.B. Narvik, loc. cit., pp. 42, 44, 45, 48.

The new line held while the Allied command prepared the final assault on Narvik.

The Advance of the 2d Mountain Division Toward Narvik

On 4 May, the day the German troops advancing north of Trondheim reached Grong and Namsos, Group XXI issued orders, based on an estimate of weak enemy forces to the north, giving the 2d Mountain Division the mission of pushing northward from Grong via Mosjöen to Bodö and from there attempting to establish overland contact with the force at Narvik. The straight-line distance to Narvik was about 300 miles through thinly settled, snow-covered, mountainous territory deeply cut by the fiords. The roads were poor, not continuous, and for the last 85 miles nonexistent. On the 4th Generalleutnant Valentin Feurstein, Commanding General, 2d Mountain Division, arrived at Trondheim where the troops immediately at his disposal amounted to two battalions plus one company of mountain infantry, one battery of mountain artillery, and an engineer platoon. The main force of the 2d Mountain Division, which had begun leaving Germany at the end of April, was still in transit. Motorized units and the mountain regiment which had executed the landing at Trondheim were to be attached to Feurstein's force as they became available.[22]

On the Allied side the prospect of a German advance northward was regarded with the strongest misgivings because of the possibility that reinforcements could be brought to Narvik but, above all, because the reach of the German Air Force would be extended toward the vulnerable Allied bases in the north. The intention was to delay and, if possible, stall the German advance. At the time of the evacuation of Namsos it had been proposed that part of the force withdraw overland, fighting a rearguard action between Grong and Mosjöen; but the plan was dropped after the command at Namsos insisted that the terrain was impassable. Instead, 100 Chasseurs Alpins were transferred by sea from Namsos to Mosjöen. The Allied plan as it finally developed was to create centers of resistance at Mosjöen, and Bodö, and, since the operations at Åndalsnes and Namsos had demonstrated the dangers of committing large forces without air protection, it was decided to employ only small, self-sufficient units. Beginning in mid-April, five Independent Companies of 20 officers and 270 men each had been created. They were expected to live off the country and engage the cooperation of the local population in guerilla warfare. Brought from England, two companies landed at Mosjöen replacing the Chasseurs Alpins; one landed at Mo and two at Bodö, where they joined a company of Scots

---

[22] *Gruppe XXI, Ia, an Kdr. 2. Geb. Div., 6.5.40 (muendlich 4.5.1700)*, in *Anlagenband 6 zum KTB. 2 u. 3, 1.4.–8.5.40.* AOK 20 E 279/6.

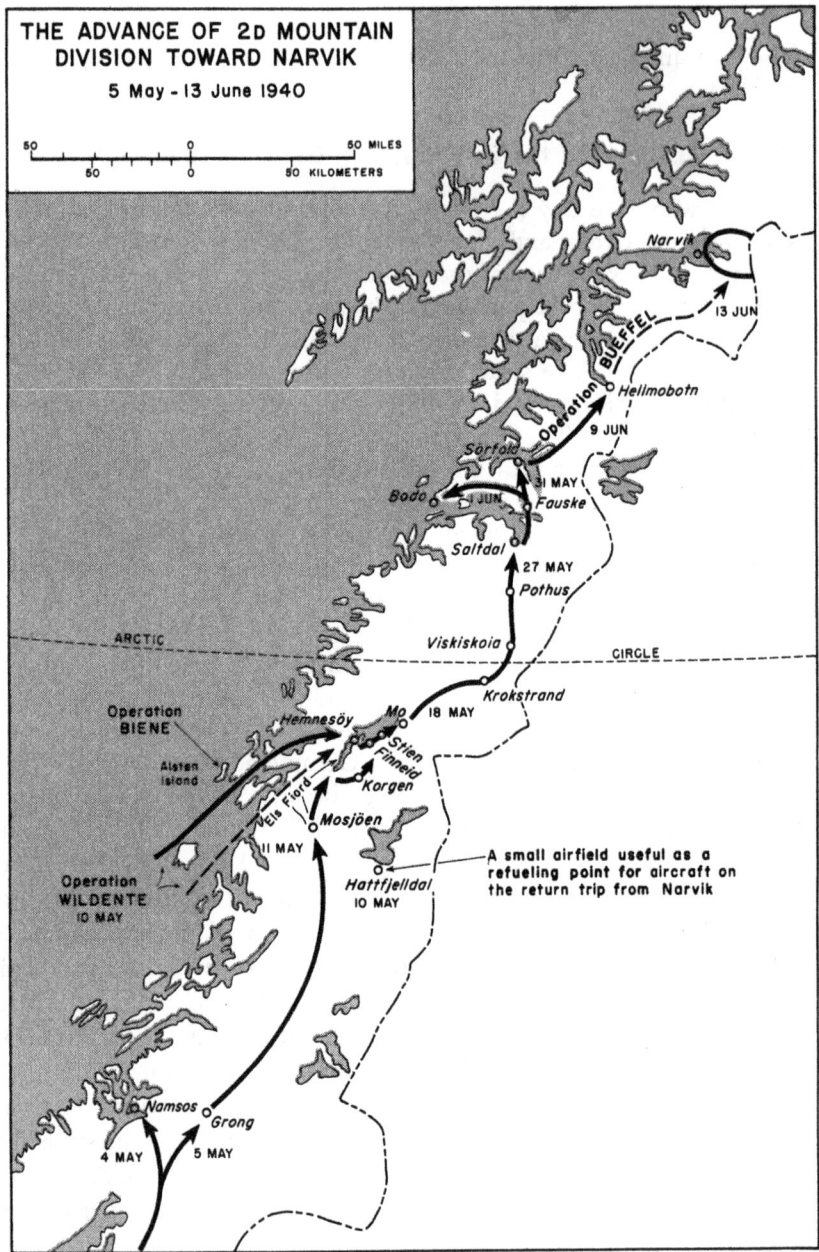

Map 8

Guards sent from the Narvik area. The Norwegian troops at hand amounted to one reserve battalion and one battalion which was withdrawing from Grong to Mosjöen.[23]

Starting from Grong on 5 May the German mountain troops covered nearly 90 miles in four days over terrain which the British command

[23] Derry, *op. cit.*, pp. 166, 168, 177–79. Roskill, *op. cit.*, p. 191.

at Namsos had judged to be impassable. On the morning of the 10th British and Norwegian troops staged brief resistance 10 miles south of Mosjöen and then withdrew to positions beyond the town with the intention of fighting a series of delaying actions between Mosjöen and Mo. That afternoon the Germans executed operation WILDENTE. Aboard the coastal steamer *Nord Norge* a company was taken from Trondheim to the Hemnesöy Peninsula in the fiord at Mo. Seaplanes brought in another half company. The landing was a success despite the fact that it was contested at the quay by British troops and that the steamer was sunk by two British destroyers which appeared on the scene. The operation apparently was dictated mainly by the peculiarities of the geography of northern Norway. The road north from Mosjöen ended at Elsfiorden on the Els Fiord, and the Hemnesöy Peninsula dominated the water route to Mo. A road via Korgen and Finneid to Mo was separated from the Mosjöen–Elsfiorden road by a high ridge and was dominated at Finneid by the Hemnesöy. WILDENTE opened the route to Mo for the Germans, but it also came as a calamity for the British companies at Mosjöen since it cut their route of retreat and ended all plans for contesting the ground north of Mosjöen to Mo. The British abandoned their positions and were evacuated by ship to Bodö while the Norwegian battalion, which was forced to abandon most of its equipment, retreated overland to Mo,[24] where the British managed to hold open the road through Finneid past the Hemnesöy Peninsula just long enough for the battalion to pass through.

On the 11th the German column entered Mosjöen and received orders to advance as quickly as possible to Hemnesöy. By the 15th the Germans were in Elsfiorden; and, while an attempt was made to improvise a ferry for transport to Finneid, three and a half companies worked their way across the mountains from Elsfiorden to Korgen and thence along the road to Finneid. The British, in the meantime, had brought three companies of Scots Guards to Mo in addition to the Independent Company already there and had established a strong defensive position at Stien, eight miles northeast of Finneid. After assembling their forces at Finneid on the 16th and 17th, the Germans went over to the attack on the afternoon of the 17th. Finding the British position protected by a small river, the Germans marched eastward and attacked the left flank while parachute troops were dropped to develop a secondary flank attack. The fighting continued throughout the short night, and the British began to fall back about 0200. During the night the British units

---

[24] *Holzinger, Hauptman 1./138, Gefechtsbericht des Unternehmens Wildente vom 8.4.1940 2230 bis zum 15.5.1940 1900 Uhr, 17.5.40 and Rudolf, Oberleutnant 7./138, Gefechtsbericht des Unternehmens "Wildente" vom 10.5. 1600 Uhr bis 11.5. 0300 Uhr, in Anlagenband 13 zum Ktb. 2 u. 3, 20.5.–31.5.40.* AOK 20 E 279/13. *Gruppe XXI, Taegliche Meldungen, loc. cit.,* p. 92. Derry, *op. cit.,* pp. 180–82.

Waiting to attack, German troops fighting in mountainous terrain take cover behind a rock.

received orders to retire north of Mo, and at 2000 on the 18th the Germans occupied the town.[25]

To hold Bodö and the territory north of Mo, the British had two infantry battalions, four Independent Companies, and two batteries of artillery at Bodö and a battalion of Scots Guards (brought up to strength by reinforcements from Bodö) and an Independent Company in the vicinity of Mo, a total of about 4,500 men. Of Norwegian troops, there were approximately a battalion in the Mo area and a battalion (transferred from Bardufoss) at Bodö.[26] The German force under General Feurstein, which changed almost daily as new elements arrived, on 15 May consisted of six battalions of mountain infantry, four batteries of artillery, a divisional reconnaissance battalion, an engineer battalion, a company of motorcycle troops, a bicycle squadron, a mortar battery, and a platoon of tanks. The German troops probably totaled about 6,000 men, but not all were committed in the assault.[27]

The Scots Guards fought the first delaying action north of Mo in the vicinity of Krokstrand. The Independent Company had been taken out of action and withdrawn northward, and reinforcements were slow in arriving because of delays in assembling the forces at Bodö occasioned by the sinking of a transport and the grounding of a cruiser carrying

[25] *2. Geb. Div., Bericht ueber das Vorgehen der Gruppe Sorko von Elsfiorden nach Mo und die Gefechte bei Stien und Andfiskaanen, 19.5.40,* in *Anlagenband 12 zum Ktb. 2 u. 3, 9.5.–19.5.40.* AOK 20 E 279/12. Derry, *op. cit.,* pp. 182–86.
[26] Derry, *op. cit.,* pp. 187–92 and 214–15. Roskill, *op. cit.,* p. 192.
[27] *Gruppe XXI, Kraefteeinsatz bei 2. Geb. Div. amd 10.5.,* 14.5.40 and *Gruppe XXI, Bis 15.5. sind Gruppe Feurstein angefuehrt, 15.5.50,* in *Anlagenband 19 zum Ktb. Nr. 2 u. 3, Kriegsgliederungen 15.4.–25.5.40.* AOK 20 E 279/19.

troops. The positions at Krokstrand could only be held for a matter of hours, and on the 23d a fresh Independent Company attempted a new stand at Viskiskoia. It, too, failed the next afternoon when the Germans developed a flank attack which drove back the Independent Company. The Scots Guards and other units were then ordered to withdraw as fresh troops had occupied positions farther north at Pothus. There an infantry battalion and two Independent Companies with some Norwegian troops managed to hold from the morning of the 25th until 1900 on the 26th. At Pothus for the first time the British troops had the support of two fighter aircraft operating from a newly constructed airstrip at Bodö.[28]

On 25 May, while the fighting was in progress at Pothus, the immediate evacuation of Bodö was ordered. The Allies had decided a day earlier to close out their operation against Narvik and therefore saw no need to continue tying down the 2d Mountain Division.[29] In a week, the British units, with the Germans close behind, fell back to Bodö, completing the evacuation on 31 May.[30] At Fauske the German force split. One column pushed westward toward Bodö while the other continued the northward advance toward Sörfold. The Germans entered Bodö on the morning of 1 June and reached Sörfold on the following day.[31] At Sörfold the forward elements of the 2d Mountain Division were still 85 miles from Narvik, and from there north the route lay through a sparsely settled, pathless mountain wilderness.

Defeat and Victory

On 24 May the Allied Command in London decided that, because of the disastrous situation in France where the battle around Dunkerque was entering its final stage, the Narvik operation would have to be halted but that the city was to be captured first in order to cover the evacuation and ensure destruction of the port.[32] The final assault, originally planned for the 21st, was postponed until the 27th, largely to gain the advantage of land-based air support from the airfield at Bardufoss which came into use on the 21st and where, finally, two squadrons of fighters and a squadron of naval amphibians were based. The attack, preceded by a cruiser and destroyer bombardment, was to be launched straight across the Rombaks Fiord from Öyjord, a distance of about one mile. It would be carried out by two battalions of the Foreign Legion and one Norwegian battalion supported by two tanks and the fire of three batteries of artillery stationed at Öyjord. Simultaneously the Polish battalions would launch thrusts against Ankenes and toward the

---

[28] Derry, *op. cit.*, pp. 189–92.
[29] Roskill, *op. cit.*, p. 192.
[30] Derry, *op. cit.*, pp. 213–15.
[31] *Gruppe XXI, Taegliche Meldungen, loc. cit.*, pp. 134–40.
[32] Churchill, Vol. I, p. 652.

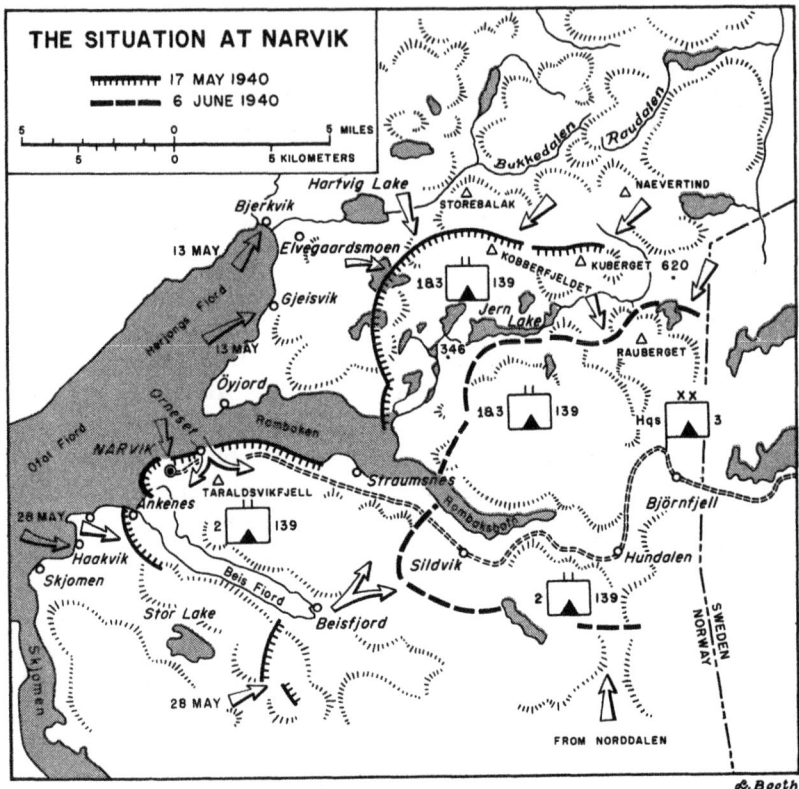

Map 9

head of the Beis Fiord while the French and Norwegians kept up pressure on the northern front. Later a sweeping attack from the south was to cut the railroad in the German rear.[33]

The bombardment began at 2340 on the 27th, and the landing followed promptly at midnight. Coming ashore at Orneset, east of Narvik, the troops attempted to work their way around the slope of the Taraldsvikfjell and gain control of the western approaches to the city. The Germans, holding the higher ground on the mountain, staged a strong resistance and at one time drove the assault force back almost to the beach. By holding the Taraldsvikfjell they were able to prevent the French and Norwegian battalions from driving straight across the tip of the peninsula before the troops in Narvik could withdraw along the shore of the Beis Fiord. This they accomplished before noon on the 28th.

At the same time the troops at Ankenes fell back across the Beis Fiord, losing some of their boats in the process, and joined the withdrawal. The

---

[33] Derry, *op. cit.*, p. 208.

Polish thrust toward the head of the fiord was held up long enough to prevent the cutting off of the troops withdrawing from Narvik. At night the Poles made contact with elements of the Foreign Legion in Beisfiord Village, but by then the Germans had taken up positions to the north and east.

Although the first German reports mentioned Allied tanks in the attack on Narvik, it appears that both of the tanks became bogged down on the beach and were not brought into action. On the morning of the 28th German dive bombers damaged the antiaircraft cruiser *Cairo,* and during the succeeding days German aircraft bombed the Allied bases at Harstad and Skaanland and brought Narvik under heavy air attack.[34]

After the Allied troops had taken Narvik they pushed eastward along the railroad where they had the benefit of supporting fire from warships in the fiord. On the 30th they began developing a secondary attack from the south where a force in approximately battalion strength moved northeastward across the base of the Narvik Peninsula, endangering Sildvik on the railroad and threatening to cut off all the German troops farther west. Although Dietl averted that danger by throwing a company of parachute troops into the area, there still remained the possibility that the Allies might try a similar flanking movement farther east. By the 30th Dietl's stocks of rations and ammunition were rapidly dwindling since bad weather had (for three days) prevented supply flights. The supply situation was to become worse as the bad weather persisted.

The next morning the Norwegians resumed their attack on the right flank of the northern front, where the relative quiet of the past few days had facilitated the German withdrawal from Narvik. After the attack increased in strength throughout the day, forcing the Germans off the height (Hill 620) which had formed the eastern anchor of their line, Dietl decided to withdraw to a shorter line in order to make some reserves available which might be used to stem the threat in the north were it to continue to develop. On 1 June he drew the left flank of the northern front back to the western slope of the Rauberget and pulled the front on the Narvik Peninsula back about a mile, making possible the formation of one company of reserves for each battalion. With minor changes that line was to hold until the end of the campaign.[35]

On 30 May Group XXI informed Dietl that Hitler had decided the Narvik force was to be supported by all possible means. While awaiting the support, which would become effective in five or six days, Dietl was to hold out as best he could, giving up the railroad if necessary. Hitler had ordered the OKL to make strong elements of the 7th Air Division available. They were to be committed in conjunction with a

---

[34] *3. Geb. Div., K.T.B. Narvik, loc. cit.,* pp. 55–58. Derry *op. cit.,* pp. 209–11 and 217. Dietl, *op. cit.,* pp. 161–68. *Gruppe XXI, Taegliche Meldungen, loc. cit.,* p. 130.
[35] *3. Geb. Div., Taegliche Meldungen, loc. cit.,* pp. 158–64.

planned naval operation off the north coast of Norway (Operation JUNO. See pp. 104–108 below).[36]

The Air Force had for two weeks past displayed increasing reluctance to participate in the reinforcement of Narvik. On 16 May Hitler had ordered Goering to provide gliders for the transport of troops to Narvik. Group XXI readied 600 mountain troops; but, after successive delays, Goering on the 29th ordered all the gliders held at Aalborg. A Hitler decision on the following day reduced the number of gliders made available to six, and those were not committed.[37] The newly promised reinforcements, it was decided by 4 June, were to consist of two parachute battalions, a total of 1,800 men, to be brought in over a period of a week. On 5 June Group XXI promised an additional 1,000 mountain troops with parachute training in the near future. None of the intended reinforcements were delivered before the end of the campaign.[38]

At the beginning of June the OKW planned a new operation for the relief of Narvik under the cover-name NAUMBURG. On 4 June it informed Group XXI that the intention was to land a strong force in the Lyngen Fiord, 90 miles north of Narvik, and from there to drive southward to attack the rear of the enemy at Narvik. Simultaneously the Air Force would take the airfield at Bardufoss, about 60 miles north of Narvik, and use it to support the advance. The OKH would furnish about 6,000 troops and a dozen tanks to be transported from Germany in the fast liners *Bremen* and *Europa*.[39] Both Group XXI and the Navy believed the operation could succeed, but the Navy thought that the two liners, after being escorted to the landing area by warships left at Trondheim following Operation JUNO, could not be brought back to Germany but would either have to be abandoned or sent to Base North on the Soviet arctic coast.[40] On 7 June the OKW was planning to execute the operation about 14 days later.[41]

Of the German schemes for bringing aid to Narvik, the one which came closest to fruition was Operation BUEFFEL, conducted by the 2d Mountain Division. In the last week of May the division had assembled a picked force of 2,500 of its best mountaineers, men who could be ex-

[36] *Gruppe XXI, Ia, Nr. 1056/40, an Gruppe Narvik, 31.5.40* and *OKW, WFA, L, an Gruppe XXI, 31.5.40*, in *Anlagenband 13 zum Ktb. 2 u. 3, 20.5.–31.5.40*. AOK 20 E 279/13. *Gruppe XXI, Ia, Nr. 1040/40, an Gruppe Narvik, 30.5.40*, in *Anlagenband 10 zum Ktb. Nr. 2 u. 3, 27.5.–4.6.40*. AOK 20 E 279/10.
[37] *OKW, Abt. L. Nr. 0037/40, an Gruppe XXI, 17.5.40*, in *Anlagenband 8 zum Ktb. Nr. 2 u. 3, 17.5.–26.5.40*. AOK 20 E 279/8. *Gruppe XXI, Ia, Nr. 1021/40, an Chef OKW, 29.5.40* and *OKW, Abt. L, an Gruppe XXI, 30.5.40*, in *Anlagenband 10 zum Ktb. 2 u. 2, 27.5.–4.6.40*. AOK 20 E 279/10.
[38] *Gruppe XXI, an Gruppe Narvik, 5.6.40*, in *Anlagenband 14 zum Ktb., 2 u. 3, 1.6.–14.6.40*. AOK 20 E 279/14.
[39] *Gruppe XXI, Ia, Nr. 284/40, Fuehrerweisung vom 5.6.40*, in *Gruppe XXI-Drontheim, Unternehmen "Naumburg."* AOK 20 D 279/28.
[40] *Fuehrer Conferences*, 1940, I, p. 52.
[41] *OKW, Heimatstab Nord, Ia, Aktennotiz ueber Ferngespraech Oberst d. G. Warlimont-Major i. G. v. Tippelskirch am 7 Juni 1940*, in *Gruppe XXI-Drontheim, Unternehmen "Naumburg."* AOK 20 E 279/28.

pected to make the final arduous march to Narvik and on arrival be capable of engaging in combat. The march, expected to take ten days, began at Sörfold on 2 June and continued according to schedule as the troops pushed onward in rain, snow, and fog through mud and melting snow. The terrain ruled out the use of either pack animals or vehicles, and supply was entirely by air drop. Heavy weapons and ammunition were to be dropped shortly before the detachment reached Narvik. On 9 June, after the Allies evacuated Narvik, the advance halted slightly short of the halfway point at Hellmobotn. A token force in platoon strength continued on to Narvik where it arrived on the 13th. In his final report the commanding officer stated that, without doubt, had the situation required it, the entire detachment could have completed the march and been capable of going into combat.[42]

While the Germans prepared measures for the relief of Narvik, the main concern of the Allied command was to keep the evacuation of its 24,500 men secret until the convoys were at sea. Some supplies, including guns and tanks, were shipped out before the end of May; and the first group of troopships loaded 15,000 men on the 4th, 5th, and 6th of June and sailed on the 7th. The second group took aboard most of the remaining troops on the 7th and 8th and left its rendezvous area on the morning of the 9th. The rear guard at Harstad went aboard the cruiser *Southhampton* at 0900 on the 8th.[43]

At the last minute the Norwegian Government, which had been kept in the dark about the evacuation until late on 1 June, attempted to salvage at least a remnant of its territory by diplomatic means. As early as mid-April there had, apparently at German instigation, been talk of neutralizing Narvik. At the end of the month the project became known as the Mowinckel Plan after the former Norwegian Prime Minister L. Mowinckel suggested it to the Swedish Foreign Minister in Stockholm. The Swedes took it up but got no encouragement from the belligerents until after 1 June when, with the evacuation impending, the Norwegians approached the Swedish Government. The Germans, despite their desperate position at Narvik, accorded the matter dilatory treatment. After the Swedish Minister directly proposed the neutralization of Narvik in a conference on 4 June the State Secretary in the German Foreign Ministry deduced that the Allies were about to evacuate, but the OKW apparently did not share that impression. As late as 7 June the OKW was busy planning Operation NAUMBURG, which could not have been executed before the last week of the month.[44]

[42] 2. Geb. Div., Ia., Nr. 66/40, an Gruppe XXI, Ia. 18.6.40 and Gruppe Obstlt. v. Hengl, Bericht ueber das Unternehmen Bueffel, 15.6.40, in Anlagenband 15 zum Ktb. Nr. 2 u. 3, Erfahrungsberichte d. Gruppe XXI. AOK 20 E 279/15.
[43] Derry op. cit., pp. 218–21.
[44] Derry, op. cit., pp. 173–76. Hubatsch, op. cit., p. 253.

During the first week of June Dietl's sole objective was to hold a bridgehead along the Swedish border, no matter how limited, until reinforcements could be brought in and the relief operation had time to take effect. His stocks of ammunition were running low. Almost continuous bad weather after the end of May prevented air supply and imposed hardships on his troops who had no shelter in their new positions, but it hampered Allied operations as well, with the result that the front remained relatively quiet. The Allied evacuation came as a surprise and was not discovered until about 1700 on June 8th. Thereafter the Germans quickly reoccupied Narvik. On the following day the Norwegian Command signed an armistice which ended the fighting in Norway.[45]

After the armistice the Germans quickly established a firm hold on northern Norway. In mid-May, to support the advance of the 2d Mountain Division, they had begun opening a sea route north of Trondheim. Several small Norwegian bases on the coast and on offshore islands were occupied, and at the end of the month the 181st Division began Operation BIENE, directed against a British communications and intelligence center on Alsten Island.[46] By 8 June the coastal waters were open to German shipping as far north as Fauske, and at the middle of the month the cruiser *Nuernberg* and two steamers transported the second infantry regiment and the artillery regiment of the 3d Mountain Division to Narvik and Tromsö.[47]

Operation JUNO

By mid-May the German warships damaged in the April operations had been repaired. The *Scharnhorst*, the *Hipper*, and the *Nuernberg* were on training cruises in the Baltic, and the *Gneisenau* was scheduled for a shakedown cruise at the end of the month. On 16 May the Naval Staff decided that, at the beginning of June, the battleships and cruisers could start operating in the sea area between Norway and the Shetlands and northward as a diversion and to create difficulties for Allied supply movements. During the following days a wide divergence of opinion developed between the Naval Staff on the one hand and the operating commands, Naval Group West and Fleet Command, on the other. The operating commands wanted to conserve their forces and believed the chances of success too small to warrant risking the few German heavy ships in operations in and beyond the Shetlands–Norway passage. But Admiral Raeder and the Naval Staff, probably believing

[45] *3. Geb. Div., K.T.B. Narvik, loc. cit.*, pp. 63–74. *Gruppe XXI, Ia, an OKW, L, 9.6.40, in Anlagenband 14 zum Ktb. 2 u. 3, 1.6.–14.6.40.* AOK 20 E 279/14.
[46] *Gruppe XXI, Abt. Ia, Nr. 178/40, Operationsbefehl, 25.5.40, in Anlagenband 9 zum Ktb. 2 u. 3., 17.5.–25.5.40.* AOK 20 E 279/9.
[47] *Gruppe XXI, Ia, Nr. 354/40, Befehl fuer Transport der Restteile 3. Geb. Division nach Nordnorwegen, 13.6.40, in Anlagenband 14 zum Ktb. 2 u. 3, 1.6.–14.6.40.* AOK 20 E 279/14.

the war was drawing to a close, insisted on adopting aggressive methods to prove the worth of the Navy and assure its future development.[48]

On 21 May Raeder informed Hitler that the *Scharnhorst* and the *Hipper* would be ready for new missions on about 27 May and that the *Gneisenau* would be ready at the beginning of June. His plan was for the ships to operate in the northern North Sea and the Arctic Ocean to relieve the German land operations in northern Norway and to defend the Skagerrak and southern Norway by threatening communications between the British Isles and Norway. Operations using Trondheim as a base were to be begun later.[49] He also ordered the possibility of again using submarines in the Narvik area investigated, but the Commanding Admiral, Submarines, strongly advised against it since the brightness of the nights and the enemy's favorable opportunities for patrol indicated only slight prospects of success.[50]

On 24 May, with the situation at Narvik deteriorating rapidly, the Naval Staff dropped its plans for harassing the Allies' supply lines and began to consider means of bringing direct relief to the force at Narvik. It concluded that the situation at sea was favorable and that a sortie into West Fiord as far as Narvik or into Vaags Fiord as far as Harstad was entirely feasible. On the following day it ordered Naval Group West to plan an operation along those lines and time it as early as possible, sometime after June 2. Group XXI would designate promising shore targets. On the 27th Hitler added the mission of opening and protecting a coastal supply line for the 2d Mountain Division in the Trondheim–Mo–Bodö area.[51]

The order for the operation, to be carried out under the code name JUNO by the battleships *Scharnhorst* and *Gneisenau*, the cruiser *Hipper*, and four destroyers, was issued on 29 May. The first and main assignment was a surprise penetration into And Fiord and Vaags Fiord to Harstad and destruction of the bases, transports, and warships found there. If reconnaissance reports showed that a sortie into West Fiord and Ofot Fiord, possibly as far as Narvik, appeared to offer better prospects of success, that was to be carried out as the main assignment. The additional task, protection of supply transport from Trondheim to Bodö, could be carried out either simultaneously with the main assignment or after its excution. Trondheim was to be used as a base. The Naval Staff indicated that it was thinking not only of a single strike against a specific target but also of continuing operations which would be carried out over a longer period.[52] The order as delivered to the Commanding Admiral, Fleet, Admiral Wilhelm Marschall, set specific missions; but in a verbal discussion with Marschall on 31 May Raeder

[48] *Naval War Diary,* Vol. 9, pp. 119, 141, 153, 190.
[49] *Fuehrer Conferences,* 1940, I, p. 50.
[50] *Naval War Diary,* Vol. 9, p. 201.
[51] *Naval War Diary,* Vol. 9, pp. 218–19 and 237.
[52] *Naval War Diary,* Vol. 9, pp. 275ff.

couched the requirements in more general terms, which may have been the cause of a serious divergence of views regarding execution of the operation which later developed between the Commanding Admiral, Fleet, and the Naval Staff.[53]

At 0800 on 4 June the warships steamed out of Kiel. Four supply ships had been dispatched under minesweeper escort to Trondheim; and two tankers, from which the warships would refuel at sea, were on route to the rendezvous points in north Norwegian waters. A day earlier observations of lively transport traffic toward Narvik had led the Naval Staff to surmise that the Allies were building up their strength at Narvik in order to gain a victory there to counterbalance the defeat in Flanders.[54] On the 6th the Germans estimated the British naval forces in the north Norwegian area at 2 battleships, 1 aircraft carrier, 4 cruisers, and 15 destroyers. (Actually Lord Cork's force for the evacuation amounted only to 2 aircraft carriers, 3 cruisers, and 10 destroyers.)[55] With no other intelligence or reconnaissance reports at his disposal, Admiral Marschall decided on the 6th to time his attack on Harstad for the night of the 8/9th.[56] On the evening of the 6th the warships met the tanker *Dithmarschen* at a position halfway between Norway and Iceland and began refueling operations which lasted for 24 hours.

On the night of the 7th, the refueling completed, Marschall assembled his commanders at a conference aboard the flagship. In the morning air reconnaissance had spotted a convoy steaming southward from Narvik. A second message, received during the conference, reported three more groups of ships at sea. From the westward movement of the ships Marschall concluded that the British were evacuating Narvik and decided that the convoys offered valuable targets.[57] Naval Group West and the Naval Staff had not drawn the same conclusion and on being informed at 0500 on the 8th of Marschall's intention to attack the convoys instructed him that his main assignment was still to strike at Harstad. An attack on the convoys by the *Hipper* and the destroyers was left to his discretion, although it was believed that such a move would reveal the presence of the warships prematurely.[58]

Meanwhile, at 0600, the warships had come across the tanker *Oil Pioneer* and the trawler *Juniper* and had sunk both before they could transmit radio signals. Throughout the morning the search for the convoys continued, and the *Scharnhorst* and the *Hipper* launched their planes. These reported a convoy consisting of a cruiser and a merchant ship to the south and an armed merchant ship and a hospital ship to the north. The *Hipper* set a course to intercept the merchant ship while

---

[53] Assmann, *Campaign in Norway*, p. 70.
[54] *Naval War Diary*, Vol. 10, p. 20.
[55] Assmann, *Campaign in Norway*, p. 71. Roskill, *op. cit.*, p. 193.
[56] Derry, *op. cit.*, p. 222.
[57] Assmann, *Campaign in Norway*, pp. 71ff.
[58] *Naval War Diary*, Vol. 10, p. 68.

the battleships began a search for the convoy. The merchant ship, which proved to be the troop transport *Orama*, traveling empty except for 100 German prisoners, was sunk and its last radio signals were successfully jammed. The hospital ship *Atlantis* was not attacked. Observing the regulations, it did not transmit a report; therefore, the presence of the German ships was not revealed until 24 hours later when the *Atlantis* gave a visual message to the battleship *Valiant*.

Shortly after 1300 Marschall released the *Hipper* and the four destroyers to Trondheim for refueling and to take over the task of opening a route for Army supplies along the coast from Trondheim to Bodö. At about the same time Marschall decided to abandon the search for the convoy and to proceed with the battleships into the Harstad-Tromsö area where radio intercepts indicated the presence of two British aircraft carriers. At 1645 the masthead of a warship was sighted which on closer approach was identified as a large aircraft carrier, the *Glorious*, escorted by two destroyers, later identified as the *Ardent* and the *Acasta*. The *Glorious*, proceeding to Scapa independently because it was short of fuel, had no security patrols in the air. The German ships opened fire three quarters of an hour later, and the first shells put an end to attempts to arm and launch the carrier's torpedo bombers. In an action lasting about an hour and a half the Germans sank the carrier and both destroyers; but, shortly before the end, the *Acasta*, the last to go down, secured a torpedo hit aft on the *Scharnhorst* which put the after turret out of action and flooded two engine rooms. Again the British ships failed to give the alarm. Messages from the *Glorious* were jammed, and neither of the destroyers attempted to use its radio, with the result that the first news of the battle came on the afternoon of the following day when the German claims were broadcast.[59]

With the damage to the *Scharnhorst* reported as serious and her speed reduced to 20 knots, Marschall broke off the operation and intended to steer for home immediately but Naval Group West ordered him to put into Trondheim instead, where the ships arrived on the afternoon of the 9th. The first action reports brought expressions of satisfaction from the Naval Staff which dispatched the cruiser *Nuernberg* to join the operation; but on the 9th Marschall's conduct of the operation was subjected to severe criticism. The Naval Staff, apparently still not aware that the Allied evacuation had ended on the night of 8-9 June, maintained that the admiral should have adhered to the plan to attack Harstad and that the encounter with the *Glorious* was a piece of pure luck. In the belief that the evacuation was still in progress it ordered Marschall, on the afternoon of the 9th, to resume operations as soon as possible, if necessary with the *Gneisenau* alone. The next morning Marschall put to sea with the *Gneisenau*, the *Hipper*, and the destroyers

---

[59] Assmann, *Campaign in Norway*, pp. 72–73.

but returned to Trondheim that night on instructions from Naval Group West.

During the succeeding days the Naval Staff, which continued to urge aggressive action while the admiral wanted to conserve his limited forces, became increasingly critical of the inactivity of the Fleet. Finally, Marschall requested relief on the grounds of illness, which occasioned further delays until 20 June when the new Commanding Admiral, Vizeadmiral Guenther Luetjens, sailed at 1600 with the *Gneisenau*, the *Hipper*, and one destroyer for a thrust into northern waters and the Iceland area. Seven hours later the *Gneisenau* was hit by a torpedo from a British submarine, whereupon the ships put back into Trondheim. With both of its battleships damaged (the *Scharnhorst* had started home on the 20th) the Naval Staff regarded its hopes for operations in the northern waters as completely frustrated. After temporary repairs had been made, the *Gneisenau* with the *Hipper*, the *Nuernberg*, and the destroyers returned to Kiel on 28 July.[60]

While JUNO was still in progress the OKW had ordered conversion of the liners *Bremen* and *Europa* as troopships completed with the intention of using them in a projected occupation of Iceland, to be executed under the code name IKARUS. The Naval Staff saw no advantages in the occupation since Germany could not control the sea around Iceland and use of the island as a naval base was out of the question; but it believed the operation, although risky, was technically possible if it were timed for after September, when the period of longer nights set in. The damage the *Scharnhorst* and the *Gneisenau* had suffered off Norway, however, reduced the prospects of an early execution, and IKARUS was shelved as a more ambitious undertaking, the invasion of England, came to the fore.[61]

---

[60] *Naval War Diary,* Vol. 10, pp. 68–69, 77, 78, 103, 116, 171, 182–83. Hubatsch, *op. cit.,* pp. 241ff.
[61] *Fuehrer Conferences,* 1940, I, pp. 55, 60. *Naval War Diary,* Vol. 10, pp. 103, 153.

Chapter 6

The Campaign in Norway—Summary

In comparison with the expenditures of men and matériel which became commonplace later in the war the Norwegian campaign was minor. It cost Germany 1,317 killed, 1,604 wounded, and 2,375 lost at sea or otherwise missing. The British lost 1,896 men in ground fighting and upwards of 2,500 more at sea. The Norwegian losses numbered 1,335 men and those of the French and Poles 530. The campaign cost the German Air Force 127 combat aircraft as opposed to 87 Allied planes according to German estimates, which do not include the 25 planes which went down with the aircraft carrier *Glorious*. In the fighting at sea Germany sacrificed 1 heavy and 2 light cruisers, 10 destroyers, 1 torpedo boat, 6 submarines, and 15 small craft. The British lost 1 aircraft carrier, 1 cruiser, 1 antiaircraft cruiser, 7 destroyers, and 4 submarines while the French and Poles lost 1 destroyer and 1 submarine each.[1] Of the losses the only ones of major significance were those sustained by the German Navy. It had lost the new heavy cruiser *Bluecher;* and at the end of June, after the *Scharnhorst* and the *Gneisenau* had been damaged, Germany had only 1 heavy cruiser, 2 light cruisers, and 4 destroyers fit for action. In the anxious days of the summer of 1940 this was a source of some comfort to the British. Winston Churchill has described it as a "fact of major importance potentially affecting the whole future of the war." [2] On the other hand, the Norwegian campaign constituted the high point in the German Navy's exploitation of its surface forces.

As an isolated military operation the German occupation of Norway was an outstanding success. Carried out in the teeth of vastly superior British sea power, it was, as Hitler said, "not only bold, but one of the sauciest undertakings in the history of modern warfare." [3] Well planned and skillfully executed, it showed the Wehrmacht at its best; nevertheless, some of the faults which were later to contribute greatly to the German defeat were already present, although not yet prominent enough to in-

---

[1] *Die Berichte des Oberkommandos der Wehrmacht, 1 September 1939 bis 31 Dezember 1940* (Berlin, 1941), p. 247. Derry, *op. cit.*, p. 230.
[2] Churchill, *op. cit.*, vol. 1, p. 657.
[3] *Gruppe XXI, Notiz fuer das Kriegstagebuch, 1.4.40,* in *Anlagenband 1 zum K.T.B. Nr. 1, Anlagen 1–52, 2.20.–18.4.40.* AOK 20 E 180/7.

fluence the outcome of the campaign. For success the operation depended heavily on daring and surprise combined with lack of preparedness and indecision on the part of the enemy. Those elements won campaigns but were not enough to win the war. The campaign also revealed two serious defects in Hitler's personal leadership: his tendency to lose his nerve in a crisis and his persistent meddling in the details of operations.

To some extent WESERUEBUNG gave evidence of Hitler's fatal weakness, his inability to keep his commitments within the bounds of his resources. Most German authorities still contend that Germany's strategic interests in Scandinavia and the existence of Allied intentions to open an offensive there created a compelling necessity for German action; but two who qualify as experts of the first rank have concluded that WESERUEBUNG was not the sole solution for Germany and probably not the best. General der Artillerie a.D. Walter Warlimont has pointed out that even if the Allies had been able to establish themselves in Norway they would have been forced to relinquish their hold there once the invasion of France started and that, if it were still necessary, the occupation of Norway could have been accomplished much more cheaply after the campaign in France [4] Professor Walther Hubatsch in his history of the Norwegian campaign reaches essentially the same conclusion and adds the observation that Germany "undoubtedly" had the strength at that time to force the Allies back out of Scandinavia. He observes, also, that in Scandinavia the Allies would have had to contend with opposition from the Soviet Union as well as Germany.[5] These views find further support in the official British historian's statement that "given the political situation of 1939–40 British intervention in some form was inevitable; and given the paucity of our then resources in men and arms, a more or less calamitous issue from it was likewise inevitable." [6] Of course, the clock cannot be set back, and the function of history is not to speculate on what might have been; still, although the contentions of Warlimont and Hubatsch may benefit from hindsight, they reflect a strong body of opinion which existed in the German Command at the time and which, in essence, opposed the then growing tendency to plunge in with a full-scale offensive at any point which was or might be threatened. It needs also to be pointed out in this connection that the counter-argument, namely, that Germany acted out of compulsion, rests in large part on the reading of a cause and effect relationship into a coincidence.

To return to the firmer ground of tangible gains, WESERUEBUNG brought Germany control of its supply line for Swedish iron ore (later also for Finnish nickel), a number of new naval and air bases, and some other economic advantages, mostly minor, such as the local production

---

[4] *Walter Warlimont, Gutachten zu der Kriegstagebuch-Ausarbeitung OKW/WFSt "Der noerdliche Kriegssachauplatz,"* p. 19.   MS # C–099 p. 1.   OCMH.

[5] Hubatsch, *op. cit.,* pp. 261ff.

[6] Derry, *op. cit.,* p. 246.

of Norwegian metals and ores. The naval and air bases somewhat improved the German position with respect to the British Isles, increased the chances to break out into the Atlantic with raiders, and later made possible air and sea attacks on the Allied Murmansk convoys. A decisive improvement, particularly in the naval situation, was not achieved. Germany could still be shut off from the open sea, and for the Navy the losses in ships sustained during WESERUEBUNG offset the advantages gained in the bases.

From the point of view of military operations two features of the Norwegian campaign stand out: (1) it was the first joint operation involving all three branches of the armed forces, and (2) it proved that, under certain circumstances, superior air power could be used to neutralize superior sea power.

As an armed forces operation, the campaign revealed that neither side had developed a command organization suited to the direction of large-scale joint operations. On the German side a projected armed forces command gave way at an early stage to independent service commands coordinated at the highest level by Hitler and the OKW and depending at the tactical level on cooperation between the individual commanders. The British had to cope with a divided command of their own forces plus the frictions, disagreements, and suspicions which arose out of the effort to conduct combined operations involving Norwegian, French, and Polish contingents. On the whole, the Germans managed to achieve the greater degree of coordination, partly, no doubt, because the difficulties they faced were fewer.

The power of the German Air Force was dramatically demonstrated when, on 18 April, the cruiser *Suffolk,* which had shelled the airfield at Stavanger, returned to Scapa Flow with her quarter-deck awash after being subjected to seven hours of almost continuous air attacks.[7] A week earlier Admiral Forbes had decided to leave the waters around southern Norway mostly to submarines because of German air superiority.[8] That decision had virtually assured the safety of the Germans' supply line from their home base. While the Luftwaffe was not able to carry out its strategic mission to the extent of preventing enemy landings in Norway, it was effective in keeping the Allies from establishing secure bases and contributed greatly toward forcing their subsequent withdrawal. The tactical support of ground troops could be carried out unopposed and, hence, was very successful, although, particularly at Narvik, it was one of the sources of friction between the Army, which wanted close support of its troops, and the Air Force, which wanted to concentrate on the more rewarding targets at sea.

One aspect of the Norwegian campaign which seemed to have great importance at the time was the appearance of the so-called Fifth Col-

---

[7] Derry, *op. cit.,* p. 74.
[8] Roskill, *op. cit.,* p. 171.

umn.   The name "Quisling" eventually became a generic term applied to that species of traitor who made himself a willing tool of the invader. The Fifth Column, long regarded as one of the Nazis' most effective weapons, was, in fact, a negligible factor in the campaign.   The idea of boring from within may have appealed to Hitler and Rosenberg, but the preservation of secrecy alone forbade its being incorporated into the military plan.   Quisling was from the first a source of political embarrassment and a military liability in that he contributed greatly to the failure of the intended "peaceful" occupation.   Probably the chief significance of the Fifth Column in Norway and elsewhere was that it was a phantasm which could be blown up beyond any relationship to reality in the minds of a people caught in a disastrous war for which they were not prepared either militarily or psychologically.

PART TWO

OPERATIONS IN FINLAND

Chapter 7

Plans and Preparations

The Change of Course in German-Finnish Relations

The Winter War of 1939–1940 left Finland independent but teetering on the brink of disaster. Its economy, already shattered by the war, had to bear the strain of 400,000 refugees from territory annexed by the Soviet Union. Strategically, the peace treaty created favorable conditions for a new Soviet attack. In the south the border was pushed northwestward, away from the Karelian Isthmus and Lake Ladoga where the Finns had been able to put up their strongest resistance during the war. The acquisition of Salla and some territory around it gave the Soviet Union an entering wedge for a drive across the waist of Finland to the head of the Gulf of Bothnia; and the railroad which Finland was forced under the treaty to build from Kemiyärvi to Salla (Kuolayärvi)—while the Soviet Union completed a stretch from Salla to Kandalaksha on the Murmansk Railroad—would facilitate either Soviet military operations or an economic penetration of northern Finland. In the far north possession of the western half of the Rybatchiy Peninsula enabled Soviet forces to dominate the entrance to Pechenga, while, in the south, occupation of Hanko gave the Russians a naval base and a strong beachhead in the heart of Finland west of Helsinki.[1] The German occupation of Norway completed the physical isolation of Finland by putting an end to such modest prospects of Western intervention as had existed during the Winter War, and the fall of France brought political isolation as well by making Germany the dominant power on the Continent and Great Britain a suppliant for the favor of Stalin.

In June 1940, while the Allies were going down to defeat in Norway and France, the Soviet Union, setting to work to gather in its share of

---

[1] *Der russisch-finnische Krieg, Anlagenband zum T.B. AOK Norwegen, Ic.* AOK 20594/15.

the spoils, occupied Lithuania, Latvia, and Estonia and subjected Finland to renewed pressure. It began early in the month with a demand for the return of all property, both public and private, which the Finns had removed from Hanko before the Soviet occupation. That was followed by a demand for either Soviet control of the nickel mining concession at Pechenga or operation of the mining company in partnership with Finland. Pechenga, where a Canadian firm held the concession, had been left to Finland after the Winter War solely out of regard for a British reaction, which in June no longer had to be feared. In July Soviet insistence on demilitarization of the Åland Islands and the right to send trains across Finnish territory to Hanko increased the tension. Finland submitted with regard to the property and demilitarization questions and agreed to negotiate on the remaining two demands.[2]

Meanwhile, the Finns, thus threatened, began to pin their hopes on the then seemingly remote possibility that help might yet be secured from Germany. On 4 July the Finnish Foreign Minister told the German Minister that sentiment friendly to Germany was developing in the population in "avalanche proportions" and that efforts were underway to form a government oriented exclusively toward Berlin. Public opinion, he said, was influenced strongly by the idea that Finland with the aid of German arms could, in a few months, recover the territories lost to Russia. The German Minister replied that he would regard as objectionable the formation of a government onesidedly favorable to Germany since Germany intended to respect its agreements with Russia; it would be preferable, he suggested, to form a government which cooperated with Germany secretly while outwardly maintaining an attitude of reserve. Two days later he was admonished from Berlin to avoid such statements as the last because they might arouse "false hopes."[3]

Nevertheless, two occurrences during the summer were to result in a radical change of the official German attitude toward Finland. In July the I.G. Farben concern contracted for 60 percent of the Pechenga nickel ore production, thus assuring Germany of an adequate supply of that strategic metal and giving Germany an interest in the preservation of Finland. Even more important for Finland—and the world—Hitler at the end of July ordered planning begun for a campaign against the Soviet Union.[4] Naturally, Finland came under consideration as a potential ally.

German interest in the Pechenga ore became apparent in the plans and military dispositions affecting Finland that the Germans initiated in August. At the end of July the Soviet Union ushered in a new period

[2] Mannerheim, *op. cit.*, pp. 422–24.
[3] Bluecher tel. to Foreign Ministry, No. 398, 4 July 1940 and Woermann to Bluecher, No. 310, 6 July. U. S. Department of State, German Foreign Ministry Records, B 19/B003639.
[4] Helmuth Greiner, *Das Unternehmen "Barbarossa,"* p. 12. MS # C–065i. OCMH.

of crisis in Eastern Europe with the occupation of Bessarabia. Communist demonstrations in Helsinki and a Russian charge that the Finns were attempting to suppress the Soviet-supported Association for Peace and Friendship With the Soviet Union, which had been founded in Finland after the Winter War, appeared to indicate that Finland's turn was next. German intelligence concluded that the Soviet Union would begin military operations against Finland in mid-August.[5] On 13 August Hitler ordered a strengthening of the land, sea, and air forces in the northernmost parts of Norway. The 2d Mountain Division was to be shifted from Trondheim to the Kirkenes area. For the event of a Soviet attack on Finland he gave the Mountain Corps Norway (the 2d and 3d Mountain Divisions under the command of General Dietl, formed in June 1940) and the 2d Mountain Division the task of preparing, under the cover-name RENNTIER, an operation which had as its objectives the speedy occupation of Pechenga and the nickel mines at Kolosyoki and defense of the northern Norwegian fiords against possible landings.[6]

The first open sign of a shift in German policy toward Finland came on 18 August when Lt. Col. Joseph Veltjens, as Goering's personal emissary, made contact with Finland's Marshal Mannerheim and secured permission for the transport of German Air Force supplies and personnel across Finnish territory from the head of the Gulf of Bothnia to Kirkenes. Simultaneously representing Goering in his capacity as director of the German Four Year Plan, Veltjens also secured an option on the nickel mining concession at Pechenga. The Air Force move was followed on 22 September by a transit agreement covering supplies of all the armed services and in November by a transport arrangement for troops returning on furlough to Germany from northern Norway.[7] In conjunction with the transit agreements and as a result of a favorable report on the Finnish Army which Hitler received from the German Military Attaché in Helsinki, Germany undertook to supply arms to the Finns.[8] The shipments began in August when Germany released stocks of military equipment and supplies originally destined for Finland which had been impounded during the occupation of Norway.[9]

To the Government of the Soviet Union the German Foreign Ministry explained the transit agreements as a temporary aid in strengthening the Norwegian defenses against a British attack. The Soviet Govern-

[5] *Ibid.*, p. 12. *Halder Diary*, Vol. IV, p. 137. Helmuth Greiner, *Aufzeichnungen ueber die Lagebesprechungen bei der Abteilung Landesverteidigung vom 8 August 1940 bis zum 25 Juni 1941*, p. 8. MS # C–065i. OCMH.

[6] *OKW, WFSt, Abt. L, Nr. 33230/40, Norwegen, 16.8.40* and *Geb. Korps Norwegen, Chefs Nr. 82/40, "Renntier," 7.9.40,* in *Gruppe XXI, "Renntier," 16.8–7.9.40.* AOK 20 20844/1. MS # C–065i, p. 13.

[7] MS # C–065i, p. 14. Mannerheim, *op. cit.,* pp. 425–27. *Heimatstab Nord des W. B. Norwegen, Nr. 3229/40, Urlaeubertransport durch Finnland, 24.11.1940,* in *Taetigkeitsberichte der Gruppe XXI, November 1940.* AOK 20 12564/1.

[8] *Halder Diary,* Vol. IV, p. 149, 153, 158.

[9] Wipert von Bluecher, *Gesandter zwischen Diktatur und Demokratie* (Wiesbaden: Limes Verlag, 1951), p. 198.

ment accepted the explanation without comment but did not long conceal its growing suspicion.   On 1 November Anastas I. Mikoyan, Peoples Commissar for Foreign Trade, complained that the Germans were unwilling to deliver war matériel to the Soviet Union, yet were making deliveries to Finland and other countries.[10]   In Finland the agreements brought new hope.   Marshal Mannerheim, in his memoirs, stated that but for the transit agreements Finland would have fallen victim to the Soviet Union during the fall of 1940.[11]

The extent of Soviet concern over the new German-Finnish relationship became clear at the time of the visit of Soviet Foreign Minister Vyacheslav M. Molotov to Berlin in mid-November.   Molotov stated that the Nazi-Soviet Pact of the previous year could be regarded as fulfilled, except for one point, namely, Finland.   The Finnish question was still unsolved, and he asked Hitler to tell him whether the Nazi-Soviet Pact, as far as it concerned Finland, was still in force; the Soviet Government could find no grounds for a change.   Hitler replied that Germany had no political interest in Finland but needed the deliveries of Finnish nickel and lumber and, above all, did not want a new conflict in the Baltic Sea area.   He painted a picture of Swedish involvement and British, or even United States, intervention.   A Baltic conflict, he declared, would place a heavy strain on German-Russian relations and on the great collaboration planned for the future.

Molotov asked for withdrawal of German troops from Finland, a promise that Germany would not support Finnish anti-Soviet demonstrations, and, above all, concurrence in the Soviet desire to proceed with a settlement of the Finnish question in keeping with the 1939 treaty.   The settlement, he implied, could be carried out without war as had those involving Bessarabia and the Baltic States.   Sidetracking the discussion, the German Foreign Minister, Ribbentrop, replied that there was actually no reason for making an issue of the Finnish question. Strategically, the peace treaty with Finland met all of Russia's wishes, and whatever disturbances had arisen as a result of the German troop movements would subside as soon as the transports ended.   Hitler added that both sides agreed in principle that Finland belonged in the Russian sphere of influence and thereupon dismissed the problem as purely theoretical.[12]   Actually, in this conference, which marked the beginning of the end of German-Soviet collaboration, nothing was less theoretical; Hitler warned the Russians to stay out of Finland, and the warning, however grudgingly, was heeded.

The Molotov visit to Berlin produced a mild crisis in German-Finnish relations.   The Finns became apprehensive over the possibility that the Germans and Russians might have gotten together to engineer another

---

[10] U.S. Department of State, *Nazi-Soviet Relations, 1939–1941* (Washington, 1948), pp. 188, 198, 202, 204, 217.
[11] Mannerheim, *op. cit.,* p. 427.
[12] *Nazi-Soviet Relations,* pp. 217–47.

116

division of the spoils in Eastern Europe; their anxiety in that respect was heightened by a misunderstanding regarding the German option on the nickel mining concession. The Finnish Government had assumed that Germany, in defense of its option, would make itself a third party to the negotiations with Russia on that matter and so deflect some of the pressure from Finland; consequently, the Finns were thoroughly dismayed when, as the Russians began pushing their claims in October, the German Government declared that it had no interest in the ownership of the mines. Actually, the German Foreign Office did not learn until the end of October that an option existed and then found that its hands were tied since it had assured the Russians in July that Germany's interest in the mines did not go beyond securing enough of the ore output to meet German requirements.[13]

On 23 November, to allay the misgivings of the Finns, Veltjens went to Helsinki a second time. He was instructed to say that nothing had been decided during the Molotov visit which made it necessary for Finland to adopt an "unnecessarily yielding" attitude in its negotiations with the Soviet Union. The German refusal to enter into the negotiations concerning the mining concession, he was to explain, meant only that Germany regarded the decision as one which was entirely up to Finland—to the extent of also recognizing Finland's right to keep the concession for itself if it so desired. To bolster the Finns' confidence, he was instructed to say the Russians were aware that Germany in the existing situation regarded new "complications" in the north as undesirable.[14] Several days later the German Minister in Helsinki was told to use the same words of encouragement in his talks with members of the Finnish Government and to add that it was believed the Soviet Government would keep the German attitude in mind in the future conduct of its relations with Finland.[15]

The Russians' dissatisfaction with the outcome of the Berlin talks was underscored on 26 November when Molotov informed the German Ambassador in Moscow that the Soviet Union would join the Three Power Pact (one of the matters discussed in Berlin) provided certain conditions were met. First on the list was "that the German troops be immediately withdrawn from Finland, which under the compact of 1939 belongs to the Soviet Union's sphere of influence." The Soviet Union promised "to ensure peaceful relations with Finland" and to protect German economic interests there.[16] In the succeeding months the Germans avoided giving a direct reply, and at the end of March 1941 Ribbentrop told the Japanese Foreign Minister that Germany

[13] *Weiszaecker, Aufzeichnung,* 30 Oct 40. U.S. Department of State, German Foreign Ministry Records, B 19/B003819–21.
[14] *Wiehl, an deutsche Botschaft Moskau, W 5394,* 24 Nov 40. U.S. Department of State, German Foreign Ministry Records, B 19/B003881.
[15] *Ribbentrop, an Gesandtschaft Helsinki, Nr. 29, 29.11.40.* U.S. Department of State, German Foreign Ministry Records, B 19/B003889.
[16] *Nazi–Soviet Relations,* p. 258.

would not attempt to bring the Soviet Union into the pact "for some time" since the Russians had set conditions which were irreconcilable with the German point of view, particularly concerning Finland and Turkey (Molotov had also asked that Russia be given control of the Dardanelles).[17]

In December 1940 German and Soviet attention was drawn to Finland by the Finish presidential election. For the Finns the chief consideration was to elect a man acceptable to Germany, and early in the month the German Foreign Ministry decided to support the candidature of T. M. Kivimaki, then Finnish Minister in Berlin. Subsequently, the Soviet Union informed the Finnish Government that the election of certain individuals, among them Kivimaki, would be regarded "as not serving the interests of Soviet-Finnish relations."[18] On learning of the Soviet move the Germans decided against encouraging the Finns to elect a candidate whom the Russians opposed and switched their support to Risto Ryti, whom they suspected of being pro-British but who was considered preferable to a weak compromise candidate.[19] At the end of the month Ryti was elected and subsequently held office until 1 August 1944.

At the New Year's reception for the diplomatic corps in Berlin the Finnish Minister greeted the German Secretary of State in the Foreign Office, Ernst von Weizsaecker, with the statement that in his homeland people were now more calm since they believed that in a future conflict with Russia they could not stand alone. Weizsaeker replied that the Russians were certainly taking into account the German desire for no new unrest in the north.[20] As the new year began, however, it was soon revealed that Finland had not yet entirely weathered the storm.

In mid-January the Russians renewed their demand for the mining concession and threatened, if an agreement were not reached quickly, "to bring order into the situation by the application of certain means."[21] For a time it appeared that Germany would either have to intervene openly or to advise the Finns to give in, but the Foreign Ministry decided, instead, to encourage the Finns secretly and give them indirect help in staving off a showdown by muddying the waters of the negotiations with various demands for guarantees with respect to delivery of the ore contracted for by Germany. Those tactics succeeded, and, although the Russians angrily broke off the negotiations before the end of the month and stopped their exports to Finland, an open breach did not follow.

---

[17] *Nazi–Soviet Relations*, p. 304.
[18] *U. St. S. Pol., Dg. Pol., Nr. 710, 4.12.40. Schmidt, Notiz fuer RAM, 12.12.40.* U.S. Department of State, German Foreign Ministry Records, B 19/B003913.
[19] *Weizsaecker, an Gesandtschaft Helsinki, fuer Gesandten, Nr. 737, 17.12.40.* U.S. Department of State, German Foreign Ministry Records, B 19/B003918.
[20] *Weizsaecker, No. 925, 31.12.40.* U.S. Department of State, German Foreign Ministry Records, B 19/B003945.
[21] *Wiehl, Aufzeichnung, 19.1.41.* U.S. Department of State, German Foreign Ministry Records, B 19/B003955.

Hitler indicated in his meeting with Mussolini at the Berghof on 18–20 January that, if necessary, Germany would have gone further in supporting Finland. The Russians, he said, had agreed to let Germany have the necessary nickel supplies but would not hold to their agreement any longer than suited them; therefore, he could not permit further Soviet encroachments in Finland.[22]

In February, when another crisis appeared to be in the making, the Finns attempted, through the military attachés, to secure direct German diplomatic support; but the Foreign Ministry on 19 February informed the OKW that the negotiations between Finland and Russia were being followed closely and that there was no danger of the Russians' using force.[23] In March the Russians again broke off the negotiations briefly, but their tendency in the spring of 1941, as they came into serious conflict with Germany in the Balkans, was to relax the pressure on Finland; and in April the Soviet Minister in Helsinki was replaced by a more tactful and moderate diplomat.

The winter of 1940–1941 also saw the establishment of contact between the Finnish and German general staffs. In December Kenraalimajuri Paavo Talvela conferred with Goering and Halder, and in January the Finnish Chief of Staff, Kenraaliluutnanti Erik Heinrichs, went to Berlin. At the end of February Col. Erich Buschenhagen, Chief of Staff, Army of Norway (Group XXI, redesignated in December 1940), visited Helsinki and toured northern Finland. Those meetings, which will be discussed in more detail later, dealt with "hypothetical" cases. As far as can be determined, no commitments were made on either side; still, they provided the Germans with information useful in their planning for an invasion of the Soviet Union and the Finns with more than a hint that they could expect to be drawn into collaboration with Germany.

In the spring, as a result of a little comedy of errors, the German-Finnish *rapprochement* was given additional concrete expression. Late in February SS-Brigadefuehrer Gottlob Berger informed the German Foreign Ministry that 700 Finns had applied at the Legation in Helsinki for enlistment in the SS and that Reichsfuehrer-SS Heinrich Himmler had given permission for their acceptance. On 1 March Berger announced that he intended in the next day or two to send a doctor to Helsinki to begin the physical examinations. Since no word of these intentions had been mentioned to the Finns, the Foreign Ministry asked Berger to postpone action while it hustled the Finnish Minister in Berlin off to Helsinki to get the opinion of his Government.[24] In the meantime, an inquiry to the Helsinki Legation brought the somewhat startled reply

---

[22] MS # C–065i, p. 81.
[23] MS # C–065k, pp. 216, 221, 230, 231.
[24] *St. S., U.St. S. Pol., Pol. VI 806, 22.2.41 and Grundherr, Aufzeichnung, 1.3.41.* U.S. Department of State, German Foreign Ministry Records, B 19/B004040 and B 19/B004047.

119

that the number of men who had applied was not 700 but less than two dozen, and they wanted to join the Army, not the SS. A check with Berger then revealed that his information had come from a Swedish citizen who had since been jailed in Sweden and had destroyed his alleged list of 700 names.[25] By the time these facts were established the Finnish Minister had returned with the information that his Government and Mannerheim were "basically friendly" to the idea of recruiting a Finnish unit for service in Germany and believed it would revive the feeling of military association which had existed between the two countries in the past. They preferred the creation of a unit similar to the 27th Royal Prussian Jaeger Battalion, which during World War I had served as the cradle of the Finnish officer corps and had given the country all of its ranking officers except Mannerheim and one or two others who served in the Czarist Russian Army. But they had no particular objection to the SS as long as the Finns were given status separate from that of the collaborator units which the SS was then recruiting in the occupied countries.[26] The German Foreign Ministry, for its part, was reluctant to embark on a project which would give open evidence of German-Finnish collaboration. At the same time, it was forced to save face for the SS. During the remainder of March it worked out an agreement whereby the Finns undertook to recruit about 1,000 men through an ostensibly private committee. The recruiting was completed in two months, and the battalion subsequently formed served in the SS-Panzer Grenadier Division "Wiking" on the Eastern Front, mostly in the Ukraine, until July 1943 when it returned to Finland and was disbanded.[27]

In the last months before the appointed time for reckoning with the Soviet Union one of the German concerns was to keep the friendship with Finland from ripening too rapidly. For the Germans a fairly nebulous relationship was advantageous. The Finns, on the other hand, not having the Germans' knowledge of the course which events were likely to take in the near future, did not attempt to disguise their desire to slip under the German wing formally and openly if necessary. On 2 April the Finnish Foreign Minister, Rolf Witting, told the German Minister that the Russo-Finnish War had revealed Finland's inability to stand alone against its large neighbor. The Swedish assistance had proved insufficient, and help from Great Britain (in the future) was out of the question. The generally accepted opinion in Finland, he stated, was that the only country which could give Finland real protection

---

[25] *Gesandtschaft Helsinki, Nr. 153, 11.3.41.* and *Grundherr, Fernschreiben an Sonderzug Heinrich, 14.3.41.* U.S. Department of State, German Foreign Ministry Records, B 19/B004068 and B004075.
[26] *Grundherr, Aufzeichnung, Pol. VI 1181, 17.3.41.* U.S. Department of State, German Foreign Ministry Records, B 19/B004088.
[27] *Bluecher, Nr. 193, 24.3.41* and *Bluecher, Nr. 204, 29.3.41.* U.S. Department of State, German Foreign Ministry Records, B 19/B004098 and B 19/B004105. Mannerheim, *op. cit.,* p. 433.

against the Soviet Union was Germany.[28]   This consideration, he indicated, was the determining element in his policy.   Several weeks earlier he had hinted that in connection with the recruiting for the SS "Finland might be able to march into the Three Power Pact."   To keep the conversation from proceeding any further along that line the German Minister had changed the subject.[29]   That Witting's suggestion was not taken up redounded in the long run to Finland's advantage since in a few months the country was to find its position as an independent cobelligerent preferable to 'that of a German ally.

As it was, Witting did not have long to wait for the culmination of his policy.   On 28 May Minister Karl Schnurre, Hitler's personal envoy, called on the Finnish President and, after telling him that the existing tension between Germany and Russia could lead to war, asked that one or several Finnish military experts be sent to Germany to be informed on the situation.[30]   A hypothetical tone was to be maintained for a while yet, but as the Finnish military delegation emplaned for Salzburg on 24 May no one could doubt that the stage was being set for the final act.

Planning for Combined Operations

The BARBAROSSA Directive (The Strategic Plan)

In conferences with his military advisors on 21 and 31 July 1940 Hitler set in motion the planning for an operation against the Soviet Union.[31]   Whether Finland could be used as an ally, he said, remained to be seen. (His own estimation of Finland remained low until 22 August when a report on the Finnish Army from the Military Attaché in Helsinki induced him to reverse his opinion.)   One of the political objectives he foresaw was an expansion of Finland to the White Sea.[32]

From the outset it was clear that Finland offered, at the most, three operational possibilities: an attack on the Murmansk Railroad, the occupation of Pechenga, and an attack across the southeastern border into the Russian right flank.   Generalmajor Erich Marcks, author of the first (5 August) plan of operations submitted to the OKH after the July conferences, recognized the significance of the Murmansk Railroad as a link between Great Britain and the Soviet Union.   But Marcks envisioned a heavy concentration of German forces in the central and southern sectors, leaving northern Russia, Leningrad, and—therefore—

[28] *Gesandtschaft Helsinki, Tgb. Nr. 58/41, Potlitik des finnischen Aussenministers,* 2.4.41.   U.S. Department of State, German Foreign Ministry Records, E 295447/1.
[29] *Gesandtschaft Helsinki, Nr. 153, 11.3.41.*   U.S. Department of State, German Foreign Ministry Documents, B 19/B004068.
[30] Mannerheim, *op. cit.,* p. 434.
[31] For a more detailed account of the planning for the attack on Russia see Department of the Army Pamphlet No. 20–261a, *The German Campaign in Russia, Planning and Operations (1940–1942).*
[32] *Halder Diary,* Vol. IV, pp. 128, 149.

Finland out of the first and main assault phase of the campaign. He recommended postponing the decision on whether or not to make a bid for Finnish participation in the form of an attack on the Murmansk Railroad to a later stage of the operation.[33] The second possibility, the occupation of Pechenga, was placed firmly on the German agenda in mid-August, when Hitler ordered planning begun for Operation RENN-TIER. The third possibility came under consideration in a plan which the National Defense Branch, OKW, submitted to the OKW operations chief, Jodl, on 19 September. The OKW planners proposed a stronger northward thrust by the German Army and, consequently, a larger role for Finland. All available German and Finnish forces were to be massed on the southeastern border of Finland for an attack either across the Isthmus of Karelia toward Leningrad or east of Lake Ladoga toward Tikhvin. The intention was to assist the advance of the German northern army group toward Leningrad.[34] That plan possessed the advantage of tying the operations out of Finland in with the German main effort, but it was impaired by political and transportation difficulties which would prevent concentration of German troops in southern Finland prior to the attack.

At a conference with Hitler on 5 December Brauchitsch and Halder presented a preliminary plan, based on the staff work which had been done thus far, for a campaign in Russia. Hitler approved it, and on the following day Jodl instructed the National Defense Branch to prepare a directive on that basis. From the record of the conference, which is incomplete, it can only be determined that Hitler indicated the participation of Finland was to be counted on, and mention was made of sending one division by rail from Narvik across Sweden to operate in conjunction with the 2d Mountain Division in northern Finland.[35] A more complete statement of the plan, as it existed at that time, is contained in the record of a conference on 7 December between Halder and Falkenhorst. Preparations were to be made for an offensive by four divisions from Norway, one division going overland to Pechenga, another proceeding to Finland by rail from Narvik, and two divisions crossing Sweden by rail from central Norway. The force, as appears from a conference a week later between Halder and Buschenhagen, was to launch two attacks, one in the north in the Pechenga area and the other farther south in the vicinity of Salla.[36]

---

[33] *AOK 18, Abt. Ia. Nr. 167/40, Operationsentwurf Ost, 5.8.40,* in *Vorbereitungen, Aufmarsch Ost I.* AOK 18 17562/8.

[34] Gotthard Heinrici, *Der Feldzug in Russland, Ueberblick ueber die Jahre 1941–1942,* p. 65. MS # T–6 (Neufassung). OCMH.

[35] Helmuth Greiner, *Entwuerfe zum Kriegstagebuch des Wehrmachtfuehrungsstabes (Abteilung Landesverteidigung) vom 1.12.1940–24.3.1941,* pp. 29–34. MS # C–065k. OCMH.. *Halder Diary,* Vol. V, p. 51. The entry in the *Halder Diary* can be read as "two mountain divisions," but in the light of other evidence it appears that "the 2d Mountain Division" is the correct reading.

[36] *Halder Diary,* Vol. V, pp. 54, 60.

On 18 December Hitler signed Directive No. 21, the strategic plan for Operation BARBAROSSA. The directive, which the OKW issued as the basis for operational planning by the services, reads as follows regarding operations in Finland:

II. *Prospective Allies and their Mission*

Romania's and Finland's active participation in the war against Soviet Russia is to be anticipated; they will provide contingents on either wing of our ground forces.

In due course the Armed Forces High Command will approach these two countries and make arrangements as to the manner in which their military contingents will be placed under German command at the time of their intervention.

Finland will cover the concentration of the German Force North (elements of Group XXI) which will be transferred from Norway, and the Finnish troops will operate in conjunction with this force. Moreover, Finland will have to neutralize Hanko.

It may be assumed that, by the start of the campaign at the latest, there will be a possibility of using the Swedish railroads and highways for the transfer of the German Force North.

III. *The Campaign Plans*

During the Russian Campaign, Group XXI will continue to consider the protection of Norway as its primary mission. Any excess forces available beyond the scope of this mission will be committed primarily in the north (Mountain Corps) to secure the Petsamo region and its ore mines as well as the highway connecting Petsamo with Oulu (Arctic Highway). Together with Finnish contingents these forces will subsequently thrust toward the Murmansk Railway in an attempt to prevent supplies from reaching the Murmansk area by land.

Whether an operation by a stronger German force—consisting of two to three divisions which would jump off from the region around and south of Rovaniemi—can be executed, will depend on Sweden's willingness to make its railroads available for such a concentration of German units.

The bulk of the Finnish Army will coordinate its operations with the advance of the German north wing. Its principal mission will be to tie down the maximum Russian forces by an attack west of or on both sides of Lake Ladoga and to seize Hanko.[37]

In short, Directive No. 21 provided for the occupation and defense of Pechenga, essentially Operation RENNTIER; thrusts toward Murmansk and the railroad as had been suggested in the Marcks Plan, only using German troops; and an operation similar to that which the National Defense Branch had proposed to be executed by the Finns along their southern border. It should be noted that at this stage Murmansk, as far as the Germans were concerned, by no means had the strategic importance it was later to attain. In the light of the German expec-

---

[37] *I.M.T.,* Doc. 446–PS.

tation of victory within three to four months—too short a time for significant aid to come to the Soviet Union through Murmansk—the operation against that port was an unnecessary diversion of forces. That it was planned at all seems to be traceable to Hitler's particular, almost fearful, concern for areas where the British might establish even a temporary foothold.

The presence of the Finnish General Talvela in Berlin in mid-December raises the possibility of Finnish participation in the formulation of Directive No. 21. From the existing evidence, it appears that the visit was largely, though—at least from the German point of view—not entirely, coincidental. Talvela's mission was to maintain the personal contact between Mannerheim and Goering which Veltjens had established in his two trips to Helsinki. In talks with Goering and Halder he described the Finnish political and military situation and, in particular, attempted to enlist German support for a political union of Finland and Sweden. The idea of a Swedish-Finnish union ran counter to Hitler's intention of keeping the northern European states dependent on Germany; Goering, therefore, stated that Germany was interested in Finland only as an independent nation, not as a Swedish province. That matters of more positive interest to Germany were at least touched on is indicated in Halder's request for information regarding the time the Finns would need to mobilize—"inconspicuously"—for an attack toward the southeast.[38]

The Army of Norway Staff Study SILBERFUCHS

At the end of December, on the basis of the oral instructions given to Falkenhorst and Buschenhagen, the Army of Norway understood its task as a broadening of the theoretical preparations already underway for RENNTIER. The considerations were to take into account a force expanded to approximately four divisions and a thrust through to the White Sea in the vicinity of Kandalaksha for the purpose of cutting off and taking possession of the Kola Peninsula.[39] On 16 January 1941 von Brauchitsch, in addition, instructed Falkenhorst to prepare a study which would include a German-Finnish advance southeastward into the Lake Ladoga–Lake Onega–White Sea area and proposals with respect to command and supply arrangements.[40]

On 27 January the Army of Norway completed the requested study under the cover-name SILBERFUCHS. The main burden of the attack

---

[38] *Aufzeichnung, Ministerialdirektor Weihl, Nr. 15/40, an Herrn Reichsaussenminister, 20.12.1940.* U.S. Department of State, German Foreign Ministry Records, B 19/B003932. *Halder Diary,* Vol. V, p. 62.

[39] *AOK Norwegen, Taetigkeitsbericht des Armee-Oberkommandos Norwegen, Abt. Ia in der Zeit vom 1.12.–31.12.40,* in *Taetigkeitsberichte des Armee-Oberkommandos Norwegen, Dez. 1940.* AOK 20 12564/2.

[40] *A.O.K. Norwegen, Taetigkeitsbericht des Armee-Oberkommandos Norwegen, Abt. Ia in der Zeit vom 1.1.–31.1.41,* in *Taetigkeitsberichte des Armee-Oberkommandos Norwegen, Jan. 1940.* AOK 20 12564/3. *Halder Diary,* Vol. V, p. 73.

would fall on the Finnish Army which would have to provide security for the south coast including the Åland Islands, defend its border northwest of Lake Ladoga with relatively weak forces, and mass its main force for an attack east of Lake Ladoga toward the Svir River. The main German attack would be directed along the railroad Rovaniemi–Salla–Kandalaksha to the White Sea to cut off the Russian forces on the Kola Peninsula. The forces employed would be the XXXVI Corps, composed of two infantry divisions and the SS-Kampfgruppe "Nord," and the Finnish III Corps, with at least two divisions.[41] SS-Kampfgruppe "Nord," reinforced by a machine gun battalion, an artillery battalion, an antitank battalion, one or two companies of engineers (all motorized), and a battalion of tanks, was to provide mobile advanced security for the assembly of the infantry divisions. Part of the Finnish troops would be used for a secondary attack from Suomussalmi via Ukhta toward Kem. On reaching the Murmansk Railroad at Kandalaksha part of the German force would turn north and, in collaboration with one reinforced mountain division advancing on Murmansk from Pechenga, destroy the Russian units on the Kola Peninsula and take possession of Murmansk and Polyarnyy. The mass of the German force, if possible linking up with the Finns advancing toward Kem, would push southward behind the eastern wing of the Finnish Army. Future operations, either east or west of Lake Onega, were to be determined later.

The operation depended on Sweden's permitting the use of its territory for troop and supply transports. The Army of Norway would supply all of the German units, leaving about five divisions for the defense of Norway; construction, supply, and communications troops and a large number of horse-drawn and motor vehicles would have to be furnished from Germany. The Finns were expected to claim the overall command since their troops would be in the majority.[42]

The Army Operation Order

At the end of January the OKH implemented Directive No. 21 with an operation order, the *Aufmarschanweisung* BARBAROSSA, which Hitler approved on 3 February. In that order the defense of Norway remained the most important task of the Army of Norway. Forces in excess of those needed in Norway could be used in Finland, where, until the Finns entered the war, the mission would be to secure the Pechenga region. After the Finns entered the war one of two courses would be pursued. The first was identical with the Army of Norway SILBERFUCHS proposal: a drive to Kandalaksha by two or three German divisions with attached Finnish contingents, destruction of the Russian forces on the Kola

---

[41] The Finnish corps designation used here is that of 15 June 1941 when the V Corps became the III Corps.

[42] *A.O.K. Norwegen, Ia, Nr. 3/41, Studie ueber Operationsabsicht "Silberfuchs," 27.1.41,* in *"Silberfuchs" Bd. I, 10.1.–8.5.41.* AOK 20 20844/4.

Peninsula in collaboration with German troops advancing on Murmansk from Pechenga, and a shift of the German main force southward to aid the operations of the Finnish Army. The second was an alternative in the event that Sweden refused to permit troop movements across its territory. In that case only one attack would be launched—from Pechenga eastward, with the objective of taking Polyarnyy, Murmansk, and the railroad.

The mission of the Finnish Army would be to take Hanko, cover the deployment of German forces in northern Finland, and—at the latest, when German Army Group North crossed the Dvina River— begin an offensive on both sides of Lake Ladoga with the weight of the attack, if possible, east of the lake.[43] The original Finnish preference, apparently, was for a limited operation west of Lake Ladoga to recover the strategically and economically valuable territory on the Isthmus of Karelia which had been lost to Russia in the Winter War. The Germans, on the other hand, wanted a sweep around the eastern shore of the lake to cut off Leningrad by a junction of the Finnish Army with the Army Group North in the Volkhov–Tikhvin area.

The statement of the Finnish mission was based on a conversation Halder had had on 30 January with the Finnish Chief of Staff, General Heinrichs, who brought an answer to the question Halder had asked Talvela a month earlier (Finland could mobilize "quietly" but not without attracting some attention) and added the information that the Finns would be able to attack with five divisions west of Lake Ladoga, three divisions east of Lake Ladoga, and two divisions against Hanko. The Finnish participation in the planning, again, was indirect. Hitler ordered on 3 February that Finland and the other potential allies could be approached only after it was no longer possible to disguise the German intentions.[44]

On 11 February the OKH informed the Army of Norway that only part of the rear area personnel and vehicles requested in its SILBERFUCHS study could be supplied and that the SS-Kampfgruppe "Nord" was not to be used in the projected operation.[45] Taking those limitations into account, the Army of Norway was to investigate and report on the possibility of executing its operation in accordance with the OKH *Aufmarschanweisung*.[46] The Army of Norway replied that the occupation of Pechenga could be carried out quickly at any time, but the destruction of the Russian forces defending Murmansk could not be accomplished

---

[43] *OKH, GenStdH, Op. Abt. (IN), Nr. 050/41, Aufmarschanweisung "Barbarossa," 31.1.41, in AOK Norwegen, Ia, Aufmarschanweisung "Barbarossa," 31.1.–23.7.41.* AOK 20 20844/3.

[44] *OKW, WFSt, 44089, Besprechung ueber Fall "Barbarossa" und "Sonnenblume," 3.2.41,* (no folder title). OKW/1938. *Halder Diary,* Vol. V, p. 85.

[45] The SS-Kampfgruppe "Nord" was composed of the 6th and 7th SS Death's-Head Regiments. It was a police unit and had just begun military training; however, it was the only unit in the Army of Norway command which was motorized.

[46] *OKH, GenStdH, Op. Abt. (IN), Nr. 150/41, an A.O.K. Norwegen, 11.2.41,* in *"Silberfuchs" Bd. I, 10.1.–8.5.41.* AOK 20 20844/4.

unless Sweden permitted full use of its territory for troop and supply movements. An operation from Pechenga alone was not possible because a strong force could not be assembled in the far north and the operational possibilities, in any case, were poor. The Army of Norway proposed to go ahead along the lines suggested in its SILBERFUCHS study, but, because of the limitations on rear area personnel and vehicles, it would no longer be able to plan a turn south in support of the Finnish Army. Operations directed toward the south could not be contemplated until a base of supply had been created at Kandalaksha.[47] On 2 March the OKH accepted the Army of Norway proposal as a basis for further planning.[48]

At the end of February Colonel Buschenhagen, Chief of Staff, Army of Norway, renewed contact with the Finnish General Staff in Helsinki and toured northern Finland. Buschenhagen, who emphasized that all the considerations were purely theoretical and no conclusions should be drawn, learned that the Finns regarded Pechenga as too remote to be defended with the forces at their command but would welcome and support German operations there. They anticipated, as had been the case in the Winter War, a Russian thrust via Kandalaksha and Salla aimed at cutting the route to Sweden and would greatly appreciate German assistance in that area. They believed they could cover the assembly of the German force in the Rovaniemi–Salla area and had one to two divisions of III Corps available for the purpose. Their war aims were limited: they wanted to win back what had been lost in the Winter War and might go as far as the line Lake Ladoga–Lake Onega–White Sea, but beyond that they had no aspirations.[49]

The Revised Army Operation Order

Early in March the British Navy inadvertently ushered in a new stage in the planning. On the morning of 4 March, two British cruisers and five destroyers appeared off Svolvaer in the Lofotens. After shelling the town and sinking several ships in the harbor, they sent a landing party ashore which took about 200 German merchant seamen and 20 soldiers prisoner. A number of Norwegian civilians went along with the British voluntarily.[50]

Although the raid had no military importance it aroused in Hitler's mind an overwhelming concern for the defense of Norway, which led him, at a conference on 12 March, to reappraise the situation in the

[47] A.O.K. Norwegen, Ia, Nr. 10/40, an OKH, GenStdH, Op. Abt., 13.2.41, in "Silberfuchs" Bd. I, 10.1.–8.5.41. AOK 20 20844/4.
[48] OKH, GenStdH, Op. Abt. (IN), Nr. 188/41, an A.O.K. Norwegen, 2.3.41, in "Silberfuchs" Bd. I, 10.1.–8.5.41. AOK 20 20844/4.
[49] Deutsche Gesandtschaft, Der Militaerattaché, Helsingfors, 22.2.41, (no folder title). H 27/43.
[50] W. B. Norwegen, Ia, Nr. 710/41, Bericht ueber die Vorgaenge in Svolvaer am 4.3.1941, in Taetigkeitsberichte des AOK Norwegen fuer Monat Maerz 1941. AOK 20 12564/5.

Scandinavian area. The British, he declared, if they wanted a chance at victory, would have to take the offensive when the campaign against the Soviet Union began. Norway, because of its long, broken coastline and poor internal lines of communication, was their best target. They would probably attempt numerous small raids which might, however, evolve into a major operation; therefore, the paramount task of the Army of Norway was to provide airtight security for Norway. The Norwegian defenses were to be strengthened by 160 batteries of artillery suitable for coastal defense and one to two garrison divisions, and it would no longer be possible to release nearly 40 percent of the forces in Norway for BARBAROSSA. Since the attitude of Sweden in the transit question appeared doubtful, other possibilities with respect to assembly and designation of objectives for the operation would have to be investigated.[51]

After the conference the OKH revised the *Aufmarschanweisung* BARBAROSSA in the light of the new requirements stated by Hitler. The defensive mission in Norway was stressed: the additional batteries for coastal defense were to be emplaced by mid-May, and existing troop strength was not only not to be reduced by withdrawals for BARBAROSSA but actually to be increased in the Kirkenes–Narvik area. As for the offensive mission, Pechenga was to be occupied and defended at the time BARBAROSSA began—under certain circumstances (a Soviet attack on Finland) even earlier. Murmansk was to be hemmed in but occupied only in the further course of operations, if sufficient forces were available; the operation against Murmansk was thereby reduced somewhat in scope and its execution made tentative.[52]

One of the further consequences of the Svolvaer raid was that Falkenhorst, who as Armed Forces Commander, Norway, was subordinate to the OKW but as Commanding General, Army of Norway, was tactically subordinate to the OKH, was placed under the command of the OKW in both capacities. That left the Army of Norway under the OKW in Norway and under the OKH with respect to its participation in BARBAROSSA, a situation which was remedied later in the month by giving the OKW control of planning and operations in Finland.[53]

The Army of Norway Operation Orders

During March the Army of Norway virtually suspended planning while awaiting clarification of its mission. In the course of the month the concentration of the 2d Mountain Division in the area around Kirkenes for RENNTIER began; and the first elements of SS-Kampfgruppe

[51] *Ausfuehrungen des Fuehrers auf dem Berghof am 12.3.1941 zur Lage,* in *AOK Norwegen, Ia, Chefsachen allgemein, 21.9.40–1.5.42.* AOK 20 35641.
[52] *OKH, GenStdH, Op. Abt. (IN), Nr. 050/41, Aufmarschanweisung "Barbarossa," 21.1.41,* in *A.O.K. Norwegen, Ia, Aufmarschanweisung "Barbarossa," 31.1.–23.7.41.* AOK 20 20844/3.
[53] *Chef OKW, Nr. 44266/41, Abschrift von Fernschreiben, 5.3.41* (no folder title). OKW/175. *Halder Diary,* Vol. VI, p. 29.

"Nord" were readied for transport, allegedly as replacements, via Sweden to northern Norway, where it was to assemble near Kirkenes. From there it could proceed southward through Finland along the Arctic Ocean Highway avoiding the use of Swedish territory in the assembly for BARBAROSSA. The Kampfgruppe had to be reincluded in the operation because, as the only major motorized force available to the Army of Norway, it alone was capable of making the long overland march from Kirkenes to Rovaniemi.[54]

On 7 April an OKW directive implementing the revised *Aufmarschanweisung* provided a basis for resumption of the planning. The reinforced 2d Mountain Division was to be held ready for the occupation of Pechenga, but with a proviso that the forces defending the Narvik–Kirkenes sector not be reduced below 18 battalions. Whether, after security had been provided for the northern Norwegian coast and Pechenga, enough strength could be mustered for a thrust to Polyarnyy to close Kola Bay depended on a number of conditions which could not be foreseen, but the necessary preparations were to be made and as many troops as possible assembled. The operation to cut off Murmansk from the south would have Kandalaksha Bay as its first objective; its further conduct would depend on the situation. For the assembly the Swedish railroads would presumably not be available; therefore, the OKH would dispatch one infantry division by sea to Finland, while the Army of Norway sent the XXXVI Corps Headquarters and attached elements, also by sea, from Norway. If Sweden granted transit rights after the start of BARBAROSSA, an additional division would be dispatched from southern Norway. The over-all command of operations out of Finland would be offered to Mannerheim.[55]

On 17 April the Army of Norway submitted its plan of operations to the OKW and on the 18th and 20th issued operation orders to the Mountain Corps Norway and the XXXVI Corps. The enemy strength was estimated at five infantry divisions and one or two weak armored units. (In the intelligence conferences at the OKW on 5 and 6 June the distribution of enemy forces was estimated as follows: one division in the Murmansk area, one division at Salla, one—possibly a second— division at Kandalaksha, one division in the vicinity of Kem, and one division—possibly two—at Arkhangel'sk.)[56]

The Mountain Corps Norway was given a defensive mission and two offensive missions. As Commander in the Polar Region, the Commanding General, Mountain Corps Norway, Dietl, was responsible

---

[54] *A.O.K. Norwegen, Taetigkeitsbericht des Armee-Oberkommandos Norwegen, Abt. Ia in der Zeit vom 1.3.–31.3.41. in Taetigkeitsberichte des Armee-Oberkommandos Norwegen, Maerz 1941.* AOK 20 12564/5.

[55] *OKW, WFSt, Abt. L (I Op.). Nr. 44355/41, Weisung an den Wehrmachtsbefehlshaber Norwegen ueber seine Aufgaben im Fall "Barbarossa," 7.4.41,* (no folder title). OKW 1838.

[56] *A.O.K. Norwegen, Abt. Ic, Nr. 110/41, Ic Besprechung beim OKW v. 5.6.– 6.6.41, in "Silberfuchs" Bd. II, 4.5.–18.6.41.* AOK 20 20844/5.

for the defense of Norway north of Narvik. For that task he had, aside from naval units and coastal artillery, the 199th Infantry Division, the 9th SS-Regiment, three machine gun battalions, a police battalion, and (proposed) a bicycle battalion—essentially the 18 battalions Hitler demanded. The first of the offensive missions, Operation RENNTIER, was to be prepared in such a manner that Pechenga could be occupied at any time, at the latest three days after receipt of an appropriate order. The second, under the code name PLATINFUCHS, would be launched either after RENNTIER or directly from Norway, in which case it would include the occupation of Pechenga. It would take the form of an advance along the arctic coast to Port Vladimir and Polyarnyy with the objective of closing Kola Bay above Murmansk. Whether Kola Bay could then be crossed and Murmansk occupied would depend on the situation and terrain conditions found on reaching Polyarnyy. The forces to be employed were the 2d and 3d Mountain Divisions, a communications battalion, a construction battalion, an antiaircraft battalion (less 2 batteries), two batteries of 105-mm. guns, and a *Nebelwerfer* (rocket launcher) battery.[57]

The XXXVI Corps was to execute the main German attack, the operation against Kandalaksha, code-named POLARFUCHS. The corps would consist of the 169th Infantry Division, SS-Kampfgruppe "Nord," the Finnish 6th Division (detached from the Finnish III Corps), two battalions of tanks, two motorized artillery battalions, two construction battalions, a bridge-construction battalion, a heavy weapons battalion, a communications battalion, two batteries of antiaircraft artillery, and a *Nebelwerfer* battery. After assembling its forces east of Rovaniemi, the XXXVI Corps would direct the weight of its attack along the road Rovaniemi–Kandalaksha, enveloping and reducing the Russian border strong point at Salla and then pressing on to Kandalaksha. Once Kandalaksha was taken it would become necessary to provide security against an attack from the south, push northward along the railroad, and take Murmansk in conjunction with the operations of the Mountain Corps Norway.

Because of uncertainty concerning the scale of Finnish participation, the April order to the XXXVI Corps was in part tentative. The Army of Norway proposed a secondary attack, probably by the Finnish 6th Division to be launched from Kuusamo, 65 miles south of Salla, via Kesten'ga to Loukhi on the Murmansk railroad and reconnaissance via Ukhta toward Kem.[58] The Commanding General, XXXVI Corps, General der Kavallerie Hans Feige, tentatively suggested employing his main force in the southern attack in order to strike northward behind Salla at Kayrala, where the Salla–Kandalaksha road passed be-

---

[57] *A.O.K. Norwegen, Ia, Nr. 14/41, Operationsanweisung fuer das Geb. Korps Norwegen, 18.4.41,* in "Silberfuchs" Bd. I, 10.1.–8.5.41. AOK 20 20844/4.
[58] *A.O.K. Norwegen, Ia, Nr. 53/41, Operationsanweisung fuer das Hoehere Kommando XXXVI, 20.4.41,* in "Silberfuchs" Bd. I, 10.1.–8.5.41. AOK 20 20844/4.

tween two lakes and over a line of commanding hills, and at the crossing of the Tuntsa River. Such a maneuver, he thought, would deny the Russians the possibility of executing a defense in depth; but he was aware that the road and terrain conditions spoke against a sweeping envelopment.[59]

On June 11, after the Finnish participation had been made final, the Army of Norway issued a supplement to its April order and an operation order for the Finnish III Corps which would be attached to the German forces. The III Corps (one division plus border guards, the second division being attached to the XXXVI Corps) would provide offensive flank security south of the XXXVI Corps zone. It would attack from the vicinity of Suomussalmi via Ukhta toward Kem with its main force and send a secondary force from Ukhta via Kesten'ga to Loukhi. The Finnish 6th Division advance from the vicinity of Kuusamo, instead of being directed toward Loukhi, would be turned northeastward behind Salla toward the Tuntsa River near Allakurtti. Both the XXXVI Corps and the III Corps were to come under the command of Headquarters, Army of Norway, which would be established at Rovaniemi to direct Operation SILBERFUCHS—all German and Finnish operations out of Finland north of the line Oulu–Belomorsk.[60]

The roles of the Navy and Air Force in Operation SILBERFUCHS were to be limited. The Navy even expected to have to halt supply shipping along the arctic coast until Russian naval supremacy in the Arctic Ocean could be overcome. It saw the occupation of Polyarnyy and Murmansk as the most likely means of reducing the effectiveness of Russian and possible British naval operations. For that reason Admiral Raeder had insisted from the first on the occupation of Murmansk as one of the Navy's primary requirements.[61] The Fifth Air Force (Norway) retained about 200 combat planes for its primary mission, the defense of Norway, and made the following available for SILBERFUCHS:

Long-range reconnaissance	one flight	3
Dive Bombers	one group	30
Bombers	one squadron	10
Fighters	one squadron	10
Reconnaissance planes attached to AOK Norway		7
Total		60

[59] Hoeheres Kommando z. b. V. XXXVI, Der Befehlshaber, Ia, 510/41, in "Silberfuchs" Bd. I, 10.1.–8.5.41. AOK 20 20844/4.
[60] A.O.K. Norwegen, Ia, Nr. 148/41, Operationsanweisung fuer das V. finnische Armee-Korps, 10.6.41, in "Silberfuchs" Bd. II, 4.5.–18.6.41. AOK 20 20844/5. A.O.K. Norwegen, Ia, Nr. 53/41, Operationsanweisung Hoeh. Kdo. XXXVI., 11.6.41, in "Silberfuchs" Bd. I, 10.1.–8.5.41. AOK 20 20844/4. A.O.K. Norwegen, Ia, Kriegstagebuch, 3.6.41–13.1.42, 2 Jul 41. AOK 20 35198/1.
[61] Admiral Norwegen, B Nr. 20, Vorgang: 1 Skl. I op. 262/41 v. 6.3.41, Betrifft: Fall "Barbarossa," 25.3.41, in "Silberfuchs" Bd. I, 10.1.–8.5.41. AOK 20 20844/4. Die Seekriegsleitung und die Vorgeschichte des Feldzuges gegen Russland, pp. 22, 25. H 22/439.

That modest force was to operate against Soviet naval units in the Arctic Ocean, provide close support for the Army of Norway, and carry out a variety of other missions including destruction of the port facilities at Polyarnyy and Murmansk, interdiction of troop movements on the Murmansk Railroad, destruction of Soviet air installations, and destruction of locks in the Baltic–White Sea Canal (which the Navy insisted on to prevent the transfer of Soviet light naval units from the Baltic to the White Sea).[62]

The German–Finnish Conversations, May–June 1941

On 25 May the OKW opened three days of conferences with a Finnish military delegation headed by General Heinrichs and including the chiefs of operations, mobilization, supply, and the chief of staff of the Finnish Navy. In his opening remarks Jodl depicted the forthcoming attack on the Soviet Union as a preventive operation. Germany, he said, had a friendly treaty relationship with the Soviet Union which was economically advantageous; opposed to that was an unprovoked Soviet concentration of forces on the German border which was forcing Germany to take appropriate countermeasures. Germany intended to clarify the situation through political channels in the immediate future. If that were to prove impossible, a military solution would almost certainly become necessary in order not to allow the Soviet Union to choose its own time.[63] The course of the war could be predicted with certainty: participation of many small states in a crusade against Bolshevism and, especially, the superiority of the German armed forces would, after certain territories had been taken, reduce the Soviet Union to military impotence. The Soviet collapse would come earliest in the north. The chief task of the Finns, Jodl explained, would be to tie down Russian forces in the Lake Ladoga area. A bloody breakthrough battle was not demanded since the Soviet front would collapse of itself as German Army Group North advanced.

On the following day Halder took a different tack and asked for the creation of a strong striking force which could attack either east or west of Lake Ladoga depending on the development of the situation. He anticipated that the Finnish attack would begin about 14 days after the Germans launched BARBAROSSA. After the conference the OKW explained that Jodl had only set forth the minimum expectation. The Finns, for their part, indicated that the Lake Ladoga area was of greatest interest to them; therefore, they would not confine themselves to waiting but would attack.

---

[62] *Luftflottenkommando 5, Fuehrungsabteilung Ia, Br. Nr. 88/41, Weisung fuer den Kampf im Falle "Barbarossa," 12.6.41,* in *"Silberfuchs" Bd. II, 4.5.–81.6.41.* AOK 20 20844/5.

[63] This preventive war argument was revived by the defense at the Nuremberg War Crimes Trials. It does not appear to have been used in 1941 as anything more than a convenient excuse.

The Finns wanted to concentrate all of their strength on the Lake Ladoga front and argued against detaching a corps to participate in the German advance toward Kandalaksha. For the same reason they wanted the Germans to assume responsibility for the reduction of Hanko. Those questions, along with others relating to the exact direction of the Finnish main effort and the time of mobilization, were left undecided for the time being. Since the military delegation lacked authority to make any commitments—but Heinrichs pointed out that its presence indicated the Finnish position—the conversations were adjourned to 3 June, when they were to be resumed in Helsinki.[64]

In the meeting of 25 May Jodl stated that Falkenhorst would command in northern and central Finland (SILBERFUCHS) and Marshal Mannerheim would command in the south on the Ladoga front. Mannerheim would be in direct touch with the OKH. This represented a departure from the earlier German intention, expressed as late as 28 April in a preliminary plan for the conversations with the Finns, to offer the over-all command in Finland to Mannerheim.[65] The reasons for the decision to institute separate commands in Finland are not clear. One, probably, was the desire of the OKW to command in an active theater. Another might have been the fact that Mannerheim could be brought into the planning only at a very late stage, too late for him to assume command at the start of the campaign. That possibility is to some extent supported by Mannerheim's statement that late in June 1941—after operations had begun—he was tentatively approached on the subject of assuming full command in Finland.[66] In any case, as far as the success of Operation SILBERFUCHS was concerned, the division of command was not serious, since the operation was, as Halder characterized it, merely an "expedition" not fundamentally related either to BARBAROSSA or to the Finnish operations in the south. What was serious was that the Germans, when they established independent German and Finnish commands, compounded their more basic error of failing to bring Mannerheim under their direct control by preliminary agreement and so lost all hope of keeping him in hand and laid themselves open to the dangers of coalition warfare.

According to Clausewitz the worst possible situation is that in which two independent commanders find themselves operating in the same theater of war. Why the Germans fell into that trap is not easily dis-

---

[64] OKW, WFSt, Abt. L. (I Op.), Nr. 44793/31, Protokoll ueber die Besprechung mit den Vertretern der finnischen Wehrmacht am 25.5.41 in Salzburg, 25.5.41, OKW, Abt. Ausland, Nr. 183/41, 28.5.41; and Buschenhagen, Lfd. Nr. 51/41, 28.5.41, an AOK Norwegen, in "Silberfuchs" Bd. II, 4.5.–18.6.41. AOK 20 20844/5. OKH, GenStdH, Op. Abt. (IN), Nr. 991/41, Protokoll ueber die deutsch–finnischen Besprechungen am 26.5.41, in Chefsachen Fremde Heere Ost, Bd. I. H 3/1.
[65] OKW, Abt. L, Nr. 44594/41, Vorschlag fuer die Vorbereitung der Besprechungen ueber Beteiligung Finnlands am Unternehmen "Barbarossa," 28.4.41, (no folder title). OKW/1938.
[66] Mannerheim, op. cit., p. 450.

covered. In Directive No. 21 the OKW was given the task of approaching Finland and Romania and arranging "the manner in which their military contingents will be placed under German command at the time of their intervention"; but there is no indication of an attempt at any time to carry out the order with respect to Finland. Probably in the prevailing optimism of 1941 it was not thought possible that a situation could develop which would undermine the Finns' will to collaborate; moreover, for a short, victorious campaign in which Finland, after all, was only expected to stage a diversion on the outer flank, a tight integration of the Finnish forces was not necessary and could entail unwanted obligations with respect to reinforcements and supplies.

When the talks resumed on 3 June Colonels Buschenhagen and Eberhard Kinzel, representing the OKW and the OKH respectively, found the Finnish General Staff prepared to accept the German May proposals. The Finnish main force would be assembled in such a manner that, depending on the wishes of the OKH, an attack could be launched either east or west of Lake Ladoga on five days' notice. The attack east of the lake, which the Finns recognized as the most advantageous militarily, would be opened by a force of five infantry divisions and a mixed infantry and cavalry division. Up to seven additional divisions were to be employed later as they became available. Heinrichs warned that it would be wrong to expect too much of the Finnish Army. The Svir River was the objective, but it could be reached only under exceedingly favorable circumstances.

The III Corps (two divisions) and the Pechenga Detachment (three companies and a battery of artillery) would be attached to the Army of Norway. The Finns undertook to occupy the Åland Islands and seal off Hanko, but they wanted the attack on Hanko to be executed by a German division brought in from Norway.

For the event that Germany and the Soviet Union reached a peaceful settlement Finland wanted a guaranty of its independence, if possible with its old boundaries, and economic assistance. Also in the political sphere, Heinrichs cautioned that any attempt to install a "Quisling-type" government in Finland would put an immediate end to the German-Finnish collaboration.[67]

On 14 June, three days before the Finnish general mobilization began, the President of Finland and the Foreign Affairs Committee of the Parliament approved the military arrangements.[68] On the following day the Finns submitted an urgent request that, before ordering the mobilization, they be given either an assurance that war would ensue

[67] A.O.K. Norwegen, Der Chef des Generalstabes, Nr. 140/41, Ergebnis der deutsch-finnischen Besprechungen in Helsinki, 3.–5.6.1941, in "Silberfuchs," Bd. II, 4.5.–18.6.41. AOK 20 20844/5. Fremde Heere Ost, Chef, Nr. 74/41, Protokoll ueber die Besprechungen in Finnland vom 3.–6. Juni 1941, in Chefsachen Fremde Heere Ost, Bd. I. H 3/1.
[68] Mil. Att., Nr. 78/41, fuer OKW Fuehrungsamt, 15.6.41, in Chefsachen, Bd. 1941. H 27/43.

Commanding General, Army of Norway, Generaloberst Nikolaus von Falkenhorst, right, walking through the woods with Generalmajor Erich Buschenhagen, left, and Kenraaliluutnantti Paal Oesterman. (Photo taken after 1 August 1941, when Buschenhagen was promoted to Generalmajor.)

or a binding promise that, in the event of a peaceful settlement, the political desires they had stated earlier would be met. In reply Keitel authorized the Military Attaché to state that "the demands and conditions raised by Finland concerning the measures to be taken are to be regarded as fulfilled." [69] The general mobilization was ordered on 17 June.

Colonel Buschenhagen, accompanied by General der Infanterie Waldemar Erfurth, returned to Helsinki by plane on the afternoon of 13 June. Two days later Buschenhagen established the Headquarters, Army of Norway in Finland, at Rovaniemi, and control of the Finnish III Corps passed to the Army of Norway. In order to avoid attracting Russian attention Falkenhorst remained in Norway another week, arriving in Rovaniemi on 21 June. Thereafter the Army of Norway maintained two headquarters more than a thousand miles apart. The greater part of its staff remained in Norway, and supplementary staff sections were improvised for the direction of operations out of Finland. General Erfurth as Chief, Liaison Staff North, was attached to Mannerheim's headquarters as the representative of the OKW and the OKH in Finland. At the request of the Finns a Finnish general officer had also been assigned to the OKH.

---

[69] *OKW, WFSt, an Abt. Ausl., 15.6.41,* (no folder title). OKW/1972 *Buschenhagen, an OKW fuer Gen. Jodl, 15.6.41,* in *Chefsachen, Bd. 1941.* H 27/43.

The two questions still to be settled were those regarding the exact time and place of the Finnish attack. Apparently they had been left undecided not because of the scruples of the Finns but because the Germans did not want to reveal the starting date for their own operations against the Soviet Union and because the OKH desired a slight delay in order to be able to time the Finnish attack properly in relation to the progress of the German Army Group North. On 16 June Erfurth informed the OKH that General Heinrichs, on instructions from Mannerheim, had asked that the Finnish main operation not begin until two or three days after the start of SILBERFUCHS because, as Erfurth wrote, "The Finns want to create the impression among their own people and people's representatives of being drawn in by the course of events."[70] The OKH replied that the timing of the Finnish operation would depend on the development of the battle on the German front, but the Finnish request would be kept in mind.[71]

When the German armies marched into Russia on 22 June Finland declared its neutrality, which it maintained officially until the night of 25 June. After severe Soviet air attacks on the cities of southern Finland on the 25th, the Premier informed a secret session of Parliament that the nation, having been attacked, was proceeding to defend itself with all means, and was, therefore, at war.[72] On the previous night with German operations in the Soviet Union going according to schedule, the OKH had made its decision regarding the location of the Finnish attack and had instructed Erfurth to tell the Finns that they were to prepare for an operation east of Lake Ladoga by at least six divisions with the weight of the attack on the left and the objective set at a distance. Five days later the Finns submitted a plan of attack which fulfilled the German requirements. On 4 July with the Army Group North drawing up to the Dvina River, the last major natural obstacle before Leningrad, and no serious resistance anticipated, Halder decided that the time had come to set the date for the Finnish attack. Taking into account the Finns' desire for five to seven days' advance notice, the first day of operations was to be 10 July.[73]

---

[70] *Erfurth, an OKH Attache Abteilung, fuer GenStdH, Op. Abt., 16.6.41,* in *Chefsachen Bd. 1941.* H 27/43.

[71] *OKH, Att. Abt. (z.b.V.), GenStdH, 130/41, an den deutschen Militaerattaché in Helsingfors,* in *Chefsachen Bd. 1941.* H 27/43.

[72] On 24 June Finland had agreed to permit German aircraft to take off from Finnish territory for operations against the Soviet Union and to permit ground reconnaissance by the Army of Norway units across the Finnish–Soviet border as of midnight that day. *Verbindungsstab Nord, Ia 77/41, an A.O.K. Norwegen, Bef. St. Finnland,* in *A.O.K. Norwegen, K.T.B., Anlagenband 1.* AOK 20 19070/2.

[73] *Halder Diary,* Vol. VI, pp. 144, 156, 175, 189.

Chapter 8

Operation SILBERFUCHS (I)

Concentration of Forces

The concentration of the Army of Norway forces for SILBERFUCHS was itself an undertaking of major proportions. In the far north, the Mountain Corps Norway had to move the 3d Mountain Division from Narvik to Kirkenes and bring in from southern Norway the 199th Infantry Division and the staff of the 702d Infantry Division plus miscellaneous units amounting to several battalions. The 2d Mountain Division was already in the Kirkenes area. At the same time the SS-Kampfgruppe "Nord," coming through Sweden, had to be transported from Narvik to Kirkenes. The sea afforded the only practicable means of transportation since Reichsstrasse 50, completed from Narvik to Kirkenes in the fall of 1940, at first could not be kept clear of snow and in June was rendered useless by the thaw. The road south of Narvik was blocked in numerous places by ice in the ferry crossings of the fiords.[1] Transfer of the 199th Infantry Division and the staff of the 702d Infantry Division was completed at the end of May; but the last elements of the 3d Mountain Division did not reach their assembly area south of Kirkenes until 17 June; and assembly of the SS-Kampfgruppe was completed on 6 June, barely in time to begin the march southward through Finland along the Arctic Ocean Highway to Rovaniemi on the 7th.[2]

The assault force of the Mountain Corps Norway (the 2d and 3d Mountain Divisions plus service troops) numbered 27,500 men.[3] For its supplies the Mountain Corps Norway was to draw on a one year's stockpile which Hitler, in the fall of 1940, had ordered accumulated in Norway. Supplies were to be brought into the zone of operations by ship as far as possible; in emergencies they were to come overland from Narvik via Reichsstrasse 50.[4]

---

[1] *AOK Norwegen, Taetigkeitsbericht des Armee-Oberkommandos Norwegen, Abt. Ia in der Zeit vom 1.5–31.5.1941*, in *Taetigkeitsberichte des Armee-Oberkommando Norwegen, Mai 1941.* AOK 20 12564/7.

[2] *Generalkommando Gebirgskorps Norwegen, Ia, Taetigkeitsbericht fuer Monat Juni 1941, 1.7.1941.* AOK 20 14030/3.

[3] *AOK Norwegen, O. Qu., Qu. 1, "Silberfuchs," 9.5.41*, in "Silberfuchs" Bd. II, *4.5.–18.6.41.* AOK 20 20844/5.

[4] *AOK Norwegen O. Qu., Qu. 1, Nr. 326/41, Besondere Anordnungen fuer die Versorgung zum Operationsbefehl fuer das Geb. Korps Norwegen, 13.5.41*, in g. Kdos. Chefsache Gebirgskorps Norwegen Ia/Ost, 19.5.–23.12.41. AOK 20 26373/1.

Transfer of the main force of the XXXVI Corps to Finland was accomplished in two sea transport operations: BLAUFUCHS 1 (169th Division, 20,000 men, from Stettin to Oulu) and BLAUFUCHS 2 (Headquarters, XXXVI Corps, and corps troops, 10,600 men, Oslo to Oulu). The first ships sailed on 5 June, and operations were completed on 14 June. The 8,000 men of the SS-Kampfgruppe reached Rovaniemi on 10 June. These troop movements were carried out under the guise of a relief operation for northern Norway; and the XXXVI Corps was ordered not to turn eastward from the line Oulu–Rovaniemi–Arctic Ocean Highway until 18 June, the date on which it was considered no longer possible to conceal the forthcoming attack on Russia. With its movement thus restricted it became impossible for the XXXVI Corps to draw up to the Finnish eastern border in time to open an offensive on 22 June, BARBAROSSA Day. The XXXVI Corps, exclusive of attached Finnish units, totaled 40,600 troops. The corps was initially provided with rations for three months, ammunition for two to three months, and motor fuel for two months. The management of supplies for Finland as well as Norway was in the hands of the Heimatstab Nord, renamed, in June 1941, Heimatstab Uebersee.[5]

For the defense of Norway, the Army of Norway retained seven divisions organized into the LXX Corps (three divisions, headquarters in Oslo), the XXXIII Corps (two divisions, headquarters at Trondheim), and the Territorial Staff of the Mountain Corps Norway (two divisions, headquarters at Alta).[6] It had also 160 batteries of army coastal artillery, 56 batteries of naval coastal artillery, 6 police battalions, an SS-Regiment, and 3 motorized machine gun battalions. The troops in Norway numbered about 150,000.[7] In conjunction with the concentration of forces for the attack on Russia the units in Norway were assigned to Operation HARPUNE NORD, an elaborately staged deception intended to make it appear that the invasion of England was next on the German timetable. In Norway, Denmark, and France (HARPUNE SUED) the Germans went through the motions of preparing an amphibious attack on England timed for about 1 August 1941.[8]

---

[5] *OKW, WFSt, Abt. L. (I Op.), Anlage 1, Zeitplan "Barbarossa," 5.6.41; OKW, WFSt, Abt. L. (I Op.). Nr. 44803/41, an W.B. Norwegen, 26.5.41; AOK Norwegen, O. Qu. Qu. 1, 6/41, "Silberfuchs," in "Silberfuchs" Bd. II, 4.5.–18.6.41. AOK 20 20844/5. AOK Norwegen O. Qu., Qu. 1, Nr. 326/41, Besondere Anordnungen fuer die Versorgung zum Operationsbefehl "Polarfuchs" (Hoeh. Kdo. XXXVI), 14.5.41, in g. kdos, Chefsache Gebirgskorps Norwegen, Ia/Ost, 19.5.– 23.12.41. AOK 20 26373/1. 169. I.D., Fuehrungsabt, in Kriegstagebuch Nr. 2, Teil 1, 1.6.–9.9.41, 6, 7, 11 June 1941. 169 I.D. 20291/2.*

[6] On 28 June the Territorial Staff was detached from the Mountain Corps Norway and made directly subordinate to the Army of Norway, Headquarters Oslo. Henceforth it was designated as Provisional Corps "Nagy."

[7] *OKH, GenStdH, Org. Abt., Sicherungskraefte Norwegen (geplanter Stand vom 1.6.41), 8.5.41. H 1/381b.*

[8] *AOK Norwegen, Ia, Nr. 6/41, Operationsbefehl Nr. 1 fuer die Vorbereitung der Unternehmung "Harpune," in Taetigkeitsberichte fuer Monat Mai. AOK 20 12564/7.*

On 22 June, when the German armies in the south crossed the Soviet frontier, the Mountain Corps Norway, unopposed, executed RENNTIER with the 2d Mountain Division taking up positions in the Liinahamari–Pechenga area and the 3d Mountain Division along a line extending farther south to the vicinity of Luostari.[9]   On the same day the Army of Norway ordered the attack across the Finnish-Russian border to be begun on 29 June by the Mountain Corps Norway, on 1 July at 0200 by the Finnish III Corps, and on 1 July 1600 by the XXXVI Corps.[10] Staggered timing was employed for the purpose of making air support available for the initial assault in each corps sector.   The aircraft had to shift from their main bases at Kirkenes and Banak to Rovaniemi for missions in the XXXVI Corps area.   Beginning on 23 June they flew missions against Murmansk and Salla.   The Russians retaliated with attacks on Pechenga, Kemiyärvi, and Rovaniemi.

On 23 June negotiations for the transit of one division across Sweden from southern Norway to Finland began in Stockholm.   The Swedish Government gave its consent two days later, and OKW ordered the 163d Infantry Division to begin moving out of Oslo on the 26th.   The division was replaced in Norway by the 710th Infantry Division from Germany.   Contrary to the earlier intention of committing the 163d Division at Hanko, the OKW ordered it attached immediately to the Finnish Army as Mannerheim's reserve for operations in the Lake Ladoga area.[11]

The concentration of German forces in northern Finland clearly revealed the serious and in most respects insuperable problems with respect to its communications lines which would confront Army of Norway in the forthcoming campaign.   From its main base in Norway the army had four tenuous routes of access to Finland: (1) The sea route around the northern tip of Norway to Kirkenes and Pechenga. It could not be protected against British or Russian naval attack and at the entrance to Pechenga harbor passed within range of Russian artillery on the Rybatchiy Peninsula.   (2) Reichsstrasse 50 from Narvik to Kirkenes.   In 1941 the road did not have an all-weather surface, and the snow removal techniques were inadequate.   (3) The land routes, road (one) and railroad, through Sweden.   For the use of these, permission, which was granted more and more reluctantly after June 1941, had to be secured from the Swedish Government.   (4) The sea route through the Baltic.   While the Baltic Sea was relatively safe for shipping, the Finnish ports at the head of the Gulf of Bothnia had low capacities and were icebound during four to five months of the year;

---

[9] *Saturn Geier, Ia, Nr. 409/41, Morgenmeldung 22.6.41* and *Saturn Geier, Ia, Nr. 418/41, Morgenmeldung 25.6.41,* in *Geb. Korps Norwegen, Ia, Taetigkeitsbericht fuer Monat Juni 1941, 1.7.41.*   AOK 20 14030/3.

[10] *AOK Norwegen, Abt. Ia, Nr. 111/41, Armeebefehl, 22.6.41* in *g.kdos. Chefsache Gebirgskorps Norwegen, Ia/Ost, 19.5–23.12.41.*   AOK 20 26373/1.

[11] *AOK Norwegen, Befehlsstelle Finnland, Ia, Kriegstagebuch, 3.6.41–13.1.42.* (hereafter referred to as *A.O.K. Norwegen, K.T.B.*) 23–30 June. AOK 20 35198/1.

moreover, Germany lacked the merchant vessels to maintain simultaneous traffic to Norway, the arctic ports, and in the Baltic.

Aside from being less vulnerable, the army's lines of communication inside Finland were no better. It had one single-track railroad running along the coast of the Gulf of Bothnia from Oulu to Kemi and thence north to Rovaniemi and Kemiyärvi with a connecting line to the Swedish border east of Tornio. Rolling stock was scarce, and, because the Finnish railroads were built to the Russian gauge, German equipment could not be supplied immediately. For the same reason rail shipments from Sweden had to be transloaded at the border. Since the Finnish engines burned wood, their hauling capacity was low, and it required 70 to 80 trains to move one German division. On the average, the Army of Norway could count on no more than three trains a day from Oulu to Rovaniemi. The road net in northern Finland was thin. Few of the roads could be called improved even in a relative sense, and very few of the bridges were capable of carrying heavy military equipment. In the north, the Arctic Ocean Highway was the sole link between Rovaniemi and Pechenga. As such it was of major importance to Army of Norway operations in Finland, but it, too, had been built to meet the limited requirements of Finnish internal traffic. As a supply route its usefulness was marginal, since, on the 600-mile round trip from Rovaniemi to Pechenga, trucks nearly consumed the weight of their payloads in gasoline.[12]

PLATINFUCHS (Operations of Mountain Corps Norway)

Harsh climate and forbidding terrain were the distinguishing features of the Mountain Corps Norway zone of operations. At Pechenga Bay the influence of the Gulf Stream is still strong enough to permit a lush summer vegetation—grasses, bushes, and a few trees—near the bay and along the Pechenga River valley. East of Pechenga the coast is bare; the rock surface is gouged and molded into a wild jumble of rises and depressions; giant boulders, rocks, and gravel supply the texture of the landscape. In the valleys, many of which have no outlets, the melting snows have formed hundreds of lakes. This belt of rocky tundra varies in width from less than ten miles near Pechenga to 25 or 30 miles in the vicinity of Kola Bay where the effect of the Gulf Stream rapidly diminishes, although it keeps the bay and the port of Murmansk open throughout the year. Inland the tundra gradually shades off into the coniferous forests of the taiga. The winter, which on this inhospitable coast lasts from October to May, is a succession of arctic storms and blizzards; but the temperature (low $-13°$ Fahrenheit) does not reach the extremes frequently recorded farther south ($-45°$ in southern Lapland and $-40°$ in Karelia and southern Finland). The summer brings

---

[12] General der Infanterie a.D. Erich Buschenhagen, Comments on Part II of *The German Northern Theater of Operations, 1940–1945*, May 1957.

an average of 40 days with a mean temperature over 50°.   Even though the daytime temperature occasionally rises into the 80's, on the heights and in protected spots in the valleys patches of snow and ice often last through the summer.   In summer, winds off the ocean drive in banks of fog which blanket the coast for periods ranging from a few hours to weeks at a time.

After completing Operation RENNTIER on 22 June, the Mountain Corps Norway assembled its two divisions (each consisting of two rifle regiments and a regiment of artillery) along the Arctic Ocean Highway. The objective of the ensuing Operation PLATINFUCHS (as stated in the corps order), scheduled to begin on 29 June, was Murmansk, 56 miles east of the Soviet Finnish border.   Dietl intended to strike with the 2d Mountain Division along the coast via Titovka, Bol'shaya Zapadnaya Litsa, and Ura Guba to Polyarnyy near the mouth of Kola Bay and with the 3d Mountain Division southeastward via Motovka to Murmansk.   For the purpose the 2d Mountain Division was assembled around Pechenga while the 3d Mountain Division took up positions in the vicinity of Luostari.

The objective of the first phase of PLATINFUCHS was the line Motovka–Bol'shaya Zapadnaya Litsa.   On its left flank the 2d Mountain Division was to commit one regiment which, after sealing off the neck of the Rybatchiy Peninsula with one battalion, would thrust southeastward through Titovka to Bol'shaya Zapadnaya Litsa.   The main force of the division, one reinforced regiment, was to strike southeastward from Pechenga to the road Titovka–Bol'shaya Zapadnaya Litsa, running just east of the Zapadnaya Litsa River.   The 3d Mountain Division, with one regiment in the assault, would attack past Chapr Lake toward Motovka.   Fifty-five miles farther south the Finnish "Ivalo" Battalion (Pechenga Detachment) would stage a diversionary attack north of the Lutto River to tie down Soviet forces in the vicinity of Ristikent.[13]

To the Litsa River

At 0300 on 29 June the attack began without air support in a heavy morning fog.   Within three hours the 3d Mountain Division was ferrying troops across the Titovka, and the units of the 2d Mountain Division had reported good progress.   Before noon the entire situation was changed by a discovery that the roads shown on the maps between the Titovka River valley and Motovka and from Motovka to Bol'shaya Zapadnaya Litsa did not exist.   The Mountain Corps Norway, concluding that it could not supply two divisions moving on parallel courses

---

[13] *Gen. Kdo. Gebirgskorps Norwegen, Ia, Nr. 98/41, Befehl fuer die Bereitstellung und den Angriff des Geb. Korps Norwegen am 29.6.–25.6.41, in Gebirgskorps Norwegen, K.T.B. 1. Anlagenband 1.   XIX AK 15085/2.*

over pathless tundra, immediately stopped the advance of the 3d Mountain Division, ordering its main force to pull back to the Arctic Ocean Highway and move into the Pechenga area behind the 2d Mountain Division. Of the one regiment already on the Titovka River, two battalions were ordered to proceed northward along the river valley into the 2d Mountain Division zone while one battalion executed a sweeping arc northeastward to make contact with the right flank regiment of the 2d Mountain Division on a road connecting the Titovka and Litsa Rivers about five miles inland from the coast. That road proved hardly worthy of the name although it was the northern segment of the main route to Kola Bay.[14]

Before the end of the first day's fighting, the terrain, bad maps, and unsatisfactory aerial reconnaissance had forced the Mountain Corps Norway to revise its plan of operations. While the 3d Mountain Division assembled behind the right wing of the 2d Mountain Division, the right regiment of the latter supported by a battalion of the 3d Mountain Division would push down the road to the Litsa bridge, seven miles southwest of Bol'shaya Zapadnaya Litsa. The bridge and the road from there to Kola Bay, at least, offered a new operational possibility since they had not been positively identified before the operation began.[15]

On the 30th the left flank regiment of the 2d Mountain Division took Titovka with one battalion, but its remaining two battalions were tied down in heavy fighting at the neck of the Rybatchiy Peninsula where the Russians landed reinforcements on the eastern shore in the vicinity of Kutovaya, supporting the landings with destroyer fire. The right flank regiment pushed a battalion through to the west bank of the Litsa River on the following day, while fighting continued around Kutovaya. It was becoming clear that the task facing the Mountain Corps Norway was more difficult than had been anticipated. In the Murmansk region the Russians had two full divisions, of which two regiments were digging in to hold the Litsa River line.[16] Another regiment with at least one battalion of artillery was identified on the Rybatchiy Peninsula. Contrary to the original German assumption, these were no mediocre units; ably led, they fought with skill and determination; and they had the advantage of air superiority, since the Fifth Air Force, already inferior in numbers, was forced to shift its operations back and forth between the Mountain Corps area and that of the XXXVI Corps in the south. In addition, the German attack, thrown off balance by initial errors with regard to the location of roads, was slowed down by

---

[14] *Gebirgskorps Norwegen, Ia, Kriegstagebuch Russland 1, 19.6.–31.12.41* (hereafter referred to as *G.K.N., K.T.B. 1.*), 29 Jun 41. XIX AK 15085/1.

[15] *Gen. Kdo. Gebirgskorps Norwegen, Nr. 140/41, Korpsbefehl fuer die Fortsetzung der Operationen nach Osten, 29.6.41,* in *Gebirgskorps Norwegen Ia, Kriegstagebuch Russland 1, Anlagenband 1.* XIX AK 15085/2.

[16] The 14th and 52d Rifle Divisions of the Fourteenth Army, which with approximately six and one-half divisions was holding the sector from Murmansk to Belomorsk.

THE FIRST ATTACK ACROSS
THE LITSA
1 June - 6 July 1941

GERMAN MOVEMENT
MOUNTAIN UNIT
RUSSIAN UNIT

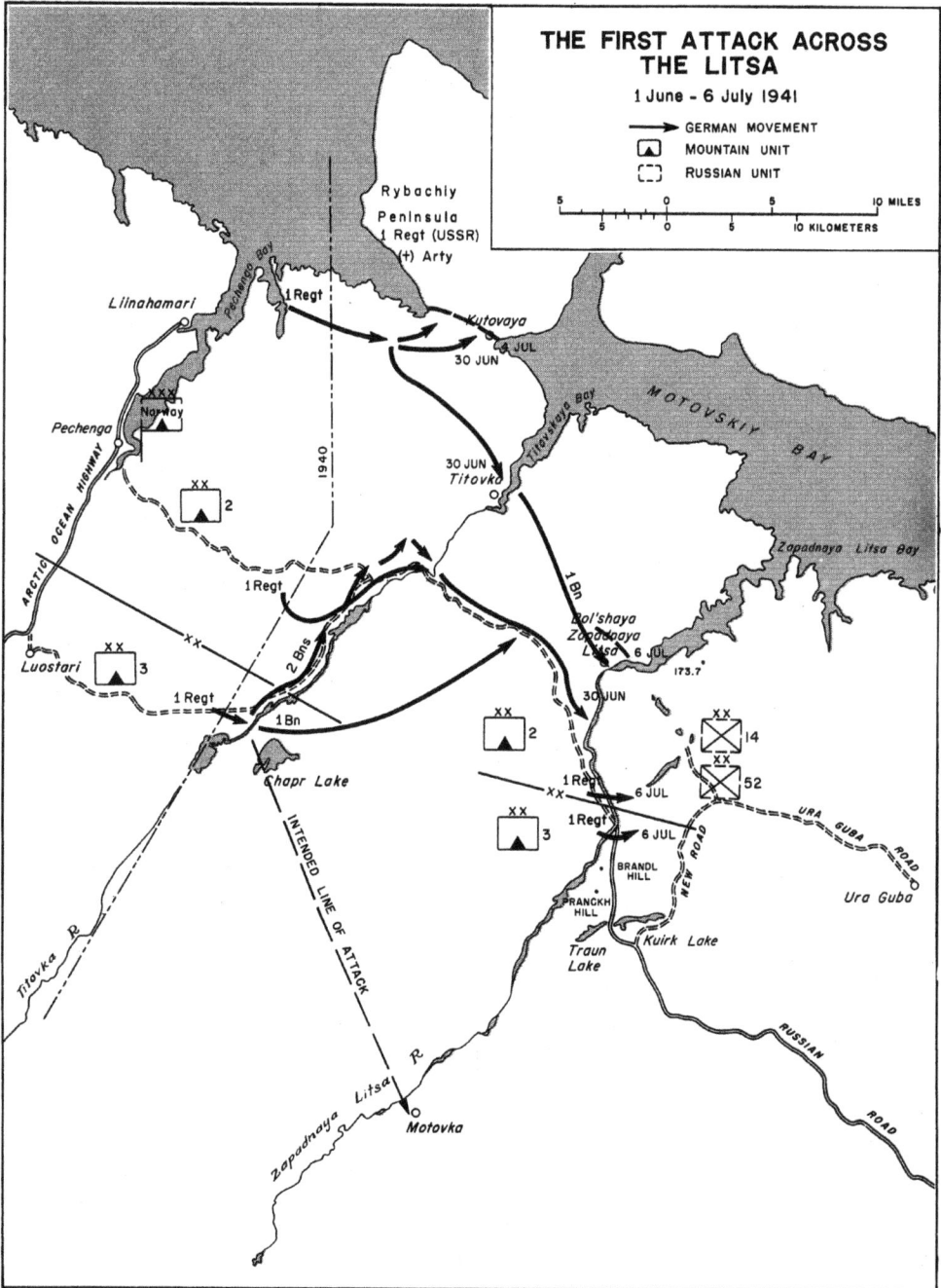

5   0   5   10 MILES

5   0   5   10 KILOMETERS

Rybachiy
Peninsula
1 Regt (USSR)
(+) Arty

Liinahamari

Pechenga Bay

1 Regt

Kutovaya
4 JUL
30 JUN

MOTOVSKIY   BAY

XXX
Norway

Pechenga

XX
2

1940

30 JUN
Titovka

Titovka Bay

Zapadnaya Litsa Bay

ARCTIC OCEAN HIGHWAY

1 Regt

2 Bns

1 Bn

Bol'shaya
Zapadnaya
Litsa   6 JUL

173.7

XX
3
Luostari

XX

1 Regt

1 Bn

30 JUN

XX
2

1 Regt
6 JUL

XX
14

XX
52

URA   GUBA   ROAD

Chapr Lake

XX

1 Regt   6 JUL

Ura Guba

INTENDED LINE OF ATTACK

XX
3

1 Regt

BRANDL
HILL

NEW ROAD

Titovka R.

PRANCKH
HILL

Traun
Lake

Kuirk Lake

RUSSIAN

Zapadnaya Litsa R.

Motovka

ROAD

Map 10

R. Booth

Tundra in the Pechenga-Litsa River area.

exceptionally difficult terrain. It was found that even mountain troops could not move at a rate exceeding one kilometer per hour.[17]

By 4 July the Rybatchiy Peninsula was sealed off, but two battalions, rather than one as originally intended, were required to hold the line. On the same day one company succeeded in crossing the Litsa east of Bol'shaya Zapadnaya Litsa. Meanwhile, the Mountain Corps Norway planned an attack across the river for 6 July. The 2d Mountain Division moved up to the west bank of the river from Bol'shaya Zapadnaya Litsa to the Litsa bridge, while the 3d Mountain Division took up positions at and south of the bridge. The main thrust was to be at the bridge and southeastward along the road. The 2d Mountain Division would commit a regiment north of the bridge and the 3d Mountain Division a regiment south of the bridge. After the river had been crossed the attack was to proceed along the road.[18]

Although hampered by the terrain—the 3d Mountain Division was able to get only one battalion in position on the river—the attack was launched as planned on the morning of the 6th because the 2d Mountain Division assembly area was exposed to enemy artillery fire. In the face of determined resistance the attack did not get rolling until late in the

---

[17] *Gen. Kdo. Gebirgskorps Norwegen, Ia, Nr. 300/41, Erfahrungsbericht ueber den bisherigen Osteinsatz im Eismeergebiet, 12.12.41* (folder). AOK 20 36037/2. *A.O.K. 20 Ic, Feindlage 3.7.41, in A.O.K. 20 Ic, Anlagen zum K.T.B. I.* AOK 20 25353/1. *G.K.N., K.T.B. 1,* 1 Jul 41.

[18] *Gen. Kdo. Gebirgskorps Norwegen, Ia, 156/41, Befehl fuer Bereitstellung und Angriff des Geb. Korps ueber die Liza am 6.7.41, in Gebirgskorps Norwegen, Ia, Kriegstagebuch Russland 1, Anlagenband 1.* XIX AK 15085/2. *G.K.N., K.T.B. I,* 4 Jul 41.

day, and at the end of the day the 2d Mountain Division had only one battalion across the river while the 3d Mountain Division had established two battalions in a bridgehead slightly more than a mile wide. In the meantime, two Soviet transports, escorted by two destroyers and a cruiser, had steamed to the head of Litsa Bay, landing a battalion on the north shore and another on the south shore, forcing the 2d Mountain Division to screen the left flank of the corps with one battalion. Shortly before midnight the corps chief of staff informed Army of Norway Headquarters that, with Russian landings in progress, the flank of the corps was endangered and operations across the Litsa could not be continued. The troops east of the Litsa held their positions on the 7th, but after beating off strong counterattacks during the night they were ordered back to the west bank on the following morning. Reporting on the situation to the Army of Norway Dietl demanded increased air support and stated that he could not proceed without reinforcements of at least a regiment and, preferably, a division.[19]

While the Mountain Corps Norway was engaged on the Litsa, Hitler became preoccupied with his old fear of a British landing and demanded a strengthening of the security forces around Pechenga. The Navy undertook to station a flotilla of five destroyers at Kirkenes, and the Mountain Corps Norway detached an infantry battalion and three batteries of artillery to form a mobile defense force. The necessity to provide forces for defense of Pechenga, the line on the Rybatchiy Peninsula, and flank defense between Titovka and Bol'shaya Zapadnaya Litsa was draining the strength of Dietl's corps. On 7 July the OKW ordered the Army of Norway to transfer some troops from the XXXVI Corps and to explore the possibility of getting Finnish troops as a means of enabling Dietl to reassemble his assault force. The Army of Norway furnished a motorized machine gun battalion, and on 9 July prevailed upon Mannerheim to release the Finnish 14th Regiment, less one battalion, for employment in the Pechenga area.[20]

Stalemate on the Litsa

After his troops had withdrawn behind the Litsa Dietl's first intention was to launch the 3d Mountain Division in a second attack at the bridge and along the road. Whether the attack could be carried out was doubtful from the first since supplies for the division had to be brought up by pack mules, of which, owing to losses through exhaustion, barely enough were available to transport rations, not to mention ammunition. The plan had to be dropped entirely on 10 July after a dispatch rider carrying orders for the attack missed a regimental headquarters near Kutovaya

[19] G.K.N., K.T.B. 1, 7 and 8 Jul 41.
[20] OKW, WFSt, Abt. L. (I Op.), Nr. 441165/41, an A.O.K. Norwegen, Bef. St. Finnland, 7.7.41, in A.O.K. Norwegen, K.T.B., Anlagenband 1. AOK 20 19070/2. G.K.N., K.T.B. 1, 4–8 Jul 41. A.O.K. Norwegen, K.T.B., 8 Jul 41.

and drove his motorcycle into the Russian lines. Two days later Dietl shifted the weight of the attack to the left flank of the corps. There the 2d Mountain Division was to attack eastward from the vicinity of Bol'shaya Zapadnaya Litsa to the chain of lakes lying in a rough arc about six miles behind the river. It would then turn south in the rear of the Soviet forces defending the river's west bank to create favorable conditions for an attack at the bridge by the 3d Mountain Division. With one division advancing west of the road and the other east of it the corps then intended to push seven miles south of the bridge to where the road passed through the narrows between Kuirk Lake and an unnamed lake to the west which the Germans called Traun Lake.[21] This was no sweeping envelopment of the type the Germans usually favored but an operation tailored to the limitations imposed by arctic terrain, where infantry, at best, moved slowly and its supplies slower still.

At the end of the first day of operations, 13 July, the 2d Mountain Division, with seven battalions across the Litsa east of Bol'shaya Zapadnaya Litsa, gained about two miles. On the following day enemy resistance became noticeably stronger, and Russian ships were again observed landing troops on the north shore of Litsa Bay. With shipping movements and landings reported at several points along the Motovskiy and Litsa Bays, the Chief of Staff, Mountain Corps Norway, concluded on the morning of the 15th that operations would have to be halted until the threat to the left flank had been eliminated. The attack continued throughout the day, penetrating the chain of lakes at one point, but the prospects were not good. On the 16th the Russians threw strong counterattacks against the bridgehead from the south and southeast and attacked along the line sealing off the Rybatchiy Peninsula. The supply situation was deteriorating rapidly in the bridgehead and in the 3d Mountain Division zone as well since the division had a regiment, which it had formerly depended on for hauling supplies, committed in the bridgehead. At noon the next day corps told the Army of Norway it could no longer continue the advance toward Murmansk; it intended to reduce the size of the bridgehead in order to gain enough troops to mop up the Russian forces which had landed north of Litsa Bay. Dietl believed he could not resume his offensive unless he received at least one additional division.[22]

On the 18th, the 2d Mountain Division drew its troops on the bridgehead back to a line extending from a waterfall three and one-half miles south of Bol'shaya Zapadnaya Litsa to the shore of Litsa Bay two miles east of the settlement. The 3d Mountain Division established a line on the west bank of the river from the waterfall to a point two and one-half miles south of the bridge. With Soviet troops already ashore

---

[21] *Gen. Kdo. Gebirgskorps Norwegen, Ia, Nr. 165/41, Befehl fuer erneuten Angriff des Gebirgskorps ueber die Liza, 17.7.41,* in *Gebirgskorps Norwegen, K.T.B. 1, Anlagenband 1.* XIX AK 15085/2.
[22] *G.K.N., K.T.B. 1,* 13–18 Jul 41. *A.O.K. Norwegen K.T.B.,* 17 and 18 Jul 41.

north of Litsa Bay and landings reported on the south shore of Titovka Bay, the corps faced a prospect of defending an almost continuous front 36 miles long from the western shore of the Rybatchiy Peninsula through Titovka and Bol'shaya Zapadnaya Litsa to the right flank of the 3d Mountain Division on the Litsa.[23]

On the 21st Dietl conferred with Falkenhorst, Buschenhagen, and the Commanding Admiral, Norway. They agreed that, with winter weather expected to set in within eight to ten weeks, the Mountain Corps could not be left where it was; it would either have to push through to Murmansk or pull back into Finland. The Navy, although two submarines were to be stationed at Kirkenes in addition to the five destroyers, could not promise to accomplish much against Soviet movements by sea because of the distances involved and the Russians' naval superiority. Falkenhorst thought it would be possible to scrape together an equivalent of three regiments quickly in Norway, but there Hitler's strictures against weakening the Norwegian defenses, particularly in the north, still stood.[24]

Two days later the Army of Norway informed Dietl that he could have two battalions from Norway and ordered him to resume the offensive. Taking stock of his forces Dietl found that both of his divisions had one regiment already seriously run down; three battalions were tied down on the northern flank between Titovka and Bol'shaya Zapadnaya Litsa and were barely holding the enemy; and the 2d Mountain Division, fighting off repeated heavy attacks on the bridgehead, had proposed withdrawing behind the Litsa. On the 24th he told army that with two fresh battalions he could only undertake to clean out the right flank north of Litsa Bay.[25]

On the same day, at the request of the OKW, the Army of Norway undertook to review the situation of its three corps. The OKW proposed that if the operations of the XXXVI Corps and the Finnish III Corps did not look promising it be considered whether the XXXVI Corps attack could be canceled and forces shifted north to reinforce the Mountain Corps and enable it to take Murmansk. The Army of Norway replied that the Finnish III Corps operation appeared to offer the best chance of cutting the Murmansk Railroad at an early date. The prospects of the XXXVI Corps did not look good, but if it went over to the defensive the Russians would be able to draw out troops to throw against either the Finnish III Corps or the Mountain Corps Norway. The Mountain Corps, the Army of Norway believed, could still reach

[23] Gen. Kdo. Gebirgskorps Norwegen, Ia, Nr. 180/41, Befehl fuer vorlaeufige Abwehr an der Liza, 18.7.41, in Gebirgskorps Norwegen, K.T.B. 1, Anlagenband 1. XIX AK 15085/2.
[24] AOK Norwegen Ia, Nr. 231/41, an OKW, WFSt, Abt. L, in Silberfuchs Bd. III, 12.6.41–10.1.42. AOK 20 20844/6. A.O.K. Norwegen K.T.B., 21 Jul 41.
[25] G.K.N., K.T.B. 1, 23 and 24 Jul 41. A.O.K. Norwegen K.T.B., 23 Jul 41.

THE SECOND ATTACK ACROSS
THE LITSA
13-17 July 1941

GERMAN FRONT LINE

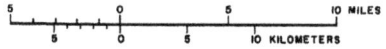

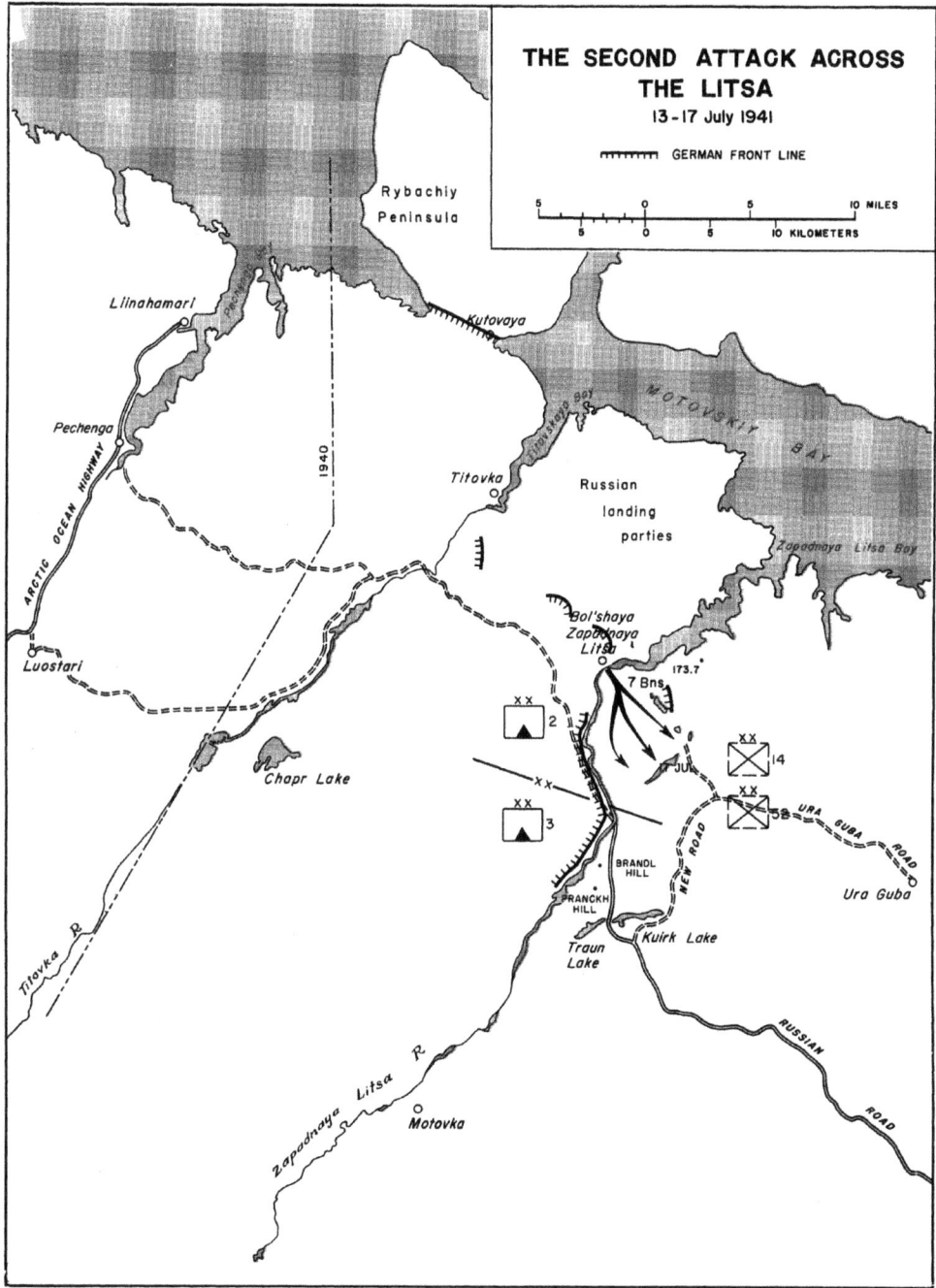

5   0   5   10 MILES

5   0   5   10 KILOMETERS

Rybachiy
Peninsula

Liinahamari

Kutovaya

MOTOVSKIY   BAY

Pechenga

1940

Titovka

Russian
landing
parties

Zapadnaya Litsa Bay

Arctic Ocean Highway

Luostari

Bol'shaya
Zapadnaya
Litsa

173.7

7 Bns

XX
2

XX
4

Chapr Lake

XX
3

NEW ROAD

URA GUBA   ROAD

Ura Guba

BRANDL
HILL

PRANCKH
HILL

Traun
Lake

Kuirk Lake

RUSSIAN

Titovka R.

ROAD

Zapadnaya Litsa R.

Motovka

Map 11

R. Booth

Murmansk if an additional mountain division were brought in within four weeks.[26]

During the last week of July Russian pressure continued strong, particularly against the bridgehead; and on the 30th British carrier-based aircraft bombed and strafed Liinahamari and Pechenga.[27] The Mountain Corps Norway, meanwhile, brought four battalions into position for a push northeastward from the line Titovka–Bol'shaya Zapadnaya Litsa. The attack, which began on 2 August, progressed rapidly since the Russians had made the mistake of spreading their two battalions thinly along a ten-mile front. By the 5th one battalion had been wiped out and the other, after suffering heavy losses, evacuated to the south shore of Litsa Bay. The threat to the corps flank had been eliminated; and with that the fury of the Russian attacks along the Litsa also abated, indicating that the Russians were shifting to the defensive.[28]

On 30 July Hitler ordered the 6th Mountain Division transferred to the Mountain Corps Norway, but the division was in Greece and at best could not make the move before the second half of September.[29] The Army of Norway, noting that early signs of autumn had already appeared in northern Finland, believed quick action was necessary and asked for at least two regiments from Norway to get the Mountain Corps in motion before the 6th Mountain Division arrived. This request Hitler refused on 5 August, maintaining that there would still be time in September to reopen the attack. But a week later, after Generalmajor Walter Warlimont, Chief of the National Defense Branch, OKW, had investigated the situation of the Mountain Corps Norway on the spot, Hitler changed his mind and permitted the 388th Infantry Regiment and the 9th SS-Infantry Regiment to be withdrawn from Norway so that the Mountain Corps could resume its advance.[30]

During the rest of August, while the two fresh regiments were being brought up, the Mountain Corps Norway planned a new attack across the Litsa with the objective of creating favorable conditions for a rapid drive toward Murmansk after the 6th Mountain Division arrived. Dietl proposed essentially to repeat the pattern of the last July attack: the

[26] *OKW, WFSt, Abt. L (I Op.), Nr. 441255/41, an A.O.K. Norwegen, Bef. St. Finnland 24.7.41 and A.O.K. Norwegen, Bef. St. Finnland, Ia, Nr. 44/41, Lagebeurteilung vom 24.7.*, in *A.O.K. Norwegen, K.T.B. Anlagenband 1.* AOK 20 19070/2.
[27] In July the Finnish "Ivalo" Battalion had advanced to within 12 miles of Ristikent. After a number of small but sharp engagements with the Russians it fell back at the end of the month to the Akka river near the Finnish-Soviet border and thereafter engaged chiefly in patrol activity. The battalion had accomplished its mission of tying down Soviet forces southeast of Murmansk. *Batl. Ivalo, Abschrift von Funkspruch Nr. 153, [1.1.42],* in *Gebirgskorps Norwegen, Kriegstagebuch Russland 1, Anlagenband 2,* XIX AK 15085/4.
[28] *G.K.N., K.T.B. 1,* 25 Jul–5 Aug 41.
[29] *OKW, WFSt, Abt. L (1 Op.) Nr. 441298/41, an A.O.K. Norwegen, 31.7.41,* in *Silberfuchs Bd. III, 16.6.41–10.1.42.* AOK 20 20844/6.
[30] *OKW, WFSt, Abt. L (I Op.). Nr. 441325/41, an AOK Norwegen Bef. St. Finnland, 5.8.41, and OKW, WFSt, Abt. L (I Op.). Nr. 441375/41, an AOK Norwegen, Bef. St. Finnland, 13.8.41,* in *Silberfuchs Bd. III, 16.6.41–10.1.42.* AOK 20 20844/6. *A.O.K. Norwegen, K.T.B.,* 5 and 12 Aug 41.

3d Mountain Division would attack frontally across the river while the 2d Mountain Division pushed south from the bridgehead in the rear of the Russian positions. The objective would be to inflict heavy losses and soften up the enemy rather than to gain ground. The Army of Norway, on the other hand, proposed a thrust directed around the Russian flank from the right flank of the 3d Mountain Division. The thinking at army headquarters was based on experiences of the XXXVI Corps and the 163d Division which had shown the Russians in prepared positions to be particularly insensitive to frontal attacks—invariably they sat tight, forcing the attacking troops to chew through the positions one by one. Against this Dietl argued that, in an arctic wilderness of bare rock hilltops and swampy valleys, envelopments could not gain momentum and quickly bogged down. Taking into account the disadvantages of both courses, the Army of Norway still preferred an envelopment. The final decision came on 25 August when the Commanding General, 3d Mountain Division, concluded that recent improvements in the Russian positions had reduced the prospects for success of a frontal attack and that he could shift his main force several miles farther south for a thrust around the enemy flank.[31]

The Last Attempt

Planning for the new attack centered on three roads: the Russian Road (road names are those used by the Germans), which was the main road to Kola Bay and had been the objective of the July operations of the 3d Mountain Division; the New Road, which branched off from the Russian Road seven miles south of the Litsa Bridge in the narrows between Kuirk and Traun Lakes and ran northward about ten miles to a junction with the Ura Guba Road; and the Ura Guba Road—over most of its length not much more than a path—which after joining the New Road ran up to the positions facing the 2d Mountain Division bridgehead. These roads were the supply routes for the Soviet front on the Litsa. What was perhaps even more important for German operations, the New Road, in particular, if it could be reached, provided a route of march behind the Russian lines.

The Mountain Corps intended to mass two regiments, one mountain regiment and the 9th SS-Regiment, on the left flank of the 2d Mountain Division in the bridgehead, push due east for about two miles, and then swing south behind the chain of lakes to the junction of the Ura Guba and New Roads. The 3d Mountain Division would assemble two regiments south of its right flank for a thrust around the Russian left to the fork of the Russian and New Roads and northward along the New Road until it made contact with the 2d Mountain Division

[31] *Gen. Kdo. Gebirgskorps Norwegen, Ia, Besuch des Kd. Generals im Raume der 3. Geb. Div. am 24.7.41,* in *Kriegstagebuch Russland 1, Anlagenband 2.* XIX AK 15085/4. *G.K.N., K.T.B. 1,* 14, 18, 19, 22, and 25 Aug 41. *A.O.K. Norwegen, K.T.B.,* 18 and 22 Aug 41.

near the junction with the Ura Guba Road. With one regiment, the attached 388th Infantry Regiment, the 3d Mountain Division would launch a secondary attack frontally across the Litsa to take two prominent heights, Pranckh Hill and Brandl Hill, two miles south of the bridge. Having taken the heights, which were the anchor of the Soviet left flank, the regiment would continue east and join the advance along the New Road. The attack was to begin on 8 September.[32]

As the Mountain Corps Norway completed its preparations an ominous new development was already exerting influence on the potential outcome of the operation. On 30 August, off the Norwegian north coast, a Russian submarine sank two transports carrying replacements for the Mountain Corps Norway. Seeing the handwriting on the wall, the Army of Norway immediately ordered Dietl to be prepared to carry out his advance on Murmansk without awaiting the arrival of the entire 6th Mountain Division, part of which was scheduled to go by sea. That the division would be seriously delayed became obvious on 7 September when British naval vessels attacked a convoy carrying troops in the vicinity of North Cape. The transports managed to hide in a fiord, but their escort, the artillery training ship *Bremse*, was sunk.[33]

Even without regard to doubts concerning the timely arrival of the 6th Mountain Division, the assessment of the forthcoming Mountain Corps Norway operation was strongly pessimistic. On 4 September at army headquarters Buschenhagen informed Jodl, operations chief of the OKW, that the attack was regarded as particularly difficult and that whether Murmansk could be reached before winter depended on the results of the first few days. The army already thought it might be better to use the 6th Mountain Division in the advance on Kandalaksha were it not for Hitler's express desire to take Murmansk as soon as possible. On the following day Dietl told Jodl that, even if the impending attack and subsequent advance on Murmansk were completely successful, it would hardly be possible to reach the west shore of Kola Bay before winter set in (early October). He doubted whether the forces at hand, including the 6th Mountain Division, would be sufficient to accomplish a crossing to the east shore and occupy Murmansk. Moreover, even if the corps reached Murmansk, it could not hope to bring in supplies during the winter either overland from Pechenga or by sea; therefore, the railroad north from Kandalaksha would have to be taken and put into operation if Murmansk were to be held. That the railroad could be secured was entirely uncertain. Jodl could only suggest that the projected attack be carried out leaving the questions whether to continue on to

[32] *Gen. Kdo. Gebirgskorps Norwegen, Ia, Nr. 185/41, Befehl zum Angriff des Korps am 6.9., 1.8.41,* in *Kriegstagebuch Russland 1, Anlagenband 1.* XIX AK 15085/2. *Gen. Kdo. Gebirgskorps Norwegen, Ia, Lagenkarten 20.u.25., 18.8. u. 7.9.41* in *Kriegstagebuch Russland 1, Anlagenband 3.* XIX AK 15085/5. *G.K.N., K.T.B. 1,* 27 Aug and 5 Sep 41.
[33] *G.K.N., K.T.B. 1,* 31 Aug 41. *A.O.K. Norwegen, K.T.B.,* 30 and 31 Aug, 7 Sep 41.

Murmansk, hold the line reached, or fall back into Finland for Hitler to decide after its conclusion.[34]

After jumping off as scheduled on 8 September, the divisions by afternoon reported good progress on both flanks. The 2d Mountain Division had broken out of the bridgehead with its left-flank units and had taken Hill 173.7 from which its attack was to swing south. At the same time the right flank regiment of the 3d Mountain Division had pushed to within a mile and a half of the Kuirk Lake narrows.

The 388th Infantry Regiment's attack across the Litsa, however, had failed completely. Two battalions of the regiment crossed the river and made rapid progress up the slopes of Pranckh Hill and Brandl Hill, but, as soon as the artillery preparation lifted, the Russians began to fire from positions which had been bypassed in the hasty advance. Two companies moving up in column formation were caught in fire from both sides. By early afternoon their situation was desperate, and the regimental commander asked permission to pull his troops back behind the river as the only means of avoiding complete destruction of his regiment, which had already suffered 60 percent losses in one battalion. Late in the day the regiment withdrew to the left bank of the Litsa. How good a chance had been lost became clear after it was learned that a large number of Russian troops had been bivouacked in the open behind the two hills.

The danger of a too rapid advance by inexperienced troops was demonstrated for a second time that day in the 2d Mountain Division sector. Two battalions of the 9th SS-Regiment staged a quick sweep which carried them over and beyond Hill 173.7, but later, when bypassed Russians opened fire in the rear and those in front counterattacked with mortar and artillery support, the SS-men broke and ran. One battalion commander left the field, and the other recovered control of his troops only after the 2d Mountain Division had committed mountain troops to regain the lost ground.[35]

On the second day, after the 2d Mountain Division had managed to push about three miles to the south, the Russians tied it down in heavy counterattacks. With one regiment in the assault and one in reserve and holding the flanks, the 3d Mountain Division advanced to within 300 yards of the Russian Road–New Road fork but there ran into prepared positions, held by approximately a regiment, and had to halt while it brought up artillery and supplies. On the 10th, while Russian counterattacks tied down both divisions, the 3d Mountain Division estimated it would need another 24 hours to bring up supplies. Early the next morning Falkenhorst was on the phone wanting to know the reason

[34] *G.K.N., K.T.B. 1,* 5 Sep 41. *A.O.K. Norwegen, K.T.B.,* 4 Sep 41.
[35] *Gen. Kdo. Gebirgskorps Norwegen, Ia, Besuch des Kd. Generals im Raum der 3. Geb. Div., 10.9.41,* and *Besprechung Kd. General mit Gen. Mjr. Schlemmer am Div. Gef. Stand, 11.9.41,* in *Kriegstagebuch Russland 1, Anlagenband 2.* XIX AK 15085/4. *G.K.N., K.T.B. 1,* 8 and 10 Sep 41.

THE LAST ATTACK ACROSS
THE LITSA

8-20 September 1941

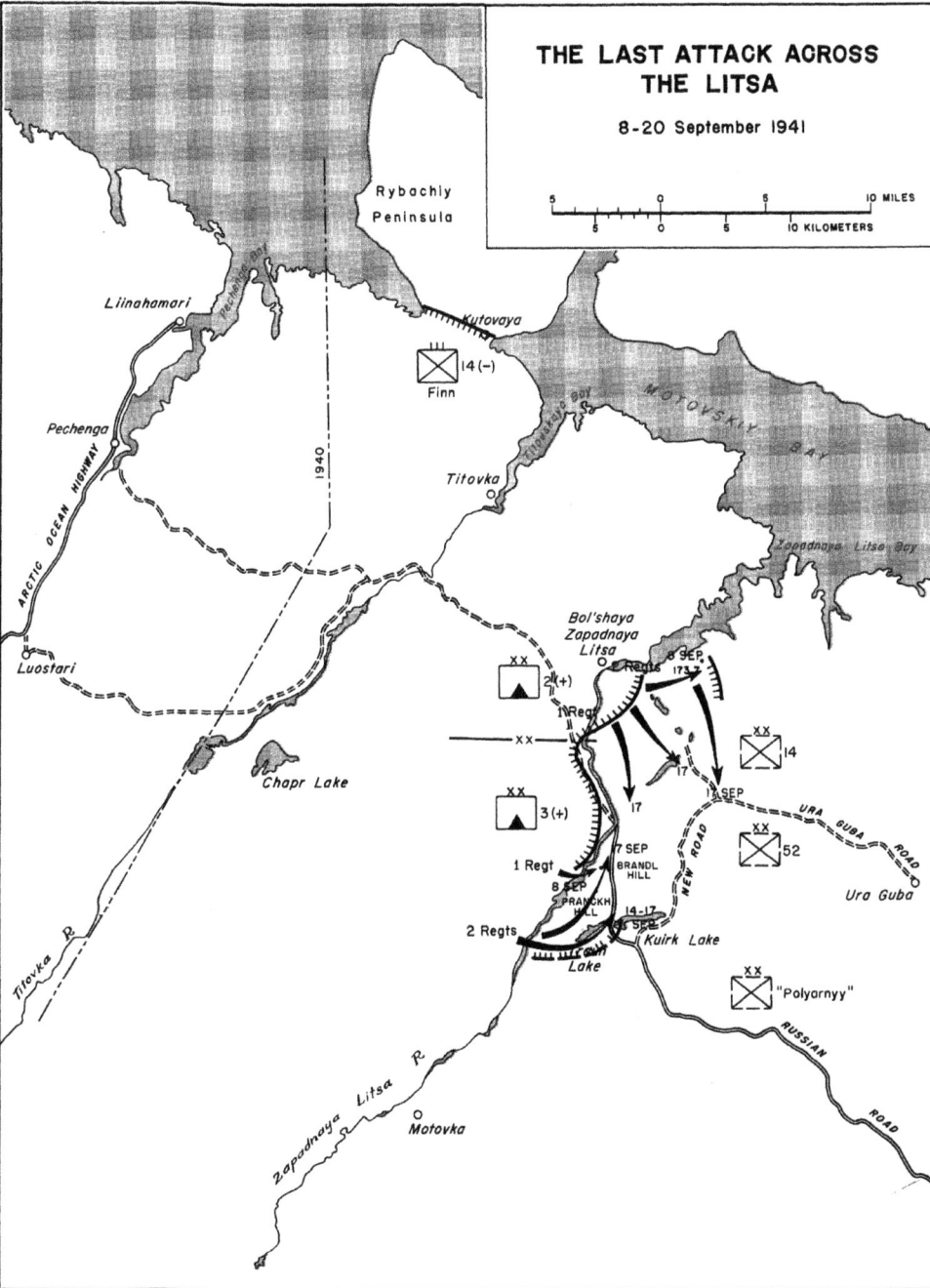

Rybachly
Peninsula

Liinahamari

Kutovaya

14 (-)
Finn

Pechenga

Titovka

MOTOVSKIY BAY

1940

Zapadnaya Litsa Bay

Luostari

Bol'shaya
Zapadnaya
Litsa

9 SEP

Regts

173

ARCTIC OCEAN HIGHWAY

2 (+)

1 Regt

17

14

URA GUBA ROAD

Chapr Lake

3 (+)

17

9 SEP

52

Ura Guba

1 Regt

7 SEP
BRANDL
HILL

NEW ROAD

8 SEP
FRANCKH
HILL

2 Regts

14-17
SEP

Kuirk Lake

Lake

"Polyarnyy"

Titovka R.

RUSSIAN ROAD

Zapadnaya Litsa R.

Motovka

Map 12

R. Booth

Engineer using jackhammer to break up rocks for the construction of positions on the Litsa River front.

for the delay. Dietl replied that under existing terrain conditions all movement and preparation was slow and time consuming.

On the 12th the 2d Mountain Division resumed its attack southward gaining about a mile, most of which it lost again during the night when the Russians counterattacked. Still not ready, the 3d Mountain Division set its attack for the 13th and then had to postpone it for another twenty-four hours when the Russians attacked just as the division was about to jump off. Ammunition was running low in both divisions since pack animals were the only form of transport to the forward positions, and they could carry only about enough to sustain defensive operations. On the 14th the 3d Mountain Division threw both of its regiments into the attack and at nightfall had possession of the lake narrows; but by then the strain of fighting for a week in cold, rainy weather was telling on both divisions, and for the next two days they limited themselves to local attacks and patrol activity.[36]

As the Mountain Corps operation proceeded at a desultory pace developments elsewhere were deciding its outcome. After the loss of two freighters off the north coast of Norway on 12 and 13 September, the Army of Norway learned on the 13th that all shipping to ports east of North Cape had been halted. On the same day the supply officer of

---

[36] *G.K.N., K.T.B. 1,* 8–16 Sep 41.

the Mountain Corps Norway reported that the ammunition on hand amounted to about one and one-half basic loads; there were enough rations to last until the end of September; and the motor fuel stored at Pechenga was enough for nine days with another nine days' supply at Kirkenes.[37]

The Army of Norway, concluding that the arrival of the 6th Mountain Division would increase the supply difficulties of the Mountain Corps and that the prospects of taking Murmansk were not good in any case, proposed to divert the division to the attack on Kandalaksha. Hitler, however, in a conference with Falkenhorst at Fuehrer Headquarters on the 15th, decided that, although the intention of reaching Murmansk in the current year would have to be abandoned, the attack in progress should be allowed to run its course while the 6th Mountain Division moved up and prepared to relieve the 2d and 3d Mountain Divisions. The 6th Mountain Division would hold the line during the winter and be in a favorable position to resume the drive on Murmansk in the spring.[38]

After Falkenhorst's visit to Fuehrer Headquarters, Hitler and Jodl proposed that the Navy employ its battleships to clear the sea lanes around the arctic coast of Norway. Raeder refused to do so, arguing that the enemy could always muster superior forces against battleships used on defensive missions.[39] The Germans assumed that the British had found their weak spot and were making a determined effort to block the arctic sea route. From the British side the situation was viewed quite differently. On 23 July, in response to Russian calls for help, the Admiralty had sent out a token force of two aircraft carriers, two cruisers, and six destroyers. At the end of the month the aircraft raided Kirkenes, Pechenga, and Liinahamari; but, since the losses of planes were high and no shipping was encountered at sea, the operation was deemed unprofitable and the force returned to Scapa. A second force of two cruisers and two destroyers sailed on 19 August to evacuate the inhabitants of Spitzbergen and destroy the coal mines. The cruisers of that force on their way home encountered and sank the *Bremse*. At the end of August two cruisers and an aircraft carrier escorted an old carrier and a freighter loaded with fighter planes to Arkhangel'sk. On the return trip in early September they sank one freighter off Norway, but this result was regarded as hardly justifying the effort expended. A greater danger to German shipping in September came from 11 submarines which the Russians had stationed off the north Norwegian coast. Nevertheless, in assessing the situation on 14 September Falkenhorst concluded that, while the submarine threat could be reduced by

---

[37] Gen. Kdo. Gebirgskorps Norwegen, Ia, *Vortrag des Quartiermeisters beim Chef des Stabes ueber die Versorgungslage am 13.9.41*, in *Kriegstagebuch Russland 1, Anlagenband 2.* XIX AK 15085/4.
[38] *A.O.K. Norwegen, K.T.B.*, 13, 15, and 17 Sep 41.
[39] *Fuehrer Conferences*, 1941, II, pp. 34 and 51ff.

reinforcing the subchaser and escort forces, the British surface vessels posed an insuperable problem. The British, intent mainly on the political objective of giving the Russians a visible show of support, had accomplished more than they knew.[40]

On 18 September Dietl and the army chief of staff decided that the Mountain Corps offensive would have to be halted. It was not producing the desired results; and the prospects looked poor since the Russians, in addition to replacing the losses of their two divisions at the front, had, according to intelligence reports received during the last two or three days, succeeded in creating a third division, the so-called "Polyarnyy" Division, composed of sailors, prisoners, and labor camp inmates. Above all, the attack would have to be stopped because of the supply situation. Buschenhagen again raised the possibility of using the 6th Mountain Division in the operation against Kandalaksha, but Dietl replied that his corps was completely worn out and would not get through the winter unless it were relieved.[41]

In the meantime the Mountain Corps Norway offensive was approaching the point of collapse. On 17 September the 3d Mountain Division took Pranckh Hill and Brandl Hill in an attack from the south. On the same day, a new Russian regiment was reported approaching the southern flank of the division. After fighting off heavy Russian counterattacks on the 18th, the Commanding General, 3d Mountain Division, on the following morning informed corps headquarters that the Russians had brought up reinforcements: two regiments of the "Polyarnyy" Division had been identified on the division front. The Russians were attacking continuously, and losses were mounting hourly. The long front, extending in a salient from the Litsa to the lake narrows and back to the Litsa again in the vicinity of Pranckh and Brandl Hills, could only be thinly held. In fact, the division commander could not guarantee that it could be held at all. To avoid complete destruction of his division, he requested permission to withdraw to the west bank of the river. Although the situation was perhaps not as serious as he thought, since the regiments of the "Polyarnyy" Division had no more than a total strength of 1,000 men each, that was not known at the time; and Dietl at noon reluctantly agreed to let the division withdraw.[42]

By the morning of the 24th the 3d Mountain Division held only Pranckh Hill and Brandl Hill east of the river, and those were given up two days later. On the 21st the Army of Norway canceled the offensive, with the exception that the 2d Mountain Division operations were to continue as far as was necessary to acquire good defensive positions for

[40] *A.O.K. Norwegen, Bef. St. Finnland, Ia, Nr. 64/41, Beurteilung der Lage am 14.9.41,* in *Silberfuchs, Br. III, 12.6.41–10.1.42.* AOK 20 20844/6. Roskill, *op. cit.,* pp. 488–90 and 493.

[41] *A.O.K. Norwegen, Bef. St. Finnland, Abt. Ic, Az. D 11, Nr. 1438/41, Feindlage vom 18.9.–2.10.41,* in *A.O.K. Norwegen, Ic, Anlagen zum K.T.B. 1.* AOK 20 25353/1. *G.K.N., K.T.B. 1,* 18 Sep 41. *A.O.K. Norwegen, K.T.B.,* 18 Sep 41.

[42] *G.K.N., K.T.B. 1,* 17–19 Sep 41.

the winter. Two days later a Fuehrer Directive confirmed the army order. In the directive Hitler raised the question whether it might still be possible to occupy the western half of the Rybatchiy Peninsula before winter. Both army and corps answered that, while such an undertaking might remove the danger of Russian artillery fire in the entrance to the harbor at Pechenga, it would also lengthen the front and should not be attempted. Thereafter the Mountain Corps Norway settled down to constructing winter positions. In mid-October the 6th Mountain Division moved up to take over the line while the 2d Mountain Division withdrew to the vicinity of Pechenga and the 3d Mountain Division, which had been in the arctic since April 1940, moved into southern Finland on the first stage of its return to Germany.

The decision to transfer the 3d Mountain Division out of Finland was made without reference to the demands of the tactical situation and was completely determined by political considerations. In the general decline of morale which followed the setbacks suffered during the summer campaign the division was particularly affected. One of the then current rumors had it that the 3d Mountain Division was being kept in the arctic as part of a plot to exterminate the Austrians. (Most of the division personnel was Austrian.) Finally, one of the soldiers who was a Nazi Party member complained to the party authorities; and, since there were at the same time signs of unrest in the Austrian provinces, the matter was taken through party channels to Hitler, who ordered the division transferred.[43]

Summary

In a two and one-half months' campaign, at a cost of 10,290 casualties, the Mountain Corps Norway had advanced about 15 miles. With respect to the attainment of its objective, Murmansk, it was not appreciably better off at the end of the campaign than it had been at the beginning. Operation PLATINFUCHS had misfired.

PLATINFUCHS could be said to have run its course by 17 July when Dietl reported that with the forces at its disposal the Mountain Corps Norway could no longer execute its mission. The failure of the operation to a certain extent resulted logically from the terms under which it was conceived. Because of Hitler's insistence on maintaining the defenses of Norway at full strength, the force for PLATINFUCHS had been determined by what could be spared in Norway and not by the requirements of the operation. For that reason expectations concerning the outcome of PLATINFUCHS had remained vague. The Army of Norway set Polyarnyy as a definite objective and left the occupation of Murmansk

---

[43] General der Infanterie a.D. Erich Buschenhagen, Comments on Part II of *The German Northern Theater of Operations, 1940–1945*, May 1957. *G.K.N., K.T.B. 1*, 24–26 and 29 Sep 41; 13 and 25 Oct 41. *A.O.K. Norwegen, K.T.B.*, 23, 24, and 29 Sep 41; 18 Nov 41.

for a later decision, which corresponded approximately to Hitler's instructions that Murmansk was to be hemmed in and occupied in the further course of operations if sufficient forces were available. The OKW directive of 7 April was completely indefinite, stating only that it remained to be seen whether enough strength could be mustered for a thrust to Polyarnyy after security had been provided for northern Norway and Pechenga. On 15 May, after Dietl had reported that expert opinion in the Scandinavian countries considered the terrain between Pechenga and Murmansk completely unsuitable for military operations in summer, Jodl had replied that all the difficulties were known to the OKW, that only the occupation of Pechenga was desired as a certainty, and that anything beyond that would be considered a gift.[44]

Nevertheless, it had been assumed that the occupation of Murmansk would be a likely outcome of PLATINFUCHS and that, in any event, the Mountain Corps Norway would be master of the situation militarily. No one anticipated that the corps would be fought to a standstill before it had achieved a position which could be considered even remotely promising. This error resulted from a false appraisal of the enemy and the terrain. Contrary to expectations, the Russians fought with skill and determination, proving themselves to be masters in the construction of defensive positions and nerveless in the tenacity with which they held their ground. Moreover, not even Dietl, despite his warning to Jodl, was fully aware of the extent to which the terrain would influence operations by braking the momentum of even limited attacks and by affording an endless succession of excellent defensive positions. Added to this was faulty knowledge of the local geography. One road which had been counted on for use was nonexistent, and the other was hardly more than a path west of the Litsa, a state of affairs made doubly serious by the fact that the Russians had a sea route and a reasonably good road from Kola Bay to the Litsa.

The second and final phase of the Mountain Corps Norway operations was primarily an attempt to revive PLATINFUCHS by building the strength of the corps up to a level commensurate with the requirements of its mission, which Hitler then for the first time definitely made the capture of Murmansk. It failed when the closing of the sea route around northern Norway delayed the arrival of the 6th Mountain Division and brought the Mountain Corps to the verge of paralysis. The two roads, Reichsstrasse 50 from Narvik (400 miles) and the Arctic Ocean Highway from Rovaniemi (300 miles), were both of very limited capacity. The Russians, on the other hand, had the Murmansk Railroad which they were able to use to bring up replacements and to begin creating a

[44] *Gen. Kdo. Gebirgskorps Norwegen, Ia, Sonderanlage zum Taetigkeitsbericht April, Mai, Juni 1941,* in *Gebirgskorps Norwegen, Kriegstagebuch Russland 1, Anlagenband 30,* XIX AK 15085/33.

new division.[45]   The collapse of the Mountain Corps supply line, however, did not take place before the corps, employing two fresh—if not first-rate—regiments, had been stopped dead in its tracks for a third time by the Russian line on the Litsa.   Dietl himself concluded that the Russians, drawing on their seemingly inexhaustible manpower reserves and exploiting the highly favorable terrain for a defense in depth, would have prevented his breaking through to Murmansk even with the 6th Mountain Division.[46]

---

[45] In September 1941 Hitler ordered his construction chief, Dr. Fritz Todt, to build a narrow gauge railroad from Rovaniemi to Pechenga using Russian prisoners of war as labor.   The project was first postponed because of the impossibility of laying a roadbed over arctic ground in winter and was then dropped when it was learned that the railroad would have to be built all the way from the Gulf of Bothnia because the Finnish line below Rovaniemi did not have the capacity to sustain a new line in the north.   Instead, the Germans began building a road from the Porsanger Fiord in Norway to Ivalo on the Arctic Ocean Highway.   It was to play an important part in the 1944 withdrawal from Finland.

[46] Letter Dietl to Jodl 23 Sep 41 in Dietl, op. cit., pp. 231ff.

Chapter 9

Operation SILBERFUCHS (II)

POLARFUCHS (Operations of XXXVI Corps and Finnish III Corps)

Thirty miles above the Arctic Circle, in the point of a flattened spearhead formed by the Finnish-Soviet border of 1940, lay Salla, flanked on the north by the Kuola River, which joins the westward flowing Salla River at the western edge of the settlement, and on the south by the 2,000-foot-high Salla Mountain. The bare slopes of the mountain afforded a clear field of observation across the tangled evergreen forest stretching up to and beyond the border three miles to the west. By June 1941 the Soviet Union had completed a railroad from Kandalaksha to the border; the Finnish connecting line to Kemiyärvi was not finished but was being pushed rapidly as the Finns gained enthusiasm from the knowledge that the railroad could now be put to a use quite different from that which the Russians had intended. In their 15 months' occupation the Russians had fortified the border and the flank approaches to Salla, making it a major defensive strongpoint held by an infantry division (the 122d Rifle Division) and, according to German estimates, 50 tanks.

In the last week of June the Army of Norway main force, the XXXVI Corps, assembled its two German divisions opposite Salla. The Finnish 6th Division was already in position north of Kuusamo. The corps planned to take Salla in a double envelopment and so open the way for a quick thrust to the Murmansk Railroad at Kandalaksha. It placed the weight of its initial attack on the north flank, where the 169th Infantry Division was to commit three combat teams of approximately regimental strength. The first would advance along the Tennio River eight miles north of Salla where it would screen the corps' left flank and become the northern arm of a second pincers directed against Kayrala. The second was positioned five miles north of Salla for a thrust southeastward to the Salla–Korya road and then south along the road to complete the encirclement. The third, stationed on and north of the Savukoski–Salla road, would mount a frontal attack against the border fortifications. On the south flank of the corps, the two regiments of the SS-Division "Nord' would cross the border along and

157

south of the Rovaniemi–Kandalaksha road and advance up to and behind Salla from the south.[1] The Finnish 6th Division, crossing the border 45 miles south of Salla and advancing northwestward, was to send a detachment to attack Kayrala from the south while its main force thrust deep in the Russian rear toward Allakurtti.[2]

The Finnish III Corps, on the Army of Norway right flank, in June 1941 held a 60-mile front between Kuusamo and Suomussalmi. In the last two weeks of the month the corps reorganized its one division (the 3d) into two groups, Group F and Group J, each with one rifle regiment and a small number of attached troops including border guards. The corps held one regiment in reserve and had at its disposal one German tank company and a battalion detached from the Finnish 6th Division. Group J assembled south of Kuusamo for an attack in the direction of Kesten'ga while Group F, its first objective Ukhta, drew its forces together east of Suomussalmi. The ultimate objectives of III Corps were Loukhi and Kem on the Murmansk Railroad.[3]

As the XXXVI Corps and the III Corps prepared for the attack, one great doubt remained: it concerned the military capability, if any, of the SS-Division. Its officers of all ranks had no more military training than they had been able to absorb during a short course of lectures and demonstrations given them in the previous winter. The division had fired its artillery only once, and proficiency in the use of small arms was so low that provision had to be made for target practice while the division moved up to the front. The march from northern Norway had been so poorly executed and revealed such a profound ignorance of military procedures that it resulted in the relief of the commanding general and his operations officer. The new commanding general, after looking over his troops, reported on 23 June that he could not assume responsibility for committing them in battle. The Commanding General, XXXVI Corps, Feige, was reluctant to use the SS-Division against Salla and did so only at the insistence of the Army of Norway which was more optimistic than the corps in its assessment of the SS-Division and held a lower opinion of the enemy's defensive capabilities.[4]

Salla

Two hours after midnight on 1 July the Finnish 6th Division crossed the border near the northwestern tip of Pana Lake. At 1600, after a

---

[1] The SS-Kampfgruppe was renamed SS-Division "Nord" in June 1941.
[2] Gen. Kdo. XXXVI A.K., K.T.B., Nr. 3 (9.5.–2.9.1941) Textband, Einsatz in Nordfinnland (hereafter cited as XXXVI A.K., K.T.B., 3), 16 Jun 41. XXXVI AK 22102/3. Gen. Kdo. XXXVI A.K., Ia, Nr. 654/41, Korpsbefehl fuer den Angriff am Y-Tag, 27.6.41, in XXXVI A.K., K.T.B. 3, Anlagenband A 1. XXXVI AK 22102/4.
[3] III AKE, No. 10/III/3b, Dem Chef des Gen. Stabes, Abloesungsstab A.O.K. Norwegen, 18.6.41, in Anlagen zum K.T.B. des III finn. A.K., 10.6.–31.12.41. III finn AK 19654/2. III Armeekorps Stab, Nr. 2/III/2b/L5616, Entfaltungsbefehl des AK, 17.6.41., in A.O.K. Norwegen, Anlagen zum K.T.B., Band I. AOK 20 19070/2. A.O.K. Norwegen, K.T.B., 16 and 25 Jun 41.
[4] XXXVI A.K., K.T.B. 3, 9 May–29 Jun 41 (passim).

ten-minute preparatory bombardment by a dive-bomber group, the SS-Division and the 169th Division began their advance. The timing of the attacks demonstrated one of the peculiarities of arctic warfare: with 24 hours of summer daylight the distinction between night and day did not exist, and the two German divisions were able to open their attack late in the afternoon, thus gaining the advantage of having the sun at their backs. The day was hot, with the temperature in the high 80's, which brought out swarms of mosquitos. After the air bombardment Salla and Salla Mountain disappeared in clouds of smoke, and the artillery fire soon started numerous forest fires which reduced visibility and in places threatened to block the advance of the troops.

Before midnight the XXXVI Corps had a clear indication of the kind of opposition it was going to meet. The right-flank regiment of the 169th Division, advancing on the border fortifications on either side of the Savukoski–Salla road with two battalions, was stopped about 500 yards east of the border and was then thrown back by a sharp counterattack which touched off a brief panic in the rear echelon of the German regiment. That brought to a quick end the planned frontal attack on Salla. The regiment in the center, on the other hand, had made good progress and at the end of the day was drawing up to the Salla–Korya road. Along the Tennio River the left-flank regiment had gained about two miles.

Shortly after midnight the question concerning the effectiveness of SS-Division "Nord" was answered: SS stragglers came streaming past corps headquarters on the Rovaniemi–Salla road, and the corps artillery commander urgently requested the SS-Division to clear its men out of his artillery positions. On the division front confusion reigned; the operations officer could give the positions of only two of his six battalions. Later in the morning, after the division commander had declared his troops incapable of continuing the attack, Feige ordered the division to assemble on the border and take up defensive positions. Meeting the SS general at corps headquarters several hours later, Falkenhorst with heavy irony "congratulated him on the behavior of his troops." [5]

The second day also brought a crisis in the 169th Division area. The Russians, seeing an encirclement developing, counterattacked against the center regiment and, with tank and air support, forced it back off the road. In the morning the division sent up a battalion of infantry and a company of tanks (one company was already committed) and later in the day drew on the divisional reserve for another battalion of infantry. By mid-afternoon the division had concluded that it could not take Salla with one regiment and decided to abandon the projected advance of the left-flank regiment to Kayrala, ordering it instead to turn south along the Salla–Korya road.

---

[5] *XXXVI A.K., K.T.B. 3*, 2 Jul 41.

Mountain troops picking their way through the forest east of Salla. Note edelweis badge of the mountain troops on cap of man in foreground.

On the following day, while the left regiment moved south, the center regiment regained the road and pushed down to the Kuola River. The division, meanwhile, had decided also to commit its third regiment in the river crossing and assault on Salla. The wearing effect of unending daylight was beginning to tell on the troops as they worked their way into position north of the river during the next two days in preparation for a crossing on 6 July.

Early on the morning of the 4th the XXXVI Corps headquarters staff witnessed an astonishing scene as the motorized SS-Division came streaming down the road toward Rovaniemi swearing Russian tanks were at its heels. For several hours the corps staff, including the chief of staff and Feige himself, were out on the road getting the SS-men headed back toward the front. Some of the vehicles were stopped and turned back at the Army of Norway advanced headquarters halfway down the road toward Kemiyärvi, and a few went the full 50 miles to Kemiyärvi where an SS-man urged the local commandant to blow up the bridge across the Kemi River to hold up the Russian tanks which he claimed were in hot pursuit. It was later learned that the division, hearing tanks start up behind the Russian positions had called for artillery fire, which led the Russians to retaliate in kind. The commanding general, convinced that the Russians were attacking and having no confidence in his troops, had ordered a withdrawal which rapidly became a full-scale panic.

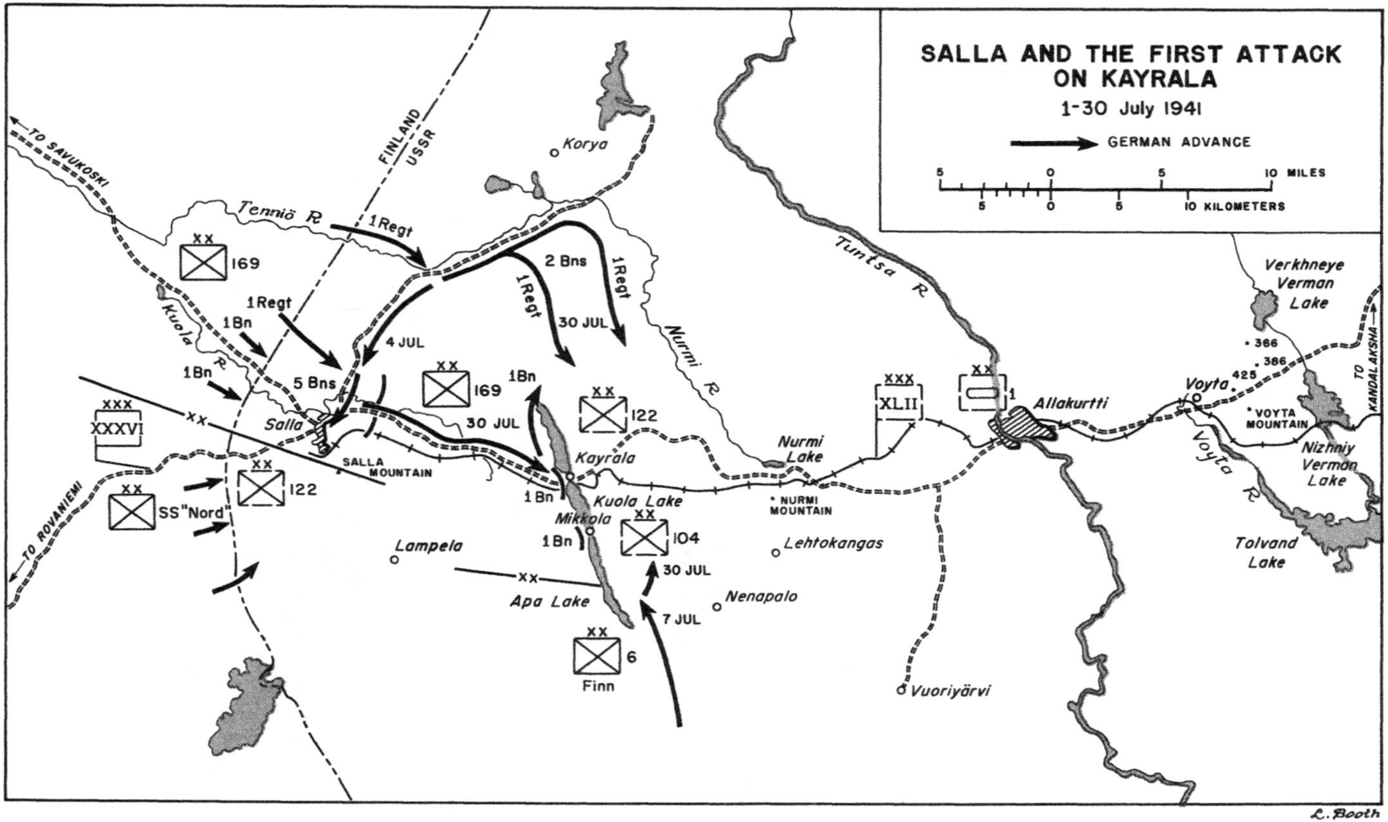
SALLA AND THE FIRST ATTACK ON KAYRALA
1-30 July 1941
GERMAN ADVANCE
5 0 5 10 MILES
5 0 5 10 KILOMETERS
TO SAVUKOSKI
TO ROVANIEMI
TO KANDALAKSHA
FINLAND
USSR
Korya
Tenniö R
Kuola R
Tuntsa R
Nurmi R
Voyta R
1Regt
2 Bns
1Regt
1Regt
30 JUL
1Bn
1Bn
4 JUL
5 Bns
1Bn
30 JUL
169
169
122
122
104
6
Finn
SS"Nord"
XXXVI
XLII
1
Salla
SALLA MOUNTAIN
Kayrala
Kuola Lake
Mikkola
1Bn
1Bn
30 JUL
7 JUL
Lampela
Apa Lake
Nenapalo
Lehtokangas
NURMI MOUNTAIN
Nurmi Lake
Vuoriyärvi
Allakurtti
Voyta
366
386
425
VOYTA MOUNTAIN
Verkhneye Verman Lake
Nizhniy Verman Lake
Tolvand Lake
L. Booth

Map 13

With the SS-Division proved completely unreliable, it was not only impossible to complete the encirclement of Salla but necessary as well to shore up the stationary front on the border. Falkenhorst first offered the entire army reserve, a Finnish battalion, an SS battalion, and a motorized machine gun battalion, but then changed his mind and sent only the motorized machine gun battalion. Feige asked for a regiment of the 163d Infantry Division, which was completing its move through Sweden, and learned for the first time that the division had been given to Mannerheim and it would take high-level negotiations to get a regiment back from the Finns. The next day, sooner than had been expected, Hitler approved the transfer of the regiment. The OKH, which had counted on the 163d Division to give weight to Mannerheim's forthcoming offensive east of Lake Ladoga, was in no wise pleased by the decision, and Halder commented on it acidly as clearly demonstrating the questionable nature of the whole Murmansk operation.[6]

The collapse of the SS-Division "Nord" also brought into question the further operations of the Finnish 6th Division. In order to prevent the division from becoming exposed to a Russian attack in isolation and to assist the 169th Division, which henceforth would have to carry the burden of the attack alone, Feige ordered it to abandon its thrust toward Allakurtti and turn due north toward Kayrala. On 6 July Feige thought it would be best to draw the SS-Division out of the line altogether and set it up in a training camp behind the front, but that was no longer possible since Hitler had personally ordered the division to stay at the front.[7]

By early morning on 6 July the 169th Division was ready to launch its final assault across the Kuola River and into Salla from the east. It had a regimental combat team of five battalions and two tank companies along the river west of the Salla–Korya road, another with two battalions east of the road, and two battalions at the disposal of the division. The division hoped, by swinging south behind Salla to the eastern slope of Salla Mountain, to be able still to trap the Russian force. With dive bomber and artillery support, the attack made progress against stubborn resistance, and at noon the right-flank regiment was within a half mile of Salla after knocking out 16 Russian tanks in one hour and losing most of its own. The division, having committed all of its reserves, saw no chance of drawing a line south to Salla Mountain. Five hours later the right regiment entered Salla and was promptly thrown into a withdrawal which stopped only after the commanding general and his two regimental commanders intervened in person.

---

[6] *Halder Diary,* Vol. VI, p. 191.

[7] The behavior of SS-Division "Nord" was a major annoyance to Hitler and probably something of a blow to Himmler, who touted his Waffen-SS divisions with their imposing names, "Liebstandarte Adolf Hitler," "Das Reich," "Totenkopf," "Wiking," and "Nord," as the very cream of the German fighting forces.

During the night the German situation remained precarious, and on the following morning the division became concerned over reports of a Russian column with tanks moving west from Kayrala. Resuming the attack at 1500 on the 7th, the division made little progress until shortly before midnight when it became clear that the Russians were withdrawing southeastward toward Lampela. Moving into Salla during the morning against rear-guard resistance the division captured the artillery equipment of a division and brought its total of tanks destroyed or captured to 50, but the mass of the 122d Rifle Division had slipped away through the open southern arc of the encirclement. The XXXVI Corps was inclined to look on the taking of Salla as a first-rate achievement under the circumstances. Falkenhorst was not so pleased and on viewing the scene of action commented that he could have taken the positions facing the SS-Division with recruits.[8]

Leaving the SS-Division to pursue the Russians in the direction of Lampela, the 169th Division had to turn east immediately in order, if possible, to prevent the enemy from making another stand at the narrows of Kayrala and Mikkola where the Kuola Lake–Apa Lake chain lay like a ten-mile-long moat across the road. At the same time the XXXVI Corps learned that it would have to give up the motorized machine gun battalion, its only fresh motorized unit, which was being transferred to the Mountain Corps Norway . The Finnish 6th Division was already pushing northward along the east shore of Apa Lake, but it had been forced to leave all its artillery behind on the long march through the wilderness. Early on the morning of the 9th a battalion of the 169th Division advanced to within a mile and a half of Kayrala where it was stopped by artillery fire. That night a regiment of the Finnish division cut the road and railroad three miles east of the lakes but had to fall back to the south under Russian pressure from both sides.

Stalemate at Kayrala

After a frontal attack by one battalion at Kayrala and a second at Mikkola failed on 10 July it became clear that the Russians were ready to make another stand. The 104th Rifle Division, which had not yet been in action, was holding the narrows, and the 122d Rifle Division was regrouping behind the lake. The XLII Corps headquarters, if not already in command, would appear within the next few days; and the 1st Tank Division, which had had units at Salla, was located at or west of Allakurtti.[9]

---

[8] 169. I.D., Fuehrungs-Abt, Kriegstagebuch Nr. 2, Teil 1, 1.6–9.9.1941 (hereafter referred to as 169.I.D., K.T.B. 2, Teil 1), 1–8 Jul 41. 169 ID 20291/2. A.O.K. Norwegen, K.T.B., 1–8 Jul 1941. XXXVI A.K., K.T.B. 3, 1–8 Jul 41.

[9] The 1st Tank Division was composed of two tank regiments, a motorized infantry regiment, and—probably—a motorized howitzer regiment. On about 1 August the tank regiments were withdrawn to the front before Leningrad. A.O.K. Norwegen, Bef. St. Finnland, Ic, Az D 11, Nr. 791/41, Feindlage 3.8–11.8.41, in A.O.K. Norwegen, Ic Anlagen zum K.T.B. I. AOK 20 25353/1.

Anticipating stronger resistance than at Salla and having only two effective divisions, the XXXVI Corps planned to execute a shallow double envelopment with the limited objective of opening the lake narrows. Assigning the main effort to the 169th Division, it intended to send one regiment by way of the Salla–Korya road to a point north and east of the lake chain for a thrust into the enemy's right flank, two battalions directly around the northern tip of Kuola Lake, and single battalions in feigned frontal attacks on Kayrala and Mikkola. The Finnish 6th Division, still without artillery support except for that which could be given from the 169th Division and corps positions on the road, would come up from the south, east of Apa Lake.

A delaying factor in the operation was the problem of bringing the regiment on the northern flank into position. Using the Salla–Korya road, it could get behind the Russian lines but at a point eight miles north of the tip of Kuola Lake. It would then have to work its way south across wooded, hilly, almost mountainous country to the Russian flank defenses established at right angles to the lake chain, take those positions, and jump off southward behind the lake. The regiment began to meet resistance as soon as it turned south off the road.

In the first of what was during the next two weeks to grow into a series of sharp, sometimes acrimonious, differences of opinion with the XXXVI Corps, the Army of Norway asked for a deeper envelopment extending east of the Nurmi River to make certain that the Russian divisions were trapped and destroyed. That task the XXXVI Corps declared to be beyond its strength. Instead, it revised its plan for operations on the northern wing, sending up an additional regiment plus two reserve battalions from the newly arrived 324th Infantry Regiment (163d Infantry Division) and extending its flank to the west bank of the Nurmi River.

The first task was to cut a road through forests, bogs, and fields of boulders for each of the left-flank regiments. On 16 July Falkenhorst appeared at the front testily wanting to know what was taking so long. In the course of his explanation the corps operations officer broached one matter which was troubling the corps more and more. The German soldier, as he put it, had lost his instinct for forest fighting; he felt insecure and attempted to crash his way through places where he should have proceeded with stealth. In this respect the Russians and Finns were far superior. Falkenhorst replied with heavy sarcasm that he would then have to report to Hitler that "XXXVI Corps cannot attack because it is 'degenerate.' " [10] His impatience was not unjustified, however. In the past three or four days twelve Soviet transports had landed reinforcements at Kandalaksha that were moving up to Allakurtti and Kayrala (probably also to Murmansk) by road and railroad. German planes had succeeded in destroying only one convoy returning empty

---

[10] *XXXVI A.K., K.T.B. 3*, 16 Jul 41.

Half-tracked motorcycles pulling antitank guns on a corduroy road.

from Allakurtti. While the new arrivals were not a full division as was at first feared, they were enough to restore the 122d Rifle Division to full strength.

The effect of the reinforcements was felt immediately as the enemy became more active, thrusting against the regiments on the north flank and threatening the Finnish 6th Division east of Apa Lake. While the Army of Norway urged an immediate attack as the only solution, the XXXVI Corps became more pessimistic. It knew the Russians to be superior in numbers and was particularly worried about the 1st Tank Division, which was reported to have some heavy tanks. On 21 July the commander of the 169th Division declared that his left-flank regiments could accomplish only the first two phases of their assignment, the march to the tip of Kuola Lake and the taking of the Russian flank defense line. The third, a thrust to the Kayrala–Allakurtti road, would be beyond their strength.

On 23 July Falkenhorst went out to look over the 169th Division left flank for himself. In a one-sided conversation he gave the commanding general the following estimates: of the enemy—two or three regiments, badly beaten at Salla, which were gaining time to recover by the delays of the division; of the terrain—a few hills over which everything necessary could be carried; of the roads—boulevards compared to those with which Dietl had to contend; of the division staff—living too close to the troops.[11] Later in the day he dashed off a summary of his impressions to Feige: troops supposedly building a road were lying about

[11] *169. I.D., Kommandeur, Besuch des Herrn Oberbefehlshaber, 23.7.1941,* in *XXXVI A.K., Anlagenband A 2.* XXXVI AK 22102/5.

in hammocks sunning themselves;[12] there was talk of "defense" and "stationary warfare," ideas which if they did not vanish immediately would force him to ask the OKW for some more energetic commanders; the time for long memorandums and estimates of the situation had passed. Feige was "directed to report the day and hour on which the corps will begin the attack with its divisions." [13] Under the influence of this stinging communication Feige immediately set the attack for 2300 on 26 July.

After a last-minute appeal to Hitler secured dive bomber support, which until then had all been assigned to the inactive Mountain Corps Norway sector, the attack began on time.[14] Of the two regiments on the 169th Division's left flank one ran into a Soviet attack launched simultaneously and could not get out of its starting positions; the other gained about a mile before it was pinned down. The Finnish 6th Division, which was to tie down the enemy until the 169th Division had broken through the northern flank defenses, gained some ground and then was thrown back. Shortly before noon on the 27th Feige informed the Army of Norway that by continuing the attack he could soften up the enemy but not achieve a decisive success. Buschenhagen replied that the attack had to continue because Hitler had ordered that the Murmansk Railroad must be reached in at least one place. In the afternoon the two reserve battalions were thrown in on the northern flank without result.

Before noon on the following day the attack had bogged down completely, and the Army of Norway ordered the XXXVI Corps to tie down the enemy with limited attacks in order to prevent him from shifting troops to the Mountain Corps Norway or Finnish III Corps sectors. To the OKW, army reported that the attack was stalled and could not be resumed without an additional division.[15] On the 30th Hitler confirmed the action already taken by the Army of Norway and ordered the XXXVI

---

[12] Unknowingly he had come upon another of the peculiarities of arctic warfare: because heat (in July 1941 the temperature rose above 85° Fahrenheit on 12 days, twice reaching 97°) and mosquitos made work virtually impossible during the normal daytime hours, the division had been doing its road building during the nights, which were light but cool and free of mosquitos.

[13] Three days later the army chief of staff explained that impatient expressions should not be taken personally; army was under pressure from Fuehrer Headquarters. *O.B., A.O.K., Norwegen, an den Kom. Gen. des Hoeh. Kdos. XXXVI, 23.7.41* and *Gen. Kdo. XXXVI A.K., Ia., Ferngespraech Kom. Gen. XXXVI A.K. mit Chef des Stabes A.O.K. am 27.4.41*, in *XXXVI A.K., Anlagenband A 2.* XXXVI A.K. 22102/5.

[14] In order to preserve the striking power of its limited forces the Fifth Air Force had been ordered to maintain a clear-cut main effort at all times. Since the air units were not subordinate to the Army of Norway and often operated according to their own tactical conceptions, co-ordination of air and ground operations was difficult, particularly in the light of the fact that the Commanding General, Fifth Air Force, kept his headquarters in Oslo. General der Infanterie a.D. Erich Buschenhagen, Comments on Part II of *The German Northern Theater of Operations, 1940–1945*, May 1957.

[15] *A.O.K. Norwegen, Bef. St. Finnland, Ia, Nr. 46/41, Lagebeurteilung vom 28.7.1941*, in *A.O.K. Norwegen, Anlagen zum K.T.B., Band I.* AOK 20 19070/2.

Corps attack closed down.   In one month the XXXVI Corps had advanced slightly more than 13 miles at a cost of 5,500 casualities.   The 169th Infantry Division, with 3,296 casualities, was reduced to an effective strength of 9,782 officers and men.[16]

Finnish III Corps Operations in July and August 1941

The Fuehrer Directive of 31 July ordered the Army of Norway to shift its main effort to the Finnish III Corps zone and the drive to Loukhi, leaving only as many troops with the XXXVI Corps as were necessary for defense and to create an impression of further offensive intentions.[17]   The directive, in the main, confirmed measures already taken by the Army of Norway.   Since mid-July Falkenhorst had believed that the Murmansk Railroad could be reached most quickly at Loukhi, and on the 19th he had committed a regiment and an artillery battalion of the SS-Division "Nord" to the III Corps attack in that direction.   On the 29th and 30th he sent an additional infantry battalion and an artillery battalion of the SS-Division to the III Corps.

Concluding the Fuehrer Directive, Hitler added that, were the drive toward Loukhi also to lose its momentum, all German troops were to be withdrawn and sent to the Army of Karelia.   In fact, he wanted the Army of Norway to prepare immediately to commit forces in support of the Army of Karelia.   It appeared that Hitler was considering stopping for good the German operations in the XXXVI Corps and Finnish III Corps zones, but he did not revert to this aspect of the directive again.   His reference to immediate support for the Army of Karelia was later clarified and limited to the 324th Infantry Regiment, which the OKH wanted returned to the 163d Infantry Division and which the Army of Norway continued to insist it could not spare.[18]

On 1 July, following the Army of Norway plan, the III Corps had sent Group J (one regiment) across the border east of Kuusamo in the direction Kesten'ga–Loukhi and Group F east of Suomussalmi in the direction Ukhta–Kem.   In accordance with the Army of Norway instructions the corps placed its main effort in the Group F sector, committing its reserve regiment there for a converging attack by two regiments on Voynitsa (Vuoninnen) 12 miles east of the border.   The corps sector was held by the Russian 54th Rifle Division, which at first divided its forces about equally to defend Kesten'ga and Ukhta.[19]

[16] *A.O.K. Norwegen, K.T.B., 10–31 Jul 41.   XXXVI A.K., K.T.B. 3, 10 Jul–1 Aug 41.   169 I.D., K.T.B. 2, Teil 1, 10–13 Jul 41.*
[17] *OKW, WFSt, Abt. L (I Op.), Nr. 441298/41, an A.O.K. Norwegen, Bef. St. Finnland, 31.7.41* and *OKW, WFSt, Abt. L (I Op.). Nr. 1325/41 an A.O.K. Norwegen, Bef. St. Finnland, 2.8.41,* in *A.O.K. Norwegen, Anlagen zum K.T.B., Band I.* AOK 20 19070/2.
[18] *Ibid.*
[19] *A.O.K. Norwegen, Ia, Nr. 148/41, Operationsanweisung fuer das V. finnische Armee-Korps, 10.6.41; III AKE, No. 10/III/3b, dem Chef des Gen. Stabes Abloesungsstab A.O.K. Norwegen, 18.6.41;* and *Gen. Kdo. III A.K., Nr. 501/III/3b, Befehl des A.K., 23.7.41,* in *Anlagen zum K.T.B. des III. finn. A.K. 10.6.–31.12.41.* Finnland 19654/2.

The III Corps offensive made good initial progress against weak resistance. By 5 July Group J was in Makarely, 17 miles east of the border, and the right-flank regiment of Group F had marched 28 miles to Pon'ga Guba. On the 10th, as Group J drew up to Tungozero, the two regiments of Group F in the south encountered a center of resistance at Voynitsa which they encircled and wiped out during the next nine days. By the 19th, Group J was on the Sof'yanga, an eight-mile long channel connecting Pya Lake and Top Lake. It was a major obstacle, strongly defended, which could not be taken without careful preparation; but the Group J commander was optimistic. Once in the narrows between the lakes he could advance to Kesten'ga without worrying about his flanks, and from Kesten'ga to Loukhi there were 42 miles of improved road.

Visiting Group J on 18 July, Buschenhagen, the army chief of staff, was astonished at the rapidity of its advance (some 40 miles) and noted with surprise that the Finns had built a road all the way. Experienced in forest warfare, the Finns had several times broken the enemy's defensive efforts by rapid thrusts at his flanks and rear, which often could be developed into *mottis*—small tight encirclements, sometimes several at the same time. These were particularly effective in the forest where the more sweeping encirclements favored by the Germans were difficult to establish and nearly impossible to draw sufficiently tight to prevent the enemy's escape. On the basis of Buschenhagen's observations the Army of Norway decided to send the SS regiment and artillery battalion already mentioned to Group J and to shift the III Corps main effort from Group F to Group J. In compliance Kenraalimajuri H. Siilasvuo, Commanding General, III Corps, began drawing two battalions out of the Group F sector for transfer to the north flank.[20]

While Group J prepared to cross the Sof'yanga, Group F resumed its advance to Ukhta. After cleaning out several small pockets east of Voynitsa, which yielded prisoners and enemy equipment, it reached Korpiyärvi on the 23d. From there, during the next five days, it advanced in two columns, one along the north shore of Sredneye Kuyto Lake and the other along the Korpiyärvi–Ukhta road, to the Yeldanka Lake line, 12 miles northwest of Ukhta.

On 30 July Group J began its assault across the Sof'yanga and sent one battalion by boat over the western tip of Top Lake to land in the Russian rear. On the same day the Army of Norway decided to commit additional SS troops in the Group J zone to protect its open northern flank between the lakes and the border.[21] In three days'

---

[20] *A.O.K. Norwegen, K.T.B.,* 1–19 Jul 41.
[21] At this time the first appearances of the Soviet partisans were arousing growing concern throughout the Army of Norway area. The partisans, in reality small, roving detachments of Russian troops (50–100 men), were being reported from the Mountain Corps Norway zone southward. There is no record of their having achieved any noteworthy successes.

OPERATIONS OF GROUP F
UKHTA
July - November 1941

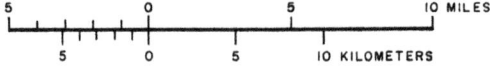

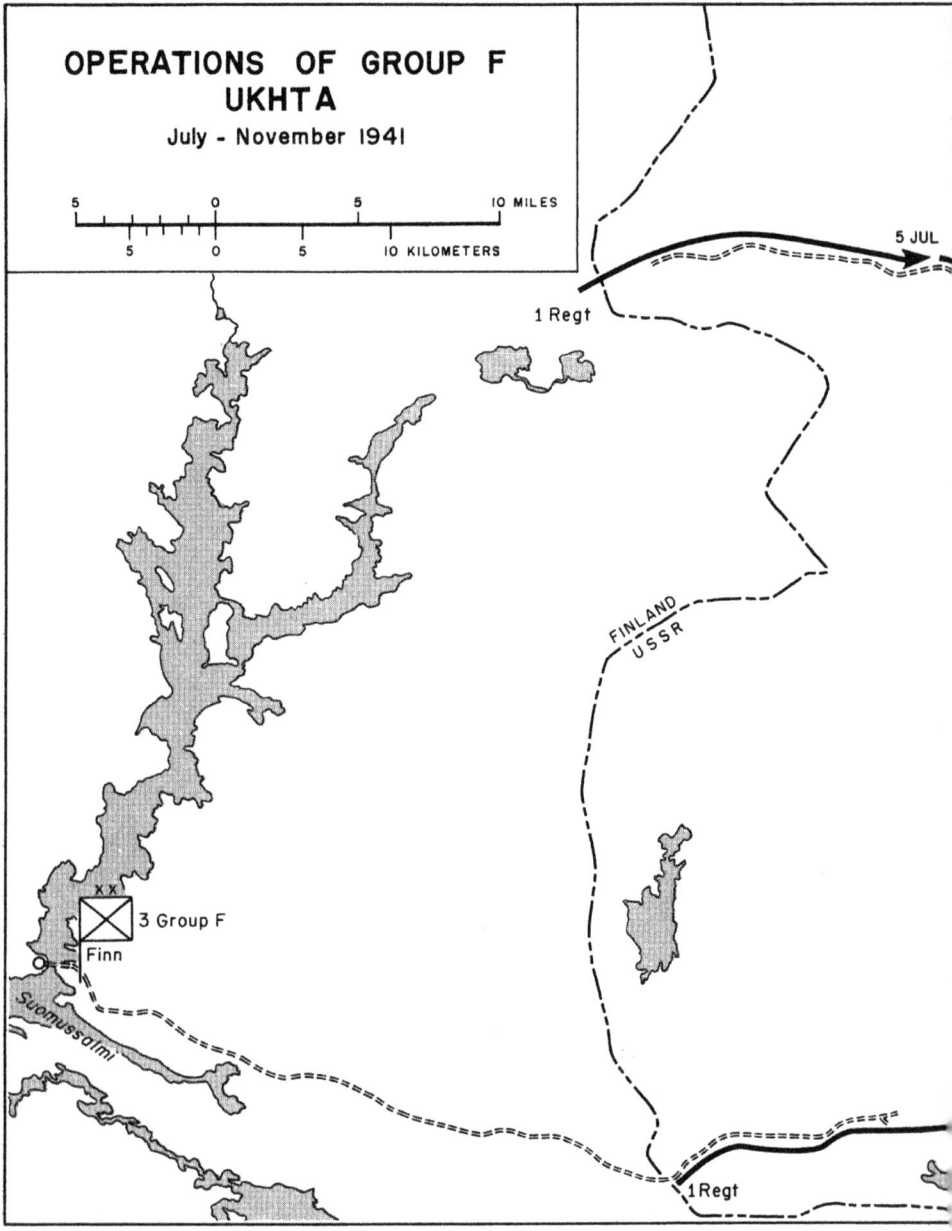

5	0	5	10 MILES

5	0	5	10 KILOMETERS

5 JUL

1 Regt

FINLAND
USSR

XX
3 Group F
Finn

Suomussalmi

1 Regt

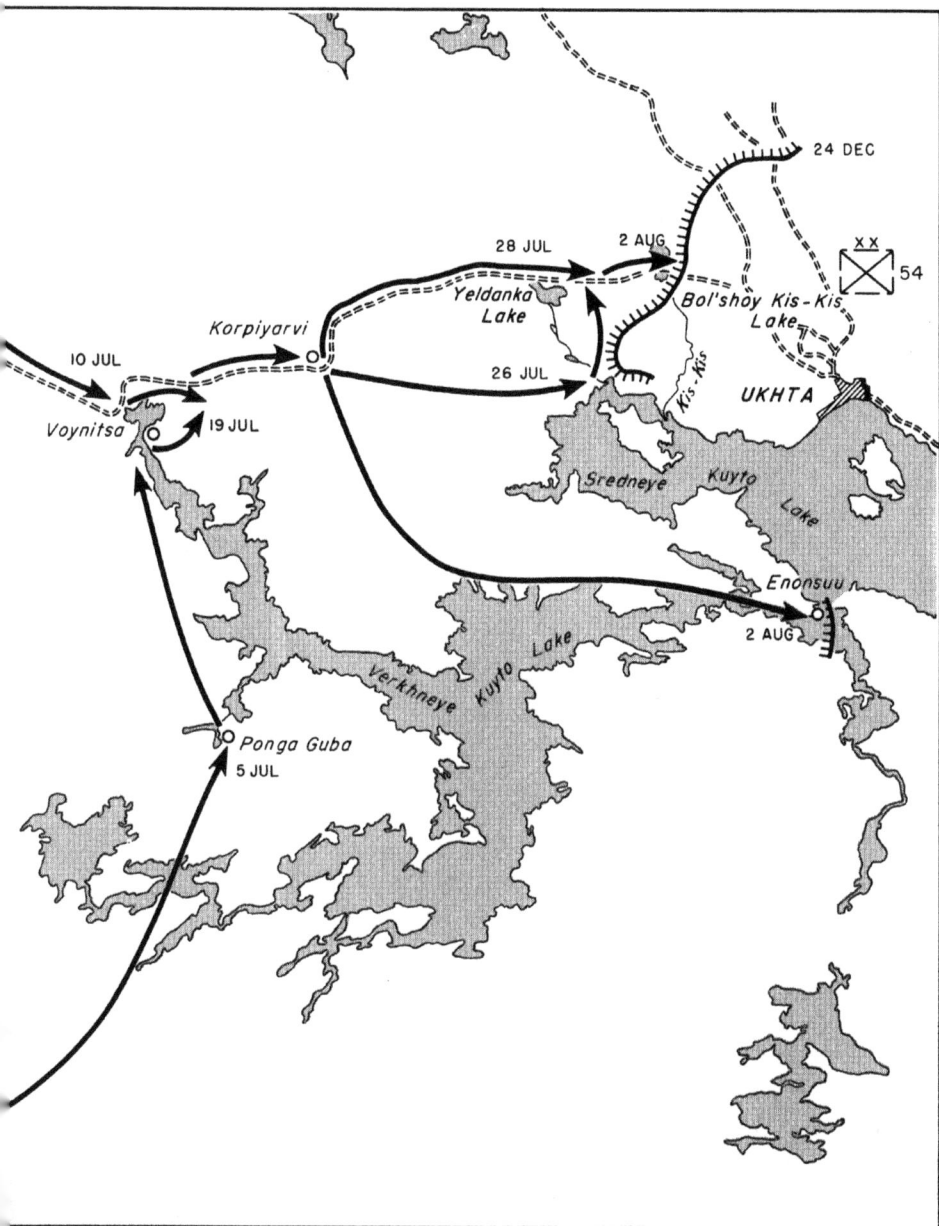

24 DEC

2 AUG

28 JUL

XX
54

Korpiyarvi

10 JUL

Yeldanka
Lake

Bol'shoy Kis-Kis
Lake

Voynitsa

19 JUL

26 JUL

Kis-Kis

UKHTA

Sredneye   Kuyto

Lake

Enonsuu

Verkhneye   Kuyto   Lake

2 AUG

Ponga Guba

5 JUL

R. Booth

fighting Group J broke the Russian resistance on the Sof'yanga and on the night of 7 August reached Kesten'ga. The Russians were throwing in what were believed to be their last reserves, 500 forced laborers and another 600 troops drawn from the headquarters guard of the Fourteenth Army and a replacement battalion at Murmansk.[22]

By 11 August the Finnish regiment of Group J, following the railroad embankment of the Kesten'ga spur line, was just south of the narrows between Yelovoye Lake and Lebedevo Lake, 20 miles southwest of Loukhi. Heavy resistance on the road and between the road and railroad behind the advance regiment forced a halt. On the 14th the movement of enemy truck convoys westward from Loukhi confirmed the impression which had been gained from frantic Russian radio traffic two days earlier that the 88th Rifle Division was being rushed in from Arkhangel'sk. In the course of the next two days the Russian resistance stiffened markedly.

Meanwhile, Group F in the south, having become stalled at the Kis Kis River line on the Korpiyärvi–Ukhta road, had gone over to attempting a deep envelopment from the north, which was meeting resistance at all points, and from the south around the southern shore of Sredneye Kuyto Lake. In the south it reached Enonsuu, directly across from Ukhta, on 2 August and sent patrols as far as Lu'salma. On the 19th, after a week of probing attacks which registered no significant gains, the Army of Norway ordered the operation halted in order to shift more weight to the attack toward Loukhi, and a battalion was drawn out for transfer north.

In the Group J sector the enemy showed signs of weakening; but the strength of the SS and Finnish troops was also declining. In the last week of August they trapped a Russian regiment south of the railroad and behind the advanced Finnish positions but were unable to destroy it, and the fight moved northward across the railroad as the SS-men and Finns attempted to tighten the ring and starve the Russians out. On 25 August General Siilasvuo informed the Army of Norway that his troops were exhausted and that he did not consider it possible to carry out his mission—a quick thrust to Loukhi—with his existing forces. He requested a fresh Finnish division, accustomed to forest warfare.[23]

Four days later Falkenhorst and Buschenhagen met with Siilasvuo at Kuusamo. The Finnish general reported that Group J was stalled. His 6 Finnish and 3 SS battalions faced a total of at least 13 Russian battalions, and 2 of the SS battalions together had an effective strength of no more than 280 men. There was a danger that the Russians would be able to strike southward to Kesten'ga and bring about the collapse of the Group J positions. Siilasvuo also considered it an error to have

[22] A.O.K. Norwegen, Bef. St. Finnland, Ic Az D 11, Nr. 791/41, Feindlage 3.8.–11.8.41, in Ic Anlagen zum K.T.B. I. AOK 20 25353/1.
[23] III A.K., Nr. 1024 a/III, dem O.B. des A.O.K. Norwegen, 25.8.41, in A.O.K Norwegen, Anlagen zum K.T.B., Band I. AOK 20 19070/2.

stopped the attack on Ukhta since there Group F was exposed in highly unsatisfactory positions. Falkenhorst decided that the attack on Ukhta would be resumed while Group J made every effort to hold in place. To assist in overcoming the immediate dangers, Group J would be given a motorized machine gun battalion and the remainder of the SS-Division infantry (2 battalions). When the situation of the XXXVI Corps permitted, army would also send one regiment of the Finnish 6th Division. It was expected that on the arrival of that regiment the push toward Loukhi could be resumed.[24]

Encirclement at Kayrala–Mikkola

On 3 August the XXXVI Corps ordered its divisions to tie down the enemy opposite them and to create favorable conditions for resumption of the advance after reinforcements arrived. That order was immediately superseded by an army order instructing the XXXVI Corps to prepare to resume its offensive with the main effort on the southern flank (Finnish 6th Division) and stating that reinforcements could not be counted on for the time being.[25] During the succeeding days, the XXXVI Corps several times renewed its requests for added forces. Feige argued that the Army of Norway main effort logically belonged in the XXXVI Corps sector since there alone was the movement of supplies by road and railroad assured and since it was necessary to take and hold Kandalaksha in order to maintain a German occupation of Murmansk. Cutting the railroad at Loukhi, he believed, could have no decisive effect because the Russians would still hold the vital Kandalaksha—Murmansk line and would have contact with Arkhangel'sk by way of the White Sea.[26] The Army of Norway, on the other hand, despite the fact that it wanted the XXXVI Corps to resume its offensive, saw the best chance for immediate results in the attack on Loukhi and the best future prospects in the planned Mountain Corps Norway offensive. Therefore, the two fresh regiments which Feige wanted— and thought he had been promised—were given to the Mountain Corps Norway. To a large extent, no doubt, the Army of Norway was influenced by the peculiarity of its mission which made the Murmansk Railroad less a strategic objective than a matter of prestige, with the result that the cutting of the railroad as soon as possible and the early occupation of Murmansk became goals worth striving for even at the expense of sound tactical procedure.

Encouraged by the withdrawal of the armored elements of the 1st Tank Division, the Army of Norway wanted the XXXVI Corps to execute a deep envelopment reaching up to the road and railroad imme-

[24] *A.O.K. Norwegen, K.T.B.,* 19 Jul–29 Aug 41.
[25] *Gen. Kdo. XXXVI, Ia, Nr. 802/41, Korpsbefehl, 3.8.41* and *A.O.K. Norwegen, Ia, Nr. 51.41, Armeebefehl, 2.8.41,* in *XXXVI A.K., Anlagenband A 2.* XXXVI AK 22102/5.
[26] *XXXVI A.K., K.T.B. 3,* 8 Aug 41.

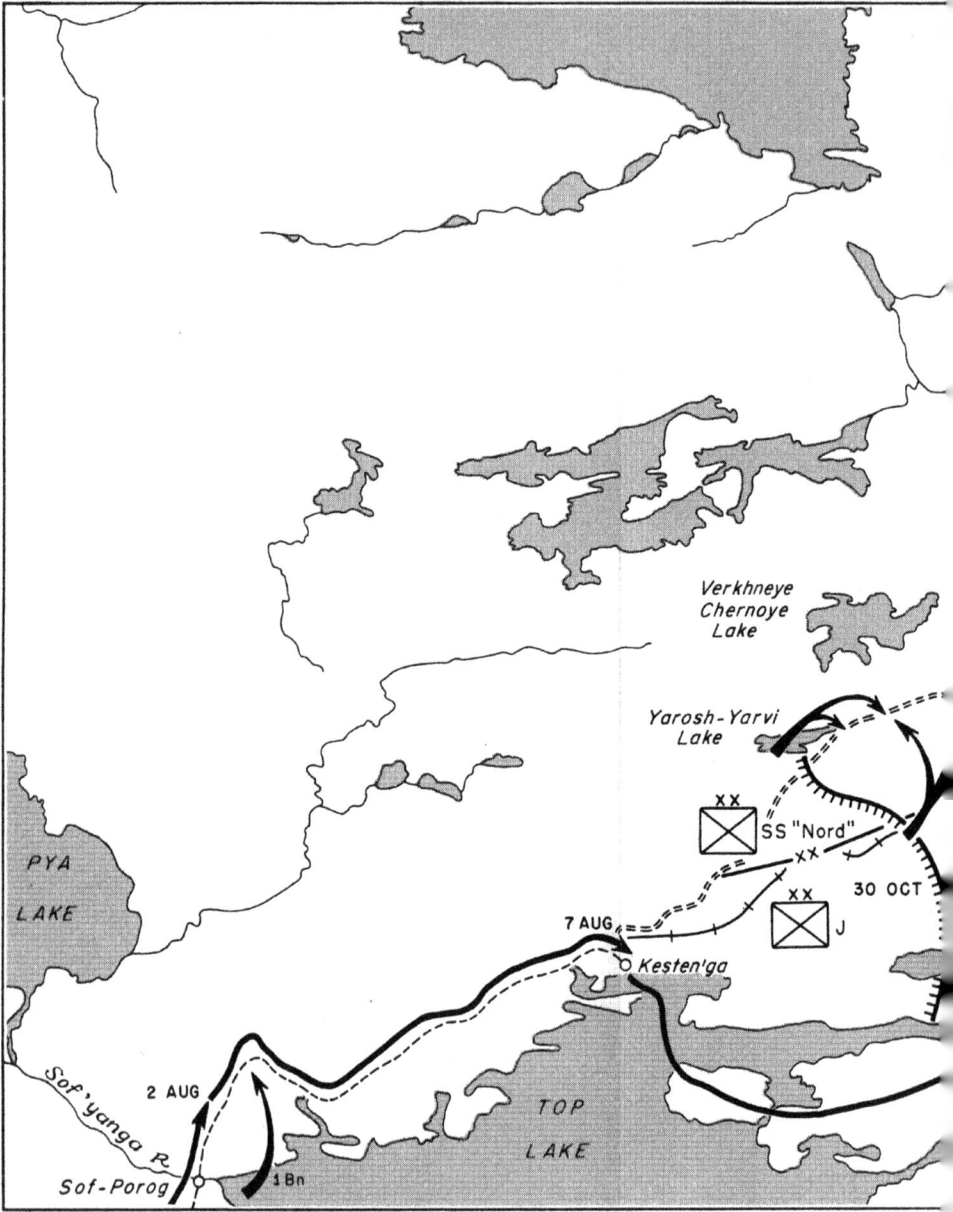

PYA
LAKE

Verkhneye
Chernoye
Lake

Yarosh-Yarvi
Lake

SS "Nord"

30 OCT

7 AUG

Kesten'ga

J

Sof'yanga R.

2 AUG

Sof-Porog

1 Bn

TOP
LAKE

Bol'shoye Severnoye
Lake

_lovoye
_ake

Lebedevo
Lake

Verkhneye
Lake

XX
88

7 NOV

XX
"Polyarnyy"

_ol'shoye Lagi-Yarvi
Lake

Maloye Lagi-Yarvi
Lake

Loukhi

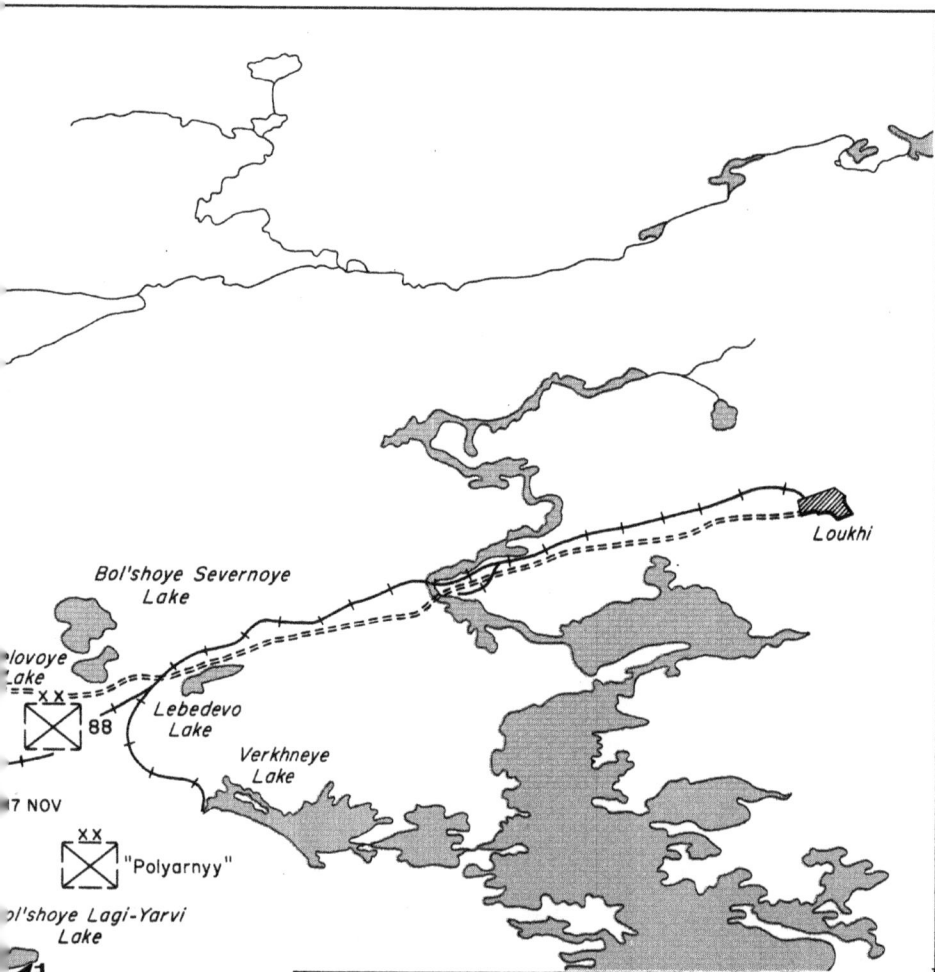

GROUP J AND SS "NORD"-LOUKHI

June - November 1941

⊤⊤⊤⊤⊤⊤⊤⊤⊤⊤⊤⊤⊤	FRONT LINE 30 OCT 1941
⊤⊤⊤ ⊤⊤⊤ ⊤⊤⊤	FRONT LINE 17 NOV 1941

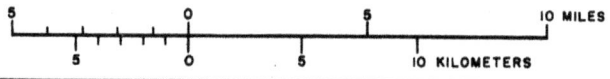

5   0   5   10 MILES

5   0   5   10 KILOMETERS

L. Booth

diately west of Allakurtti.[27]   That, the XXXVI Corps insisted, was impossible, both because of the terrain and because of insufficient forces. It set, instead, Nurmi Lake and Nurmi Mountain, about halfway between Kayrala and Allakurtti, as the easternmost objectives.   The XXXVI Corps intended "to stake everything on one card"—the thrust of the Finnish 6th Division to Nurmi Mountain.   The 169th Division front would be stripped to an absolute minimum of strength in order to gain enough troops to take over the Finnish 6th Division defensive positions, provide approximately one German regiment as corps reserve (in addition to one Finnish regiment), and form a combat team of two battalions plus six companies of mixed SS, engineer, and construction troops.   The combat team, crossing the Nurmi River behind the left wing of the 169th Division, would push southeastward toward Nurmi Lake as the right arm of the envelopment.   The Finnish 6th Division would direct its main force, one regiment with two regiments in reserve, toward Nurmi Mountain where it would block the road and railroad. As flank proetction one regiment would strike eastward to Vuoriyärvi and then north along the road to Allakurtti.[28]

Regrouping for the attack proved to be a task of major proportions. A road (completed on 14 August) had to be built from Lampela to the southern end of Apa Lake to carry the artillery into the Finnish 6th Division zone.   Meanwhile, the 169th Division troops being transferred had to be pulled out through Salla into Finland, sent south to the point where the Finnish 6th Division had crossed the border, and thence northward along the original Finnish 6th Division route, a march of 110 miles to cover a straight-line distance of 18 miles.   Very probably, however, this roundabout movement aided in deceiving the enemy, for the Russians continued to concentrate their probing attacks and patrol activity on the northern flank.

During the regroupment, relations between Falkenhorst and Feige did not improve.   At corps headquarters on the 15th, Falkenhorst remarked that battalion-for-battalion the sides were equal, a statement that Feige interpreted as an attempt to make his earlier insistence on two fresh regiments appear superfluous, if not frivolous.   The Russians, he countered, were maintaining a constant flow of replacements while the replacement situation of the Germans and Finns was extremely precarious.[29]

Early on 19 August, in heavy rain and fog, the Finnish 6th Division jumped off.   Its main column, meeting light resistance, reached Lehto-

[27] See footnote 9 above.
[28] *Gen. Kdo. XXXVI A.K., Ia, Nr. 843/41, Korpsbefehl, 12.8.41* and *Gen. Kdo. XXXVI A.K., Ia, 858/41, Korpsbefehl fuer den Angriff am X-Tag, 15.8.41,* in *XXXVI A.K., Anlagenband A 2.* XXXVI AK 22102/5.
[29] Between 30 June and 15 September the 169th Division received 3,100 replacements and sustained 5,300 casualties.   No statistics are available for the Finnish 6th Division. *169.I.D., Ia, Nr. 488/41, Ausserordentlicher Zustandsbericht, 17.9.41,* in *XXXVI A.K., K.T.B., 3.9.–17.9.1941.* XXXVI AK 23305. *XXXVI A.K., K.T.B. 3,* 4–15 Aug 41.

kangas in the late afternoon; but the Finnish regiment on the right made slow progress against heavy resistance, and the German regiment on the left barely got out of its starting positions. The XXXVI Corps expected counterattacks, but they did not come. Surprise had been achieved, and the Finnish main force was able to reach and cut the road and railroad between Nurmi Lake and Nurmi Mountain on the following day. To strengthen the main thrust, the XXXVI Corps committed one of its reserve regiments and assigned the other to the Finnish 6th Division for use when needed. By the 22d the Finns had established five battalions in defensive positions across the road to hold the Russians attempting to break out eastward. It had become urgently necessary to close the ring from the north where the left enveloping force was making slow progress east of the Nurmi River; therefore, to lend weight to the advance, the 169th Division reduced its holding positions once more and sent two infantry battalions and an artillery battalion east of the river.

A Russian radio message intercepted during the night of the 22d spoke of a "complete encirclement." On the following day the Finnish 6th Division committed its last reserve regiment to extend the right arm of the encirclement northward; meanwhile, the Russians were escaping over a previously undetected road north of Nurmi Lake, which the northern enveloping force did not reach and cut until the 25th. On the 24th the Finnish regiment on the right took Vuoriyärvi, and on the following day a break in the weather permitted the first bomber and dive bomber attacks on the retreating Russians.

On 25 August it was apparent that a clear-cut victory was in the making. The Russians were streaming eastward in disorder past Nurmi Lake, and an SS battalion pushed through the narrows at Kayrala. The Russian defenses north and south of the lakes were collapsing. By the 27th the encirclement battle was over and the pursuit in progress. The success was somewhat dimmed by the fact that, although the Russians had been forced to abandon almost all their vehicles and equipment, most of the troops escaped owing to the Germans' inability to close the ring from the north.[30]

To the Verman Line

While the Russians in bloody fighting managed to keep the jaws of the pincers apart northeast of Nurmi Lake during the morning of 27 August, the XXXVI Corps hastily regrouped, returning its detached units to the 169th Division and attaching three SS battalions to the Finnish 6th Division, and ordered a relentless pursuit in the direction of Allakurtti. At the end of the day advance parties were within four miles of Allakurtti on the road and on the railroad, but the Russians had fallen back to prepared positions and held a bridgehead around the western outskirts of

[30] A.O.K. Norwegen, K.T.B., 19–27 Aug 41. XXXVI A.K., K.T.B. 19–27 Aug 41. 169.I.D., K.T.B. 2, Teil 1, 19–27 Aug 41.

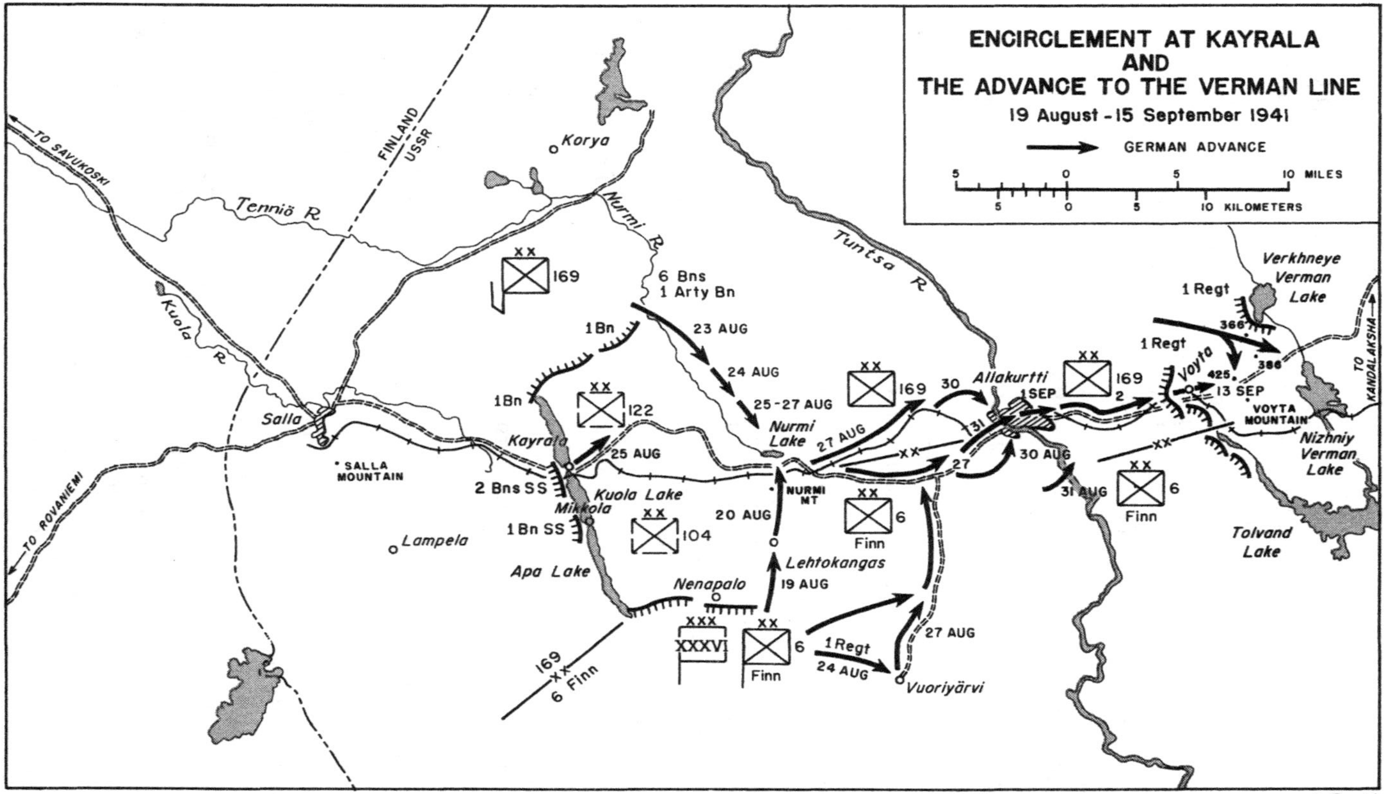
ENCIRCLEMENT AT KAYRALA
AND
THE ADVANCE TO THE VERMAN LINE
19 August - 15 September 1941
GERMAN ADVANCE
5 0 5 10 MILES
5 0 5 10 KILOMETERS
TO SAVUKOSKI
TO ROVANIEMI
TO KANDALAKSHA
FINLAND
USSR
Korya
Tenniö R
Kuola R
Nurmi R
Tuntsa R
Salla
SALLA MOUNTAIN
Lampela
Kayrala
Kuola Lake
Mikkola
Apa Lake
Nenapalo
Lehtokangas
Vuoriyärvi
Nurmi Lake
NURMI MT
Allakurtti
Voyta
VOYTA MOUNTAIN
Verkhneye Verman Lake
Nizhniy Verman Lake
Tolvand Lake
169
122
104
XXXVI
6 Finn
6 Bns
1 Arty Bn
1 Bn
2 Bns SS
1 Bn SS
1 Regt
23 AUG
24 AUG
25-27 AUG
25 AUG
20 AUG
19 AUG
27 AUG
24 AUG
30
31
27
1 SEP
30 AUG
31 AUG
13 SEP
366
386
425
R. Booth

Map 16

the town. Attacking the bridgehead frontally and on both flanks, the corps made small progress until late on the 30th when it forced the Russians back to the eastern bank of the Tuntsa River. On the next day a regiment of the 169th Division, having found a foot bridge the Russians had overlooked when they blew up the road and railroad bridges, crossed into the eastern section of Allakurtti. After another day of fighting at the eastern edge of town, the Russians on the night of 1 September suddenly fell back, leaving the way open to the Voyta River, six miles to the east. As the XXXVI Corps drew up to the Voyta on the 2d, the Army of Norway pulled out the last two battalions of the 7th SS-Regiment for transfer to the Finnish III Corps; and the battalion of the 9th SS-Regiment, which had been attached late in the Kayrala operation, was ordered returned to the Mountain Corps Norway.[31]

With reduced strength, the XXXVI Corps faced the Voyta River Line, the pre-1940 Soviet border fortifications, manned in the critical center sector—lying astride the road and railroad—by the motorized regiment of the 1st Tank Division and on the flanks by the remnants of four regiments of the 104th and 122d Rifle Divisions. The motorized regiment had been attached to the 104th Rifle Division but had been located outside the Kayrala encirclement and, therefore, was reasonably fresh. From Kandalaksha the Russians were bringing up replacements, reportedly 8,000—many of them prisoners and labor camp inmates—by 15 September.[32] The XXXVI Corps ranged its forces along the river, the 169th Division on the north and the Finnish 6th Division on the south.

On the afternoon of 6 September the corps opened a frontal attack across the river with four regiments and sent one regiment in a wide enveloping sweep around the northern flank of the fortified line to Hill 366, southwest of the northern Verman Lake. The frontal attack was promptly stopped dead except on the right flank of the 169th Division where one regiment established a small bridgehead south of the road. The enveloping thrust progressed rapidly up to Hill 366, but there the regimental commander discovered that the hill which reconnaissance two days earlier had reported unoccupied was in fact fortified and strongly held. The regiment found itself in an extremely precarious situation, tied down in heavy fighting, and isolated five miles behind the enemy lines. From this, during the next several days, there developed a heated exchange of demands and accusations between corps headquarters and the regimental commander—the best in the XXXVI Corps, who had won the Knight's Cross of the Iron Cross in the fighting at Salla. The acrimony resulted in part from the immediate crisis but was even more a symptom of the exhaustion overtaking the corps.

---

[31] *XXXVI A.K., K.T.B. 3*, 27 Aug–2 Sep 41. *A.O.K. Norwegen, K.T.B.*, 28 Aug–2 Sep 41.
[32] *A.O.K. Norwegen, Bef. St. Finnland, Ic, Az D 11, Nr. 1260/41, Feindlage vom 7.9.–17.9.41*, in *A.O.K. Norwegen, Ic Anlagen zum K.T.B. I.* AOK 20 25353/1.

Motorcycle stuck in the thick mud on a road on the XXXVI Corps front.

On the next day, in cloudburst-like rainstorms, the attack made no progress. That night the XXXVI Corps intercepted a radio message transmitted by an NKVD station ordering the Voyta positions held at all costs, even in encirclement. Knowing the Russian tenacity in holding prepared positions, corps immediately decided to abandon the frontal attack and concentrate on the enveloping left flank. But the regiment there was in trouble. On the 7th it had taken Hill 366 and reported taking Hill 386 a mile farther south, but on the following morning it developed that Hill 386 had not been taken. The regimental commander, his agitation increasing throughout the day, repeatedly called for more men and artillery support. Corps ordered an additional regiment to join the attack and began sending up a Finnish regiment to cover the exposed flank northeast of Hill 366. At this critical stage the XXXVI Corps had no air support. The Army of Norway had only three dive bombers available at Rovaniemi, the rest of the planes being assigned to the Mountain Corps Norway operation in progress on the Litsa.

The attack remained stalled north of Hill 386 for two days. When the hill was taken on the 10th, the XXXVI Corps ordered the new regiment to push south to the road and then east to the Verman River and the original regiment to turn west past Lysaya Mountain and bring about the collapse of the Voyta fortifications by an attack from the rear. The latter regiment hesitated for almost a day and moved out only after Feige intervened personally. On the 11th the 169th Division pushed a battalion across the Voyta at the road, and after another day's fighting established contact with the regiment coming from the east. With the road open, artillery and tanks could move up to the Verman River, but south of the road the Russians clung to their positions and had to be driven out piecemeal by the Finnish 6th Division in another week's fighting. On 15 September they briefly threatened the entire corps front by retaking Hill 366.

When this last crisis had passed, the XXXVI Corps found itself facing the Verman Line, more prepared positions strung along the Verman River, anchored on the north on the Verkhneye Verman Lake and in the south on Lake Tolvand, with the Russians still holding bridge-heads around the road and railroad.[33] In the Verman Line the 104th and 122d Rifle Divisions were regrouping. During the next two weeks, with 5,000 replacements, they would be brought up to 80 percent of strength. Between the Verman Line and Kandalaksha the Russians had, since June, been using forced labor, mostly women, to build at least three more fortified lines.[34]

On 13 September the Army of Norway informed the XXXVI Corps that it intended to shift the army main effort to the XXXVI Corps zone— the Mountain Corps Norway operation on the Litsa was faltering. This proposal the XXXVI Corps characterized as "grotesque" and "hardly calculated to arouse confidence in the higher leadership." The corps was worn out. It had sustained 9,463 casualties since the beginning of the campaign, 2,549 of them after 1 September.[35] The 169th Division was judged no longer capable of executing even a defensive mission. In his situation estimate of 16 September, Feige maintained that two good opportunities for exploiting the successes of the XXXVI

[33] A.O.K. Norwegen, K.T.B., 2–15 Sep 41. Gen. Kdo. XXXVI A.K., Kriegstage-buch mit Anlagen, 3.9–17.9.41. XXXVI AK 23305.
[34] A.O.K. Norwegen, Bef. St. Finnland, Ic, Az D 11, Nr. 1260/41, Feindlage vom 18.9.–2.10.41, in A.O.K. Norwegen, Ic Anlagen zum K.T.B. I. AOK 20 25353/1.
[35] Gen Kdo. XXXVI, Ia, an A.O.K. Norwegen, Bef. St. Finnland, 16.9.41, in 23305.

Corps had been lost for lack of sufficient troops—once immediately after the encirclement of Kayrala and again on 15 September in front of the Verman Line, when, Feige said, "the door to Kandalaksha stood open." The XXXVI Corps could go no farther on its own power, and, as each day passed, the enemy regained strength. A push to Kandalaksha was still possible, but it would take at least one mountain division and one more Finnish division. Even so, since the Russians had time to recover their equilibrium, it would be, as it had been so far, a matter of fighting from line to line.[36]

The XXXVI Corps saw the fault as lying entirely with the Army of Norway, which was not the case. On 25 August Falkenhorst had asked the OKW for the remaining two regiments of the 163d Infantry Division to exploit the victory at Kayrala but had received no reply. In the conference with Jodl on 4 September Buschenhagen had proposed diverting the 6th Mountain Division to the XXXVI Corps, but at that time Hitler was intent on using the division to take Murmansk as soon as possible. Ten days later, at Fuehrer Headquarters, Falkenhorst had asked for permission to use both the 6th Mountain Division and the 163d Infantry Division in the XXXVI Corps zone. The mountain division was refused. Hitler had promised a decision on the 163d Division in three to four days depending on the outcome of the operations around Leningrad, which at that time were believed to be in their final phase. The XXXVI Corps, he had ordered, was to continue its advance "if at all possible." [37]

On 17 September the Army of Norway instructed Feige to establish a defensive line on the Verman and rest his troops by thirds. All army could promise was the Schuetzenverband Oslo, a regimental headquarters with two battalions, which was on its way from Norway.[38] Feige noted bitterly that the troops as well as the staff believed the exertions of the corps had been in vain and that another good opportunity to bring the march on Kandalaksha to a successful conclusion had been missed. He predicted that the corps had seen its last major action, for the Lapland winter was approaching.[39]

Five days later, on 22 September, Fuehrer Directive No. 36 ordered the XXXVI Corps to make all preparations for resuming the offensive toward Kandalaksha in the first half of October. The Finnish High Command would be asked to send the 163d Division in time. The operations of the Finnish III Corps were to be stopped and all the troops freed transferred to the XXXVI Corps.[40] But as the month drew to

---

[36] *Hoeh. Kdo. XXXVI, der Befehlshaber, Lage am 15.9.41, 16.9.41, XXXVI A.K., K.T.B. 3 Anlagenband G.* XXXVI AK 22102/11.

[37] *A.O.K. Norwegen, K.T.B.,* 25 Aug, 4, 13, 15, and 17 Sep 41.

[38] *A.O.K. Norwegen, K.T.B.,* 17 Sep 41.

[39] *Gen. Kdo. XXXVI A.K., Kriegstagebuch mit Anlagen, 3.9.–17.9.41,* 17 Sep 41. XXXVI AK 23305.

[40] *Der Fuehrer und Oberbefehlshaber der Wehrmacht, WFSt, Abt. L (I Op), Weisung Nr. 36, 22.9.41,* in *A.O.K Norwegen, Anlagen zum K.T.B., Band II.* AOK 20 19070/3.

German submarine in a northern fiord.

its end the prospects of getting the 163d Division dimmed. On 5 October, after learning that the 163d Division could not be expected in less than four to five weeks, the Army of Norway postponed the XXXVI Corps operation until winter and began drawing out troops with the intention of reviving operations in the Finnish III Corps zone.[41]

The OKW, on 8 October, answered the Army of Norway report on its new intentions with an order to stop all operations. A call to Jodl at OKW brought the explanation that the total situation on the main Russian front had changed so greatly that the military collapse of the Soviet Union in the foreseeable future appeared "not unlikely." [42] Two days later Fuehrer Directive No. 37 confirmed the OKW order and Jodl's remarks. It stated that, in the light of the Army of Norway reports on the condition of its troops and its operational possibilities and since the defeat or destruction of the mass of the Soviet Armed Forces on the main front made it unnecessary to tie down Russian forces in Finland any longer, the Army of Norway operations would be stopped. The army's chief missions for the immediate future were to protect the nickel mines and prepare to take Murmansk and the Rybatchiy Peninsula during the winter. German and Finnish units would be exchanged by the XXXVI Corps and the III Corps so that Mannerheim could take over the III Corps and proceed with his planned reorganization of the Finnish Army.[43]

---

[41] *A.O.K. Norwegen, Bef. St. Finnland, Ia, Nr. 81/41, an OKW, WFSt, Abt. L, 7.10.41,* in *A.O.K. Norwegen, Anlagen zum K.T.B., Band II.* AOK 20 19070/3.

[42] Army Group Center had just closed the Bryansk and Vyazma pockets and was launching its final drive on Moscow.

[43] *Der Fuehrer und Oberste Befehlshaber der Wehrmacht, WFSt, Abt. L (I Op.), Nr. 441696/41, Weisung 37, 10.10.41,* in *A.O.K. Norwegen, Anlagen zum K.T.B., Band II.* AOK 20 19070/3.

Finnish III Corps Final Operations

During the first half of September the situation of the III Corps continued to deteriorate. Group F reopened its offensive and was immediately stopped by the Russians, who, after the arrival of the 88th Rifle Division, had been able to assemble two full regiments, an artillery regiment, and the 54th Rifle Division headquarters in the Ukhta area. Group J and SS-"Nord" under constant pressure from the 88th Rifle Division—joined in mid-September by the Independent Brigade Grivnin (one regiment of the 54th Division and the Special Regiment "Murmansk")—had to abandon the advanced positions south of Yelovoye Lake and fall back to a line eight miles east of Kesten'ga. After the Russians achieved local breakthroughs and threatened to force a further withdrawal, the Army of Norway on 9 September asked for an additional Finnish regiment. Erfurth refused to transmit the request to Mannerheim, stating that the Finnish political situation made it inopportune.[44] On the 12th, in order to create some sort of reserve for the III Corps, the Army of Norway pulled the SS-Reconnaissance Battalion out of the XXXVI Corps Sector and ordered the transfer of the regimental staff and one battalion of the Finnish 14th Regiment from Pechenga. A second appeal to Mannerheim for a regiment brought a refusal tempered by a promise of 2,800 replacements.[45]

When the last elements of SS-Division "Nord" were transferred to the III Corps in early September, Falkenhorst insisted that the division be assigned a sector under its own commander. Siilasvuo, preferring to keep the SS under the command of Group J, protested; but Falkenhorst could not allow a Finnish colonel to command a German division while its own headquarters stood idly by. The SS-Division had to some extent found itself but was still far from reliable. At the middle of the month Siilasvuo again asked that the SS-Division staff be taken out so that he could assign the troops according to their capabilities. He had given the SS the best sector, which was subsequently reduced several times until it comprised barely one-third of the line, but the SS still could not fight off enemy attacks without help. Falkenhorst refused, and the III Corps in the future had to adjust its operations to take into account this element of weakness.[46]

After his trip to Fuehrer Headquarters on 14 September Falkenhorst received instructions, later confirmed in Directive 36, to stop the Group F attack on Ukhta and permit Group J and SS-"Nord" to go over to the defensive, shortening their front if necessary. Toward the end of the month, after the Russian pressure had suddenly slacked off and

---

[44] See below, ch. 10, pp. 16ff.
[45] *A.O.K. Norwegen, K.T.B.,* 1–16 Sep 41.
[46] *Gen. Kdo. III A.K., Nr. 138/III/2.b., an das A.O.K., 19.9.41,* in *A.O.K. Norwegen, Anlagen zum K.T.B., Band III.* AOK 20 19070/3. *A.O.K. Norwegen, K.T.B.,* 2 and 19 Sep 41.

prisoner of war interrogations revealed poor morale among the Russians in the Kesten'ga–Loukhi area, the III Corps asked for reinforcements and proposed to take up its advance to Loukhi. Since the prospects of getting the XXXVI Corps back into motion had dwindled to almost nothing, the Army of Norway immediately offered a regiment of the Finnish 6th Division, the Schuetzenverband Oslo, the 9th SS-Regiment from the Mountain Corps Norway, a regiment of artillery and the remaining battalion of the Finnish 14th Regiment. On 6 October the Army of Norway gave orders for the attack—which it had to cancel two days later when the OKW ordered all operations stopped. The planned troop shifts were halted, but the 9th SS-Regiment and the battalion of the Finnish 14th Regiment were held in the III Corps zone at the disposal of the Army of Norway.[47]

At exactly the time Hitler canceled the Army of Norway operations the situation on the left flank of the III Corps was changing from favorable to downright tempting. The Independent Brigade Grivnin had been dissolved. One of its regiments was identified later opposite the XXXVI Corps and the other had moved south, possibly to the 54th Rifle Division. On 11 October Falkenhorst and Siilasvuo met and decided that the changed situation offered good prospects for an attack but that, in the light of Hitler's order, it would have to be limited to an effort to improve the positions of Group J and SS-"Nord." Twelve days later, Siilasvuo reported that he believed the attack to improve his positions would be a complete success. Falkenhorst revealed the direction his thoughts were taking when he asked whether, in a favorable situation, a thrust straight through to Loukhi was possible. Siilasvuo replied that it was. The Army of Norway had already ordered the 9th SS-Regiment to Kuusamo and a regiment of the Finnish 6th Division, an infantry battalion and a *Nebelwerfer* battery from the XXXVI Corps to the III Corps.[48]

The III Corps set as its objective the Yelovoye Lake–Verkhneye Lake Line. The SS-Division would tie down the Russians on its front between the road and railroad, and Group F (three Finnish regiments and the 9th SS-Regiment) would break through along the railroad turning north to trap the enemy on the SS-Division front. In the south an independent detachment of two battalions would skirt the Russian left flank toward Verkhneye Lake.[49] On 30 October the attack began, and in two days the III Corps had encircled a Russian regiment opposite the SS-Division front. The III Corps on 3 November reported its intention to destroy the regiment as quickly as possible and push on to the narrows north of Lebedevo Lake, but during the

---

[47] *A.O.K. Norwegen, K.T.B.,* 17 Sep–8 Oct 41.
[48] *A.O.K. Norwegen, K.T.B.,* 11–23 Oct 41.
[49] *Gen. Kdo. III A.K., Nr. 411/III/3.b., Korpsbefehl ueber Angriffsvorbereitungen, 20.10.41* and *Gen. Kdo. III A.K., Nr. 465/III/3.b., Angriffsbefehl des Korps, 25.10.41,* in *A.O.K. Norwegen, Anlagen zum K.T.B., Band II.* AOK 20 19070/3.

following days the operation took a strange turn as Siilasvuo insisted on mopping up the pocket before resuming his advance.[50]

On the 9th in a sharply worded telegram the OKW called for a report on the situation and intentions with respect to the III Corps and pointed out that Fuehrer Directive No. 37 had ordered operations on this sector of the front limited to defense. The Army of Norway replied that two regiments of the 88th Rifle Division had been virtually destroyed, and the narrows between Lebedevo Lake and Yelovoye Lake could be taken as a springboard for future operations against Loukhi.[51] On the same day Erfurth informed the Army of Norway that Mannerheim wanted to proceed with the reorganization of the Finnish Army and asked that the III Corps go over to the defensive as soon as possible. To an inquiry whether "as soon as possible" meant "immediately" Erfurth replied that Mannerheim left the exact time up to the Army of Norway, but he was in a hurry to get on with the reorganization.[52] On the 15th Buschenhagen went to Helsinki for a conference with General Warlimont of the OKW. Warlimont emphasized that the OKW took a dim view of the III Corps operation: the Finns wanted control of their troops in order to proceed with the reorganization, and Himmler wanted SS-"Nord," for which he intended to substitute other SS units, sent home. Warlimont demanded that the first German troops be drawn out of the III Corps sector by 1 December at the latest.[53]

In the meantime, beginning on 7 November, the Russians had moved the "Polyarnyy" Division, renamed the 186th Rifle Division, to the III Corps front. It was regarded as no great threat since it numbered no more than 2,600 men.[54] On 13 November the III Corps completed mopping up the pocket. The corps counted 3,000 Russian dead and took 2,600 prisoners.

But Siilasvuo made no move toward continuing the operation, and on the 16th he reported that his corps was facing 17 enemy battalions, which led him to conclude that a further attack would produce no results. The commanders of SS-"Nord" and Group J, both of whom believed

---

[50] *A.O.K. Norwegen, K.T.B.,* 3 Nov 41. *Dtsch. V.O. beim III. (finn.) A.K., Bericht ueber die Einstellung des Angriffs III. (finn.) A.K. Mitte November 1941,* in *A.O.K. Norwegen, Ia, Chefsachen, 2.6.41–18.11.41.* AOK 20 20844/2.
[51] *OKW, WFSt, Abt. L (I Op.), Nr. 441898/41, an A.O.K. Norwegen, Bef. St. Finnland, 9.11.41* in *A.O.K. Norwegen, Anlagen zum K.T.B., Bd. II.* AOK 20 19070/3. *A.O.K. Norwegen, K.T.B.,* 9 Nov 41.
[52] *Verbindungsstab Nord, Ia., Nr. 97/41 an A.O.K. Norwegen, Bef. St. Finnland, 9.11.41* and *Verbindungsstab Nord, Ia, Nr. 100/41, an A.O.K. Norwegen, Bef. St. Finnland, 10.11.41,* in *A.O.K. Norwegen, Anlagen zum K.T.B., Band II.* AOK 20 19070/3.
[53] *A.O.K. Norwegen, Bef. St. Finnland, O. Qu., Qu. 1, Nr. 343/41, Besprechung zwischen General Warlimont und General Buschenhagen in Helsinki am 15.11.41, 30.11.41,* in *A.O.K. Norwegen, Anlagen zum K.T.B., Band II.* AOK 20 19070/3.
[54] *A.O.K. Norwegen, Bef. St. Finnland, Ic, Az D 11, Nr. 2054/41, Feindlage vom 10–25.11.41,* in *A.O.K. Norwegen, Ic Anlagen zum K.T.B. I.* AOK 20 25353/1.

the prospects for continuing the operation were good, objected to his estimate of the situation. Nevertheless, on the following day he informed Group J that the attack was canceled, and on the 18th he told the Army of Norway flatly that he was not in a position to continue the operation and would hold the existing line.[55] The Army of Norway, influenced by the Finnish attitude and that of the OKW as expressed by Warlimont, had already decided to abandon the operation, and it instructed the III Corps to take up defensive positions.[56]

Reports from the German liaison officers with the III Corps and Group J revealed that as late as 18 November the commander of Group J had considered his force fully capable of continuing the attack and had stated that both he and his regimental commanders wanted to do so. Siilasvuo, on the other hand, had since the closing of the pocket in the first days of November shown signs of not intending to continue the advance and had begun building defensive positions even before the pocket was wiped out.[57] Falkenhorst thought Siilasvuo's remarkable behavior could be traced to recent United States peace moves directed at Finland.[58]

Falkenhorst's suspicion was well founded. On 27 October the United States Government had submitted a strong note to President Ryti in which it demanded that Finland stop all offensive operations and withdraw to the 1939 border and issued the specific warning that "should material of war sent from the United States to Soviet Territory in the north by way of the Arctic Ocean be attacked on route either presumably or even allegedly from territory under Finnish control in the present state of opinion in the United States such an incident must be expected to bring about an instant crisis in relations between Finland and the United States."[59] During the next few weeks relations between the United States and Finland drifted dangerously close to a breach. Although Ryti indignantly rejected the American demands, Finland certainly did not want, in those perilous days, to have a Finnish corps under German command posing the only serious threat to the Murmansk Railroad. The Germans were beginning to experience the frustrations of coalition warfare.

---

[55] *Generalkommando III A.K., Nr. 652/III/3.b., an Herrn Oberbefehlshaber der Armee Norwegen, 18.11.41,* in *A.O.K. Norwegen, Ia, Chefsachen, 2.6.41–18.11.41.* AOK 20 20844/2.

[56] *A.O.K. Norwegen, K.T.B.,* 16–18 Nov 41.

[57] *Verbindungsoffz Gruppe J, Notiz zum Kriegstagebuch, 20.11.41* and *Dtsch. V.O. beim III. (finn.) A.K., Bericht ueber die Einstellung des Angriffs III. (finn.) A.K. Mitte November 1941, 20.11.41,* in *A.O.K. Norwegen, Ia, Chefsachen, 2.6.41–18.11.41.* AOK 20 20844/2.

[58] Marginal note on *Dtsch. V.O. beim III. (finn.) A.K., Bericht ueber die Einstellung des Angriffs III. (finn.) A.K. Mitte November 1941,* in *A.O.K. Norwegen, Ia, Chefsachen, 2.6.41.–18.11.41.* AOK 20 20844/2.

[59] Bluecher, tel. to Foreign Ministry, No. 1204, 28.10.41. U.S. Department of State, German Foreign Ministry Records. William L. Langer and S. Everett Gleason, *The Undeclared War, 1940–1941* (New York: Harper and Brothers, 1953), p. 831.

The Army of Lapland

In the first implementing instructions for Fuehrer Directive No. 37, issued on 7 November 1941, the OKW announced that, as soon as the transfer of command could be arranged, the Headquarters, Army of Norway, would return to Norway and Dietl would establish the Headquarters, Army of Lapland, to assume command of the German force in Finland.[60] That Falkenhorst would in the end himself become a casualty of the 1941 campaign, if not inevitable, was certainly predictable. Aside from his being to some extent tagged as a "hard-luck" general by the course of events in his sector, Falkenhorst had since the start of the campaign been subjected to a number of influences which, on the one hand, made him something less than master in his own house and, on the other, ensured that he would be saddled with most of the blame for failures. The Fifth Air Force, for instance, was an independent command; moreover, it could always depend on Goering to secure its views a favorable hearing in the highest places. Similarly, the SS-Division and Finnish III Corps had direct channels to Himmler and Mannerheim. Mannerheim's headquarters, in close contact with the OKW through the German Liaison Staff North, while officially maintaining an air of detachment, kept a close and critical eye on the Army of Norway operations. Far from the least significant of the influences operating against Falkenhorst was that which Dietl himself exerted. Dietl was one of the few generals whom Hitler liked and trusted; furthermore, the defense of Narvik in 1940 had apparently convinced Hitler that Dietl possessed special endowments of luck and the ability to master adversity. As a consequence, Hitler from the outset was inclined to place more confidence in Dietl than in Falkenhorst; and, after the advance out of Finland slowed down, he relied increasingly on the hope that Dietl might accomplish a second "miracle of Narvik." [61]

The change of command in Finland promised several advantages. Dietl was very popular with both the German troops and the Finns, and his taking command could be expected to raise the morale of the troops and help regain the confidence of the Finnish people. The appointment alone would be taken as a promise of victories to come. His soldierly qualities and personal charm augured well for his future relations with Mannerheim. Perhaps most important of all, the creation of a separate German command made it possible to offer Mannerheim the over-all command in Finland and so, possibly, secure more aid from the Finnish Army in future operations against the Murmansk Railroad.

---

[60] *OKW, WFSt, Abt. L (I Op.), Nr. 441861/41, Durchfuehrungsbestimmungen Nr. 1 zur Weisung 37, 7.11.41,* in *AOK Norwegen, Anlagen zum K.T.B., Band II.* AOK 20 19070/3.
[61] General der Infanterie a. D. Erich Buschenhagen, Comments on Part II of *The German Northern Theater of Operations, 1940–1945,* May 1957.

At the mid-November conference in Helsinki Warlimont told Erfurth that this could be the ultimate purpose of the change of command in Finland.[62] Mannerheim stated in his memoirs that an offer was made to him in the winter of 1941–42.[63]

Strangely enough, it was Dietl who objected most seriously to his own appointment. His talent, he knew, lay principally in the direct command of troops at the front, and he doubted his ability to assume the more remote responsibilities of an army commander. On being briefed at army headquarters, he became aware, apparently for the first time, of the tactical and command problems which Falkenhorst had faced; and, on 24 November, in a letter to Jodl he asked that his appointment as Commanding General, Army of Lapland, be canceled. In the first week of December, he was called to the Fuehrer Headquarters where Hitler and Jodl in a combined effort persuaded him not to relinquish the command.[64]

SILBERFUCHS in Retrospect

After three and one-half months of fighting, at a cost of 21,501 German and more than 5,000 Finnish casualties, the Army of Norway was thoroughly bogged down in all three of its corps sectors, and the prospects for a successful offensive in the future were dim indeed.[65] The outcome of SILBERFUCHS pleased no one—except the Russians. The Finns, civilian populace and Army High Command alike, had been watching the Army of Norway performance with growing dissillusionment since mid-summer.[66]

The failure of SILBERFUCHS has most frequently been laid to dispersal of forces and its concomitant, inability to achieve a clear-cut main effort at any one point. Throughout the campaign Feige argued, from premises which were both tactically and strategically correct, that the main effort should be placed in the XXXVI Corps area. After his last attempt to cross the Litsa, Dietl complained to Jodl that the Army of

[62] General der Infanterie a. D. Waldemar Erfurth, Comments on Part II of *The German Northern Theater of Operations, 1940–1945*, 6 May 1957.

[63] Mannerheim, *op. cit.*, p. 472.

[64] *Dietl an Jodl, 24.11.41*, in *AOK Norwegen, Anlagen zum K.T.B., Band II.* AOK 20 19070/3. *Dietl an Chef des Stabes AOK Norwegen, 1.12.41*, in "*Silberfuchs*" *Bd. III, 12.6.41–10.1.42.* AOK 20 20844/6. General der Infanterie a. D. Erich Buschenhagen, Comments on Part II of *The German Northern Theater of Operations, 1940–1945*, May 1957.

[65] The casualty figures used are those of 29 September for the Germans and 10 September for the Finns. The losses of the SS-Division "Nord" and the Finnish III Corps during October and November probably added about 1,500 to 2,000 to the totals. The Army of Norway casualties were only a small part of the total German losses of 564,727 on the Eastern Front during the same period, but proportionately they were somewhat greater than those for the entire operation (19.83 percent for the Army of Norway and 16.61 percent for all armies on the Eastern Front). *AOK Norwegen, Bef. St. Finnland, Ia, Nr. 1632/41 an OKW, WFSt, Abt. L, 29.9.41*, in *AOK Norwegen, Anlagen zum K.T.B. Band II.* AOK 20 19070/3. *Halder Diary*, Vol. VII, p. 124.

[66] *Halder Diary*, Vol., p. 16.

Norway had failed to establish a main effort at one point and attack there with superior forces.[67]   Later he lent support to Feige's contention when he told Hitler that, because of terrain and other defensive advantages of the enemy, operations in the Mountain Corps Norway sector should be suspended "for good" and an attempt made to create a main effort opposite Kandalaksha.[68]   Since the war Erfurth has suggested that the Army of Norway several times failed to carry out OKW orders aimed at creating a main effort in one or the other of the army sectors.[69]

To evaluate these criticisms it is necessary to re-examine the groundwork of Operation SILBERFUCHS.   In the first place, the objective of the Army of Norway was political and psychological rather than strategic; that is, Hitler, although he did not expect that the British would be able to bring decisive or even substantial aid, wanted to take Murmansk to prevent their bringing *any* aid to the Soviet Union.   There is some reason for believing that the operation was directed more against Great Britain, to demonstrate its isolation and helplessness, than against the Soviet Union.   Under those circumstances it became worthwhile to disregard sound tactics and attempt to stage a quick march along the arctic coast to Murmansk.   Second, the Army of Norway operations were merely subsidiary to the German main effort—in the opinion of the OKH, even superfluous.   They were deliberately begun with limited forces and, quite correctly, substantial new forces were refused in order not to detract from the possibility of achieving a decision on the main Russian front.[70]   Third, the Army of Norway had two defensive missions: to protect the nickel mines at Pechenga, which Hitler consistently rated as more important than the capture of Murmansk; and to defend the waist of Finland at Salla, which was indispensable to the existence of Finland.   The original dispersal of the Army of Norway forces was therefore justified, and after the forces were committed it was impossible to close down any one of the sectors completely even though offensive operations there had become unprofitable.

The criticisms must also be viewed in the light of the tactical problems faced by the Army of Norway.   SILBERFUCHS began—or nearly began—with clearly defined main effort in the proper place, the XXXVI Corps zone.   With the 163d Infantry Division, which was not expected to be held up long at Hanko, the corps would have had four divisions;

---

[67] Dietl to Jodl, 27 Sep 41 in Dietl, *op. cit.*, p. 232.

[68] *Vortragspunkte fuer Herrn Kommandierenden General, 21.11.41*, in *Gebirgskorps Norwegen, K.T.B. 1, Anlagenband 2.* XIX AK 15085/4. *Dietl an Jodl, 24.11.41*, in *A.O.K. Norwegen, Anlagen zum K.T.B., Band II.* AOK 20 19070/3.

[69] Waldemar Erfurth, "*Das Problem der Murman-Bahn*," Part I, in *Wehrwissenschaftliche Rundschau*, June 1952.

[70] In this connection it must be considered whether Hitler's concern for the defense of Norway, where he held seven divisions while operations in Finland languished, was not excessive.   He did eventually consent to part with two regiments and some odds and ends.   But their performance seemingly lent weight to his argument that the Norwegian garrison troops were not suited to the demands of warfare in Karelia and Kola.

but Hitler's decision to give the 163d Division to Mannerheim and the collapse of the SS-Division reduced the corps' strength by half. Falkenhorst should probably have foreseen the latter disaster; but there was a major extenuating factor in that the SS-Division was the only motorized unit available to him. His decision in July to stage the main effort in the Mountain Corps Norway sector proved later to be an error of major proportions; nevertheless, it was partially justified at the time by the extremely slow start of the XXXVI Corps. Moreover, the situation of the Mountain Corps was thought at the time to be so precarious that the corps could not be left where it was; it could only go forward or back, and to pull back would have opened the Rybatchiy Peninsula and made the holding of Pechenga doubtful. By 4 September, before Dietl's final attack, the Army of Norway was prepared to shift the 6th Mountain Division to the strategically more important Kandalaksha operation, but then Hitler was intent on Murmansk.

Erfurth's charge that the Army of Norway failed to carry out instructions aimed at creating a definite main effort rests mainly on two orders. One was the OKW order of 7 July, which instructed Falkenhorst to transfer troops from the XXXVI Corps to the Mountain Corps Norway after Salla had been taken. The other was the Fuehrer Directive of 30 July, which stopped the XXXVI Corps offensive, ordered the Army of Norway to concentrate its efforts in the Mountain Corps and the III Corps sectors, and proposed that, should the III Corps offensive also stall, the troops freed were to be transferred to the Army of Karelia.[71] The 7 July order carried no specific intent to create a main effort. It merely recognized the fact that it had become necessary to restore Dietl's original striking force, which was being dissipated in defensive missions behind the front at Pechenga and the Rybatchiy Peninsula, particularly as a result of Hitler's growing fear of a British landing. The intent of the later Fuehrer Directive is less clear. In halting the XXXVI Corps and strengthening the Mountain Corps Norway and the III Corps it only confirmed measures which the Army of Norway had recommended and had already begun putting into effect. The provision regarding a shift of forces to the Army of Karelia was new; whether or not it resulted from an intention to stop the XXXVI Corps permanently and the III Corps eventually as well cannot be determined. That Falkenhorst deliberately ignored it is certain; that he put the XXXVI Corps back into motion as a means of forestalling its taking effect is likely. Still, it must also be pointed out that the directive itself probably did not reflect a firm intention on the part of the OKW since no supplementary orders were issued. In this context, too, it is necessary to view the question of halting operations by one or another of the corps and establishing a main effort elsewhere in the light of the tactical situation of the Army of

---

[71] Erfurth, "*Das Problem der Murman-Bahn,*" Part I, *loc. cit.*

Norway. Falkenhorst maintained consistently and correctly that to relax the pressure at any one point meant giving the Russians an opportunity to exploit the superior maneuverability which the Murmansk Railroad afforded them to pull out troops and shift them to one of the other sectors. With the troops at its disposal the Army of Norway could not create a true main effort anywhere without defeating its own ends in the process and could not shut down any single sector without creating a potential threat elsewhere.

In the last analysis, it can be said that, while the tactical direction of the Army of Norway operations, particularly the decision to build a main effort in the Mountain Corps zone, was not above reproach, the outcome of SILBERFUCHS was primarily determined by the failure to commit a force commensurate in strength with the demands of its mission. The most significant contributory element was Russian possession of the Murmansk Railroad. This made it possible for the Russian Fourteenth Army to move troops and replacements laterally behind the lines at will while poor lines of communication forced the three Army of Norway corps to fight in isolation. Nearly as important were the tremendous defensive potentialities of the terrain, the German troops' lack of training and inclination for arctic warfare, and the ability of the Russians to bring in reinforcements and replace their losses, when necessary, by drawing on the numerous prison camps of Kola and Karelia.

Chapter 10

Finland's War

Operations in 1941

The Finns at the beginning of their 1941–1944 war with the Soviet Union, which Mannerheim has called the Continuation War to emphasize its direct antecedents in the Winter War of 1939–1940, faced their gigantic adversary with confidence and renewed strength. A year and a half earlier they had fought alone; in June 1941 they stood at the side of the world's strongest military power. Moreover, their own military situation had improved. They had tested leadership and experienced troops who, man for man, had proved themselves superior to the enemy. Improved mobilization procedures assured the Army of approximately twice as many operational units as had been available at the outbreak of war in 1939. Supply dumps and arsenals emptied during the Winter War had been restocked, mostly with German weapons; and it had been possible to increase the firepower of the infantry through employment of larger numbers of automatic weapons, antitank guns, and heavy mortars. The artillery had heavy batteries which had been almost entirely lacking in the Winter War; and the Air Force had been strengthened somewhat.[1] In the first weeks of war the country mobilized nearly 500,000 men for its armed forces, 30,000 for military road and bridge construction, and 80,000 *Lottas* (women auxiliaries), a tremendous force for a nation of four million, and one which, as was quickly demonstrated, it could not maintain indefinitely.[2]

In the last week of June Mannerheim moved his headquarters to Mikkeli, the old town from which he had also directed the Winter War. The German Liaison Staff North took up quarters nearby. In accordance with the operations plan completed and submitted to the OKH on 28 June he deployed his units along the border south of the line Oulu–Belomorsk. In the north to close the gap between the Army of Norway right flank and the Finnish main force the 14th Division was stationed

---

[1] Mannerheim, *op. cit.*, p. 443.
[2] *OKW, WFSt, Abt. L I H Op., Nr. 44151/41, Oberbefehlshaber der finnischen Wehrmacht an Herrn Generalfeldmarschall Keitel, 29.8.41, in A.O.K. Norwegen, Ia., Chefsachen, 2.6.–18.11.41.* AOK 20 20844/2.

188

Finnish Lotta *on aircraft spotting duty.*

on either side of Lieksa. The main force, Army of Karelia, under Mannerheim's chief of staff, General Heinrichs, occupied a line extending from Ilomantsi on the north to a point opposite the narrows between Yanis Lake and Lake Ladoga. The Army of Karelia consisted of Group O (one cavalry brigade and the 1st and 2d Jaeger Brigades) on the left, the VI Corps (11th Division and 5th Division) in the center, and the VII Corps (19th Division and 7th Division) on the right. The 1st Division was the army reserve. The front between the Army of Karelia right flank and the Gulf of Finland was held by the II Corps (2d, 18th, and 15th Divisions) on the left and the IV Corps (8th, 10th, 12th, and 4th Divisions) on the right. The 17th Division was committed to seal off Hanko. After its arrival in the first days of July Mannerheim stationed the German 163d Infantry Division (less one regiment) at Joensuu as his reserve.[3]

The Soviet forces opposite the Finnish Army were attached to Marshal Klimenti Voroshilov's Northwest Front. North of Lake Ladoga, in the Army of Karelia sector, the Soviet Seventh Army had three divisions in the line and one in reserve. On the Isthmus of Karelia, opposite the Finnish II and IV Corps, the Soviet Twenty-third Army had four divisions in the fortifications along the border and two to three divisions in reserve. The Russian garrison at Hanko consisted of two rifle brigades plus fortification, railway, and air defense units. By the first week of July, German successes on the main front had forced the Russians to weaken their concentration against Finland; nearly all of the reserves were pulled out, leaving only seven divisions and the two brigades at Hanko to oppose the Finnish Army. When Mannerheim opened his offensive he had a clear 3 : 1 numerical superiority and the assurance that the Soviet main force would remain tied down on the German front.[4]

The Finnish plan was to strike on either side of Yanis Lake, split the Russian main force, and then advance east of Lake Ladoga with the Army of Karelia via Olonets to Lodeynoye Pole on the Svir River. The II Corps would defend the border but hold itself ready to advance on order into the Elisenvara–Khitola area and, in the further course of operations, thrust toward Lakhdenpokh'ya on the northwest shore of Lake Ladoga. The IV Corps would hold on the border, and the 14th Division would advance toward Reboly and Lendery.[5]

Ladoga–Karelia

The Finnish offensive began on 10 July with the Army of Karelia main effort in the VI Corps zone north of Yanis Lake between Vyartsilya and Korpisel'kya. At Korpisel'kya the attack struck a soft spot in the Russian line and, with the help of a Jaeger brigade from Group O, quickly achieved a breakthrough.[6] After occupying Kokkari and the village of Tolvayärvi on the 12th, the Jaeger brigade turned south toward Muanto, which it took two days later. Continuing its advance on the 15th it cut the east-west railroad at Loymola and in another quick thrust on the following day reached Koirinoya on the east shore of Lake Ladoga.

---

[3] Mannerheim, *op. cit.*, pp. 445–47. Erfurth, *op. cit.*, pp. 17ff.

[4] Mannerheim, *op. cit.*, pp. 444, 447.

[5] *Verbindungsstab Nord, Ia, Nr. 183/41, Auszug aus den Operationsanweisungen fuer Kar. Armee, 1.7.41,* in *A.O.K. Norwegen, Tagesmeldungen, Band I.* AOK 20 19070/12.

[6] The Finnish Jaeger brigades were light infantry equipped with bicycles for summer operations. They were highly mobile, and in broken, wooded terrain they could perform the spearhead functions ordinarily assigned to armored and motorized columns in more open country. Their performance impressed the Germans, and Falkenhorst paid them the compliment of repeatedly trying to get one of them for employment on the Army of Norway front.

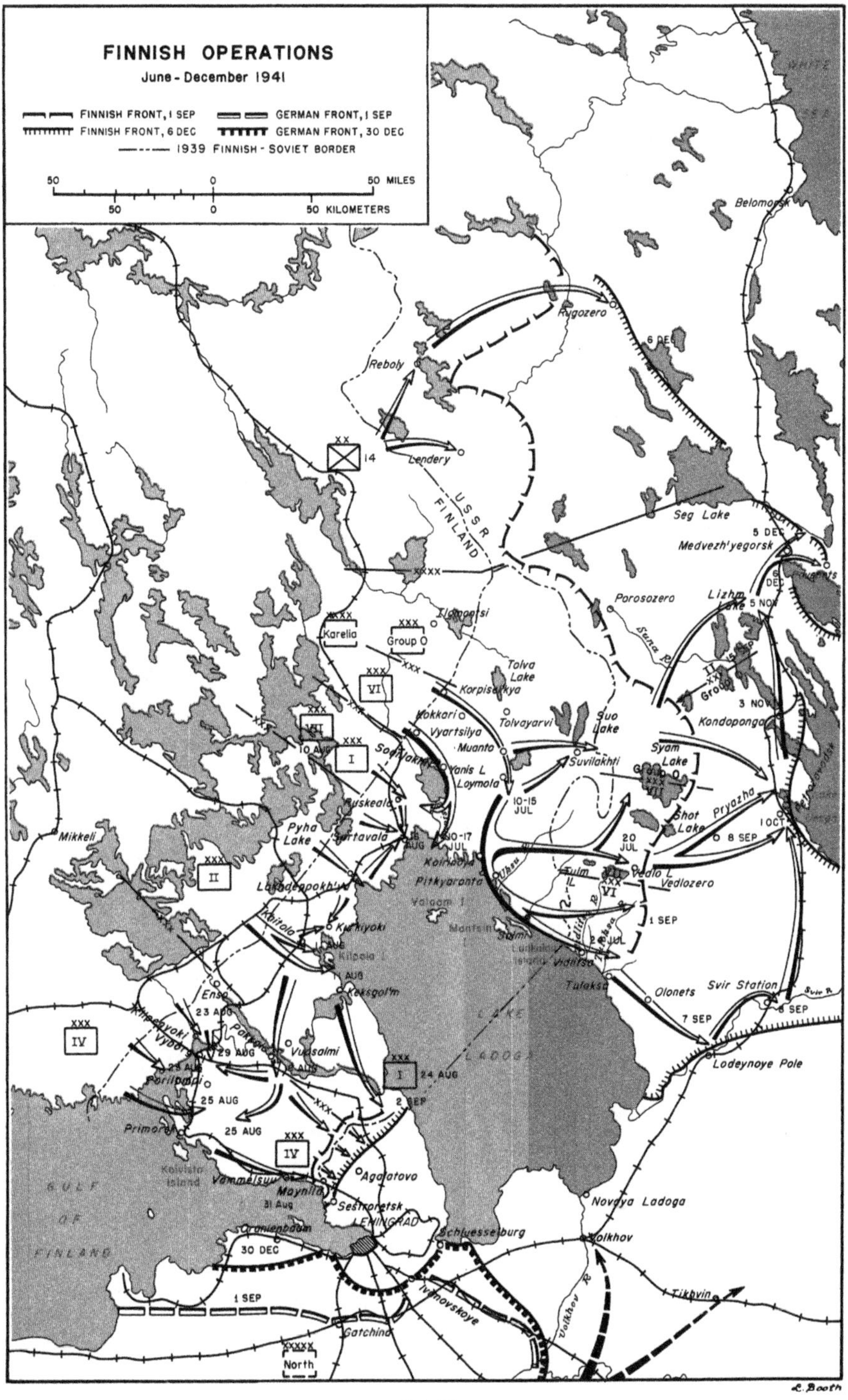

FINNISH OPERATIONS
June - December 1941

FINNISH FRONT, 1 SEP   GERMAN FRONT, 1 SEP
FINNISH FRONT, 6 DEC   GERMAN FRONT, 30 DEC
—·—·— 1939 FINNISH - SOVIET BORDER

50   0   50 MILES
50   0   50 KILOMETERS

Map 17

With that the Russians in the vicinity of Sortavala were cut off from the east.   The Finns had covered 65 miles in six days.

Meanwhile, the VI Corps right-flank units going by way of Vyartsilya had been slowed down in hill country off the east shore of Yanis Lake near Soanlakhti, and the VII Corps, which had been expected to sweep west of Yanis Lake, had met heavy resistance and gained little ground. On the 16th, Russian resistance at Soanlakhti collapsed, and on the following day the Finns reached the Yanis River where they set up a defense line facing west.   At the same time Mannerheim ordered the 1st Division out of reserve to protect the eastern flank at Loymola and shifted the 17th Division from Hanko to the vicinity of Vyartsilya.   The front at Hanko was held thereafter only by coastal defense units and a Swedish volunteer battalion.   On the 16th Mannerheim committed the 163d Division on the east flank to take Suvilakhti, the road and railroad junction at the southern tip of Suo Lake.

The VI Corps, with orders to continue southward, sent one column east via Kyaznyasel'ka to Tulm Lake on the 20th while the main force pushed south along the shore of Lake Ladoga and took Salmi on the 21st after three days of heavy fighting.   On the following day the VI Corps occupied Mansila on the pre-1940 border, and by the 24th had reached the line of the Tuloksa River where Mannerheim ordered it to stop.   On the night of the 24th the Russians landed a brigade on the islands of Mantsin and Lunkulan west of Salmi and threw a heavy counterattack against the Tuloksa River line.   The Russian assaults failed, but fighting continued heavy throughout the rest of July and early August as the Finns went over to the defensive.

On the Army of Karelia left flank the German 163d Division ran into trouble in the lake country north of the Loymola–Suvilakhti rail line.   The VI Corps, trying to help, sent a column from the Tulm Lake area which on 26 July cut the railroad behind Suvilakhti north of Shot Lake, but at the end of the month the 163d Division was thoroughly bogged down.   It was feeling the absence of its third regiment acutely and clearly needed reinforcements.   Mannerheim ordered in Group O and its two brigades.

The VII Corps on the Army of Karelia right flank had kept the Russians west of Yanis Lake under constant pressure and at the end of July stood at Ruskeala.   At the same time one division detached from the VI Corps had established a holding line along the Yanis River from Lake Ladoga to Yanis Lake.   The Russians, hemmed in on two sides, were forced back toward Sortavala; and favorable conditions for cleaning out the northwest shore of Lake Ladoga were created.

On 31 July the II Corps began an offensive from its line on the border between the Vuoksi River and Pyhä Lake.   Its objective was to take the railroad junction at Khitola and cut the Russian communications in the Sortavala area.   Mannerheim held the 10th Division, detached from the IV Corps, in reserve. The offensive made good progress, and on 5 August Mannerheim threw in the 10th Division, which in a quick thrust reached the shore of Lake Ladoga near Lakhdenpokh'ya. Khitola fell to the main force on the 11th while a flanking column reached Lake Ladoga between Khitola and Keksgol'm on the same day. The Russians between Khitola and Yanis Lake were split into two groups: one of about two divisions was forced back to the vicinity of Kurkiyoki; and the other, slightly smaller, held out in Sortavala. The Russians at Kurkiyoki withdrew to Kilpola Island, close to the coast; from there they were evacuated by boat in mid-August.

Before closing in on Sortavala Mannerheim shifted VII Corps Headquarters east to take command of the sector between the 163d Division and the VI Corps and placed the VII Corps troops under the newly created I Corps. The I Corps then pushed in on Sortavala, taking the old Finnish city on 16 August. Most of the Russians escaped to Valaam Island, later to be pulled back to the Leningrad area. The offensive on the northwest shore of Lake Ladoga had been a brilliant tactical success, but was still a disappointment since neither the Finnish nor the German Air Force, which at that time had a squadron of Ju 88's ranging over Lake Ladoga as far north as Valaam Island, was able to prevent the Russian evacuations.[7]

The Karelian Isthmus

During the first half of August the Finnish plan of operations underwent a fundamental change. As early as 14 July Erfurth had reported a certain resistance on Mannerheim's part to the idea of an offensive east of Lake Ladoga; this the OKH dismissed as mostly a product of Erfurth's imagination. However, on 2 August, when the OKH asked the Finns to resume their offensive east of Lake Ladoga toward Lodeynoye Pole in conjunction with the final drive toward Leningrad which the Army Group North would launch within a week or so, Mannerheim refused, saying he could not resume operations east of the lake until the 163d Division had executed its mission of taking Suvilakhti. The OKH attempted to put pressure on the 163d Division but, when it became apparent that no quick action could be expected in that direction, turned to Mannerheim on 10 August with a second proposal: that he help by staging an offensive toward Leningrad on the Isthmus of Karelia. Mannerheim agreed.[8]

There is reason to suspect that the idea of an operation on the Isthmus of Karelia was not unwelcome to Mannerheim and that he may, in fact, have deliberately forced the appearance of such a con-

[7] Mannherheim, *op. cit.*, pp. 445–49. Erfurth, *op. cit.*, pp. 26–32.
[8] *Chefgruppe Verb. Stab Nord, Ia, Nr. 284/41, Auszug aus Weisung des OKH an Verb. Stab Nord, OKH, GenStdH, Op. Abt. (Ia), Nr. 40722/41*, in 163d. I.D., *Ia Anlagen zum Kriegstagebuch, Band II*. 163 ID 16260/19. Erfurth, *op. cit.*, pp. 34ff.

tingency.[9]   In his entire conduct of the war Mannerheim demonstrated that he was interested above all in the former Finnish territories and, secondly, in what might be called the Finnish Irredenta in Eastern Karelia.   Toward adventurous sallies into the wide-open spaces of Russia in support of the German strategy he was cold.   Mannerheim was also, as the Germans more than once noted, a pessimist, which made him remarkably sensitive to even temporarily untoward shifts in the course of events; therefore his opposition to an operation east of Lake Ladoga could also have been influenced by a negative assessment of the performance of the Army Group North.

The mission of Generalfeldmarschall Wilhelm Ritter von Leeb's Army Group North was to cut off Leningrad and establish contact with the Finns in the Lake Ladoga area.   Starting from East Prussia the army group made rapid progress through the Baltic States; but Voroshilov, who had no intention of attempting a stand in the recently annexed territories, pulled his forces back in good order.   As a result, there was a noticeable absence of the gigantic encirclement battles characteristic of the other areas of the Eastern Front.   On crossing into the Soviet Union proper in early July the Army Group North began to meet stiffer resistance, and at about the same time the constant expansion of the front reduced Leeb's ability to maintain a clear-cut main effort.   Between Lake Ilmen and Lake Peipus the terrain proved unsuitable for tanks, and for several weeks after mid-July progress fell off to a crawl.   In this situation Leeb undertook to organize a final thrust, timed for the second week of August, out of the sector west of Lake Ilmen to Leningrad.   Hitler, who at that time regarded Leningrad as his most important objective, wanted to detach the Third Panzer Group (army) from the Army Group Center to lend weight to the attack but was dissuaded and ended by sending one armored corps.   It was to aid this attack, begun on 10 August, that the OKH urged Mannerheim to reopen his offensive east of Lake Ladoga.   Mannerheim, understandably, preferred to await further developments.[10]

With the situation on the northwest shore of Lake Ladoga well in hand, Mannerheim on 13 August ordered the II Corps to turn south

---

[9] Generalleutnant Erwin Engelbrecht, Commanding General, 163d Infantry Division, recorded a conversation he had with General Talvela, Commanding General, VI Corps, on 2 September 1941 which lends some support to this supposition. Talvela said he regretted that his sector had been left completely inactive for the past several weeks even though he had repeatedly tried to get permission to resume the attack.   He regretted the inactivity the more since the impact of his first advance had thrown the Russians into a panic which in his opinion would have made it "positively easy" at that time to push to the Svir and, possibly, create a bridgehead across it.   The entire advance to the Tuloksa River line, he said, had cost the VI Corps 3,500 casualties; the period of inaction since had cost as many. *163. I.D., Kommandeur, Unterhaltung des Div.-Kdeurs. mit finnischen General Talvela Kdr. des VI A. K. ueber taktisches Geschehen, 2.9.41,* in 163 I.D., Ia Anlagen, Band III.   163 ID 1620/21.
[10] *H. Gr. Nord, Kriegstagebuch, 22.6.–31.8.41, passim.*   H. Gr. Nord 75128/1. *Halder Diary,* VI, pp. 249, 251, 254; VII, pp. 9, 15, 18, 33.   *Der Fuehrer und Oberste Befehlshaber der Wehrmacht, WFSt, Abt. L (I Op.), Nr. 441230/41, Weisung Nr. 33, 19.7.41* and *Nr. 441298/41, Weisung Nr. 34, 30.7.41.*   OKW/1938.

toward Pakkola at the narrowest point of the Vuoksi River. There on the 18th the Finns crossed the river north of the town. Their familiarity with the terrain of their former territory was paying dividends; the crossing almost exactly duplicated an exercise which they had held at the same place during the 1939 war games. In short order they established a large bridgehead south of the Vuoksi from which they could strike at the rear of the Russian troops opposite the IV Corps on the border. At the same time the left flank of the II Corps, pushing south via Keksgol'm, cleared the river line east to Lake Ladoga.

On 22 August the IV Corps began its offensive. The Russians had started blowing up their border fortifications a day earlier, and the first phase of the attack took the form of a pursuit in which the IV Corps reached the line Vilyoki–Kilpenyoki on the 23d. A simultaneous thrust out of the II Corps bridgehead had carried to within eight miles of Vyborg. The Russians, who had three divisions in the Vyborg sector, intended to hold the city with one division and throw the Finns back across the Vuoksi by a drive to Pakkola with the other two. At the river they hoped to make contact with another division coming south from Kilpola Island, but the plan could not be brought to the point of execution as the Finns quickly and methodically set about encircling Vyborg. On the 25th the II Corps cut the rail line to Leningrad east of Vyborg, and on the same day a division crossed Vyborg Bay to take up positions astride the road and rail connection between Vyborg and Primorsk. With that the Russians in and around the city were cut off on all sides. On the 29th units of the IV Corps marched into Vyborg, and as the ring drew tighter the Russian divisions were forced into a *motti* in the forest near Porilampi. Abandoning most of their vehicles and equipment, a large group of Russians managed to break out of the encirclement and escape to the Koyvisto Islands in the Gulf of Finland, where they held out until November when they were evacuated. What remained of the *motti* was mopped up on 1 September.

By 31 August units of the IV Corps had pushed south on the Isthmus as far as Vammelsuu. That same day they took Mansila on the old border, famous as the place where, according to Russian allegations, Finnish artillery fire had precipitated the Winter War. On 24 August Mannerheim had shifted I Corps headquarters from Sortavala to the left flank on the Isthmus where, with two divisions detached from the II Corps, it undertook to clear the Ladoga side of the Isthmus south of the Vuoksi. On 2 September it also reached the old border. In a four-week offensive the Finns had retaken their lost territory on the Isthmus of Karelia.

In the Army of Karelia zone, in the last week of August, the 163d Division and Group O took Suvilakhti, and the VII Corps pushed its front into the narrows between Syam Lake and Shot Lake. On the Finnish north flank the 14th Division, operating independently, had scored a

Finnish engineers using bangalore torpedo to demolish Russian fortifications on the Isthmus of Karelia.

brilliant success by encircling a Russian division near Reboly and before the end of August advanced to Rugozero where, in early September, it was ordered to go over to the defensive.[11]

Eastern Karelia

In the latter half of August, with the Army Group North back in motion and rapidly approaching Leningrad, the question of the fate of that city came to the fore in German planning. In the advance planning for BARBAROSSA and the occupation of Russia, Hitler, whose knowledge of the economic geography of the Soviet Union may have been somewhat wanting, decided that the population of the Ukraine and southern Russia was worth preserving for the sake of industrial and raw materials production and because it could produce an agricultural surplus. The north imported food, and, therefore, in order to prevent its draining off the agricultural surplus of the south, which he intended to divert to Germany, he decided that the population there would have to be reduced by some millions, principally through the natural process of starvation. Leningrad he regarded as both a symbol of the Russian nation (which he intended to destroy for all time) and a concentration of several million useless mouths to feed.

Starting from the premise that the city would in no case be occupied, he and his advisers in the OKW turned to the problem of how to deal with the city. One thought was to hem it in as closely as possible, surround it with an electrified fence and machine guns, and leave the popu-

---

[11] Mannerheim, *op. cit.*, pp. 446, 449, and 452ff. Erfurth, *op. cit.*, pp. 31ff. and 35.

lation to starve.   Another was to let out the women and children and shove them across the Russian lines to create confusion behind the enemy's front.   This was regarded as a good idea in theory but difficult to execute and likely not to be effective since the Russians themselves were insensitive to things of that sort.

It was certain that the city would be leveled to the ground and the population removed.   Since the Finns had expressed a desire to have the Neva as a boundary, all the territory north of the river would go to them.   While awaiting a final decision on how to deal with Leningrad, the Army Group North was to encircle the city but not enter it and not accept a surrender if it were offered.   The OKH was uneasy, fearing for the moral effects on its troops should they be called upon to slaughter unarmed civilians by the thousands.   It favored a compromise solution which would let starvation and destruction do their work as far as possible within the city and then permit the last desperate remnants of the noncombatants to filter through the German lines and disperse across the countryside.[12]

To isolate Leningrad, Army Group North planned to cross the Neva River near Schluesselburg, make contact with the Finns, and establish a line between the city and the western shore of Lake Ladoga.   It intended also to push via Volkhov and join the Army of Karelia in the vicinity of the Svir River.   It wanted the Finns to advance south of their old border on the Isthmus of Karelia and south of the Svir to meet the German spearheads.   These proposals Keitel, in a letter written on 22 August, laid before Mannerheim.[13]

The approach drew a gloomy reply from Mannerheim.   He explained that with 16 percent of its population devoted exclusively to military duties Finland was having serious difficulty in maintaining its economy.   Moreover, the casualty rate was markedly higher than it had been in the Winter War.   During August he had abolished the fourth platoon in every infantry company, and in September he intended to disband a division to acquire replacements.   He was most reluctant to consider the idea of an offensive across the old border on the Karelian Isthmus since he believed the pre-1939 Russian fortifications there were extremely strong and, he recommended, could best be taken by a German attack from the rear.   On the Isthmus of Olonets he intended to resume his advance to the Svir but anticipated strong resistance and thought that if the Svir were reached it would be very difficult to continue on across the river.

In his memoirs Mannerheim maintains that he accepted command

---

[12] *OKW, WFSt, Abt. L (I Op.), Nr. 002119/41, Vortragsnotiz Leningrad, 21.9.41.* OKW/1938.   *H. Gr. Nord, Kriegstagebuch, 22.6.–31.8.41,* 29 Aug 41, and *passim* in succeeding volumes of the *K.T.B.*   H. Gr. Nord 75128/1.

[13] *H. Gr. Nord, Kriegstagebuch, 22.6.–31.8.41,* 22 Aug 41.   H. Gr. Nord 75128/1. *Der Chef des Oberkommandos der Wehrmacht, Nr. 44 1418/41, WFSt, Abt. L, an Sr. Exzellenz, Herrn Generalfeldmarschall Mannerheim, 22.841,* in *A.O.K. Norwegen, Chefsachen 2.6.–18.11.41.*   AOK 20 20844/2.

196

The President of Finland, Risto Ryti (in civilian clothes), inspecting an antiaircraft unit, 1941.

of the Finnish Army in 1941 only on the condition that he never be required to lead an offensive against Leningrad. One of the earliest and strongest Soviet arguments against the existence of an independent Finland was that the second city of the Soviet Union, Leningrad, would thereby be threatened. He therefore believed that Finland should not take any action which might lend substance to that argument, which could be revived by the Russians after the war. On receiving Keitel's letter, he states, he showed it to President Ryti, reminding him of the condition under which he had taken command and expressing the conviction that to cross the Svir would be contrary to Finland's interests. Ryti agreed.[14]

In a conversation with the Finnish Acting Chief of Staff, Maj. Gen. E. F. Hanell, Erfurth assembled some explanatory impressions and information concerning Mannerheim's intentions. Hanell said that Mannerheim had recently been besieged by requests from the President and Cabinet to be careful in expending the manpower of the country.[15]

---

[14] Mannerheim, *op. cit.*, p. 454. *OKW, WFSt, Abt. L, Nr. 441451/41, Oberbefehlshaber der finnischen Wehrmacht an Herrn Generalfeldmarschall Keitel, 26.8.41, in A.O.K. Norwegen, Chefsachen 2.6.–18.11.41.* AOK 20 20844/2.

[15] The German Minister to Finland, Wipert von Bluecher, at the time reported that two parties were developing within the Cabinet. One wanted to continue the offensives; the other, which Ryti seemed to favor, thought the time had come to go over to defensive warfare, wanted to stop at the old border on the Isthmus of Karelia, and wanted to rein in on Mannerheim's offensive plans for Eastern Karelia. This proved to be merely a passing phase, and Cabinet sentiment almost immediately swung back in favor of aggressive pursuit of the war. Bluecher, tel. to Foreign Ministry No. 866, 1.9.41. Serial 260. U.S. Department of State, German Foreign Ministry Records. Bluecher, *op. cit.*, pp. 246ff.

Leading industrialists had sounded urgent warnings that with nearly all the men on military duty an economic collapse was in the offing. As far as the offensives on either side of Lake Ladoga were concerned, the Finnish Constitution required the Commander in Chief to secure permission from the Government for operations beyond the national boundaries. Such permission had only been given for the sector east of Lake Ladoga, and there only to the Svir River. But Hanell did not doubt that permission could also be secured for the Isthmus of Karelia if Mannerheim seriously requested it. He suggested that such a request would be forthcoming when "the German Army rapped loudly and clearly on the door of Leningrad." On the matter of an offensive east of Lake Ladoga Mannerheim had given his word and would keep it. As far as the question of crossing the Svir was concerned his attitude would become more positive as the German armies drew closer. He appeared to fear that the Army Group North would stop on the Volkhov River and leave it to him to negotiate the entire distance between the Svir and the Volkhov. Erfurth thought that Mannerheim's native pessimism had temporarily gotten the best of him and recommended the award of a German decoration to aid in restoring his morale.[16]

In the German High Command Mannerheim's apparently wavering confidence in his ally had a disquieting effect. The OKH immediately instructed the Army Group North that, aside from operational considerations, German prestige demanded a junction with the Finns as early as possible. As soon as the situation in any way permitted, even before Leningrad was completely encircled, the army group was to divert forces in the direction of Lodeynoye Pole.[17]

At the end of August, one Army Group North division reached the Neva at Ivanovskoye where it cut the last rail line out of the city and was in a position to interdict traffic on the river.[18] On 1 September Mannerheim told Erfurth that he had secured permission from Ryti to cross the border on the west side of the Karelian Isthmus as far as the line Sestroretsk–Agalatovo.[19] Two days later when Keitel, at Army Group North headquarters, told Leeb of this decision Leeb maintained that a mile or two of territory more or less was not important but that it was absolutely essential to have the Finns tie down the Russian divisions on their front. Otherwise the Russians could pull out troops to throw against his own line drawing up to Leningrad, and a difficult situation would ensue.[20]

On 4 September the operations chief of the OKW, Jodl, flew to Mikkeli carrying all three classes of the Iron Cross to Mannerheim.

[16] General der Infanterie Erfurth, an OKW, WFSt, Abt. L., 26.8.41, in A.O.K. Norwegen, Chefsachen 2.6.–18.11.41. AOK 20 20844/2.
[17] H. Gr. Nord, Kriegstagebuch, 22.6.–31.8.41, 28 Aug 41. H. Gr. Nord 75128/1.
[18] H. Gr. Nord Kriegstagebuch, 22.6.–31.8.41, 30 Aug 41.. H. Gr. Nord 75128/1.
[19] Verbindungsstab Nord, Ia, Nr. 840/41, an OKW, WFSt, Abt. L, 1.9.41, in OKH, GenStdH, Op. Abt., I/N, Band II, Finnland. H 22/227.
[20] H. Gr. Nord, Kriegstagebuch, 1.–30.9.41, 3 Sep 41. H. Gr. Nord 22506.

The Marshal, according to the account in his memoirs, remained cool toward Jodl's pleading for an offensive on the Isthmus but, in order to avoid tension and not jeopardize the negotiations for 15,000 tons of grain which were then in progress, did promise to try a push off the right flank—which was never executed. Nevertheless, at the time, the Germans believed Jodl's mission was a complete success. Mannerheim had, in fact, promised to cross the border along the entire front on the Isthmus and advance up to the Russian permanent fortifications. On the right flank he would go as far as Sestroretsk and, if possible, Agalatovo. Three weeks later he informed Keitel that he had advanced beyond the border approximately to the depths promised. To some extent Mannerheim was temporizing. To cross the border, which zigzagged erratically, in itself had no particular military significance; and whether the mere appearance of Finnish troops before the main Russian fortifications would tie down the enemy as effectively as the Army Group North desired was problematical. But these were considerations of which the Germans were also aware. The Jodl visit also brought the encouraging news that the Finnish advance to the Svir would begin that same day.[21]

On 4 September the Army of Karelia was deployed as follows: Group O (one cavalry brigade and one Jaeger brigade) on the left flank from the border to the north shore of Syam Lake with the mass of the corps just north of the lake; the VII Corps (two divisions) in the center between Syam Lake and Vedlo Lake east of both; the VI Corps (three divisions and a Jaeger brigade) on the right flank between Vedlo Lake and the mouth of the Tuloksa. The 163d Division was in the VI Corps zone but was the Commander in Chief's reserve and was used only for flank protection along the Ladoga shore.[22]

The offensive began on the night of the 4th with an artillery barrage, the heaviest staged by the Finns thus far in the war, which paved the way for a VI Corps breakthrough on the Tuloksa Line. Within three days the VI Corps reached the Svir opposite Lodeynoye Pole, and on the 8th the Jaeger brigade cut the Murmansk Railroad at Svir Station. On the same day the VII Corps took the important road junction at Krasnaya Pryazha. By the middle of the month the Army of Karelia had possession of the entire length of the Svir and was developing a converging attack on Petrozavodsk, the capital of the Karelo-Finnish SSR.

While the 1st Jaeger Brigade approached the city from the south along the Murmansk Railroad the VII Corps sent one division on a daring and strenuous march through the forests between the railroad and the Pryazha–Petrozavodsk road and a second column along the road.

---

[21] Mannerheim, *op. cit.*, p. 455. Erfurth, op. cit., pp. 36ff. *Verbindungsstab Nord, Ia, Nr. 84/41, Oberbefehlshaber der Wehrmacht an Herrn Generalfeldmarschall Keitel, 25.9.41, in A.O.K. Norwegen, Chefsachen 2.6.–18.11.41.* AOK 20 20844/2. *Verbindungsstab Nord, Ia, Nr. 871/41, an OKW, WFSt, Abt. L, 4.9.41, in OKH, Gen StdH, Op. Abt. I/N, Band II, Finnland.* H 22/227.
[22] *Verbindungsstab Nord, Lage am 4.9. Vormittags.* Map, uncatalogued.

Group O, aided later by the II Corps transferred from the Isthmus of Karelia, pressed in from the northwest. After two weeks of fighting, the city fell on 1 October. The Russians had withdrawn across Lake Onega. The VI Corps had in the meantime crossed the Svir at its Lake Onega end, creating a bridgehead about 12 miles deep and 60 miles wide in order to gain better defensive positions. Despite the signs of a very early winter—which was to have fateful consequences for the German armies in the south—Mannerheim decided to strike northward from Petrozavodsk toward Medvezh'yegorsk.[23]

In September, while the Army of Karelia was establishing itself on the Svir, the Army Group North was engaged in the vicinity of Leningrad. In the first week of the month it had a spearhead on the Neva at Ivanovskoye, but from there the front on the left dipped sharply south of Leningrad, touching the Gulf of Finland west of Oranienbaum; on the right it dropped off southeast to the Volkhov River and thence south. On 6 September Hitler decided that the time had come to resume the drive on Moscow. The Army Group North would lose the Fourth Panzer Group and have to close in on Leningrad as best it could; its only remaining larger mechanized unit, the XXXIX Corps, was earmarked for a push across the Volkhov toward the Svir.

On the 8th Schluesselburg fell, giving the army group control of the upper reaches of the Neva to Lake Ladoga. Leeb had already protested that to send the XXXIX Corps east of the Volkhov would be a dissipation of strength; and on the 10th the OKH ordered him to advance across the Neva west of Leningrad and make contact with the Finns on the Isthmus of Karelia, leaving the Volkhov–Svir operation in abeyance until more troops became available. That solution quickly proved illusory as the Russians staged strong counterattacks at Schluesselburg and along the Svir. On the 15th Leeb reported to the OKH that the enemy was drawing troops off the Finnish front to throw against the Army Group North. If the Finns were to reopen their offensive on the Isthmus, he said, the battle of Leningrad could be decided in a few days. Otherwise, the time when a crossing of the Neva might be undertaken could not even be predicted. Three days later, in response to a second call for Finnish help, Halder assured Leeb that the Finnish High Command intended to resume its attacks on both sides of Lake Ladoga—on the Isthmus as soon as the Army Group North crossed the Neva and south of the Svir as soon as the effects of a German drive in that direction became perceptible.[24]

In the middle of the month Keitel took up his correspondence with Mannerheim again, asking the Marshal to station the 163d Division near the mouth of the Svir and permit it, when the time came, to cross

---

[23] Mannerheim, *op. cit.*, pp. 458ff. and 461. Erfurth, *op. cit.*, pp. 37ff.
[24] *H. Gr. Nord, Kriegstagebuch, 1.–30.9.41,* 6–10, 15, and 18 Sep 41. H. Gr. Nord 22506. *Der Fuehrer und Oberste Befehlshaber der Wehrmacht, OKW, WFSt, Abt. L (I Op.), Nr. 441492/41, Weisung Nr. 35, 6.9.41. OKW/1938.*

the river and advance to meet the projected thrust of the Army Group North.[25] Mannerheim agreed, although he later insisted that the timing of the jump-off be his. The question of the Finns' own intentions had remained unanswered since the Jodl visit, and, although Keitel did not revert to it directly, Mannerheim undertook to clear the air in a long letter written on 25 September. His practiced eye had probably detected the doubtful elements in the Army Group North situation, even though the Germans, as he said later, had not informed him of their decision to pull out the Fourth Panzer Group. Moreover, Keitel's communication was hardly calculated to inspire confidence since it dealt mainly with explanations for the failures of the Army of Norway and suggested that the Army Group North, for the time being, would not be able to mount offensives either across the Neva or in the direction of the Svir.[26] The Marshall informed Keitel of his intention to take Petrozavodsk and Medvezh'yegorsk. After that his chief concern would be to alleviate the nation's serious manpower problem by reorganizing the Army, converting the divisions into brigades, and returning the surplus men to the civilian economy. He refused to consider advancing beyond his existing lines on the Svir and the Isthmus of Karelia.[27]

At the end of September, although Russian counterattacks continued heavy, the Army Group North managed to stabilize its front east of Leningrad. In the first week of October, when the successes of the Army Group Center made it appear that the enemy would be forced to pull out troops in the north for the defense of Moscow, Leeb began taking the XXXIX Corps (two panzer and two motorized divisions) out of the line near Schluesselburg and readying it for a thrust to the east. On 14 October, though there was still no sign that the Russians were reducing their forces opposite the army group, Hitler ordered Leeb to attack eastward via Chudovo and Tikhvin with the objective of enveloping the Russians south of Lake Ladoga and making contact with the Army of Karelia along the line Tikhvin–Lodeynoye Pole.

Two days later the XXXIX Corps headed eastward from Chudovo. The Russians offered strong resistance, and after the first two or three days the fall rains overtook the operation. Before the end of the first week the panzer divisions were leaving their tanks behind, bogged down on muddy roads. On 24 October Hitler wanted to cancel the operation,

---

[25] The idea of using the 163d Division had come earlier in the month from Erfurth, who seeing Mannerheim's growing reluctance to consider crossing the Svir thought a thrust by the German division might draw the Finns after it. *Verbindungsstab Nord, Ia, Nr 836/41 and Nr. 69/41, an OKW, WFSt, Abt. L, 31.8.41 and 15.9.41, in OKH, GenStdH, Op. Abt., I/N, Band II, Finnland.* H 22/227.
[26] *OKW, WFSt, Abt. L (I Op.), Nr. 002046/41, Abschrift von Fernschreiben Chef OKW an Feldmarschall Mannerheim, 14.9.41 and Der Chef des Oberkommandos der Wehrmacht, WFSt, Abt. L, Nr. 441580/41, an den Oberbefehlshaber der finnischen Wehrmacht Feldmarschall Mannerheim, 22.9.41, in A.O.K. Norwegen, Chefsachen 2.6.–18.11.41.* AOK 20 20844/2. *Mannerheim, op. cit.,* p. 457.
[27] *Verbindgungsstab Nord, Ia, Nr. 84/41, Oberbefehlshaber der finnischen Wehrmacht an Herrn Generalfeldmarschall Keitel, 25.9.41, in A.O.K. Norwegen, Chefsachen 2.6.–18.11.41.* AOK 20 20844/2.

and only the efforts of the OKH kept him from issuing such an order. Called to Fuehrer Headquarters Leeb spoke in favor of going ahead but did not himself believe it would be possible to do more than take Tikhvin.[28]

After two more weeks, during which it inched forward to within six miles of Tikhvin, the XXXIX Corps on 8 November planned a final quick thrust to the city. If it failed the operation was to be halted until conditions improved. It succeeded, and on the 9th one division could be turned northwestward from Tikhvin along the railroad toward Volkhov. At the end of the month, however, the Russians had nearly encircled the Germans at Tikhvin, and it became necessary to throw in two additional divisions to hold the flanks of the salient.[29]

On 1 December in assessing its situation the Army Group North concluded that the question of a junction with the Finns could not be taken under consideration for the present. Whether or not Tikhvin could be held depended on the enemy's ability to bring up more troops; the advance toward Volkhov would have to be stopped for lack of forces. Two days later the Commanding General, XXXIX Corps, reported that he could not hold Tikhvin much longer, and on the 7th Leeb ordered him to prepare to withdraw as soon as Hitler gave permission. At the same time both Halder and Keitel called to warn against a withdrawal—Hitler was determined to hold Tikhvin. Keitel claimed that the Finns were prepared to establish contact from their side. In his order of the 8th stopping offensive operations on the Eastern Front Hitler instructed the Army Group North to hold at Tikhvin and be ready to mop up south of Lake Ladoga and meet the Army of Karelia as soon as reinforcements could be brought up. Three days later he postponed further offensive operations until 1942.[30]

At the front events were overruling Hitler even before his orders could be issued. On the 7th Leeb intended to order the evacuation of Tikhvin, where the XXXIX Corps was fighting in driving snow and below zero temperatures, but was asked to hold up his order until Keitel and Jodl, closeted with Hitler, could secure a decision. Reluctantly, Hitler agreed, insisting that the road and railroad out of the city to Volkhov and Leningrad continue to be held. On the 9th Tikhvin was evacuated. Leeb saw no solution other than to pull back behind the Volkhov. For six more days Hitler insisted on holding as far forward as possible. Not until the 15th, after Leeb told him complete destruction of the XXXIX Corps was the sole alternative, did he agree to a withdrawal behind the river. By the 24th the Army Group North had its troops back be-

[28] H. Gr. Nord, Kriegstagebuch, 1.–30.10.41, passim. H. Gr. Nord 22927.
[29] H. Gr. Nord, Kriegstagebuch, 1.–30.11.41, passim. H. Gr. Nord 75128/3a.
[30] OKH, GenStdH, Op. Abt. (Ia), Nr. 1693/41, Weisung fuer die Aufgaben des Ostheeres im Winter 1941/42, 8.12.41 and Der Fuehrer und Oberste Befehlshaber der Wehrmacht, OKW, WFSt, Abt. L. (I Op.), Nr. 442090/41, Weisung Nr. 39, 8.12.41. OKW/1938. H. Gr. Nord, Kriegstagebuch, 1.–31.12.41, 1–7 Dec 41. H. Gr. Nord 75128/4a.

hind the Volkhov, where Hitler ordered the line held "to the last man." [31]

On the day before the Army Group North gave up Tikhvin the Army of Karelia completed its operations in Eastern Karelia. The weather had also acted as a brake on Finnish operations. In October, advancing from the south and west, the Army of Karelia pushed the Russians back toward Medvezh'yegorsk. On 19 October the II Corps cleared the line of the Suna River. On 3 November the attack force coming from the south took Kondoponga, and two days later the two forces met north of Lizhm Lake. Then the onslaught of winter slowed the advance, and at mid-November it appeared that the troops' offensive strength was exhausted. In a last, almost desperate, push the Finns took Medvezh'yegorsk on 5 December, Povenets the following day, and on the 8th cleaned out a large *motti* south of Medvezh'yegorsk. They then established a defensive line on the Maaselkä, the drainage divide between the White Sea and the Gulf of Finland running across the narrows between the northern tip of Lake Onega and Seg Lake. With that, active operations ceased all along the Finnish front, and Mannerheim began releasing the older age groups in the Army.[32]

Cobelligerents and Brothers-in-Arms

The German-Russian conflict was a fight to the death between Hitler and Stalin, two of the outstanding international villains of all time. Geography and the proved rapacity of the Soviet Government forced Finland to regard one of them as her savior at exactly the time that her traditional friends in the West, Great Britain and the United States, were trying to keep the other on his feet. The situation might have been less painful had Finland not accumulated a great fund of sympathy in the West during the Winter War and had it not been able to show a large amount of justice in its cause against the Soviet Union. To save what they could of their credit with the democracies, to avoid falling completely under the influence of Germany, and yet to preserve their existence as a nation, the Finns were forced to equivocate, claiming for themselves an exceptional status as cobelligerents and speaking of their German friends as brothers-in-arms rather than allies. These semantic distinctions, which on the surface only created a somewhat ludicrous picture of tiny Finland fighting the Soviet Union and professing itself mildly surprised to find the Germans there too, in fact were evidence of forces which were to influence Finland's entire conduct of war. It must be said to the credit of the Germans that it was mainly their unusual and, for themselves, unprofitable re-

[31] H. Gr. Nord, Kriegstagebuch, 1.–31.41, 7–24 Dec 41. H. Gr. Nord 75128/4a. Der Fuehrer und Oberste Befehlshaber der Wehrmacht, WFSt, Abt. L (I Op.), Nr. 442182/41, 16.12.41. OKW/1938.

[32] On 3 December the Russians had evacuated Hanko. Mannerheim, op. cit., pp. 461, 466. Erfurth, op. cit., pp. 38–40.

straint which allowed the Finns to play an independent game to the extent that they did.

The true expectations with which the Finns entered the war are difficult to determine. As a small nation caught in the center of a great struggle they could not afford the luxury of consistency any more than could the Great Powers. Their announced war aims were limited to recovery of the lost territories; that they expected to take a good deal more is certain. Bellicose utterances by Mannerheim and others, particularly during the early months of the war, are not hard to find.[33] The most extreme statement of Finnish war aims was that which Ryti gave to Hitler's personal envoy Schnurre in October 1941: Finland wanted the entire Kola Peninsula and all of Soviet Karelia with a border on the White Sea to the Gulf of Onega, thence southward to the southern tip of Lake Onega, along the Svir River, the south shore of Lake Ladoga, and along the Neva River to its mouth. Ryti agreed with the Germans that Leningrad would have to disappear as a center of population and industry. He thought a small part of the city might be preserved as something in the nature of a German trading post.[34] Later he also told the German Minister that Finland did not want to have a common border with Russia in the future and asked that Germany annex all the territory from the Arkhangel'sk region south.[35]

Still, even in the heady, victorious months of 1941, a realistic appraisal of its own strength and a deep-seated popular conviction that Finland should not allow itself to be drawn into a war against the democracies to some extent restrained Finnish ambitions.[36] To these were added recurring qualms occasioned by distaste for the Nazi-German Government and lingering suspicions concerning its ultimate intentions with regard to Finland. The element of indecision in Finnish policy was heightened by knowledge of the fact that neither Great Britain nor

---

[33] On 3 June 1941 Heinrichs gave the German military representatives a *pro memoria* which opened as follows:

"The Commander in Chief wishes to take this opportunity to say that the interest called forth by these discussions is in no way purely operational or military-technical in nature.

"The idea [destruction of the Soviet Union] which forms the basis of the propositions communicated to him by the highest echelons of the German leadership must arouse joy in the Finnish soldier's heart and is regarded here as a historic sign of a great future." Heinrichs added orally that "for the first and probably the last time in Finland's thousand-year history the great moment has come in which the Finnish people can free itself for all time from the pressure of its hereditary enemy." *A.O.K. Norwegen der Chef des Generalstabes, Nr. 140/41, Ergebnis der deutsch-finnischen Besprechungen in Helsinki, 3.–5.6.41, in "Silberfuchs" Bd. II, 4.5.41–18.6.41.* AOK 20 20844/5. *Fremde Heere Ost, Chef, Nr. 74/41, Protokoll ueber die Besprechungen in Finnland vom 3.–6. Juni 1941, 10.6.41, in Chefsachen Fremde Heere Ost, Bd. I.* H 3/1. See also Langer and Gleason, *The Undeclared War,* p. 827.

[34] Schnurre, *Aufzeichnung,* 31.10.41. Serial 260. U.S. Department of State, German Foreign Ministry Records.

[35] Bluecher, Tel. to Foreign Office, 11.9.41. Serial 260. U.S. Department of State, German Foreign Ministry Records.

[36] Bluecher, Tel. to Foreign Ministry, Nr. 659, 22.7.41. Serial 260. U.S. Department of State, German Foreign Ministry Records.

the United States was entirely comfortable in its new-found friendship with Stalin.

The first clear-cut crisis in relations with the West came in July 1941 after Ribbentrop, the German Foreign Minister, on the 9th demanded that Finland break diplomatic relations with Great Britain.[37] The Germans contended that the 53-man British mission in Helsinki was acting as an intelligence center for the Soviet Union. Although the British no doubt intended to use their Helsinki Ministry to the benefit of the Russians as far as they could, Ribbentrop's demand can probably be traced more directly to Hitler's determination to prevent even token demonstrations of British-Soviet collaboration. Its immediate motivation is to be found in Stalin's reference to British and American aid in his 3 July speech and in the negotiations which were to produce the British-Soviet Agreement of 12 July 1941.[38]

The Finns, who were counting on a short war and obviously hoped to avoid crucial diplomatic developments, tried to delay their decision but were forced by repeated German urgings to inform the German Minister on 22 July that the Cabinet had empowered the Foreign Minister "to carry the matter with England as far as a breach of diplomatic relations."[39] The Finnish Government still wanted the decisive move to come from the British side, but the British betrayed no such inclination; consequently, on 28 July Finland declared its intention to close its legation in London "until further notice" and asked what the British intended to do. The question was decided three days later when British carrier aircraft bombed Pechenga: Finland promptly withdrew its mission, and the British were forced to do the same.[40]

The United States State Department, in the meantime, had adopted a waiting attitude, to some extent based on the hope that Finland, as its official statements seemed to indicate, would not carry the war beyond its old borders. In mid-August the Soviet Union, anxious to reduce the forces committed against Finland, authorized the State Department to inform Finland of its willingness to make peace, with territorial concessions. On 18 August Under Secretary of State Sumner Welles communicated the offer to the Finnish Minister in Washington in fairly explicit terms, but Helsinki made no reply.[41]

Enraged at his peace offer's having been ignored, Stalin began demanding that Britain either stop the Finns or declare war. Under this pressure the British Government on 22 September warned Finland

---

[37] Ribbentrop, Tel. to German Ministry, Helsinki, No. 630, 9.7.41. Serial 260. U.S. Department of State, German Foreign Ministry Records.
[38] Langer and Gleason, *The Undeclared War*, pp. 535ff. Bluecher, *op. cit.*, p. 236.
[39] Bluecher, Tel. to Foreign Ministry, No. 659, 22.7.41. Serial 260. U.S. Department of State, German Foreign Ministry Records.
[40] Langer and Gleason, *The Undeclared War*, 551. Mannerheim, *op. cit.*, p. 451.
[41] Langer and Gleason, *The Undeclared War*, pp. 550 and 826ff. *Documents on American Foreign Relations* (Boston: World Peace Foundation, 1942), Vol. IV, p. 642.

through the Norwegian Legation in Helsinki against invading purely Russian territory.[42] On 3 October Secretary of State Cordell Hull, to reinforce the British warning, told the Finnish Minister that although the United States was glad to see Finland recover her lost territory the important question was whether Finland would be content to stop there.[43]

As the German advance on Moscow progressed during October, the United States State Department became more and more worried about the Murmansk supply route and at the end of the month decided to take a forceful step. The note of 27 October has already been cited above in its relation to Falkenhorst's last attempt to take Loukhi. The intention had been to issue a pointed warning; but, through a mistake in transmission, an earlier, stronger version of the note, virtually demanding that Finland end hostilities and pull back to the 1939 border, was sent. While the Finnish Government delayed its reply, the State Department in early November published its records of the August peace offer. In a long note on 11 November the Finnish Government recapitulated its grievances against the Soviet Union, characterized the peace offer as neither "an offer of mediation, or even . . . a recommendation, on the part of the United States, but . . . merely a piece of information," and refused to enter into "any engagements that would . . . imperil . . . her national security by artificial suspension or annulment of fully justified military operations." [44]

The American moves begun by the 27 October note, aside from their possible effect on the last German attempt to cut the Murmansk Railroad, did succeed in muddying the water of German-Finnish relations somewhat. The Finns had been slow in informing their German friends of the August peace move and had apparently never given them a very complete version. In any case, publication of the record automatically brought the solidity of the German-Finnish cooperation into question. Germany immediately began urging Finland to become a signatory of the Anti-Comintern Pact which was to be renewed at the end of November.

While adherence to the Anti-Comintern Pact, which as the Finns frequently pointed out later had been in force throughout the period of the German-Soviet alliance, would not bring a real change in Finland's relationship to Germany, both the Finns and Germans were aware that it could significantly influence the nation's already delicate relations with the Western Powers; but Finland was in no position to refuse. Aside from the matter of the peace move, relations with Germany had soured slightly over Finnish resistance to German attempts at getting control

---

[42] In another of the peculiarities of the German-Finnish relationship Finland·maintained diplomatic relations with the exiled government of Norway and, in fact, more than once let its displeasure with the German conduct of affairs in occupied Norway be known.

[43] *Documents on American Foreign Relations*, Vol. IV, p. 643.

[44] *Documents on American Foreign Relations*, Vol. IV, pp. 642–51. Langer and Gleason, *The Undeclared War*, pp. 830–33.

of the Pechenga nickel concession for I. G. Farben.[45]   Moreover, Finland had been forced at the end of October to ask Germany for 175,000 tons of grain to tide its population over the winter and for 100 to 150 locomotives and 4,000 to 8,000 railroad cars to keep its transportation system operating.   The Finnish railroads, which had a low hauling capacity to start with, had deteriorated rapidly after the outbreak of war and by November 1941 were on the verge of a complete breakdown. Since the transportation crisis also endangered the Army of Norway, the request, while it demonstrated Finland's dependence on Germany, was not one the Germans could use as a bargaining point.   On 21 November Keitel promised to ship 55 locomotives and 900 cars immediately. He could not promise more until overland contact had been established between the German and Finnish armies.[46]

Unable to avoid signing the Anti-Comintern Pact, the Finns naturally desired to have the event go off as unobtrusively as possible; but the Germans would be satisfied with nothing less than having Foreign Minister Witting come to Berlin in person.   The Finns' worst fears were realized the moment Witting stepped off his plane at Tempelhof Airport almost literally into the arms of a fully uniformed Ribbentrop backed up by a battalion of assorted dignitaries.   On the following day (25 November), after Witting signed the pact in company with the Italian Foreign Minister and the Japanese Ambassador, Ribbentrop gave him the full guest-of-honor treatment.   That evening his colleagues in Helsinki were on the phone trying to get him home posthaste, but his departure was delayed another two days as he waited for an audience with Hitler.   On the 27th, after one of Hitler's hour-long, rambling harangues, he emplaned for Helsinki.   Hitler had promised him the Kola Peninsula and the desired border.   He had assured him that Germany would provide the grain requested and had again raised the question of Finland's mineral resources, particularly nickel, in the exploitation of which, he said, Germany wanted to participate.[47]   On 19 December Germany agreed to furnish 75,000 tons of grain before the end of February 1942 and a total of 260,000 tons before the next harvest.[48]

---

[45] Hitler's representative, Schnurre, had proposed that the control of Nikkeli O. Y. be 80 percent German and 20 percent Finnish.   The Finns, who in view of the original Canadian-British concession and the Russian claims wanted to keep the question of ownership open until after the war, had taken the course of indirect resistance, complaining to Falkenhorst and emphasizing the necessity of not endangering the wartime production of ore.   *V.O., Wi Rue Amt, A.O.K. Norwegen, Bef. St. Finnland, an OKW, Wi Rue Amt, Stab Ia, 6.11.41* and *V.O., WI Rue Amt, A.O.K. Norwegen, Bef. St. Finnland, an OKW Wi Rue Amt, Ia, 9.11.41,* in *A.O.K. Norwegen, Anlagen zum K.T.B., Band II.*   AOK 20 19070/3.

[46] *AOK Norwegen, Bef. St. Finnland, Nr. 101/41, an OKW, WFSt, Abt. L, 4.11.41,* in *AOK Norwegen, Anlagen zum K.T.B., Band II.*   AOK 20 19070/2. *Der Chef des Oberkommandos der Wehrmacht, Nr. 441979/41, WFSt, Abt. L, (I Op.), an Se. Exzellenz Generalfeldmarschall Freiherr von Mannerheim, 21.11.41,* in *OKH, GenStdH, Op. Abt. I/N, Band II, Finnland.*   H 22/227.

[47] Bluecher, *op. cit.,* pp. 260–62.

[48] *Dir. Ha. Pol., Aufzeichnung,* No. 226, 19.12.41.   Serial 1260.   U.S. Department of State.   German Foreign Ministry Records.

Arriving in Helsinki on 28 November, Witting found himself confronted with a British ultimatum. Through the United States Legation the British Government informed the Finns that it would be obliged to declare war, "unless by December 5 the Finnish Government cease military operations and withdraw from all active participation in hostilities." [49] The British note was in one sense less stringent than that of 22 September: it did not insist on Finland's giving up territory already taken. A day later in a private letter to Mannerheim, Churchill suggested that it would be sufficient if Finland quietly ceased operations and held what she had.[50] The British move was not prompted by Witting's recent activity in Berlin but, rather, was a direct—and somewhat embarassed—response to demands from Stalin which could no longer be sidestepped. The Finnish reply was not sent until after Great Britain had declared war on 6 December. It only expressed surprise that the British could find anything in Finland's attitude which would give them cause to declare war.[51] For the Finnish people the blow was softened by an announcement on the same day that their troops had taken Medvezh'-yegorsk and that the Parliament had formally annexed the reconquered territories.[52]

A Thrust to Belomorsk

On 25 September, at the same time that he refused to carry farther the Finnish offensives on the Svir and the Isthmus of Karelia, Mannerheim laid before the OKW a proposal for a winter offensive directed against Belomorsk.[53] He thought that after Leningrad had fallen he would be able to spare eight or nine brigades for such an operation. He also suggested that the German and Finnish troops of the III Corps and the XXXVI Corps be exchanged and the advances toward Kandalaksha and Loukhi then continued.[54]

Hitler's headquarters took up Mannerheim's proposal immediately. It was the more welcome in that it seemed to offer a fresh start for the nearly moribund operation against the Murmansk Railroad. In the Fuehrer Directive No. 37, closing down the Army of Norway summer offensive, Hitler simultaneously ordered Falkenhorst to prepare a winter drive to Kandalaksha in conjunction with a Finnish advance to Belomorsk and, possibly, to Loukhi. Keitel on 13 October informed Mannerheim that the directive had been issued. The attacks on Belomorsk and

---

[49] *Documents on American Foreign Relations,* Vol. IV, p. 640.
[50] Mannerheim, *op. cit.,* pp. 463ff.
[51] *Documents on American Foreign Policy,* Vol. IV, pp. 641ff.
[52] Mannerheim, *op. cit.,* p. 465.
[53] That the Belomorsk–Obozerskaya bypass, carrying Murmansk Railroad traffic eastward to Moscow, was in operation did not become known to the Germans and Finns until after the start of operations in Russia. Its existence greatly reduced the strategic importance of the Finns' cutting the Belomorsk–Leningrad section of the line.
[54] *Verbindungsstab Nord, Ia, Nr. 84/41, Oberbefehlshaber der finnischen Wehrmacht an Herrn Generalfeldmarschall Keitel, 25.9.41,* in *A.O.K. Norwegen, Ia, Chefsachen, 2.6.–18.11.41.* AOK 20 20844/2.

Loukhi would be the responsibility of the Finnish command, and Falkenhorst would direct the advance to Kandalaksha.[55]

Army of Norway headquarters received the idea of a winter offensive without enthusiasm. The army reported that operations against Kandalaksha in winter using the ordinary infantry divisions of the XXXVI Corps, which had almost no trained skiers, were hardly possible. In fact, if the line on the Verman River were to be held, the XXXVI Corps would have to keep at least two regiments of the Finnish 6th Division as mobile protection for its flanks.[56] Falkenhorst insisted that for a winter operation against Kandalaksha he would need at least two mountain divisions and one or two Finnish brigades since he did not believe he could employ the existing divisions of the XXXVI Corps as anything more than reserves. To meet Falkenhorst's demands, the OKW offered him the 5th and 7th Mountain Divisions—the former was in Crete and the latter was yet to be formed in Germany out of a standard infantry division—and transmitted a request to Mannerheim for two Finnish brigades. The XXXVI Corps was immediately redesignated the XXXVI Mountain Corps. Its divisions were to be retrained in mountain and winter warfare on the spot.[57]

In mid-November the Army of Norway learned that because of the Finnish railroad situation not more than one of the new mountain divisions could be brought in, and that not before the end of March. Since 1 March was regarded as the latest starting date if the spring thaw were to be avoided, Falkenhorst reported, "It can be said with certainty that the planned operation against Kandalaksha cannot be executed during the winter." [58] The OKW, no longer placing much confidence in Falkenhorst, ordered Dietl as the future commanding general to make a personal reconnaissance and report directly to Fuehrer Headquarters. On 24 November Dietl telegraphed ahead to Jodl that he concurred with the Army of Norway in regarding the planned attack as impossible to execute because of the transportation and supply problems. In any case, as an experienced officer of mountain troops, he had serious doubts about using troops that were not completely trained and acclimated for winter warfare in the Arctic.[59] As an alternative the Army of Norway proposed a combined German-Finnish advance to Belomorsk and thence

[55] *Der Fuehrer und Oberste Befehlshaber der Wehrmacht, OKW, WFSt, Abt. L (I Op.), Nr. 441696/41, Weisung Nr. 37, 10.10, 41,* in *A.O.K. Norwegen, Anlagen zum K.T.B., Band II.* AOK 20 19070/3. *Der Chef des Oberkommandos der Wehrmacht, WFSt, Abt. L, Nr. 441707/41, 13.10.41,* in *A.O.K. Norwegen, Ia. Chefsachen, 2.6.–18.11.41.* AOK 20 20844/2.
[56] *A.O.K. Norwegen, Bef. St. Finnland, Ia, Nr. 86/41, an OKW, WFSt, Abt. L, 13.10.41,* in *A.O.K. Norwegen, Anlagen zum K.T.B. Band II.* AOK 20 19070/3.
[57] *OKW, WFSt, Abt. L (I Op.), Nr. 441861/41, Durchfuehrungsbestimmungen Nr. 1 zur Weisung Nr. 37, 7.11.41,* in *A.O.K. Norwegen, Anlagen zum K.T.B., Band II.* AOK 20 19070/3.
[58] *A.O.K., Norwegen, Bef. St. Finnland, Ia, Nr. 2382/41, an OKW, WFSt, Abt. L, 21.11.41,* in *A.O.K. Norwegen, Anlagen zum K.T.B., Band II.* AOK 20 19070/3.
[59] Tel. Dietl to Jodl [no heading or title], 24.11.41, in *A.O.K. Norwegen, Anlagen zum K.T.B., Band II.* AOK 20 19070/3.

eastward along the railroad to Obozerskaya, thereby cutting off both Murmansk and Arkhangel'sk.[60]

In the meantime, the OKW was waiting for Mannerheim's answer to a Keitel letter of 21 November outlining the German plans. Writing on 4 December, after an illness had forced him to put off his reply, Mannerheim characterized the early cutting of the Murmansk Railroad as a matter of greatest importance. But his proposal of September, he pointed out, had been predicated on the assumption that Leningrad would fall and contact would be established on the Svir in a matter of a few weeks. Since then more than two months had passed; the condition of his troops had deteriorated, and the war was creating internal difficulties for Finland. The attack on Kandalaksha, he believed, would have to begin on 1 March at the latest. "If the situation in any way permitted," Finnish troops would begin an advance toward Belomorsk at the same time.[61] Erfurth interpreted the Mannerheim letter as, at least in part, an attempt to speed up the German efforts at achieving a junction on the Isthmus of Karelia and the Svir. In a conversation he had with the Marshal at the end of November the latter had said that the Murmansk Railroad would have to be taken during the winter—and the sooner the better. Erfurth believed the Finns were still genuinely anxious to get the railroad into their and German hands in the hope that it would then disappear as a political problem between them and the Western Powers.[62]

On 14 December, following a staff conference at Finnish Headquarters, Mannerheim and Falkenhorst met at Rovaniemi. Because of the railroad situation, which he described as catastrophic, and other difficulties, Mannerheim took a dim view of the prospects of a Kandalaksha operation—so dim, according to Falkenhorst, that he was unwilling to risk Finnish troops in the operation. Nevertheless, Mannerheim stated, the declarations of war by Great Britain and the United States (the latter against Germany but not Finland) had given the Murmansk Railroad greatly increased significance, and it would have to be cut. He thought Belomorsk was the key point and proposed a converging attack from the south and west by combined German and Finnish forces. The OKW promptly accepted the new Mannerheim proposal and offered him the 7th Mountain Division for the operation.[63]

---

[60] *A.O.K. Norwegen, K.T.B.*, 26 Nov 41.

[61] *Oberbefehlshaber der finnischen Wehrmacht an Herrn Generalfeldmarschall Keitel, 4.12.41*, in *OKH, GenStdH, Op. Abt. I/N, Band II, Finnland.* H 22/227.

[62] It is worth noting with reference to the criticisms leveled at Falkenhorst's conduct of the summer operations that at this time both Mannerheim and Erfurth believed that attacks would have to be launched simultaneously not only at Belomorsk and Kandalaksha but across the Litsa toward Murmansk as well in order to prevent the Russians from exploiting the tactical advantages of the Murmansk Railroad. *Der Kommandeur Verbindungsstab Nord, an OKH, GenStdH, Op. Abt., 25.11.41* and *Verbindungsstab Nord, Ia, Nr. 119/41, an OKH, Op. Abt., 5.12.41*, in *OKH, GenStdH, Op. Abt. I/N, Band II, Finnland.* H 22/227.

[63] *A.O.K. Norwegen, K.T.B.*, 13, 14, 16 and 20 Dec 41. *Verbindungsstab Nord, Ia, an OKH, GenStdH, Op. Abt., 15.12.41* in *OKH, GenStdH, Op. Abt. I/N, Band II, Finnland.* H 22/227.

It was not long before Mannerheim, watching the Soviet winter offensive develop, had changed his mind. On 20 January 1942 Erfurth reported that the question of a Belomorsk operation was completely up in the air and Mannerheim would not make a positive decision unless the situation on the German front, particularly in the Leningrad area, improved. Erfurth could only recommend that all possible means of persuasion be brought to bear on the Marshal. Mannerheim's officers, he thought, were less pessimistic, but none of them had any influence.[64] In response Keitel wrote to Mannerheim, telling him that the Russians were wearing themselves out in their attacks on the German front and before spring would have no more reserves. "This," he told the Marshal, "can be expected also to help your intended operation in the direction of Sorokka [Belomorsk]." [65]

In the first week of February Dietl, by then the commanding general of the newly constituted Army of Lapland, discussed the Belomorsk operation with Mannerheim. Mannerheim avoided a direct refusal, repeatedly stating that things would be different if the Germans were to take Leningrad, but left no doubt that in the existing situation he would not stage a winter offensive. Erfurth, who reported on the conference to the OKW, concluded that, in addition to his negative assessment of the military situation, Mannerheim was influenced by the internal politics of Finland. He and Ryti had for months promised the people that the end was in sight and that only a small additional effort would be needed. An offensive against Belomorsk would far exceed what the population had been led to expect. Above all, Mannerheim could not undertake such an operation if it were possible that he might be dealt a setback.[66]

On 3 February Mannerheim answered Keitel's letter saying that, if the general situation did not take a favorable turn soon, he doubted whether he would be able to make troops available for a winter operation against Belomorsk, but he would not give up the idea.[67] Erfurth commented that by a "favorable turn" Mannerheim meant that Leningrad would have to be taken before he would undertake any further offensive operations. He needed the fall of Leningrad in order to make troops available and for the sake of morale at home; moreover, recently, as inquiries from the Finnish Chief of Staff revealed, he had become worried that the German spring offensive would be concentrated in the Ukraine and the northern sector of the Eastern Front would be left to

[64] *Verbindungsstab Nord, Ia, Nr. 13/41, nachr. OKH, Chef des GenStdH, 20.1.41,* in *OKH, GenStdH, Op. Abt. I/N, Band II, Finnland.* H 22/227.
[65] *Der Chef des Oberkommandos der Wehrmacht, Nr. 55208/42, an den Oberbefehlshaber der finnischen Wehrmacht Herrn Feldmarschall Freiherr Mannerheim, 26.1.42,* in *OKH, GenStdH, Op. Abt. I/N, Band II, Finnland.* H 22/227.
[66] *Verbindungsstab Nord, Ia, Nr. 20/42, an OKW, WFSt, Abt. L. 2.2.42,* in *OKH, GenStdH, Op. Abt. I/N, Band II, Finnland.* H 22/227.
[67] *Verbindungsstab Nord, Ia, Nr. 24/42, an OKH, GenStdH, Op. Abt., 3.2.41,* in *OKH, GenStdH, Op. Abt. I/N, Band II, Finnland.* H 22/227.

languish. As far as Mannerheim's keeping the Belomorsk operation in mind was concerned, Erfurth believed it was merely intended to give his letter a courteous tone and could not be taken as a promise either for the present or the future.[68]

---

[68] *Verbindungsstab Nord, Ia, Nr. 25/42, an OKH, Op. Abt., 9.2.42, in OKH, GenStdH, Op. Abt. I/N, Band II, Finnland.* H 22/227.

Chapter 11

The Northern Theater in 1942

Norway

Falkenhorst Returns to Norway

On 14 January 1942 the Army of Lapland formally assumed command of the German forces in Finland. Falkenhorst had been ordered to Oslo two weeks earlier. During the last weeks of 1941 Norway had suddenly moved back into the forefront of German strategic considerations. In his first order implementing Fuehrer Directive No. 37 Hitler, who always regarded Norway as the apple of his eye, had projected a sizable strengthening of the fortifications and forces there; but his decision at that time to establish separate commands in Norway and Finland stemmed more directly from disappointment with the outcome of Operation SILBERFUCHS.[1] The United States entry into the war brought what had been fairly vague apprehensions, mostly on Hitler's part, into sharp focus.

On 25 December the OKW, citing information which indicated that Great Britain and the United States were planning a major operation in the Scandinavian area, ordered an immediate reevaluation of the situation in Norway to determine whether a large-scale invasion could be beaten off. Falkenhorst's estimate was negative. He asked for 12,000 replacements to bring his divisions up to strength and approximately three additional divisions to give the defense depth.[2]

At that moment the British Navy, as it had earlier in the year, unwittingly took a hand in the German considerations. On the morning of 27 December a cruiser and destroyer force shelled and staged brief landings on Vest-Vågöy, in the Lofotens, and Målöy, at the mouth of Nord Fiord south of Trondheim.[3] While the landings appeared to be

[1] *OKW, WFSt, Abt. L. (I Op.), Nr. 441861/41, Durchfuehrungsbestimmungen Nr. 1 zur Weisung 37, 7.11.41, in A.O.K. Norwegen, Anlagen zum K.T.B., Band II.* AOK 20 19070/3.

[2] *OKW, WFSt, Abt. L. (I Op.), Nr. 003157/41, an A.O.K. Norwegen, 25.12.41, in A.O.K 20, Chefsachen allgemein, 21.9.40–1.5.42.* AOK 20 35641. *W.B. Norwegen, Ia, Nr. 5129/41, Beurteilung der militaerischen Lage in Norwegen, 25.12.41, in A.O.K. Norwegen, Anlagen zum K.T.B., Band III.* AOK 20 19070/4.

[3] *A.O.K. Norwegen, Ia. Taetigkeitsbericht des Armeeoberkommandos Norwegen in der Zeit vom 1.–31.12.41, in Taetigkeitsberichte fuer den Monat Dezember 1941.* AOK 20 19648/2.

merely disruptive in purpose, the OKW feared that they might also have been staged to feel for weak spots where the British could gain a foothold from which to interdict German shipping along the Norwegian coast. As a result, Falkenhorst had been ordered back to Norway immediately.[4]

At the end of the month Hitler told Keitel and Raeder: "If the British go about things properly they will attack northern Norway at several points. In an all-out attack by their fleet and ground troops, they will try to displace us there, take Narvik if possible, and thus exert pressure on Sweden and Finland." He wanted all the German battleships stationed in Norway and proposed having the *Scharnhorst*, the *Gneisenau*, and the heavy cruiser *Prinz Eugen*, which were bottled up at Brest, break through the English Channel for the purpose.[5] Three weeks later in a conference with Raeder he stated that recent reports had convinced him that Great Britain and the United States were bent on attacking northern Norway in order to bring about a decisive turn in the course of the war. He expected attempts in the near future to seize numerous points along the coast from Trondheim to Kirkenes and a full-scale offensive in the spring. He claimed to have positive proof that Sweden had been promised Narvik and the ore deposits at Pechenga and would therefore participate on the side of the Western Powers. Norway he described as "the zone of destiny in this war," and he demanded unconditional compliance with all of his demands concerning that area. The Navy, he insisted, would have to employ "each and every vessel in Norway." The order for "each and every vessel" at first included all of the submarines. The Naval Staff was pleased and relieved to learn, on 23 January, that Hitler had been impressed by a report on submarine accomplishments off the coast of the United States and had decided to leave the submarines there.[6]

The question of Sweden's intentions had worried the Germans since the start of the campaign against the Soviet Union. They had hoped and, to some extent, expected that Sweden would be drawn into the "crusade against Bolshevism" at least as a silent partner; but Sweden, after allowing the 163d Infantry Division to cross its territory from Norway in June 1941, had sharply restricted its assistance to the German forces. In his report to the OKW at the end of the year Falkenhorst had characterized Sweden's attitude in the event of a British-American landing in Norway as "at best uncertain." The Naval Staff, on the other hand, at the same time concluded that Swedish assistance, which took the form of food, war matériel, and credits for Finland and railroad transportation, protection of shipping, and improvement of the ore facilities at Luleå for Germany, was a "not inconsiderable accomplishment." In general, the German military authorities did not regard

[4] *OKW, WFSt, Op., Nr. 442268/41, an W.B. Norwegen, 28.12.41,* in *A.O.K. 20, Chefsachen allgemein, 21.9.41–1.5.42.* AOK 20 35641.
[5] *Fuehrer Conferences, 1941,* II, p. 94.
[6] *Fuehrer Conferences, 1942,* p. 6. *Naval War Diary,* Vol. 29, pp. 207, 217, 228.

German railway gun in Norway.

the threat from Sweden as acute except, as the Naval Staff stated it, in the event of "a big British operation which is successful." [7]

The OKW and the Armed Forces Commander, Norway (Falkenhorst), in January 1942 worked on the assumption that Norway as a key point of the European defense system could become a scene of major operations during 1942. They thought a full-scale attack during the winter was unlikely but did not rule out the possibility of local landings aimed at interdicting coastal shipping. A major offensive in the spring, they thought, had to be taken into consideration. Falkenhorst was promised 12,000 replacements, 20 "fortress" battalions (older men armed with captured weapons) with a total of 18,000 men, and the 3d Mountain Division by early spring. In addition, he was instructed to begin setting up an armored unit, later designated as the 25th Panzer Division. [8]

Still worried, in early February, Hitler dispatched Generalfeldmarschall Wilhelm List, the Armed Forces Commander Southeast (Balkans), to inspect the defenses in Finland and Norway and gave him broad authority to investigate the measures taken by the Army, Navy, Air Force, and civilian authorities. List recommended construction of additional defensive installations on the coast and in the interior,

[7] *W.B. Norwegen, Ia, Nr. 5129/41, Beurteilung der militaerischen Lage in Norwegen, 25.12.41,* in *A.O.K. Norwegen, Anlagen zum K.T.B., Band II.* AOK 20 19070/4. *Naval War Diary,* Vol. 28, p. 136 and Vol. 29, p. 228.
[8] *OKH, GenStdH, Org. Abt., Nr. 128/42, Vortragsnotiz, 11.1.42,* in *Norwegen, 8.1.42–22.2.44, Teil 1.* H 22/106, *OKW, WFSt, Op. Nr. 00226/42, Kampfanweisung fuer die Verteidigung Norwegens, Ia, Nr. 12/42, Weisung fuer die Verteidigung Norwegens, 27.1.42,* in *A.O.K 20, Chefsachen allgemein, 21.9.40–1.5.42.* AOK 20 35641.

strengthening of the coast artillery, creation of three new divisional commands to take over the garrisons at Alta, Tromsö, and Stavanger, improvement of the roads in the north, and establishment of dependable communications between local detachments of the three services.[9] The command arrangements, he believed, could be left as they were. Hitler had thought of unifying the Northern Theater under an armed forces commander and had Generalfeldmarschall Albert Kesselring in mind for the post.[10]

In March Hitler issued Fuehrer Directive No. 40 with the objective of creating responsible over-all commands in each of the European areas at least with respect to defense of the coasts. He assigned the preparation and execution of coastal defense in Norway to the Armed Forces Commander, Norway, and in northern Finland to the Commanding General, Army of Lapland. Operationally the Air Force and Navy units remained under their respective high commands, but they were ordered to "respond to the requirements of the Armed Forces Commander within the bounds of their ability." [11] In practice the order only increased Falkenhorst's authority slightly since each of the services, and the Navy in particular, insisted on its own interpretation. It also did not settle the question of relations between the Armed Forces Commander and Reichskommissar, Terboven.

Meanwhile, under the cover of the long winter nights, the Navy was transferring its heavy ships to Norway. The battleship *Tirpitz,* first to go, docked in Trondheim on 16 January. The Naval Staff had been planning the transfer since November 1941, mainly for the effect it would have of tying down British heavy naval units.[12] Japan's entry into the war and Hitler's alarm over the Norwegian defenses enhanced the advantages of the shift. The move was a success. Churchill, in January 1941, believed that if the *Tirpitz* could be removed from the scene the world naval situation would be changed and the Allies could regain naval supremacy in the Pacific.[13]

The *Tirpitz* was the German Navy's most formidable ship. With a displacement of 42,000 tons and eight 15-inch guns in its main batteries, it was a potential match for any vessel afloat. The other two German battleships, sometimes called battle cruisers, the *Scharnhorst* and the *Gneisenau,* were lighter (31,000 tons) and mounted 11-inch guns. The *Scheer* and the *Luetzow* (11,000 tons), the so-called pocket battleships, carried 11-inch guns, but actually were heavy cruisers, as were the newer 8-inch cruisers *Prinz Eugen* and *Hipper* (14,000 tons).

[9] *OKH, GenStdH, Org. Abt., Nr. 1584/42, Bericht des Generalfeldmarschall List, 5.4.41, in Norwegen, 8.1.42–22.2.44, Teil I.* H 22/106.
[10] *Halder Diary,* VII, p. 230. *Naval War Diary,* Vol. 29, p. 207.
[11] *Der Fuehrer und Oberste Befehlshaber der Wehrmacht, OKW, WFSt, Op. Nr. 001031/42, 23.3.42, in Weisungen OKW, Fuehrer, 12.2.42–23.3.44, Band 3.*
[12] *Fuehrer Conferences,* 1941, Vol. II, p. 55.
[13] Winston Churchill, *The Second World War* (Boston: Houghton Mifflin Company, 1950), Vol. IV, p. 112.

In the second week of February the *Scharnhorst*, the *Gneisenau*, and the *Prinz Eugen* broke through the Channel, reaching Germany on the 13th. Both battleships were damaged by mines, and the *Gneisenau* sustained severe damage during an air raid on Kiel later in the month. The *Prinz Eugen* with the *Scheer* proceeded to Norway, docking at Trondheim on the 23d; but the *Prinz Eugen*'s rudder was blown off by a torpedo hit on the way, and the ship had to be returned to Germany for repairs. In March and April the *Hipper* and the *Luetzow* moved to Norway. In May the Navy had 1 battleship, 3 heavy cruisers, 8 destroyers, 4 torpedo boats, and 20 submarines stationed along the Norwegian coast at Trondheim, Narvik, and Kirkenes.[14] That strong force, aside from its potential defensive value, posed a threat to the British and American arctic convoys. Nevertheless, it constituted an unprofitable diversion of strength. Churchill has said that he was glad to have the German ships out of the way in Norway at the time the U-boat war in the Atlantic was in its most dangerous phase.[15]

At the end of April the Army of Norway had five infantry divisions, two security divisions, three area garrisons under divisional commands, and the 3d Mountain Division, which arrived during the month. The replacements and 20 fortress battalions had been incorporated into the divisions, and the 25th Panzer Division was being organized.[16] The army intended to bring the total of heavy coast artillery batteries up to 152 before 1 August and to begin work on another 66 artillery batteries, 2 torpedo batteries, and 21 depth charge projectors. In June Hitler ordered his armaments minister to convert Reichsstrasse 50 into an all-weather road and to begin building a single-track railroad from Mo via Fauske and Narvik to Kirkenes.[17]

During the spring and summer the Armed Forces Command, Norway, lived in a state of recurrent alarm. Every convoy sailing from Iceland to the Russian arctic ports was regarded as a possible invasion force, and "reliable" reports of impending landings came in almost daily. Actually, the chances of a British-American operation in the north were remote. The British version of Project SLEDGEHAMMER, early in the year, envisioned large-scale raiding operations along the coast of Europe from northern Norway to the Bay of Biscay, but SLEDGEHAMMER rapidly evolved into a plan to establish a beachhead in France. As an alternative Churchill brought forward Operation JUPITER. He envisioned landings at Pechenga and Banak as a means of operating in direct con-

[14] *OKW, WFSt, Op. (M), Nr. 55598/42, Vortragsnotiz, 1.4.42* and *OKW, WFSt, Op. (M), Nr. 55717/42, Vortragsnotiz, 22.4.42. OKW/119. Naval War Diary,* Vol. 30, pp. 137, 245, 275, 286; Vol. 31, p. 211; Vol. 33, p. 332.

[15] Churchill, *op. cit.*, Vol. IV, p. 256.

[13] *AOK Norwegen, Ia, Taetigkeitsberichte* for the months January to May 1942. AOK 20 29362/1–5.

[17] *OKH, GenStdH, Op. Abt. (V), Vortragsnotiz Betr. Ausbau Norwegen, 5.4.42* and *OKW, WFSt, Qu. (III), Nr. 002050/42, 18.6.42, in Norwegen, 8.1.42–22.2.44, Teil I.* H 22/106.

junction with the Russians and of removing from the scene the bases which were threatening the arctic convoys, but his plan aroused no enthusiasm either among his own military advisers or in the United States. His intention was to land a division at Pechenga and take the airfield at Banak near the head of Porsanger Fiord with one brigade. The operation would not have been as easy as Churchill seems to have thought. At Banak the Allied troops would have encountered units in division strength. Within bombing distance of Banak and Pechenga the Germans had four airfields, and at Pechenga they had taken strong defensive measures which will be described in more detail later in this chapter.[18]

In the early fall, when intelligence reports indicated an Allied operation against Norway was unlikely before mid-winter, German anxiety subsided slightly. The 3d Mountain Division was transferred to the Army Group North, and the OKW planned to exchange the troops of three Norway divisions for those of three burned-out divisions from the Eastern Front, reducing the divisions to two regiments each in the process.[19] The Navy strengthened its force slightly by sending the light cruiser *Koeln* north and in November dispatched the light cruiser *Nuernberg* to replace the *Scheer,* which returned to Germany. Tension began building up again almost immediately. In October the Army of Norway warned that further enemy landings (like the Dieppe raid of August 1942) were to be considered an absolute certainty. A landing in Norway was described as most dangerous because it could lead to a reversal of policy on the part of Sweden and because, even if limited to the offshore islands, it could succeed in cutting the supply line to northern Norway and Finland.[20]

As 1942 drew to a close, fear of an Allied landing in Norway and its possible effect on the attitude of Sweden grew. On 16 November, commenting on reports that the Swedish Government was strongly impressed by the recent events in North Africa, Hitler declared that for the coming spring he regarded "unqualified security in the Northern Area" as more important than a far-reaching offensive in Russia. To strengthen the Norwegian defenses he stopped all exchanges of troops with the Eastern Front and ordered a tank battalion from Finland and an engineer battalion from the Army Group North transferred to the Army of Norway immediately. He also earmarked the 5th Mountain

---

[18] Churchill, *op. cit.,* Vol. IV, pp. 256, 323ff, 350, 447ff, 448. Maurice Matloff and Edwin M. Snell, *Strategic Planning for Coalition Warfare 1941–1942* (Washington, 1953), pp. 100, 189, 235, 244.

[19] *A.O.K. Norwegen, Ia, Taetigkeitsbericht des Armeeoberkommandos Norwegen in der Zeit vom 1–30.9.42,* in *Taetigkeitsberichte fuer den Monat September 1942.* A.O.K. 20 29362/9.

[20] *A.O.K. Norwegen, Ia, Nr. 45/42, Ausbau der Kanal–und Atlantikkueste, 10.10.42,* in *A.O.K. Norwegen, Chefsachen zum K.T.B., 5.5.42–4.9.42.* AOK 20 45273.

Division for Norway as soon as the Army Group North could spare it and promised one of the Air Force field divisions then being formed.[21]

In December, through Finnish Army Headquarters, the Army of Norway received information concerning an alleged Allied plan to stage a landing on the narrow "neck" of Norway, somewhere between Trondheim and Narvik, for the purpose of splitting the German forces in Scandinavia. The Allies also expected, it was said, that the Germans, fighting with their backs against the Swedish border, would demand permission to cross Swedish territory which the Swedes were almost certain to refuse. If the Germans resorted to force, Sweden would join the Allies and a second front would be created in Scandinavia. After analyzing the information the Army of Norway concluded that the most likely place for a landing would be in the Bodö area and the most likely time in March or April 1943. At the end of the year Falkenhorst retrospectively described the rumors of an invasion in 1942 as "mere attempts to deceive and mislead." "On the other hand," he concluded, "the report of a new operation planned for 1943 appears reliable." [22]

The Civil Administration

Although popular rejection of the German rule in Norway was quick in coming and relentless, optimists among the German observers had predicted before the start of the Russian campaign that as operations against the Soviet Union progressed and clearly demonstrated the invincibility of German arms, a favorable turn in Norwegian opinion was to be expected. Those predictions had been promptly disproved. In September 1941 the Army of Norway reported that 90 percent of the population was convinced the British would win ultimately despite the German victories in the east. At the end of the year, the Army of Norway reported that the mass of the population was "in sharp opposition to Germany." [23]

The year 1942 brought to an end the last German hopes of achieving a *modus vivendi* with the Norwegian people. It was Reichskommissar Terboven who placed the stamp of finality on the failure of German policy. He had come to Norway in 1940 determined to rule, permanently and alone. His first step had been to eliminate competition and undercut Quisling by easing the representatives of Rosenberg's ministry out of the country. In September 1940, disposing of the fiction of an independent government, he abolished all the Norwegian political par-

[21] Helmut Greiner, *Aufzeichnungen ueber die Lagevortraege und Besprechungen im Fuehrer Hauptquartier vom 12 August 1942 bis 17 Maerz 1943*, p. 67. MS # C–065a. OCMH. *OKW, WFSt, Op. Nr. 004354/42, an W.B. Norwegen, 17.11.42*, in *Norwegen, 8.1.42–22.2.44, Teil I*. H 22/106.

[22] *A.O.K. Norwegen, Ia, Taetigkeitsbericht des Armeeoberkommandos Norwegen in der Zeit vom 1–31.12.42* and *W.B. Norwegen, Ic/Ia, Nr. 5600/42, Operationen gegen Norwegen, 29.12.42*, in *Taetigkeitsberichte fuer den Monat Dezember 1942*, AOK 20 29362/13.

[23] *AOK Norwegen, Ia, Taetigkeitsberichte* for the months of June, September, October, and November 1941. AOK 20 13386/1 and 4; 18856/1 and 19648/1.

ties except Quisling's National Union Party. He apparently promised Quisling, somewhat vaguely, that he would be permitted to form a government as soon as his party developed some popular support. Since the party did not gain strength and Terboven demonstrated at every turn that he had no intention of relinquishing any of his power, Quisling was rapidly reduced to the futile pursuit of showering Hitler and Rosenberg with carping letters. In the fall of 1940 Terboven created a chairmanless and virtually powerless committee of 13 State Councilors, 10 of them Quisling men. A year later when he renamed the councilors ministers, the Army of Norway reported that the population was not impressed.[24] Because Quisling retained some influence with Hitler and Rosenberg, it was not possible to shunt him aside entirely. On 1 February 1942 Terboven reinstated him as Minister President but kept in his own hands the supreme executive power and required that all laws and ordinances have the prior approval of the Reichskommissar.[25] A feeble entity from the start, the second Quisling government eight months later lost its last political asset, a vague and already hollow claim that it could function as a true Norwegian Government. On the night of 5 October 1942, after an act of sabotage had been discovered in an important industrial installation, Terboven without informing Quisling declared a state of emergency in the Trondheim area. On his own authority he had 10 prominent men arrested and shot the following day as an expiatory measure and another 24 men executed within the next few days as indirect accomplices in the crime. That highhanded act of terror branded Quisling forever as a spineless puppet and killed all prospects of effective collaboration between the Norwegian and German authorities.[26]

By 1942 repression was firmly established as the principal instrument of German policy in Norway. How little success it had was demonstrated during the year when the Norwegians began to supplement their well-organized passive resistance with sabotage and other active measures. Terboven, who bore the responsibility for maintaining order within the country, knew only one answer—more repression. In that respect, he did not reach his high point until February 1945 when he proposed to arrest and have shot numbers of influential businessmen as "intellectual instigators and accomplices" of the resistance. The measure, fortunately, was never approved.

Relations between Terboven and Falkenhorst were marked by wariness tinged with mutual suspicion. As Armed Forces Commander in an occupied country which might any day become the scene of active hostilities Falkenhorst could not help but regard the presence of an inde-

---

[24] *AOK Norwegen, Ia, Taetigkeitsbericht* for the month of October 1941. AOK 20 18856/1.
[25] International Military Tribunal, Vol. VI, p. 515.
[26] General der Infanterie a.D Erich Buschenhagen, Comments on Part II of *The German Northern Theater of Operations, 1940–1945,* July 1957.

pendent civilian administrator, who claimed equal if not superior rank, as a nuisance and potential danger. Terboven, on the other hand, was torn between the ambition to establish himself as clearly superior to the military commander and the nagging fear that in a crisis he might himself be shouldered aside. To Falkenhorst and his staff the poor state of German relations with the Norwegian people had been a source of irritation ever since April 1940. For purely practical military reasons they had wanted from the first to avoid stirring up any kind of resistance. The appointment of Terboven, an advocate of severity, had, in a sense, been a repudiation of their policy, and subsequently they had kept track of his failures with a certain perverse relish.

While Falkenhorst, in the tradition of the German Army, diligently kept to his own sphere of responsibility, the Navy, from time to time, challenged Terboven's position directly. Both Raeder and the Commanding Admiral, Norway, Generaladmiral Hermann Boehm, favored supporting Quisling and the National Union Party with a view toward completing a peace treaty through them which would leave Norway nominally neutral and independent but fully committed to cooperation with Germany. Raeder urged Hitler to appoint Boehm Armed Forces Commander, Norway, or name him to replace Terboven so that the policy envisioned by the Navy might be put into effect. In October 1942 Hitler decided against the Navy and ordered that for the duration of the war no negotiations were to be conducted concerning either an interim or final conclusion of peace between Germany and Norway.[27]

Operations in Finland

With the question of its future operations completely undecided, the main task of the Army of Lapland in the winter of 1941–42 was to regroup and return its attached Finnish units to Mannerheim's command. Since the Marshal had refused to assume responsibility for the Finnish III Corps sector, two additional German divisions, the 5th and 7th Mountain Divisions, were to be brought in. In the far north, the Mountain Corps Norway, under Generalleutnant Ferdinand Schoerner, formerly Commanding General, 6th Mountain Division, had one division, the 6th Mountain, in the Litsa line and the 2d Mountain Division plus the 193d Infantry Regiment in reserve near Pechenga while the line at the neck of the Rybatchiy Peninsula was held by the 288th Infantry Regiment plus one battalion of the 2d Mountain Division. Schoerner was a particularly energetic and determined officer. He gained a reputation for displaying those qualities best in adverse situations, with the result that in later commands on the Eastern Front he rose rapidly, being promoted to field marshal in the last month of the war. His ruthless generalship, especially in the later stages of the war, earned him the enmity of his own troops, and he became the most un-

---

[27] *Ibid.*

Winter position on the Verman line.

popular general in the German Army. During the first winter in Lapland, he demonstrated his disdain for adversity by admonishing his troops to live by the slogan "The Arctic Does Not Exist" (*Arktis ist nicht*).

On the Verman River the XXXVI Corps, renamed the XXXVI Mountain Corps, under General der Infanterie Karl F. Weisenberger, who had replaced General Feige in November 1941, held its front with the 169th Infantry Division, the 324th Infantry Regiment (163d Division), and the 139th Mountain Regiment (detached from the 3d Mountain Division). The Finnish 6th Division was pulled out of the front and on 15 February left the Army of Lapland zone. The Finnish III Corps had SS-Division "Nord" and Finnish Division J east of Kesten'ga and the Finnish 3d Division at Ukhta. The former Group J had been raised to divisional strength in the fall of 1941 by the addition of the 14th Regiment and a regiment of the Finnish 6th Division. SS-"Nord," reduced to a strength of three infantry battalions, was reinforced by two motorized machine gun battalions. The 9th SS-Regiment, which had been pulled out in December for return to Germany, reached Reval just in time to be thrown into the Army Group North front during the Soviet winter offensive. In January 1942 the Army of Lapland was promised five fortress battalions for defense of the Kirkenes–Pechenga area, and in mid-January the first elements of the 7th Mountain Division debarked at Hanko. At the end of the month ice closed the Finnish ports, stopping all further transport operations until spring.[28]

---

[28] *A.O.K. Lappland, Ia, Org., Nr. 301/42, Kriegsgliederung, 30.1.42,* in *Anlagenband I zum K.T.B. A.O.K. Lappland.* AOK 20 19692/2. *A.O.K. Lappland, Ia, K.T.B. 1,* 14, 20, 22, and 31 Jan; 15 Feb 42. AOK 20 19692/1.

Mannerheim's reorganization of the Finnish Army was to be less thoroughgoing than he had planned. In January 1942 the Army of Karelia headquarters was disbanded, and Heinrichs returned to his post as Army Chief of Staff. The Finnish line was divided into three "groups" or "fronts": the Maaselkä Front, the Aunus Front (Isthmus of Olonets—in Finnish "Aunus"), and the Isthmus Front (Isthmus of Karelia). During the winter more than 100,000 older men were released from the Army, but the planned conversion of divisions into brigades proceeded slowly and was finally abandoned in May after two divisions had been converted.[29]

The front in Finland remained relatively quite throughout the winter except on the Maaselkä Front where the Russians staged several probing attacks. In late March the Finns captured Suursaari (Gogland), an island in the Gulf of Finland south of Helsinki. Suursaari was valuable for the air defense of Finland and in blockading Leningrad. It had been occupied by a small Finnish force in December 1941 and retaken by the Russians. On 1 April the Finns also took Tytärsaari, a smaller island 12 miles to the south, which they turned over several days later to a German garrison. On 11 April the Russians began an offensive against the Svir bridgehead which they broke off without result ten days later.[30]

In late winter the Army of Lapland's prospects of resuming offensive operations in the near future declined. On 2 March one regiment of the 7th Mountain Division awaiting shipment to Finland was transferred temporarily to the Army Group North, and a week later it was followed by one regiment of the 5th Mountain Division. At the end of February the OKW informed Dietl that his main mission in the foreseeable future would be defense of the Pechenga area, particularly against sea-borne landings. Since the Russians on the Rybatchiy Peninsula posed a standing threat there, he was to prepare a plan for taking the peninsula, but the timing was left entirely open. In mid-March the Army of Lapland, on orders from Hitler, transferred three battalions to the Mountain Corps Norway to provide mobile defensive units for the Finnish arctic coast. On 2 April, visiting Dietl at Rovaniemi, Mannerheim again said that he could not advance to Belomorsk while the Russians held Leningrad. Because of the terrain, he did not believe such an operation possible before the next winter in any case.[31]

The Soviet Spring Offensive

After the fall of 1941 the Russians gradually strengthened their forces opposing the Army of Lapland. In the late fall they created the Karelian Front (army group) to direct operations from Murmansk to Lake

---

[29] Mannerheim, *op. cit.*, p. 470. Erfurth, *op. cit.* p. 74.
[30] Mannerheim, *op. cit.*, pp. 469, 473. Erfurth, *op. cit.*, p. 72.
[31] *A.O.K. Lappland, Ia, K.T.B. 1*, 21 Feb; 2, 10, and 15 Mar; 2 Apr. 42. AOK 20 19692/1.

Snow-covered road in northern Finland. Note dead saplings placed to indicate outline of road.

Onega. The Fourteenth Army took over the zone from Murmansk to Kandalaksha, and in April 1942 headquarters of the Twenty-sixth Army took command in the sector opposite the Finnish III Corps. On 1 April the Russians had two divisions, two brigades, three border regiments, and two machine gun battalions opposing the Mountain Corps Norway; two divisions, one border regiment, and two ski battalions opposite the XXXVI Mountain Corps; and two divisions, two brigades, three ski battalions, and a border regiment opposite the III Corps.[32] In April they moved in two new divisions opposite the III Corps and two ski brigades opposite the Mountain Corps Norway, at the same time bringing the ski battalions already in the XXXVI Mountain Corps and the III Corps areas up to brigade strength.

The Army of Lapland was late in detecting the Soviet preparations. On 13 April the III Corps canceled attack plans of its own when aerial reconnaissance reported 700–800 cars in the Loukhi railroad yards, but because of bad weather the army detected the actual build-up at the front only off the southern flank of the Mountain Corps Norway. Until two days after the attack began Dietl believed that the Russians would not undertake a large-scale operation with the spring thaw imminent. But the Russians apparently expected to derive two advantages from the thaw: they intended to gain their first objective before it set in strongly enough to stop operations and thereafter expected to be safe from counterattacks for several weeks; and they believed it would make

---

[32] (*Geb.*) *A.O.K. 20, Ic, Taetigkeitsbericht fuer die Zeit vom 1.4.–31.12.42, 6.3.43.* AOK 20 27252/19. Situation map 13 Apr 42 in *Taetigkeitsbericht der Abt Ic, Karel.-Front u. Feindlagenkarten vom XIX A.K.* AOK 20 27252/22.

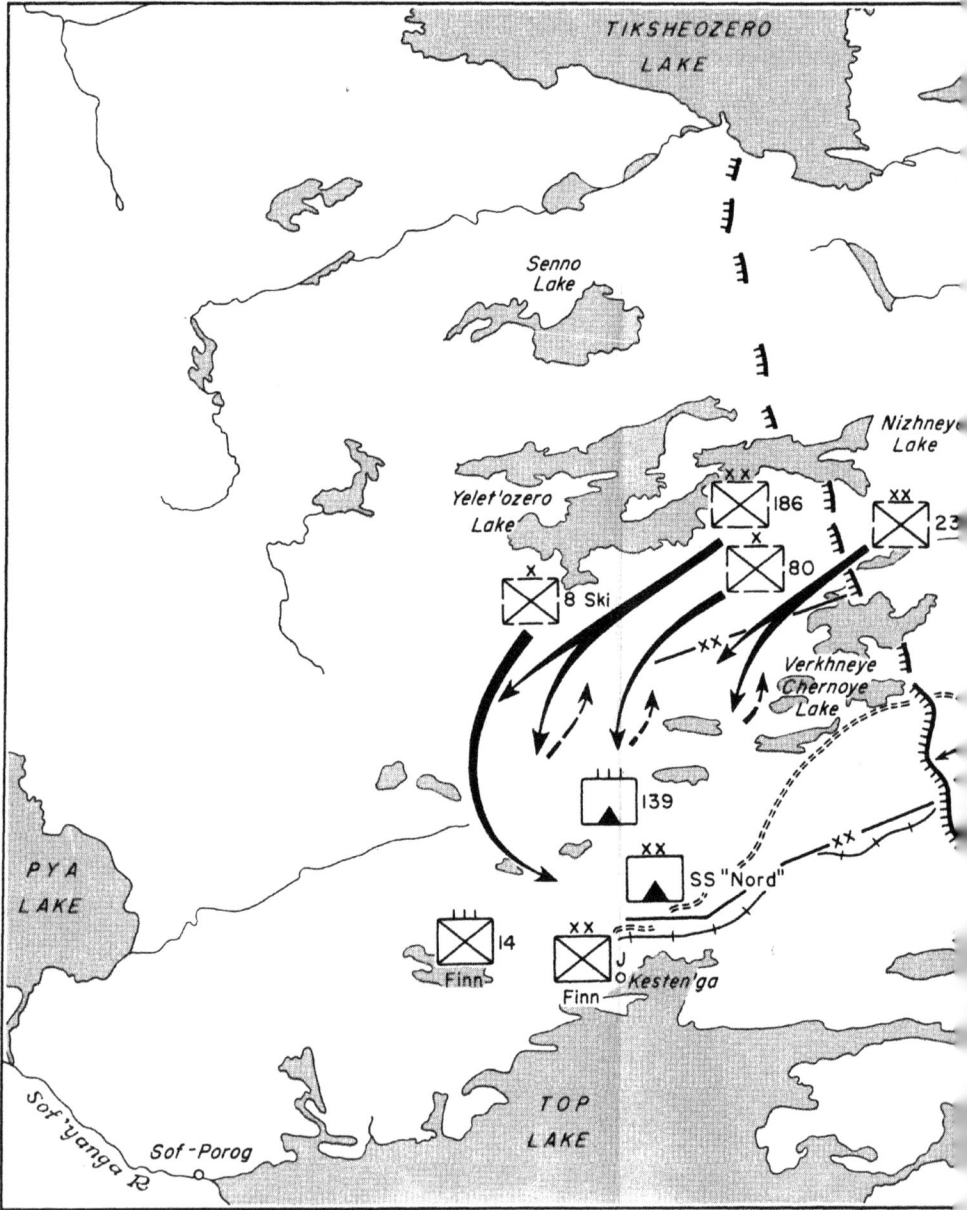

TIKSHEOZERO LAKE

Senno Lake

Nizhneye Lake

Yelet'ozero Lake

X X
186

X X
23

X
80

X
8 Ski

X X

Verkhneye Chernoye Lake

139

X X
SS "Nord"

PYA LAKE

14
Finn

X X
J
Finn

Kesten'ga

TOP LAKE

Sof'yanga R.

Sof-Porog

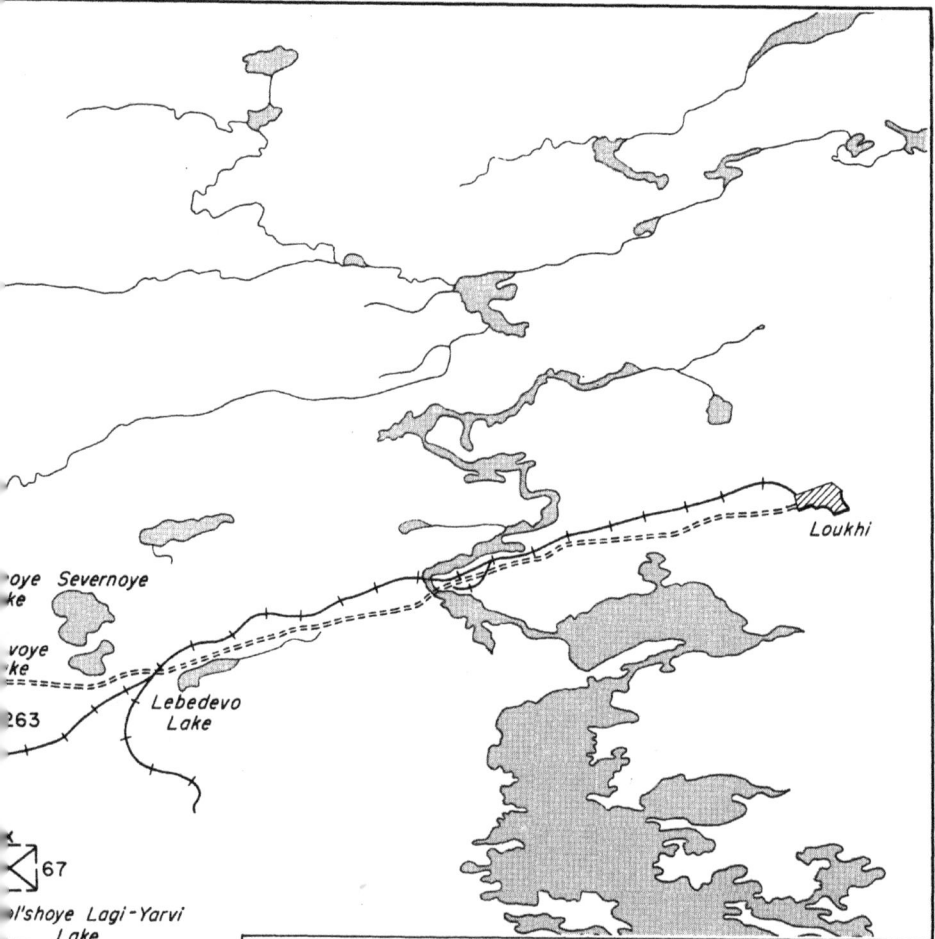

oye Severnoye
ke

voye
ke

263

Lebedevo
Lake

67

l'shoye Lagi-Yarvi
Lake

Loukhi

SOVIET OFFENSIVE
IN THE KESTEN'GA-LOUKHI SECTOR
24 April-23 May 1942

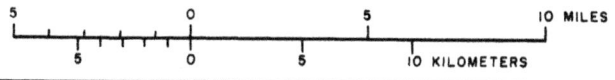

5   0   5   10 MILES

5   0   5   10 KILOMETERS

L. Booth

the III Corps' 250-mile-long supply line impassable while, for their own supplies, they had the use of a rail line up to the front.[33]

The Russians launched their offensive on 24 April with a thrust by the 23d Guards Division and the 8th Ski Brigade against the thinly held left flank of the III Corps east of Kesten'ga. Later in the day frontal attacks on the center and a second enveloping thrust on the right flank gave it added force. On the 26th the left flank of the III Corps cracked, and at the same time with more information on the extent of the Soviet build-up available it became clear that the offensive was intended as a decisive stroke to smash the corps' front and force it back west of Kesten'ga. The Army of Lapland had in reserve only one tank battalion equipped with obsolete Panzer I's and a company of the Brandenburg Regiment (specialists trained for sabotage operations behind the enemy lines). Those it threw in along with the entire XXXVI Mountain Corps reserve, one battalion. The III Corps brought up an additional battalion from the Ukhta sector. The Fifth Air Force, which had orders to concentrate on the Arctic shipping and the Murmansk Railroad except in a crisis, ordered its fighters and dive bombers to begin shifting from Banak and Kirkenes to Kemi behind the III Corps front.

On 27 April the Soviet Fourteenth Army opened an offensive on the Litsa. It began during the day with a heavy attack on the 6th Mountain Division right flank by the 10th Guards Division and a secondary thrust against the left flank on the bridgehead by the 14th Rifle Division. That night the 12th Naval Brigade landed on the west shore of Litsa Bay and began to push down on the open flank. This last move came as a complete surprise to the Mountain Corps Norway and might have had considerable success if it had been executed in greater strength. At the turn of the month the worst snow storm of the year stalled operations on both sides in the Litsa area for several days.[34]

With Russian spearheads standing due north of Kesten'ga, Dietl on 1 May asked Mannerheim for the Finnish 12th Brigade (formerly the 6th Division) to reinforce the III Corps. Mannerheim, unwilling to tie down the brigade in what threatened to develop into a long, drawn-out operation, refused but offered instead to give the Army of Lapland the 163d Infantry Division and take over the Ukhta sector after a German corps relieved III Corps. The offer promised little help in the immediate situation, but Dietl decided to accept since in the long run he would gain a division and get rid of responsibility for the front at Ukhta.[35]

---

[33] A.O.K. *Lappland, Ia, K.T.B., Band I, Nr. 2,* 12, 13, 26 Apr 42. AOK 20 27252/1. A.O.K. *Lappland, Ia, Op., Nr. 1750/42, Zusammenfassender Bericht ueber die Abwehrkaempfe der Armee Lappland vom 24.4.–23.5.42,* in *Anlagenband VII zum K.T.B. Nr. 2 A.O.K. Lappland.* AOK 20 27252/7.
[34] *Gen. Kdo. Geb.-Korps Norwegen, Ia, Nr. 965/42, Bericht ueber die Abwehrkaempfe des Gebirgskorps gegen die russische Umfassungsoperation v. 27.4.–16.5.42,* in *Anlagenband VI zum K.T.B. A.O.K. Lappland.* AOK 20 27252/6.
[35] A.O.K. *Lappland, Ia, K.T.B., Band I, Nr. 2,* 1 and 4 May 42. AOK 20 27252/1.

In the first days of May the Soviet Twenty-Sixth Army brought up fresh units, the 186th Rifle Division and the 80th Rifle Brigade, to add weight to the envelopment of the III Corps' left wing. The Army of Lapland ordered the remaining two battalions of the 139th Mountain Regiment down from the XXXVI Mountain Corps, and the III Corps brought in another battalion from Ukhta. By pulling two battalions out of the right flank the III Corps managed to oppose the Russian two divisions and two brigades with nine battalions. On 3 May the Russians sent the 8th Ski Brigade and a regiment of the 186th Rifle Division in a wide sweep to the west and south in an attempt to cut the road behind Kesten'ga. The III Corps proposed pulling out of Kesten'ga and the positions east of the town to establish a new line in the narrows between Pya Lake and Top Lake, but Dietl, believing a withdrawal would entail too great losses of men and supplies, ordered the corps to hold even if it should be cut off.

On 5 May the 8th Ski Brigade and the regiment of the 186th Rifle Division came within two miles of the road running west of Kesten'ga and had advance parties out almost to the road; but in the swamps northwest of the town the attack lost momentum. In the next two days the Germans and Finns were able to encircle the two Russian units and virtually wipe them out. The 8th Ski Brigade was reduced to a total strength of 367 men. By 6 May the Army of Lapland and the III Corps concluded that the crisis on the north flank had passed. The defense had been successful, at least partly as a consequence of the Russians' failure to employ their vastly superior numbers effectively. They had dissipated their strength in un-co-ordinated attacks by single divisions, with the result that the 186th Rifle Division and the 23d Guards Division were reduced to between 30 and 40 percent of strength, the 80th Rifle Brigade was almost as bad off, and the 8th Ski Brigade was nearly destroyed. At the end the political officers (Politruks) were often no longer able to drive their men into battle. On the 7th, certain that the Russians could not mount another attack without fresh units, Dietl decided to counterattack.[36]

The fighting on the Litsa front never reached a crisis like that in the III Corps area, but the situation there was believed to be potentially more serious because of the supposed danger of a United States-British landing on the arctic coast. On 9 May Dietl and Schoerner decided to risk everything for the sake of a quick decision. The entire 2d Mountain Division, parts of which had moved up already, was ordered to the front, and the coastal defenses between Tana Fiord and Pechenga Bay

---

[36] *A.O.K. Lappland, Ia, Op. Nr. 1750/42, Zusammenfassender Bericht ueber die Abwehrkaempfe der Armee Lappland vom 24.4.–23.5.42, 4.6.42,* in *Anlagenband VII zum K.T.B. Nr. 2, A.O.K. Lappland.* AOK 20 27252/7. *A.O.K. Lappland, Ia, K.T.B., Band I, Nr. 2,* 1–7 May 1942. AOK 20 27252/1. *III A.K., No. 408/Adj.,* [Report on defensive battles in the Kesten'ga–Luokhi sector], *28.5.42,* in *Anlagenband VI zum K.T.B., A.O.K. Lappland.* AOK 20 27252/6.

THE SOVIET OFFENSIVE
ON THE LITSA
27 April - 14 May 1942

German Front Line
Russian Movement

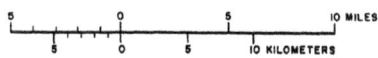

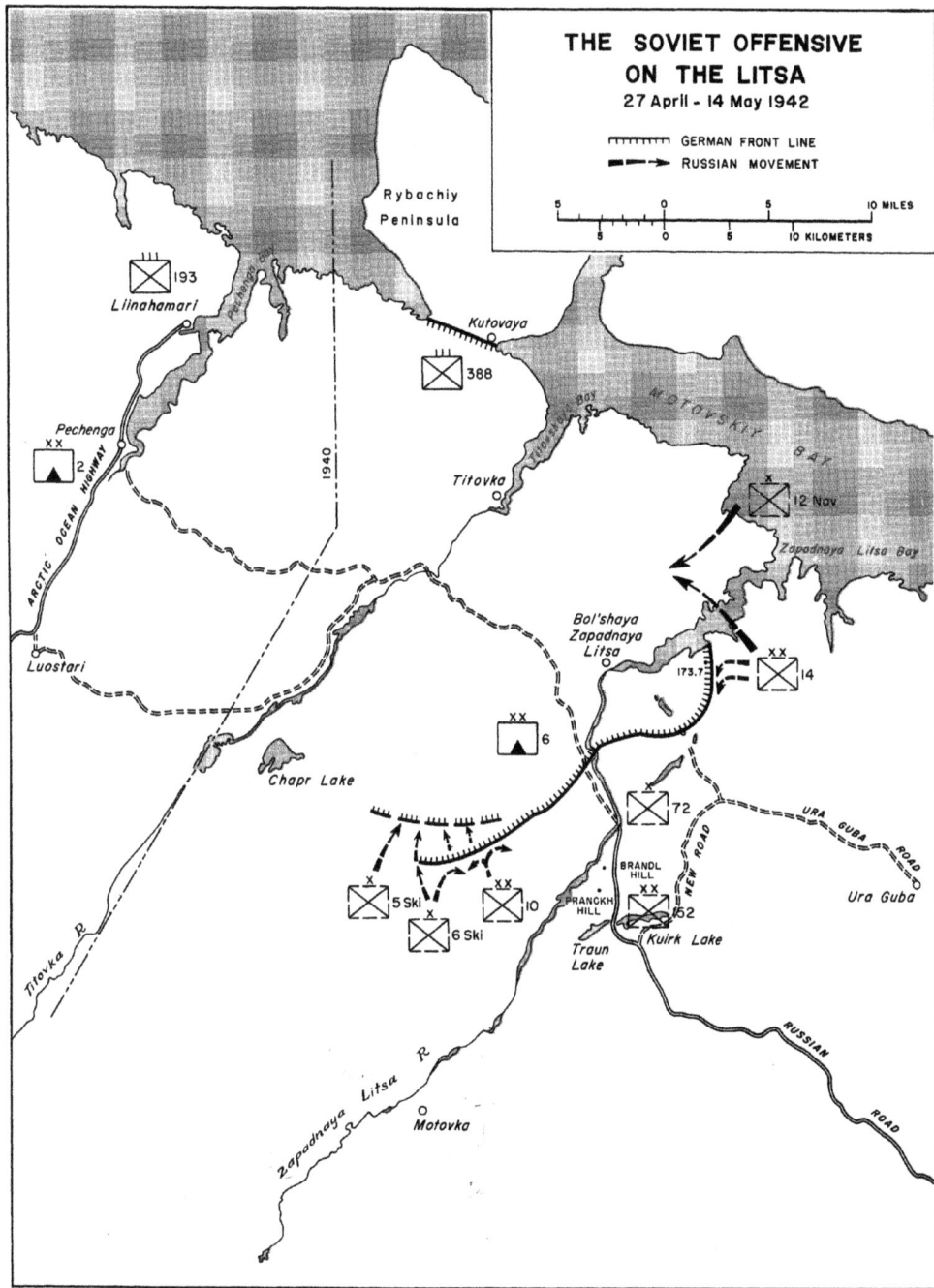

5   0   5   10 MILES
5   0   5   10 KILOMETERS

Rybachiy
Peninsula

Liinahamari   193

Kutovaya

388

MOTOVSKIY BAY

Pechenga   2

Titovka   12 Nov

1940   Zapadnaya Litsa Bay

Luostari   Bol'shaya
               Zapadnaya
               Litsa
               173.7   14

Chapr Lake   6

                            72   URA GUBA ROAD

                            NEW ROAD

               5 Ski   10   BRANDL
                             HILL   Ura Guba
               6 Ski   PRANCKH
                        HILL   52
Titovka R.   Traun   Kuirk Lake
                        Lake

                                 RUSSIAN ROAD

Zapadnaya Litsa R.

Motovka

Map 19   L. Booth

were stripped down to four battalions. But even before the last reserves were in the line the situation suddenly changed. On 14 May the 12th Naval Brigade, its over-water supply lines under constant dive-bomber harrassment, found its positions on the west shore of Litsa Bay untenable and withdrew. Thereafter the Russians, although they had brought up a fresh division in the past week, also ceased their attacks on the southern flank, and on 15 May the Mountain Corps Norway regained its original positions along the entire front.

North of Kesten'ga spring thaws delayed the III Corps counterattack until 15 May. Meanwhile, the Russians, characteristically, had thrown up elaborate field fortifications. When a flanking attack by three Finnish battalions became bogged down in impassable terrain, the Germans had to resort to a series of frontal attacks which finally breached the Russian line on 21 May. Russian resistance collapsed, and the III Corps had almost regained its original line when, on 23 May, contrary to orders from the Army of Lapland, Siilasvuo stopped the advance.[37]

The last week and a half of operations north of Kesten'ga had seen a recurrence of tension between the German and Finnish commanders. The Army of Lapland noted on 23 May, "In the course of the last three weeks the army has received the growing impression that the Commanding General, III Corps, either on his own initiative or on instructions from higher Finnish authorities, is avoiding all decisions which could involve Finnish troops in serious fighting." The German liaison officer with the III Corps reported that German troops had made all the major attacks since 15 May, and the Army of Lapland recorded that Siilasvuo had repeatedly issued orders on his own authority which he knew the Army of Lapland would not automatically approve, the last of those being his order to break off the operation.

Although the III Corps had not regained the best defensive positions at several points, Dietl decided to let Siilasvuo's decision stand, particularly since he saw an immediate danger that the Finns would pull out and leave the German troops stranded. On the 23d he issued an order limiting Siilasvuo's authority with regard to withdrawing troops from the line; but on the following day, disregarding that order, the III Corps ordered all Finnish battalions out of the German sector of the front and demanded that within three days the Germans return all horses and wagons borrowed from the Finns. The last measure would have cut off the Germans without supplies, and Dietl had to appeal to Siilasvuo in the name of "brotherhood-in-arms" not to leave the German units in a hopeless position.[38]

Although the Finnish liaison officer with the Army of Lapland assured

[37] A.O.K. Lappland, Ia, Op. Nr. 1750/42, Zusammenfassender Bericht ueber die Abwerhrkaempfe der Armee Lappland, loc. cit. A.O.K. Lappland, Ia, K.T.B., Band I, Nr. 2, 15–23 May 1942. AOK 20 27252/1.
[38] A.O.K. Lappland, Ia, K.T.B., Band I, Nr. 2, 22–25 May 1942. AOK 20 27252/1.

him that the Finnish High Command had exerted no pressure on the III Corps to spare its Finnish troops or to get them out quickly, Dietl ordered the German troops made independent of Finnish support as fast as possible and asked the OKW to speed up transfer of the 7th Mountain Division. However, Hitler had just decided that elements of the 7th Mountain Division would have to remain with the Army Group North temporarily.

On 3 June a working staff of the XVIII Mountain Corps arrived, and Dietl proposed having the corps take over the Kesten'ga sector at the middle of the month, but Siilasvuo refused to relinquish his command unless the majority of the Finnish troops were out of the area by then. On the 18th Mannerheim agreed to an exchange at the end of the month provided the 14th Regiment and elements of the 3d Division were returned to him. With agreement finally reached, the XVIII Mountain Corps, under General der Gebirgstruppe Franz Boehme, took command at Kesten'ga on 3 July. One Finnish regiment remained in the corps sector until mid-September, when it was relieved by the last elements of the 7th Mountain Division.[39]

The defensive battles east of Kesten'ga and on the Litsa were clearcut victories for the Germans and Finns. The III Corps claimed to have counted 15,000 Russian dead in the front lines and maintained that enemy losses behind the lines from artillery fire and aerial bombardment were also high. The 85th Independent Brigade, for instance, was smashed by dive bombers before it could reach the front. The Mountain Corps Norway claimed 8,000 enemy killed. The total German and Finnish casualties were 3,200 on the Litsa and 2,500 in the III Corps sector. Still, the suddenness with which the Russians broke off their operations came as a surprise, since, with a fresh division, the 152d "Ural" Division, on the Litsa, and, reportedly, 20,000 replacements at Loukhi, they had the potential for a second try. Their initial heavy losses no doubt figured largely in the decision to abandon both offensives, as did the fact that, with their timetable thrown off schedule, the oncoming thaw reduced their prospects of success. In the opinion of the Army of Norway one result of the successful defense ranked above all others; namely, that in the far north for some time to come the danger of a Russian thrust in conjunction with a British-American landing was removed.[40]

[39] *A.O.K. Lappland, Ia, K.T.B., Band 2, Nr. 2, 3, 5, 7,* and 18 Jun 42. AOK 20 27252/2. *A.O.K. Lappland, Ia, K.T.B., Band 2, Nr. 3,* 17 Sep 42. AOK 20 27252/3.
[40] III A.K., No. 408/Adj., [Report on defensive battles in the Kesten'ga–Loukhi sector], 28.5.42 and *Gen. Kdo. Geb-Korps Norwegen, Ia, Nr. 965/42, Bericht ueber die Abwehrkaempfe des Gebirgskorps Norwegen gegen die russische Umfassungsoperation v. 27.4.–16.5.42,* in *Anlagenband VI zum K.T.B. A.O.K. Lappland.* AOK 20 27252/6. *A.O.K. Lappland, Ia, Op. Nr. 1750/42, Zusammenfassender Bericht ueber die Abwehrkaempfe der Armee Lappland vom 24.4.–23.5.42, 4.6.42,* in *Anlagenband VII zum K.T.B. Nr. 2, A.O.K. Lappland.* AOK 20 27252/7.

The new Marshal of Finland, Baron Carl Gustaf Mannerheim (left) is congratulated on the occasion of his 75th birthday by Generaloberst Edward Dietl; center background is Generaloberst Hans-Juergen Stumpff.

Abortive Plans

In late April, a day before the Russians began their spring offensive, the Army of Lapland informed the OKW that, since its promised reinforcement would not be completed until fall, it considered offensive operations during the summer impracticable. A month later, in its directive for the Army of Lapland operations in the summer, the OKW accepted that estimate and set only two specific tasks for the army: to restore the situation east of Kesten'ga, regaining the old defense line; and to move all troops that could be spared from the first assignment to the Mountain Corps Norway. The army main effort henceforth would be in the Mountain Corps sector, where the primary mission would be defense against United States-British invasion attempts. The OKW pointed out that it considered the Rybatchiy Peninsula of greatest importance for the conduct of the war in the far north and that preparations for taking the peninsula would have to be continued. Since it could not foresee the time when the troop and supply situations would make such an operation possible, the date was left open—possibly the late summer of 1942 or the late winter of 1942–43.[41]

On 4 June Hitler and Keitel flew to Imola to pay their respects to Mannerheim on his seventy-fifth birthday. The visit was not entirely

---

[41] *OKW, K.T.B. Ob. d. Wehrmacht,* 1 Apr–30 Jun 42, 23 Apr and 16 May 42. International Military Tribunal Doc. 1807–PS. *OKW, WFSt, Op. Nr. 55798/42, Weisung fuer die weitere Kampfuehrung des AOK Lappland, 16.5.42,* in *Anlagenband VI zum K.T.B. A.O.K. Lappland.* AOK 20 27253/6.

welcome to the Finns since it gave a substantial jolt to their already strained relations with the United States and resulted in a breach of consular relations two weeks later. During the German visit Dietl told Hitler that the Army of Lapland did not have enough troops to take the Rybatchiy Peninsula or to hold it if it were taken. Hitler was reluctant to abandon the operation and ordered preparations continued, instructing the Fifth Air Force to ready all its ground installations in the area for very strong forces. The proposed operation against Belomorsk also came under consideration, and Keitel reported later that the Finns had said they were sorry they had not been able to execute the operation during the past winter because Belomorsk was of special importance to them not only militarily but for the purpose of establishing their postwar frontier. They did not consider the operation possible during the summer but had it under consideration for the next winter.[42]

After the Russians fell back from Kesten'ga the front became quiet. In June the Army of Lapland finished moving its five fortress battalions to the arctic coast, and during July and August it pushed work on the coast artillery, emplacing 21 batteries in the zone between Tana Fiord and Pechenga Bay. At the end of summer, Headquarters, 210th Infantry Division, was brought in to command the fortress battalions and coast artillery. At the end of June the Army of Lapland was redesignated as the Twentieth Mountain Army. In July the XVIII Mountain Corps staged a small attack to recover a commanding height off its left flank which had been left in Russian hands when Siilasvuo stopped the III Corps operations. Otherwise, the Germans and Russians both contented themselves with harassment, which for the most part took the form of starting forest fires in each other's areas. White phosphorus shells easily ignited the evergreen trees, and the fires occasionally burned across mine fields or threatened installations causing serious temporary inconvenience.[43]

The only summer activity which came near having strategic significance was Operation KLABAUTERMANN, which the German Navy and Air Force conducted from Finnish bases on the shore of Lake Ladoga. The idea of using small boats to interdict Soviet traffic on Lake Ladoga had occurred to Hitler in the fall of 1941, too late to be put into effect. It was revived in the spring of 1942 after Finnish reports indicated that the Russians were evacuating Leningrad. Hitler feared that the Russians might pull out of Leningrad entirely; in that case, the northern sector of the front would no longer be important to them, and they would be able to transfer troops to another part of the front. Conse-

---

[42] On his birthday Mannerheim was named Marshal of Finland, and during the visit Hitler advanced Dietl to the rank of Generaloberst. *OKW, K.T.B. Ob. d. Wehrmacht, 1 Apr–30 Jun 42, 5 Jun 42.* I.M.T., Doc. 1807–PS.

[43] In June, also, transfer of the 163d Infantry Division to the XXXVI Mountain Corps zone was completed, and SS-Division "Nord" was renamed SS-Mountain Division "Nord." A.O.K. *Lappland, Ia, K.T.B., Band 2, Nr. 2, passim.* AOK 20 27252/2 (*Geb*) *A.O.K. 20, Ia, K.T.B., Band 3, Nr. 2, 1 Sep 42.* AOK 20 27252/3.

quently, he ordered the evacuation "combated with all means." [44] By 1 July the Navy had German and Italian PT boats ready for action on the lake.   The Air Force brought in its craft a month later.   Both claimed the over-all command and so further impaired the operation, which was already hampered by lack of air cover and the hazards of operating on the shallow lake.[45] KLABAUTERMANN dragged on until 6 November when the German crews and equipment were withdrawn. The Russians, in the meantime, had completed their evacuation as planned, using boats to carry supplies and military equipment from Novaya Ladoga to the Isthmus and bringing back nonessential civilians on the return trips.[46]

In June it appeared that the Twentieth Mountain Army's next mission would be occupation of the Rybatchiy Peninsula, planning for which was then given the code name WIESENGRUND.   Since Mannerheim was about to take over the Ukhta sector, releasing the 5th Mountain Division for other tasks, the troop problem appeared to be solved.   In the first week of July, however, the OKW informed Dietl that the 5th Mountain Division could not be transferred to the Pechenga area because it was impossible to bring up enough supplies for another full-strength division there.   The OKW intended "in the long run" to send in enough "static" troops (without horses and vehicles) to relieve the 6th Mountain Division on the Litsa, freeing it and the 2d Mountain Division for WIESENGRUND.   Dietl protested immediately that the Litsa line was no place for scantily equipped, third-rate troops, and with that WIESENGRUND was shelved.[47]

Having still, potentially, a division to spare, Dietl returned immediately to the idea of a double thrust to the Murmansk Railroad, by the XXXVI Mountain Corps to Kandalaksha and by the Finnish Army to Belomorsk. In conferences with Erfurth on 8 and 9 July and with Jodl on the 13th the project was further developed, and after Jodl carried it back to Fuehrer Headquarters Hitler gave it his approval in Fuehrer Directive No. 44 of 21 July 1952.   The Twentieth Mountain Army was to prepare to take Kandalaksha in the fall and was assured that to free the required Finnish forces Leningrad would be taken in September at the latest and the 5th Mountain Division would be in Finland by the end of September.   Hitler warned that defense of the Pechenga nickel mines remained the army's most important task and required maintenance of sufficient reserves at all times.   He also officially canceled WIESENGRUND

---

[44] *OKW, K.T.B. Ob. d. Wehrmacht,* 1 Apr–30 Jun 42, 26 May 42.   I.M.T. Doc. 1807–PS.

[45] The Air Force claim stemmed from its possession of the Siebel-ferries, twin-hulled landing craft mounting a small caliber antiaircraft gun, which had been invented by an Air Force colonel.   The dispute is a good example of the tendency of each of the German services to arrogate to itself any function for which it could establish even a remotely defensible claim.

[46] Erfurth, *op. cit.,* pp. 75, 94–96.

[47] *(Geb.) AOK 20, Ia, Op. Nr. 1405/42, an Geb.-Korps Norwegen, 3.7.42, in Anlagenband VIII zum K.T.B. Nr. 2, (Geb.) AOK 20.   AOK 20 27252/8.*

for 1942 but ordered preparations continued in such a fashion that it could be executed in the spring of 1943 on eight weeks' notice. The Kandalaksha operation was assigned the code name LACHSFANG.[48]

The XXXVI Mountain Corps initiated planning for LACHSFANG on 22 July. Success, it was believed, hinged on two requirements, a quick breakthrough on the Verman line, and, subsequently, a rapid thrust toward Kandalaksha before the enemy could make another stand. The XXXVI Mountain Corps intended to smash the Verman positions by punching through with one infantry division along the road and another along the railroad. A mountain division would sweep around the north flank and push eastward to prevent the enemy's organizing a second line farther back. The corps planned to employ 80,000 troops, just twice the number used in the 1941 summer operations; and the Fifth Air Force agreed to provide 60 dive bombers, 9 fighters, and 9 bombers, more planes than had been available for the entire SILBERFUCHS Operation in 1941. Time was an essential element. Operations could be continued up to 1 December but after that would become impossible because of deep snow and short periods of daylight. The late winter, mid-March to mid-April, afforded a second, but less favorable, possibility since the German infantry divisions were not trained for winter operations in the Arctic. The XXXVI Mountain Corps believed it would need four weeks for LACHSFANG and wanted to time the operation to end in mid-November since then the length of daylight would be less than seven hours and an hour a week would be lost thereafter.[49]

Because a simultaneous Finnish operation against Bēlomorsk was considered indispensable, Erfurth sounded out the Finnish reaction to Fuehrer Directive No. 44. Heinrichs, Mannerheim's chief of staff, indicated that the Finnish attitude was "positive"; but Leningrad would have to be taken first. The Finnish Command also regarded it "as necessary" that the left flank of the Army Group North be advanced east to the middle Svir. The first condition was expected, but the second came as a surprise. At the OKH the Germans told Mannerheim's representative, Talvela, that, if the Marshal intended to insist on it as a prerequisite, LACHSFANG would have to be dropped. Avoiding a firm commitment, Mannerheim in August sent Heinrichs to Fuehrer Headquarters to straighten the matter out orally. Having entered a caveat, the Finns proposed to employ eight divisions and an armored division (activated in July 1942) in an attack northeastward from the Maaselkä Front. Again, time was a critical element, since four of the divisions would have to come from the Isthmus Front, and redeployment, because

[48] Der Fuehrer, OKW, WFSt, Op., Nr. 551275/42, Weisung Nr. 44, 21.7.42, in Weisungen OKW, Fuehrer, 12.2.42–23.3.44, Band 3.
[49] Gen. Kdo. XXXVI (Geb.) A.K., Fuehrungsabteilung, K.T.B. u. Anlagen zu "Lachsfang," 22.7.–31.10.42. XXXVI AK 29155/1. Gen. Kdo. XXXVI (Geb.) A.K., Qu., Unterlagen fuer "Lachsfang," 1.8.–22.8.42. XXXVI AK 29155/2.

of poor roads, could not be accomplished in less than three to four weeks after the fall of Leningrad.[50]

The German and Finnish LACHSFANG operations gave strong promise of success, but whether or not they could be executed depended entirely on events in the Army Group North sector. In Fuehrer Directive No. 45 of 23 July 1942 Hitler ordered the army group to be prepared to execute Operation NORDLICHT, the capture of Leningrad, by September. He promised five divisions and heavy siege artillery from the Eleventh Army, which had completed its operations in the Crimea, since the Army Group North, which had been slighted in favor of the summer offensive by the southern army groups, already had its forces spread thin over an extensive front. The Eighteenth Army, in the Leningrad zone, believed NORDLICHT would require from two to three months for execution. Because 13 Soviet rifle divisions and 3 tank brigades (exclusive of those opposite the Finns) were known to be in the Leningrad area, the Army Group North set its own troop requirements at 18 divisions. With 5 divisions from the Eleventh Army and 5 of its own, it still anticipated a deficit of 8 divisions.[51]

On 8 August Generalfeldmarschall Georg von Kuechler, who had replaced Leeb as commanding general of the army group, reported on NORDLICHT at Fuehrer Headquarters. He pointed out that the Russians already outnumbered his own troops nearly two to one and asked for new divisions from the OKH. Hitler replied that he could not give divisions he did not have and that he had already made artillery available on a scale not seen in warfare since the World War I battle of Verdun.[52] To the question of how much time was required, Kuechler replied that he expected to complete NORDLICHT by the end of October. Jodl, who was also present, interjected that it would have to be ended sooner since it was not an end in itself but a preparation for LACHSFANG.[53] Hitler then set 10 September as the latest starting date for NORDLICHT.

That the conference satisfied no one was clear immediately, and Jodl at one point suggested turning the operation over to Generalfeldmar-

---

[50] *OKH, GenStdH, Op. Abt. IN, Operationen gegen die Murmanbahn, 5.8.42* and *Der Kdr. d. Verb. Stab Nord, Nr. 46/42, Kampffuehrung in Nordfinnland, 2.8.42,* in *OKH, GenStdH, Op. Abt. IN, Band II, Finnland.* H 22/227. *OKW, WFSt, Op. (H), Nr. 55139/42, Abschrift von Fernschreiben Gen. Erfurth, 10.8.42.* OKW/119. Erfurth, *op. cit.,* pp. 83ff.

[51] *Der Fuehrer, OKW, WFSt, Op. Nr. 551258/42, Weisung Nr. 45, 23.7.42,* in *Weisungen OKW, Fuehrer, 12.2.42–23.3.44, Band 3.* H. Gr. Nord, Ia, K.T.B., 20, 23, 26 Jul 42. H. Gr. Nord 75128/11.

[52] He was moving up the siege artillery which had been used at Sevastopol, a total of 817 guns (280 batteries), in calibers ranging from 75 millimeters to 800 millimeters. In the 800-mm. caliber (31.5 inches) there was one gun, with 46 rounds of ammunition. "Dora," as it was called, required its own antiaircraft batteries and special police protection. Among the other heavy pieces were two 600-mm., two 420-mm., and six 400-mm. howitzers—in fact, as Hitler claimed, a powerful array of artillery.

[53] *OKH, Gen Qu., Qu. 3/Mun., Nr. 02364/42, Vortragsnotiz, Munitions-Aufmarsch fuer "Nordlicht," 26.8.42,* min. *OKH, GenStdH, Op. Abt. IN, Band II, Teil I.* H 22/224. H. Gr. Nord, Ia, K.T.B., 8 Aug 42. H. Gr. Nord 75128/13.

schall Fritz Erich von Manstein, who as Commanding General, Eleventh Army, had achieved a brilliant success in the siege of Sevastopol. Although the idea appeared to make no impression on Hitler at the moment, two weeks later he announced his intention to give Manstein and the Eleventh Army staff command of NORDLICHT. The Army Group North protested that, with the plan already worked out by the Eighteenth Army and the starting date three weeks away, a change of command would only create confusion; but Hitler, having made up his mind, was determined to have Manstein.

If he expected a more optimistic approach to NORDLICHT he was mistaken. In his first conference with Kuechler, on 28 August, Manstein said that he did not believe massive air and artillery bombardment could be counted on to break the Russian resistance. Sevastopol, he pointed out, had demonstrated the Russians' relative immunity to terrorization by heavy bombardment. He believed NORDLICHT would be difficult and preferred an attack from the Finnish Isthmus Front. In any event, he thought the attack would have to be made from both fronts.[54]

In the meantime, another difficulty had arisen. The Army Group North would have to release the 5th Mountain Division before 15 August if it was to participate in LACHSFANG on schedule. That Kuechler declared impossible because he had no reserves with which to relieve the division and could not risk further weakening his front on the Volkhov. The problem went up to Hitler, who mulled it over for a week and at the last minute, on 15 August, decided to leave the 5th Mountain Division with the Army Group North and transfer the 3d Mountain Division from Norway to Finland instead.[55]

On 27 August, as Kuechler had feared, the Russians demonstrated that they held most of the trumps. They opened an offensive from the east immediately south of Lake Ladoga, striking at the so-called "bottleneck," the extreme left flank of the Army Group North where its fronts facing east and facing Leningrad stood back-to-back only a few miles apart. Their offensive threatened, potentially at least, to reestablish land contact with Leningrad; and within a day or two they had achieved local breakthroughs. Hitler was furious but helpless as he watched his own plans for an offensive evaporate.[56]

On the last day of the month the OKW had to divert the 3d Mountain Division, which already had elements at sea, from Finland to the Army Group North; and the Eighteenth Army reported that, with the Russian offensive certain to be the major concern for weeks, NORDLICHT had become a completely indefinite affair. A day later the OKW and OKH drew the necessary conclusions: they canceled LACHSFANG for

[54] *H. Gr. Nord, Ia, K.T.B.*, 8, 21 and 28 Aug 42. H. Gr. Nord 75128/13.
[55] *H. Gr. Nord, Ia, K.T.B.*, 10 Aug 42. H. Gr. Nord 75128/13. *OKW, WFSt, Op. Nr. 002820/42, 15.8.42*, in *Weisungen* OKW, *Fuehrer, 12.2.42–23.3.44, Band 3.*
[56] *H. Gr. Nord, Ia, K.T.B.*, 27–31 Aug 42. H. Gr. Nord 75128/13.

1942 and made NORDLICHT dependent on the situation in the bottleneck, the ability to assemble enough forces, and the weather.[57] Informing Mannerheim of these decisions, the OKW requested his participation in NORDLICHT.   The Finnish reply on 4 September stated that the Finnish Army Headquarters did not refuse "in principle" to participate in NORDLICHT but described the possibilities as "extremely limited." [58]

The prospects for NORDLICHT were not bright. The fighting to restore the Army Group North's left flank lasted until mid-October, and the German High Command, from Hitler on down, was more chary of being caught off balance by the Russian winter than it had been a year earlier. On 1 October the OKH, because of the impending fall rains, postponed the operation until frost had set in, and three weeks later it made the postponement indefinite and ordered that the assembled artillery was to be used to inch the line around Leningrad forward gradually with as small a commitment of troops as possible. At the end of the month the Eleventh Army was placed under the direct control of the OKH and put into the line between the Army Group North and the Army Group Center. NORDLICHT, although still ostensibly on the agenda, had ceased to be even a remote possibility.[59]

With NORDLICHT out of the picture, the OKW informed Dietl that it would no longer be possible to create the necessary conditions for carrying out the Finnish LACHSFANG in the late winter of 1942–1943; therefore, all LACHSFANG operations were canceled.   The OKW intended to give the Twentieth Mountain Army an additional division in the coming spring which might be used to execute LACHSFANG during the summer of 1943. The army main effort for the immediate future was placed in the Mountain Corps Norway (in November redesignated the XIX Mountain Corps) zone, but there also no special measures were to be instituted for the time being.[60]   In December Hitler ordered the strength of the Twentieth Mountain Army, which then stood at 172,200 men, increased by an Air Force field regiment and a police regiment.[61]

Operations Against the Arctic Convoys

Although the British had been sending small convoys and single ships to Murmansk and Arkhangel'sk since the summer of 1941 and began large convoy movements shortly after the Beaverbrook-Harriman Mis-

---

[57] H. Gr. Nord, Ia, K.T.B., 31 Aug and 1 Sep 42. H. Gr. Nord 75128/13 and 14. OKW, WFSt, Op., Nr. 55149/42, an GenStdH, Op. Abt., 5.9.42, in OKH, GenStdH, Op. Abt. IN, Band 2, Teil II. H 22/225.
[58] General der Infanterie a.D. Waldemar Erfurth, Comments on Part II of The German Northern Theater of Operations 1940–45, June 1957.
[59] H. Gr. Nord, Ia, K.T.B., 1, 20, and 30 Oct 42. H. Gr. Nord 75128/15.
[60] OKW, WFSt, Op. (H), Nr. 551796/42, an (Geb.) AOK 20, 29.10.42, in Weisungen OKW, Fuehrer, 12.2.42–23.3.44, Band 3.
[61] (Geb.) AOK 20, Ia, Nr. 3376/42 and OKH, GenStdH, Org. Abt., 12.11.42, in Anlagenband XII zum K.T.B. Nr. 2 (Geb.) AOK 20. AOK 20 27252/12. (Geb.) AOK 20, Ia, K.T.B., Band 3, Nr. 2, 24 Nov and 14 Dec 42. AOK 20 27252/3.

sion of October 1941, the German response was slow. This can probably be traced to Hitler's preoccupation, particularly in the early winter of 1941–42, with more crucial problems elsewhere. In February 1942 the Navy had 12 submarines in Norwegian waters, 6 for coastal defense and 6 for operations against convoys.[62] The *Tirpitz,* the *Scheer,* and the *Prinz Eugen* (damaged) were there, and their presence alone had an effect on Allied actions; but the Navy had no immediate intention of employing them directly against the convoys, partly because a fuel oil shortage ruled out extensive cruises by the big ships. The Fifth Air Force at the same time had a combat strength of 60 twin-engine bombers, 30 dive bombers, 30 single-engine fighters, and 15 naval floatplane torpedo-bombers.[63] Generaloberst Hans-Juergen Stumpff, Commanding General, Fifth Air Force, had moved his headquarters to Kemi, Finland, in the fall of 1941. He remained there during the winter, directing the main air effort against Murmansk and the railroad. The uninterrupted darkness of the arctic winter made air operations against shipping targets at sea unprofitable in any case.[64]

In early March the Naval Staff, believing that the mere presence of the *Tirpitz* in Trondheim would not fully achieve the desired effect of tying down enemy naval forces, decided to send the battleship against Convoy PQ 12, which was then at sea northeast of Iceland.[65] The *Tirpitz* and five destroyers put out on 6 March. After failing to find the convoy in three days' cruising, they were ordered back on the 9th. The sortie had been a halfhearted venture from the start because of the Naval Staff's reluctance to risk losing the battleship. Raeder concluded that anticonvoy operations were too dangerous for heavy vessels without aircraft carrier escort, and he doubted whether they were justified in view of the ships' main task, the defense against landings.[66] The sole result of the *Tirpitz* operation was a decision to speed up work on the aircraft carrier *Graf Zeppelin,* which, even so, could not be ready before late 1943.

---

[62] *Naval War Diary,* Vol. 30, p. 91.
[63] *The Rise and Fall of the German Air Force,* p. 113.
[64] The Fifth Air Force for a time employed geologists in an effort to locate spots along the railroad where bombing might set off landslides and bury large stretches of track. The attempt was based on a piece of knowledge regarding arctic geology which the Germans had acquired at some cost. At the end of September 1941 a Soviet bomber, striking at the Mountain Corps Norway's only bridge across the Pechenga River, had dropped a stick of bombs which missed the bridge but by their concussion caved in both banks of the river, completely burying the bridge, and damming the river. It was found that at the site of the catastrophe a layer of glacial drift (sand and rocks) had been laid down over a substratum of oceanic sediment. The latter, having never dried out, remained extremely unstable. Wherever it was cut, as by a river, it sustained its own weight and that of the glacial drift above it only in the most precarious sort of equilibrium. Similar conditions were known to exist throughout northern Finland and the Kola Peninsula, but the Germans did not succeed in exploiting them in their attacks on the Murmansk Railroad.
[65] Convoys sailing east to Russian arctic ports were given PQ numbers, those returning QP numbers.
[66] *Naval War Diary,* Vol. 31, pp. 20, 53, 56, 75, 81, 85.

In mid-March, after a dozen PQ convoys had made the run to Murmansk in comparative safety, Hitler issued the first order for intensive anticonvoy operations. Stating that the convoys could be used both to maintain Russia's capacity for resistance and for staging a landing on the German-held arctic coast, he ordered the sea traffic, "which so far has hardly been touched," interdicted. The Navy was to increase its U-boat commitment, and the Air Force to strengthen its long-range reconnaissance and bomber forces and to move up torpedo-bombers. The Air Force was to keep Murmansk under constant bombardment, reconnoiter the sea area between Bear Island and the Murman Coast, and operate against convoys and enemy warships.[67]

The first result of the Hitler order was a Fifth Air Force proposal to occupy Spitzbergen and use the airfield there to attack the convoys from both sides. The Army of Norway thought a battalion, which would take along supplies for one year, would be enough to hold the island, but the OKW believed an occupation would tie down too much naval and air strength in defensive operations without offering any decisive advantages since, during nearly all of the year, the pack ice forced convoys to pass within 300 miles of German air bases in Norway. On 22 March Hitler decided against the proposal.[68]

In April PQ 13 and PQ 14 sailed, but bad weather and the spring thaw, which temporarily rendered the northern airfields unusable, hampered German operations. PQ 14 encountered pack ice north of Iceland, and 14 of its 23 ships turned back. PQ 13 lost 5 ships out of 19, and the *Trinidad*, one of the cruiser escorts, was torpedoed and later sank. German destroyers were sent out but because of inadequate reconnaissance could not make contact with the convoy. Again the Germans were fearful of risking their ships against a superior enemy force.[69]

By late April the build-up Hitler had ordered was taking effect. The Navy had 20 submarines stationed in Norway, 8 for defense and 12 for use against convoys; and the Air Force had moved in 12 newly converted twin-engine torpedo-bombers (He. 111). On 2 May nine torpedo-bombers on their first mission in the Arctic attacked PQ 15 and reported three sinkings. At the end of the month submarine operations, except against isolated, unescorted ships, became too dangerous because of the increased length of daylight, but the air build-up continued. On 27 May 100 twin-engine Ju. 88's and a number of He. 111 torpedo-bombers attacked PQ 16 and claimed 9 sinkings. The operations against PQ 16 showed that high-level dive bombing combined with

---

[67] *Der Fuehrer und Oberste Befehlshaber der Wehrmacht, OKW, WFSt, Op. (M), Nr. 55493/42, 14.3.42.* OKW/119.
[68] *OKW, WFSt, Op., Nr. 55518/42, Vortragnotiz, 13.3.42* and *OKW, WFSt, Op. (M), Nr. 55537/42, Betr.: Spitzbergen, 22.3.42.* OKW/119. *W.B. Norwegen, Ia, Nr. 16/42, an OKW, WFSt (Op), 13.3.42, in AOK Norwegen, Chefsachen allgemein, 21.9.40–1.5.42.* AOK 20 35641.
[69] Churchill, *op. cit.*, Vol. IV, p. 257. *Naval War Diary*, Vol. 32, pp. 13–18 and 30 Apr 42.

torpedo attacks launched from just above water level could dissipate and confuse the convoy defenses.[70]

In early June agents reported PQ 17 forming off the southwest coast of Iceland. With that much advance warning and 24-hour daylight in the arctic area to assure good reconnaissance, the Navy planned another attempt to get its heavy vessels into action. The *Luetzow*, the *Scheer*, and six destroyers were to go to Alta Fiord, and the *Tirpitz*, the *Hipper*, and six destroyers were to be posted in the West Fiord. After PQ 17 left Iceland on 27 June, the Navy learned that aside from cruisers and destroyers it had also to contend with a remote escort of two battleships and an aircraft carrier. It then altered the plan and ordered all the ships to Alta Fiord where German air superiority would be sufficient to drive off the enemy's heavy ships. In making the shift the *Luetzow* ran aground, damaging its bottom. Similar mishaps temporarily disabled four of the destroyers.

As PQ 17 approached the Spitzbergen–Bear Island passage the time to strike had come, but the battleships and aircraft carrier posed a standing threat, and on 4 July the Naval Staff decided a strike would be impossible. On the following day its confidence revived when the battleships, aircraft carriers, and cruisers were sighted steering west. They were under orders, of which the Germans were unaware, not to advance into the zone of German air dominance east of Spitzbergen–Bear Island unless the *Tirpitz* put in an appearance. The Naval Staff decided to let the operation begin, but Hitler interposed a strong injunction against risking an attack unless the enemy carrier had been located and eliminated. In the afternoon the *Tirpitz*, the *Scheer*, the *Hipper*, and eight destroyers put out from Alta Fiord, only to be ordered back a few hours later when enemy radio traffic indicated that they had been sighted.

Reviewing the operation Raeder concluded that to attack convoys with heavy ships was rendered difficult by Hitler's insistence on avoiding losses or setbacks at all cost. PQ 17, he maintained, offered an opportunity which had never occurred before and was not likely to appear again; therefore it was probable that the big ships would never be used against convoys. Undoubtedly, Hitler's excessive concern with preserving strong naval forces for the defense of Norway made him overly cautious where the battleships were concerned; nevertheless, Raeder's own stanch adherence to the "fleet in being" theory probably played a greater part in the decision to call off the operation than the admiral was willing to admit after the opportunity had been lost.[71]

---

[70] Generalmajor a.D. Hans-Detlev Herhudt von Rohden, *"Die Kampffuehrung der Luftlotte 5 in Norwegen, 1942."* Von Rohden 4376–408. Naval War Diary, Vol. 34, 27 May 1942. *Rise and Fall of the German Air Force*, pp. 113ff.
[71] *Naval War Diary*, Vol. 35, pp. 36ff, 57, 70–72, and 97. *Fuehrer Conferences, 1942*, pp. 86 and 91–93. Churchill, *op. cit.*, Vol. IV, pp. 263–65.

Although the Navy hesitated, the Fifth Air Force was in a position to strike with devastating power. By the time PQ 17 sailed, Stumpff had assembled, in the vicinity of North Cape, 103 twin-engine bombers (Ju. 88), 42 twin-engine torpedo-bombers (He. 111), 15 floatplane torpedo-bombers (He. 115), 30 dive bombers (Ju. 87), and 74 long-range reconnaissance planes (FW. 200, Ju. 88, and BV. 138), a total of 264 combat aircraft. On 2 July reconnaissance reported the position and course of PQ 17, and on the 4th the bombers and torpedo-planes began their attack, claiming four sinkings in the first strike. During the day, the cruisers turned back, and that night the Admiralty ordered the destroyers back, instructing the nearly defenseless merchant ships to disperse. Thereafter the planes of the Fifth Air Force hunted down scattered elements of PQ 17 almost at leisure. The Germans claimed destruction of the convoy down to its last ship; the British figures concede a loss of 23 ships out of 34.[72]

The PQ 17 disaster led the British Admiralty to propose stopping convoy traffic in the Arctic until after the period of long daylight. Stalin protested violently. As a compromise, after an interval of nearly two months, PQ 18 sailed in early September. The Fifth Air Force had increased its torpedo-bomber strength to 92 planes, and the Navy was prepared to commit as many as 12 submarines. The *Tirpitz,* the *Scheer,* the *Hipper,* and the *Koeln* were readied for a sortie against PQ 18 or westbound QP 14, which was expected at the same time, were an opportunity to occur. Again there was a fly in the ointment, an aircraft carrier escort. The Navy organized 7 submarines into a special group *Traegertod* (carrier's death), and the Fifth Air Force decided to direct its main effort against the carrier.

On 13 September, as PQ 18 entered the Spitzbergen–Bear Island passage, a submarine fired two torpedoes at the carrier and missed. On the same day the Fifth Air Force opened its attack with a strike by 56 bombers. The bombers found they could not approach the carrier which was strongly defended by its own aircraft. They also found it difficult to get at the merchant ships, which maintained a tight formation inside a screen of 12 destroyers. On the 14th 54 bombers repeated the attempt. The attacks continued until 19 September but with diminishing success because of bad weather. The British announced a loss of 13 ships out of 40, which approximately agrees with German estimates. The price was also high for the Fifth Air Force which lost 20 bombers in the first two strikes. When the carrier continued on past Spitzbergen with PQ 18 and then picked up QP 14 on the return trip, the battleship sortie was abandoned. In fact, even the submarines were instructed to avoid QP 14 since experience with PQ 18 had demon-

[72] *Rise and Fall of the German Air Force,* p. 114. Churchill, *op. cit.,* Vol. IV, pp. 263–65. Rohden, "*Die Kampffuehrung der Luftflotte 5 in Norwegen, 1942.*" Von Rohden 4376–408.

strated that attacks on convoys with surface and air protection were too
risky.[73]

After PQ 18 put in at Arkhangel'sk, thus mollifying Stalin for the
time being, arctic convoys were again suspended. Shipping requirements of the North African invasion helped to justify the suspension.
The landings in North Africa on 8 November also had a significant influence on the disposition of German anticonvoy forces. All of the
Fifth Air Force's torpedo-bombers and most of its twin-engine bombers
had to be shifted to the Mediterranean, leaving only the slow floatplanes,
some dive bombers, and the long-range reconnaissance units. With the
winter darkness setting in and conditions for air operations becoming
poor the loss had no great immediate significance. What was important
was that the German Air Force would never again be able to muster
similar strength in the Arctic.[74]

In December, taking advantage of the season, the arctic convoys were
resumed; and the German Navy, in what was to prove a fateful decision,
planned another attempt at bringing its heavy vessels into action. The
Hipper, the Luetzow, and five destroyers were stationed in Alta Fiord.
On 30 December the task force put to sea after a submarine reported
Convoy JW 51 B south of Bear Island (JW 51 A had passed earlier in
the month without being sighted).[75] Early the next morning the German ships approached the convoy and were immediately engaged by
the destroyer escort. The Luetzow managed to bring the merchantmen
under fire briefly at long range; but, when two British cruisers appeared,
damaging the Hipper with their first salvo, the Germans promptly broke
off the action in accordance with their standing orders not to risk the
ships against equal or superior forces. The operation ended as a total
failure with the merchant ships scarcely touched. The Germans lost
one destroyer and the British a destroyer and a minesweeper.

The Navy had planned the sortie as a routine operation, dependent
for its outcome largely on luck. It learned too late that Hitler, who was
having troubles in North Africa and at Stalingrad among other places,
had been counting on a major victory and was enraged by the failure.
On 6 January 1943 Hitler called in Raeder and after a harangue on
the poor performance of the German Navy in all wars since 1866, announced his intention to take the battleships out of commission. Raeder,
as the chief exponent of the big ships, offered his resignation and proposed Doenitz, the submarine specialist, as his successor. Both were
immediately accepted, and at the end of the month Hitler ordered all

---

[73] *Rise and Fall of the German Air Force,* p. 115. *Naval War Diary,* Vol. 37, pp.
143, 153, 165, 176, 212, and 224ff. Rohden, *"Die Kampffuehrung der Luftflotte
5 in Norwegen, 1942."* Rohden 4376–408.
[74] *Rise and Fall of the German Air Force,* p. 115.
[75] After PQ 18 the arctic convoys were given JW numbers eastbound and RA
numbers westbound, starting with 51.

vessels larger than destroyers decommissioned. In February Doenitz succeeded in getting the order reversed to the extent of allowing the *Tirpitz* and the *Luetzow* (and later the *Scharnhorst*) to remain in Norway; nevertheless, the sortie against JW 51 A had clearly been a near-fatal blow to the German high seas fleet.[76]

---

[76] *Naval War Diary,* Vol. 40, pp. 5, 12, 31; Vol. 41, pp. 3, 18, 100, 463, 465; and Vol. 42, pp. 202, 410.

Chapter 12

In the Backwater of War

The Stagnant Front

The new year, 1943, dawned bleak on the Eastern Front. In the south, at Stalingrad, the fate of the German Sixth Army was sealed; and in the north, on 12 January, the Russians opened an offensive to drive a wedge between Lake Ladoga and the left flank of the Army Group North. In six days they broke through, pushed the Army Group North back from the lake, and reestablished land contact with Leningrad. Although the Army Group North, in heavy fighting that lasted two and one-half months and cost the Russians some 270,000 men, managed to restrict the Russian gain to a corridor six miles wide, which could be brought under artillery fire and so constituted only a token relief of Leningrad, the development had a severe psychological effect in Finland.[1] It brought an immediate reaction from Mannerheim in the form of a request to Dietl for return of four of the five (later also the fifth) Finnish battalions still with the Twentieth Mountain Army. Dietl was reluctant to part with the battalions since their personnel, mostly native to northern Finland, far surpassed German troops at the vital task of protecting the open flanks of his corps. Moreover, it was clear that, since the number of troops involved was small, Mannerheim's request was primarily an expression, thinly disguised, of declining confidence in his German "brothers-in-arms." The OKW, probably believing that the situation would not be helped by descending to a squabble over battalions, ordered the Twentieth Mountain Army to return four of the battalions as quickly as replacements could be found, retaining only the fifth, the "Ivalo" Battalion, which was essential for the defense of Pechenga.[2]

As far as German planning for operations in Finland was concerned, the withdrawal south of Lake Ladoga and Mannerheim's reaction to it only confirmed the correctness of decisions already made. A conference

---

[1] *H. Gr. Nord, Ia, 13000/44, Der Feldzug gegen die Sowjet-Union der Heeresgruppe Nord, Kriegsjahr 1943, 24.12.44.*
[2] *(Geb.) AOK 20, Ia, Nr. 133/43, an OKW, WFSt, 29.1.43, in K.T.B. Nr. 2, Anlagenband I.* AOK 20 36560/2. *(Geb.) AOK 20, Ia, Kriegstagebuch Nr. 2, Erstausfertigung, 13 and 16 Feb 43.* AOK 20 36560/1.

at Fuehrer Headquarters on 14 January had decided that there was almost no chance of the Twentieth Mountain Army's being given an offensive mission in the year 1943. In the north it was not strong enough to take and hold the Rybatchiy Peninsula. An operation against Kandalaksha would require a simultaneous Finnish drive to Belomorsk, which was not expected, and at least an additional division plus two regiments for the Twentieth Mountain Army, which could not be spared elsewhere. The Twentieth Mountain Army was to remain prepared to beat off a British-American landing which might be aided by a Russian offensive or Swedish intervention.[3] In spite of the strained situation on the main front, the OKW did not intend to pull troops out of the Twentieth Mountain Army sector.

The conference had come to a thoroughly negative estimate of Finnish capabilities. The strength of the Finns, it had concluded, had been overestimated. They had no inclination for a large-scale offensive; more serious still, if the Russians launched a major attack against them, setbacks were to be expected. Their defenses were poorly constructed, they had few reserves, and their army was not imbued with the spirit of holding to the last man. Their greatest asset, it was decided, was the terrain, which made a Russian attack unlikely in the foreseeable future.[4]

While the Germans were engaged in writing off Finland as a positive element in their military situation, the Finns were taking a long, cold look at the whole war. On 3 February, the day after the Sixth Army surrendered at Stalingrad, Mannerheim, Ryti, and several members of the Cabinet, meeting at Mikkeli, concluded that the war had passed a decisive turning point and that for Finland it had become necessary to get out at the first opportunity. Six days later, in a secret session, Parliament was informed that Germany could no longer win and that Finland, tied to Germany for the immediate future at least, would have to accustom itself to thinking in terms of another Treaty of Moscow (1940).[5]

What appeared to be a ray of hope for Finland was not long in coming. The re-election of Ryti in mid-February provided an opportunity for changing the Cabinet; and Dr. Henrik Ramsay, who was reputed to have connections in Great Britain and the United States, replaced Witting as Foreign Minister. To the new Foreign Minister the United States State Department on 20 March transmitted an offer to establish contact between Finland and the Soviet Union.

New to diplomacy and certainly not acquainted with the personality of Ribbentrop, Ramsay decided to take the matter to Berlin in the hope of paving the way for Finland's withdrawal from the war by a friendly agreement. Ribbentrop, dispelling his illusions in short order, told him

---

[3] For estimates of Swedish intentions, see below, pp. 252ff.
[4] (Geb.) AOK 20, Ia, Zeitenfolge des O.B.-Besuchs beim Fuehrer und Obersten Befehlshaber, 14.1.43, in K.T.B. Nr. 2, Anlagenband I. AOK 20 36560/2.
[5] Mannerheim, op. cit., pp. 491ff.

that Germany was also fighting the war for Finland and the German people would not appreciate having Finland "cast come-hither looks" at the Russians. He then confronted Ramsay with two demands: the first for a prompt rejection of the United States offer and the second for a public declaration that Finland would not negotiate a separate peace. The first was not too painful to meet since subsequent developments revealed that the United States merely intended to establish direct contact between the parties, not to mediate. But the second, if complied with, would have meant abandoning the independent status as a cobelligerent which Finland had claimed since the start of the war. The Finnish Government delayed until 16 May when the Prime Minister gave a speech in which he stated that Finland would fight to the end rather than throw itself on the mercy of its eastern neighbor. The text was transmitted to Berlin with an explanation that it constituted the official Finnish attitude. The Finns had gone far enough to avoid jeopardizing their badly needed imports from Germany but not far enough to please Ribbentrop who called home for two months his minister in Helsinki.[6]

In mid-March, to coordinate planning for the entire Scandinavian area, the Operations Staff, OKW, called in the Chief of Staff, Twentieth Mountain Army, and the Operations Officer, Army of Norway. It was agreed that a landing by British-American forces on the north coast of Norway or Finland was possible, but that they could succeed in driving the Germans out of Scandinavia only if the landing were accompanied by a simultaneous Soviet offensive, which the OKW regarded as improbable because of mistrust among the Allies. The Twentieth Mountain Army considered a Soviet offensive of any kind unlikely; it had reported a month earlier that the Russians had drawn at least three rifle divisions and two rifle brigades out of their front in the north, an indication that they neither expected nor planned an attack. As a basis for planning, the OKW proposed it could be assumed Finland's status would not change unless a Soviet offensive directly threatened southern Finland or a successful British-American landing brought Sweden into the war against Germany.

Describing the position of Finland, the Chief of Staff, Twentieth Mountain Army, stated that, since Stalingrad, opinion in Finland had decidedly shifted against Germany, and the Finnish Government no longer believed in a German victory. Pessimism was particularly strong in Mannerheim's headquarters, at least partly the result, he believed, of the dark picture General Talvela, then liaison officer at the OKH, was painting of the German situation. The Finns, he thought, were preparing to shift their course, and only a great German victory in the summer of 1943 could prevent their making a determined effort to defect. Whether Finland could get an acceptable peace was another question since it did not appear that either Great Britain or the United

⁶ Bluecher, *op. cit.*, pp. 320–34. Mannerheim, *op. cit.*, pp. 493ff.

States would be able to offer any substantial guarantees, and without them Finland would be completely at the mercy of the Soviet Union. The Chief of the Operations Staff, OKW, Jodl, on the other hand, stated the belief that the Finns, while protecting their own national interest, would keep faith with Germany. To counteract the pessimism he proposed to ask that Talvela be recalled. For the future, he expected an operation against Leningrad, planned for the summer, to have a beneficial effect "on the entire northern area." [7]

While the highest headquarters in Germany and Finland were attempting to discover which way the wind would blow, the front from the Gulf of Finland to Litsa Bay was dead quiet, a condition which had persisted with very minor interruptions since the Soviet spring offensive of 1942. At one point the Twentieth Mountain Army and the OKW found themselves engaged in a desultory argument over whether the army front should be designated as "the front without combat activity" (*Front ohne Kampfhandlungen*), which the OKW had adopted, or as "the front without extensive combat activity" (*Front ohne groessere Kampfhandlungen*), which the Twentieth Mountain Army favored on the grounds that numbers of casualties were still being reported.

In the far north the greatest problem of the XIX Mountain Corps, because it remained dependent on the sea route around Norway, was supply; but even that affected the building up of reserves rather than current needs. The front on the Litsa which had been the scene of the 1941 and 1942 fighting had been built up into a strong line of interconnecting strong points. Because construction was difficult in the rocky terrain, completely satisfactory positions there could not be completed until the summer of 1944. The troops were housed in huts behind the line, which, except in emergencies, was manned by a skeleton force. The climate imposed hardships but, at the same time, was responsible for an extraordinarily low sickness rate. South of the Litsa front a screening line of strong points, at intervals of 1 to 3 miles in the north but 8, 10, and more miles over most of its length, extended to the level of Ivalo. Between the flanks of the XIX Mountain Corps and the XXXVI Mountain Corps the front was open for a distance of one hundred miles and more. On the coast the Divisionsgruppe Rossi had been created to defend the Pechenga area while the 210th Infantry Division was responsible for the zone east to the Army of Norway boundary. The nickel mines were the most remarkable installation in the XIX Mountain Corps area. At Hitler's order, the processing installations and power plants were being moved underground or into bomb-proof concrete structures as quickly as those could be built. A

---

[7] (*Geb.*) *AOK 20, Ia, Besprechungsnotiz anlaesslich der Anwesenheit des Chefs des Gen.-St. (Geb.) AOK 20, Generalmajor Jodl, im OKW vom 16.–17.3.43*, in (*Geb.*) *AOK 20, Ia, K.T.B. Nr. 2, Anlagenband III.* AOK 20 36560/4. *OKW, WFSt, K.T.B.*, 18 Feb and 10 Mar 43. International Military Tribunal, Doc. 1789–PS.

Troop quarters on the Litsa front.

regiment of infantry with artillery guarded the mines, which reputedly had stronger antiaircraft defenses than any other spot on the Eastern Front.[8]

The XXXVI Mountain Corps, in a line which had not changed since the fall of 1941, and the XVIII Mountain Corps had constructed strong positions on their immediate fronts with screens of strong points off the flanks. Lumber was available in plentiful supply, and the troops were housed in barracks. Conditions were similar on the Finnish Army front, where the Finns' skill in carpentry had produced structures which were not only serviceable but often decorative as well. All in all, the forces in Finland were on a near peacetime basis.

The quiet was ominous for it signified that the enemy believed the fate of the Twentieth Mountain Army and the Finnish nation was sealed and that he was biding his time before bringing down the final curtain. In Finland all eyes were turned south to the main front where the two vital questions were whether the German armies could establish a line that would hold and whether the Army Group North, in particular, could keep its grip on Leningrad. Both were questions of life or death for Finland, the latter being of the greatest immediate importance because, once Leningrad had been liberated, the Russians could turn north on the Isthmus of Karelia, strike at the heart of Finland, and knock her out of the war regardless of what happened elsewhere. The danger was heightened by the fact that, aside from the city's strategic significance in relation to Finland, the Soviet Union had made Leningrad a national symbol and its liberation a matter of prestige.

---

[8] Generalleutnant, a.D. Hans Degen, *Dreieinhalb Jahre Polarkrieg.* MS D–337. OCMH.

Knowing the importance of Leningrad to Finland and, therefore, to the entire German position in Scandinavia, Hitler on 13 March ordered the Army Group North to prepare an operation, timed for late summer, for the capture of Leningrad.[9] Even at the time it was issued, Hitler's order rested on a questionable assumption—that the Army Group North, which was completely on the defensive, would be able to regain the initiative long enough to stage an offensive. The army group itself reported that the enemy had two operational possibilities which he was certain to pursue to the limit of his ability in 1943. The first was to push the Germans back from Leningrad, as he had already attempted during the winter. The other was to strike south of Lake Ilmen at the junction of the Army Groups North and Center, split the two German forces, and drive the Army Group North back against the Baltic coast.[10] There was no real certainty that the Army Group North could prevent him from doing either.

During the relatively quiet months of the spring Kuechler's staff planned Operation PARKPLATZ, the taking of Leningrad. Much of the siege artillery brought up in 1942 was still in the army group area, but reinforcements of eight or nine divisions would be needed, and those could not be made available until after the Army Group South had completed Operation ZITTADELLE to pinch off the giant salient which had remained west of Kursk after the winter battles.[11]

ZITTADELLE was launched on 5 July only to be stopped within a week. It was then turned into a crushing defeat by a massive Soviet counter-offensive which broke through the German line on the Donets River at the end of the month and in the next two months was to drive the Army Group South back from the Donets to the Dnepr. Once their offensive was rolling in the south the Russians turned to the north and on 22 July opened a second full-scale attempt to free Leningrad.[12] With a catastrophe brewing in the south and another possible in the north, the OKH on 31 July ordered the Army Group North to set up a special staff for the purpose of laying out a line of defensive positions along the Narva River and the west shore of Lake Peipus, 125 miles southwest of Leningrad.[13] Operation PARKPLATZ was forgotten.

In Finland, as the summer passed, apprehension grew. In July the Finnish SS-battalion was returned to Finland at Mannerheim's request and disbanded. During the same month, Finland rejected a Soviet oral offer to discuss peace, delivered through its legation in Stockholm.

[9] OKH, GenStdH, Op. Abt., Nr. 430 163/43, Operationsbefehl Nr. 5, 13.3.43. OKW, WFSt, K.T.B., 17 Mar 43. International Military Tribunal, Doc. 1786–PS.
[10] Oberkommando Heeresgruppe Nord, Ia, Nr. 037/42, Beurteilung der Lage der Heeresgruppe Nord, 18.4.43, in OKH, GenStdH, Op. Abt., I/N, Band I, Nord. H 22/223.
[11] OKH, GenStdH, Op. Abt. I/N, Parkplatz. H 22/281.
[12] H. Gr. Nord, Ia, 13000/44, Der Feldzug gegen die Sowjet-Union der Heeresgruppe Nord, Kriegsjahr 1943, 24.12.44.
[13] OKH, GenStdH, Op. Abt., Nr. 430493, an H. Gr. Nord, 2.8.43–[31.7.43 orally], in OKH, GenStdH, Op. Abt., I/N, Band I, Nord. H 22/223.

About the same time, the Finns, through their legation in Lisbon, informed the United States that they would not join in resistance to a United States invasion of northern Norway.[14]   In August, with the tide clearly turned against Germany in the south, three members of Parliament delivered to Ryti a petition signed by 33 prominent men in which it was stated that Finland was slipping into a dangerous situation.   The President was asked to take steps toward restoring good relations and mutual confidence with the United States and toward getting Finland out of the war.[15]   Later in the month publication of the contents of the petition in a Swedish newspaper touched off a press and public discussion which heavily favored a separate peace.

With anxiety already growing, Finland in September was threatened with the development which it feared most.   The Army Group North, after a month of Soviet attacks, was holding around Leningrad by the skin of its teeth and was working desperately to build the so-called PANTHER Position, the Narva River–Lake Peipus line.   Even to the inexperienced observer it was clear that a withdrawal, which was already the decision of choice, might at any moment be forced on the army group.

Replying to an OKW request for an opinion, the Twentieth Mountain Army on 14 September stated that the Army Group North should not be pulled back under any circumstances.   The Finns, the army memorandum went on, already felt betrayed because the capture of Leningrad had been repeatedly promised and never carried out, even in times when, in their opinion, it had been possible.   Once the Army Group North fell back to Lake Peipus the Finnish Aunus and Maaselkä Fronts would project into Soviet territory like a spearhead and have to be withdrawn under circumstances which made the establishment of a tenable line to the rear doubtful at best.   More than likely, a shift in governments would result, bringing to power a regime oriented toward Russia.   If the Russians then offered bearable peace conditions Finland would leave the war and the Twentieth Mountain Army would have to find its way out of Finland, an undertaking which in wintertime over the poor roads of northern Finland and Norway would be extremely hazardous.[16]   A week later the Finnish Government warned, through both the German Minister in Helsinki and their own Minister in Berlin, that a withdrawal from the area south and west of Leningrad would have the most serious consequences for Finland.[17]   At the end of the

---

[14] Mannerheim, *op. cit.*, pp. 497ff.
[15] *Auswaertiges Amt, No. Pol. VI 1091, an das Oberkommando der Wehrmacht, 30.8.43, in OKW, Ag. Ausland, Akte Finnland.   OKW/1040.*
[16] *(Geb.) AOK 20, Ia, Nr. 12/43, an OKW, WFSt, z. Hd. Gen. d. Art. Jodl, 14.9.43, in Anlagen zum Chefsachen-K.T.B., (Geb.) AOK 20, Ia, 1.7.43–31.12.43.* AOK 20 43871/10.
[17] *Auswaertiges Amt, Pol. VI 9259, an das Oberkommando der Wehrmacht, 22.9.43, in OKW, Ag. Ausland, Akte Finnland.   OKW/1040.* Bluecher, *op. cit.*, p. 341.

month, the Commanding General, XXXVI Mountain Corps, reported after a trip to Helsinki that fear of a withdrawal from Leningrad dominated Finnish thinking.[18]

The tragic element in the Finnish situation was heightened by the fact that at no time in the war had local tactical conditions been more favorable for a Finnish-German offensive. The Finnish Minister of Defense told the Commanding General, XXXVI Mountain Corps, that on its front Finland had roughly 400,000 men while the Russians opposite them numbered between 160,000 and 180,000.[19] The Twentieth Mountain Army had over 170,000 combat troops facing approximately 90,000 Russians. The Finns' refusal to exploit that clear 2:1 superiority drew some criticism from the German side, both at the time and after the war. The German opinion was that Finland did not want to risk a complete breach with the United States.[20] In reality, there was no way an offensive out of Finland could have permanently influenced the course of events. The Murmansk Railroad could possibly have been cut, but by then it was no longer vital to the Russian war effort; Soviet production had increased and supplies from the West were moving through the Persian Gulf. A strong Finnish thrust on the Isthmus of Karelia, which might have relieved the situation of the Army Group North temporarily, would in the long run have been suicidal for the Finnish nation.

On 24 September the Russian pressure south of Leningrad slacked off, but unmistakable signs of trouble had cropped up on the Army Group North–Army Group Center boundary east of Nevel.[21] A successful breakthrough there, properly exploited, threatened to bring about a collapse of the entire Army Group North front.

On 28 September the Twentieth Mountain Army received Fuehrer Directive No. 50. By way of explanation Hitler stated that the situation of the Army Group North was "completely stabilized," that the danger point on the Army Group North–Army Group Center boundary was being reinforced, but that in order to be prepared for unfavorable developments the army group was constructing positions on the Narva River–Lake Peipus line. It had also become necessary to take measures in anticipation of Finland's possible withdrawal from the war.[22] In that case the mission of the Twentieth Mountain Army would be to swing the XXXVI Mountain Corps and the XVIII Mountain Corps back

---

[18] *Der Kommandierende General des XXXVI (Geb.) A.K., Ia, Nr. 252/43, Militaerpolitische Eindruecke auf meiner Suedfinnlandreise, 28.9.43,* in *Anlagen zum Chefsachen-K.T.B., (Geb.) AOK 20, Ia, 11.7.43–31.12.43.* AOK 20 43871/10.
[19] *Ibid.*
[20] Erfurth, *op. cit.,* p. 119. Dietl, *op. cit.,* p. 259.
[21] *H. Gr. Nord, Ia, 13000/44, Der Feldzug gegen die Sowjet-Union der Heeres-gruppe Nord, Kriegsjahr 1943, 24.12.44.*
[22] The Operations Staff, OKW, had told Hitler three days earlier that signs of a peace move in Finland were increasing and a complete shift on the part of Finland was to be expected if the Army Group North fell back. *OKW, WFSt, K.T.B.,* 28 Sep 43. International Military Tribunal, Doc. 1790–PS.

to a line across northern Finland south of Ivalo and defend the nickel mining region as long as might be necessary. When the time came, the Twentieth Mountain Army would be given two additional divisions from the Army of Norway. Construction and supply preparations were to begin immediately.[23]

On 6 October the expected Soviet offensive east of Nevel began, and in three days the flanks of the Army Group North and the Army Group Center had lost contact. In that dangerous situation Mannerheim reverted to a request which he had raised tentatively and been persuaded to withdraw earlier: he asked permission to begin preparing defensive positions behind the Twentieth Mountain Army lines for the event of a German withdrawal from Finland. This signal mark of failing confidence led Erfurth to ask that the OKW send a top-level representative immediately.[24] On the 14th Jodl flew to Helsinki and in two days of conferences with Mannerheim and the Finnish Minister of Defense described the war situation as seen from the German side. The defection of Italy, he explained, was not significant militarily since that nation had never constituted an element of strength in the alliance. As far as an invasion of France was concerned, Germany would welcome it as an opportunity to deal Great Britain and the United States a resounding defeat, put an end to second front plans, and free troops for the Eastern Front. At Leningrad, he admitted, the situation was dangerous; and there had been a thought of pulling the northern flank back; but, out of consideration for Finland, Germany had abstained from following that course. Germany, he let it be known, was aware of Finnish efforts to get out of the war and took the attitude that no nation could ask another to risk destruction for its sake; but, he pointed out, Finland's future in the clutches of Stalin would not be bright.[25]

While not concurring in all of the points of his analysis, the Finns were impressed by Jodl's presentation—and by a letter Jodl brought with him in which Hitler took Ryti to task over the lack of discipline in Finnish internal policy and the unfriendly attitude of the Finnish press toward Germany.[26] Under both these influences the Finnish Minister of Defense a week later promised Dietl the "truest brotherhood in arms" and assured him that the newspaper talk of a separate peace was groundless. Jodl, he said, had explained the total situation "openly and completely." [27] At the end of the month Ryti replied to Hitler in a letter, which, while it contained no specific commitments, was taken to be positive in tone.[28]

[23] OKW, WFSt, Op., Nr. 662375/43, Weisung Nr. 50, 28.9.43 in Anlagen zum Chefsachen-K.T.B., (Geb.) AOK 20, Ia, 1.7.43–31.12.43. AOK 20 43871/10.
[24] OKW, WFSt, K.T.B., 15 Oct 43. I.M.T., Doc. 1790–PS.
[25] Mannerheim, op. cit., pp. 498ff.
[26] Dietl, op. cit., p. 261.
[27] (Geb.) AOK 20, Ia, Aktennotiz ueber die Besprechung mit dem finnischen Verteidigungsminister, General der Infanterie Walden, 25.10.43, in (Geb.) AOK 20, Ia, K.T.B., Anlagenband Oktober 1943. AOK 20 43871/5.
[28] OKW, WFSt, K.T.B., 30 Oct 43. I.M.T., Doc. 1790.

While Jodl was in Mikkeli the Twentieth Mountain Army took the opportunity to raise its objections to Directive 50. Even though the army, possessing an eight to nine months' stockpile of fuel, rations, and ammunition, was the best supplied of the German armies, it saw no prospect of being able to hold out in northern Finland for a prolonged period. Neither the Navy nor the Air Force, it believed, was capable of preventing the enemy's cutting its sea supply lines around Norway and at the same time interdicting the ore traffic. The army saw itself stranded, dissipating its supplies in an effort to hold mines which could not be exploited. Jodl and the OKW agreed with the army position in general but did not believe it would be possible, in any event, to withdraw across the Baltic Sea, as the Twentieth Mountain Army proposed, and did not want to risk giving up the mines prematurely.[29]

After the Jodl mission, as the year drew to a close, it appeared that a measure of stability had been restored in German-Finnish relations, and Hitler ordered that Directive 50 be regarded for the time being as a stand-by measure. The balance was delicate. In late October Mannerheim renewed his request for permission to lay out defensive positions behind the German lines, and in November Finland resumed its contact with the Soviet Union.[30] In the fighting around Nevel, the Army Group North was being spared complete disaster as much through lack of daring and imagination on the part of the Soviet leadership as through its own efforts. The Nevel operation had been staged to tie down German forces in the north while the main Soviet offensive proceeded in the south; therefore, the Russians were slow in exploiting their breakthrough. At the end of October and again in December the Army Group North warned that, if the enemy succeeded in expanding the breakthrough at Nevel, the PANTHER Position would be outflanked and the entire army group front would collapse.[31] Toward the end of December Hitler began seriously to consider taking Army Group North back to the PANTHER Position in order to gain a dozen or so divisions for the southern flank of the Eastern Front where the Russians were threatening the Crimea and were about to retake the iron and manganese mines at Krivoi Rog and Nikopol. While such a move would place greater pressure on the Finnish front, he believed the Finns would still have to fight and might thus even afford some relief for the German main front. But to lose more ground in southern Russia, he thought, might bring Turkey into the war and so add to the burden on Germany.

---

[29] (Geb.) AOK 20, Ia, Besprechungspunkte zwischen Chef OKW/WFSt und Chef (Geb.) AOK 20 am 14.10.43 in Mikkeli, in Anlagen zum Chefsachen-K.T.B., (Geb.) AOK 20, Ia, 1.7.43–31.12.43. AOK 20 43871/10. OKW, WFSt, K.T.B., 19 Oct 43. I.M.T., Doc. 1790-PS.

[30] OKW, WFSt, K.T.B., 25 Oct and 16 Dec 43. I.M.T., Doc. 1790-PS. Mannerheim, op. cit., p. 500.

[31] H. Gr. Nord., Ia, 154/43, Beurteilung der Lage, 28.10.42, and OKH, GenStdH, Op. Abt., I/N, Nr. 430765/43, Abschrift von Fernschreiben, Beurteilung der Lage der H. Gr. Nord vom 13.12.43, in OKH, GenStdH, Op. Abt., I/N, Band I, Nord. H 22/223.

On 31 December the OKW drafted a letter warning Mannerheim of the proposed withdrawal, but in the following days Hitler became preoccupied with second thoughts. Before long, the plan vanished in the onrush of events.[32]

Norway, 1943

The Problem of a Defensive Strategy for Scandinavia

In the early months of 1943 Hitler's chronic fear of an invasion of Norway, reinforced by recent events in North Africa and by the growing hostility of Sweden, continued unabated. The North African landings appeared to indicate that the Allies were committed to a strategy of attacking on the periphery of Europe, which made Norway a likely next target. Sweden, regarded with lingering suspicion since the summer of 1941 when it refused to join Hitler's "crusade against Bolshevism," became a new source of apprehension in 1942 as its policy toward Germany stiffened in direct proportion to the increasing danger of Allied landings in Scandinavia.

On the question of where the invasion might take place the German command was in general agreement. Both Hitler and Falkenhorst remained deeply impressed by the report on Allied planning which had come to them through Finnish sources in December 1942, not only because it seemed reliable but also because it offered in fact the greatest prospects of success at the lowest cost. Falkenhorst believed that landings in Denmark, southern Norway, at Trondheim, or at Narvik would be considered too costly; he thought the Allies' objective would not be to retake Norway but rather, by an attack probably somewhere between Narvik and Trondheim, to interdict German traffic to the Polar area and to influence the Swedish and Finnish attitudes.[33] The Operations Branch, OKW, thought a further objective of such an operation might be to establish contact with the Swedes and with their tolerance or support cross northern Sweden via Tornio to attack in the rear of the Twentieth Mountain Army.[34]

The possible Swedish intentions with regard to such an operation were described as "obscure." Most disturbing was the knowledge that Sweden might very well be able to decide the issue by passive measures alone. At the turn of the year 1942–43, reliable attaché reports indi-

[32] *Stenogr. Dienst im F.H.Qu., Fragment Nr. 11, Besprechung mit Gen. Oberst Zeitzler vom 29.12.43. OKW, WFSt, K.T.B.,* 31 Dec 43. I.M.T. Doc. 1790–PS.
[33] *AOK Norwegen, Ia, Nr. 773/43, Notiz fuer Vortrag bei WFSt,* [date of entry] 6.3.43, in *Taetigkeitsberichte Monat Februar 1943.* AOK 20 34698/2. *Der Chef des Generalstabes der Armee Norwegen, Ia, Nr. 15/43, Besprechung der operativen Aufgaben, 21.3.43,* in *Taetigkeitsberichte Monat Maerz 1943.* AOK 20 34698/3.
[34] *OKW, WFSt, K.T.B.,* 10 Mar 43. International Military Tribunal, Doc. 1786–PS.

cated that at the time of a landing Sweden would stop all German transit across its territory and return to strict neutrality. It was assumed that in the further course of events Sweden would not aid the Germans but might support the Allies. To the Germans loss of the transit privileges, together with the halting of sea traffic along the Norwegian coast certain to result from any landing, meant that all Army of Norway units at and north of Narvik and the XIX Mountain Corps in Finland would be isolated and serious supply problems would be created for central and southern Norway. To be prepared for such an emergency the OKW on 5 January reaffirmed an order issued a year earlier for the establishment of reserve stockpiles of eight to nine months' supplies in the Narvik–north Finland zone.[35]

In early February the OKW took under consideration the question of operational reserves for the Army of Norway. Three months before, Hitler had stated the intention of making one, possibly two, additional divisions available for Norway. On 5 February the OKW decided to send six fortress battalions to release one division for the army reserve and, if possible, also to transfer a mountain division to Norway. It also concluded that the Armed Forces Commander, Norway, would have to be given a directive covering the possibility of Sweden's entrance into the war and that the Air Force would have to begin its ground preparation for such an eventuality immediately.[36] That a written directive was issued is unlikely since the Operations Branch, OKW, returned to the same question a month later; but that the Army of Norway received instructions in some form to include Sweden in its considerations regarding the defense of Norway is indicated in orders which it issued early in February.

On 10 February Generalleutnant Rudolf Bamler, Chief of Staff, Army of Norway, signed two top secret orders. One was sent to the LXX Corps and the XXXIII Corps directing them to take under consideration that each might—while retaining full responsibility for the defense of its sector of the Norwegian coast—be required to release one division as army reserves "for other purposes." The XXXIII Corps was to be prepared to give up a second infantry division in exchange for an Air Force field division.[37] The second went to Generalleutnant Adolf von Schell, Commanding General, 25th Panzer Division, instructing him as follows:

In order to be prepared for the possibility that Anglo-Saxon forces in a large-scale attack on Scandinavia may thrust into Sweden or land airborne forces there and that Sweden cannot or does not wish to defend

[35] OKW, WFSt, K.T.B., 5 Jan 43. I.M.T., Doc. 1786–PS.
[36] OKW, WFSt, K.T.B., 5 Feb 43. I.M.T., Doc. 1786–PS.
[37] AOK Norwegen, Ia, Nr. 2/43, an Gen. Kdo. LXX A.K., Gen Kdo. XXXIII A.K., Kdr. 25. Pz. Div. (nachrichtlich), 8.2.43, in Taetigkeitsberichte Monat Februar 1943. AOK 20 34698/2.

its territory the 25th Panzer Division is to work out a study on the following basis:

1.) The enemy, after successes in the Arctic area, has crossed the Swedish border in the direction of Kiruna and has taken the airfields of southern Sweden with strong air forces and airborne troops. The Swedish Armed Forces have offered scattered resistance but can be expected to stop all operations in a short time on orders from their government. How the Swedish forces will respond to a German invasion is undetermined.

2.) Own intention—to prevent the enemy advancing from Narvik to Kiruna and the airborne forces from completing the occupation of Sweden and to take southern Sweden as a German base of operations.

The operations necessary for this purpose should be conceived with the greatest daring on the assumption that the Swedish Armed Forces will, at least, not offer unified resistance and will not be in complete agreement with the decision of their government to offer no resistance to the Anglo-Saxons but to oppose the Germans.

3.) Execution of the operation. Two possibilities are to be given consideration:

a. An advance eastward from the Trondheim area via Östersund to the Gulf of Bothnia in order to prevent the enemy forces in northern Sweden from making contact with those in the south and to create the preconditions for the destruction of the enemy in southern Sweden.

b. An advance eastward from the Oslo area into the area north of Stockholm including the occupation of Stockholm in order rapidly thereafter to take possession of the airfields located south of the general line Oslo–Stockholm.

For the operation, Schell was told he could count on having the 25th Panzer Division, one infantry division in the vicinity of Trondheim, another near Oslo, and strong air and airborne support.[38]

During the remainder of February and the first weeks of March, the chances that the Army of Norway would be able seriously to institute new operational planning did not look bright. Russian successes at Stalingrad and elsewhere on the Eastern Front and mounting Allied pressure in North Africa had created an acute manpower shortage in early 1943 which left the OKW with nothing to spare for the Army of Norway. After the 14th Air Force Field Division, which had begun leaving Germany in December 1942, assembled in southern Norway in February, the OKW did not return to its intention expressed earlier of also sending a mountain division. On 1 March the Army of Norway had a strength of 10 infantry divisions plus the 14th Air Force Field Division, still being equipped and trained, and the 25th Panzer Division, so far not much more than an agglomeration of small motorized and

---

[38] *AOK Norwegen, Ia, Nr. 3/43, an den Kommandeur der 25. Pz. Div., 10.2.43,* in *Taetigkeitsberichte Monat Februar 1943.* AOK 20 34698/2.

armored detachments.[39]   With its existing strength—considerably watered down by exchanges with the Eastern Front in the previous year—the army considered itself hardly capable of doing more than maintaining its static defenses along the Norwegian coast, particularly since a partially successful British raid in January 1943 brought renewed demands from Hitler for an airtight defense of the coast.   In March, to achieve a degree of mobility, it began moving the 14th Air Force Field Division into the Namsos–Bodö area to take over the coastal positions of the 196th Infantry Division while the latter pulled back to act as a reserve force in that, as it was believed, threatened area.   At the same time the scattered elements of the 25th Panzer Division were assembled in southern Norway, northeast of Oslo, to provide the nucleus of an operational reserve.

On 8 March the Operations Staff, OKW, turned again to the question of the "obscure attitude of the Swedish Government" and proposed to issue an order instructing Falkenhorst to determine what measures might become necessary if Sweden were to intervene on the side of the enemy.   It wanted to suggest as a basis mobile defensive tactics to prevent a junction of Allied and Swedish forces and the "exploitation of every opportunity" to operate offensively across the Swedish border for the purpose of "nipping in the bud any Swedish attempts to attack." That order did not get Jodl's approval, and two days later a second was drawn up, this time instructing the Armed Forces Commander, Norway, and the Commanding General, Twentieth Mountain Army, to prepare jointly a short study concerning the conduct of operations in the entire Scandinavian area "for the event that the military and political situation there might change."   Contrary to the earlier intention, it was proposed that the Army of Norway and the Twentieth Mountain Army maintain contact with each other and prevent a junction of the Allies and Swedes but "avoid even the appearance of encroaching on Swedish sovereignty." No additional forces were foreseen for either army.   On orders from Hitler that directive was not issued, though its contents were apparently communicated orally to the Chief of Staff, Twentieth Mountain Army, and the Operations Officer, Army of Norway on 16 March.[40]

---

[39] After the 25th Panzer Division was activated in Norway in early 1942, progress in bringing it up to strength had been slow.   In March 1943 it was just beginning to receive some German Mark III and IV tanks, but, for the most part, its tank armament consisted of obsolete German Mark II's and French Hotchkiss and Suoma tanks.   It had a ration strength, probably somewhat higher than the actual strength, of 11,000 men.

When he took command of the division in early January 1943 Schell reported that "everything" was still missing.   The tanks and artillery were too weak and the troops untrained.   He proposed to conduct training in the following three directions:
1.   To combat an enemy landed in Norway,
2.   To fight against Sweden, [tactics—] break through and then, where successful, thrust deep regardless of neighboring columns,
3.   To fight under normal tank conditions.
25. Pz. Div., Kommandeur, Tgb. Nr. 1/43, Lage der Division, 6.1.43, in AOK Norwegen Ia, Chefsachen zum K.T.B., 5.5.42–4.9.43.   AOK 20 45273.
[40] OKW, WFSt, K.T.B., 3 Mar 43. I.M.T., Doc. 1786–PS. Walter Warlimont, Commentary on the OKW War Diary, pp. 224ff. OCMH.

Both Hitler and Jodl were obviously anxious to avoid offering Sweden any provocation at that time, especially since militarily they were not in a position to accept the consequences; but it was quickly demonstrated that the latter condition was one which Hitler, at least, did not intend to tolerate indefinitely. In his weekly report for the first week of March Falkenhorst requested that, since it appeared that the mountain division which he had been promised would not be forthcoming, an attempt at least be made to give him several fortress battalions. The Operations Staff, OKW, believed that it would not be possible to create fortress battalions for Norway. On 13 March, in discussing the matter with Hitler, Jodl learned that Hitler was still determined to reinforce the Army of Norway, intending to send six fortress battalions as soon as possible and planning to learn from the Army Chief of Staff whether it might not be possible, after all, to release a mountain division for Norway from the Eastern Front. Hitler also stated an intention to equip the 25th Panzer Division with "the heaviest assault weapons, ones against which Sweden possesses no means of defense." [41]

By the time the Chief of Staff, Twentieth Mountain Army, and the Operations Officer, Army of Norway, arrived at Fuehrer Headquarters on 16 March the terms of the discussion, as foreseen by the Operations Staff, OKW, on 10 March, had already changed somewhat in view of Hitler's renewed insistence on reinforcing the Army of Norway. The Operations Officer, Army of Norway, Col. Bernard von Lossberg, reported that the Army of Norway considered Allied landings possible in two areas, namely, between Trondheim and Narvik and between Alta Fiord and Tana Fiord. The first was considered the more likely, particularly by Jodl, who expressed the opinion then current in the Operations Branch, OKW, that mutual suspicion and mistrust would prevent collaboration of the Western Powers and Russia in the far north. Concerning the question of cooperation between the Army of Norway and the Twentieth Mountain Army in dealing with a landing, the indications were that the Twentieth Mountain Army would not be able to give substantial help because its forces were nearly all committed at the front. It was suggested that the Twentieth Mountain Army attempt to create an operational reserve of one division by reducing the divisions of the XXXVI Mountain Corps to two regiments each. (The Twentieth Mountain Army rejected this solution a day or two later.) With regard to operational reserves for the Army of Norway, Jodl indicated that the army would be given the 295th Infantry Division, a reactivated Stalingrad division, and that the 25th Panzer Division would be built up;

[41] *OKW, WFSt, K.T.B.*, 13 Mar 43. I.M.T., Doc. 1786–PS. *W.B. Norwegen, Ia, Nr. 792/43, Woechentlicher Lagebericht, 9.3.43,* in *Taetigkeitsberichte fuer den Monat Maerz 1943.* AOK 20 34698/3.

but all he promised for the division in the near future was 500 trucks.[42]

In the week following the conference Hitler intervened again to increase and speed up the reinforcements for the Army of Norway. Quite suddenly, the tide of the war seemed once more to be turning in his favor. The Army Group Center had completed a planned withdrawal which shortened its front by several hundred kilometers. In the Ukraine, Manstein, in a counterattack which had retaken Kharkov, was dealing the Russians a thumping defeat which ended their winter offensive. As Manstein's army group began consolidating its front, Hitler, for the first time in many months, found himself with divisions to spare, not enough to contemplate another offensive like those of 1941 and 1942 but sufficient for an attempt at regaining the initiative in limited areas of the Eastern Front and for strengthening the German position in Scandinavia.

On 23 March the OKW informed Falkenhorst that the 295th Infantry Division would be brought up to a strength of two regiments plus eight fortress battalions, an engineer battalion, and a communications unit. The 25th Panzer Division was to be brought up to full strength before the end of June. It would be given ten Panzer IV's five self-propelled assault guns, and ten heavy antitank guns per month during April, May, and June. Three of the fortress battalions Falkenhorst planned to station in southern Norway and in the far north to create local reserves. The remaining five, plus two already on hand, he intended to leave with the 295th Infantry Division which would move into the Trondheim area where it would release the 181st Infantry Division for the reserve.[43]

During the last week of March Schell put the finishing touches on his "Operational Study, Sweden," which he submitted to the Army of Norway on 6 April. His first concern was to devise tactics suitable to the terrain of Sweden and capable of execution with relatively weak forces. Deciding that an attack through the mountains of western Sweden would have to follow the roads and valleys, he chose to rely on the shock effect of a swift, almost reckless, advance. He proposed to echelon his tanks and infantry in such a manner that, by leapfrogging, fresh spearheads could take over at intervals, enabling the advance to continue at high speed day and night. This was in part an adaptation of the tactics developed during the advance north through central Norway in the spring of 1940. The conditions were similar, long narrow valleys with steep slopes, and a lightly armed enemy presumed to have neither modern armor nor

---

[42] *OKW, WFSt, K.T.B.*, 16 Mar 43. I.M.T., Doc. 1786–PS. *Helmut Greiner, Aufzeichmungen ueber die Lagevortraege und Besprechungen im Fuehrer Hauptquartier vom 12 August bis 17 Maerz 1943, p. 117.* MS # C–065a. OCMH. *AOK Norwegen, Ia, Taetigkeitsbericht der Abteilung Ia fuer den Monat Maerz 1943*, in *Taetigkeitsberichte fuer den Monat Maerz 1943.* AOK 20 34698/3. (Geb.) *AOK 20, Ia, Besprechungsnotiz anlaesslich der Anwesenheit des Chefs des Gen.-St. (Geb.) AOK 20, Generalmajor Jodl, im OKW vom 16–17.3.43.* AOK 20 36560/4.

[43] *OKW, WFSt, Op. Nr. 001355/43, an W.B. Norwegen, 23.3.43* and *AOK Norwegen, Ia, Nr. 7038/43, an OKH (Org. Abt.), 29.3.43, in Taetigkeitsberichte fuer den Monat Maerz 1943.* AOK 20 34698/3.

heavy antitank weapons. "It can be expected," he wrote, "that the enemy, unaccustomed to battle and, in any case, not credited with a high degree of enthusiasm for combat, will not be able to hold against this method of operation with heavy and armored weapons, particularly, if it is possible—as planned—to appear where least expected."

Judging the Swedish main forces to be distributed in three concentrations of three to four divisions each—one near Östersund, one in the vicinity of Stockholm, and the other northwest of Vänern Lake—he presented the following two plans of operations in accordance with Paragraph 3 of the army order:

Operation I. The Swedish divisions at Östersund were relatively isolated and could not be reinforced from the south without impairing the defenses there. They could be reached by two roads, one running due east from Trondheim and the other northeast from Röros. Schell proposed sending one infantry division along the Trondheim–Östersund route and a panzer division northeastward from Röros. After Östersund had been taken it would be a simple matter to continue the advance to the Gulf of Bothnia. Operation I could be executed within the limits set by the Army of Norway and leave a division to spare. Although it would also drive a wedge between the presumed Allied forces, it was a partial solution, and further operations would be required in the south.

Operation II. In the south the problem was to take Stockholm, by far the most important strategic objective in Sweden, and at the same time eliminate the Vänern Lake divisions with the smallest possible expenditure of effort. The most direct route with the best roads ran due east from Oslo past the northern shore of Vänern Lake; but it crossed three lines of fortifications: one along the border, the second running north from the northwestern tip of Vänern Lake, and the third—the outer ring of the Stockholm defenses—anchored on the northeastern tip of the lake. Schell, therefore, proposed to place his jump-off point in the Tryssil area farther north, where two long, parallel river valleys ran southeastward around and behind the first two lines of Swedish defenses.

On the left flank, one division, preferably motorized, would advance southeastward to Falun while one panzer division following the northernmost of the valleys, that of the Väster-Dalälven, would take Ludvika. At Falun and Ludvika the divisions would break through the outer Stockholm defenses, that in the north continuing on to Upsala and that in the south to Västeras. Depending on the circumstances, the divisions could then either close in directly on Stockholm or move out to the coast north and south of the city. A decisive battle could be expected at the inner Stockholm defense ring, in the vicinity of Avesta.

In the southern valley, that of the Klarälven, one infantry division would advance to Filipstad. There it was expected to be able to turn east toward Stockholm but might be drawn off into the fighting north of Vänern Lake. On its right a second infantry division would cross the border and roll up the Swedish Vänern Lake defenses from the north.

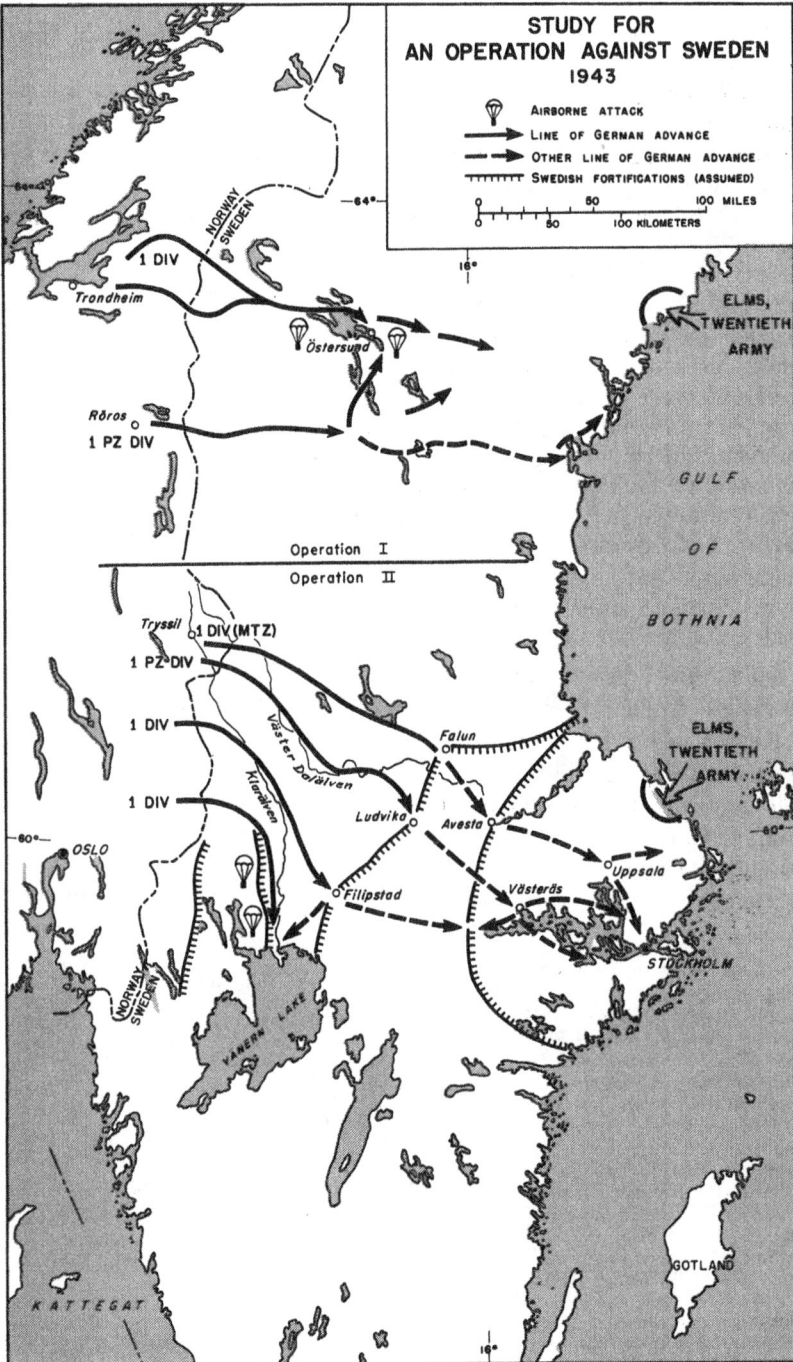

STUDY FOR
AN OPERATION AGAINST SWEDEN
1943

AIRBORNE ATTACK
LINE OF GERMAN ADVANCE
OTHER LINE OF GERMAN ADVANCE
SWEDISH FORTIFICATIONS (ASSUMED)

0   50   100 MILES
0   50   100 KILOMETERS

Map 20

259

The operation would also require several small parachute landings and small amphibious landings on the southwest coast and north of Stockholm to distract and tie down the enemy.[44]

Schell foresaw that the Swedish command could assemble three to four divisions south of Filipstad and three divisions in the vicinity of Avesta and then, by counterattacking northwestward via Filipstad and across the line Falun–Ludvika, block the German advance. "But," he concluded, "such an operation would require rapid decisions, great daring, lightning execution, and great flexibility in the high and intermediate leadership, which are not expected of the Swedes." Another inconvenient possibility was that the Vänern Lake divisions would remain in their prepared positions north and northwest of the lake. This would force the German division taking Filipstad to turn southwestward and make necessary commitment of an additional division to continue the advance toward Stockholm. If, on the other hand, the Swedish Vänern Lake group withdrew southwest of the lake or pulled back into the outer ring of Stockholm defenses, the operation could proceed as planned. Evaluating all the possibilities, Schell decided that the Vänern Lake divisions would probably attempt to take up new positions facing north and northeast but that the speed and daring of the German advance would prevent their devising a viable scheme of operations until it was too late; therefore, the extra division would not be needed.[45]

On 8 April Lossberg, Operations Officer, Army of Norway, completed his review of the Schell study with the comment, "A speedy occupation of Sweden will require a combination of Operations I and II and forces adequate for the purpose." [46] That those forces would be available was still far from certain, and at the middle of the month the Operations Staff, OKW, again raised the possibility of exchanging three Norway divisions for Eastern Front divisions. That intention was soon dropped. At the end of the month, Hitler, reaffirming his determination to create

---

[44] In its issue of 26 June 1946 the Soviet Army newspaper *Krasnaya Svesda* devoted a full page to Operation POLARFUCHS, a German plan for the invasion of Sweden dating from the spring of 1943. The article based on alleged revelations by Bamler, after the war a prisoner of war in Russia, described an operation requiring from 17 to 19 divisions directed eastward from the Swedish-Norwegian border and landings along the Baltic coast and on Gotland. As described, the operation would have required every division the Germans had in Norway plus reinforcements of two to four divisions. Even then it could not have been executed, inasmuch as the majority of the divisions in Norway were static divisions, ones without either equipment or training for mobile operations.

From the point of view of tactics the Bamler article is also questionable. The main effort is placed in the Östersund area with a secondary attack directed frontally against the Swedish positions west of Vänern Lake. There is also mention of a landing in divisional strength on Gotland, an undertaking which would have been a pointless diversion of strength.

The code-name POLARFUCHS probably originated with this article. It does not appear in the German records, and that it would have been used is unlikely since the Army of Norway had already executed an Operation POLARFUCHS—the XXXVI Corps offensive in 1941.

[45] 25. *Panzer-Division, Kommandeur, Nr. 3/43, Operative Studie Schweden, 31.3.43.* AOK 20 63905.

[46] *Ibid.*

strong operational reserves for the Army of Norway, announced the creation of three new divisions. Two of them were to be static divisions: one formed in Germany by 1 July; the other formed in Norway by 1 August using cadres from the existing divisions and replacements from Germany. They were to release two infantry divisions for the army reserve. The third division was to be a panzer division formed by 15 September out of elements from the Eastern Front.[47] When the terms of this order were met, the army would have an operational reserve of four infantry and two panzer divisions, enough to reinforce the Narvik–Trondheim area and to execute an operation in the sense of the Schell study.[48]

The Army of Norway reported that it intended to use the two static divisions to release the 214th and 269th Infantry Divisions and that it intended to station the six reserve divisions in such a manner "that, on the one hand, they will have, at least, elements in position to support the coastal defenses and, on the other, be favorably situated in the event that the army is to receive new missions." [49] In mid-May the Army of Norway requested a corps and a panzer corps headquarters to command the reserves. At the same time it reported that it had created a reserve of one reinforced regiment in the Narvik area.[50]

Meanwhile, the Naval Staff had taken the possibility of a conflict with Sweden under consideration. In May it submitted its considerations to the OKW. It foresaw no great tactical problems. The main mission of the Navy would be to trap the Swedish Navy in port by blocking the major harbors, particularly Stockholm, Goteborg, and Karlskrona, with mines on the night before the attack. The Baltic Training Fleet, four cruisers and a World War I battleship, would be able to deal with any vessels which managed to put to sea. The Navy believed that the Swedish destroyers (11), submarines (23), and torpedo boats (12) would constitute a worthwhile accretion of strength for the German Navy if they could be captured intact. The heavier Swedish units it regarded as too far out-of-date to be worth serious consideration either as opponents or as booty.

Although the Navy's only special request was for two months' advance

---

[47] *AOK Norwegen, Ia, Nr. 1161/43, an OKW, WFSt, (Op.), 12.4.43; AOK Norwegen, Ia, Nr. 1161/43, II Ang., 16.4.43;* and *OKW, WFSt, Op. (H), Nr. 002069/43, an W.B. Norwegen, 30.4.43,* in *Taetigkeitsberichte Monat Maerz 1943.* AOK 20 34698/4.

[48] Norway itself was considered unsuitable for large-scale armored operations. In February 1943 the Army of Norway had reported that a panzer division in Norway was "actually a luxury" since tanks could be used only in certain localities. *AOK Norwegen, Ia, Nr. 773/43, Notiz fuer Vortrag bei WFSt, 6.3.43,* in *Taetigkeitsberichte Monat Februar 1943.* AOK 20 34698/2.

[49] The reserves were to be stationed as follows: two panzer divisions in the Sarpsborg–Halden areas, the 214th Division west of Oslo, the 269th Division east of Lillehammer, the 181st Division at and northeast of Dombaas, and the 196th Division in the vicinity of Steinkjer (headquarters and one regiment) and Bodö (one regiment).

[50] *AOK Norwegen, Ia, Nr. 25/43, an OKW, WFSt. (Op.), 5.5.43; AOK Norwegen, Ia, Nr. 1438/43, 14.5.43,* in *Taetigkeitsberichte Monat Mai 1943.* AOK 20 34698/5.

notice to put the Baltic Fleet on a full war footing, it anticipated several dangerous developments which, in its view, cast doubt on the wisdom of an operation against Sweden. The most serious of those was possible loss of the Baltic Sea as a submarine training area. Others of importance were disruption of supply shipments to Finland, loss of the Swedish iron ore, and loss of transit across Swedish territory to Norway. In expressing those fears the Navy was concerned with the possibility that, if Sweden were not subdued very quickly, American and British air forces might intervene and the Russian naval units bottled up at Leningrad might break out, turning the Baltic Sea into a major zone of operations.

The Navy was also apparently worried that an outright preventive operation might be attempted and listed, as an additional danger in a conflict with Sweden, the creation of conditions favorable to an Allied landing in Scandinavia.[51] The Navy again expressed its apprehension on that score on 23 May when the Naval Staff warned the Foreign Ministry, which was then about to open crucial negotiations with Sweden concerning the transit agreements, that a conflict with Sweden might paralyze the submarine fleet. The Naval Staff emphasized that the capture of Leningrad and elimination of Soviet naval forces in the Baltic would, from the naval point of view, have to come before any operation against Sweden.[52]

While the Navy was recording its doubts, the transport and relief movements for the Army of Norway swung into high gear. The 14th Air Force Field Division at the end of April completed the relief of the 196th Infantry Division. Elements of the 295th Infantry Division began arriving in Norway in May, and by the end of June transfer of the division was nearly completed. During May and June formation of a static division (the 274th Infantry Division) in Norway proceeded on schedule. Most remarkable was the transformation of the 25th Panzer Division from a collection of odds and ends into a powerfully equipped (for Scandinavian conditions) panzer division. By the end of June the division had been completely re-equipped with German artillery and small arms; it had received well over 1,000 trucks and other vehicles; and its strength (ration strength) stood at 21,000 men. It had 7 Mark II tanks, 41 Mark III's, 16 Mark IV's, 40 Hotchkiss (French), 15 Suomas (French), and 15 self-propelled assault guns.[53]

---

[51] *OKM, B. Nr. 1 SKL B 1568/43, Kurze Betrachtung zum Kriegsfall mit Schweden und zu den dabei auftretenden Aufgaben der Kriegsmarine (Stand Mai 1943)*, in *Kriegstagebuch der Seekriegsleitung Teil C, Band III*.

[52] *Naval War Diary*, Vol. 45, p. 261.

[53] In July additional shipments of tanks brought the totals up to 14 Mark II's, 62 Mark III's, and 26 Mark IV's. *AOK Norwegen, Ia, Taetigkeitsbericht der Abt. Ia, fuer den Monat Juni 1943*, in *Taetigkeitsberichte Monat Juni 1943*. AOK 20 40216/1. *AOK Norwegen, Ia, Nr. 1676/43, Truppengliederung, 16.6.43*, in *Taetigkeitsberichte Monat Juni 1943*. AOK 20 40216/1. *AOK Norwegen, Ia, Nr. 2410/43, Truppengliederung, 19.8.43*, in *Taetigkeitsberichte Monat August 1943*. AOK 20 40216/3. *AOK Norwegen, O. Qu., Qu. 1, Taetigkeitsbericht April 1943, Taetigkeitsbericht Mai 1943, Taetigkeitsbericht Juni 1943*, and *Taetigkeitsbericht Juli 1943*. AOK 20 33279/1 and 2, 34298, and 34421.

On 21 June Falkenhorst informed the XXXIII Corps, the LXX Corps, and the 25th Panzer Division that in September the army reserves would be fully assembled and that he intended then to conduct fall maneuvers on a large scale for the purpose of giving instruction in the *"Skandinavien Taktik."* He delegated the planning and direction of the maneuvers to Schell.[54] To supplement the army order, Schell issued a summary of the terrain estimate and tactical recommendations in his study for an operation against Sweden as a guide in preparing for the maneuvers.[55]

In July the build-up of reserves and planning for the fall maneuvers progressed, but in the lengthening shadow of ominous events on other fronts. The first of those was the catastrophic failure of the offensive against the Kursk salient in southern Russia. Its direct effect on the Northern Theater was to end all hopes that Leningrad would be taken; most important, it demonstrated that, far from operating offensively, the German armies in the east would not even be able to tie down the Russians in positional warfare during the summer of 1943. The disaster in Russia was accompanied by rapid deterioration of the German position in the Mediterranean and by growing concern over possible Allied landings in the Balkans or on the Channel coast. At the end of the month the OKW informed the Army of Norway that the infantry division promised from Germany would not be available and that the panzer division would not arrive by September.[56]

In August Hitler could no longer afford the luxury of a strong operational reserve in Norway. At the middle of the month, with the Army Group South retreating in the Ukraine and Italy about to defect, he ordered the 25th Panzer Division to the Channel coast at top speed.[57] Two weeks later the Army of Norway recorded in its monthly activity report that orders for the fall maneuvers had been issued but "were rendered, in part, purposeless by the transfer of 25th Panzer Division." [58] In September the 181st Division was transferred to the Balkans, and in the last week of the month, when the remnants of the reserve conducted maneuvers, they were limited to regimental and battalion exercises tailored to situations which might arise in the defense of the Norwegian coast.

In what has the earmarks of a post-mortem on the planning which had been conducted in the first half of the year, Bamler in December

---

[54] *AOK Norwegen, Ia, Nr. 1800/43, 21.6.43*, in *Taetigkeitsberichte Monat Juni 1943.* AOK 20 40216/1.
[55] *25. Panzer-Division, Kommandeur, Tgb. Nr. 333/43, Theoretische Grundlagen fuer die Entwicklung eines skandinavischen Kampfverfahrens, 26.5.43*, in *Taetigkeitsberichte Monat Juni 1943.* AOK 20 40216/1.
[56] *AOK Norwegen, Ia, Taetigkeitsbericht der Abteilung Ia fuer den Monat Juli 1943*, in *Taetigkeitsberichte Monat Juli 1943.* AOK 20 40216/2.
[57] *OKW, WFSt, Op. (H), Nr. 004550/43, an W.B. Norwegen, 21.8.43*, in *Taetigkeitsberichte Monat August 1943.* AOK 20 40216/3.
[58] *AOK Norwegen, Ia, Taetigkeitsbericht der Abt, Ia fuer den Monat August 1943*, in *Taetigkeitsberichte Monat August 1943.* AOK 20 40216/3.

1943 presented the following tactical problem to the Army of Norway corps chiefs of staff: The enemy had staged successful landings in central Norway near Trondheim and in Denmark. He had landed airborne forces in Sweden and would attempt to gain direct contact with Sweden by taking Denmark. Sweden remained neutral but would defend her border against the Germans. The core of the problem was to mount a clear-cut main effort against one of the threats.

Most of the officers chose an operation against Sweden; but, in his critique, Bamler rejected that solution. He and Falkenhorst, he said, were agreed that the main effort would have to be in central Norway. Sweden might come later, after the enemy in Norway had been eliminated, but as long as the Army of Norway had no more than two divisions in reserve an invasion of Sweden would be certain to bog down. If a full panzer corps were on hand, he concluded, the situation might be different.[59]

Internal Affairs and the Situation at the End of the Year

During 1943, in keeping with Hitler's determination to deny the Western Powers as much as a foothold in Europe, the Army of Norway continued its endless program of expanding and improving the Norwegian defenses. The most ambitious projects, such as emplacement of heavy naval guns, were the responsibility of Einsatzgruppe Wiking of the Organisation Todt, which employed Germans, Norwegians, and large numbers of Russian prisoners of war as labor.[60] In the summer of 1943 Einsatzgruppe Wiking completed the first block of bombproof submarine pens at Trondheim and had others under construction there and at Bergen. Later in the year it finished winterproofing the Reichsstrasse 50 as far as Lakselv on Porsanger Fiord. In previous years even the most modern snow removal equipment had been unable to cope with the tremendous snow falls produced by the collision of maritime and arctic air masses along the Norwegian arctic coast. It had been necessary to build snowplow stations at 5- to 10-mile intervals and to construct several snow tunnels, one of them nearly five miles long. The wood for the tunnels and for the giant snow fences which skirted the road over much of its length had to be brought in from the south.[61]

In 1943 Einsatzgruppe Wiking began work on Germany's largest and most expensive project in Norway, the Arctic Railroad. Hitler

[59] *Der Chef des Generalstabes der Armee Norwegen, Abt. Ia, Nr. 69/43, Besprechung der operativen Aufgabe, 13.12.43,* in *Taetigkeitsberichte Monat Dezember 1943.* AOK 20 40216/6.

[60] The Organisation Todt bore the name of the former Reich Minister for Arms and Munitions, Dr. Fritz Todt, who was killed in 1942. Regarded as Germany's construction genius, he had founded the Organisation Todt which during the war directed large-scale military construction throughout occupied Europe. Einsatzgruppe Wiking was a subordinate establishment for Norway and Denmark (for a short time in 1944 also Finland).

[61] Franz Xaver Dorsch, *Organisation Todt,* p. 45–59. MS # P–037. OCMH.

Snow tunnel on Reichsstrasse 50.

had become convinced that a railroad between Trondheim and Narvik, which would provide a secure route for supply and ore traffic, could be built in two years.   He intended at first also to carry the construction north to Kirkenes.   Falkenhorst protested repeatedly that the railroad, which would require 145,000 Russian prisoners as labor and—according to the Army of Norway estimates—take four to six years to build, would place an unbearable strain on his limited transportation facilities and would delay all other defensive preparations in Norway.[62]   But in the face of repeated protests from the Army of Norway Hitler agreed only to postpone the work north of Narvik and to allow that between Trondheim and Narvik to proceed "as fast as possible" rather than at a fixed high speed.   The technical difficulties of building the Arctic Railroad were tremendous.   It would have required some 40 miles of tunnels, and over long stretches roads first had to be built to bring in equipment and material.   At the end of 1944 Einsatzgruppe Wiking with vast expenditures of manpower (40,000 to 50,000 Russian prisoners of war) and material—which could have been put to better use elsewhere—had brought it about one-third of the way toward completion.   As late as mid-April 1945 Hitler gave the construction equal priority with the warships of the Navy in the allotment of motor fuel and coal, both of which were then running desperately short in Norway.[63]

---

[62] *AOK Norwegen, Ia, Taetigkeitsbericht fuer den Monat Januar 1943*, in *Taetigkeitsberichte Monat January 1943*.   AOK 20 34698/1.   *AOK Norwegen, Ia, Nr. 467/43, Anruf Min. Rat Henne, 13.2.43*, in *Taetigkeitsberichte Monat Februar 1943.* AOK 20 34698/2.

[63] Dorsch, *Organisation Todt*, p. 49.   (Geb.) AOK 20 (OKW/W.B. Norw.), Ia, *Nr. 2459/45, Eisenbahnbau Nordnorwegen, 16.4.45*, in *K.T.B. Anlagenband 1.4.–30.4.45.*   AOK 20 75036/5.

In 1943 a major obstacle to successful organization of the Norwegian defenses cropped up in the form of the person of Reichskommissar Terboven. In accordance with standard German practice, the Army of Norway claimed the full powers of the executive in a zone of active operations. In the army view, once Norway became the scene of active hostilities on more than a limited scale, all administrative authority would automatically pass to Falkenhorst, and Terboven would take his departture. To the Reichskommissar, already annoyed by the authority which Fuehrer Directive No. 40 had conferred on Falkenhorst in matters relating to defense, the mere existence of such a possibility was unbearably irksome. He countered with a plan of his own to create a so-called *Sicherungsbereich* (Security Zone) in southeastern Norway around Oslo. There he intended to assemble all the SS and police units in Norway and, in the event of an invasion, retain the governmental authority using the police and SS as a defense force. This state within a state, conceived solely for the purpose of satisfying Terboven's vanity was patently ridiculous; but Hitler and Himmler, who never let slip an opportunity to extend the influence of the SS, regarded it with some favor. Against such opposition the Army of Norway, and the OKW as well, had to proceed cautiously. The Terboven plan, which should have been rejected out of hand, remained the subject of lengthy negotiations which dragged on until the end of the war.[64]

In the summer of 1943 the far from cordial relations between Terboven and Falkenhorst took a turn for the worse. In July Terboven claimed to have knowledge that many of the able-bodied Norwegians escaping to Sweden for military training were former Norwegian officers. Because of these violations of the paroles given in June 1940, he demanded that all the former Norwegian officers be taken into custody. Falkenhorst agreed in principle but refused to make troops available "for a purely police action."[65] Enraged, Terboven complained to Fuehrer Headquarters that "the Armed Forces are obviously trying to avoid openly making themselves guilty of an unfriendly action."[66] Hitler instructed the OKW to order the Armed Forces to carry out the arrests. The officers were taken into custody on 17 August.[67]

During the second half of 1943 Denmark returned to a position of prominence in the Northern Theater. At the end of August, in order to stamp out a wave of strikes, Germany declared martial law in Denmark. In protest, the king and government ceased exercising their functions. The German forces disarmed the Danish Army and Navy;

---

[64] *W.B. Norwegen, Ia, Nr. 1375/43, an OKW, WFSt, 4.5.43*, in *Taetigkeitsberichte Monat Mai 1943*. AOK 20 34698/5. *W.B. Norwegen, Ia, Nr. 28/43* [personal letter Bamler to Warlimont], *15.5.43*. OKW/119. *OKW, WFSt, K.T.B.*, 17 Aug 43. I.M.T., Doc. 1786–PS.

[65] *W.B. Norwegen, Ic/Qu., Nr. 3652/43, Festnahme ehem. norwegischer Offiziere, 7.7.43*. OKW/119.

[66] *Terboven an Herrn Reichsleiter Martin Bormann, Fuehrerhauptquartier, 10.7.43*. OKW/119.

[67] *OKW, WFSt, K.T.B.*, 17 Aug 43. I.M.T. Doc. 1786–PS.

and the SS, taking advantage of the situation, moved in to arrest the Danish Jews, some of whom escaped and found asylum in Sweden. Thereafter German control of Denmark was tightened. The Army of Norway expressed concern that the disturbances in Denmark and increasing hostility in Sweden could provide the impulse for an Allied invasion of Jutland and southern Sweden.[68] Late in the year the German forces in Denmark were increased by two divisions to six divisions and 130,000 men.[69]

At the year's end, the Army of Norway, with 12 divisions plus the Panzer Division Norway, totaled 314,000 men. Of those, the 196th and 214th Divisions, the last of the army reserves, were on standby orders for transfer to other theaters. The Panzer Division Norway, composed of odds and ends left behind by the 25th Panzer Division, had a strength of about a regiment and was armed with 47 Mark III tanks left in Norway because they were equipped with unsatisfactory transmissions. In the last months of the year the Army of Norway repeatedly urged that a full panzer division be stationed in Norway for the sake of its deterrent effect on Sweden. As a result of stockpiling throughout the year, the Army of Norway was in a position to conduct large-scale operations for eight to nine months with the supplies on hand.[70]

On 28 December the Operations Staff, OKW, recorded Hitler's prediction for 1944 as follows: "Along with a landing in the West, the Fuehrer definitely expects one in Norway. Were Germany eventually to collapse, the British could not tolerate having the Russians suddenly appear in Narvik. In order to forestall that, the British will, in the Fuehrer's opinion, take the risk of an attack against Norway in addition to an attack in the west." [71]

The Arctic Convoys

After the disastrous December 1942 attack on JW.51B responsibility for the conduct of anticonvoy operations passed entirely to the submarines, of which 21, a far from negligible force, were employed. Between January and March 1943 the British sent two more convoys, totaling 42 ships, and 6 ships sailing independently on the northern run. Eight ships were lost. Another 5 ships were lost out of 36 returning empty from Russian ports. In April the Admiralty decided to suspend convoy traffic in the Arctic until autumn and the return of long nights.[72]

In June 1943 a British-Norwegian landing party took the German weather station on Spitzbergen. The Germans at first feared that a

---

[68] *W.B. Norwegen, Ia, Nr. 2604/43, Woechentlicher Lagebericht, Stichtag: 30.8.1943*, in *Taetigkeitsberichte Monat August 1943*. AOK 20 40216/3.

[69] *OKW, WFSt, K.T.B.*, 31 Dec 43. I.M.T. Doc. 1786–PS.

[70] *AOK Norwegen, Ia, Nr. 3687/43, Truppengliederung des Armee-Oberkommandos Norwegen, 1.12.43*, in *Taetigkeitsberichte Monat Dezember 1943*. AOK 20 40216/7. *OKW, WFSt, K.T.B.*, 31 Dec 43. International Military Tribunal Doc. 1790–PS.

[71] *OKW, WFSt, K.T.B.*, 28 Dec. 43. I.M.T. Doc. 1790–PS.

[72] Churchill, *op. cit.*, Vol. V, pp. 256–58.

naval and air base to protect the convoys would be established. When it became known that the British and Norwegians had only set up a weather station, the German Navy planned to counter with a landing of its own. The *Tirpitz,* the *Scharnhorst,* and nine destroyers were readied in Alta Fiord, and in the first week of September they took aboard 600 Army of Norway troops. That battleship support for the operation was superfluous was known, but the Navy from the start was more interested in showing the crews some action to keep up their morale than it was in the military results of the Spitzbergen raid, which were expected to be slight in any case. It may have been haunted by the memory of 1918 when the sailors at Kiel after years of inactivity mutinied and touched off a revolution.

On 8 September Operation ZITRONELLA, Spitzbergen, was carried off according to plan, encountering no resistance worthy of mention.[73] Most of the Norwegian garrison escaped to the mountains and began rebuilding within a few days. In mid-October a United States-British task group brought in reinforcements and new equipment.[74] The Naval Staff concluded on 9 September, "What is important is not the relatively small tactical success but that our heavy units could be put into action again at long last. It has also reminded friend and foe of the strategic importance which the presence of these naval units represents when related to the war situation in general." [75]

In less than two weeks the Navy had cause to regret its "reminder" concerning the presence of the battleships. The *Tirpitz,* in particular, the British had never forgotten, since its existence alone forced them to keep battleships, which could have been used more profitably elsewhere, in home waters. Goaded by ZITRONELLA, the British Navy dispatched six midget submarines against the *Tirpitz.* Three were lost at sea, but three reached Alta Fiord, and two managed to slip through the entrance of the battleship's antisubmarine net, which had been left open to permit small boat traffic to a teletype station ashore. The mines they planted beneath the battleship failed to sink it but seriously damaged its steering gear and propeller shafts. With no dock in Norway capable of berthing the giant and a three-knot-per-mile tow to Germany an open invitation to disaster, the Navy decided to undertake the repairs on the spot. The most optimistic estimate was that they would require six months.[76]

In November the convoy traffic resumed. After the first convoy had passed without losing a single ship, the German Navy found itself confronted with exactly the same dilemma it had faced a year earlier.

[73] *Naval War Diary,* Vol. 46, p. 245 and Vol. 49, pp. 49, 129.
[74] Samuel Eliot Morison, *History of United States Naval Operations in World War II* (Boston: Little, Brown and Company, 1956), Vol. X, p. 231.
[75] *Naval War Diary,* Vol. 49, p. 129.
[76] Morison, *op. cit.,* Vol. X, p. 231. *Naval War Diary,* Vol. 49, p. 321 and Vol. 50, p. 30.

German submarine on arctic patrol.

Surface operations against the convoys were risky and promised little, but there was a need to demonstrate the value of the capital ships and a moral obligation not to keep powerful vessels lying idle while supplies to be used against the hard-pressed troops on the Eastern Front were being transported to Russia. On 2 December the Naval Staff decided that the *Scharnhorst* would have to be used against the convoys during the dark months.

After waiting out most of the month, aerial reconnaissance on 23 December located a convoy, escorted by cruisers and destroyers, steaming northeastward toward Bear Island. The Fifth Air Force reported that it had no planes suitable for use against the convoy and refused further reconnaissance unless the Navy intended to take action. On the following day the Navy decided to commit the *Scharnhorst* and detailed five destroyers as a scouting force for the battleship. With six hours of twilight but no more than 45 minutes of light suitable for accurate gunnery, the *Scharnhorst* would have to time its attack for about an hour before noon. If enemy battleships put in an appearance the operation was to be broken off and the ships returned to port.

On the morning of the 25th, the Naval Group North, reporting that high winds had grounded the reconnaissance planes and made it doubtful whether the destroyers could put to sea, recommended canceling the sortie. The Naval Staff, however—on the grounds that no heavy units had been detected in the convoy escort, that the possibility of surprise existed, and that the critical situation of the Army in Russia justified the risk—decided it could not cancel. If the destroyers could not operate, the *Scharnhorst* would have to be sent out alone. At 1900 on Christmas Day the *Scharnhorst* and the destroyers left Alta Fiord.

At 0730 on the 26th Konteradmiral Erich Bey, commanding in the *Scharnhorst,* dispatched the destroyers in a reconnaissance line to locate the convoy. An hour and a half later the convoy covering force of three cruisers picked up the *Scharnhorst* on radar and after closing the range opened fire. Without returning the fire the *Scharnhorst* altered course, and shortly thereafter the radar contact was lost. To reinforce the cruisers 4 destroyers were detached from the convoy escort of 14; but, most important, 125 miles away to the southwest the battleship *Duke of York* with a cruiser and 4 destroyers had been alerted and was coming up fast. The presence of the *Duke of York* remained unknown to the Germans.

At noon the cruisers reestablished radar contact, and some minutes later in a brisk exchange of fire both sides scored hits before the *Scharnhorst* again broke off action. At 1418 Admiral Bey ordered the destroyers, which had not been able to locate the merchant ships, to return to base. Apparently, he intended to withdraw with the *Scharnhorst* at the same time.

Meanwhile, the cruisers maintained radar contact, keeping just out of visual range. Aided by frequent reports from the shadowing cruisers, the *Duke of York* closed in rapidly, coming within radar range at 1617 and taking the *Scharnhorst* completely by surprise with the first 14-inch salvo fired at 1650. Outnumbered and outgunned, but, with a rated speed of 31 knots, faster than the British battleship and cruisers, the *Scharnhorst* reversed course and attempted to withdraw. For more than an hour, in a running battle, it looked as though she might escape, but at 1819 she reported receiving radar-directed fire at a range of more than 10 miles. Shortly thereafter, her speed began to drop off. At 1825 Admiral Bey sent his final message: "To the Fuehrer—We will fight to the last shell."

An hour later, after the 77th salvo, the *Duke of York* ceased firing and sent in two cruisers and the destroyers to deliver torpedo attacks. Together they fired 55 torpedoes, leaving the *Scharnhorst* dead in the water shrouded in a dense cloud of smoke. At 1945 the battleship exploded and sank, taking down with her all but 36 of the nearly 2,000 men in her crew.[77]

The Naval Staff blamed the loss of the *Scharnhorst* on superior British radar and inadequate German aerial reconnaissance. Slight comfort as it might have been, the sinking confirmed a prediction Hitler had made in March 1943. At a conference in which Doenitz argued for keeping the battleships in commission, Hitler had complained that the history of the surface fleet had been nothing but a series of defeats, beginning with the *Graf Spee*. The large ships, he had insisted, were a thing

[77] *Naval War Diary,* Vol. 50, pp. 16, 233, 254, 264, 279, 281, 294–312. Morison, *op. cit.,* Vol. X, pp. 236–43. Churchill, *op. cit.,* Vol. V, p. 275.

of the past, and he preferred having the steel and nickel contained in them to sending them into action again. When Doenitz undertook to find a suitable target for the ships within three months, he had replied, "Even if it should require six months, you will then return and be forced to admit that I was right." [78]

---

[78] *Fuehrer Conferences,* 1943, p. 14.

Chapter 13

Finland Leaves the War

The Stagnant Front, January to June 1944

After a year of maintaining an increasingly precarious grip on Leningrad, the Army Group North in January 1944 saw the handwriting on the wall. At the turn of the year both the army group and the Chief of Staff, OKH, argued for an immediate withdrawal to the PANTHER Line as the sole means of forestalling a disaster. Hitler, worried about the effects on Finland and the consequences of Russia's gaining egress to the Baltic Sea, delayed the decision. The Russians, for their part, were not yet ready to exploit the strategic possibilities of their salient at Nevel. On 14 January they began an offensive against the Eighteenth Army, concentrating on the Oranienbaum and Leningrad sectors and on the anchor of the army right flank at Novgorod. For two days it appeared that another defensive battle was developing which the army group might be able to weather as it had those in the previous year, but by the 17th the Russians had broken out of the Oranienbaum pocket and were rapidly encircling Novgorod. On the following day Kuechler was forced to order withdrawals from the shore of the Gulf of Finland between Oranienbaum and Leningrad and from the advanced positions east of Leningrad.

On the 19th the Soviet Union announced the liberation of Leningrad as a major victory. Of greater tactical importance were the establishment of contact between the Oranienbaum garrison and the Soviet main forces and the encirclement of Novgorod. To gain reserves, Kuechler asked permission to shorten his line east of Leningrad and to evacuate Novgorod, which would soon fall in any case. Hitler agreed reluctantly and then tried to take back his consent but was told that the orders had been given and could not be recalled. Even before the withdrawal began, Kuechler was convinced that he could not make a stand anywhere east of the PANTHER Line. Hitler, maintaining that the Army Group North was not capable of judging what constituted a crisis, refused to give ground except locally and piecemeal. Finally, on 30 January, with the Eighteenth Army down to an infantry strength of 17,000 men and after Kuechler twice went to Fuehrer Headquarters to argue with Hitler in person, he ordered the army group to pull back to the Luga River line. This line existed for the most part only on paper, and the Soviets had already penetrated it at one point. On the following day Hitler dismissed Kuechler and placed Generaloberst Walter Model in command of the Army Group North.[1]

By the end of the month it had become necessary for the OKW to take up the subject of the Army Group North with Mannerheim. He was told of the intention to hold the Luga line and was asked to suggest how Germany might help in strengthening the Finnish front to compensate for the increased Soviet threat.[2] In response, on 1 February, the Marshal proposed that the Twentieth Mountain Army extend its right flank south to take in the Ukhta sector, which would release one Finnish division.

Informed of this request, Dietl, irritated by recent Finnish protests against even the smallest withdrawals of German troops from Finland, objected strenuously. He insisted that it was a waste of manpower to tie down additional German troops on a secondary front in Finland and that Finland, "through greater efforts in the sense of total war," was entirely capable of creating a reserve division out of its own resources "without laying claims on the German Army which is already carrying the entire burden." He proposed, instead, to call on Mannerheim not to raise any objections if the Twentieth Mountain Army were to offer all the troops it could spare to the Army Group North, "which is also fighting in Finland."[3] The OKW, on the other hand, having already committed itself not to reduce the strength of the Twentieth Mountain Army, was relieved to find Mannerheim's demand so modest and hastened to comply, ordering Dietl to take over Ukhta as quickly as possible.[4]

The retreat of the Army Group North had a more shattering effect in Finland than Mannerheim's response to the OKW communication indicated. On 12 February, as Russian troops threatened the city of Narva on the left flank of the PANTHER Line and under the influence of a United States note warning Finland that the longer she continued the war the more unfavorable the terms of peace would become, the Finnish Government dispatched the former prime minister and last ambassador to the Soviet Union, Dr. Juho K. Paasikivi, to Stockholm to receive the Russian peace terms from the Soviet Minister, Madame Alexandra Kollontay. The terms which Paasikivi brought back embraced restoration of the Treaty of Moscow (1940), internment of the

---

[1] *H. Gr. Nord, Kriegstagebuch, I/44*, 20–31 Jan 44. H. Gr. Nord 75128/33.
[2] *OKW, WFSt, K.T.B. Ausarbeitung, Der noerdliche Kriegsschauplatz, 1. Jan–31. Mar 1944*, 4. OKW/2040.
[3] *(Geb.) AOK 20, Ia, Nr. 5/44, an OKW, WFSt, 3.2.44*, in *Chefsachen-Anlagenband, 1.1.44–30.6.44*. AOK 20 58629/10.
[4] *OKW, WFSt, K.T.B. Ausarbeitung, Der noerdliche Kriegsschauplatz, 1. Jan–31. Mar 1944*. OKW/2040.

German troops in Finland, demobilization, and reparations. They were more stringent than had been expected, and the internment of the Twentieth Mountain Army in particular the Finns considered a technical impossibility. On 8 March the Finnish Government rejected the Soviet terms but indicated a desire to negotiate further.[5]

Since Stalin had promised Roosevelt and Churchill at Teheran in December 1943 to offer Finland a negotiated peace which would preserve her national independence, the Soviet Union did not accept the Finnish action as final and offered to receive Finnish representatives for the purpose of clarifying the terms—possibly with the intention of regaining a free hand through an irrevocable Finnish rejection. On 26 March Paasikivi and the former Foreign Minister Carl Enckell flew to Moscow where in meetings with Molotov they were given the conditions which Stalin had outlined to Roosevelt and Churchill:

1. Internment or expulsion of all German troops in Finland by the end of April.

2. Restoration of the 1940 borders.

3. Exchange of prisoners.

4. Demobilization of the Finnish Armed Forces.

5. Reparations amounting to six hundred million dollars to be paid in kind over a period of five years.

6. Pechenga to be returned to the Soviet Union.

7. The Soviet Union to relinquish its claim to Hanko (in return for Pechenga).[6]

The Finns rejected the second set of Soviet demands on 18 April. Still holding great stretches of Soviet territory and having an undefeated army in the field, they had obviously hoped to make a better bargain. Furthermore, the alarm approaching panic which had motivated Paasikivi's trip to Stockholm in February had gradually subsided as the Army Group North, under Model's command, completed its withdrawal to the PANTHER Line in the first week of March and in the succeeding weeks managed to establish a stable front there. Also important was the realization, sharply brought home by the German occupation of Hungary in March, that the German response to Finland's defection might be violent.

The Finnish peace move, unwelcome as it was, came as no surprise to the Germans. In the first stages of the Finnish-Soviet negotiations the German Government adopted an attitude of restraint since it could be assumed with some certainty that Finland was not yet ready for peace at any price, and the Soviet terms might prove to be the best remedy for the Finnish peace fever. As the situation of the Army Group North became stabilized and Finnish dismay at Stalin's terms grew, Hitler began taking steps toward forcing Finland into an unequivocal adherence to

---

[5] *Ibid.,* p. 11. Bluecher, *op. cit.,* pp. 351–56.
[6] Bluecher, *op. cit.,* p. 359. Churchill, *op. cit.,* Vol V, p. 400.

the German cause.   In March he reduced the flow of weapons to Finland, and in the first week of April he instructed Dietl to inform Mannerheim that German weapons could not be given as long as there was a possibility that they might fall into the hands of the enemy.   On 13 April, the day after the Finnish Parliament voted to refuse the Soviet terms, he ordered grain shipments to Finland halted and on the 18th stopped shipment of war matériel.   The adoption of these last two measures was not admitted to the Finns, but their effects were felt in Finland immediately.[7]

At the end of April the Finnish Chief of Staff, Heinrichs, was invited to Fuehrer Headquarters at Berchtesgaden.   There, after Keitel had taken him to task over recent Finnish policy, Jodl adopted a more friendly tone and told Heinrichs that an authoritative declaration was needed to the effect that German military equipment furnished to Finland would not fall into the hands of the Russians.[8]   In May Mannerheim attempted to fulfill the German requirement by a personal letter to Hitler.   Hitler refused to lift the embargo on the ground that the Mannerheim letter was too cautious and diplomatic in tone, but agreed to let Finland have enough weapons to continue fighting.   In early June an appeal from Heinrichs to Keitel brought another refusal, with the proviso that specific Finnish requests would be considered on an individual basis.[9]

From January to June 1944 the front zone of the Finnish Army was quiet, but in February the Russians began bringing up additional troops opposite the Twentieth Mountain Army.   By early March the number of Red Army troops in the Twentieth Mountain Army zone had risen from about 100,000 to between 147,000 and 163,000, and all signs pointed to a full-scale Russian offensive before the end of the month. The point of greatest danger was the XXXVI Mountain Corps sector where the Russians had brought up two new divisions and four brigades plus rocket launchers and artillery and had extended their right flank northwestward to gain a favorable jump-off line.[10]   On 22 March the Twentieth Mountain Army informed its corps that the Russian preparations had been completed to the point where an attack could begin at any time and ordered them to hold their lines at all costs, because the army could not abandon the positions on which it had expended two years of effort without risking disastrous losses.[11]   At Dietl's request

---

[7] *OKW, WFSt, K.T.B. Ausarbeitung, Der noerdliche Kreigsschauplatz, 1.4.–31.12.1944*, pp. 5–7.   International Military Tribunal, Doc. 1795–PS.

[8] Erfurth, *op. cit.*, p. 143.

[9] *OKW, WFSt, K.T.B., Ausarbeitung, Der noerdliche Kriegsschauplatz, 1.4.–31.12.44;* pp. 9–11.   I.M.T., Doc. 1795–PS.

[10] *(Geb.) AOK 20, Ic, Nr. 1210/44, Taetigkeitsbericht der Abteilung Ic fuer die Zeit vom 1.1.–30.6.44.*   AOK 20 58631/1.

[11] *(Geb.) AOK 20, Ia, Op., Nr. 352/44, an XVII A.K., XXXVI A.K., XIX A.K., 23.3.44,* in *K.T.B., AOK 20 Anlagen 1.3.–31.3.44.*   AOK 20 58629/4.

Mannerheim stationed the Finnish 3d Brigade and two independent battalions as reserves in the Twentieth Mountain Army area.

As March drew to a close and the spring thaws approached in April, the danger of a Soviet offensive subsided. The Twentieth Mountain Army concluded that the build-up had been associated with the Finnish-Soviet peace talks and that an offensive would have followed had the Finns accepted an armistice. In April Dietl attempted to secure Mannerheim's support for a limited offensive to remove the threat to the northern flank of the XXXVI Mountain Corps. The Marshal refused to commit Finnish troops; consequently, the Twentieth Mountain Army had to accept the existence of a precarious situation in the XXXVI Mountain Corps sector and lesser tactical disadvantages in the sectors of its other two corps as permanent.[12] By the first week of June there were no signs of impending activity anywhere on the German front in Finland, and all indications pointed to another quiet summer.

BIRKE and TANNE

The danger of Finnish defection in February 1944 immediately revived planning for the execution of Fuehrer Directive No. 50.[13] It also brought to the fore the problem of preserving German control of the Baltic Sea. With Leningrad liberated and Army Group North not likely to hold east of Narva, the stranglehold on the Soviet Baltic Fleet had already relaxed somewhat. A Finnish-Soviet armistice threatened to knock all of the props out from under German strategy in the Baltic. In neutral Finnish or in Russian hands Suursaari and Hanko would no longer serve as corks to keep the Soviet naval forces bottled up in the eastern end of the Gulf of Finland, and the Åland Islands could be used to stop the Luleå ore traffic. Once Russian naval units could roam the Baltic at will, submarine training would have to cease and the fate of the submarine fleet would be sealed.

With these considerations in mind Hitler on 16 February ordered that in the event of a Finnish change of course the Åland Islands and Suursaari were to be occupied immediately. Under the code names TANNE WEST (Åland Island) and TANNE OST (Suursaari) the OKW instituted the necessary preparations. The 416th Infantry Division, in Denmark, and a parachute regiment were earmarked for the Ålands operation, and the provision of troops for Suursaari was made a responsibility of the Army Group North. Finnish resistance was not expected. (In June, at the height of the Soviet summer offensive against Finland, the troops for the TANNE operations were placed on the alert; and at the same time, as an additional precaution, Hitler ordered all leave

---

[12] (Geb.) AOK 20, Ia, Nr. 96/44, K.T.B. Notiz ueber Besuch des Oberbefehlshabers im finnischen Hauptquartier, Mikkeli, in K.T.B., Chefsachen-Anlagenband, 1.1.–30.6.44. AOK 20 58629/10.

[13] See above, p. 249.

Reindeer patrol.

troops returning to the Twentieth Mountain Army held at Gdynia as a force for the possible occupation of Hanko.) Control of the TANNE operations remained in the hands of the OKW which assigned the tactical direction to OKM and OKL.[14]

Meanwhile, the Twentieth Mountain Army prepared a plan of operations, given the code name BIRKE, based on Fuehrer Directive No. 50. The mission of the Twentieth Mountain Army, in the event that Finland dropped out of the war, was to hold northern Finland for the sake of the nickel mines. For that purpose the army would swing its right flank back to a line running roughly from Karesuando near the Swedish border to the Arctic Ocean Highway south of Ivalo. The maneuver was to be completed in two phases. In the first phase the XXXVI Mountain Corps and the XVIII Mountain Corps would pull out of the Kandalaksha, Luokhi, and Ukhta sectors and fall back to Rovaniemi, establishing a screening front east of Rovaniemi on the line Kemiyärvi–Autinkylä which was to be held until the main force had safely passed northward through Rovaniemi. In the second phase the XXXVI Mountain Corps would proceed northward along the Arctic Ocean Highway to its new sector south of Ivalo and tie in with the right flank of the XIX Mountain Corps. The XVIII Mountain Corps would move northwestward over the Rovaniemi–Skibotten route and take up positions northeast of the Swedish border in the vicinity of Karesuando. A definitive plan for the second phase could not be made in advance because its execution depended on the season. In summer it could be

---

[14] *OKW, WFSt, K.T.B. Ausarbeitung, Der noerdliche Kriegsschauplatz, 1.1.–31.3.44,* pp. 7, 25. OKW/2040. *OKW, WFSt, K.T.B. Ausarbeitung, Der noerdliche Kriegsschauplatz, 1.4.–31.12.44.* I.M.T., Doc. 1795–PS.

carried out as described, but in winter the Finnish end of the Rovaniemi–Skibotten route was impassable. In winter, therefore, both the XXXVI Mountain Corps and the XVIII Mountain Corps would have to move north over the Arctic Ocean Highway, with the XVIII Mountain Corps continuing on into northern Norway and the XXXVI Mountain Corps providing troops to man the Karesuando positions.[15]

The drawbacks to BIRKE were numerous. The most serious of them was, as the Twentieth Mountain Army had pointed out when Fuehrer Directive No. 50 was first issued, that, were the sea route around northern Norway cut, both the ore and supply shipments would stop immediately, and thereafter the Twentieth Mountain Army could only hold out for a few months. In addition, the execution of BIRKE promised to be risky. The Twentieth Mountain Army did not have enough manpower to construct suitable positions at Ivalo and Karesuando in advance and, in any case, could not start work without revealing its intentions to the Finns. The withdrawal itself would be confined to a few roads, difficult to keep open in winter and exposed to round-the-clock air attacks in summer; and in northern Finland the army would have to establish a new front under highly unfavorable conditions of climate and terrain. A final possibility was that Sweden, whose attitude was doubtful at best, would be forced to permit transit of Russian troops as it had of German troops in 1941. The Russians could then strike at the exposed right flank of the Karesuando positions or advance to Narvik, cutting off the Twentieth Mountain Army's line of retreat. All of these considerations Dietl laid before Hitler during his last visit to Fuehrer Headquarters on 22 June 1944.[16]

The Soviet Summer Offensive

The Attack

The black day of the Finnish Army was 10 June 1944. After a massive artillery and air preparation accompanied by probing attacks on 9 June, the Soviet Twenty-first Army on the morning of the 10th concentrated the full force of its attack on the left-flank division of the Finnish IV Corps holding the western side of the front on the Isthmus of Karelia. In a massive assault three Russian divisions annihilated one regiment of the Finnish division, and before noon the Russians had broken through the Finnish front to a distance of approximately six miles.

Although there had been advance warnings the Russian offensive took the Finnish High Command by surprise. During May there had

---

[15] (Geb.) AOK 20, Ia, Op., Nr. 92/44, Armeebefehl Nr. 1 fuer die Durchfuehrung von "Birke," in K.T.B., Chefsachen-Anlagenband, 1.1.–30.6.44. AOK 20 58629/10.
[16] (Geb.) AOK 20, Ia, Nr. 231/44, Notizen fuer Vortrag beim Fuehrer, 16.6.44, in K.T.B., Chefsachen-Anlagenband, 1.1.–30.6.44. AOK 20 58629/10.

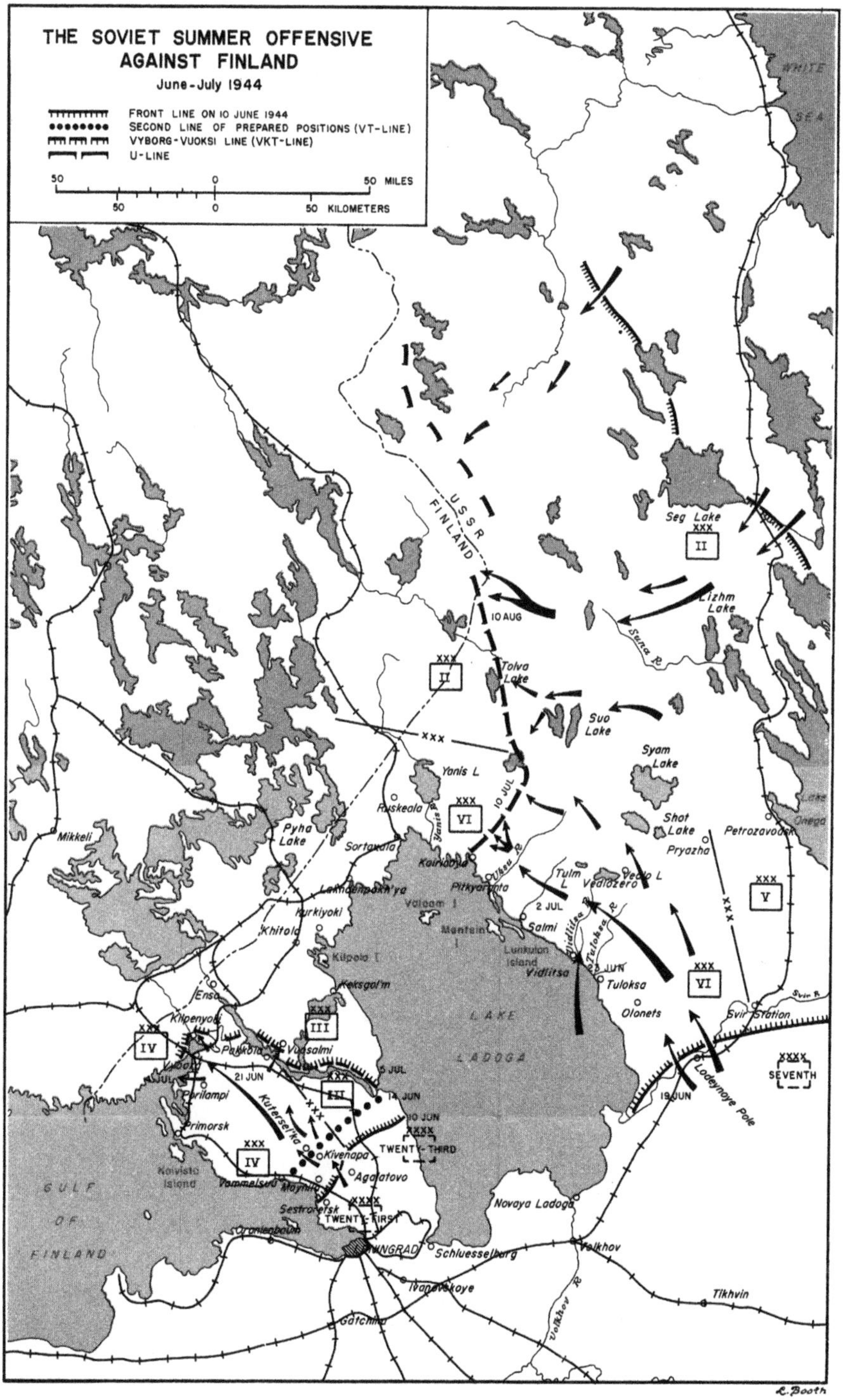
THE SOVIET SUMMER OFFENSIVE
AGAINST FINLAND
June-July 1944
FRONT LINE ON 10 JUNE 1944
SECOND LINE OF PREPARED POSITIONS (VT-LINE)
VYBORG-VUOKSI LINE (VKT-LINE)
U-LINE
50 0 50 MILES
50 0 50 KILOMETERS
WHITE SEA
USSR
FINLAND
Seg Lake
II
Lizhm Lake
10 AUG
Suna R.
Tolva Lake
Suo Lake
Syam Lake
Yanis L
10 JUL
VI
Ruskeala
Shot Lake
Petrozavodsk
Lake Onega
Pryazha
Pyha Lake
Sortavala
Mikkeli
Koirinoja
Pitkyaranta
Tulm L
Vedlozero
Vedlo L
Lahdenpokh'ya
Valaam I
Kurkiyoki
2 JUL
Salmi
V
Khitola
Mantsin I
Kilpola I
Vidlitsa
23 JUN
Tuloksa
Keksgol'm
Olonets
Enso
Svir Station
Svir R.
III
Kilpenyoki
IV
Pakkola
Vuosalmi
LAKE LADOGA
SEVENTH
21 JUN
5 JUL
Perilampi
14 JUN
19 JUN
Lodeynoye Pole
Kuterselka
10 JUN
Primorsk
TWENTY-THIRD
Kivenapa
Koivisto Island
Agalatovo
Vammelsuu
GULF OF FINLAND
Sestroretsk
TWENTY-FIRST
Novaya Ladoga
Oranienbaum
Schluesselburg
Volkhov
Ivanovskoye
Volkhov R.
Tikhvin
Gatchina
R. Booth

Map 21

been indications of an attack in the making, and on 1 June Finnish Army Intelligence warned that an offensive was to be expected within ten days. Four or five days before the attack the Russians began radio silence—an almost infallible sign. But the Army operations chief was not convinced, and his judgment carried the greatest weight with Mannerheim.[17]

When the attack began the III Corps held the left and the IV Corps the right flank of the Finnish front on the Isthmus. Together they had three divisions in the line and one brigade in reserve. In the second line stood another three divisions plus one brigade engaged in constructing fortifications. Lastly, the Finnish Armored Division was stationed east of Vyborg. On the Isthmus the Finns had three defense lines. The first of them, the front, roughly followed the old Finnish-Soviet border. The second, immediately to the rear, laid out in terrain militarily more advantageous than the first, ran in an almost straight line across the Isthmus from Vammelsuu on the Gulf of Finland to Taipale on Lake Ladoga. The third ran from Vyborg to Kuparsaari and thence along the north bank of the Vouksi River to Taipale. It had strong natural advantages but had not been placed under construction until November 1943 and was far from completion.[18] Between the third Isthmus line and the heart of Finland there was the so-called Moscow Line along the 1940 border. It had some concrete fortifications, and additional construction was in progress, but it had no natural advantages and could only be used for a last ditch stand.

Concerning the Finns' capacity for resistance the Germans had had severe doubts at least since early 1943. In June 1943 Dietl repeated his prediction made in February of that year that the Finnish Army would not be able to withstand a strong Soviet attack. The Finns, he stated, were superior to the Germans as forest fighters and in dealing with adverse conditions of terrain and climate, but they preferred to avoid pitched battles.[19] In July 1944, after the Russian summer offensive had passed its peak, an OKW observer concluded that the Finnish setbacks could be blamed, at least in part, on lack of training and neglect of fortifications. He also believed that in June 1944 the Finns had no longer expected a Russian attack and that, until the shock of the breakthrough on 10 June produced a more realistic judgment, they had a tendency, induced by their experiences in the Winter War and 1941, to underestimate the enemy. This last criticism was one from which the Germans extracted a degree of wry satisfaction since they had long felt that the Finns failed to appreciate fully the nature of Germany's problems on the Eastern Front. There was also a feeling that the Finns

---

[17] General der Infanterie a.D. Waldemar Erfurth, Comments on Part II of *The German Northern Theater of Operations, 1940–1945*, June 1957.

[18] Mannerheim, *op. cit.*, pp. 501, 507.

[19] *OKW, WFSt, Op. (H), Nr. 003072/43, Bericht ueber die Reise des Majors d.G. Jordan nach Finnland vom 7. bis 23.6.43.* OKW/56.

had failed to adapt to the conditions of total war—the near-peacetime conditions prevailing on the home front were frequently cited—and were trying to get through the war with as little inconvenience to themselves as possible.[20]

To achieve and exploit their breakthrough the Russians had assembled 10 rifle divisions and the approximate equivalent of 3 tank divisions in addition to the 3 static divisions already in the front on the Isthmus of Karelia. In the assault area their artillery reportedly numbered 300 to 400 guns per kilometer of front.[21] For striking power the Soviet command relied almost exclusively on its tremendous superiority in tanks, artillery, and aircraft. The rifle divisions were weak, averaging about 6,200 men each, and their will to fight declined rapidly after the first few days of combat. The Russian tactics, concentration on a narrow front with a tremendous commitment of matériel and—following the breakthrough—exploitation by several corps abreast, followed a pattern which the German armies on the Eastern Front had come to regard as standard.[22]

Immediately after the Russian breakthrough on 10 June it was clear that the IV Corps could not hold in front of the second line. Mannerheim gave the IV Corps a division from the reserve, a regiment of the III Corps, ordered the Armored Division to move up from Vyborg, and set in motion the transfer of one division from East Karelia and recall of the 3d Brigade from the Twentieth Mountain Army. By the 12th the IV Corps had withdrawn to the second line. The III Corps, which had not been under attack, was then also ordered back. On the same day Mannerheim ordered a division and a brigade out of East Karelia to the Isthmus and asked the OKW to release the weapons and grain which had been intended for Finland but were held in Germany by Hitler's embargo. On the following day Hitler agreed.[23]

Its chances of holding the second line slim, the Finnish High Command was forced to consider radical measures. On 13 June Heinrichs told Dietl that, if the second line were lost, the Finnish intention was to give up the Svir and Maaselkä fronts and pull back in East Karelia to a short line northeast of Lake Ladoga, thus freeing two to three additional divisions for the Isthmus. Since November 1943 work had been in progress on the so-called U-Line, the line of the Uksu River–Loimola Lake–Tolva Lake. Dietl urged the Finns to carry out that intention, but he feared that out of reluctance to give up East Karelia they would hesitate too long.[24] Later he recommended to

---

[20] *Ibid. OKW, WFSt, Op. (H), 007561/44, Reisebericht ueber Frontbesuch in Suedfinnland, 13.7.44.* OKW/56.

[21] *OKW, WFSt, Ic/II, Nr. 04451/44, Notiz zur Feindlage Finnland und (Geb.) AOK 20, 17.6.44, in Feindlage Nord.* OKW/1559. Mannerheim, *op. cit.,* p. 507.

[22] *(Geb.) AOK 20, Ia, Nr. 2624/44, Fuehrungsanordnungen Nr. 18, 21.7.44, in Taetigkeitsberichte Monat Juli 1944.* AOK 20 65635/3.

[23] Erfurth, *op. cit.,* p. 187. Mannerheim, *op. cit.,* p. 508.

[24] *(Geb.) AOK 20, Ia, Nr. 229/44, an OKW, WFSt, Herrn Generaloberst Jodl, 14.6.44, in K.T.B., Chefsachen-Anlagenband, 1.1.–30.6.44.* AOK 20 58629/10.

Hitler that German policy be to tie the Finns to Germany by giving them as much support as possible and to hold them to complete operational measures, not allowing them to dissipate their strength in attempts to hang on in East Karelia. On the shorter line, he thought, Finland might hold out indefinitely, which would assure preservation of Finland and, at the same time, spare the Twentieth Mountain Army the necessity of executing Operation BIRKE.[25]

While Dietl was at Mikkeli the second line on the Isthmus was already under attack. It held for a day; but on 14 June the Russians brought up their heavy weapons and, since—as a captured map later revealed—they had reconnoitered the second line in detail before the offensive began, were able to attack in force immediately. Overwhelming the Finns a second time with the weight of their artillery fire and tanks, they broke through the second line at the village of Kutersel'ka and by 15 June had smashed the Finnish front on an eight-mile stretch from Kutersel'ka to the coast. By then it was apparent that the Russians' main effort would be directed along the railroad line to Vyborg. The Finns had virtually no hope of stopping them short of the city and were worried by the danger that they could reach and close the seventeen-mile-wide narrows between Vyborg and the Vuoksi River before III and IV Corps could be withdrawn. Such a maneuver would in all probability be decisive, for it would end all hopes of holding the Vyborg–Vuoksi line and would force the III and IV Corps to withdraw northward across the Vuoksi and, because there was only one bridge across the river, abandon much of their heavy equipment on the way.

On 16 June Mannerheim ordered the withdrawal to the Vyborg–Vuoksi Line. On the 20th, after four more days of heavy fighting, the IV Corps, under continuing Russian pressure, moved into the line between Vyborg and the river while the III Corps established itself on the north bank of the Vuoksi and held a bridgehead on the south bank across from Vuosalmi. Once again the Finnish Army stood on the line where it had stopped the Russians in 1940. The withdrawal had gone better than might have been expected, chiefly because the Russians, rigidly intent on the city of Vyborg, failed to strike toward the Vyborg–Vuoksi narrows. But the Finns still had no cause for optimism. The Russian forces on the Isthmus had been gradually increased to 20 rifle divisions, 4 tank brigades, 5 to 6 tank regiments, and 4 self-propelled assault gun regiments. Against these the Finns, drawing on the last units which could be spared from East Karelia, could assemble no more than 10 divisions and 4 brigades.[26]

---

[25] (Geb.) AOK 20 Ia, Nr. 231/44, Notizen fuer Vortag beim Fuehrer, 16.6.44, in K.T.B., Chefsachen-Anlagenband, 1.1.–30.6.44. AOK 20 58629/10.
[26] Mannerheim, op. cit., p. 511. OKW, WFSt, K.T.B. Ausarbeitung, Der noerdliche Kriegsschauplatz, 1.4.–31.12.44, pp. 18–22. I.M.T. Doc. 1795–PS.

Political Developments and German Aid

The military crisis resulting from loss of the second line on the Isthmus inevitably brought a political crisis in its wake. On 18 June the Finnish Cabinet held a long meeting. Concerning its results the German Minister could only secure evasive answers. On the evening of the 19th Heinrichs asked Erfurth whether Germany was willing to provide aid other than weapons, specifically six divisions to take over the front in East Karelia and release Finnish troops for the Isthmus. Mannerheim repeated this request on the following day. At about the same time the Finns reestablished contact with the Soviet Government.

In Germany the necessity for extending help to Finland had already been recognized and accepted even though the Germans themselves faced a dangerous situation in Normandy and expected the greatest Soviet offensive of the war to break loose any day. Hitler lifted the embargo on shipments to Finland on 13 June, and on the 19th torpedo boats delivered 9,000 *Panzerfaust* (antitank grenades). Three days later 5,000 *Panzerschreck* (bazookas) were airlifted to Finland. To give the six divisions Mannerheim requested was impossible, but on the 20th the OKW informed him that Germany was ready to give every kind of help if the Finnish Army was actually determined to hold the Vyborg–Vuoksi Line. Aside from weapons and supplies, the Germans offered the 122d Infantry Division, a self-propelled assault gun brigade (the 303d), and air units consisting of a fighter group and a ground attack close support group (Stukas) plus one squadron. The ground troops were drawn from the Army Group North and the air units from the Fifth Air Force in Finland and the First Air Force with the Army Group North. The aircraft were transferred immediately and on 21 June flew 940 support missions for the Finnish Army.[27]

Although the German aid was offered and, in part, delivered without a prior commitment on Finland's part, its price was well known to both parties. On 21 June Mannerheim informed Hitler that Finland was prepared to establish closer ties with Germany, and on the following day Ribbentrop flew to Helsinki to conduct the negotiations in person.[28] That the Foreign Minister himself undertook the mission indicated a determination to bind Finland to Germany unequivocally. For this reason his unannounced appearance in Finland, aside from being a surprise, aroused dismay in the Finnish Government.

The negotiations, which Ribbentrop conducted in the high-pressure manner for which he was noted, did not go smoothly. Both sides recognized that in view of the strong sentiment for peace, which had already resulted in a movement to bring to power a government under Paasikivi, the Finns could not give a declaration which had to be ratified

---

[27] *OKW, WFSt, K.T.B. Ausarbeitung, Der noerdliche Kriegsschauplatz, 1.4.–31.12.44,* pp. 22 and 27–29. I.M.T., Doc. 1795–PS.
[28] *Ibid.* p. 24.

by Parliament. The Germans offered to compromise and accepted a declaration signed by the President.[29]   On 23 June the German position was strengthened when the Soviet Government informed the Finns that it would not open negotiations until the President and Foreign Minister declared in writing that Finland was ready to capitulate and turned to the Soviet Union with an appeal for peace.[30]   On the 24th Ryti and Ramsay conferred with Mannerheim at Mikkeli, and on the next day Hitler added pressure with a directive which stated categorically that a public clarification of Finland's attitude was to be secured.   If such a clarification could not be achieved, support for Finland would stop.[31] Late on the night of 26 June Ryti called in Ribbentrop and handed him a letter in which he stated that he, as President of Finland, would not make peace with the Soviet Union without the consent of the German Government and that he would not permit any government appointed by him or any other persons to conduct armistice or peace talks or negotiations serving those purposes without German consent.[32]

Ribbentrop returned to Germany in triumph, but with a contract which was unenforceable by any means at Germany's command.   The end result of his mission was to obscure the obvious generosity of German aid extended at a time when it could scarcely be spared and to arouse, instead, in the minds of the Finns a feeling that they had been made victims of blackmail in their hour of greatest need.   While this cannot be said to have affected materially future Finnish actions, it went far toward relieving any moral qualms they might have had concerning the course they were about to pursue.

Within a week after the Ryti letter was signed the United States broke off diplomatic relations with Finland.   The Finnish Minister in Washington and his principal aides had already been handed their passports and ordered out of the country in June.   Although this was a severe blow, the fact that a declaration of war did not follow could, in the long run, be regarded as a major accomplishment of Finnish diplomacy: Finland had weathered the war without an irrevocable break in its ties with the democracies.

The oppressive atmosphere surrounding the June negotiations was deepened by Dietl's death on 23 June.   He had conferred with Hitler on the previous day and was returning to Finland when his plane crashed in the Austrian Alps.   The accident was kept secret for several days for fear of its effect on the negotiations.   On 28 June Generaloberst Lothar Rendulic took command of the Twentieth Mountain Army.

For the Finns the June negotiations had one purpose—to secure assistance in stopping the Russian offensive.   The Ryti letter achieved that purpose, but the aid that came was less than the Finns expected.

---

[29] Bluecher, *op. cit.*, p. 371.
[30] Mannerheim, *op. cit.*, p. 513.
[31] Bluecher, *op. cit.*, p. 372.
[32] Bluecher, *op. cit.*, p. 372.

It was in fact less than the Germans had intended to give, for, in the meantime, the massive Russian offensive against the Army Group Center which began on 22 June had imposed a nearly overwhelming drain on German resources. The 303d Self-propelled Assault Gun Brigade reached Finland on 23 June, and the 122d Infantry Division arrived five days later. But a second assault gun brigade intended for Finland had to be diverted to the Army Group Center at the last minute, and a corps headquarters to command the German units in Finland, although pulled out of the southern sector of the Eastern Front, was never sent.[33] German weapons and supplies, including some tanks and heavy equipment, continued to flow to Finland. The *Panzerfaust* and *Panzerschreck,* once they had been proved effective, greatly increased the Finns' ability to withstand Russian tank attacks and played a major role in restoring the confidence of the Finnish Army.

The Last Phase

On 21 June the Russians occupied Vyborg, which the Finns had evacuated a day earlier. Although there had been no intention to defend the old city, its loss was a blow to Finnish morale. Between Vyborg and the Vuoksi, Russian pressure continued heavy, and on 25 June they threw ten divisions reinforced by assault artillery against the front near Repola, penetrating the line to a distance of some two and one-half miles. In four days of heavy fighting the Finns managed to seal off the penetration but without restoring their former front. The Russians remained in possession of a salient which was the more dangerous in that it brought them close to terrain favorable for armored operations.[34]

On 16 June Mannerheim had issued orders for withdrawal from East Karelia. The intention was to pull back gradually from the Svir and Maaselkä lines to the general line Uksa River–Suo Lake–Poros Lake.[35] At the last minute, as the withdrawal was starting, the OKW tried without success to persuade him not to give up East Karelia.[36] In this respect the OKW directly contradicted the advice which Dietl had given. Its decision to do so probably rested on several considerations. In the first place, it had become an obsession with Hitler never to give ground voluntarily. Even more important in this instance was the fact that in giving up East Karelia the Finns would lose their principal war gain, their last lever for bargaining with the Soviet Union, and, consequently, their motivation for remaining in the war. Furthermore, with a major

[33] *OKW, WFSt, K.T.B. Ausarbeitung, Der noerdliche Kriegsschauplatz, 1.4.–31.12.44,* pp. 29–30. I.M.T. Doc. 1795–PS.
[34] Mannerheim, *op. cit.,* p. 515. *OKW, WFSt, K.T.B. Ausarbeitung, der noerdliche Kriegsschauplatz, 1.4.–31.12.44,* p. 31. I.M.T., Doc. 1795–PS.
[35] *(Geb.) AOK 20, Ia, Nr. 234/44, 17.6.44,* in *K.T.B., Chefsachen Anlagenband, 1.1.–30.6.44.* AOK 20 58629/10.
[36] *OKW, WFSt, K.T.B. Ausarbeitung, Der noerdliche Kriegsschauplatz, 1.4.–31.12.44,* p. 30. I.M.T., Doc. 1795–PS.

offensive in the offing on the Eastern Front, it could be assumed that the Russians would stop short of an all-out effort at a decision in Finland. The OKW line of reasoning had much to recommend it—from the German point of view but not from the Finnish. The Finns had no taste for desperate gambles and, for that matter, although they seemed to be acting in agreement with Dietl's recommendations, neither had they any enthusiasm for last stands in the *Goetterdaemmerung* vein.

In the Maaselkä and Aunus (Svir) Fronts the Finns had a total of four divisions and two brigades. Opposite them stood eleven Russian divisions and six brigades. By evacuating their large bridgehead south of the Svir on 18 June they escaped a Russian attack which began the following day, but thereafter the withdrawal went less smoothly than had been expected. The Russians kept up an aggressive pursuit and, by crossing the Svir on either side of Lodeynoye Pole and staging a landing on the Ladoga shore between Tuloksa and Vidlitsa, threatened to push the Finnish divisions back into the wilderness on the eastern side of the Isthmus of Olonets. On 30 June the Finns evacuated Petrozavodsk, and two days later they pulled out of Salmi. By 10 July the Finnish divisions were in the U-Line. With Russian pressure continuing strong, the Finns were by no means certain that they could hold the front, and they began work on new positions between Yanis Lake and Lake Ladoga. A further withdrawal to the Moscow Line also came under consideration.[37]

In the first days of July the Finns were given a short respite, at least on the Isthmus of Karelia. On the 4th the Russians occupied the islands in Vyborg Bay and attempted a landing on the north shore. There they ran into the 122d Infantry Division, which was moving up, and were thrown back. At the same time they attacked the Finnish bridgehead south of Vuosalmi, but otherwise they confined themselves to local attacks and regrouping, giving the Finns an opportunity to strengthen their defenses.[38]

In the Finnish High Command concern for the future was growing, particularly with respect to manpower. At the end of June casualties had reached 18,000, of which only 12,000 could be replaced. On 1 July Mannerheim asked for a second German division and additional self-propelled assault gun units. When Hitler countered with nothing more than a promise to build the assault gun battalion of the 122d Infantry Division up to brigade strength Mannerheim protested that in advising his Government to accept the German proposals during the June negotiations he had assumed a heavy responsibility; if the German units were not forthcoming, not only would the military situation deteriorate, but his political prestige would be destroyed. Hitler, in

---

[37] Mannerheim, *op. cit.*, p. 518. Erfurth, *op. cit.*, pp. 192, 194, 199, 207. *OKW, WFSt, Op. (H), Nr. 007561/44, Reisebericht ueber Frontbesuch in Suedfinnland, 13.7.44.* OKW/56.
[38] Erfurth, *op. cit.*, p. 199.

reply, offered one self-propelled assault gun brigade before 10 July, another to be sent later, and tanks, assault guns, antitank guns, and artillery.[39]

In the second week of July the Finns were forced to give up their positions on the right bank of the Vuoksi south of Vuosalmi. The Russians, in turn, gained a bridgehead of their own on the north bank. Lacking the strength to eliminate the bridgehead, the Finns had to undertake to contain it. Despite this dangerous development and continued heavy fighting which brought the number of Finnish casualties up to 32,000 by the 11th, the fronts on both sides of Lake Ladoga were beginning to stabilize. By 15 July the Finns had detected signs—confirmed several days later—that, although the Russian strength on the Isthmus had risen to 26 rifle divisions and 12 to 14 tank brigades, the first-rate guard units were being pulled out and replaced with garrison troops. It could be expected that the tempo of the offensive would be reduced.[40]

While the Finns achieved a degree of equilibrium in the second half of the month, the Army Groups North and Center were experiencing a full-scale disaster. In three weeks the Russian offensive had driven the Army Group Center back into Poland and nearly to the border of East Prussia. By mid-July the time had come to pull the Army Group North back behind the Dvina or see it cut off and isolated in the Baltic States. Hitler's solution was to place Schoerner, then a Generaloberst, in command of the army group with orders to hold the old PANTHER Line between Narva and Pskov at all costs.[41]

On 17 July Hitler dispatched one of the self-propelled assault gun brigades promised the Finns to the Eastern Front instead and sent the second one east also on the following day. These decisions were not communicated to Mannerheim until several days later—after the Soviet troop withdrawals from the front in Finland had been confirmed.[42]

To the Finns the fate of the Army Group North was nearly as momentous as that of their own Army. Once the Baltic coast was in Russian hands their supply lines to Germany, on which they depended for much of their food and almost all of their military supplies, could be cut. The loss of Pskov on 23 July and of Narva on the 27th were staggering blows for them. The shock was intensified when, two days after the fall of Narva, Hitler ordered the 122d Infantry Division back to the Army Group North. Mannerheim asked that the division leave via Hanko rather than Helsinki in order to avoid alarming the people. The OKW explained that the deciding factor had been the relative

---

[39] *OKW, WFSt, K.T.B. Ausarbeitung, Der noerdliche Kriegsschauplatz, 1.4–31.12.44*, pp. 31ff. I.M.T., Doc. 1795–PS.
[40] *Ibid.*, pp. 32–34. Erfurth, *op. cit.*, p. 203.
[41] Kurt von Tippelskirsch, *Geschichte des zweiten Weltkriegs* (Bonn: Atheneaum-Verlag, 1951), pp. 530–42.
[42] *OKW, WFSt, K.T.B. Ausarbeitung, Der noerdliche Kriegsschauplatz, 1.4.–31.12.44*, pp. 33ff. I.M.T., Doc. 1795–PS.

quiet on the Finnish front and assured him that he could count on German help in any new crisis, but under the circumstances these explanations must have had a decidedly empty ring.[43]

Armistice

In a secret meeting on 28 July in Mannerheim's country house at Sairala, Ryti announced his intention to resign and urged Mannerheim to accept the presidency of Finland. Three days later the resignation was submitted, and Parliament drafted a law, passed unanimously on 4 August, elevating Mannerheim to the presidency without the formality of an election. With that, the stage was set for a repudiation of the Ryti-Ribbentrop agreement and a new approach to the Soviet Union.

To the Germans Ryti's resignation came as a surprise. They assumed that the shift would not be advantageous to Germany. Although they saw a possibility that Mannerheim might intend to rally the national will to resist, it appeared more likely that he would assume the role of a peacemaker. Apprehensive, but powerless to exercise any real influence over the course of Finnish policy, the Germans in near-panic hastened to reassure Mannerheim. On 3 August, in response to a Finnish inquiry concerning the situation in the Baltic area, the OKW ordered the Commanding General, Army Group North, Schoerner, to report to Mannerheim in person immediately. Keitel was to follow in a few days. The Schoerner visit surprised nearly everyone, including Schoerner himself who asked Erfurth why he had been rushed off to Helsinki in such head-over-heels fashion. The Finns took Schoerner's sudden appearance as a sign of nervousness and as a too obvious attempt to court Mannerheim.[44]

To draw even mildly encouraging conclusions from the situation of the Army Group North required a man of Schoerner's zeal and determination. Although Narva and Pskov had fallen, most of the Narva–Peipus line was still in German hands; but, at the turn of the month, the Russians had thrust through to the Baltic near Mitau cutting off and isolating the army group. The ominous nature of this development was underscored when the Lufthansa suspended air traffic between Germany and Finland. Direct telephone communications had been broken several days earlier. Undaunted, Schoerner promised that the Baltic area would absolutely be held; the Army Group North would be supplied by air and by sea; and armored forces from East Prussia would restore the land contact.[45] Remarkably enough, largely as a result of the combined wills of Schoerner and Hitler pitted against the logic of events, the promise was kept; but, even though Schoerner left Manner-

---

[43] *Ibid.,* p. 35.
[44] General der Infanterie a.D. Waldemar Erfurth, Comments on Part II of *The German Northern Theater of Operations, 1940–1945,* June 1957.
[45] *Ibid.,* pp. 36–38. Erfurth, *op. cit.,* pp. 207, 210, 211ff.

heim with the impression that his report had had a positive effect, it appears that his success, if any, was transitory. Still, the German determination—more specifically, that of Hitler and Schoerner with an assist from the Navy in the interest of submarine warfare—to hold the Baltic shore at all costs was of very material benefit to Finland, not in encouraging the nation to remain in the war but in affording it an opportunity to make peace before it was completely isolated.

With the Army Group North making its stand on the shores of the Narva River and Lake Peipus and with the Soviet summer offensive degenerating into local attacks on the Isthmus of Karelia, the military position of Finland in August was, if only for the time being, as favorable as even a confirmed optimist would have dared predict a month or so earlier. Between mid-July and mid-August the Russians reduced their forces on the Isthmus by 10 rifle divisions and 5 tank brigades. On 10 August in East Karelia the Finnish Army ended its last major operation in World War II with a victory when the 14th Division, the 21st Brigade, and the Cavalry Brigade trapped and nearly destroyed 2 Russian divisions in a pocket east of Ilomantsi.[46] It appeared that as in the Winter War, although the Soviet Union could claim a victory, its offensive had failed, largely for the same reasons—underestimation of the Finnish capacity to resist and rigid, unimaginative Soviet tactical leadership.

Mannerheim believed that in their eagerness to destroy Finland the Russians betrayed their promise to the Western Powers to assist the Normandy landings and weakened their own offensives against the Army Groups Center and North.[47] In the absence of reliable Soviet sources no definite conclusions concerning their intentions can be drawn. It is unlikely that the offensive against Finland was undertaken with deliberate disregard for a promise to aid the landings in Normandy with an offensive in the east. The offensive in Finland was a secondary effort and was probably staged to fill in time while Stalin waited, first, to see whether the Allies would actually invade the Continent and, then, to make certain that the invasion was in earnest and had prospects of success. Probably, the success of the invasion influenced Stalin to give up his excursion into Finland and to devote all of his efforts to the race for Berlin.

By the time Keitel went to Helsinki (17 August), carrying an oak leaf cluster for Mannerheim and a Knight's Cross of the Iron Cross for Heinrichs, the German situation offered little to sustain even his indomitable optimism. The Allied breakout in Normandy had succeeded, and the liberation of Paris was only days away. In southern France the Allies were rapidly developing a secondary offensive. In Italy the Germans were driven back to the Gothic Line; in the East the Rus-

---

[46] Erfurth, *op. cit.*, p. 216.
[47] Mannerheim, *op. cit.*, pp. 519–22.

sians stood on the outskirts of Warsaw. The end for Germany suddenly seemed very close, much closer than it actually was.

Mannerheim, for his part, took the Keitel visit as an opportunity to
clear the air, possibly not so much for the Germans' benefit as to open
the way for a new approach to Moscow. The 60,000 casualties incurred during the summer, he said, had been replaced, but Finland
could not endure a second bloodletting on that scale. Turning to what
was probably also uppermost in Keitel's mind, the status of the Ryti-
Ribbentrop agreement, he stated that Ryti, in a desperate situation,
had made a contract which proved highly unpopular. Finland believed that Ryti's resignation nullified that contract. Keitel, taken
aback by that blunt statement, in order to protect Germany's legal interests, rejected it stating that he was not empowered to receive political
communications.[48]

In Finland, after the middle of the month, signs of the approaching
end mushroomed on all sides. Peace sentiment increased with every
passing day, and rumors of all sorts gained currency. In this atmosphere the report that Rumania had sued for peace struck like a bombshell. On 25 August, through its legation in Stockholm, Finland asked
whether the Soviet Government would receive a Finnish peace delegation. An accompanying verbal note informed the Soviet Government
that Mannerheim had told Keitel he did not consider himself bound
by the Ryti-Ribbentrop agreement.[49] Official notice that Finland had
repudiated the agreement was not sent to Germany until the following
day.[50]

In its reply on 29 August the Soviet Government made its willingness
to receive a delegation contingent upon the prior fulfillment of two conditions: that Finland immediately break off relations with Germany
and that Finland order all German troops to leave its territory within
two weeks, at the latest by 15 September, and, in case of the Germans'
failure to comply, take steps to intern them. The Finnish Parliament
accepted the conditions on 2 September, and on the same day approved
a government motion to break off relations with Germany.

The Finnish decision came as somewhat of a surprise to the Germans.
Although the German Minister in Helsinki had been informed on 31
August that negotiations were in progress, it was expected that the Soviet
terms would prove unacceptable. Several times in the past a glance at
the Soviet terms had proved the best means of inhibiting the Finnish
sentiment for peace. On 2 September, in a last minute, heavy-handed
effort to give impetus to a repetition of that pattern, Rendulic called on
Mannerheim and emphasized in particular that the Russian demands

---

[48] Mannerheim, *op. cit.*, p. 524. Erfurth, *op. cit.*, p. 217. Bluecher, *op. cit.*,
pp. 395ff.
[49] *OKW, WFSt, K.T.B. Ausarbeitung, Der noerdliche Kriegsschauplatz, 1.4.–
31.12.44*, p. 47. I.M.T., Doc. 1795–PS.
[50] Erfurth, *op. cit.*, p. 220.

might bring about a conflict between German and Finnish troops which, he maintained, would result in 90 percent losses on both sides since the best soldiers in Europe would be opposing each other.[51]

Two problems which worried the Finnish leadership as the end approached proved less serious than they might have been. The first of these was the danger of an economic collapse when German assistance stopped. It was solved in August when Sweden agreed to cover the requirements of grain and some other foodstuffs for a six-month period. The second, the possibility that some elements of the population, particularly in the Army, would refuse to accept the peace and would create internal dissension or throw their lot in with the Germans, although it occasioned some apprehension, never actually arose. During the last months, the Germans had toyed with a number of ideas for keeping Finnish resistance alive by extralegal means. In June, when he went to Helsinki, Ribbentrop had proposed, somewhat wildly, that the German Minister find a thousand reliable men to take over the government.[52] At the same time, Hitler had instructed Dietl to draw Finnish troops into the Twentieth Mountain Army in the event of a separate peace.[53] Later Rendulic suggested that the German infantry division and assault gun brigade in southern Finland be used as a nucleus around which a resistance movement could be built and in August proposed General Talvela as a man who might be persuaded to lead the resistance.[54] None of these projects passed beyond the talking stage, and one that was later tried, reactivation of the traditional Finnish 27th Jaeger Battalion (in the German Army), attracted only a scattering of volunteers.[55] The overwhelming majority of the Finnish population was willing to follow its government, and the Finnish Government had been careful throughout the war to prevent the emergence of possible Quislings.

Having met the Soviet conditions, the Finns appointed an armistice delegation—which, as it developed, would have to negotiate the terms of peace as well—headed by Minister President Antti Hackzell. Mannerheim undertook to explain the Finnish action in a personal letter to Hitler in which he expressed gratitude for the German help and loyal brotherhood-in-arms and stated that, while Germany could never be completely destroyed, the Finns could, both as a people and a nation; therefore, Finland had to make peace in order to preserve its existence. Next, he turned to Stalin, proposing a cease fire to prevent further

---

[51] (GEB.) AOK 20, Der Oberbefehlshaber, Ia, Nr. 356/44, an OKW, WFSt, 4.9.44, in K.T.B., Chefsachenanlagen, 1.7.–18.12.44. AOK 20 65635/12.
[52] Bluecher, op. cit., p. 369.
[53] OKW, WFSt, K.T.B. Ausarbeitung, Der noerdliche Kriegsschauplatz, 1.4.–31.12.44, p. 43. I.M.T., Doc. 1795–PS.
[54] (Geb.) AOK 20, Ia, Nr. 1010/44, Notiz fuer Besprechung O.B. mit Chef OKW, 14.8.44, in K.T.B., Chefsachenanlagen, 1.7.–18.12. AOK 20 65635/12.
[55] OKW, WFSt, K.T.B. Ausarbeitung, Der noerdliche Kriegsschauplatz, 1.4.–31.12.44, p. 54. I.M.T., Doc. 1795–PS.

bloodshed while the negotiations were in progress. Both sides accepted 0700 on 4 September as the time; but, although the Finns stopped their operations on time, the Russians, either through a mistake or to underscore their victory, let theirs run another 24 hours.[56]

The delegation reached Moscow on 7 September, but the Soviet Government delayed a week before presenting its terms. Restoration of the 1940 border was a foregone conclusion. In addition, the Russians demanded the entire Pechenga region and, in place of Hanko, a fifty-year lease on Porkkala, which would give them a base astride the main rail and road routes to southwestern Finland within artillery range of Helsinki. The reparations were set at $300,000,000 to be paid in goods over a five-year period. The Finnish Army was to withdraw to the 1940 border within five days and be reduced to peacetime strength within two and one-half months. The Soviet Union was to be granted the right to use Finnish ports, airfields, and merchant shipping for the duration of the war against Germany; and a Soviet commission would supervise execution of the armistice, which was to become effective on the day it was signed.[57]

On 18 September the Finnish Cabinet took the terms under consideration but could not reach an agreement. The Russians, meanwhile, demanded that the signing be completed by noon of the following day. Early on the morning of the 19th, after the Army informed the Cabinet that under the most favorable circumstances Finland could not continue the war for more than another three months, the Parliament gave its approval. In Moscow the Finnish delegation signed the armistice shortly before noon, before it had received the official authorization.[58]

---

[56] Mannerheim, *op. cit.*, pp. 525, 529, 530.
[57] Mannerheim, *op. cit.*, pp. 531, 543ff.
[58] Mannerheim, *op. cit.*, pp. 532ff.

Chapter 14

The Undefeated Army

TANNE and BIRKE

Finland's appeal for an armistice left the Germans in a state of painful indecision, mostly because all of the possible courses of action appeared to be little more than invitations to disaster. Although the Twentieth Mountain Army remained committed to execution of Operation BIRKE, for the sake of the nickel mines, it had no assurance that it would succeed in establishing a line in the north which could be held, not to mention the near certainty that sooner or later the army's sea supply line would be cut and its downfall would then become inevitable. On the other hand, a continuous withdrawal through the arctic regions of Finland into Norway, with winter only weeks away, presented even greater risks. The TANNE operations, too, presented more disadvantages than advantages. TANNE WEST had been in doubt almost since its inception because of Sweden's interest in the Åland Islands and the necessity for avoiding any provocation which might result in loss of the Swedish sources of iron ore and ballbearings. On 3 September Hitler decided to abandon TANNE WEST since it had also developed that the division from Denmark could not be spared.[1] On the same day the Navy, which was responsible for TANNE OST, reported that the operation could not be executed because only untrained troops were available.[2]

On 6 September BIRKE began. The intention to hold northern Finland was not revealed to the Finns, and the operation was to be conducted at a deliberate pace which would give enough time for movement of the army's supplies and at all times keep the XVIII Mountain Corps and the XXXVI Mountain Corps in a position to deal effectively with a Russian or Finnish pursuit. The first step, on 6 September, was to begin pulling the XVIII Mountain Corps troops east of Kesten'ga back to the Sof'yanga Position—a move which had been in preparation

---

[1] *OKW, WFSt, K.T.B. Ausarbeitung, Der noerdliche Kriegsschauplatz*, pp. 46, 52. I.M.T., Doc. 1795–PS.
[2] *Naval War Diary*, Vol. 61, p. 58.

for several months and would have been carried out even if Finland had stayed in the war.[3]

The army's chief concern was for its open right flank and the army boundary on the right flank of the XVIII Mountain Corps. After learning that the Finns were moving two divisions north, avowedly for the purpose of preventing the development of a vacuum between the Finnish Army and the Twentieth Mountain Army which the Russians might exploit, Rendulic on 3 September detached sufficient motorized units from the XXXVI Mountain Corps and the XVIII Mountain Corps to create two reinforced regiments. These, designated Kampfgruppe West and Kampfgruppe Ost, were stationed in the vicinity of Oulu and Hyrynsalmi to prevent the Finns from moving in behind the army. The concern for the army boundary was allayed, for the time being at least, when the Finnish 14th Division, on the Finnish left flank, promised to maintain contact until the XVIII Mountain Corps had accomplished its withdrawal behind the Finnish border.

What would happen after that was a question on which Finnish and German opinion differed sharply. The Finns maintained that the Russians would not advance beyond the 1940 border. They contended that, once the Twentieth Mountain Army had successfully disengaged, the withdrawal would become purely a technical matter of moving troops and supplies. Rendulic, on the other hand, believed the Finns either had lost touch with reality or were being deliberately dishonest. That the Russians would respect the border, he thought, was extremely unlikely. Much more likely was that they intended to occupy all of Finland north of the line Tornio–Suomussalmi, essentially the Twentieth Mountain Army zone. In the light of that assumption, which, it must be said, was the only safe one, the German withdrawal had to be conducted according to tactical principles and as if it were being undertaken on enemy rather than friendly or neutral territory.[4]

The first trouble for the Twentieth Mountain Army came in the XXXVI Mountain Corps zone. The westward extension of their right flank which the Russians had been working on since early in the year gave ample evidence that they intended to trap and destroy the XXXVI Mountain Corps.[5] Although aware of that, the corps had to time its movements not only according to its own situation but also in a manner that would allow the XVIII Mountain Corps to pass through Rovaniemi behind it.

---

[3] The XVIII Mountain Corps, under General der Infanterie Friedrich Hochbaum, had the 6th SS-Mountain Division "Nord" and the Divisionsgruppe Kraeutler (the 139th Regiment, formerly of the 3d Mountain Division, two ski battalions, and an artillery regiment) in the Kesten'ga sector and the 7th Mountain Division in the Ukhta sector.

[4] (Geb.) AOK 20, Ia, Kriegstagebuch, 1.9.–18.12.44, 6 Sep 44 et passim. AOK 20 65635/2.

[5] The XXXVI Mountain Corps, with the 163d and 169th Divisions, was commanded by General der Gebirgstruppe Emil Vogel.

The danger point in the XXXVI Mountain Corps zone developed in the vicinity of Korya northeast of Salla at the terminus of the road running down to Salla which the Germans had used in their own attack on Salla in the summer of 1941. The appearance of Russian troops there on 7 September came as a complete surprise. Surprise changed to dismay when the Germans learned that the Russians had also brought up tanks over terrain that until then had been considered virtually impassable for infantry. In the following days, after assembling a reindeer brigade and elements of a tank brigade with T 34 tanks, the Russians gained a foothold on the road and threatened to advance on Salla where they could have cut off the retreat of the entire corps. Events of the succeeding weeks indicated that bringing the tanks into position had required a tremendous effort which could not be maintained long enough to make full tactical use of them. Their appearance nevertheless had a serious psychological impact on the German troops and led the army and corps commands to consider that the enemy might be planning more radical measures than had been expected.[6]

With its rear endangered, the XXXVI Mountain Corps began to evacuate the Verman Line on the night of 9 September. The Russians had already sent a force due south from the Korya area and on 11 September reached and cut the main road from Salla east of the Kayrala Lake narrows. Fortunately, the corps had built an alternate road which swung south from Allakurtti through Vuoriyärvi and thence via Mikkola back to the main road west of Kayrala. Traffic proceeded over that route almost without interruption until the main road was reopened on 13 September. On the 14th the last elements of the XXXVI Mountain Corps passed through Allakurtti, and, although the Russians had augmented their northern envelopment with a secondary thrust against the southern flank in the direction of Vuoriyärvi, the withdrawal proceeded in good order.

In the light of the apparent seriousness of the Russian effort the XXXVI Mountain Corps revised its plan of withdrawal. Instead of routing all its troops along the main road via Salla and Kemiyärvi to Rovaniemi, it intended to shift two-thirds of the 169th Division northwestward to Savukoski to block a possible Russian attempt to strike at the Arctic Ocean Highway between Rovaniemi and Ivalo. In the meantime, the corps still had to hold for about ten days at Kayrala and in the vicinity of Korya in order to keep control of Salla until the XVIII Mountain Corps withdrawal had made sufficient progress farther south. On 24 September, after evacuating the bridgehead east of Kayrala, the XXXVI Mountain Corps set in motion a quick withdrawal through Salla to Markayärvi and Savukoski. The Russian pursuit stopped at Salla.[7]

[6] *Ibid.*, 7 and 8 Sep 44. Erfurth, *op. cit.*, p. 246. Hoelter, *op. cit.*, pp. 34ff.
[7] *(Geb.) AOK 20, Ia, Kriegstagebuch, 1.9.–18.12.44*, 11, 12, 13, 16, and 24 Sep 44. AOK 20 65635/2. Hoelter, *op. cit.*, p. 36.

While the XXXVI Mountain Corps fought its way back into Finland, the evacuation in the south proceeded with hardly a hitch. On 10 September the 6th SS-Mountain Division and Divisionsgruppe Kraeutler were firmly established in the Sof'yanga Position, and the 7th Mountain Division began its withdrawal from Ukhta. At the middle of the month the XVIII Mountain Corps divisions moved into their switch positions west of the 1940 Finnish border. Four Russian divisions followed up to the border and stopped.[8]

Until the middle of the month the XVIII Mountain Corps carefully maintained contact with the Finnish left flank, for its own protection and in the hope that Finland might yet reject the Soviet terms and resume the war on Germany's side. On 17 September Rendulic regarded the relationships between Finland and the Soviet Union on the one hand and Germany and Finland on the other as so undecided that he ordered all retrograde movements stopped. The next day, after Finland had signed the armistice, he revoked the order and gave the XVIII Mountain Corps permission to break contact with the Finns.[9]

The evacuation of excess personnel and supplies through the Finnish Baltic ports began in the first week of September. On the 6th the 303d Self-propelled Assault Gun Brigade went aboard ship in Helsinki, and by the 13th all Germans including the legation and liaison staffs were out of southern Finland. At Oulu and Kemi on the Gulf of Bothnia the Twentieth Mountain Army, in part using ships loaned by the Finns, loaded 4,049 troops, 3,336 wounded, and 42,144 tons of supplies, leaving about 106,000 tons of supplies which later had to be destroyed. Oulu was evacuated on 15 September, and the last ships departed from Kemi on the 21st.[10]

As 15 September, the last day of the period of grace allowed for a voluntary German evacuation, drew near, relations between the Twentieth Mountain Army and the Finns remained friendly. Rendulic ordered his troops to behave "loyally" toward the Finns, and the Finnish liaison officer at army headquarters disclosed that Finland was willing to "make compromises" although it wanted to create the impression "outside" that it had broken with Germany completely.[11] On 13 September the Finns informed the Twentieth Mountain Army that they would order all railroad rolling stock between Rovaniemi and Salla moved west of Rovaniemi on the 14th but would do nothing if the Germans took over the equipment. Between Rovaniemi and Oulu, they intended to keep the railroad in operation until the end of the

---

[8] *OKW, WFSt, K.T.B. Ausarbeitung, Der noerdliche Kriegsschauplatz, 4.4.–31.12.44*, p. 57. I.M.T. Doc. 1795–PS.
[9] *(Geb.) AOK 20, Ia, Kriegstagebuch, 1.9.–18.12.44*, 17 and 18 Sep 44. AOK 20 65635/2.
[10] *OKW, WFSt, K.T.B. Ausarbeitung, Der noerdliche Kriegsschauplatz, 1.4.–31.12.44*, pp. 55, 57, 71. I.M.T., Doc. 1795–PS.
[11] *(Geb.) AOK 20, Ia, Kriegstagebuch, 1.9.–18.12.44*, 14 Sep 44. AOK 20 65635/2.

month for the evacuation of Finnish civilians and would haul 60 cars of German supplies a day. The Twentieth Mountain Army, in return, agreed to turn Oulu over to the Finnish troops on the 15th.[12]

The first break in this spirit of mutual accommodation came from the German side. In the second week of September the OKM suddenly changed its estimate of the prospects for TANNE OST after the naval liaison officer on Suursaari reported that the Finnish commandant of the island had said he would never fire on German troops. Doenitz expressed the opinion that so important a place as Suursaari could not be allowed to fall to the Russians without a fight and asked for reconsideration of TANNE OST. The Naval Staff thereupon proposed to execute the operation no later than 15 September, since it appeared from the liaison officer's reports that the Finns would not offer resistance and might evacuate the island as early as the 12th. On 11 September, after the naval liaison officer reported that the Finnish commandant had declared he would not fight the Germans even if ordered to do so, Hitler ordered preparations for the operation speeded up. Two days later the time was set at 0200 on the 15th.

With a mixed force of naval and army personnel of approximately regimental strength taken aboard at Reval, a Navy task force executed the landing on schedule on the morning of the 15th. After the first wave of 1,400 men was ashore, the Finns opened fire, and shortly after daylight the Russians intervened with heavy air strikes. The second wave, which consisted mostly of naval personnel not trained for assault operations, could not be landed. After as many troops as possible had been taken off the island, the operation had to be canceled.[13] The Finns claimed to have taken 700 prisoners.[14]

TANNE OST was so complete a fiasco that the Naval Staff, contrary to its usual custom, never investigated—or at least did not record—the causes of its error. For a time it appeared that the indirect consequences of the operation might prove even more serious than the tactical debacle itself. The Finnish Government immediately ordered all Finnish ships in the Baltic Sea to put into Swedish or Finnish ports, with the result that 13,000 tons of Twentieth Mountain Army supplies being returned to Germany were lost.[15] Mannerheim also retaliated on 15 September with a demand that Rendulic immediately give up all the territory south of the general line Oulu–Suomussalmi and the entire Baltic shore from Oulu to the Swedish border.[16]

---

[12] (Geb.) AOK 20, Ia, Nr. 1194/44, Fortsetzung der Besprechungen mit dem Sonderbeauftragten des Oberkommandos der finn. Wehrmacht am 12.9. abends, 13.9.44, in K.T.B. Anlagenband, 1.9.–15.9.44. AOK 20 65635/5.

[13] Naval War Diary, Vol. 61, pp. 156, 231, 255, 333, 393.

[14] Mannerheim, op. cit., p. 531.

[15] OKW, WFSt, K.T.B. Ausarbeitung, Der noerdliche Kriegsschauplatz, 1.4.–31.12.44, p. 71. I.M.T., Doc. 1795–PS.

[16] (Geb.) AOK 20, Ia, Aktennotiz 15.9.44, in K.T.B. Anlagenband 1.9.–15.9.44. AOK 20 65635/5.

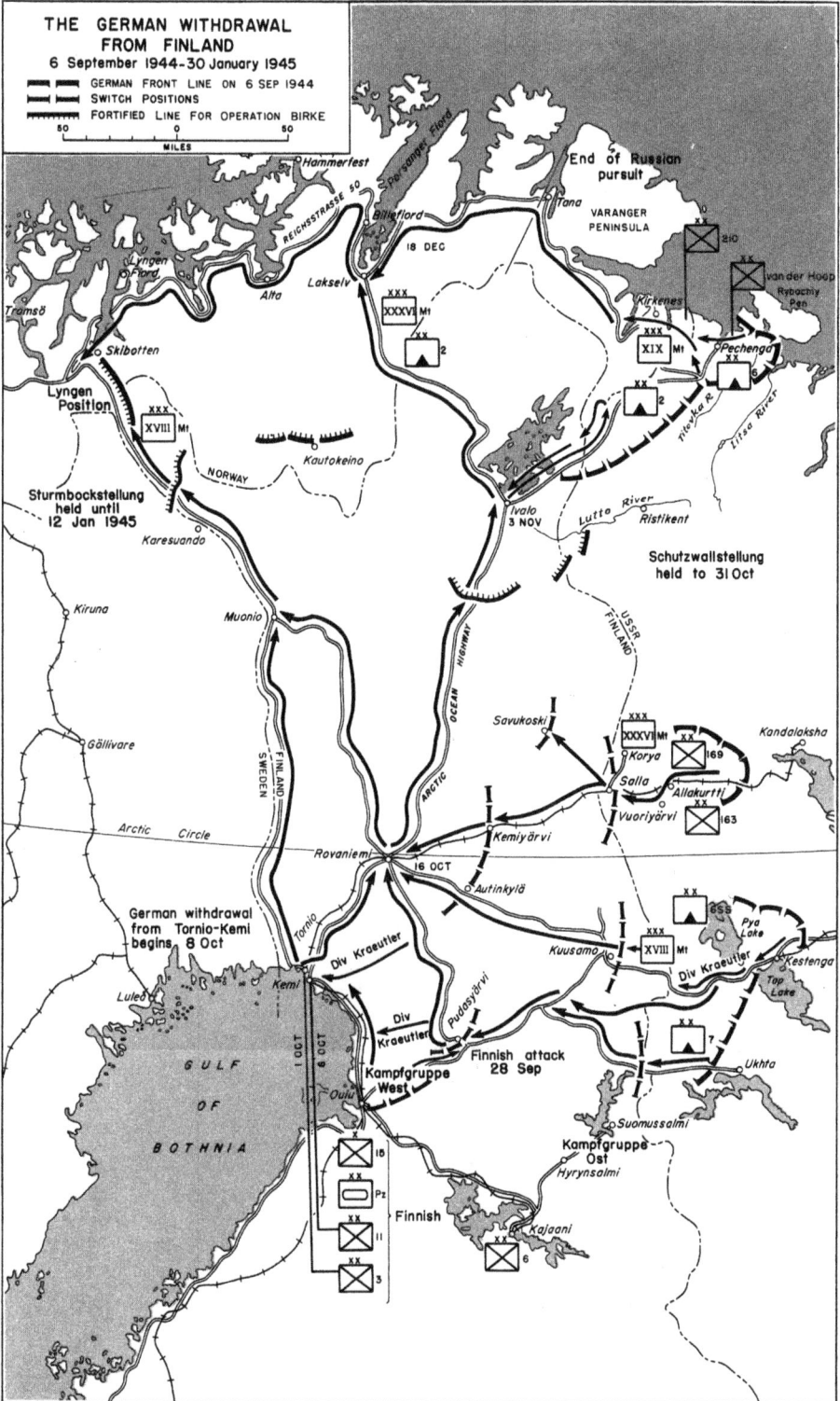

THE GERMAN WITHDRAWAL
FROM FINLAND
6 September 1944-30 January 1945

GERMAN FRONT LINE ON 6 SEP 1944
SWITCH POSITIONS
FORTIFIED LINE FOR OPERATION BIRKE

50   0   50
MILES

Map 22

Although the Finnish Government raised a cry of treachery, the Finns probably regarded the Suursaari incident as something of a stroke of good fortune since it supplied overt evidence to refute Russian charges of collusion between Finland and Germany. That Finland did not regard it as a cause for open hostilities was demonstrated during the next few days. Rendulic, convinced—by the Finnish liaison officer's failure to deny a direct accusation—that a Russian desire to open a route to the Swedish border in preparation for a possible advance across northern Sweden to Narvik lay behind the Finnish pressure for evacuation of the Baltic shore, rejected Mannerheim's demand but declared his willingness to negotiate for a gradual withdrawal.[17]

Within two days the Twentieth Mountain Army and the Finnish Army Headquarters formulated an agreement whereby the Finnish troops would execute what the Finnish operations chief described as "fall maneuvers" designed to avoid clashes between the Germans and Finns while at the same time enabling Finland to report progress "of the advance" to the Russians. The Finns agreed to permit German destruction of all roads, railroads, and bridges, particularly since those measures would help justify the slow Finnish advance to the Russians. They also promised not to rebuild the railroad bridges and to build the road bridges strong enough to carry only supplies, not tanks. The Twentieth Mountain Army agreed to provide Finnish Headquarters with two days' advance notice of its movements. The Finnish liaison officer also proposed that, in the event Finland were forced to declare war against Germany, he be interned and then allowed to continue to function. The question which remained unanswered was how long the Finns could keep their side of the bargain. Rendulic observed that, although they did not want to fight the Germans, the Finns were determined to have peace at any price and would accept all Soviet demands.[18]

Having struck a bargain with the Finns, the Twentieth Mountain Army proceeded with its redeployment. On the right flank Divisionsgruppe Kraeutler, screened on the east by the 7th Mountain Division, moved west across the waist of Finland to take over the coastal sector between Tornio and Oulu where it would give ground in the south gradually, drawing back to a bridgehead southeast of Kemi in the first week of October. Kampfgruppe Ost, holding around Oulu, would fall back to Pudasyärvi where it would converge with the 7th Mountain Division, which would hold Pudasyärvi until the first week of October and then fall back slowly to Rovaniemi.[19]

---

[17] *Ibid.*
[18] (*Geb.*) *AOK 20, Ia, Besprechung des O.B. mit dem Sonderbeauftragten des finn. H.Q. Obstl. Haahti, 18.9.44* and (*Geb.*) *AOK 20, Ia, Nr. 1290/44, an OKW, WFSt, 20.9.44,* in *K.T.B. Anlagenband, 16.9.–31.9.44.* AOK 20 65635/6.
[19] (*Geb.*) *AOK 20, Ia, Nr. 409/44, Armeebefehl fuer die Fortsetzung der Bewegungen ab 23.9.44, 22.9.44,* in *Chefsachenanlagen 1.7.–18.12.44.* AOK 20 65635/12.

South of the army boundary, Mannerheim, who had moved the Finnish 6th Division to Kajaani and the 15th Brigade to the Oulu area earlier in the month, stationed a border Jaeger brigade at Kajaani and the Finnish Armored Division, the 3d Division, and the 11th Division at Oulu, where General Siilasvuo established his headquarters as Commanding General of the Finnish Lapland forces.[20]

For ten days the "fall maneuvers" proceeded exactly according to plan. On 26 September the Twentieth Mountain Army reported that the Finns were following from phase line to phase line according to the agreement and at the same time leaving so much no-man's land between the two forces that exchanges of fire were hardly possible. The Finnish Armored Division was committed along the Oulu–Kemi road, the worst possible route for an armored force because of the many river crossings. The army also regarded it as favorable that most of the Finnish units were the ones which had earlier fought side by side with the Germans.[21] The German troops were destroying all bridges and ferries as they passed, sometimes while the Finns stood by and watched.[22] The sole cause for concern was—how long before the Russians became suspicious? The answer was to come in two days.

On the morning of 28 September, after having opened fire briefly, a Finnish battalion commander demanded that the 7th Mountain Division evacuate Pudasyärvi before nightfall. The Twentieth Mountain Army at first dismissed the incident as merely a display of excessive zeal on the part of the local commander. When the Finns refused to negotiate, Rendulic, later in the day, gave the 7th Mountain Division permission to return fire if necessary and, shortly before midnight, presented Siilasvuo with an ultimatum demanding that the Finnish forces reaffirm their intention to observe the previous agreements or accept the consequences of open hostilities. During the following two days the Finns increased their pressure at Pudasyärvi, capturing a German platoon there on 30 September. At the same time there were incidents in Tornio and Kemi, touched off by Finnish troops who had been left in the Twentieth Mountain Army area to supervise the civilian evacuation and guard industrial installations.[23] The Russians, apparently, had dropped a hint that they were ready to give "assistance" if the Finns failed to execute the armistice terms with sufficient determination.

[20] Mannerheim, *op. cit.,* pp. 528, 535.
[21] One fact overlooked in this assumption was that the 3d, 6th, and 11th Divisions were sent north probably not because they had had close contact with the Germans but rather for the far better reason that they were composed of men recruited from the Twentieth Mountain Army zone. Their commander, Siilasvuo, although he had commanded a corps under the Twentieth Mountain Army for nearly a year, had toward the end displayed anything but a pro-German bias.
[22] (*Geb.*) *AOK 20, Ia, Nr. 1349/44, an OKW, WFSt, 26.9.44,* in *K.T.B. Anlagenband, 16.9.–31.9.44.* AOK 20 65635/6.
[23] (*Geb.*) *AOK 20, Ia, Kriegstagebuch, 1.9.–18.12.44,* 28–30 Sep 44. AOK 20 65635/2.

At Suomussalmi and Kuusamo Russian troops had already crossed the border.

By 1 October open fighting had broken out in Kemi and at Tornio, where the Finns took possession of the road and railroad bridges. During the day the Finnish 3d Division, coming by sea from Oulu, began disembarking at Tornio. The OKW saw a parallel between the Tornio bridges and the Allied attack on the Rhine bridges in Holland and insisted that they be retaken. Rendulic, although not sharing the OKW opinion regarding the importance of the bridges, instituted measures to regain control of the situation in the Kemi–Tornio area.

At the outset Divisionsgruppe Kraeutler had only one infantry battalion, two battalions of artillery, and miscellaneous supply troops with which to defend Tornio, Kemi, and about sixty miles of coastline. At the first sign of a crisis it was given the Kampfgruppe West, approximately a regiment, which had been withdrawing through Pudasyärvi with the 7th Mountain Division. On 2 October Rendulic furnished two additional infantry battalions and ordered the Machine Gun Ski Brigade, which was already moving northward from Rovaniemi, into the Divisionsgruppe Kraeutler sector.[24]

The army had to attempt to check the Finns without delaying its own withdrawal. After the army quartermaster reported on 2 October that all the supplies had been evacuated from Rovaniemi, it was not necessary to protect the town longer than the few days needed by the remaining elements of the XXXVI Mountain Corps and the 6th SS-Mountain Division passing through. Rendulic, therefore, ordered Divisionsgruppe Kraeutler to concentrate on pushing the Finns back into Tornio, but stated that retaking of the town itself was not necessary. The 7th Mountain Division was to hold near Pudasyärvi until the 6th SS-Mountain Division and the 163d Infantry Division had reached Rovaniemi and turned north.[25]

Late on the night of 2 October, after the term had been extended several hours at the Finnish liaison officer's request, the Finns rejected Rendulic's ultimatum of 28 September. In his reply Siilasvuo stated that no agreements contrary to the Soviet-Finnish armistice terms had ever been made and that any exchanges of information which might have been made with individuals were not binding on the Finnish troop leadership.[26] On the following day Rendulic declared that the army would henceforth operate against the Finns "without restraint." Abandoning the policy, which had so far been carefully observed, of limiting property destruction to roads, railroads, and bridges, he ordered, "As

---

[24] The Machine Gun Ski Brigade had been the chief component of Kampfgruppe Ost. It had been formed earlier in the year, out of three motorized machine gun battalions plus some infantry, to provide a mobile reserve for the Twentieth Army.
[25] *Ibid.,* 2 Oct 44.
[26] *Generalleutnant Siilasvuo, Bfh. d. finnischen Gruppe Lappland an dem O.B. der 20. (Geb.) Armee, 2.10.44,* in *K.T.B. Anlagenband, 1.10.–15.10.44.* AOK 20 65635/7.

of now, all cover, installations, and objects of use to the enemy are to be destroyed." [27] The taking of hostages, which had started a few days earlier, began in earnest; but the hostages were all released several days later on orders from the OKW, which also ordered that Finnish soldiers and civilians in the army zone were to be treated as internees rather than as prisoners of war.[28] This display of moderation was occasioned chiefly by concern for public opinion in Sweden, where hostility to Germany had increased alarmingly since the outbreak of hostilities with the Finns.

At Tornio, on 3 October, the main force of the Divisionsgruppe Kraeutler made some progress against the Finnish beachhead, but it was clear that, with the Finnish Armored Division pushing rapidly along the coast toward Kemi, the operation would have to be completed or abandoned within a few days. By the following day the Divisionsgruppe had been forced back to a bridgehead east of Kemi. On 5 October, with the pressure against Kemi strong and progress slow against Tornio, army headquarters decided that the attack on Tornio would have to be stopped on the evening of the 6th and the withdrawal from Tornio and Kemi begun on the 7th. Part of the Divisionsgruppe would fall back along the Swedish border toward Muonio, while the rest would fight a delaying action along the Kemi–Rovaniemi road. On 6 October the Finns landed a second division, the 11th, at Tornio, and Rendulic confirmed his order for the withdrawal. The next day, the Finns, resorting to their *motti* tactics, encircled a German force north of Tornio, and the withdrawal had to be postponed for twenty-four hours while the encirclement was being broken.

Beginning on 8 October the Divisionsgruppe Kraeutler and the 7th Mountain Division withdrew northward through Lapland, giving up Rovaniemi on the 16th.[29] The main objective of the Finnish offensive, to disprove Russian accusations of bad faith, had been achieved at Tornio and Kemi, where foreign journalists were on hand to witness the fighting. Although the Finnish troops maintained a close pursuit, they did not seriously interfere in German operations again.

NORDLICHT

Although the OKW and the Twentieth Mountain Army had clearly recognized the dangers of Operation BIRKE from the time Fuehrer Directive No. 50 was issued in the fall of 1943, the Finnish capitulation, coming late in the year, made it appear that the alternative, a withdrawal behind the Lyngen Position, the short line across northern Nor-

---

[27] (Geb.) AOK 20, Ia, Kriegstagebuch, 1.9.–18.12.44, 3 Oct 44. AOK 20 65635/2.
[28] Auswaertiges Amt Nr. 882, an OKW, Herrn Generaloberst Jodl, 6.10.44 and OKW, WFSt, Qu. 2 (Nord), Nr. 0012133/44, an O.B. (Geb.) AOK 20, 9.10.44. OKW/138.2.
[29] (Geb.) AOK 20, Ia, Kriegstagebuch, 1.9.–18.12.44, 3–10 Oct 44. AOK 20 65635/2.

German ships at nickel ore docks, Kirkenes.

way between the Lyngen Fiord and the northern tip of Sweden, might well be impossible. On 18 September the opinion in the OKW was that the army would have to be taken back to the Lyngen Position but that this move would probably not be possible before June 1945. A day later, however, Rendulic was instructed also to take into account the "highly unfavorable possibility" that the operation would have to be executed in winter.

With the dilemma thus completely unsolved, the Operations Staff, OKW, at the end of the month undertook a review of the entire strategic position in Scandinavia and Finland. The review was necessitated by the situation of the Twentieth Mountain Army and by a new element— the loss of the submarine bases on the French coast and the consequent vast increase in the importance of the Norwegian bases, particularly in view of the intention to resume large-scale submarine warfare with new types equipped with snorkels and hydrogen peroxide engines. The OKW believed that the British air and naval forces formerly committed against the French bases would be transferred north, lured by the submarine bases, the vulnerable sea supply lines of the Twentieth Mountain Army, and the desire to prevent the Russians from gaining a foothold in northern Scandinavia. The Twentieth Mountain Army, the OKW concluded, would have to be pulled back before the expected British offensive developed or be left to take heavy losses. To hold northern Finland no longer appeared worthwhile in any case since Dr. Albert Speer, the war production chief, had recently stated that the stockpile of nickel in Germany was adequate. On the other hand, to take the Twentieth Mountain Army back into Norway would strengthen the defenses there, relieve the strain on coastal shipping, and provide forces for defense of the Narvik area against Sweden. On 3 October, after these considerations had been presented in the form of a balance sheet, Hitler approved a pullback to the Lyngen Position. In the following two days the OKW issued the preliminary orders and assigned the code name NORDLICHT.[30]

Tactically, NORDLICHT was an extension of BIRKE with the added problems of setting the XIX Mountain Corps in motion and evacuating the army's six- to eight-months' stockpile of supplies. As an expedition by an army of some 200,000 men with all their equipment and supplies across the arctic territory in winter it had no parallel in military history. The season was already far advanced. Reichsstrasse 50 between Lakselv and Kirkenes was normally considered impassable because of snow between 1 October and 1 June; and, even though the fall of 1944 was unusually mild, the XIX Mountain Corps would need luck and would have to be west of Lakselv by 15 November at the latest. The XXXVI Mountain Corps was more fortunate, having an all-weather road from Ivalo to Lakselv. The XVIII Mountain Corps roads, about half completed between Skibotten and Muonio and unimproved between Muonio and Rovaniemi, had a low carrying capacity, which was in part compensated for by the corps' having the most direct route to Lyngen Fiord.

While the weather and roads posed technical problems which exceeded all previous experience, the tactical situation was certain to be dangerous and could at any moment become catastrophic. The Finns, already following close on the heels of the XXXVI and the XVIII Mountain Corps could, potentially, stage offensives with superior forces against both, and the Russians could be depended on not to let the XIX Mountain Corps get away without a fight. Their final objectives could not be predicted. Would they try to waylay the XXXVI Mountain Corps at Ivalo? Would they follow into Norway? Would they attempt to cut the entire army off by taking Narvik? The least that could be expected was a close pursuit down to the Lyngen Position. From all appearances British and American intervention was only slightly less certain than trouble with the Russians. Reichsstrasse 50, broken by numerous ferry crossings and running immediately along the coast for long stretches, was temptingly vulnerable to naval and air attacks. Not to be taken lightly either was the danger from Sweden, which, having abrogated its trade agreements with Germany, appeared to be veering toward open hostility. The Twentieth Mountain Army was already under standing orders to avoid any incidents which could be interpreted as provocation, a difficult task since the XVIII Mountain Corps' route

---

[30] *OKW, WFSt, K.T.B. Ausarbeitung, Der noerdliche Kriegsschauplatz, 1.4.– 31.12.44*, pp. 63–66. I.M.T., Doc 1795–PS.

Camouflaged supply trail in the Tundra.

of march took it directly along the Swedish border for several hundred miles.

How the first phase of NORDLICHT would be executed was determined by the Russians who, after a build-up which the Germans had watched apprehensively since mid-September, opened their offensive against the XIX Mountain Corps on 7 October. The XIX Mountain Corps, under General der Gebirgstruppe Ferdinand Jodl, stood in the line it had held since the late summer of 1941. On the left flank the 6th Mountain Division held the strongly fortified Litsa front, and on the right the 2d Mountain Division manned the line of strongpoints. The Divisions-gruppe van der Hoop held the line across the neck of the Rybatchiy Peninsula and provided security for the Pechenga area.[31] The fortress battalions of the 210th Infantry Division were ranged along the coast between Pechenga Bay and Kirkenes. In September Rendulic had moved the Bicycle Reconnaissance Brigade "Norway," detached from the Army of Norway, into the corps zone and had intended also to send the Machine Gun Ski Brigade, which at the end of the month he had to divert to Tornio instead. Opposite the XIX Mountain Corps the Russian main force, under Headquarters, Fourteenth Army, had been expanded to form three corps with a total of some six divisions and eight brigades. It was supported on the Rybatchiy Peninsula by at least two naval brigades and an indeterminate number of other troops.[32] Facing this formidable build-up the XIX Mountain Corps

---

[31] The Divisionsgruppe van der Hoop was the former Divisionsgruppe Rossi. General Rossi died in the plane crash which killed Dietl.

[32] (Geb.) *AOK 20, Ia, Kriegstagebuch, 1.9.–18.12.44,* 20 Sep 44. AOK 20 65635/2.

could not resort to evasive action, as the XXXVI Mountain Corps had, but was forced to make a stand at the front for the sake of the tremendous stockpiles of supplies and equipment which were just beginning to be evacuated through Pechenga and Kirkenes.

On the morning of 7 October the Russian IC Assault Corps, with an estimated four divisions massed on a narrow front, hit the 2d Mountain Division strongpoint line immediately south of Chapr Lake, which lay astride the 2d Mountain Division–6th Mountain Division boundary. The attack, with artillery, air, and tank support, quickly swept over several of the strongpoints and before noon had almost reached the Titovka River on the Finnish-Soviet border. The 2d Mountain Division was badly shaken, and the Bicycle Reconnaissance Brigade was ordered out of reserve to throw up defensive positions on both sides of Lan Road, the division's supply road which joined the Arctic Ocean Highway at Luostari. On the following day while the 2d Mountain Division fell back to the Lan positions, the Twentieth Mountain Army ordered that the enemy must be prevented from gaining a foothold on the Arctic Ocean Highway and gave permission to pull the 6th Mountain Division back from the Litsa to gain troops.

On 9 October the Russians shifted their attack south and their CXXVI Light Corps gained ground toward the Arctic Ocean Highway around the right flank of the 2d Mountain Division. The attack along Lan Road continued heavy, and a dangerous situation developed as the left flank of the 2d Mountain Division was driven back, leaving a gap between it and the right flank of the 6th Mountain Division. The Twentieth Mountain Army issued orders dispatching a regiment of the 163d Infantry Division, a machine gun battalion, and an SS battalion to the XIX Mountain Corps area.

The 10th brought a series of crises. Beginning shortly before midnight, Russian troops from the Rybatchiy Peninsula landed on the mainland west of the peninsula and in the course of the day turned the left flank of Divisionsgruppe van der Hoop, forcing it away from the neck of the peninsula. At the 2d Mountain Division–6th Mountain Division border, IC Assault Corps sent two regiments due north through the gap to cut the Russian Road, the 6th Mountain Division's main route to Pechenga. Off the right flank of the 2d Mountain Division, troops of the CXXVI Light Corps made good their threat of the day before and established themselves on the Arctic Ocean Highway five miles west of Luostari. The Twentieth Mountain Army ordered the 6th Mountain Division to clear the Russian Road and fall back to the line Pechenga–Luostari and ordered immediate destruction of the Kolosyoki nickel works. The 163d Infantry Division, still on the Rovaniemi–Salla road, was routed toward the XIX Mountain Corps at top speed, and the army recalled the Machine Gun Ski Brigade from Divisionsgruppe Kraeutler.

THE SOVIET OFFENSIVE AGAINST
XIX MT CORPS
7-28 October 1944

††††††† GERMAN POSITION, DATE INDICATED

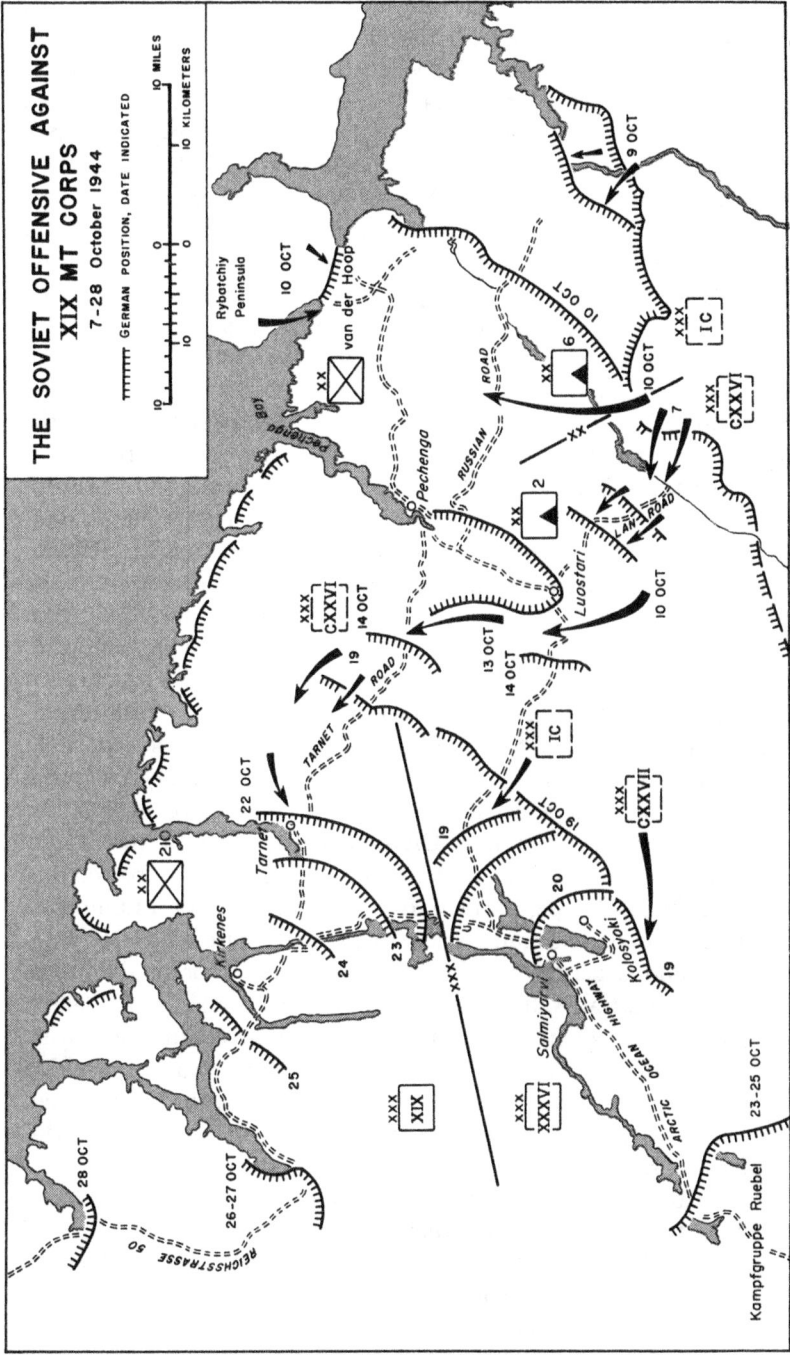

10 MILES

10 KILOMETERS

L. Booth

Map 23

During the next two days the 6th Mountain Division cleared the Russian Road and, together with the Divisionsgruppe van der Hoop, fell back to a bridgehead east of Pechenga. The 2d Mountain Division held the road junction at Luostari. West of the Russians, who held about five miles of the Arctic Ocean Highway, Kampfgruppe Ruebel, a regiment and three battalions under the Commanding General, 163d Division, Generalleutnant Karl Ruebel, threw up a screening line.

On 13 October, while Kampfgruppe Ruebel and the 2d Mountain Division attempted unsuccessfully to drive the Russians off the highway, the CXXVI Light Corps sent a strong detachment north and cut the Taarnet Road, the direct road between Pechenga and Kirkenes. With that the 2d and 6th Mountain Divisions and the Divisionsgruppe van der Hoop were isolated. To save the situation it became necessary to give up Luostari and Pechenga, turn the divisions west to reopen the Taarnet Road, and then fall back behind the Norwegian border.[33]

In one week the Russians had brought about the collapse of a front on which the Germans had lavished three years of planning and labor. For the Germans the blow was intensified by the fact that the Russian offensive was conducted with complete disregard for the assumption the Twentieth Mountain Army had accepted as doctrine since 1941: that the arctic terrain made rapid movement of large forces impossible and, in particular, ruled out tank operations. This made the army appear in large degree a victim of its own misconception; but a closer examination does not sustain that conclusion. On the German side the 1941 experience and three years of inactivity had undoubtedly produced some complacency and a decline of readiness for combat which the rapid collapse of the 2d Mountain Division clearly demonstrated. They had probably also overlooked the changes three years of occupation had produced in the landscape, particularly the appearance of a number of relatively good roads and numerous paths which invited an attempt to employ tanks and larger troop units. Nevertheless, their original assumption was only partially disproved, since the Russians, employing a vastly superior force of specially trained troops with skillful and daring leadership against an opponent whose chief desire was to avoid a decisive engagement, failed—just as the Mountain Corps Norway had in 1941—to achieve their main objective, to trap and destroy the XIX Mountain Corps.

On 15 October Rendulic, Jodl (XIX Mountain Corps), and Ruebel conferred at the Kampfgruppe Ruebel Headquarters. They decided that, when the Taarnet Road was reopened, the 2d Mountain Division, which had not yet recovered from the shock of the original attack, would be transferred south behind the Kampfgruppe Ruebel to rest and re-

---

[33] *XIX (Geb.) A.K., Kurzbericht ueber die Kampfhandlungen im Petsamo-und Varangerraum vom 7.10.44, 5.11.44*, in Gen. Jodl, Kampfbericht–Petsamo. AOK 20 75034/1. *(Geb.) AOK 20, Ia, Kriegstagebuch, 1.9.–18.12.44*, 7–14 Oct 44. AOK 20 65635/2.

group. The remaining units of the XIX Mountain Corps would screen Kirkenes until the supplies were evacuated; and Headquarters XXXVI Mountain Corps would take over the Kampfgruppe Ruebel, which was being rapidly brought up to a strength of nearly two divisions. The fate of the army depended on Kampfgruppe Ruebel. It would have to hold northeast of Kolosyoki until the Kirkenes defenses were completed in order to prevent the Russians from gaining a foothold on the road, which had been built to carry ore to Kirkenes, and would also have to prevent the Russians from striking southward along the Arctic Ocean Highway to Ivalo.

Also present at the meeting was General der Gebirgstruppe Georg Ritter von Hengl, a former commanding general of the XIX Mountain Corps, who in his capacity as head of the National Socialist Leadership Staff, OKH, brought a message of encouragement from Hitler. Hengl maintained that Jodl (OKW) had said the emphasis of the XIX Mountain Corps operations should be on saving the troops and concern for the supplies was secondary. Since this report contradicted all previous orders, a call was put through to Jodl at the OKW, who said that the Hengl communication was "distorted" but himself only provided the somewhat oracular explanation that, if it were a question of sacrificing troops for supplies, then it was expected that the army's first concern would be for the troops. In a second call two hours later, the army chief of staff pointed out that implementing the OKW orders for evacuation of all supplies would necessarily involve attrition of forces, particularly on the part of the Kampfgruppe Ruebel, and asked for replacement supplies from Germany. These, he was informed, were impossible to provide, since rations and ammunition were "rare commodities" in Germany, and the discussion therewith ended where it had begun.[34]

Meanwhile, activity at the front subsided slightly as the Russians regrouped. On 18 October, anticipating resumption of the Russian offensive within 24 hours, the Twentieth Mountain Army gave the Kampfgruppe Ruebel permission to fall back to Salmiyärvi within three days and, since that move would open the nickel road to Kirkenes, ordered the 6th Mountain Division to take over defense of the southern approaches to Kirkenes at the same time. When these operations were completed the XIX Mountain Corps and the Kampfgruppe Ruebel would be separated and facing in opposite directions, and the XXXVI Mountain Corps would assume control of the Kampfgruppe Ruebel.

The Russian attack began as expected on 19 October, with the main effort directed against Kampfgruppe Ruebel. Although the Kampfgruppe drew back along the Arctic Ocean Highway and escaped the full force of the IC Assault Corps attack, its situation became precarious a

---

[34] (Geb.) AOK 20 Reisebericht des O.B., 15.10.44. in K.T.B. Anlagenband, 1.10.–15.10.44. AOK 20 65635/7. (Geb.) AOK 20, Ia, Kriegstagebuch, 1.9.–18.12.44, 15 Oct 44. AOK 20 65635/2.

day later as the CXXVII Light Corps thrust around the right flank and threatened to cut the highway behind the Kampfgruppe. To keep his line of retreat open, Ruebel was forced, during the next three days, to fall back to the Kaskama Lake narrows. After that the Russian pressure gradually slackened, and the Kampfgruppe was able to fall back rapidly to Ivalo.

Simultaneously with the attack on the Kampfgruppe Ruebel, the CXXVI Light Corps advanced against the 6th Mountain Division screening Kirkenes. In the face of three-to-one superiority the division had no hope of stopping the advance. Worse still, the CXXVI Light Corps directed its main effort at Taarnet, where the hydroelectric plants supplying power to Kirkenes were located. On 22 October, with those installations already in the front lines, the Twentieth Mountain Army, informing the OKW that the ships in Kirkenes could no longer be supplied with water for their boilers, requested permission to stop the evacuation and operate according to the tactical situation. After several hours' delay, permission was granted, and thereafter the corps elements east of Kirkenes fell back rapidly, the last units passing west onto Reichsstrasse 50 on the 24th. After minor rear guard actions on the 27th and 28th, the Russian pursuit slowed down as the XIX Mountain Corps withdrew in the direction of Lakselv. Of the corps' supplies, one third (45,000 tons) were saved; the rest were destroyed or fell into the hands of the Russians.[35]

On 26 October the evacuation of the Varanger Peninsula began. The Russians followed as far as Tana Fiord. Ahead of the XIX Mountain Corps, between Lakselv and Skibotten, two divisions of the LXXI corps, transferred to the Twentieth Mountain Army in mid-October, provided security for the vulnerable points on Reichsstrasse 50 and began preparations for demolition of the road after the main force had passed. Hitler, intent on preventing either the Russians or the free Norwegian Government from gaining a foothold north of Lyngen Fiord, ordered a scorched earth policy. The civilian population was to be evacuated, mostly in small boats to avoid overloading Reichsstrasse 50.

The evacuation began as a voluntary measure, but where the population refused to comply, the Germans used force. Usually the simple expedient of burning down the houses was sufficient. The total of those evacuated was estimated at 43,000. The population of Kirkenes (10,000) had to be left behind for tactical reasons, and 8,500 nomadic Laps were exempted. Otherwise, Rendulic reported in December, only 200 persons managed to escape; and these, with his usual thoroughness in such matters, he promised to hunt down.[36]

---

[35] (Geb.) *AOK 20, Ia, Kriegstagebuch, 1.9.–18.12.44*, 16–28 Oct 44. AOK 20 65635/2.

[36] (Geb.) *AOK 20, 0. Qu/Qu. 1, Nr. 5001/44, Bericht ueber Evakuierung Nordnorwegens, 15.12.44.* OKW 138/2.

In the XXXVI Mountain Corps zone, after the middle of October, the 169th Division occupied the Schutzwallstellung, the positions prepared south of Ivalo for Operation BIRKE. To the east in the direction of Lutto and Ristikent the corps established a screening line. There, on 21 October, it experienced a brief alarm when radio intelligence reported identification of the Soviet Nineteenth Army Headquarters and three divisions in the Lutto Valley; but ground reconnaissance soon revealed that the radio traffic was merely a deception.[37] After the units of the former Kampfgruppe Ruebel had passed through Ivalo toward Lakselv, the XXXVI Mountain Corps abandoned the Lutto positions on 30 October, and began its withdrawal from the Schutzwallstellung on the following day. On 2 November the 2d Mountain Division entered Reichsstrasse 50 at Lakselv to begin the final stage of the withdrawal by the main forces of the XIX and the XXXVI Mountain Corps. Next day the rear guard of the 169th Division evacuated Ivalo.[38]

The XVIII Mountain Corps, after holding Muonio until the large ammunition dump there had been evacuated, began (on 29 October) falling back to the Sturmbockstellung west of Karesuando. There, in the positions constructed for BIRKE, the 7th Mountain Division took over the task of holding the narrow strip of Finnish territory projecting northwestward between Sweden and Norway as a temporary flank protection for the Lyngen Position and the troops moving west on Reichsstrasse 50. The 139th Brigade was stationed off the left flank in Norwegian territory at Kautokeino.

On 18 December, as the rear guard on Reichsstrasse 50 passed Billefiord, the 139th Brigade began pulling back from Kautokeino. In the Sturmbockstellung the 7th Mountain Division held its positions with negligible interference from the Finns until 12 January 1945. On that date it began a leisurely march back to the Lyngen Position, which by then had been completed and was held by troops of the 6th Mountain Division.

At the end of January NORDLICHT was terminated, although the code name NORDLICHT continued to be used until May 1945 for the passage through Norway of the Twentieth Mountain Army troops being returned to Germany. At the extreme northwestern tip of Finland a few square miles of Finnish territory which had been included in the Lyngen Position remained in German hands until the last week of April 1945. East of Lyngen Fiord the Norwegian Finnmark was empty except for small German detachments at Hammerfest and Alta which continued evacuating supplies until February 1945. In January the Norwegian Government sent in a token force of police from England and Sweden.

---

[37] (Geb.) AOK 20, Ia. Nr. 467/44 an Gen. Kdo. XXXVI (Geb.) A.K., 21.10.44, in Chefsachenanlagen, 1.7.–18.12.44. AOK 20 65635/12.
[38] OKW, WFSt, K.T.B. Ausarbeitung, Der noerdliche Kriegsschauplatz, 1.4.–31.12.44, p. 75. I.M.T., Doc. 1795–PS.

Subsequently, the Russians gradually withdrew, leaving only a detachment at Kirkenes.[39]

Although Operation NORDLICHT constituted an outstanding display of skill and endurance on the part of the troops and leadership of the Twentieth Mountain Army, luck was also a significant element in its success. While the casualties (22,236) were nearly as many as those sustained during SILBERFUCHS in 1941, they fell far below the numbers that had become routine for other German armies. Of the dangers and threats which had been anticipated, none materialized. The weather was as favorable as could have been expected in the Arctic, and winter set in much later than usual that year. Most fortunate of all, NORDLICHT was executed at exactly the time when the resources of both the Russians and the West were committed to their limits on the main fronts, with the result that the Russian effort, in the final analysis, was modest and the British and Americans did not put in an appearance at all.

Norway and Surrender

The year 1944 passed for the Army of Norway, as the previous two had, in waiting for an invasion that did not come. At mid-year its strength stood at 372,000 men, but before the end of summer it had lost about 80,000 through the transfer of three divisions and miscellaneous smaller contingents to shore up the tottering fronts in Russia and France. In the fall, forced by the hostile attitude of Sweden to deploy units along the Swedish border opposite Oslo and Trondheim, the army briefly experienced a personnel shortage.[40]

Active warfare was confined to the air and sea, as the British raided the ports and coastal shipping and the German submarines doggedly harassed the arctic convoys. After the *Scharnhorst* sinking, Doenitz stationed 24 submarines in the Arctic, but sinkings declined sharply and submarine losses increased after the British began using American-built escort aircraft carriers to protect the convoys. After the loss of the French ports, Bergen and Trondheim became the main bases for submarine warfare in the Atlantic, but the fleet of revolutionary new-type submarines which they were to serve never appeared.[41]

During the year the *Tirpitz* continued to perform its functions of tying down heavy units of the British Navy and forcing it to provide extra strong cover for the convoys to Russia, but the giant battleship's days were numbered. As soon as its repairs were completed in the spring of 1944 an air attack on 2 March which scored 16 direct hits put the

[39] *OKW, WFSt, K.T.B. Ausarbeitung, Der noerdliche Kriegsschauplatz 1.4.– 31.12.44,* p. 76. I.M.T., Doc. 1795–PS. *(Geb.) AOK 20, Ia, Kriegstagebuch, 1.9.–18.12.44,* 24 Oct 44 *et passim.* AOK 20 65635/2. *(Geb.) AOK 20, Ia, Kriegstagebuch, 19.12.44–5.18.45,* 19 Dec 44 *et passim.* AOK 20 75038/2.
[40] *OKW, WFSt, K.T.B. Ausarbeitung, Der noerdliche Kriegsschauplatz, 1.4.– 31.12.44,* pp. 85, 92. I.M.T., Doc. 1795–PS.
[41] Morison, *op. cit.,* Vol. X, pp. 305–14.

The Tirpitz *in a northern fiord.*

ship out of action for another four months. After two more strikes, in July and August, failed, the British Air Force on 15 September launched two squadrons of Lancaster bombers carrying six-ton armor-piercing bombs from a field near Arkhangel'sk. Over Alta Fiord they found the *Tirpitz* already hidden in smoke from generators ranged along the shore, but they managed to score one hit which badly mangled the ship's bow. Since the repairs would require nine months, the *Tirpitz* was then transferred to Tromsö to act as a stationary floating battery off the left flank of the Lyngen Position.[42] On 28 October the Lancasters tried again from a base in Scotland but came over the target just as a cloud bank moved in and, forced to bomb through the clouds, secured no hits. Two weeks later, on 12 November, they struck once more. Coming in from the east, they achieved complete surprise. In three minutes, after receiving two direct hits and four near misses, the *Tirpitz* capsized, her superstructure grounding in the shallow water of the harbor and her bottom projecting above the surface.[43] The Naval Staff believed that the Lancasters had been able to come in undetected because they had made the flight over neutral Swedish territory.

Operation NORDLICHT inevitably brought with it a reshuffling of command and troop dispositions in Norway. In October the OKW transferred control of the LXXI Corps and northern Norway including the Narvik area to the Twentieth Mountain Army. On 18 December, in accordance with orders which Hitler had issued earlier, Rendulic

---

[42] *OKW, WFSt, K.T.B. Ausarbeitung, Der noerdliche Kriegsschauplatz, 1.4.–31.12.44,* pp. 89–91. I.M.T., Doc. 1795–PS.
[43] David Woodward, *The Tirpitz and the Battle for the North Atlantic* (New York: Berkley Publishing Corp., 1953), pp. 151–58.

took over as Armed Forces Commander, Norway, and Falkenhorst returned to Germany. The Twentieth Mountain Army absorbed the Army of Norway, and in the Narvik–Lyngen Fiord area the Armeeabteilung Narvik, composed of the XIX Mountain Corps and the LXXI Corps, was created under the command of Headquarters, XIX Mountain Corps. Headquarters, XXXVI Mountain Corps, assumed command of the troops on the Swedish border.

During the winter the main task of the Twentieth Mountain Army was to return as many units as could be spared to Germany. The 6th SS-Mountain Division began embarking at Oslo in mid-November and in the next five months the 2d Mountain, 163d, 169th, and 199th Divisions followed. Already slowed down by the necessity for moving the divisions by road from Lyngen Fiord to Mo, the transfers were reduced to a crawl in March when coal stocks ran low, and the Norwegian railroads had to run on wood. The last division scheduled to go, the 7th Mountain Division, became bogged down south of Trondheim in late April.

From January to May 1945, while the German armies on the mainland were being ground to pieces, the Twentieth Mountain Army was on a near-peacetime basis. Even the rumors, predictions and premonitions of an invasion subsided. General der Gebirgstruppe Franz Boehme, who replaced Rendulic as Armed Forces Commander, Norway, in January when the latter was transferred to the command of the Army Group North, complained that he found some units still observing Sunday as a holiday. Although he condemned the practice as a "regrettable failure to appreciate our total situation," he had little to recommend other than that the day be used for National Socialist Leadership courses or athletic competitions.[44] An OKW observer had described Norway at the end of 1944 as one of the most peaceful spots in Europe, and so it remained to the end of the war despite a gradual increase in sabotage and resistance activity.

In the dull days of late winter Reichskommissar Terboven, as he had done once or twice before, provided a certain amount of serio-comic relief. Falkenhorst, in June 1943, had persuaded the Reichskommissar to drop his demand for a private zone of operations by promising that if and when an invasion came he could remain in office and continue to exercise his authority outside the immediate combat zones.[45] After thinking the matter over during the intervening months, Terboven, in March 1945, came to the conclusion that an invasion would leave very little of Norway which could be excluded from the combat zone. This thought he communicated to Boehme, who agreed and suggested that, when the time came, he take over the post of chief of military govern-

---

[44] *Der Oberbefehlshaber der 20. (Geb.) Armee und Wehrmachtbefehlshaber Norwegen, Ia, 1010/45, 7.2.45,* in *K.T.B. Anlagenband 1.2.–28.2.45.* AOK 20 75036/3.
[45] *OKW, WFSt, K.T.B. Ausarbeitung, Der noerdliche Kriegsschauplatz, 1.4.–31.12.44,* p. 83. I.M.T., Doc. 1795–PS.

ment under the Armed Forces Commander. Terboven countered with a suggestion that he be made Boehme's deputy in all except tactical matters. He wanted to begin immediately devoting his "energies" to inspiring the troops and giving them the benefit of his personal and moral support, functions which he also intended to perform after the fighting had begun. In the OKW, where at the moment there was no desire to establish closer ties between the Wehrmacht and the party, Terboven's proposal struck like a bomb. It raised visions of every Gauleiter in Germany attempting to foist himself on the Army as a species of political commissar. As usual, Terboven had Hitler's approval "in principle," and it took the combined efforts of Keitel and Jodl to stave off this last-minute attempt to revise the German military system.[46]

In the spring, while the war burned itself out on the mainland, the Twentieth Mountain Army stood by, helpless, but still a source of lingering concern to the Allied Supreme Command, which regarded Norway as a possible locale for a desperate last stand.[47] The army itself had no such plans and, after Doenitz became Head of State, was ordered, on 4 April, to avoid all incidents which might give provocation to the Western Powers.[48]

After the German surrender in Denmark on 5 May, Obergruppen-fuehrer Walter Schellenberg, who had earlier established contacts in Sweden as part of an attempt to cast his boss, Himmler, in the role of peacemaker, appeared in Stockholm where he persuaded the Swedish Government to offer to intern the Twentieth Mountain Army and all the German personnel in Norway with the exception of Terboven and Quisling. Although Schellenberg had plenipotentiary powers from Doenitz, Boehme, who had told Doenitz in an interview on 5 May that the Twentieth Mountain Army and the other Wehrmacht elements in Norway were ready for any task "within the limits of their strength" and had come off with the impression that Doenitz regarded the force in Norway as a valuable lever for bargaining with the Allies, refused to meet the intermediaries on the ground that his mission, the defense of Norway, had not changed.[49] On 8 May, the day after the uncondi-tional surrender was announced, the OKW informed Boehme that in-dependent negotiations with Sweden would be regarded as a breach of the capitulation terms and would "have the most severe consequences for the entire German people."[50] On the same day representatives of Gen-

[46] W.B.N., Ia, Nr. 1910/45, Ernennung des Reichskommissars zum Vertreter des Wehrmachtbefehlshabers, 19.3.45 and W.B.N., Ia, 1771/45, an Chef WFSt, 14.3.45. OKW/138.2.
[47] John Ehrman, Grand Strategy (London, 1956), Vol. VI, pp. 147ff.
[48] OKW, WFSt, an W.B. Norwegen, W.B. Daenemark, 4.5.45, in WFSt, Befehle an die Truppe (Kapitulation). OKW/6.
[49] (Geb.) AOK 20 Ia, Nr. 48/45, an OKW, Gen. Feldm. Keitel, 6.5.45, in Chefs-achen–K.T.B., 1.1.–7.5.54. AOK 20 75038/5a. (Geb.) AOK 20 (OKW B Norw.), Ia, Nr. 2860/45, in (Geb.) AOK 20, Ia, Verschiedenes, Jan–Juni 1945. AOK 20 75038/6.
[50] OKW, WFSt, Nr. 0010063/45, an Oberbefehlshaber (Geb.) AOK 20, 8.5.45, in K.T.B. Anlagenband, 1.4.–30.4.45. AOK 20 75036/5.

eral Sir Andrew Thorne's Scottish Command arrived in Oslo to deliver orders for the surrender.

Terboven committed suicide in his bunker on the day of the capitulation. Quisling refused a last-minute chance to escape to Spain, choosing, instead, to "defend his convictions" before a Norwegian court. He was executed in the Akershus Fortress at Oslo on 23 October 1945.

In announcing the surrender Boehme described his army as one which "no enemy had dared to attack" and which bowed to the dictates of its enemies only to serve the total national interest.[51] The full meaning of unconditional surrender was not appreciated until after the Allied instructions had arrived. Protesting to the OKW on 10 May, Boehme denounced the capitulation terms as "unbearably severe." The German troops were being reduced to an "immobile, defenseless mass of humanity," while the Russian prisoners of war were being treated with "incomprehensible esteem." The demand that the army arrest the SS and party officials was "dishonorable." He concluded with, "Woe to the vanquished." [52]

---

[51] *Boehme, General der Gebirgstruppe und Wehrmachtsbefehlshaber Norwegen, "Soldaten in Norwegen," in K.T.B. Anlagenband 1.4.–30.4.45.* AOK 20 75036/5.
[52] *(Geb.) AOK 20 (OKWBN), Ia, an OKW, WFSt, 19.5.45, in WFSt, Befehle an die Truppe (Kapitulation).* OKW/6.

Chapter 15

Conclusion

In warfare there are occasional blind alleys, and for Germany in World War II the Northern Theater was one of those. Of the two major strategic objectives which the theater presented, expansion of the base for naval operations and interdiction of traffic through the port of Murmansk, one could not be exploited and the other was never attained. The remaining advantages which accrued to Germany were not great enough to divert enemy attention from more promising targets elsewhere; consequently, the theater remained quiescent during most of its existence and eventually collapsed as a result of German defeats on the mainland.

Norway, which a reinforced corps had conquered, took an army plus vast expenditures of matériel to defend. After 1941 a second army was tied down in Finland. Both of those armies were effectively side-tracked as far as any influence on the outcome of the war was concerned. Whether this diversion of force was either necessary or justifiable was debated from the very inception of the plan for WESERUEBUNG. Since the war German opinion on the question has been divided, but the arguments on both sides invariably center on specific strategic considerations. When a balance is cast they lead only to the conclusion that the Northern Theater was both essential to Germany's conduct of the war and a stone around its neck. In attempting to determine the relative importance of either, one immediately becomes involved in an endless chain of futile second-guessing. The answer, of course, is that the causes of Germany's failure in World War II are not to be found in the specifics of strategy or tactics—not even Hitler's—but in the fallacy of attempting to satisfy boundless ambitions with limited means.

In occupying Norway and northern Finland Germany acquired economic assets of first-rate importance to its war effort, the Swedish iron and Finnish nickel. It also gained bases which were useful for submarine warfare in general and which were essential to the operations against the Allied convoys to Russia. A further advantage that Hitler, at least, ranked above all the others was the protection of Germany's northern flank. All of these were valuable, and yet none of them had a discernible influence on the outcome of the war.

The most frequent criticism directed against Hitler's conduct of operations in the Northern Theater, and in Norway particularly, is that he poured in troops and material there on a scale which far surpassed the need and drained strength from more active theaters. His exaggerated concern for an invasion of that area was one of his major errors as a strategist, besides being a first-class example of the malfunctioning of his intuition. On the other hand, if Norway was to be defended, the commitment of forces there had to be large, although not as large, perhaps, as it was. By nature the German position in Norway was weak: a long coastline had to be defended against an enemy who had naval superiority; and poor internal lines of communication ruled out a mobile defense. A static defense was the most reliable solution and that cost men and matériel.

The crucial error of German strategy in the Northern Theater was the failure to cut the northern sea route to the Soviet Union. In 1941 its importance was not fully recognized, and the mistake could not be rectified later. Furthermore as General Buschenhagen has pointed out, the failure to stage an adequate offensive against the Murmansk Railroad, serious as it was, was fundamentally less significant than the error in strategy that left Arkhangel'sk, which could be kept open throughout most of the year, completely out of consideration. An operation to cut the railroad at Belomorsk, followed by an advance to Arkhangel'sk, would have completely closed the northern route and dealt the Soviet Union a severe blow. It would probably also have made possible a stabilization of the situation in northern Europe which, in the light of their predominantly defensive interest there, would have been entirely to the Germans' advantage.

Another error which had a most baneful effect on operations in the northern theater was the failure to take Leningrad. It appears that the city could have been taken in September 1941 had it not been for Hitler's wild and pointless determination to wipe it out entirely. The capture of Leningrad would probably have made a German-Finnish drive toward Belomorsk and Arkhangel'sk possible. It would certainly have greatly strengthened the position of the Finnish Army and paved the way for further combined operations. Above all, once the issue had been decided at Leningrad, the Russians might have turned their attention to other sectors of the front, enabling the Army Group North and the Finnish Army to establish relatively stable positions in their areas.

The poorly defined and inherently unstable partnership with Finland contributed greatly to the atmosphere of frustration which prevailed throughout the history of the Northern Theater. The Finns could have performed two services of major strategic significance, assistance in the capture of Leningrad and participation in an operation against the

Murmansk Railroad; both of these they refused. Long before the association was dissolved it had become a liability to both partners.

For Finland, which sacrificed heavily in men (55,000 killed, nearly 145,000 wounded) territory, and economic resources, the war was a costly experience. Finland was in part, as it claimed, a small nation caught in a war between two great powers and in part a victim of its own ambitions. That some of its territory would have become involved in the war was inevitable, and that it could have remained neutral was unlikely. In the end it emerged from the war still an independent nation, a better fate than befell many of the Soviet Union's small neighbors, some of which were not its enemies. This relatively favorable outcome can be credited in part to the fund of good will which Finland had built up in the United States and Great Britain and their continuing recognition of a certain amount of justice in the Finnish cause.

One significant historical precedent was established in the German Northern Theater: there, for the first time, major troop units conducted extended operations under arctic conditions. Although in the final battles of the war the Russians maneuvered large units with tanks more quickly and over greater distances than had previously been thought possible, the following conclusions regarding arctic warfare drawn from the German experience still apparently retain their validity:

1. In the Arctic the human element is all-important. The effectiveness of motorized and mechanized equipment is greatly reduced; the chief reliance must always be on men, not machines. Specialized training and experience are essential. The climate allows no margin of error either for the individual or for the organization as a whole.

2. The mobility of all units, large or small, is low. Maneuvers must be precisely planned and executed with the knowledge that distance can be as difficult to overcome as the enemy. Momentum is difficult to achieve and quickly lost.

3. Control of space is unimportant. Roads are difficult to build, and operations inevitably center around those few which already exist or can be constructed. One good line of communications such as the Murmansk Railroad can be decisive.

4. There is no favorable season for operations. Climate and terrain are always enemies, particularly to offensive operations. The winter is relatively favorable in one respect, namely, that the snow and ice make rapid movement by specially trained and equipped troops possible. Throughout much of the winter, however, operations must be conducted in near-total darkness. The most satisfactory period is in the late winter when the days are lengthening; but then time is limited, and operations must either be completed or abandoned at the onset of the spring thaw.

Appendix A

Rank Designations of German and Finnish General and Flag Officers

Army and Air Force

German	Finnish	United States equivalent
Reichsmarschall*.........	Suomen Marsalkka**...	None.
Generalfeldmarschall......	Sotamarsalkka***......	General of the Army and General of the Air Force.
Generaloberst............	Kenraalieversti****....	General.
General der Infanterie, der Artillerie, der Flieger, etc.	Jalkavaenkenraali [etc.].	Lieutenant General.
Generalleutnant..........	Kenraaliluutnantti.....	Major General.
Generalmajor............	Kenraalimajuri........	Brigadier General.

Navy

Grossadmiral.................................	Fleet Admiral.
Generaladmiral...............................	Admiral.
Admiral......................................	Vice Admiral.
Vizeadmiral..................................	Rear Admiral.
Konteradmiral................................	Commodore.

*Created for Goering in July 1940 and held only by him.
**Created for Mannerheim in June 1942 and held only by him.
***Held only by Mannerheim.
****No Finnish officer held an equivalent rank in World War II.

Appendix B

Chronology of Events

1939

September

1   World War II begins as German troops invade Poland.

2   Germany warns Norway to observe strict neutrality.

October

10   Raeder points out to Hitler the advantages of German naval and air bases in Norway.

November

30   Soviet forces invade Finland.

December

13   Hitler orders the question of occupying Norway investigated.

1940

January

6   Great Britain requests permission to send naval forces into Norwegian territorial waters.

10   *Studie Nord* is issued.

29   Field Marshall Mannerheim appeals for aid, and the Allies decided to send an expeditionary force in mid-March.

February

5   The Krancke Staff assembles in the OKW.

16   The *Altmark* is boarded by British naval personnel in Norwegian territorial waters.

21   Falkenhorst is appointed to direct planning for WESERUEBUNG.

March

1   The Fuehrer directive for WESERUEBUNG is issued.

12   The Soviet-Finish Winter War ends.

April

1   Hitler gives final approval on plans for WESERUEBUNG.

3   First ships of the Tanker and Export Echelons depart.

5   Great Britain agrees to execution of Operation WILFRED.

6   (Midnight) Warship Groups 1 and 2 depart.

8   The British Navy lays mines in Norwegian territorial waters (Operation WILFRED).

9   German troops land in Norway and occupy Denmark.

14   Allied landings begin in the Narvik area and at Namsos.

17   Allied landings begin at Åndalsnes.

May
2   Evacuation of Åndalsnes is completed.
3   Evacuation of Namsos is completed.
28 The Allies capture Narvik.

June
8   The Allies evacuate Narvik.
9   The Norwegian Army surrenders.

July
29 German planning for an invasion of the Soviet Union begins.

August
13 Hitler orders reinforcement of northern Norway and preparation for Operation RENNTIER (occupation of the Finnish nickel district in the event of a Soviet-Finnish conflict).
18 The German Air Force secures transit rights across Finnish territory.

September
22 The German-Finnish transit agreement is signed.

November
12 & 13 Molotov visits Berlin, and Hitler warns against renewed Soviet attack on Finland.

December
18 Hitler signs and issues Fuehrer Directive No. 21 for Operation BARBAROSSA, the invasion of the Soviet Union.

———

1941
January
27 The Army of Norway completes its staff study SILBERFUCHS for a combined German-Finnish operation against the Soviet Union.

March
4   A British naval force raids Svolvaer, and Hitler (subsequently) orders the defenses of Norway strengthened.

April
17 The Army of Norway submits its plan of operations for SILBERFUCHS to OKW.

May
25–28 German-Finnish miltary conferences at Salzburg and Berlin.

June
3   German-Finnish military conferences are resumed in Helsinki.
14 The President of Finland and the Foreign Affairs Committee of Parliament approve the results of the military conferences.
17 Finnish mobilization begins.
22 Germany declares war on the Soviet Union.
25 Finland declares war on the Soviet Union.

28   The Finnish Army completes and submits its plan of operations to the OKH.
29   The Mountain Corps Norway begins Operation PLATINFUCHS, the advance toward Murmansk.

July
1   The XXXVI Corps and the Finnish III Corps begin Operation POLARFUCHS, the advance toward Kandalaksha and Loukhi.
10   The Finnish Army opens its offensive in East Karelia.
28   Finland breaks diplomatic relations with Great Britain.

August
10   The Army Group North begins its final drive to Leningrad.
30   Elements of the Army Group North reach the Neva River, cutting the land routes out of Leningrad.

1941

September
2   Finland completes the reconquest of its former territory on the Isthmus of Karelia.
4   The Army of Karelia begins its advance to the Svir River.
8   The Army Group North captures Schluesselburg.
21   The Army of Norway cancels the Mountain Corps Norway offensive, which has become bogged down on the Litsa River.

October
10   Fuehrer Directive No. 37 stops all offensive operations in the Army of Norway zone.
14   The Army Group North begins an advance via Chudovo to Tikhvin to make contact with the Army of Karelia in the vicinity of the Svir River.

November
25   Finland signs the Anti-Comintern Pact.

December
5 & 6   Finnish troops capture Medvezh'yegorsk and Povenets, thereby ending the Finnish offensive of 1941.
6   Great Britain declares war on Finland.
15   Hitler, after long hesitation, agrees to the evacuation of Tikhvin and a withdrawal of the Army Group North troops to the Volkhov River.

1942

January
14   Dietl assumes command of German troops in Finland as Commanding General, Army of Lapland.
22   Hitler orders the defenses of Norway strengthened and instructs the Navy to employ "each and every vessel in Norway."

February

12 The German warships *Scharnhorst, Gneisenau,* and *Prinz Eugen* leave Brest and break through the English Channel.

March

6–9 The battleship *Tirpitz* searches for Convoy PQ 12 without result.

14 Hitler orders intensified naval and air action against the arctic convoys.

April

24 The Soviet spring offensive against the Finnish III Corps begins east of Kesten'ga.

27 The Soviet spring offensive against the Mountain Corps Norway begins.

May

15 The Mountain Corps Norway defensive battle concludes successfully.

23 The Finnish III Corps counterattack is halted.

July

4 The Fifth Air Force begins successful attacks on Convoy PQ 17.

21 Fuehrer Directive No. 44 authorizes planning for a combined German-Finnish thrust to Belomorsk (Operation LACHSFANG).

23 Fuehrer Directive No. 45 orders the Army Group North to capture Leningrad by September (Operation NORDLICHT).

August

27 The Russians open an offensive east of Leningrad.

October

1 Operation LACHSFANG is canceled.

December

30 & 31 A sortie by the *Hipper* and the *Luetzow* against Convoy JW 51 A fails.

1943

January

6 Hitler declares his intention to take all of the heavy ships out of commission. Admiral Raeder submits his resignation, which is accepted.

12 & 18 A Russian offensive re-establishes land contact with Leningrad.

February

9 The Finnish Parliament is informed that Germany cannot win the war.

March

17 The Army Group North is ordered to prepare an operation against Leningrad (Operation PARKPLATZ).

September
8 A German task force with the *Tirpitz* executes Operation ZITRO-
   NELLA against Spitzbergen.
22 British midget submarines damage the *Tirpitz*.
28 Fuehrer Directive No. 50 orders the Twentieth Mountain Army to
   prepare to hold northern Finland in the event that Finland leaves
   the war.

October
6 A Russian offensive begins at the junction of the Army Groups
   North and Center east of Nevel.

December
26 The *Scharnhorst* is sunk off northern Norway in action with the
   Duke of York and destroyers.

1944

January
14 The final Russian offensive to liberate Leningrad begins.
19 The liberation of Leningrad.
30 The Army Group North is given permission to withdraw to the
   Luga River line.

February
12 Paasikivi goes to Stockholm to receive the Soviet peace terms.

March
8 Finland rejects the Soviet terms.
26 Paasikivi and Enckell resume the negotiations in Moscow.

April
18 Finland rejects the second Soviet peace offer.

June
10 The Russian summer offensive against Finland begins.
26 The Ryti-Ribbentrop agreement is signed.

July
15–20 The Russian summer offensive ends.

August
4 Mannerheim is elected President of Finland.
25 Finland asks the Soviet Union to receive a peace delegation.

September
4 Finland and the Soviet Union agree to a cease fire.
6 Operation BIRKE, the withdrawal of the Twentieth Mountain Army
   to northern Finland begins.
19 Finland signs an armistice with the Soviet Union.

October
3 Hitler approves Operation NORDLICHT, the withdrawal of the
   Twentieth Mountain Army into Norway.
7 The Russians open an offensive against the XIX Mountain Corps.

November

12 The *Tirpitz* is bombed and capsizes in the harbor at Tromsö.

December

18 Rendulic assumes command in Norway and the Twentieth Mountain Army absorbs the Army of Norway.

1945

January

30 Operation NORDLICHT ends.

May

8 An Allied delegation arrives to receive the surrender of the German forces in Norway.

Appendix C

List of Major Participants

BAMLER, Rudolf, Generalleutnant; Chief of Staff Army of Norway—15 May 42–30 Apr 44.

BERGER, Gottlob, SS-Brigadefuehrer (Brigadier General).

BLUECHER, Wipert von; German Minister in Finland—1935–1944.

BOEHME, Franz, General der Gebirgstruppe; Commanding General, XVIII Mountain Corps—20 Oct 41–10 Dec 43; Armed Forces Commander, Norway, and Commanding General, Twentieth Mountain Army—18 Jan 45–8 May 45.

BOEHME, Hermann, Generaladmiral—1 Apr 41; Commanding Admiral, Norway—10 Apr 40–31 Jan 43.

BRAEUER, Curt, German Minister in Norway—1939–9 Apr 40; Minister and Plenipotentiary of the German Reich in Norway—9 Apr–17 Apr 40.

BRAUCHITSCH, Walter von, Generaloberst—4 Feb 38, Generalfeldmarschall—19 Jul 40; Commander in Chief of the German Army—4 Feb 38–19 Dec 41.

BUSCHENHAGEN, Erich, Oberst (Colonel)—1 Mar 38, Generalmajor—1 Aug 41; Chief of Staff, XXI Corps, Group XXI, and Army of Norway—Sep 39–May 42.

CARLS, Rolf, Admiral; Commanding Admiral, Baltic Sea Station—1 Nov 38–20 Sep 40; Commanding Admiral, Naval Group East—31 Oct 39–20 Sep 40; Commanding Admiral, Naval Group North—21 Sep 40–1 Mar 43.

CHURCHILL, Winston Spencer, First Lord of the Admiralty—5 Sep 39–10 May 40; Prime Minister, 10 May–Jul 45.

CORK, Lord William Henry Dudley Boyle, Admiral of the Fleet the Earl of Cork and Orrery; Naval Commander of the Narvik Expedition—10 Apr 40; Commander of all forces committed to the task of capturing Narvik—21 Apr–Jun 40 (after 7 May, also including the military forces in the Mosjöen–Bodö area).

DALADIER, Edouard, President of the French Council of Ministers and Minister of National Defense—Apr 38–Mar 40, also Minister of War and Foreign Affairs—Sep 39–Mar 40; Minister of War—Mar–May 40.

DIETL, Eduard, Generalmajor—1 Apr 39, Generalleutnant—1 Apr 40, General der Gebirgstruppe—19 Jul 40, Generaloberst—1 Jun 42; Commanding General, 3d Mountain Division—1 Sep 39–16 Jun 40; Commanding General, Mountain Corps Norway—16 Jun 40–15 Jan 42; Commanding General, Army of Lapland (after June 1942 Twentieth Mountain Army)—15 Jan 42–23 Jun 44.

DOENITZ, Karl, Konteradmiral—1939, Grossadmiral—30 Jan 43; Commanding Admiral, Submarines—1 Jan 36–1 May 45; Commander in Chief of the German Navy—30 Jan 43–1 May 45; Chief of State and Commander in Chief of the German Armed Forces—1 May 45–8 [23] May 45.

ERFURTH, Waldemar, General der Infanterie; Chief, Liaison Staff North later German General at Finnish Headquarters—13 Jun 41–6 Sep 44.

FALKENHORST, Nikolaus von, General der Infanterie—1 Oct 39, Generaloberst—19 Jul 40; Commanding General, XXI Corps—1 Sep 39–1 Mar 40; Commanding General, Group XXI—1 Mar 40–19 Dec 40; Armed Forces Commander, Norway—25 Jul 40–18 Dec 44; Commanding General, Army of Norway—19 Dec 40–18 Dec 44.

FEIGE, Hans, General der Kavallerie; Commanding General, XXXVI Corps—Jun–Nov 41.

FEURSTEIN, Valentin, Generalleutnant; Commanding General, 2d Mountain Division—1 Sep 40–4 Mar 41.

FISCHER, Hermann, Oberst (Colonel); Commanding Officer of the 340th Infantry Regiment—Apr–May 40.

FORBES, Admiral Sir Charles; Commander in Chief of the Home Fleet; Commander of naval operations in the Norwegian area—Apr–Jun 40.

FRAUENFELD, Alfred, Gauleiter; Plenipotentiary of the German Reich in Norway—Apr 40.

GEISSLER, Hans, Generalleutnant; Commanding General, X Air Corps—1939–15 Dec 40 [Norway].

GOERING, Hermann, Generalfeldmarschall—4 Feb 38, Reichsmarschall—19 Jul 40; Commander in Chief of the German Air Force.

HAGELIN, Wiljam, Quisling's representative in Germany 39–40; Minister of Commerce in Quisling's Norwegian Government of Apr 40.

HALDER, Franz, Generaloberst—19 Jul 40; Chief of the Army General Staff—1 Nov 38–24 Sep 42.

HEINRICHS, Erik, Kenraaliluutnantti—1941, Jalkavaenkenraali—1942; Chief of Staff of the Finnish Army—1939–1941; Commanding General, Army of Karelia—28 Jun 41–Jan 42; Chief of Staff of the Finnish Army—Jan 42–Jan 45; Commander in Chief of the Finnish Army—Jan 45.

HENGL, Georg Ritter von, Generalmajor—1 Apr 42, Generalleutnant—1 Jan 43, General der Gebirgstruppe—1 Jan 44; Commanding Officer, 137th Mountain Regiment—24 Feb 40–2 Mar 42; Commanding General, 2d Mountain Division—2 Mar 42–23 Oct 43; Commanding General, XIX Mountain Corps—23 Oct 43–21 Apr 44; Chief, National Socialist Leadership Staff, OKH—15 May 44.

HIMER, Kurt, Generalmajor—1940; Chief of Staff of XXXI Corps—1940; Military Plenipotentiary in Denmark—9 Apr 40.

HIMMLER, Heinrich, Reichsfuehrer-SS and Chief of the German Police—1936–1945.

HITLER, Adolf, Chancellor of the German Reich—30 Jan 33; Fuehrer and Chancellor—1934–1945; Commander in Chief of the Armed Forces—2 Aug 34–30 Apr 45; Commander in Chief of the Army—19 Dec 41–30 Apr 45.

HOCHBAUM, Friedrich, Generalleutnant—1 Jul 43, General der Infanterie—1 Sep 44; Commanding General, XVIII Mountain Corps—25 Jun 44–8 May 45.

JODL, Alfred, Generalmajor—1 Apr 39, General der Artillerie 7 Jul 40, Generaloberst—1 Feb 44; Chief of the German Armed Forces Operations Staff—Apr 38–8 [23] May 45.

JODL, Ferdinand, General der Gebirgstruppe—1 Sep 44; Commanding General, XIX Mountain Corps—15 May 44–8 May 45 (simultaneously Commanding General, Armeeabteilung Narvik—1 Dec 44–8 May 45).

KAUPISCH, Leonhard, General der Flieger; Commanding General, XXXI Corps, later Commanding General of the German Troops in Denmark—Sep 39–Jan 41.

KEITEL, Wilhelm, Generaloberst—1 Nov 38, Generalfeldmarschall—19 Jul 40; Chief of Staff of the German Armed Forces High Command—4 Feb 38–8 [13] May 45.

KIVIMAKI, T. M.: Finnish Minister in Germany—1940–1945.

KOLLONTAY, Alexandra, Soviet Minister in Sweden.

KRANCKE, Theodor, Kapitaen zur See (Captain)—1940; Chief of the first planning staff for Operation WESERUEBUNG—5 Feb–24 Feb 40; Naval representative on the staff of Group XXI—Feb–Apr 40.

KUECHLER, Georg von, Generalfeldmarschall; Commanding General, Army Group North—15 Jan 42–31 Jan 44.

LEEB, Wilhelm Ritter von; Generalfeldmarschall; Commanding General, Army Group North—1 Apr 41–16 Jan 42.

LOSSBERG, Bernhard von, Oberst (Colonel); Operations Staff, OKW—
1 Sep 39–12 Jan 42; Operations Officer, Army of Norway—
12 Jan 42–5 May 44.

LUETJENS, Guenther, Vizeadmiral; Commanding Admiral, Fleet—18
Jun 40–27 May 41.

MACKESY, P. J., Major General; Commanding General of British Troops
for Operation WILFRED: Army commanding general in the
Narvik area—Apr–5 May 40.

MANNERHEIM, Baron Carl Gustaf, Field Marshal—19 May 33, Marshal of Finland—4 Jun 42; Commander in Chief of
the Finnish Army; President of Finland—4 Aug 44–
4 Mar 46.

MANSTEIN, Fritz Erich von, Generalfeldmarschall; Commanding General, Eleventh Army—Sep 41–Nov 42.

MARCKS, Erich, Generalmajor; Chief of Staff, Eighteenth Army.

MARSCHALL, Wilhelm, Admiral; Commanding Admiral, Fleet—24
Apr–17 Jun 40.

MIKOYAN, Anastas Ivanovich, People's Commissar for Foreign Trade
of the Soviet Union—1938–1949.

MILCH, Erhard, Generaloberst—31 Oct 38; Commanding General, 5th
Air Force—12 Apr–10 May 40.

MODEL, Walter, Generaloberst; Commanding General, Army Group
North— 31 Jan–31 Mar 44.

MOLOTOV, Vyacheslav Mikhailovich, People's Commissar for Foreign
Affairs of the Soviet Union—1939–1949.

PAASIKIVI, Juho Kusti, Chairman of the Finnish delegation for negotiations with the Soviet Union—1939; Chairman of the
Finnish peace delegation in Moscow—Mar 40; Finnish
Minister in the Soviet Union—Mar 40–Jun 41; President
of Finland—6 Mar 46–1 Mar 50.

PELLENGAHR, Richard, General, 196th Infantry Division—Apr–May
40.

POHLMAN, Hartwig, Oberstleutnant (Lieutenant Colonel)—1940; Military Plenipotentiary in Norway—1 Apr 40.

QUISLING, Vidkun, Norwegian politician and official; leader of the
Norwegian Nasjonal Samling Party; holder of various
offices in the German puppet government of Norway.

RAEDER, Erich Grossadmiral—1 Apr 39; Commander in Chief of the
German Navy and Chief, Naval Staff—1 Jun 35–30 Jan 43.

RAMSAY, Henrik, Finnish Minister—Feb 43–Aug 44.

RENDULIC, Lothar, Generaloberst; Commanding General Twentieth
Mountain Army—28 Jun 44–15 Jan 45; Armed Forces
Commander, Norway—18 Dec 44–15 Jan 45.

RENTHE-FINK, Cecil von, German Minister in Denmark—1936–9 Apr
40; Minister and Plenipotentiary of the German
Reich in Denmark—9 Apr 40–1942.

REYNAUD, Paul, President of the French Council of Ministers—Mar–Jun 40; Foreign Minister—Mar–May 40.

RIBBENTROP, Joachim von, German Foreign Minister—4 Feb 38–2 May 45.

RITTER, Karl, Ambassador on special assignment in the German Foreign Ministry—1939–1945.

ROSENBERG, Alfred, Reichsleiter, Head of the Foreign Political Office of the Nazi Party (Aussenpolitisches Amt der NSDAP)—1933–1945.

RUGE, Otto, Generalmajor, Commander in Chief of the Norwegian Army—11 Apr–8 Jun 40.

RYTI, Risto Heikki, President of Finland—Dec 40–1 Aug 44.

SCHEIDT, Hans-Wilhelm, Reichsamtsleiter, Director of the Department for Northern Europe, Foreign Political Office of the Nazi Party.

SCHELL, Adolf von, Generalleutnant; Commanding General, 25th Panzer Division—1 Jan 43–15 Nov 43.

SCHNIEWIND, Otto, Vizeadmiral—1939; Chief of Staff, Naval Staff—22 Aug 39–10 Jan 41.

SCHNURRE, Karl, Minister; Head of Division W IV in the Economic Policy Department of the German Foreign Ministry—1939–1940.

SCHOERNER, Ferdinand, Generalmajor—1 Aug 40, Generalleutnant—15 Jan 42, General der Gebirgstruppe—1 Jun 42; Commanding General, 6th Mountain Division—1 Jun 40–15 Jan 42; Commanding General, Mountain Corps Norway later XIX Mountain Corps—15 Jan 42–23 Oct 43, Commanding General, Army Group North—23 Jul 44–17 Jan 45.

SIILASVUO, H., Kenraalimajuri—1941, Kenraaliluutnantti—1942; Commanding General, Finnish III Corps—Jun 41–Jun 42; commanding general of Finnish troops in northern Finland—Sep 44.

STUMPFF, Hans-Juergen, General der Flieger, Generaloberst—19 Jul 40; Commanding General, Fifth Air Force—11 May 40–5 Nov 43.

TALVELA, Paavo, Kenraalimajuri—1941, Keneraaliluutnanti—1942; Commanding General, Finnish VI Corps—Jun 41–Jan 42; Finnish General at German Headquarters—19 Jan 42–21 Feb 43; Commanding General, Maaselka Front—24 Feb 43–16 Jun 44; Commanding General, Svir Front—16 Jun–18 Jul 44; Finnish General at German He ad-quarters —Jul–6 Sep 44.

TERBOVEN, Joseph, Reichskommissar for the Occupied Norwegian Territories—24 Apr 40–5 May 45.

TODT, Fritz, Reich Minister for Arms and Munition; Plenipotentiary General for Construction Industry, Four Year Plan.

VELTJENS, Joseph; businessman and lieutenant colonel in the German Air Force who frequently acted as Goering's personal representative in military and economic negotiations.

VOGEL, Emil, Generalleutnant—1 Apr 43, General der Gebirgstruppe—9 Nov 44; Commanding General, XXXVI Mountain Corps—10 Aug 44–8 May 45.

VOROSHILOV, Klimenti, Marshal; Commanding General, Northwest Front—1941.

WARLIMONT, Walter, Colonel—1 Feb 38, Generalmajor—1 Aug 41, General der Artillerie—1 Apr 44; Chief of the National Defense Branch, OKW—1 Sep 39; Deputy Chief of the Armed Forces Operations Staff—1 Jan 42–6 Sep 44.

WEISENBERGER, Karl F., General der Infanterie; Commanding General, XXXVI Mountain Corps—29 Nov 41–10 Aug 44.

WITTING, Rolf, Finnish Foreign Minister—Mar 40–Feb 43.

WOYTASCH, Kurt, Generalmajor; Commanding General, 181st Infantry Division—1940.

ZEITZLER, Kurt, General der Infanterie—24 Sep 42, Generaloberst—1 Feb 44; Chief of the Army General Staff—25 Sep 42–20 Jul 44.

Bibliographical Note

The narrative in this volume is based in the main on German military records in the custody of the National Archives. Unfortunately, many of the documents pertaining to the 1940 Norwegian operation were destroyed in 1942 by a fire in the Potsdam Heeresarchiv. For the succeeding years the records of the field commands—the Army of Norway, the Twentieth Mountain Army, and their subordinate units—are complete and all together total several hundred volumes. It was also possible to assemble substantial numbers of Armed Forces High Command, Army High Command, Navy High Command, and Foreign Ministry documents. Copies of the German naval documents are in the custody of the Director of Naval History, U.S. Navy Department. The Foreign Ministry Documents are in the custody of the U.S. State Department.

In order to come even near adequately exploiting this large and virtually untouched collection of primary source material within the practical limits of time and space, it was necessary to concentrate on the German story. For most of the other nations involved, detailed accounts are available in their official histories: *Krigen Norge 1940* (Norway), *Suomen Sota 1941–1945* (Finland), and T. K. Derry, *The Campaign in Norway* (Great Britain). A number of works by German authors have also appeared. The most substantial of them are Walther Hubatsch, *Die deutsche Besetzung von Daenemark und Norwegen 1940* (Goettingen: "Musterschmidt," 1952); Waldemar Erfurth, *Der finnische Krieg 1941–1944* (Wiesbaden: Limes Verlag, 1950); and Wilhelm Hess, *Eismeerfront 1941* (Heidelberg: Kurt Vowinkel Verlag, 1956).

Glossary

Anti-Comintern Pact____ The treaty directed against the Soviet Union and the Communist International concluded by Germany, Italy, and Japan in November 1936.

Arctic Ocean Highway___ The road in Finnish Lapland connecting Rovaniemi and Pechenga.

Aufmarschanweisung_____ Directive for strategic concentration.

Divisionsgruppe (Divisional Group). A collection of units under a division headquarters but without the normal organization and equipment of an infantry or other type division.

Export Echelon (Ausfuhrstaffel). German supply ships disguised as merchant ships employed in the invasion of Norway.

Front (Finnish)_____ One of three "fronts" established in January 1942 on the Maaselkä, the Isthmus of Olonets, and the Isthmus of Karelia.

Front (Soviet)_____ An army group.

"fortress" battalions (Festungsbataillone)_____ Battalions, usually made up of older men and limited service men, intended for garrison and guard assignments.

Gauleiter _____ The territorial leaders of the Nazi Party.

I. G. Farben_____ German chemical manufacturing concern.

Jaeger brigade_____ Light infantry brigade.

Kampfgruppe _____ An *ad hoc* combat team of variable strength.

Karinhall _____ Goering's mansion near Berlin.

Leads _____ The channel inside the chain of islands off the Norwegian west coast.

Lufthansa _____ The German civilian air line.

Marinegruppe (N a v a l Command Group). Naval operating command, designated by area of responsibility, such as North, West, Baltic.

*motti*_____ Literally "a bundle of sticks." A type of encirclement developed by the Finnish Army for forest warfare.

Murmansk Railroad_____ The railroad connecting Leningrad and the arctic port of Murmansk completed during World War I. Rebuilt under the Soviet Government and later officially renamed the Kirov Railroad.

National Defense Branch
  (Abteilung Landesver-
  teidigung) OKW_____ The staff section of the OKW primarily concerned with war plans.

Nazi-Soviet Pact_____ The nonaggression treaty between Germany and the Soviet Union signed on 23 August 1939 and its secret protocols.

Nebelwerfer_____ Rocket projector.

Nikkeli O.Y_____ Finnish corporation controlling the nickel mines at Pechenga.

Obergruppenfuehrer_____ An SS rank equivalent to lieutenant general.

OKH (Oberkommando
  des Heeres)_____ Army High Command.

OKL (Oberkommando
  der Luftwaffe)_____ Air Force High Command.

OKM (Oberkommando
  der Kriegsmarine)_____ Navy High Command.

OKW (Oberkommando
  der Wehrmacht)_____ Armed Forces High Command.

Panzer_____ Tank.

Reichsamtsleiter_____ A German civil service rank.

Reichsfuehrer-SS_____ Heinrich Himmler's title as chief of the SS.

Reichskommissar_____ A title given to the chief administrative officers in certain of the German-occupied territories.

Reichsstrasse 50_____ The road along the northern coast of Norway between Narvik and Kirkenes completed in 1940.

SD (Sicherheitsdienst)___ The intelligence service of the SS which in 1944 assumed control of all German foreign intelligence.

SS (Schutzstaffel)_____ The elite military and police organization of the Nazi Party.

SS-Brigadefuehrer_____ An SS rank equivalent to brigadier general.

SS-Kampfgruppe_____ An SS combat organization of approximately divisional size.

Stuka (Sturtzkampfflug-
  zeug). Dive bomber.

Three Power Pact_____ The German-Italian-Japanese treaty of alliance concluded in September 1940.

Winter War_____ The Russo-Finnish conflict November 1939–March 1940.

Code Names

German

BARBAROSSA   Invasion of the Soviet Union, 22 June 1941

BIRKE   Plan for withdrawal of Twentieth Mountain Army into northern Lapland, 1944

BLAUFUCHS 1 and 2   Transfer of XXXVI Corps forces from Germany and Norway to Finland, June 1941

GELB   Invasion of France and the Low Countries, 10 May 1940

HARPUNE   Deception staged to divert attention from BARBAROSSA, May–August 1941

HARTMUT   Submarine operations in support of WESERUEBUNG, April 1940

IKARUS   Proposed occupation of Iceland, June 1940

JUNO   Fleet operations off Norway, June 1940

KLABAUTERMANN   PT Boat operations on Lake Ladoga, summer 1942

LACHSFANG   Proposed German-Finnish operations against Kandalaksha and Belomorsk, summer and fall 1942

NAUMBURG   Proposed landing in Lyngen Fiord to relieve Narvik, June 1940

NORDLICHT   Projected operations against Leningrad, fall 1942

NORDLICHT   Withdrawal of Twentieth Mountain Army from Finland, October 1944–January 1945

PANTHER Position   Narva River–Lake Peipus line of field fortifications, constructed in fall 1943

PARKPLATZ   Proposed operation against Leningrad, spring 1943

PLATINFUCHS   Operations of Mountain Corps Norway, 1941

POLARFUCHS   Operations of XXXVI Corps, 1941

POLARFUCHS   Code-name used in Soviet accounts of an alleged German plan to invade Sweden in 1943

RENNTIER   Standby plan for the occupation of Pechenga, August 1940–June 1941

SILBERFUCHS   Operations of Army of Norway and attached Finnish units out of Northern Finland, 1941

TANNE   Proposed occupation of Suursaari (TANNE OST) and the Åland Islands (TANNE WEST), 1944

WESERUEBUNG   Occupation of Norway and Denmark, 9 April 1940

WESERUEBUNG NORD   Operations in Norway, spring 1940

WESERUEBUNG SUED   Operations in Denmark, spring 1940

WIESENGRUND   Proposed occupation of the Rybatchiy Peninsula, summer 1942

WILDENTE   Air-sea landing near Mo, 10 May 1940
ZITRONELLA   Spitzbergen raid, 8 September 1943
ZITTADELLE   Operation against the Kursk salient in southern Russia, 5 July 1943

Allied

CATHERINE   Plan for sending battleships into the Baltic Sea, September 1939
HAMMER   Proposed direct operation against Trondheim, April 1940
JUPITER   Proposed occupation for Pechenga and Banak, 1942–43
PLAN R 4   Projected occupation of bases in Norway following WIL-FRED, April 1940
ROYAL MARINE   Proposed sowing of fluvial mines in the Rhine River, April 1940
SLEDGEHAMMER   Plan for large-scale raids Norway to France in 1942
WILFRED   Mining of Norwegian territorial waters, April 1940

INDEX

www.ingramcontent.com/pod-product-compliance
Lightning Source LLC
Chambersburg PA
CBHW060837100426

42814CB00016B/412/J